Biochar for Environmental Management

Biochar for Environmental Management

Science and Technology

Edited by
Johannes Lehmann and Stephen Joseph

London • Sterling, VA

First published by Earthscan in the UK and USA in 2009
Reprinted 2009

ISBN: 978-1-84407-658-1

Typeset by MapSet Ltd, Gateshead, UK
Cover design by Susanne Harris

For a full list of publications please contact:
Earthscan
Dunstan House
14a St Cross Street
London, EC1N 8XA, UK
Tel: +44 (0)20 7841 1930
Fax: +44 (0)20 7242 1474
Email: earthinfo@earthscan.co.uk
Web: **www.earthscan.co.uk**

22883 Quicksilver Drive, Sterling, VA 20166-2012, USA

Earthscan publishes in association with the International Institute for Environment and Development

A catalogue record for this book is available from the British Library

Library of Congress Cataloging-in-Publication Data

Biochar for environmental management : science and technology / edited by Johannes Lehmann and Stephen Joseph.
   p. cm.
  Includes bibliographical references and index.
  ISBN 978-1-84407-658-1 (hardback)
  1. Charcoal. 2. Soil amendments. 3. Environmental management. I. Lehmann, Johannes, Dr. II. Joseph, Stephen, 1950-
  TP331.B56 2009
  631.4'22—dc22

                                                                        2008040656

At Earthscan we strive to minimize our environmental impacts and carbon footprint through reducing waste, recycling and offsetting our CO_2 emissions, including those created through publication of this book. For more details of our environmental policy, see www.earthscan.co.uk.

This book was printed in the UK by MPG Books, an ISO 14001 accredited company. The paper used is FSC certified and the inks are vegetable based.

Mixed Sources
Product group from well-managed
forests and other controlled sources
www.fsc.org Cert no. SA-COC-1565
© 1996 Forest Stewardship Council
FSC

Contents

List of Figures, Tables and Boxes

Figures

Tables

Boxes

List of Contributors

James E. Amonette, Pacific Northwest Laboratories, Richland, WA 99352, US, email: jim.amonette@pnl.gov

Jeff A. Baldock, CSIRO Land and Water, Glen Osmond, SA 5064, Australia, email: Jeff.Baldock@csiro.au

Bhupinderpal Singh, NSW Department of Primary Industries, Forest Resources Research, PO Box 100, Beecroft, NSW 2119, Australia, email: Bp.Singh@sf.nsw.gov.au

Paul Blackwell, Department of Agriculture and Food Western Australia, Geraldton, WA 6530, Australia, email: PBlackwell@agric.wa.gov.au

Robert Brown, Department of Mechanical Engineering, Iowa State University, Ames, IA 50011, US, email: rcbrown@iastate.edu

K. Yin Chan, E. H. Graham Centre for Agricultural Innovation (alliance between NSW Department of Primary Industries and Charles Sturt University), NSW Department of Primary Industry, Locked Bag 4, Richmond, NSW 2753, Australia, email: yin.chan@dpi.nsw.gov.au

Ray Chrisman, Affiliate Facility, Forest Resources, University of Washington, Seattle, WA, email: nchrisman@chartermi.net

Mike Collins, Okura Plantations, Kerikeri, New Zealand, email: okuraplantation@gmail.com

Annette Cowie, NSW Department of Primary Industries, Forest Resources Research, PO Box 100, Beecroft, NSW 2119, Australia, email: annettc@sf.nsw.gov.au

Alan Crosky, School of Materials Science and Engineering, University of New South Wales, Sydney, Australia, email: a.crosky@unsw.edu.au

Claudia Czimczik, Department of Earth System Science, University of California, Irvine, CA 92697-3100, US, email: czimczik@uci.edu

Ken Davison, Westwood Industries, Kamloops, BC V2C 5P2 Canada, email: kdavison@westfibre.com

Thomas H. DeLuca, Ecology and Economics Research Department, The Wilderness Society, 503 West Mendenhall, Bozeman, MT 59715, US, email: tom_deluca@tws.org

Adriana Downie, School of Materials Science and Engineering, University of New South Wales, Sydney, NSW 2251, Australia; and BEST Energies Australia Pty Ltd, Somersby, NSW 2250, Australia, email: adriana@bestenergies.com.au

Tim Flannery, Macquarie University, NSW 2109, Australia, email: Tim.Flannery@textpublishing.com.au

Nikolaus Foidl, DESA, email: nfoidl@desa.com.bo

Joshua Frye, Frye Poultry, email: fryepoultry@frontiernet.net

John Gaunt, GY Associates, Harpenden, Herts, UK, AL5 2DF, email: john_gaunt@gya.co.uk

Mark Glover, Renewed Fuels, Randwick, NSW 2031, Australia, email: markg@renewed.com.au

Michael J. Gundale, Department of Forest Ecology and Management, Swedish University of Agricultural Sciences, S901-83, Umeå, Sweden, email: Michael.Gundale@svek.slu.se

Karen Hammes, Department of Geography, University of Zürich, 8057 Zürich, Switzerland, email: karen.hammes@gmail.com

Stephen Joseph, School of Materials Science and Engineering, University of New South Wales, Sydney, NSW 2251, Australia, email: s.joseph@unsw.edu.au

Stephen Kimber, NSW Department of Primary Industries, Wollongbar, NSW 2477, Australia, email: stephen.kimber@dpi.nsw.gov.au

Evelyn S. Krull, CSIRO Land and Water, Glen Osmond, SA 5064, Australia, email: evelyn.krull@csiro.au

Chih-Chun Kung, Department of Agricultural Economics, Texas A&M University, College Station, TX 77843-2124, US, email: cckung78@hotmail.com

David Laird, USDA-ARS National Soil Tilth Laboratory, Ames, IA 50011, US, email: David.Laird@ARS.USDA.GOV

Johannes Lehmann, Department of Crop and Soil Sciences, Cornell University, Ithaca, NY 14853, US, email: CL273@cornell.edu

Elisa Lopez-Capel, School of Civil Engineering and Geosciences, Newcastle University, Newcastle upon Tyne, UK, NE1 7RU, email: elisa.lopez-capel@ncl.ac.uk

M. Derek MacKenzie, Department of Renewable Resources, University of Alberta, 442 Earth Science Building, Edmonton, AB, T6G 2E3, Canada, email: M.Derek.MacKenzie@afhe.ualberta.ca

Julie Major, Department of Crop and Soil Sciences, Cornell University, Ithaca, NY 14853, US, email: jm322@cornell.edu

David A. C. Manning, School of Civil Engineering and Geosciences, Newcastle University, Newcastle upon Tyne, UK, NE1 7RU, email: david.manning@ncl.ac.uk

Bruce A. McCarl, Distinguished Professor of Agricultural Economics, Department of Agricultural Economics, Texas A&M University, College Station, TX 77843-2124, US, email: mccarl@tamu.edu

Paul Munroe, School of Materials Science and Engineering, University of New South Wales, Sydney, NSW 2251, Australia, email: p.munroe@unsw.edu.au

Cordner Peacocke, Conversion and Resource Evaluation Ltd., 29 Ardenlee Place, Belfast, Northern Ireland, BT6 8QS, email: cpeacocke@care.demon.co.uk

Peter Read, Centre for Energy Research, Massey University, Palmerston North, New Zealand, email: peter@read.org.nz

Glen Riethmuller, Department of Agriculture and Food Western Australia, Merredin, Australia, email: griethmuller@agric.wa.gov.au

Matthias C. Rillig, Freie Universität Berlin, Institut für Biologie, Altensteinstr. 6, D-14195 Berlin, Germany, email: matthias.rillig@fu-berlin.de

Ronald D. Sands, Global Change Research Institute, University of Maryland and Pacific Northwest National Laboratory, College Park, MD, email: ronald.sands@pnl.gov

Michael W. I. Schmidt, Department of Geography, University of Zürich, 8057 Zürich, Switzerland, email: michael.schmidt@geo.unizh.ch

Jan O. Skjemstad, CSIRO Land and Water, Glen Osmond, SA 5064, Australia, email: Jan.Skjemstad@csiro.au

Ronald J. Smernik, School of Earth and Environmental Sciences, University of Adelaide, Adelaide, Australia, email: ronald.smernik@adelaide.edu.au

Saran Sohi, Soil Science, Rothamsted Research, Harpenden, Herts, AL5 2JQ, UK, email: saran.sohi@bbsrc.ac.uk

Christoph Steiner, Department of Biological and Agricultural Engineering, University of Georgia, Athens GA 30602, US, email: csteiner@engr.uga.edu

Janice E. Thies, Department of Crop and Soil Sciences, Cornell University, Ithaca, NY 14853, US, email: jet25@cornell.edu

Dorisel Torres, Department of Crop and Soil Sciences, Cornell University, Ithaca, NY 14853 USA, email: dt273@cornell.edu

Lukas Van Zwieten, NSW Department of Primary Industries, Wollongbar, NSW 2477, Australia, email: lukas.van.zwieten@dpi.nsw.gov.au

May Waddington, ASSEMA, Brazil, email: may.waddington@gmail.com

Phillip Watts, Boral Ltd, Australia, email: Phillip.Watts@boral.com.au

Zhihong Xu, Centre for Forestry and Horticultural Research, School of Biomolecular and Physical Sciences, Griffith University, Nathan, QLD 4111, Australia, email: zhihong.xv@griffith.edu.ac

Edward Yeboah, CSIR-Soil Research Institute, Kwadaso, Kumasi, Ghana, email: eyeboah5@hotmail.com

Preface

An increasing number of global threats such as climate change, poverty, declining agricultural production, scarcity of water, fertilizer shortage and the resulting social and political unrest seem overwhelming. The urgency to address these threats creates an ever increasing demand for solutions that can be implemented now or at least in the near future. These solutions need to be widely implemented both locally by individuals and through large programmes in order to produce effects on a global scale. This is a daunting and urgent task that cannot be achieved by any single technology, but requires many different approaches.

One such approach is biochar for environmental management. Biochar has unique properties that make it not only a valuable soil amendment to sustainably increase soil health and productivity, but also an appropriate tool for sequestering atmospheric carbon dioxide in soils for the long term in an attempt to mitigate global warming. The recent broad interest in biochar has been chiefly stimulated by the discovery that biochar is the primary reason for the sustainable and highly fertile dark earths in the Amazon Basin, Terra Preta de Indio. Even though biochar has been used in many other places at other times, and has even been the subject of scientific investigation for at least a century, efforts have been isolated or regionally focused. The present global effort followed the demonstration that biochar has properties which sets it fundamentally apart from other organic matter in the environment.

The past two years have witnessed substantial growth in the biochar community with the founding of the International Agrichar Initiative at the World Congress of Soil Science in Philadelphia in 2006. This group formed the International Biochar Initiative (IBI) at the first international conference dedicated exclusively to biochar in Terrigal, Australia, in 2007. The International Biochar Initiative is instrumental not only in staging highly important international meetings, but also in providing a face for biochar research and outreach efforts as the authoritative organization with respect to information and policy on biochar. Over the past decade, scientific and technological information on biochar has been steadily increasing. The objectives of this first book on the subject are to capture this information in a comprehensive way in order to make it more accessible to a wider audience interested in the fundamental science behind biochar management. Biochar is a rapidly emerging area with enormous potential for growth. This publication marks the starting point of biochar as a fundamental technology.

The book is divided into four main areas:

1   the basic properties of biochar, with chapters characterizing and classifying physical, chemical and biological features that are the foundation of its behaviour in the environment;
2   biochar production and application, in order to introduce the multiple ways in which biochar systems can be imple-

mented and established, using existing and projected scenarios as templates;

3   environmental processes that are affected by biochar and that highlight element flows such as leaching or gaseous losses from soil, as well as the changes that biochar undergoes in the environment which influence its longevity and effectiveness as a management technique;

4   biochar implementation, with chapters discussing the framework for commercialization, emissions trading, the economics of biochar systems, and policy opportunities and constraints.

We are extremely grateful to the numerous referees who spent a significant amount of their time giving expert opinions that ensured the high scientific quality of this publication. In particular, we want to thank Jim Amonette, Dan Buckley, Nikolas Comerford, Gerard Cornelissen, Annette Cowie, David Crowley, K. C. Das, Tom DeLuca, Adriana Downie, John Gaunt, Bruno Glaser, Karen Hammes, Michael Hayes, William Hockaday, John Kimble, Heike Knicker, David Laird, Jens Leifeld, Michael Obersteiner, Cordner Peacocke, Tom Reed, Michael Schmidt, David Shearer, Ron Smernik, Christoph Steiner, Janice Thies, Phillip Watts, Andy Zimmerman, and several anonymous referees. We are indebted to Melanie Stiadle who proofread and formatted many of the chapters.

Sincere thanks go to Tim Hardwick, the editor at Earthscan, who believed in the importance of this topic from the start and guided us through the publication process with his expert advice. We are grateful for the financial support by the International Biochar Initiative.

Finally and most importantly, we want to thank our families and friends for all their patience with the frenzy of organizing this volume and all the late-night writing, and their full support, without which we would not have been able to put together this book.

Johannes Lehmann
Ithaca, NY
Stephen Joseph
Saratoga, CA

August 2008

Foreword

Throughout 2008, it has felt as if our future is crystallizing before our eyes. Food shortages, escalating oil prices, a melting Arctic ice cap and other climatic changes seem to make the news every week. All are potentially serious threats, and any one could be the harbinger of profound change for our global civilization. It's also become evident that the time we have to address such challenges is limited. For example, just 16 months from now, in December 2009, humanity will face what many argue is its toughest challenge ever – developing a global treaty sufficient to deal with the climate crisis. If we fail to forge an able successor to the Kyoto Protocol at this meeting in Copenhagen, we'll have to wait until 2020 for another chance, and many scientists argue that by then it will be too late.

Scientific studies confirm that our planet is warming at a rate consistent with the worst case scenario developed by the Intergovernmental Panel on Climate Change in 2001, meaning that we must make substantial inroads on our emissions in the next 20 years if we hope to avoid irreversible damage to Earth's climate system. Yet, with economic growth and the thirst for energy in China and India seemingly unstoppable, this is a task of the utmost difficulty. Furthermore, progress cannot be made at the cost of our food or energy security. What is needed in this 21st century of ours, clearly, are solutions that deal with several of our major problems at once. And they must be deliverable quickly, and at a scale able to make a real difference.

This book, I believe, provides the basic information required to implement the single most important initiative for humanity's environmental future. The biochar approach provides a uniquely powerful solution: it allows us to address food security, the fuel crisis and the climate problem, and all in an immensely practical manner. Biochar is both an extremely ancient concept and one very new to our thinking. Amazonian Indians used it to produce the Terra Preta soils of the Amazon Basin, which, 1000 years after their creation, remain more fertile than surrounding lands. Yet, few farmers living today have heard of biochar. Worse, our political debates about climate change continue in ignorance of it, while industries that could benefit immensely have barely considered it.

The key element in the biochar technologies is charcoal-making, which involves the heating of organic matter in the absence of oxygen. Rather than a single technology, biochar is a common thread running through various technological approaches, which can be varied to emphasize a particular outcome or opportunity. This book therefore describes a series of innovations whose products and outcomes are myriad and beneficial. Yet, it goes much further than that, for this work is essentially a 'how to' manual of biochar, providing expert analyses on biological, technical, economic, political and social aspects of the approach.

There are many important products of the charcoal-making processes, including a synthetic gas that can be used to generate electricity; a substitute for diesel fuel and the charcoal itself, which has the potential to sequester gigatonnes of atmospheric carbon per annum, making it the most potent engine of atmospheric cleansing we possess. Among the most valuable outcomes of the application of the biochar technologies are greatly increased economic efficiency in agriculture, enhanced crop yields, and slowing the return to the atmosphere of carbon captured by plants. The result is diverse and clean energy supplies, more food per unit of input, and climate security. In simple terms, this is what the biochar revolution offers us.

The biochar technologies described in this volume are potentially worldwide in their applicability. Grain production and many other forms of agriculture, livestock production, forestry and even the disposal of human waste will, I'm convinced, be profoundly transformed by the processes described in these pages, and the impact will be both swift and radical. The driver, at least initially, is likely to be the climate crisis. Approximately

8 per cent of all atmospheric CO_2 is absorbed by plants each year. If just a small proportion of the carbon captured by plants can be pyrolysed and transformed into charcoal, humanity's prospects will be much brighter, for this will buy us time as we struggle to make the transition to a low emissions economy.

With its careful evaluation of every aspect of biochar, this book represents a cornerstone of our future global sustainability. I'm convinced that its message is every bit as important as that of Rachel Carson's *Silent Spring*, and potentially every bit as politically powerful as Al Gore's *An Inconvenient Truth*. If it finds a wide enough readership, it will change our world forever, and very much for the better.

Tim Flannery
Sydney
August 2008

List of Abbreviations

ADE	Amazonian Dark Earths
AEC	anion exchange capacity
Al	aluminium
AM	arbuscular mycorrhizal fungi
ANOVA	analysis of variance
APEC	Asia-Pacific Economic Cooperation
As	arsenic
ASTM	American Society for Testing Materials
B	boron
BC	black carbon
BCSM	biosphere C stock management
BD	bulk density
BECS	bioenergy with carbon storage
BET	Brunauer, Emmett and Teller equation
BPCA	benzene polycarboxylic acid
BTU	British thermal unit
C	carbon
Ca	calcium
$CaCO_3$	calcium carbonate/calcite
$CaHPO_4$	calcium phosphate
CaO	calcium oxide
$Ca_{10}(PO_4)_6(OH)_2$	hydroxyapatite
CaS	calcium sulphide
$CaSO_4$	calcium sulphate/gypsum
CBA	cost-benefit analysis
CCBA	Climate, Community and Biodiversity Standards
CCX	Chicago Climate Exchange
CCS	carbon dioxide capture and storage
CDM	Clean Development Mechanism
CEC	cation exchange capacity
CH_3	methyl group
CH_4	methane
C_2H_4	ethane
CIMMYT	International Centre for Maize and Wheat Improvement
Cl	chlorine
C/N	carbon/nitrogen ratio

CO	carbon monoxide
CO_2	carbon dioxide
CO_2e	carbon dioxide equivalents
CP	cross-polarization
Cr	chromium
CrO	chromium oxide
$Cr_2O_7^{2-}$	acid dichromate
CTO	chemo-thermal oxidation
CTO-375	chemo-thermal oxidation at 375°C
Cu	copper
CV	coefficient of variation
DC-ox	dichromate oxidation
DEA	denitrification enzyme activity
Defra	UK Department for Environment, Food and Rural Affairs
DM	dry matter
DNA	deoxyribonucleic acid
DOC	dissolved organic carbon
DP	degree of polymerization
dS	deci-Siemens
DSC	differential scanning calorimetry
EC	electrical conductivity
EDS	energy-dispersive X-ray spectroscopy
EELS	electron energy loss spectroscopy
EGME	ethylene glycol monoethylene ether
EM	ectomycorrhizae
EPA	US Environmental Protection Agency
EPR	electron paramagnetic resonance
ESEM	environmental scanning electron microscope
ETS	European Union Emissions Trading Scheme
EU	European Union
Fe	iron
$FeCO_3$	siderite
Fe_2O_3	haematite
FeS	iron sulphide
FFT	fast Fourier transform
FoRTS	Forest Residues Transportation Model
FW	fresh weight
g	gram
G8	group of 8 leading industrialized nations
GC-MS	gas chromatography–mass spectrometry
GHG	greenhouse gas
GPP	gross primary productivity
GW	garden waste
GWC	greenhouse warming commitment
H	hydrogen
Ha	hectare
H/C	hydrogen/carbon ratio

HCO_3^-	hydrogen carbonate
He	iron
H_2O	water
HPO_4^{2-}	hydrogen phosphate
$H_2PO_4^-$	dihydrogen phosphate
H_3PO_4	phosphoric acid
hr	hour
H_2S	hydrogen sulphide
HSE	UK Health and Safety Executive
HTP	hydrothermal processing
HTT	highest (heat) treatment temperature
IBI	International Biochar Initiative
IPCC	Intergovernmental Panel on Climate Change
IR	infrared
IRMS	isotope ratio mass spectrometry
ISO	International Organization for Standardization
J	joule
JI	Joint Implementation
K	Kelvin
K	potassium
KCl	sylvite
KOH	potassium hydroxide
K_2S	potassium sulphide
K_2SO_4	potassium sulphate
K–W	Kruskal–Wallis statistic
L	litre
lb	pound
m	metre
MCL	maximum contaminant level
MEA	multilateral environmental agreement
Mg	magnesium
MgO	magnesium oxide
min	minute
MmBtu	million British Thermal Units
mmolc	millimol charge
Mn	manganese
MNS	mineral, nitrogen and sulphur
Mo	molybdenum
MRT	mean residence time
MWe	megawatts of electricity
N/N_2	nitrogen
Na	sodium
NaCl	sodium chloride
NaClO	sodium hypochlorite
Na_2CO_3	sodium carbonate
Na_2O	sodium oxide
NaOH	sodium hydroxide

Na_2S	sodium sulphide
NdF	nitrogen derived from fixation
NEXAFS	near-edge X-ray absorption fine structure
NGO	non-governmental organization
NH_2	amine
NH_4	ammonium
Ni	nickel
NMHC	non-methane hydrocarbons
NMR	nuclear magnetic resonance
NO	nitric oxide
N_2O	nitrous oxide
NO_3^-	nitrate
NOM	natural organic matter
NPK	nitrogen, phosphorus and potassium
NPV	net present value
NSW EPA	New South Wales Environment Protection Authority
NSW GGAS	New South Wales Greenhouse Gas Reduction Scheme
O	oxygen
O/C	oxygen/carbon ratio
OC	organic carbon
OECD	Organisation for Economic Co-operation and Development
OH	hydroxyl group
OTC	over-the-counter market
N	nitrogen
P	phosphorus
Pa	pascal
PA	pyroligneous acid
PAH	polycyclic aromatic hydrocarbon
PCB	polychlorinated biphenyl
PEL	permissible exposure limit
PGPR	plant growth promoting rhizobacteria
pH	hydrogen ion concentration
PL	poultry litter
PLFA	phospholipid fatty acid
PM	particulate matter
PO_4^{3-}	phosphate
ppm	parts per million
psi	pounds per square inch
PSRE	proton spin relaxation editing
QMS	quadrupole mass spectrometry
Rb	rubidium
RGGI	US Regional Greenhouse Gas Initiative
rpm	revolutions per minute
sec	second
S	sulphur
SAXS	small-angle X-ray scattering
SEM	scanning electron microscopy

Si	silicon
SiO_2	quartz
SIR	substrate-induced respiration
SO_4^{2-}	sulphate
SOC	soil organic carbon
SOM	soil organic matter
SSB	spinning side band
STXM	scanning transmission X-ray microscopy
t	tonne
TEM	transmission electron microscopy
TG	thermogravimetry
TGA	thermogravimetric analyser
TG-DSC	thermogravimetry and differential scanning calorimetry
Ti	titanium
TiO_2	titanium oxide
TOT/R	thermal/optical laser transmittance and reflectance
TPI	Tropical Products Institute
TSP	total suspended particulates
UK	United Kingdom
UN	United Nations
UNFCCC	United Nations Framework Convention on Climate Change
US	United States
USDA	US Department of Agriculture
UV	ultraviolet
UV-ox	oxidation using ultraviolet light
V	volt
VCS	Voluntary Carbon Standard
VM	volatile matter
VOC	volatile organic compound
VS	volatile solid
v/v	volume per volume
W	watt
WHC	water-holding capacity
wt	weight
XPS	X-ray photoelectron spectroscopy
XRD	X-ray diffraction
wt	weight
yr	year
Zn	zinc
$ZnCl_2$	zinc chloride
ZnS	zinc sulphide

SI prefixes used in this book

n	nano	$(\times 10^{-9})$
μ	micro	$(\times 10^{-6})$
m	milli	$(\times 10^{-3})$
c	centi	$(\times 10^{-2})$
d	deci	(10^{-1})
k	kilo	$(\times 10^{3})$
M	mega	$(\times 10^{6})$
G	giga	$(\times 10^{9})$
T	tera	$(\times 10^{12})$
P	peta	$(\times 10^{15})$
E	exa	$(\times 10^{18})$

Biochar for Environmental Management: An Introduction

Johannes Lehmann and Stephen Joseph

What is biochar?

Simply put, biochar is the carbon-rich product obtained when biomass, such as wood, manure or leaves, is heated in a closed container with little or no available air. In more technical terms, biochar is produced by so-called thermal decomposition of organic material under limited supply of oxygen (O_2), and at relatively low temperatures ($<700°C$). This process often mirrors the production of charcoal, which is one of the most ancient industrial technologies developed by mankind – if not the oldest (Harris, 1999). However, it distinguishes itself from charcoal and similar materials that are discussed below by the fact that biochar is produced with the intent to be applied to soil as a means of improving soil productivity, carbon (C) storage, or filtration of percolating soil water. The production process, together with the intended use, typically forms the basis for its classification and naming convention, which is discussed in the next section.

In contrast to the organic C-rich biochar, burning biomass in a fire creates ash, which mainly contains minerals such as calcium (Ca) or magnesium (Mg) and inorganic carbonates. Also, in most fires, a small portion of the vegetation is only partially burned in areas of limited O_2 supply, with a portion remaining as char (Kuhlbusch and Crutzen, 1995).

The question as to what biochar actually is from a chemical point of view rather than from a production point of view is much more difficult to answer due to the wide variety of biomass and charring conditions used. The defining property is that the organic portion of biochar has a high C content, which mainly comprises so-called aromatic compounds characterized by rings of six C atoms linked together without O or hydrogen (H), the otherwise more abundant atoms in living organic matter. If these aromatic rings were arranged in perfectly stacked and aligned sheets, this substance would be called graphite. Under temperatures that are used for making biochar, graphite does not form to any significant extent. Instead, much more

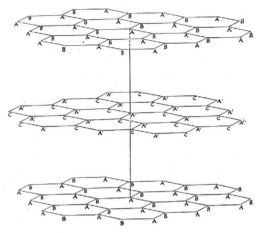

Figure 1.1 *Structure of graphite as proven for the first time by J. D. Bernal in 1924*

Source: Bernal (1924), with permission from the publisher and the estate

irregular arrangements of C will form, containing O and H and, in some cases, minerals depending upon the feedstock. Until now, biochar-type materials have largely escaped full characterization due to their complexity and variability (Schmidt and Noack, 2000). One of the first attempts to characterize the crystal structure of graphite was undertaken in the 1920s by John D. Bernal. Using X-ray diffraction, Bernal (1924) demonstrated the hexagonal structure and layering of graphene sheets in a pure graphite crystal (see Figure 1.1). The much more irregular biochar-type organic matter was only successfully investigated much later by Rosalind Franklin in the late 1940s (Franklin, 1950, 1951), and efforts to characterize the chemistry of biochar are ongoing and are discussed in detail in Chapters 2 to 4.

Biochar terminology

The term 'biochar' is a relatively recent development, emerging in conjunction with soil management and C sequestration issues (Lehmann et al, 2006). This publication establishes and uses 'biochar' as the appropriate term where charred organic matter is applied to soil in a deliberate manner, with the intent to improve soil properties. This distinguishes biochar from charcoal that is used as fuel for heat, as a filter, as a reductant in iron-making or as a colouring agent in industry or art (see historical definitions in Chapter 7).

The term 'biochar' has previously been used in connection with charcoal production (e.g., Karaosmanoglu et al, 2000; Demirbas, 2004a). The rationale for avoiding the term 'charcoal' when discussing fuel may stem from the intent to distinguish it from coal. Indeed, coal is formed very differently from charcoal and has separate chemical and physical properties, although in very specific cases the differences in properties can become

blurred (see Chapter 17). In spite of this, the term 'charcoal' is long established in popular language and the scientific literature, and will also be used in this book for charred organic matter as a source of energy.

The establishment of the term 'agrichar' is closely related to that of biochar, with the desire to apply charred organic matter to soil, but is not used further in this book. 'Biochar' is preferred here as it includes the application of charred organic matter in settings outside of agriculture, such as promoting soil remediation or other environmental services. And the term emphasizes biological origin, distinguishing it from charred plastics or other non-biological material.

'Char' is a term that is often used interchangeably with charcoal, but is sometimes applied to refer to a material that is charred to a lesser extent than charcoal, typically as a product of fire (Schmidt and Noack, 2000). The term is used in this book to refer to the charred residue of vegetation fires. Both terms, char and charcoal, are extensively employed in this volume because much of the available information on charred organic matter has been generated in studies on charcoal production for fuel and on char as a result of fires. In most instances, this body of literature provides information that is relevant to biochar management.

'Activated carbon' is a term used for biochar-type substances, as well as for coal, that have been 'activated' in various ways using, for example, steam or chemicals, often at high temperature (>700°C) (Boehm, 1994). This process is intended to increase the surface area (see Chapter 2) for use in industrial processes such as filtration.

The term 'black C' is much wider and includes all C-rich residues from fire or heat. Fossil fuels such as coal, gas and petrol, as well as biomass, can produce black C. The term includes the solid carbonaceous residue of combustion and heat, as well as the condensation products, known as soot. Black C includes the entire spectrum of charred materials, ranging from char, charcoal and biochar, to soot, graphitic black C and graphite (Schmidt and Noack, 2000).

The term 'charring' is used either in connection with making charcoal or in connection with char originating from fires.

The term 'pyrolysis' is typically used either for analytical procedures to investigate the organic chemistry of organic substances (Leinweber and Schulten, 1999) or for bioenergy systems that capture the off-gases emitted during charring and used to produce hydrogen, syngas, bio-oils, heat or electricity (Bridgwater et al, 1999). In contrast, the term 'burning' is typically used if no char remains, with the organic substrate being entirely transformed to ash that does not contain organic C. Often, substances called 'ash' in reality contain some char or biochar, significantly influencing ash properties and behaviour in technology and the environment.

Burning is very different from charring and pyrolysis, not only with respect to the solid ash residue versus biochar and related substances, but in terms of the gaseous products that are generated. Therefore, these two processes should be carefully distinguished from each other.

The terminology surrounding biochar may evolve. However, the definition provided here serves as a starting point for future development. Other terms such as gasification or liquefaction that are used in conjunction with biochar are explained elsewhere (Peacocke and Joseph, undated).

The origin of biochar management and research

While both research and development of biochar for environmental management at a global scale is a somewhat recent development, it is by no means new in certain regions and has even been the subject of scientific research for quite some time. For example, Trimble (1851) shared observations of 'evidence upon almost every farm in the county in which I live, of the effect of charcoal dust in increasing and quickening vegetation'. Early research on the effects of biochar on seedling growth (Retan, 1915)

and soil chemistry (Tryon, 1948) yielded detailed scientific information. In Japan, biochar research significantly intensified during the early 1980s (Kishimoto and Sugiura, 1980, 1985).

The use of biochar has, for some time, been recommended in various horticultural contexts – for example, as a substrate for potting mix (Santiago and Santiago, 1989). In 1927, Morley (1927) writes in the first issue of *The National Greenkeeper* that 'charcoal acts as a sponge in the soil, absorbing

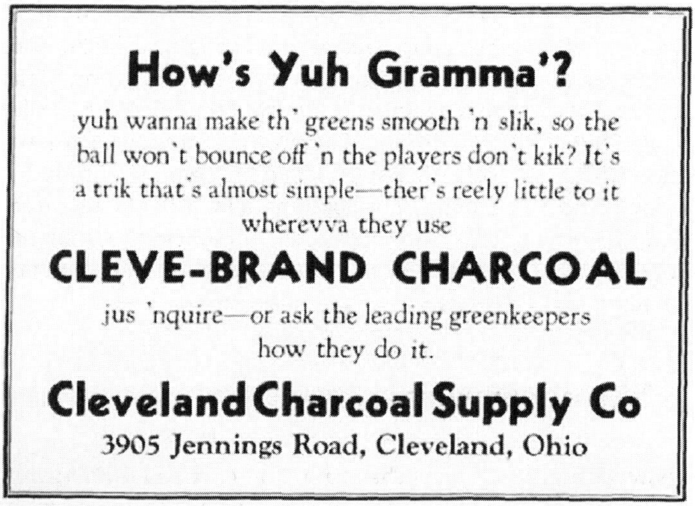

Figure 1.2 *Advertisement for biochar to be used as a soil amendment in turf greens*

Source: The National Greenkeeper (1933)

and retaining water, gases and solutions'. He even remarks that 'as a purifier of the soil and an absorber of moisture, charcoal has no equal' (Morley, 1929), and charcoal products are being marketed for turf applications in a 1933 issue of the same magazine (see Figure 1.2). Young (1804) discusses a practice of 'paring and burning' where soil is heaped onto organic matter (often peat) after setting it on fire with reportedly significant increases in farm revenue. Also, Justus Liebig describes a practice in China where waste biomass was mixed and covered with soil, and set on fire to burn over several days until a black earth is produced, which reportedly improved plant vigour (Liebig, 1878, p452). According to Ogawa (undated), biochar is described by Miyazaki as 'fire manure' in an ancient Japanese text on agriculture dating from 1697 (pp91–104). Despite these early descriptions and research, global interest in biochar only began in the past few years.

The basis for the strong recent interest in biochar is twofold. First, the discovery that biochar-type substances are the explanation for high amounts of organic C (Glaser et al, 2001) and sustained fertility in Amazonian Dark Earths locally known as Terra Preta de Indio (Lehmann et al, 2003a). Justifiably or not, biochar has, as a consequence, been frequently connected to soil management practised by ancient Amerindian populations before the arrival of Europeans, and to the development of complex civilizations in the Amazon region (Petersen et al, 2001). This proposed association has found widespread support through the appealing notion of indigenous wisdom rediscovered. Irrespective of such assumptions, fundamental scientific research of Terra Preta has also yielded important basic information on the functioning of soils, in general, and on the effects of biochar, in particular (Lehmann, 2009).

Second, over the past five years, unequivocal proof has become available showing that biochar is not only more stable than any other amendment to soil (see Chapter 11), and that it increases nutrient availability beyond a fertilizer effect (see Chapter 5; Lehmann, 2009), but that these basic properties of stability and capacity to hold nutrients are fundamentally more effective than those of other organic matter in soil. This means that biochar is not merely another type of compost or manure that improves soil properties, but is much more efficient at enhancing soil quality than any other organic soil amendment. And this ability is rooted in specific chemical and physical properties, such as the high charge density (Liang et al, 2006), that result in much greater nutrient retention (Lehmann et al, 2003b), and its particulate nature (Skjemstad et al, 1996; Lehmann et al, 2005) in combination with a specific chemical structure (Baldock and Smernik, 2002) that provides much greater resistance to microbial decay than other soil organic matter (Shindo, 1991; Cheng et al, 2008). These and similar investigations have helped to make a convincing case for biochar as a significant tool for environmental management. They have provided the break-through that has brought already existing – yet either specialized or regionally limited – biochar applications and isolated research efforts to a new level. This book is a testament to these expanding activities and their results to date.

The big picture

Four complementary and often synergistic objectives may motivate biochar applications for environmental management: soil improvement (for improved productivity as well as reduced pollution); waste management; climate change mitigation; and energy production (see Figure 1.3), which individually or in combination must have either a social or a financial benefit or both. As a result, very different biochar systems emerge on different scales (see Chapter 9). These systems may require different production systems that do or do not produce energy in addition to biochar, and range from small household units to large bioenergy power plants (see Chapter 8). The following sections provide a brief introduction into the broad areas that motivate implementation of biochar, leading to more detailed information presented in the individual chapters throughout this book.

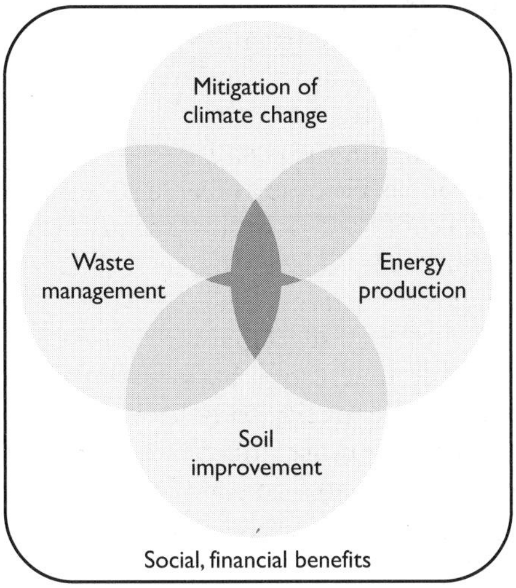

Biochar as a soil amendment

Soil improvement is not a luxury but a necessity in many regions of the world. Lack of food security is especially common in sub-Saharan Africa and South Asia, with malnutrition in 32 and 22 per cent of the total population, respectively (FAO, 2006). While malnutrition decreased in many countries worldwide from 1990–1992 to 2001–2003, many nations in Asia, Africa or Latin America have seen increases (FAO, 2006). The 'Green Revolution' initiated by Nobel Laureate Norman Borlaug at the International Centre for Maize and Wheat Improvement (CIMMYT) in Mexico during the 1940s had great success in increasing agricultural productivity in Latin America and Asia. These successes were mainly based on better agricultural technology, such as improved crop varieties, irrigation, and input of fertilizers and pesticides. Sustainable soil

Figure 1.3 *Motivation for applying biochar technology*

Source: Johannes Lehmann

management has only recently been demanded to create a 'Doubly Green Revolution' that includes conservation technologies (Tilman, 1998; Conway, 1999). Biochar provides great opportunities to turn the Green Revolution into sustainable agro-ecosystem practice. Good returns on ever more expensive inputs such as fertilizers rely on appropriate levels of soil organic matter, which can be secured by biochar soil management for the long term (Kimetu et al, 2008; Steiner et al, 2007).

Specifically in Africa, the Green Revolution has not had sufficient success (Evenson and Gollin, 2003), to a significant extent due to high costs of agrochemicals (Sanchez, 2002), among other reasons (Evenson and Gollin, 2003). Biochar provides a unique opportunity to improve soil fertility and nutrient-use efficiency using locally available and renewable materials in a sustainable way. Adoption of biochar management does not require new resources, but makes more efficient and more environmentally conscious use of existing resources. Farmers in resource-constrained agro-ecosystems are able to convert organic residues and biomass fuels into biochar without compromising energy yield while delivering rapid return on investment (see Chapter 9).

In both industrialized and developing countries, soil loss and degradation is occurring at unprecedented rates (Stocking, 2003; IAASTD, 2008), with profound consequences for soil ecosystem properties (Matson et al, 1997). In many regions, loss in soil productivity occurs despite intensive use of agrochemicals, concurrent with adverse environmental impact on soil and water resources (Foley et al, 2005; Robertson and Swinton, 2005). Biochar is able to play a major role in expanding options for sustainable soil management by improving upon existing best management practices, not only to improve soil productivity (see Chapters 5 and 12), but also to decrease environmental impact on soil and water resources (see Chapters 15 and 16). Biochar should therefore not be seen as an alternative to existing soil management, but as a valuable addition that facilitates the development of sustainable land use: creating a truly green 'Biochar Revolution'.

Biochar to manage wastes

Managing animal and crop wastes from agriculture poses a significant environmental burden that leads to pollution of ground and surface waters (Carpenter et al, 1998; Matteson and Jenkins, 2007). These wastes as well as other by-products are usable resources for pyrolysis bioenergy (Bridgwater et al, 1999; Bridgwater, 2003). Not only can energy be obtained in the process of charring, but the volume and especially weight of the waste material is significantly reduced (see Chapter 8), which is an important aspect, for example, in managing livestock wastes (Cantrell et al, 2007). Similar opportunities exist for green urban wastes or certain clean industrial wastes such as those from paper mills (see Chapter 9; Demirbas, 2002). At times, many of these waste or organic by-products offer economic opportunities, with a significant reliable source of feedstock generated at a single point location (Matteson and Jenkins, 2007). Costs and revenues associated with accepting wastes and by-products are, however, subject to market development and are difficult to predict. In addition, appropriate management of organic wastes can help in the mitigation of climate change indirectly by:

- decreasing methane emissions from landfill;
- reducing industrial energy use and emissions due to recycling and waste reduction;
- recovering energy from waste;

- enhancing C sequestration in forests due to decreased demand for virgin paper; and
- decreasing energy used in long-distance transport of waste (Ackerman, 2000).

Strict quality controls have to be applied for biochar, particularly for those produced from waste, but also from other feedstocks. Pathogens that may pose challenges to direct soil application of animal manures (Bicudo and Goyal, 2003) or sewage sludge (Westrell et al, 2004) are removed by pyrolysis, which typically operates above 350°C and is thus a valuable alternative to direct soil application. Contents of heavy metals can be a concern in sewage sludge and some specific industrial wastes, and should be avoided. However, biochar applications are, in contrast to manure or compost applications, not primarily a fertilizer, which has to be applied annually. Due to the longevity of biochar in soil, accumulation of heavy metals by repeated and regular applications over long periods of time that can occur for other soil additions may not occur with biochar.

Biochar to produce energy

Capturing energy during biochar production and, conversely, using the biochar generated during pyrolysis bioenergy production as a soil amendment is mutually beneficial for securing the production base for generating the biomass (Lehmann, 2007a), as well as for reducing overall emissions (see Chapter 18; Gaunt and Lehmann, 2008). Adding biochar to soil instead of using it as a fuel does, indeed, reduce the energy efficiency of pyrolysis bioenergy production; however, the emission reductions associated with biochar additions to soil appear to be greater than the fossil fuel offset in its use as fuel (Gaunt and Lehmann, 2008). A biochar vision is therefore especially effective in offering environmental solutions, rather than solely producing energy.

This appears to be an appropriate approach for bioenergy as a whole. In fact, bioenergy, in general, and pyrolysis, in particular, may contribute significantly to securing a future supply of green energy. However, it will, most likely, not be able to solve the energy crises and satisfy rising global demand for energy on its own. For example, Kim and Dale (2004) estimated the global potential to produce ethanol from crop waste to offset 32 per cent of gasoline consumption at the time of the study. This potential will most likely never be achieved. An assessment of the global potential of bioenergy from forestry yielded a theoretical surplus supply of 71EJ in addition to other wood needs for 2050 (Smeets and Faaij, 2006), in comparison to a worldwide energy consumption of 489EJ in 2005 (EIA, 2007). If economical and ecological constraints were applied, the projection for available wood significantly decreases (Smeets and Faaij, 2006). However, even a fraction of the global potential will be an important contribution to an overall energy solution. On its own, however, it will probably not satisfy future global energy demand.

In regions that rely on biomass energy, as is the case for most of rural Africa as well as large areas in Asia and Latin America, pyrolysis bioenergy provides opportunities for more efficient energy production than wood burning (Demirbas, 2004b). It also widens the options for the types of biomass that can be used for generating energy, going beyond wood to include, for example, crop residues. A main benefit may be that pyrolysis offers clean heat, which is needed to develop cooking technology with lower indoor pollution by smoke (Bhattacharya and Abdul Salam, 2002) than is typically generated during the burning of biomass (Bailis et al, 2005) (see Chapter 20).

Biochar to mitigate climate change

Adding biochar to soils has been described as a means of sequestering atmospheric carbon dioxide (CO_2) (Lehmann et al, 2006). For this to represent true sequestration, two requirements have to be met. First, plants have to be grown at the same rate as they are being charred because the actual step from atmospheric CO_2 to an organic C form is delivered by photosynthesis in plants. Yet, plant biomass that is formed on an annual basis typically decomposes rapidly. This decomposition releases the CO_2 that was fixed by the plants back to the atmosphere. In contrast, transforming this biomass into biochar that decomposes much more slowly diverts C from the rapid biological cycle into a much slower biochar cycle (Lehmann, 2007b). Second, the biochar needs to be truly more stable than the biomass from which it was formed. This seems to be the case and is supported by scientific evidence (see Chapter 11).

Several approaches have been taken to provide first estimates of the large-scale potential of biochar sequestration to reduce atmospheric CO_2 (Lehmann et al, 2006; Lehmann, 2007b; Laird, 2008), which will need to be vetted against economic (see Chapters 19 and 20) and ecological constraints and extended to include a full emission balance (see Chapter 18). Such emission balances require a comparison to a baseline scenario, showing what emissions have been reduced by changing to a system that utilizes biochar sequestration. Until more detailed studies based on concrete locations reach the information density required to extrapolate to the global scale, a simple comparison between global C fluxes may need to suffice to demonstrate the potential of biochar sequestration (see Figure 1.4). Almost four times more organic C is stored in the Earth's soils than in atmospheric CO_2. And every 14 years, the entire atmospheric CO_2 has cycled once through the biosphere (see Figure 1.4). Furthermore, the annual

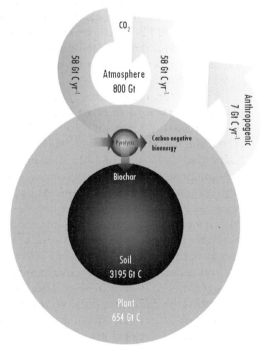

Figure 1.4 *The global carbon cycle of net primary productivity (total net photosynthesis flux from atmosphere into plants) and release to the atmosphere from soil (by microorganisms decomposing organic matter) in comparison to total amounts of carbon in soil, plant and atmosphere, and anthropogenic carbon emissions (sum of fossil fuel emissions and land-use change)*

Source: data from Sabine et al (2004)

uptake of CO_2 by plants is eight times greater than today's anthropogenic CO_2 emissions. This means that large amounts of CO_2 are cycling between atmosphere and plants on an annual basis and most of the world's organic C is already stored in soil. Diverting only a small proportion of this large amount of cycling C into a biochar cycle would make a large difference to atmospheric CO_2 concentrations, but very little difference to the global soil C storage. Diverting merely 1 per cent of annual net plant uptake into biochar would mitigate almost 10 per cent of current anthropogenic C emissions (see Chapter 18). These are important arguments to feed into a policy discussion (see Chapter 22).

Adoption of biochar for environmental management

Adopting biochar-based strategies for energy production, soil management and C sequestration relies primarily on individual companies, municipalities and farmers (see Chapter 21). But national governments and international organizations could play a critical role by facilitating the process of technological development, especially in the initial phases of research and development. Although biochar has great potential to become a critical intervention in addressing key future challenges, it is best seen as an important 'wedge', contributing to an overall portfolio of strategies, as introduced by Pacala and Socolow (2004) for climate change. Such an approach does not apply only to global warming, but also to large-scale efforts to deliver food security to more people worldwide, to produce energy and to improve waste management.

Adoption may occur in multiple sectors to varying extents because biochar systems serve to address different objectives (see Figure 1.3) and operate on different scales, and can therefore be very different from each other (see Chapter 9).

Concerns over using biomass resources that would otherwise fulfil ecosystem services or human needs have to be taken into full consideration. Possible conflicts of producing energy and biochar versus food as a consequence of massive adoption of biochar technologies have to be considered, as discussed for bioenergy in general (Müller et al, 2008). But the minimum residue cover required to protect soil surfaces also needs to be established in conjunction with biochar management of soil organic matter. While biochar will undoubtedly improve soil quality and productivity, some soil cover is required to keep water and wind erosion at a minimum. Therefore, plant residues cannot be entirely removed for biochar production. Other tasks that lie ahead are technological issues, such as refining methods for production, transportation of biochar and its application to soil, while avoiding unacceptable dust formation or health hazards (see Chapters 8 and 12). These are merely examples of questions that need to be addressed in the near future and that are discussed in more detail in individual chapters.

Much information certainly must still be gathered, and several such challenges have to be addressed (Lehmann, 2007a; Laird, 2008). But the tasks ahead are of such magnitudes that they can be solved alongside implementation. In fact, biochar research requires working under conditions of economically feasible enterprises in order to investigate the processes at the scale at which they are to be implemented. Much has already been achieved, and the basic information on which biochar for environmental management rests is available. This book documents that information and serves as the starting point for scaling up biochar management to become a global strategy.

References

Ackerman, F. (2000) 'Waste management and climate change', *Local Environment*, vol 5, pp223–229

Bailis, R., Ezzati, M. and Kammen, D. M. (2005) 'Mortality and greenhouse gas impacts of biomass and petroleum energy futures in Africa', *Science*, vol 308, pp98–103

Baldock, J. A. and Smernik, R. J. (2002) 'Chemical composition and bioavailability of thermally altered *Pinus resinosa* (Red pine) wood', *Organic Geochemistry*, vol 33, pp1093–1109

Bernal, J. D. (1924) 'The structure of graphite', *Proceedings of the Royal Society of London Series A*, vol 106, pp749–773

Bhattacharya, S. C. and Abdul Salam, P. (2002) 'Low greenhouse gas biomass options for cooking in the developing countries', *Biomass and Bioenergy*, vol 22, pp305–317

Bicudo, J. R. and Goyal, S. M. (2003) 'Pathogens and manure management systems: A review', *Environmental Technology*, vol 24, pp115–130

Boehm, H. P. (1994) 'Some aspects of the surface chemistry of carbon blacks and other carbons', *Carbon*, vol 32, pp759–769

Bridgwater, A. V. (2003) 'Renewable fuels and chemicals by thermal processing of biomass', *Chemical Engineering Journal*, vol 91, pp87–102

Bridgwater, A. V., Meier, D. and Radlein, D. (1999) 'An overview of fast pyrolysis of biomass', *Organic Geochemistry*, vol 30, pp1479–1493

Cantrell, K., Ro, K., Mahajan, D., Anjom, M. and Hunt, P. G. (2007) 'Role of thermochemical conversion in livestock waste-to-energy treatments: Obstacles and opportunities', *Industrial and Engineering Chemistry Research*, vol 46, pp8918–8927

Carpenter, S. R., Caraco, N. F., Correll, D. L., Howarth, R. W., Sharpley, A. N. and Smith, V. H. (1998) 'Nonpoint pollution of surface waters with phosphorus and nitrogen', *Ecological Applications*, vol 8, pp559–568

Cheng, C. H., Lehmann, J., Thies, J. E. and Burton, S. D. (2008) 'Stability of black carbon in soils across a climatic gradient', *Journal of Geophysical Research*, vol 113, G02027

Conway, G. (1999) *The Doubly Green Revolution*, Cornell University Press, Ithaca, NY, US

Demirbas, A. (2002) 'Utilization of urban and pulping wastes to produce synthetic fuel via pyrolysis', *Energy Sources A*, vol 24, pp205–213

Demirbas, A. (2004a) 'Determination of calorific values of bio-chars and pyro-oils from pyrolysis of beech trunkbarks', *Journal of Analytical and Applied Pyrolysis*, vol 72, pp215–219

Demirbas, A. (2004b) 'Bioenergy, global warming, and environmental impacts', *Energy Sources*, vol 26, pp225–236

EIA (US Energy Information Administration) (2007) 'International total primary energy consumption and energy intensity', Energy Information Administration, US Government, www.eia.doe.gov/pub/international/iealf/tablee1.xls, accessed 10 August 2008

Evenson, R. R. and Gollin, D. (2003) 'Assessing the impact of the green revolution, 1960 to 2000', *Science*, vol 300, pp758–762

FAO (United Nations Food and Agriculture Organization) (2006) *The State of Food Insecurity in the World*, FAO, Rome, www.fao.org/docrep/009/a0750e/a0750e00.htm, accessed 7 August 2008

Foley, J. A., DeFries, R., Asner, G. P., Barford, C., Bonan, G., Carpenter, S. R., Chapin, F. S., Coe, M. T., Daily, G. C., Gibbs, H. K., Helkowski, J. H., Holloway, T., Howard, E. A., Kucharik, C. J., Monfreda, C., Patz, J. A., Prentice, I. C., Ramankutty, N. and Snyder, P. K. (2005) 'Global consequences of land use', *Science*, vol 309, pp570–574

Franklin, R. E. (1950) 'The interpretation of diffuse X–ray diagrams of carbon', *Acta Crystallography*, vol 3, pp107–121

Franklin, R. E. (1951) 'Crystallite growth in graphitizing and non-graphitizing carbons', *Proceedings of the Royal Society of London, Series A, Mathematical and Physical Sciences*, vol 209, pp196–218

Gaunt, J. and Lehmann, J. (2008) 'Energy balance and emissions associated with biochar sequestration and pyrolysis bioenergy production', *Environmental Science and Technology*, vol 42, pp4152–4158

Glaser, B., Haumaier, L., Guggenberger, G. and
    Zech, W. (2001) 'The Terra Preta phenome-
    non: A model for sustainable agriculture in the
    humid tropics', *Naturwissenschaften*, vol 88,
    pp37–41
Harris, P. (1999) 'On charcoal', *Interdisciplinary
    Science Reviews*, vol 24, pp301–306
IAASTD (2008) *International Assessment of
    Agricultural Knowledge, Science and Technology
    for Development*, www.agassessment.org,
    accessed 8 August 2008
Karaosmanoglu, F., Isigigur-Ergundenler, A. and
    Sever, A. (2000) 'Biochar from the straw-stalk
    of rapeseed plant', *Energy and Fuels*, vol 14,
    pp336–339
Kim, S. and Dale, B. E. (2004) 'Global potential
    bioethanol production from wasted crops and
    crop residues', *Biomass and Bioenergy*, vol 26,
    pp361–375
Kimetu, J., Lehmann, J., Ngoze, S., Mugendi, D.,
    Kinyangi, J., Riha, S., Verchot, L., Recha, J. and
    Pell, A. (2008) 'Reversibility of soil productiv-
    ity decline with organic matter of differing
    quality along a degradation gradient',
    Ecosystems, vol 11, pp726–739
Kishimoto, S. and Sugiura, G. (1980) *Introduction
    to Charcoal Making on Sunday*, Sougou Kagaku
    Shuppan, Tokyo (in Japanese)
Kishimoto, S. and Sugiura, G. (1985) 'Charcoal
    as a soil conditioner', in *Symposium on Forest
    Products Research, International Achievements for
    the Future*, vol 5, pp12–23
Kuhlbusch, T. A. J. and Crutzen, P. J. (1995)
    'Toward a global estimate of black carbon in
    residues of vegetation fires representing a sink
    of atmospheric CO_2 and a source of O_2', *Global
    Biogeochemical Cycles*, vol 9, pp491–501
Laird, D. A. (2008) 'The charcoal vision: A
    win–win–win scenario for simultaneously
    producing bioenergy, permanently sequester-
    ing carbon, while improving soil and water
    quality', *Agronomy Journal*, vol 100,
    pp178–181
Lehmann, J. (2007a) 'Bio-energy in the black',
    Frontiers in Ecology and the Environment, vol 5,
    pp381–387
Lehmann, J. (2007b) 'A handful of carbon',
    Nature, vol 447, pp143–144
Lehmann, J. (2009) 'Terra preta Nova – where to
    from here?', in W. I. Woods, W. G. Teixeira, J.
    Lehmann, C. Steiner and A. WinklerPrins (eds)

Terra preta Nova: A Tribute to Wim Sombroek,
    Springer, Berlin, pp473–486
Lehmann, J., Kern, D. C., Glaser, B. and Woods,
    W. I. (2003a) *Amazonian Dark Earths: Origin,
    Properties, Management*, Kluwer Academic
    Publishers, The Netherlands
Lehmann, J., da Silva, Jr., J. P., Steiner, C., Nehls, T.,
    Zech, W. and Glaser, B. (2003b) 'Nutrient avail-
    ability and leaching in an archaeological
    Anthrosol and a Ferralsol of the Central Amazon
    basin: fertilizer, manure and charcoal amend-
    ments', *Plant and Soil*, vol 249, pp343–357
Lehmann, J., Liang, B., Solomon, D., Lerotic, M.,
    Luizão, F., Kinyangi, F., Schäfer, T., Wirick, S.
    and Jacobsen, C. (2005) 'Near-edge X-ray
    absorption fine structure (NEXAFS) spec-
    troscopy for mapping nano-scale distribution
    of organic carbon forms in soil: Application to
    black carbon particles', *Global Biogeochemical
    Cycles*, vol 19, pGB1013
Lehmann, J., Gaunt, J. and Rondon, M. (2006)
    'Bio-char sequestration in terrestrial ecosys-
    tems – a review', *Mitigation and Adaptation
    Strategies for Global Change*, vol 11, pp403–427
Leinweber, P. and Schulten, H.-R. (1999)
    'Advances in analytical pyrolysis of soil organic
    matter', *Journal of Analytical and Applied
    Pyrolysis*, vol 49, pp359–383
Liang, B., Lehmann, J., Solomon, D., Kinyangi, J.,
    Grossman, J., O'Neill, B., Skjemstad, J. O.,
    Thies, J., Luizão, F. J., Petersen, J. and Neves, E.
    G. (2006) 'Black carbon increases cation
    exchange capacity in soils', *Soil Science Society
    of America Journal*, vol 70, pp1719–1730
Liebig, J. von (1878) *Chemische Briefe*, C. F.
    Winter'sche Verlagshandlung, Leipzig and
    Heidelberg, Germany
Matson, P. A., Parton, W. J., Power, A. G. and
    Swift, M. J. (1997) 'Agricultural intensification
    and ecosystem properties', *Science*, vol 277,
    pp504–509
Matteson, G. C. and Jenkins, B. M. (2007) 'Food
    and processing residues in California: Resource
    assessment and potential for power generation',
    Bioresource Technology, vol 98, pp3098–3105
Miyazaki, Y. (1697) *Nougyou-Zennsho
    [Encyclopedia of Agriculture]*, vol 1, pp91–104,
    in 12-volume *Nihon Nousho Zenshu [Complete
    Works of Ancient Agricultural Books in Japan]*,
    Nousangyoson Bunka Kyokai, Tokyo (in
    Japanese)

Morley, J. (1927) 'Following through with grass seeds', *The National Greenkeeper*, vol 1, no 1, p15

Morley, J. (1929) 'Compost and charcoal', *The National Greenkeeper*, vol 3, no 9, pp8–26

Müller, A., Schmidhuber, J., Hoogeveen, J. and Steduto, P. (2008) 'Some insights in the effect of growing bio-energy demand on global food security and natural resources', *Water Policy*, vol 10, pp83–94

The National Greenkeeper (1933) advertisement for Cleve-Brand Charcoal, *The National Greenkeeper*, vol 7, no 2, 8 February, p10

Ogawa, M. (undated) 'Introduction to the pioneer works of charcoal uses in agriculture, forestry and others in Japan', unpublished manuscript

Pacala, S. and Socolow, R. (2004) 'Stabilization wedges: Solving the climate problem for the next 50 years with current technologies', *Science*, vol 305, pp968–972

Peacocke, C. and Joseph, S. (undated) 'Notes on terminology and technology in thermal conversion prepared for the International Biochar web site', www. Biochar-international.org/images/Terminology_and_Technology_final_vCP_sj.doc, accessed 15 August 2008

Petersen, J. B., Neves, E. and Heckenberger, M. J. (2001) 'Gift from the past: Terra Preta and prehistoric Amerindian occupation in Amazonia', in C. McEwan, C. Barreto and E. Neves (eds) *Unknown Amazonia*, British Museum Press, London, UK, pp86–105

Retan, G. A. (1915) 'Charcoal as a means of solving some nursery problems', *Forestry Quarterly*, vol 13, pp25–30

Robertson, G. P. and Swinton, S. M. (2005) 'Reconciling agricultural productivity and environmental integrity: A grand challenge for agriculture', *Frontiers in Ecology and the Environment*, vol 3, pp38–46

Sabine, C. L., Heimann, M., Artaxo, P., Bakker, D. C. E., Chen, C. T. A., Field, C. B., Gruber, N., Quéré, C. le, Prinn, R. G., Richey, J. E., Lankao, P. R., Sathaye, J. A. and Valentini, R. (2004) 'Current status and past trends of the global carbon cycle', in C. B. Field and M. R. Raupach (eds) *SCOPE 62, The Global Carbon Cycle: Integrating Humans, Climate, and the Natural World*, Island Press, Washington, DC, US, pp17–44

Sanchez, P. A. (2002) 'Soil fertility and hunger in Africa', *Science*, vol 295, pp2019–2020

Santiago, A. and Santiago, L. (1989) 'Charcoal chips as a practical substrate for container horticulture in the humid tropics', *Acta Horticulturae*, vol 238, pp141–147

Schmidt, M. W. I. and Noack, A. G. (2000) 'Black carbon in soils and sediments: Analysis, distribution, implications, and current challenges', *Global Biogeochemical Cycles*, vol 14, pp777–794

Shindo, H. (1991) 'Elementary composition, humus composition, and decomposition in soil of charred grassland plants', *Soil Science and Plant Nutrition*, vol 37, pp651–657

Skjemstad, J. O., Clarke, P., Taylor, J. A., Oades, J. M. and McClure, S. G. (1996) 'The chemistry and nature of protected carbon in soil', *Australian Journal of Soil Research*, vol 34, pp251–271

Smeets, E. M. W. and Faaij, A. P. C (2006) 'Bioenergy potentials from forestry in 2050', *Climatic Change*, vol 81, pp353–390

Steiner, C., Teixeira, W. G., Lehmann, J., Nehls, T., Macedo, J. L. V., Blum, W. E. H. and Zech, W. (2007) 'Long term effects of manure, charcoal and mineral fertilization on crop production and fertility on a highly weathered Central Amazonian upland soil', *Plant and Soil*, vol 291, pp275–290

Stocking, M. A. (2003) 'Tropical soils and food security: The next 50 years', *Science*, vol 302, pp1356–1359

Tilman, D. (1998) 'The greening of the green revolution', *Nature*, vol 396, pp211–212

Trimble, W. H. (1851) 'On charring wood', *Plough, the Loom and the Anvil*, vol 3, pp513–516

Tryon, E. H. (1948) 'Effect of charcoal on certain physical, chemical, and biological properties of forest soils', *Ecological Monographs*, vol 18, pp81–115

Westrell, T., Schönning, C., Stenström, T. A. and Ashbolt, N. J. (2004) 'QMRA (quantitative microbial risk assessment) and HACCP (hazard analysis and critical control points) for management of pathogens in wastewater and sewage sludge treatment and reuse', *Water Science and Technology*, vol 2, pp23–30

Young, A. (1804) *The Farmer's Calendar*, Richard Philips, London, UK

2

Physical Properties of Biochar

Adriana Downie, Alan Crosky and Paul Munroe

Introduction

The physical properties of biochars contribute to their function as a tool for environmental management. Their physical characteristics can be both directly and indirectly related to the way in which they affect soil systems. Soils each have their own distinct physical properties depending upon the nature of mineral and organic matter, their relative amounts and the way in which minerals and organic matter are associated (Brady and Weil, 2008). When biochar is present in the soil mixture, its contribution to the physical nature of the system may be significant, influencing depth, texture, structure, porosity and consistency through changing the bulk surface area, pore-size distribution, particle-size distribution, density and packing. Biochar's effect on soil physical properties may then have a direct impact upon plant growth because the penetration depth and availability of air and water within the root zone is determined largely by the physical make-up of soil horizons. The presence of biochar will, by affecting these physical characteristics, directly affect the soil's response to water, its aggregation, workability during soil preparation, swelling–shrinking dynamics and permeability, as well as its capacity to retain cations and its response to ambient temperature changes. In addition, indirectly, many chemical and biological aspects of soil fertility can be inferred from physical properties, such as the physical presentation of sites for chemical reactions and the provision of protective habitats for soil microbes (Brady and Weil, 2008).

This chapter focuses on the physical (structural) characteristics of freshly made biochars, relating how their qualities are influenced by both the original organic material and the processing conditions under which the biochar is made. Where possible, these physical characterizations are discussed in the context of soil systems.

Biochars: Old and new

Two approaches that one could take in examining biochars in soils include the study of biochars that have been anthropogenically or naturally incorporated within soil systems and the study of biochar made from known feed material under known conditions. Both approaches have their advantages and challenges and complement one another in developing an understanding of how the physical nature of biochars influences soil systems over time. The Black Carbon Steering Committee, for example, has developed reference materials, including wood and grass biochar produced under standardized atmospheric conditions in a pilot-scale pyrolysis oven that are intended to represent natural samples (created by forest fires) for the purpose of cross-calibration of analysis techniques (Hammes et al, 2007). As the science advances and experimental research continues, hopefully results from the two approaches will align and ancient biochar-amended soils can be more thoroughly understood to the advantage of modern agriculture.

Relevance of extended literature

There are a limited number of peer-reviewed research papers directly presenting data on the physical characterization of biochars. Some creativity, therefore, has to be applied in literature reviews, with insightful data available from papers discussing chars made for gunpowder (Gray et al, 1985) as one example. The majority of the work on pyrolysed biomass carbons (C) has been done in the interest of developing more effective activated carbons. From a physical perspective, activated carbons are black C with both high internal surface area and microporosity, and are widely used as adsorbents in separation and purification processes for gases, liquids and colloidal solids. They also often serve as catalysts and catalyst supports. Activated carbon, however, is an expensive commodity and it is unlikely that land managers will ever afford its application to soil. Activated carbons are made from char precursors, which are analogous to biochars – hence, the literature on activated carbons is often relevant to the study of biochars. The char precursors used for making activated carbon have been characterized by several research groups (Pastor-Villegas et al, 1993; Lua et al, 2004), including a range of biomass sources such as agriculture and forest residues. These precursor products are likely to be comparable to the biochars used in anthropogenically amended soils. However, some physical activation probably occurred in traditional kilns due to steam and CO_2 evolving from wet biomass feedstocks, along with some gasification due to partial oxidation with the ingress of air.

There are some characterization studies available that have endeavoured to produce synthetic chars that replicate chars produced in natural systems due to the occurrence of fire (Brown et al, 2006). However, the physical characterization of biochars has generally been performed on samples produced in reactors replicating commercial processes, which have faster heating rates and shorter residence times than traditional methods that may have been used by pre-Columbian Indians, amongst others, to produce biochar. Some characterization work has been done on traditionally made wood charcoals (see Pastor-Villegas et al, 2006); however, the reporting of these methods for biomass residues other than wood is rare. The large-scale economic manufacture of biochar will probably be carried out in modern engineered systems due to the environmental, health and safety issues associated with traditional manufacturing methods. As a result, the study of biochars made under the faster reaction times and controlled conditions of modern processing will probably be relevant for an increasing number of biochar systems (see Chapter 9) as the science moves forward.

Another consideration is that the majority of characterization work has been performed on biochars made from biomass with high C contents and low inorganic contents (ash) in order to meet the demands of the highly specified activated carbon markets. Biochar also includes products made from high-ash (inorganic) biomass feedstocks. To date, the body of physical characterization work on these types of biochars is limited but growing.

Caution on comparing data

When reviewing the literature regarding the physical characterization of biochar, care should be taken not only because experimental conditions are highly variable, but also because they are not always reported in sufficient detail. This applies to the conditions under which the samples were prepared and the conditions under which they are analysed. For example, a commonly used physical analysis technique for determining surface areas of biochars is gas sorptometry. Adsorption experimentation is only as good as the interpretation of the results and differ-

ent methods often yield very different results. Therefore, care should be taken to only compare literature values obtained by the same method. It is known that, for microporous solids, a value of surface area does not always describe a unique property of the material but, rather, depends upon how the adsorption isotherm is determined and interpreted (Marsh, 1987). Critical review of the techniques used is beyond the scope of this chapter; however, further discussion of the issues can be found in Marsh (1987), Macias-Garcia et al (2004) and many others.

Origin of biochar structure

The physical characteristics of biochar depend not only upon the starting organic material (biomass), but also upon the carbonization or pyrolysis system by which they are made (including the pre- and post-handling of the biomass and biochar). The degree of alteration of the original structures of the biomass, through microstructural rearrangement, attrition during processing, and the formation of cracks all depend upon the processing conditions to which they are exposed.

Since biochar is a term used to refer to the high-C solid formed as the result of the

pyrolysis of organic matter, the material can have originated from a diverse range of biomass materials. The original structure of most types of materials is imprinted on the biochar product (Laine et al, 1991; Wildman and Derbyshire, 1991) and, thus, has an overwhelming influence on its final physical and structural characteristics. During pyrolysis, mass is lost (mostly in the form of volatile organics) and a disproportional amount of shrinkage or volume reduction occurs. Hence, during thermal conversion, the mineral and C skeleton formed retains the rudimentary porosity and structure of the original material. The residual cellular structures of botanical origin that are present and identifiable in biochars from woods and coals of all ranks contribute the majority of the macroporosity present (Wildman and Derbyshire, 1991). Confirming this, microscopy analysis of physically activated carbon has illustrated the presence of aligned honeycomb-like groups of pores on the order of 10μm in diameter, most likely the carbonaceous skeleton from the biological capillary structure of the raw material (Laine et al, 1991). These large-sized pores serve as a feeder to lower-dimension pores (i.e. meso- and micro-pores) (Fukuyama et al, 2001; Martínez et al, 2006; Zabaniotou et al, 2008).

The chemical composition of the biomass feedstock has a direct impact upon the physical nature of the biochar produced. At temperatures above 120°C, organic materials begin to undergo some thermal decomposition, losing chemically bound moisture. Hemicelluloses are degraded at 200°C to 260°C, cellulose at 240°C to 350°C, and lignin at 280°C to 500°C (Sjöström, 1993). Therefore, the proportions of these components will influence the degree of reactivity and, hence, the degree to which the physical structure is modified during processing. The proportion of inorganic components (ash) also has implications for physical structure. Some processing conditions result in ash fusion or sintering, which can be the most dramatic change within the physical and structural composition of biochar.

Operating parameters during the pyrolysis process that influence the resultant physical properties of biochar of any given biomass feedstock include heating rate, highest treatment temperature (HTT), pressure, reaction residence time, reaction vessel (orientation, dimensions, stirring regime, catalysts, etc.), pre-treatment (drying, comminution, chemical activation, etc.), the flow rate of ancillary inputs (e.g. nitrogen, carbon dioxide, air, steam, etc.), and post-treatment (crushing, sieving, activation, etc.).

Although all of these parameters contribute to the final biochar structure, the pyrolysis HTT is expected to be the most important of the factors studied because the fundamental physical changes (i.e. the release of volatiles, the formation of intermediate melts and the volatilization of the intermediate melts) are all temperature dependent. The temperature ranges, however, under which these stages occur vary with feedstock. Heating rates and pressures are expected to have the second greatest influence since they affect the physical mass transfer of volatiles evolving at the given temperature from the reacting particles (Antal and Grønli, 2003; Biagini and Tognotti, 2003; Lua et al, 2004; Boateng, 2007).

Lua et al (2004) evaluate the relative importance of temperature, hold time, nitrogen (N_2) flow rate and heating rate during pyrolysis by assessing the standard deviations and coefficients of variation of several physical parameters (e.g. Brunauer, Emmett and Teller equation (BET) surface area, and micropore surface area and yield). They found the pyrolysis temperature to have the most significant effect, followed by pyrolysis heating rate. The N_2 flow rate and the hold (residence) time show the least effects. It should be noted that these results are only directly relevant for their given feedstock and process conditions.

On the other hand, BET surface areas of olive kernel biochars measured by Zabaniotou et al (2008) increased with increasing mass loss (burn-off), regardless of the activation temperature. This indicates that with systems that include some higher oxidative gasification conditions, the burn-off of the fixed C has the most significant effect on increasing the surface area. Indeed, the surface area depends largely upon the C mass removed during processing, creating pores in the material (Zabaniotou et al, 2008).

An additional mechanism producing the structural complexity of biochars is the occurrence of cracking. Biochar is typically laced with macro-cracks, which can be related to both feedstock properties and the rate at which carbonization is carried out (Byrne and Nagle, 1997). Wood biochar is generally broken and cracked due to shrinkage stresses developed because the surface of the material decomposes faster than its interior. Brown et al (2006) concluded that high-temperature (1000°C) surface area is controlled primarily by low-temperature (<450°C) cracking and high-temperature microstructural rearrangement. Through experimentation, they found the cracks formed to be too large and too numerous to be sealed off by microstructural rearrangement at higher carbonization temperatures (Brown et al, 2006). Byrne and Nagle (1997) have developed preparation methods for wood feedstocks based on its fundamental characteristics, such as density and strength, under which C monoliths (biochars with no cracks) can be produced for advanced applications. The importance of biochar structure for macro-scale porosity is discussed later in this chapter.

Influence of molecular structure on biochar morphology

The fundamental molecular structure of biochar creates both its surface area and porosity. Carbonaceous solid materials such as coals, charcoals, cokes, etc. contain crystalline particles (crystallites) in the order of nanometres in diameter, composed of graphite-like layers arranged turbostratically (layers are not aligned) (Warren 1941; Biscoe and Warren, 1942). The biochar structure, determined by X-ray diffraction, is essentially amorphous in nature, but contains some local crystalline structure (Qadeer et al, 1994) of highly conjugated aromatic compounds. Crystalline areas can be visualized as stacks of flat aromatic (graphene) sheets cross-linked in a random manner (Bansal et al, 1988). Similar to graphite, they are good conductors in spite of their small dimensions (Carmona and Delhaes, 1978). Thus, the microcrystallites are often referred to as the conducting phase. The other non-conducting components that complete the biochar C matrix are the aromatic-aliphatic organic compounds of complex structure (including residual volatiles), and the mineral compounds (inorganic ash) (Emmerich et al, 1987). This is complemented with the voids, formed as pores (macro-, meso- and micropores), cracks and morphologies of cellular biomass origin.

Pyrolysis processing of biomass enlarges the crystallites and makes them more ordered. This effect increases with HTT. Lua et al (2004) demonstrated, for example, that increasing the pyrolysis temperature from 250°C to 500°C increases the BET surface area due to the increasing evolution of volatiles from pistachio-nut shells, resulting in enhanced pore development in biochars. For turbostratic arrangements, the successive layer planes are disposed approximately parallel and equidistant, but rotated more or less randomly with respect to each other (see inset B, Figure 2.1) (Emmerich et al, 1987). The spacing between the planes of turbostratic regions of biochar is larger than that observed in graphite (Emmerich et al, 1987; Laine and Yunes, 1992). In spite of the two-dimensional long-range order in the directions of the graphite-like layers, materials with turbostratic structure are called non-graphitic C because there is no measurable crystallographic order in the third direction (insets B and C, Figure 2.1) (Emmerich and Luengo, 1996). Rosalind Franklin first demonstrated that some varieties of non-graphitic C are converted to graphitic C during pyrolysis, presenting crys-

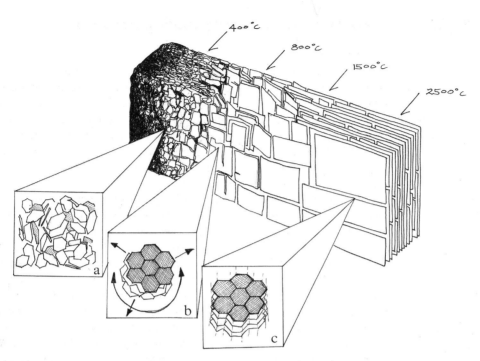

Figure 2.1 *Ideal biochar structure development with highest treatment temperature (HTT): (a) increased proportion of aromatic C, highly disordered in amorphous mass; (b) growing sheets of conjugated aromatic carbon, turbostratically arranged; (c) structure becomes graphitic with order in the third dimension*

Source: chapter authors

tallographic order in the third direction (Franklin, 1951). The pyrolysis of all biomass C will finally yield graphite when heated to 3500°C; however, some feedstocks graphitize at HTTs of less than 2000°C (Setton et al, 2002).

The surface of non-graphitized C, such as wood biochars, consists of both the faces and edges of ordered sheets (Boehm, 1994, 2002). The turbostratic linkage of these crystallites leaves random interstices (pores of various sizes). A further possible cause of micropores is from voids (holes) within hexagonal planes (Bourke et al, 2007). Heteroatoms, in particular oxygen (O), are predominantly located on the edges of ordered sheets as components of various functional groups (Boehm, 1994, 2002). The interplanar distance of graphite (0.335nm) is probably not achieved under typical pyrolysis conditions (<1000°C) due to the formation of O functional groups at the sheet edges, which through steric or electronic effects prevent the close packing of the sheets (Laine and Yunes, 1992).

Pores, of whatever origin, may become filled with tars (condensed volatiles) and other amorphous decomposition products, which may partially block the microporosity created (Bansal et al, 1988). The tars created from thermal biomass C decomposition impede the continuity of pores at low temperatures and these pores become increasingly accessible as the temperatures increase and tar components are volatilized (Pulido-Novicio et al, 2001). Mineral matter may also become occluded in the pores or exposed at the surface of the biochar particles.

Loss of structural complexity during pyrolysis

Under certain processing conditions, many research groups have reported drastic loss of structural complexity in biochar products, which is often explained by plastic deformation, melt, fusion or sintering. High heating rates, increased pressure, high HTT, high ash contents (or low ash melting points) and long retention times (in combination with high temperatures) have all been held accountable for the loss of surface area and porosity in biochar products. Of the numerous examples in the literature some typical results have been selected to demonstrate each pathway.

Rodríguez-Mirasol et al (1993) investigated the carbonization of eucalyptus kraft lignin at different temperatures and characterized the structure of the microporous biochar product. They found that partial fusion and swelling in the carbonization stage was related to the ash content (inorganic matter) in the starting material (Rodríguez-Mirasol et al, 1993). Therefore, they developed a new pre-treatment method to remove the inorganic matter by washing with diluted acidic solutions prior to carbonization in order to prevent this loss of structural complexity. High ash content is often a significant contributing factor to loss of structure. However, even in very low ash materials, such as the hazelnut shell (Aygun et al, 2003), some thermoplastic properties can be exhibited.

The lack of structure in biochars made at high heating rates has been explained by the melting of the cell structure and by plastic transformations (Biagini and Tognotti, 2003; Boateng, 2007). Cetin et al (2004) reported that at low heating rates ($20°C$ sec^{-1}), the natural porosity of pine sawdust allows a volatile release with the occurrence of no major morphological changes. However, at high heating rates ($500°C$ sec^{-1}), the cell structure is destroyed by devolatilization (Cetin et al, 2004). Biagini and Tognotti (2003) recorded the same phenomenon in their experimentation and noted the re-solidification of the solid structure and formation of more compact biochar particles (Biagini et al, 2003). They also stated that melting and swelling are more pronounced for biomass species that contain higher levels of volatile matter.

High HTT, coinciding with the ash melting points of the various biomass feedstocks, also causes decreases in structural complexity. For a pistachio-nut feedstock, Lua et al (2004) found that increasing HTT from $500°C$ to $800°C$ progressively decreased the BET surface area. They attributed this to the decomposition and softening of some volatile fractions to form an intermediate melt in the biochar structure (Lua et al, 2004). Brown et al (2006) reported similar findings with biochars made from pine. At heating rates of $30°C$ hr^{-1} and $200°C$ hr^{-1}, surface areas were found to be markedly lower at a HTT of $1000°C$ compared with those observed at lower final temperatures (Brown et al, 2006).

Increasing the reaction retention time has also been demonstrated to cause deformation in the physical structure; however, this may be the result of heat transfer rates being too slow for the solid to reach a high HTT. Guo and Lua (1998) found that at $900°C$, the high surface area of oil palm stone biochar deteriorated with increasing reaction retention time. They attributed this to both the sintering effect, followed by a shrinkage of the biochar, and realignment of the biochar structure, which resulted in reduced pores. With their reactor configuration, they found that maximum surface areas were obtained when oil palm stones were pyrolysed at $800°C$ with a retention time of three hours (Guo and Lua, 1998).

Work by Lewis (2000) with redwood has shown, however, that the pores do not collapse as suggested by Guo and Lua (1998). Lewis

(2000) provides evidence against such collapse by showing that the pores can be reopened by a CO_2 activation process in a manner that allows N_2-accessible surface area to increase from $2m^2 g^{-1}$ to $540m^2 g^{-1}$. This suggests that the pores are still present (not collapsed) and that they are only closed off at higher temperatures (Lewis, 2000).

The fusion of multiple particles, which did not occur under atmospheric conditions, has also been reported at pressures of 10bar to 20bar (Cetin et al, 2004). Cetin et al (2004) found that at these pressures, eucalyptus sawdust particles melt and fuse, losing their own distinctions. Similar results were obtained at atmospheric pressures for the fast heating rate of ~500°C min^{-1}. A number of particles fused together can form a hollow and smooth-surfaced particle (Cetin et al, 2004).

Industrial processes for altering the physical structure of biochar

Processes for increasing surface areas and porosity have been frequently investigated, driven by the many commercial applications of activated carbons that require large sorptive capacities. Although, as already highlighted, process conditions such as HTT, heating rate, etc. influence biochar's physical structure, commercially viable internal surface areas are almost always generated in high C-containing biochar precursors through physical or chemical activation.

Physical activation, which is carried out most frequently in industry, is obtained when the initial pyrolysis reactions, occurring in an inert atmosphere at moderate temperatures (400°C to 800°C), are complemented by a second stage in which the resulting biochars are subjected to a partial gasification at a higher temperature (usually >900°C) with oxidizing gases such as steam, CO_2, air or a mixture of these. This produces final products with well-developed and accessible internal pores (Bansal et al, 1988).

The activation of biochar with CO_2 involves a C–CO_2 reaction (Rodríguez-Reinoso and Molina-Sabio, 1992). This leads to the removal of C atoms or burn-off, in this way contributing to the development of a porous structure. According to Rodríguez-Reinoso et al (1992), CO_2 can open closed pores as well as widen existing pores by the activation, increasing the accessibility of the small pores to the molecules of an adsorbate. Both the surface area and the nature of porosity are significantly affected by the conditions of CO_2 activation, the extent of which depends upon the nature of the precursors (Zhang et al, 2004). Steam is suggested to play a double role: it promotes both the release of volatiles with partial devolatilization and enhances crystalline C formation (Alaya et al, 2000).

The physical and adsorptive properties of biochars depend upon activation time and quantity of steam used for activation. BET surface areas of activated olive kernel carbons were found to be increasing with activation time and temperature from a minimum value of $1339m^2 g^{-1}$ at one hour and 800°C to a maximum of $3049m^2 g^{-1}$ at four hours and 900°C (Stavropoulos, 2005). Zhang et al (2004) confirmed these trends for biochars made from oak, maize hulls and maize stover residues. They found BET surface areas of all activated carbons obtained at 700°C were lower than those obtained at 800°C (Zhang et al, 2004). With physical activation for one to two hours, surface areas were increased with activation time (Zhang et al, 2004). This expansion in surface area with increased activation time can also be explained by the increasing burn-off (mass loss) (Zabaniotou et al, 2008).

Chemical activation entails the addition of materials such as zinc salts or phosphoric acid to the C precursors (H_3PO_4, $ZnCl_2$ and alkali metal hydroxides). KOH (and NaOH) has been used for preparing activated carbons with unusually high surface areas called 'super active' carbons by some authors (Rouquerol et al, 1999). During activation, potassium (K) is intercalated and forces apart the lamellae of the crystallites that form the C structure. After washing the samples, K is eliminated, leaving free interlayer space that contributes to the porosity of the product (Marsh et al, 1984). Precursor material properties such as microcrystalline structure, reactivity and pore accessibility are shown to affect the results of these treatments. The most suitable raw materials for KOH activation are those having small-sized crystallites, medium reactivity and high accessibility to the internal pore structure (Stavropoulos, 2005).

Chemical activation offers several advantages since it is carried out in a single step, combining carbonization and activation, is performed at lower temperatures and, therefore, results in greater development of porous structure. Chemical activation methods are not, however, as common, possibly due to the possibility of generating secondary environmental pollution during disposal (Zhang et al, 2004).

Reactor type has also been demonstrated to have an influence on the physical surface and porosity of chars. Gonzalez et al (1997) conducted their investigation of CO_2 activation with both vertical and horizontal furnaces and concluded that a horizontal furnace is advantageous for micropore development.

Biochars resulting from fast pyrolysis reactors (high heating rates) have different physical properties from those made under slow pyrolysis conditions. The surface areas of switchgrass biochars made under fast pyrolysis conditions were found to be low, typically between $7.7m^2$ g^{-1} and $7.9m^2$ g^{-1} (Boateng, 2007). Further examples that are typical for fast pyrolysis, because of the high heating rates of the rather small particles (less than 1mm), were produced by a fluidized sand-bed reactor operating at approximately 500°C, with inert N_2 as the fluidizing agent (Zhang et al, 2004). Oak, maize hull and maize stover biochars exhibited low surface areas of $92m^2$ g^{-1}, $48m^2$ g^{-1}, and $38m^2$ g^{-1}, and total pore volumes of $0.1458cm^3$ g^{-1}, $0.0581cm^3$ g^{-1} and $0.0538cm^3$ g^{-1}, respectively (Zhang et al, 2004).

Gas pressure during the pyrolysis reactions also has an influence on the structure of the biochar products. For example, biochar particles that were generated at 5bar pyrolysis pressure at a heating rate of 500°C sec^{-1} to 950°C were shown to have larger cavities with thinner cell walls than biochars that were generated at atmospheric pressure. This effect was increased at 20bar (Cetin et al, 2004).

The pyrolysis system, particularly the activation method, has an influence on the physical nature of biochars. The degree of influence that it has, however, depends upon the feedstock used, with different feedstocks producing different results. For example, Pastor-Villegas et al (2006) found that the influence of the carbonization reaction method on the non-micropore structure is not significant when the raw material is eucalyptus wood, while there are considerable differences when the raw material is holm-oak wood (Pastor-Villegas et al, 2006). When studying biochars, it is essential to note the feedstock, preparation conditions and analysis methods used to ensure that meaningful conclusions are drawn which can be compared with that of other studies.

Soil surface areas and biochar

Surface area is a very important soil characteristic as it influences all of the essential functions for fertility, including water, air, nutrient cycling and microbial activity. The limited capacity of sandy soil to store water and plant nutrients is partly related to the relatively small surface area of its soil particles (Troeh and Thompson, 2005). Coarse sands have a very low specific surface of about $0.01m^2\ g^{-1}$, and fine sands about $0.1m^2\ g^{-1}$ (Troeh and Thompson, 2005). Clays have a comparatively large specific surface, ranging from $5m^2\ g^{-1}$ for kaolinite to about $750m^2\ g^{-1}$ for Na-exchanged montmorillonite. Soils containing a large fraction of clay may have high total water-holding capacities but inadequate aeration (Troeh and Thompson, 2005). High organic matter contents have been demonstrated to overcome the problem of too much water held in a clay soil, and also increase the water contents in a sandy soil (Troeh and Thompson, 2005). Indications exist that biochar will similarly change the physical nature of soil, having much of the same benefit of other organic amendments in this regard (Chan et al, 2007). Biochar specific surfaces, being generally higher than sand and comparable to or higher than clay, will therefore cause a net increase in the total soil-specific surface when added as an amendment.

The influence of biochar on microbial populations in soils is presented in Chapter 6. However, it should be noted here that soil microbial biomass commonly increases with increasing clay content under both field and laboratory conditions (Amato and Ladd, 1992; Juma, 1993; Müller and Höper, 2004), and this response is generally attributed to the increased surface area (Juma, 1993). The higher surface areas of finer-textured soils can result in increased total water content and improved physical protection from grazers. Biochar has been experimentally linked to improved soil structure or soil aeration in fine-textured soils (Kolb, 2007).

Biochar nano-porosity

The pore-size distribution of activated carbons has long been recognized as an important factor for industrial application. It is logical that this physical feature of biochars will also be of importance to their behaviour in soil processes. The relationship between total surface area and pore-size distribution is logical. As shown in Figure 2.1, as the HTT increases more structured regular spacing between the planes results. Interplanar distances also decrease with the increased ordering and organization of molecules, all of which result in larger surface areas per volume.

Micropores (known to material scientists as all pores <2nm in diameter) contribute most to the surface area of biochars and are responsible for the high adsorptive capacities for molecules of small dimensions such as gases and common solvents (Rouquerol et al, 1999). It should be noted that soil scientists refer to all pores <200nm in diameter as micro-pores; however, for the purpose of this chapter, the total pore volume of the biochar will be divided into micropores (pores of internal diameter less than 2nm), mesopores (pores of internal width between 2nm and 50nm) and macropores (pores of internal width greater than 50nm) (Rouquerol et al, 1999), as this provides a level of differentiation required to discuss molecular and structural effects. However, the importance

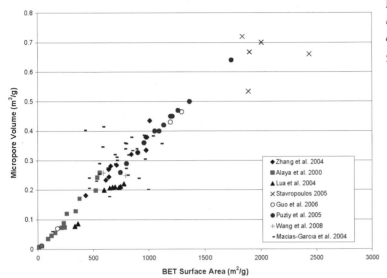

Figure 2.2 *Relationship between biochar surface area and micropore volume*

Source: chapter authors

and range of macroporosity in the context of biochar in soil systems cannot be overemphasized, and will be discussed in detail in a later section.

Figure 2.2 compiles some of the data available in the literature to demonstrate the relationship between micropore volume and total surface area of biochars. This provides evidence that pore sizes distributed in the micropore range make the greatest contribution to total surface area. The development of microporosity with higher temperatures and longer retention times has been demonstrated by several research groups (see plotted examples in Figure 2.3). Elevated temperatures provide the activation energies and longer retentions allow the time for the reactions to reach completion, leading to greater degrees of order in the structures. For example, the ratios of micropore volume to total pore volume of CO_2-activated carbons produced from maize hulls generated at 700°C were lower than those of activated carbons prepared at 800°C (Zhang et al, 2004).

The analysis of gas adsorption isotherms is the typical methodology used for assessing surface areas of C materials. The range of adsorbents, degassing regimes, temperatures, pressures and algorithms used makes comparison of literature values challenging. However, some general trends can be observed through compiling literature values (see Figure 2.3).

The surface area of biochars generally increases with increasing HTT until it reaches the temperature at which deformation occurs, resulting in subsequent decreases in surface area. A typical example is provided by Brown et al (2006), who produced biochar from pine in a laboratory oven purged with N_2 at a range of final temperatures varying from 450°C to 1000°C, and heating rates varying from 30°C hr^{-1} to 1000°C hr^{-1}. Brown et al found that independent of heating rate, maximum surface area, as measured by BET (N_2), was realized at a final temperature of 750°C. At the lowest HTT (i.e. 450°C), all of the surface areas were found to be less than 10m^2 g^{-1}, while those produced at intermediate temperatures of 600°C to 750°C had a surface area of approximately 400m^2 g^{-1} (Brown et al, 2006).

Under some conditions, a high temperature causes micropores to widen because it

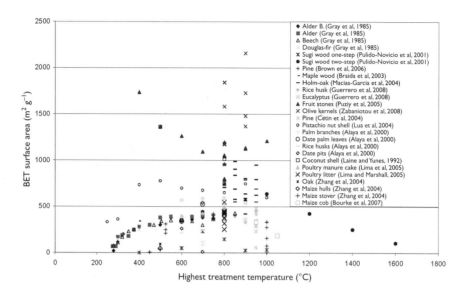

Figure 2.3 *Biochar surface area plotted against highest treatment temperature (HTT)*

Note: different methods of treatment and surface area analysis were used in each study.
Source: chapter authors

destroys the walls between adjacent pores, resulting in the enlargement of pores (Zhang et al, 2004). This leads to a decrease in the fraction of volume found in the micropore range and an increase in the total pore volume. In samples of maize hulls and maize stover, Zhang et al (2004) found microporosity to be appreciably greater after one hour of physical activation than after two hours. They proposed that the rate of pore formation exceeded that of destruction due to pore enlargement and collapse at the earlier stage and vice versa at the later stage (Zhang et al, 2004).

Heating rates also determine the extent of micropore formation. One example was provided by Cetin et al (2004), who found that biochars generated at atmospheric pressure under low heating rates mainly consisted of micropores, whereas those prepared at high heating rates were largely comprised of macropores as a result of melting (Cetin et al, 2004).

Mesopores are also present in biochar materials. These pores are of importance to many liquid–solid adsorption processes. For example, pistachio-nut shells have a mixture of micropores and mesopores, with micropores dominating, indicating that these activated carbons can be used for both gas and liquid adsorption applications (Lua et al, 2004).

Biochar macroporosity

In the past, when biochars and activated carbons were assessed mainly for their role as adsorbents, macropores (>50nm diameter) were considered to be only important as feeder pores for the transport of adsorbate molecules to the meso- and micro-pores

Table 2.1 *Surface areas and volumes of different sizes of biochar pores*

	Surface area $(m^2\,g^{-1})$	Volume $(cm^3\,g^{-1})$
Micropores	750–1360	0.2–0.5
Macropores	51–138	0.6–1.0

Source: Laine et al (1991)

(Wildman and Derbyshire, 1991). However, macro-pores are very relevant to vital soil functions such as aeration and hydrology (Troeh and Thompson, 2005). Macropores are also relevant to the movement of roots through soil and as habitats for a vast variety of soil microbes. Although micropore surface areas are significantly larger than macropore surface areas in biochars, macropore volumes can be larger than micropore volumes (see Table 2.1). It is possible that these broader volumes could result in greater functionality in soils than narrow surface areas.

As anticipated from the regular size and arrangement of plant cells in most biomass from which biochars are derived, the macropore size distribution is composed of discrete groups of pores sizes rather than a continuum (Wildman and Thompson, 1991). The obvious macroporous structure of a wood biochar imaged using a scanning electron microscope (SEM) can be seen in Figure 2.4.

To put this in perspective with typical soil particles, these discrete groups of pore diameters observed in this sample of ~5μm to 10μm, and ~100μm compare to very fine sand or silt particle sizes, and fine sand particle sizes, respectively.

Another consideration is the type of microbial communities that utilize soil pores as a preferred habitat (see Chapter 6). Microbial cells typically range in size from 0.5μm to 5μm, and consist predominantly of bacteria, fungi, actinomycetes and lichens (Lal, 2006). Algae are 2μm to 20μm (Lal, 2006). The macropores present in biochars pictured in Figure 2.4 may therefore provide suitable dimensions for clusters of microorganisms to inhabit. Chapter 6 provides more detail on microbial communities and biochar.

On the scale of soil systems, the macroporosity seen in the SEM image of a poultry litter char (see Figure 2.5), with cavities up to 500μm in the agglomerated particle, is very relevant. However, very few investigations at this scale are presented in the literature. Soil structure is defined in terms of peds, which are arrangements of primary soil particles, and soil porosity is often defined as the openness between these peds (Troeh and Thompson, 2005). The interaction and stacking of heterogenous agglomerated biochar particles and peds in the soil will have a direct impact upon the bulk soil structure.

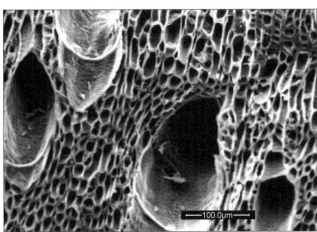

Figure 2.4 *Scanning electron microscope (SEM) image showing macroporosity of a wood-derived biochar produced by 'slow' pyrolysis: The biochar samples were chromium coated and imaged with a beam energy of 20kV on a FEI Quanta 200 environmental scanning electron microscope (ESEM)*

Source: chapter authors

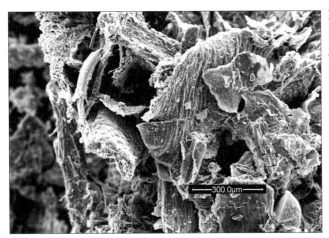

Figure 2.5 *SEM image showing macroporosity in biochar produced from poultry manure using slow pyrolysis*

Source: chapter authors

Particle-size distribution

The particle sizes of the biochar resulting from the pyrolysis of organic material are highly dependent upon the nature of the original material. Due to both shrinkage and attrition during pyrolysis, particle sizes of the organic matter feedstock are likely to be greater than the resultant biochar. In some cases, particles may agglomerate; therefore, increased particle sizes are also found (Cetin et al, 2004). Depending upon the mechanical intensity of the pyrolysis technology employed, a degree of attrition of the biomass particles will occur during processing. This is especially true in the post-handling of the material as the biochar is significantly more friable than the original biomass.

Evidence for the dependency of particle-size distribution of the biochar upon the organic matter feedstock is presented in Figure 2.6. Biochar derived from sawdust and wood chips was prepared with different pre-treatments, producing contrasting particle sizes. The pyrolysis processing, through the BEST Energies continuous slow (5°C min^{-1} to 10°C min^{-1} heating rate) pyrolysis pilot plant, resulted in an increasing proportion of particles in the smaller size distributions for both of the feedstocks, as measured by dry sieving. It can also be seen that as the pyrolysis HTT increased (450°C to 500°C to 700°C), the particle sizes tended to decrease. This may be explained by the decreasing tensile strength of the material as it is more completely reacted, resulting in less resistance to attrition during processing.

Depending upon the technology employed, biomass feedstock is prepared in different ways. The faster the heating rate required, the smaller the feedstock particles need to be to facilitate the heat and mass transfer of the pyrolysis reactions. Fast pyrolysis feedstocks, for example, are pre-processed to a fine dust or powder; therefore, the resultant biochar is very fine. Continuous slow pyrolysis technologies, which employ slower heating rates (~5°C min^{-1} to 30°C min^{-1}), can accommodate larger particles up to several centimetres in dimension. Traditional batch processes can allow weeks for the heat and mass transfer of the process to occur (see Chapter 8) and, hence, receive whole branches and logs.

The investigation by Cetin et al (2004), for example, on the first-step pyrolysis of a two-stage gasification process used biomass fuel particles with sizes between 50µm and 2000µm depending upon the reactor type and techniques used. This small size is

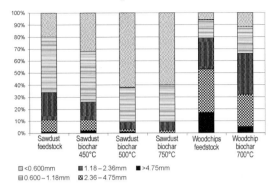

Figure 2.6 *Influence of biomass pre-treatment and HTT on the particle size distribution of different biochars*

Source: chapter authors

required to achieve the high heating rates, ranging from 500°C sec⁻¹ to extremely high heating rates of ($\approx 1 \times 10^{5}$°C sec⁻¹) and short residence times (Cetin et al, 2004).

If larger particles are used, it is possible that the reactions will be limited by the heat transfer into the particles and the mass transfer of volatiles out of the biochar. For example, in a study of the pyrolysis of oil palm stones, it was found that the biochar yields were affected by both the particle size of the stones and the maximum pyrolysis temperature (Shamsuddin and Williams, 1992). Longer retention times would perhaps have overcome the influence of the larger particle sizes.

An increase in linear shrinkage of the particles being pyrolysed can be seen to take place in conjunction with the loss of volatile matter (Emmerich and Luengo, 1996; Freitas et al, 1997). For example, as pyrolysis temperatures increase from 200°C to 1000°C, the linear shrinkage of particles was demonstrated to increase from 0 to 20 per cent for peat biochars (Freitas et al, 1997).

Cetin et al (2004) demonstrated that increasing the pyrolysis pressure (from atmospheric to 5, 10 and 20bars) leads to the formation of larger biochar particles. They accounted for this as swelling, as well as the formation of particle clusters, as a result of melting and subsequent fusion of particles (Cetin et al, 2004).

Biochar density

Two types of density of biochars can be studied: the solid density and the bulk or apparent density. Solid density is the density on a molecular level, related to the degree of packing of the C structure. Bulk density is that of the material consisting of multiple particles and includes the macroporosity within each particle and the inter-particle voids. Often, an increase in solid density is accompanied by a decrease in apparent densities as porosity develops during pyrolysis. The relationship between the two types of densities was demonstrated by Guo and Lua (1998), who reported that apparent densities increased with the development of porosities from 8.3 to 24 per cent at pyrolysis temperatures up to 800°C (Guo and Lua, 1998). However, when the temperature increased to 900°C, the apparent density of the biochar increased and the porosity decreased due to sintering. This inverse relationship between solid and apparent density was also demonstrated by Pastor-Villegas et al (2006) for eucalyptus biochar manufactured in a continuous furnace having both the lowest values of apparent density (measured as both bulk and mercury displacement) and the highest solid density value (measured by helium displacement).

The loss of volatile and condensable compounds from the unorganized phase of the biochars and the concomitant relative increase in the organized phase formed by graphite-like crystallites leads to the increase in solid density (or true density) of the

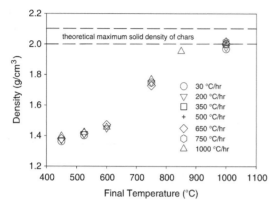

Figure 2.7 *Helium-based solid densities of biochars with HTT*

Source: Brown et al (2006)

biochars compared with their feedstocks (Emmerich et al, 1987). The maximum density of C in biochars has been reported to lie between 2.0g cm^{-3} and 2.1g cm^{-3} based on X-ray measurements (Emmett, 1948). Such values are only slightly below the density of solid graphite of 2.25g cm^{-3}. Most solid densities of biochar, however, are significantly lower than that of graphite because of residual porosity and their turbostratic structure (Oberlin, 2002), with typical values

around 1.5 g cm^{-3} to 1.7g cm^{-3} (Jankowska et al, 1991; Oberlin, 2002). Lower values such as that of a pine wood biochar collected from a natural fire site at 1.47g cm^{-3} (Brown et al, 2006) are also common. Biochars activated to produce microporosity for the adsorption of gases are denser than for those optimized to produce meso- and macro-porosity for the purification of liquids (Pan and van Staden, 1998).

The density of the biochars depends upon the nature of the starting material and the pyrolysis process (Pandolfo et al, 1994). Solid density of biochar increases with increasing process temperature and longer heating residence times, in accordance with the conversion of low-density disordered C to higher-density turbostratic C (Byrne, 1996; Kercher and Nagle, 2002). Lower amounts of volatiles, which have lower molecular weights than fixed C, and lower ash contents result in higher solid density in biochars (Jankowska et al, 1991). However, Brown et al (2006) showed that density is independent of heating rate, and found a simple and direct dependency of density upon final pyrolysis temperature (see Figure 2.7). Thus, they deduced that the He-based solid density may

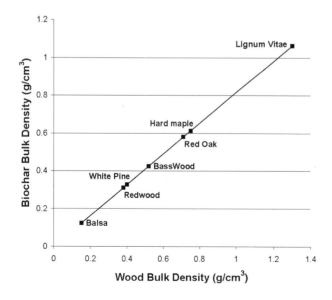

Figure 2.8 *Bulk density of wood biochar, plotted against that of its feedstock*

Note: Biochar bulk density = 0.8176 × wood bulk density. Values are for carbonization in a nitrogen atmosphere at 15°C hr-1 to 900°C.

Source: Byrne and Nagle (1997)

serve as an approximate indicator of the highest temperature experienced by any wood biochar, regardless of the exact thermal history (Brown et al, 2006). This concept may provide a useful tool for characterizing charring conditions in order to understand the production of biochars in archaeological soil such as Terra Preta and possibly provide information about their creation.

Bulk density is also an important physical feature of biochars. Pastor-Villegas et al (2006) found that the bulk densities of biochars made from different types of woods processed in different types of traditional kilns ranged from 0.30 g cm^{-3} to 0.43g cm^{-3}.

Bulk density values given in the literature for activated carbons used for gas adsorption range from 0.40g cm^{-3} to 0.50g cm^{-3}, while for activated carbons used for decolourization, the range is 0.25g cm^{-3} to 0.75g cm^{-3} (Rodríguez-Reinoso, 1997). Byrne and Nagle (1997) established a linear relationship between the bulk densities of wood and biochar made from the same material, which spans a range of species. They found that for wood pyrolysed at a heating rate of 15°C hr^{-1} to a HTT of 900°C, the carbonized wood had 82 per cent of the bulk density of the precursor wood (Byrne and Nagle, 1997).

Mechanical strength

The mechanical strength of biochar is related to its solid density. Therefore, the increased molecular order of pyrolysed biomass gives it a higher mechanical strength than the biomass feedstock from which it was derived. For example, Byrne and Nagle (1997) reported that tulip poplar wood carbonized at a HTT of 1550°C had a 28 per cent increase in strength. Mechanical strength is a characteristic used for defining the quality of

activated carbon as it relates to its ability to withstand wear and tear during use. Agricultural wastes, such as nut shells (almond, hazelnut, macadamia and walnut) and fruit stones (apricot, olive pits, etc.) are of interest as activated carbons because of their high mechanical strength and hardness. These properties can be explained by high lignin and low ash contents (Aygun et al, 2003).

Future research

The physical properties of biochar products affect many of the functional roles that they may play in environmental management applications. The large variation of physical characteristics observed in different biochar products means that some will be more effective than others in certain applications. It is important that the physical characterization of biochars is undertaken before they are experimentally applied to environmental systems, and variations in outcomes may be correlated with these features. Although the

continued examination of the influence of feedstocks and processing conditions on the physical properties of biochars is essential, an important direction for future research is to develop an understanding of how and by what mechanisms these physical characteristics of biochars influence processes in soils. Further work is also required to determine how the physical properties of biochars change over time in soil systems and how these changes influence their function.

References

Alaya, M. N., Girgis, B. S. and Mourad, W. E. (2000) 'Activated carbon from some agricultural wastes under action of one-step steam pyrolysis', *Journal of Porous Materials*, vol 7, pp509–517

Amato, M. and Ladd, J. (1992) 'Decomposition of ^{14}C-labelled glucose and legume material in soils: Properties influencing the accumulation of organic residue and microbial biomass', *Soil Biology and Biochemistry*, vol 24, pp455–464

Antal, M. J. and Grønli, M. (2003) 'The art, science, and technology of charcoal production', *Industrial Engineering and Chemical Research*, vol 42, pp1619–1640

Aygun, A., Yenisoy-Karakas, S. and Duman, I. (2003) 'Production of granular activated carbon from fruit stones and nutshells and evaluation of their physical, chemical and adsorption properties', *Microporous and Mesoporous Materials*, vol 66, pp189–195

Bansal, R. C., Donnet, J. B. and Stoeckli, F. (1988) *Active Carbon*, Marcel Dekker, New York, NY

Biagini, E. and Tognotti, L. (2003) 'Characterization of biomass chars', in *Proceedings of the Seventh International Conference on Energy for Clean Environment*, 7–10 July 2003, Lisbon, Portugal

Biscoe, J. and Warren, B. E. (1942) 'An X-ray study of carbon black', *Journal of Applied Physics*, vol 13, p364

Boateng, A. A. (2007) 'Characterization and thermal conversion of charcoal derived from fluidized-bed fast pyrolysis oil production of switchgrass', *Industrial Engineering and Chemical Research*, vol 46, pp8857–8862

Boehm, H. P. (1994) 'Some aspects of the surface chemistry of carbon blacks and other carbons', *Carbon*, vol 32, pp759–769

Boehm, H. P. (2002) 'Surface oxides on carbon and their analysis: A critical assessment', *Carbon*, vol 40, pp145–149

Bourke, J., Manley-Harris, M., Fushimi, C., Dowaki, K., Nunoura, T. and Antal, M. J. (2007) 'Do all carbonized charcoals have the same chemical structure? 2. A model of the chemical structure of carbonized charcoal', *Industrial Engineering and Chemical Research*, vol 46, pp5954–5967

Brady, N. C. and Weil, R. R. (2008) *An Introduction to the Nature and Properties of Soils*, 14th edition, Prentice Hall, Upper Saddle River, NJ

Braida W. J., Pignatello J. J., Lu, Y., Ravikovich P. I., Neimark A. V. and Xing B. (2003) 'Sorption hysteresis of benzene in charcoal particles', *Environmental Science and Technology*, vol 37, pp409–417

Brown, R. A., Kercher, A. K., Nguyen, T. H., Nagle, D. C. and Ball, W. P. (2006) 'Production and characterization of synthetic wood chars for use as surrogates for natural sorbents', *Organic Geochemistry*, vol 37, pp321–333

Byrne, C. (1996) *Polymer, Ceramic, and Carbon Composites Derived from Wood*, PhD thesis, The Johns Hopkins University, US

Byrne, C. E. and Nagle, D. C. (1997) 'Carbonized wood monoliths – characterization', *Carbon*, vol 35, pp267–273

Carmona, F. and Delhaes, P. (1978) 'Effect of density fluctuations on the physical properties of a disordered carbon', *Journal of Applied Physics*, vol 49, pp618–628

Cetin, E., Moghtaderi, B., Gupta, R. and Wall, T. F. (2004) 'Influence of pyrolysis conditions on the structure and gasification reactivity of biomass chars', *Fuel*, vol 83, pp2139–2150

Chan, K. Y., Van Zwieten, L., Meszaros, I., Downie, A. and Joseph, S. (2007) 'Agronomic values of greenwaste biochar as a soil amendment', *Australian Journal of Soil Research*, vol 45, pp629–634

Emmerich, F. G. and Luengo, C. A. (1996) 'Babassu charcoal: A sulfurless renewable thermo-reducing feedstock for steelmaking', *Biomass and Bioenergy*, vol 10, pp41–44

Emmerich, F. G., Sousa, J. C., Torriani, I. L. and Luengo C. A. (1987) 'Applications of a granular model and percolation theory to the electrical resistivity of heat treated endocarp of babassu nut', *Carbon*, vol 25, pp417–424

Emmett, P. H. (1948) 'Adsorption and pore-size measurements on charcoal and whetlerites', *Chemical Reviews*, vol 43, pp69–148

Franklin, R. E. (1951) 'Crystallite growth in graphitizing and non-graphitizing carbons', *Proceedings of the Royal Society of London, Series*

A, Mathematical and Physical Sciences, vol 209, pp196–218

Freitas, J. C. C., Cunha, A. G. and Emmerich, F. G. (1997) 'Physical and chemical properties of a Brazilian peat char as a function of HTT', *Fuel*, vol 76, pp229–232

Fukuyama, K., Kasahara, Y., Kasahara, N., Oya, A. and Nishikawa, K. (2001) 'Small-angle X-ray scattering study of the pore structure of carbon fibers prepared from a polymer blend of phenolic resin and polystyrene', *Carbon*, vol 39, pp287–290

Gonzalez, M. T., Rodríguez-Reinoso, F., Garcia, A. N. and Marcilla, A. (1997) 'CO$_2$ activation of olive stones carbonized under different experimental conditions', *Carbon*, vol 35, pp159–162

Gray, E., Marsh, H. and Robertson, J. (1985) 'Physical characteristics of charcoal for use in gunpowder', *Journal of Materials Science*, vol 20, pp597–611

Guerrero, M., Ruiz, M. P., Millera, A., Alzueta, M. and Bilbao, R. (2008) 'Characterization of biomass chars formed under different devolatilization conditions: Differences between rice husk and eucalyptus', *Energy and Fuels*, vol 22, pp1275–1284

Guo, J. and Lua, A. C. (1998) 'Characterization of chars pyrolyzed from oil palm stones for the preparation of activated carbons', *Journal of Analytical and Applied Pyrolysis*, vol 46, pp113–125

Guo, J. and Rockstraw, D. A. (2006) 'Activated carbons prepared from rice hull by one-step phosphoric acid activation', *Microporous and Mesoporous Materials*, vol 100, pp12-19

Hammes, K., Schmidt, M. W. I., Smernik, R. J., Currie, L. A., Ball, W. P., Nguyen, T. H., Louchouarn, P., Houel, S., Gustafsson, Ö., Elmquist, M., Cornelissen, G., Skjemstad, J. O., Masiello, C. A., Song, J., Peng, P. A., Mitra, S., Dunn, J. C., Hatcher, P. G., Hockaday, W. C., Smith, D. M., Hartkopf-Froder, C., Bohmer, A., Luer, B., Huebert, B. J., Amelung, W., Brodowski, S., Huang, L., Zhang, W., Gschwend, P. M., Flores-Cervantes, D. X., Largeau, C., Rouzaud, J.-N., Rumpel, C., Guggenberger, G., Kaiser, K., Rodionov, A., Gonzalez-Vila, F. J., Gonzalez-Perez, J. A., de la Rosa, J. M., Manning, D. A. C., Lopez-Capel, E. and Ding, L. (2007) 'Comparison of quantification methods to measure fire-derived (black/elemental) carbon in soils and sediments using reference materials from soil, water, sediment and the atmosphere', *Global Biogeochemical Cycles*, vol 21, pGB3016

Jankowska, H., Swiatkowski, A. and Choma, J. (1991) *Active Carbon*, Ellis Horwood, New York, NY

Juma, N. (1993) 'Interrelationships between soil structure/texture, soil biota/soil organic matter and crop production', *Geoderma*, vol 57, pp3–30

Kercher, A. K. and Nagle, D. C. (2002) 'Evaluation of carbonized medium-density fiberboard for electrical applications', *Carbon*, vol 40, pp1321–1330

Kolb, S. (2007) *Understanding the Mechanisms by which a Manure-Based Charcoal Product Affects Microbial Biomass and Activity*, PhD thesis, University of Wisconsin, Green Bay, US

Laine, J. and Yunes, S. (1992) 'Effect of the preparation method on the pore size distribution of activated carbon from coconut shell', *Carbon*, vol 30, pp601–604

Laine, J., Simoni, S. and Calles, R. (1991) 'Preparation of activated carbon from coconut shell in a small scale concurrent flow rotary kiln', *Chemical Engineering Communications*, vol 99, pp15–23

Lal, R. (2006) *Encyclopedia of Soil Science*, CRC Press, Boca Raton, FL

Lewis, A. C. (2000) *Production and Characterization of Structural Active Carbon from Wood Precursors*, PhD thesis, Department of Materials Science and Engineering, The Johns Hopkins University, US

Lima, I. M. and Marshall, W. E. (2005) 'Granular activated carbons from broiler manure: Physical, chemical and adsorptive properties', *Bioresource Technology*, vol 96, pp699–706

Lua, A. C., Yang, T. and Guo, J. (2004) 'Effects of pyrolysis conditions on the properties of activated carbons prepared from pistachio-nut shells', *Journal of Analytical and Applied Pyrolysis*, vol 72, pp279–287

Macias-García, A., Bernalte García, M. J., Díaz–Diez, M. A. and Hernandez Jimenez, A. (2004) 'Preparation of active carbons from a commercial holm-oak charcoal: Study of micro- and meso-porosity', *Wood Science and Technology*, vol 37, pp385–394

Marsh, H. (1987) 'Adsorption methods to study microporosity in coals and carbons – a critique', *Carbon*, vol 25, pp49–58

Marsh, H., Yan, D. S., O'Grady, T. M. and Wennerberg, A. (1984) 'Formation of active carbons from cokes using potassium hydroxide', *Carbon*, vol 32, pp603–611

Martínez, M. L., Torres, M. M., Guzmán, C. A. and Maestri, D. M. (2006) 'Preparation and characteristics of activated carbon from olive stones and walnut shells', *Industrial Crops and Products*, vol 23, pp23–28

Müller, T. and Höper, H. (2004) 'Soil organic matter turnover as a function of the soil clay content: Consequences for model applications', *Soil Biology and Biochemistry*, vol 36, pp877–888

Oberlin, A. (2002) 'Pyrocarbons – review', *Carbon*, vol 40, pp7–24

Pan, M. J. and van Staden, J. (1998) 'The use of charcoal in in vitro culture – a review', *Plant Growth Regulation*, vol 26, pp155–163

Pandolfo, A. G., Amini-Amoli, M. and Killingley, J. S. (1994) 'Activated carbons prepared from shells of different coconut varieties', *Carbon*, vol 32, pp1015–1019

Pastor-Villegas, J., Valenzuela-Calahorro, C., Bernalte-García, A. and Gómez-Serrano, V. (1993) 'Characterization study of char and activated carbon prepared from raw and extracted rockrose', *Carbon*, vol 31, pp1061–1069

Pastor-Villegas, J., Pastor-Valle, J. F., Meneses Rodríguez, J. M. and García, M. (2006) 'Study of commercial wood charcoals for the preparation of carbon adsorbents', *Journal of Analytical and Applied Pyrolysis*, vol 76, pp103–108

Pulido-Novicio, L., Hata, T., Kurimoto, Y., Doi, S., Ishihara, S. and Imamura, Y. (2001) 'Adsorption capacities and related characteristics of wood charcoals carbonized using a one-step or two-step process', *Journal of Wood Science*, vol 47, pp48–57

Puziy, A. M., Poddubnaya, O. I., Martínez-Alonso, A., Suarez-García, F. and Tascon, J. M. D. (2005) 'Surface chemistry of phosphorus-containing carbons of lignocellulosic origin', *Carbon*, vol 43, pp2857–2868

Qadeer, R., Hanif, J., Saleem, M. A. and Afzal, M. (1994) 'Characterization of activated charcoal', *Journal of the Chemical Society of Pakistan*, vol 16, pp229–235

Rodríguez-Mirasol, J., Cordero, T. and Rodriguez, J. J. (1993) 'Preparation and characterization of activated carbons from eucalyptus kraft lignin', *Carbon*, vol 31, pp87–95

Rodríguez-Reinoso, F. (1997) *Introduction to Carbon Technologies*, Universidad de Alicante, Alicante, Spain

Rodríguez-Reinoso, F. and Molina-Sabio, M. (1992) 'Activated carbons from lignocellulosic materials by chemical and/or physical activation: An overview', *Carbon*, vol 30, pp1111–1118

Rouquerol, F., Rouquerol, I. and Sing, K. (1999) *Adsorption by Powders and Porous Solids*, Academic Press, London, UK

Setton, R., Bernier, P. and Lefrant, S. (2002) *Carbon Molecules and Materials*, CRC Press, Boca Raton, FL

Shamsuddin, A. H. and Williams, P. T. (1992) 'Devolatilisation studies of oil-palm solid wastes by thermo-gravimetric analysis', *Journal of the Institute of Energy*, vol 65, pp31–34

Sjöström, E. (1993) *Wood Chemistry: Fundamentals and Applications*, second edition, Academic Press, San Diego, US

Stavropoulos, G. G. (2005) 'Precursor materials suitability for super activated carbons production', *Fuel Processing Technology*, vol 86, pp1165–1173

Troeh, F. R. and Thompson, L. M. (2005) *Soils and Soil Fertility*, Blackwell Publishing, Iowa, US

Wang, S.-Y., Tsai, M.-H., Lo, S.-F., Tsai, M.-J. (2008) 'Effects of manufacturing conditions on the adsorption capacity of heavy metal ions by Makino bamboo charcoal', *Bioresource Technology*

Warren, B. E. (1941) 'X-ray diffraction in random layer lattices', *Physical Review*, vol 59, pp693–698

Wildman, J. and Derbyshire, F. (1991) 'Origins and functions of macroporosity in activated carbons from coal and wood precursors', *Fuel*, vol 70, pp655–661

Zabaniotou, A., Stavropoulos, G. and Skoulou, V. (2008) 'Activated carbon from olive kernels in a two–stage process: Industrial improvement', *Bioresource Technology*, vol 99, pp320–326

Zhang, T., Walawender, W. P., Fan, L. T., Fan, M., Daugaard, D. and Brown, R. C. (2004) 'Preparation of activated carbon from forest and agricultural residues through CO_2 activation', *Chemical Engineering Journal*, vol 105, pp53–59

3

Characteristics of Biochar: Microchemical Properties

James E. Amonette and Stephen Joseph

Introduction and scope

Biochars, being derived from a variety of biological feedstocks that have been thermally degraded under a range of conditions (Chapter 8), exhibit a correspondingly large range in composition and chemistry. Due, in part, to the complex set of chemical reactions that occur during thermal processing, a large degree of chemical heterogeneity extends to the microscopic scale, even within a single biochar. Thus, in the strictest sense, each biochar made with a particular feedstock and process combination presents a unique mixture of phases and microenvironments that gives rise to a unique set of chemical properties. In some respects, the chemical complexity of biochars rivals that of incipient soils. In this chapter we focus on the chemical complexity of biochar as manifested primarily at a microscopic and molecular scale. We start by describing the biochar-formation process and how this influences the composition and nature of the solid phases, entrained oils and their organization at the microscopic level. We then proceed to discuss the range of surface chemistries exhibited by biochars in terms of functional groups and electrochemical properties. We conclude with a discussion of the influence of these properties on the sorption of aqueous species at biochar surfaces.

Formation and bulk composition

Formation

When biological material is thermally degraded in sub-stoichiometric oxygen (O) conditions, it yields a solid residue. The various definitions for this solid residue are given in Chapter 7.

A number of feedstocks and thermal degradation processes can be used to produce biochar. Potential feedstocks include all materials of biological (organic) origin,

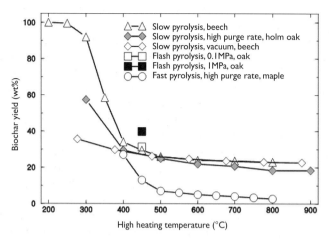

Figure 3.1 *Biochar yields for wood feedstock under different pyrolysis conditions*

Source: slow pyrolysis data from Schenkel (1999) as presented by Antal and Grønli (2003) (beech); Figueiredo et al (1989) (high purge rate, holm oak); and Demirbas (2001) (vacuum, beech). Flash pyrolysis data from Antal et al (2000) (oak). Fast pyrolysis data from Scott et al (1988) (eastern red maple).

such as manures, rendering wastes, and lignocellulosic biomass. The latter is an obvious choice as the primary feedstock because it is the most abundant biologically produced material. Thermal degradation processes include hydrothermal conversion, torrefaction, slow pyrolysis, fast pyrolysis, gasification and various permutations (Chapter 8). They are distinguished chiefly by the presence or absence of free water, feedstock residence time, availability of atmospheric O_2, heating rate, gas environment (e.g. the presence of nitrogen (N) or steam), and the temperatures and pressures used. The pyrolysis and gasification processes are described in detail in Chapter 8. Hydrothermal conversion occurs when feedstock, immersed in water, is heated at temperatures of 180°C to 250°C in a sealed vessel at autogenous pressure (0.5MPa to 1MPa) for periods of several hours to a day in length (Titirici et al, 2007a). Torrefaction involves heating the feedstock to temperatures of 200°C to 300°C at slow heating rates (<50°C min⁻¹) under an anoxic atmosphere at near-ambient pressure (Tito Ferro et al, 2004; Bergman and Kiel, 2005). Because most thermal degradation of biomass for biochar production currently involves the pyrolysis process, our discussion of the chemical aspects of biochar formation will focus on this process.

Pyrolysis of dry lignocellulosic materials involves three major parallel pathways (Shafizadeh, 1982; Varhegyi et al, 1994; Antal and Grønli, 2003):

1   a biochar- and gas-forming pathway;
2   a liquid- and tar-forming pathway; and
3   a gasification and carbonization pathway.

Competition between these pathways, whose relative rates are largely determined by the highest heat treatment temperature (HTT), volatile removal rate and particle residence time encountered during the process, controls the relative abundance of the thermal-degradation products (see Figure 3.1). In this section, we provide an overview of the chemistry occurring during the biochar-formation process, drawn, except where noted, from the reviews of Shafizadeh (1982) and Antal and Grønli (2003).

Lignocellulose degradation begins at temperatures above approximately 120°C and is dominated by the biochar- and gas-formation pathway at HTTs below 300°C. This pathway is believed to be a free-radical process initiated by homolytic cleavage of bonds. The free radicals that drive the process are initially formed by thermal action on structural O and inorganic impurities present in the feedstock. An additional source of free radicals may be from low levels of atmospheric O_2 that may be present during the initial stages of pyrolysis. Carboxyl and carbonyl groups are formed and subsequently cleaved to yield CO_2 and CO (Shafizadeh, 1982; Brennan et al, 2001). Water is also released as a result of dehydration reactions. Ultimately, some of the free-radical fragments recombine in various ways with each other and with the substrate to yield a biochar residue.

At HTTs of between 300°C and about 600°C, a different liquid- and tar-forming pathway becomes increasingly important. As a result, biochar production decreases significantly over this temperature range. The tar that is produced from cellulose is chiefly composed of anhydrosugars such as levoglucosan that are less reactive than the free-radicals generated by homolytic bond cleavage (Shafizadeh, 1982). Because of increased heat- and mass-transfer rates at these HTTs, volatilization of the anhydrosugars is also possible, thus further decreasing the potential for biochar formation. In lieu of volatilization, however, the anhydrosugars can be degraded by dehydration and fission reactions that are promoted by acidic or basic catalysts. Subsequent homolytic bond cleavage of the secondary products yields biochar. The proportion of free radicals trapped in the biochar as measured by electron paramagnetic resonance (EPR) spectroscopy also increases with HTT for a given residence time and reaches a maximum at HTTs of 500°C to 600°C (Bradbury and Shafizadeh, 1980; Degroot and Shafizadeh, 1983; Feng et al, 2004). As a result, biochars produced in this temperature range are extremely reactive towards oxidation (usually measured by O_2 chemisorption), often to the point of being pyrophoric. In general, the amount of biochar produced at HTTs of 300°C to 600°C, while substantially less than that at lower HTTs, depends largely upon the relative rates of volatilization and degradation of the anhy-

drosugars present in the tar. As heat- and mass-transfer rates (i.e. volatilization) increase, the yields of biochar decrease.

At HTTs above 600°C, heat- and mass-transfer rates are sufficiently high that a gas-forming pathway dominates, and biochar, tar and liquid formation are at a minimum. The biochar that forms initially as the substrate is being heated is carbonized, by which process more of the original O, hydrogen (H), N and sulphur (S) are removed and carbon (C) contents above 90 per cent by weight are readily obtained (Chapter 4). The number of trapped free radicals in the biochar measured by EPR spectroscopy also decreases due to defect-annealing processes at the higher temperatures (Bradbury and Shafizadeh, 1980; Feng et al, 2004), although some evidence suggests that the decrease is due to the location at the biochar surface of a greater proportion of the free radicals generated where they may react with chemisorbed O_2 and quench the EPR signal (Degroot and Shafizadeh, 1983).

Although we have focused on the primary role played by HTT, the proportion of the feedstock that is converted to biochar during pyrolysis also depends upon heating rate (inversely proportional to residence time), gas purge rate, pressure and feedstock composition. In general, lower HTTs, slower heating and purge rates, higher pressures, and greater concentrations of lignin in the substrate result in larger yields of biochar (Shafizadeh, 1982; Demirbas, 2001; Antal and Grønli, 2003).

Solid phases and their distribution

As described above, process conditions (chiefly temperature and heating rate) may cause a significant fraction of the initial carbonaceous material to be released as oily and tarry vapours during thermal degradation. At low HTTs (i.e. below 500°C), some of these vapours condense in the pores of the biochar, leading to a multi-phase substance (Schnitzer et al, 2007a, 2007b), while the majority are commonly recovered from the gas stream as bio-oil using a condensation tower. Inorganic compounds present in the feedstock undergo a similar process, with some being volatilized during thermal degradation (see Chapter 5), and the majority being retained either as discrete mineral phases or as part of the structure of the carbonaceous residue (Wornat et al, 1995).

Carbon-based phases

Several researchers have described the evolving nature of the carbonaceous residue obtained when lignocellulosic biomass is thermally degraded under various conditions (Antal and Grønli, 2003; Kercher and Nagle, 2003; Paris et al, 2005; Skodras et al, 2006; Stresov et al, 2007). As described by Paris et al (2005), four regions of change (dehydration, pyrolysis, graphene nucleation and carbonization) are observed under non-hydrothermal conditions. With very slow heating rates (approximately 2°C min^{-1}; Paris et al, 2005) and near-ambient pressure, transitions between these regions occur at about 250°C, 350°C and 600°C. At faster heating rates, these transitions occur at higher temperatures due to heat- and mass-transfer limitations. In the first region (i.e. at temperatures below 250°C), the primary changes in the feedstock are dehydration and slight depolymerization of cellulose. Little mass loss is observed. Between 250°C and 350°C, complete depolymerization (pyrolysis) of the cellulose occurs, resulting in significant mass loss by volatilization and creation of an essentially amorphous C matrix. At about 330°C, the first signs of aromatic C are seen, and above 350°C, polyaromatic graphene sheets begin to grow at the expense of the amorphous-C matrix. Above 600°C, carbonization begins, by which most of the remaining non-C atoms are removed and graphene sheets continue to grow laterally, eventually coalescing.

From a compositional standpoint, the major constituents of biomass (C, H and O) volatilize during dehydration and pyrolysis (see Chapter 4), with H and O being lost in proportionally greater amounts than C. The O and H are lost initially as water, and later as hydrocarbons, tarry vapours, H_2, CO and CO_2 (Antal and Grønli, 2003). The proportion of C in the solid phase increases from about 40 to 50 per cent by weight in the feedstock to on the order of 70 to 80 per cent by weight after pyrolysis between 250°C and 600°C. Carbonization further increases the C content to more than 90 per cent by weight except for high mineral-ash chars (Antal and Grønli, 2003).

The microstructural changes occurring during thermal degradation can be detected by a number of techniques, including transmission electron microscopy (TEM), infrared and Raman spectroscopies, electron energy loss spectroscopy (EELS), X-ray diffraction (XRD), and small-angle X-ray scattering (SAXS). The entire range of these changes is shown in SAXS patterns collected by Paris et al (2005) for slow pyrolysis of normal wood in which the initial feedstock structural features give way to a featureless profile at about 330°C, which is subsequently replaced by a new profile as the graphene sheets nucleate and coalesce at higher temperatures (see Figure 3.2).

As suggested by the extended transition from a purely amorphous C phase to one in which graphene sheets nucleate and grow, biochars produced at higher HTTs and carbonized biochars consist primarily of an intimate mixture of two solid C phases (i.e. amorphous C and graphene packets; see Chapter 2). This was first shown by Franklin (1951) using X-ray diffraction and has since been confirmed numerous times by using various structural and microscopic methods. A recent confirmation is provided by Cohen-Ofri et al (2006, 2007) using TEM (see Figure 3.3).

Building upon the work of Franklin

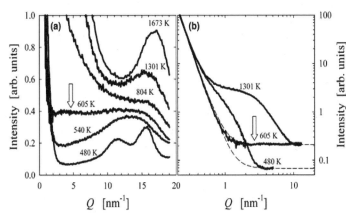

Figure 3.2 *Selected small-angle X-ray scattering (SAXS) profiles from normal wood: (a) the intensity is plotted versus the length of the scattering vector in a linear representation; and (b) for three selected profiles in a double logarithmic representation*

Note: The arrows emphasize the profile at T = 605K (330°C), which marks the almost structureless transition region between cellulose degradation and biochar formation.

Source: Reprinted from Paris et al (2005) with permission from Elsevier

(1951), a detailed quasi-percolation model describing the evolution of the graphene packets during carbonization at temperatures as high as 1400°C was developed by Kercher and Nagle (2003) using X-ray diffraction, which was supported through further observations by Paris et al (2005). The essential features of the model (see Figure 3.4) are that the number of graphene packets and their thickness remain constant as carbonization proceeds. They grow laterally at the expense of the amorphous C phase and eventually intersect with adjacent packets to provide electrical continuity through the biochar. Because the amorphous C is less dense than the aligned graphene packets, conversion creates voids in the structure, which increases the microporosity.

An analogous structural model for biochars carbonized at 950°C was presented by Bourke et al (2007). This model differed slightly from that of Kercher and Nagle (2003) by including non-graphitic rings interspersed in the nominally graphene sheets (i.e. 70 per cent aromaticity rather than 100 per cent), as well as the presence of larger multi-ring voids in the sheets. They further limited the graphene crystallite sizes in all dimensions to about 2nm, whereas Kercher and Nagle (2003) proposed packets that were more than 4nm thick and could extend laterally as far as 8.4nm.

In contrast to the relatively well-understood evolution and microstructure of biochars produced by pyrolysis and carbonization, little is known about the

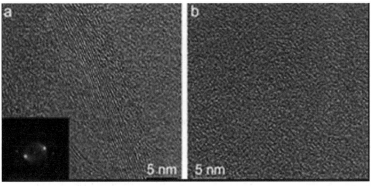

Figure 3.3 *Transmission electron microscopy (TEM) images of modern biochar samples: (a) ceratonia that contains organized and non-organized phases (inset: fast Fourier transform (FFT) of the organized region); (b) non-organized phase of Ceratonia biochar*

Source: Cohen-Ofri et al (2007). © Wiley-VCH Verlag GmbH & co. Reproduced with permission.

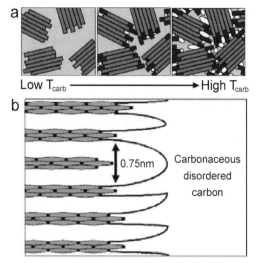

Figure 3.4 *Schematics demonstrating the concepts of the quasi-percolation model of Kercher and Nagle (2003): (a) light grey denotes the disordered carbon phase; medium grey denotes graphene sheets in large turbostratic crystallites present at low temperatures; dark grey denotes growth of the graphene sheets at higher temperatures, white denotes porosity; (b) fundamental concept of disordered C forms converting into high-density graphene sheets*

Note: In this simplistic example, the disordered C filling six graphene sheets' worth of volume can only convert into five graphene sheets' worth of material. The non-growing graphene sheet region becomes the beginning of a 0.75nm tall nanopore.

Source: reprinted from Kercher and Nagle (2003) with permission from Elsevier

conversion process and structure of biochars obtained under hydrothermal conditions (e.g. 180°C to 250°C, 0.5MPa to 1MPa). Antonietti and co-workers (Cui et al, 2006; Rothlein, 2006; Titirici et al, 2007a, 2007b) suggest that in the presence of an acidic catalyst, a 'coalification' process occurs by which water is removed from biomass to form a lignite-type product. As discussed by Titirici et al (2007a), the hydrothermal conversion approach essentially fixes the entire C into a solid phase that, similar to conventionally

produced biochar, has significant potential for C sequestration because it is more stable than the original biomass from which it was formed. Although the process yields liquid intermediate products, essentially no liquid or tar remains when the process is carried to completion and the final solid is hydrophilic (Titirici et al, 2007a).

Entrained minerals

Two factors, feedstock and process conditions, control the amount and distribution of mineral matter in biochars. The mineral ash content of feedstocks varies significantly (see Table 3.1). Woody feedstocks generally have low (<1 per cent by weight) ash contents, whereas grass, straw and grain husks, which have high silica contents, may have as much as 24 per cent by weight ash (Raveendran et al, 1995). Much of the mineral content in the feedstock is carried over into the biochar where it is concentrated due to loss of C, H and O during pyrolysis (see Chapter 5). Biochars from manures and rendering wastes typically have very high ash contents. Chicken-litter biochars, for example, can have 45 per cent mineral matter (Koutcheiko et al, 2007), and bone biochars may have as much as 84 per cent mineral matter (Purevsuren et al, 2004).

The effect of feedstock mineral-ash content on biochar yield is uncertain. Amendments of solid catalysts such as alkali carbonates and NaCl to cellulose increase biochar yields (Feng et al, 2004). Addition of iron (Fe) to lignocellulosic feedstock has a similar effect (Edye et al, 1993). Removal of mineral content (i.e. demineralization) by pre-treatment with acidic, basic or chelating solutions decreases biochar yield (Raveendran et al, 1995). These observations seem to suggest that higher mineral-ash content in the feedstock tends to increase biochar yield. However, correlations between biochar yields and the mineral-ash content of various feedstocks that have not been amended with solid catalysts are weak to non-

Table 3.1 *Ash content and elemental composition of representative feedstocks and an oak wood biochar*

Feedstock	Ash content (wt %)	Al	Ca	Fe	Mg	Na	K	P	Si
					$(mg\ kg^{-1})$				
Bagasse	2.9	—[a]	1500	130	6300	90	2700	280	17,000
Coconut coir	0.8	150	480	190	530	1800	2400	50	3000
Coconut shell	0.7	70	1500	120	390	1200	2000	90	260
Coir pith	7.1	1700	3100	840	8100	11,000	26000	1200	13,000
Maize cob	2.8	—	180	20	1700	140	9400	450	9900
Maize stalks	6.8	1900	4700	520	5900	6500	30	2100	13,000
Cotton gin waste	5.4	—	3700	750	4900	1300	7100	740	13,000
Groundnut shell	5.9	3600	13,000	1100	3500	470	18,000	280	11,000
Millet husk	18.1	—	6300	1000	11,000	1400	3900	1300	150,000
Rice husk	23.5	—	1800	530	1600	130	9100	340	220,000
Rice straw	19.8	—	4800	200	6300	5100	5400	750	170,000
Subabul wood	0.9	—	6000	610	1200	90	610	100	200
Wheat straw	11.2	2500	7700	130	4300	7900	29,000	210	44,000
Olive kernel	2.6	18,000	97,000	24,000	20,000	7900	—	—	—
Almond shell	3.4	5000	80,000	6100	14,000	5500	—	—	—
Forest residue	1.2	4900	130,000	10,000	19,000	4200	—	—	—
Saw dust	0.44	9800	170,000	29,000	27,000	10,000	—	—	—
Waste wood	8.8	4900	130,000	10,000	19,000	4200	—	—	—
Willow wood	1.1	20	3900	30	360	150	1400	340	—
Demolition wood	1.9	480	3600	350	420	670	750	60	—
Straw	17.7	5800	8600	3400	3700	3200	22000	600	—
Meat and bonemeal	10.4	7600	260,000	4900	13,000	5800	23,000	100,000	—
Oak wood biochar	0.27	1000	350,000	3400	16,000	6400	98,000	5400	4200

Note: a No data reported.

Source: Raveendran et al (1995); Skodras et al (2006); and Bourke et al (2007) (oak biochar)

existent (see the data of Raveendran et al, 1995, for untreated feedstocks).

In addition to feedstock, process conditions, chiefly HTT, and the partial pressure of O_2, steam and carbon dioxide (CO_2) control the amounts of mineral ash in biochar (Bridgwater and Boocock, 2006). During thermal degradation, potassium (K) and chlorine (Cl) ions are highly mobile and will start to vaporize at relatively low temperatures (Yu et al, 2005). Calcium (Ca) is mainly located in cell walls and bound to organic acids (Marschner, 1995). Silicon (Si) is present in the cell walls as silica or as opal phytoliths (Marschner, 1995). Both Ca and Si are released during degradation at much higher temperatures than K and Cl (Bourke, 2006). Magnesium (Mg) is both ionically and covalently bonded with organic molecules and only vaporizes at high temperatures. Phosphorus (P) and sulphur (S) are associated with complex organic compounds within the cell and are relatively stable at low degradation temperatures (see Chapter 5). N is associated with a number of different organic molecules and can be released at relatively low temperatures (Schnitzer et al, 2007b). Other elements such as Fe and manganese (Mn) exist in a number of organic and inorganic forms in the biomass and are largely retained during biochar formation (see Chapter 5).

Very little work has been carried out on the distribution and the stability of heavy metals in biochar. High mineral-ash biochars (especially chicken manure biochar and activated carbon) are known to adsorb heavy metals (Swiatkowski et al, 2004; Lima and Marshall, 2005).

Very little has been published on the distribution of mineral ash within different types of biochar. Of the inorganic elements that comprise mineral ash, most are believed to occur as discrete phases separate from the carbonaceous matrix. In some biochars, however, K and Ca are distributed throughout the matrix where they may form phenoxides (K, Ca) or simply be intercalated between graphene sheets (K) (Wornat et al, 1995).

Minerals found in biochars include sylvite (KCl), quartz (SiO_2), amorphous silica, calcite ($CaCO_3$), hydroxyapatite ($Ca_{10}(PO_4)_6(OH)_2$), and other minor phases such as Ca phosphates, anhydrite ($CaSO_4$), various nitrates, and oxides and hydroxides of Ca, Mg, aluminium (Al), titanium (Ti), Mn, zinc (Zn) or Fe. Amorphous silica is of particular interest as it typically is in the form of phytoliths that contain and protect plant C from degradation (Wilding et al, 1967; Krull et al, 2003; Smith and White, 2004; Parr and Sullivan, 2005; Parr, 2006). Crystalline silica is also of interest because it has been found in some biochars where it poses a very high-level respiratory risk.

Morphologies and distribution patterns of minerals in several different biochars are shown in Figures 3.5 to 3.9. Figure 3.5 illustrates a range of morphologies, indicating that some of the mineral phases consist of more than one mineral type. Microprobe analysis of these biochars indicates that there is a large variation of mineral content even within each particle (see Figure 3.6). Figure 3.6 illustrates the distribution of both metals and non-metals in the end grain of a wood biochar. A variety of minerals can be identified that differ greatly between different biochars (see Figures 3.7 to 3.9).

Associated oils and their distribution

Most of the literature on bio-oils (e.g. Maggi and Delmon, 1994; Bridgwater and Boocock, 1997; Guan, 2004) relates to the compounds that are released when biomass is pyrolysed. Very little analysis has taken place of the organic molecules that remain on the surface.

Schnitzer et al (2007a, 2007b) carried out a detailed analysis of the residual bio-oils on biochars derived from the fast pyrolysis of chicken manure. They found that the individual compounds identified were grouped into the following six compound classes:

1 N-heterocyclics;
2 substituted furans;
3 phenol and substituted phenols;
4 benzene and substituted benzenes;
5 carbocyclics; and
6 aliphatics.

Prominent N-heterocyclics in bio-oil were methyl- and ethyl-substituted pyrroles, pyridines, pyrimidine, pyrazines and pteridine. The alkanes and alkenes ranged from $n\text{-}C_7$ to $n\text{-}C_{18}$ and $C_{7:1}$ to $C_{18:1}$, respectively, and those in the biochar from $n\text{-}C_7$ to $n\text{-}C_{19}$ and $C_{7:1}$ to $C_{19:1}$, respectively.

Some of these compounds (e.g. butenolide) have been found to be important in the germination of native species (Dixon, 1998); others have been identified as triggering the growth of microorganisms (sesquiterpenes) (Akiyama and Hayashi, 2006); and others have been found to have biocide properties (so-called smoke vinegar) (Guan, 2004).

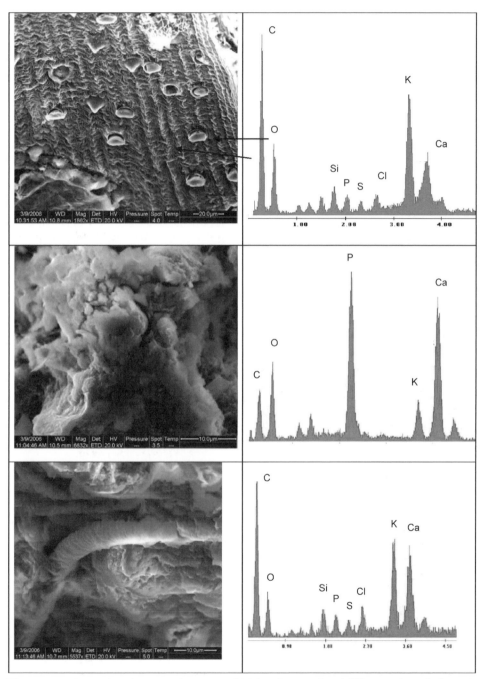

Figure 3.5 *Scanning electron microscopy (SEM) micrographs of different mineral phases in chicken manure biochar (produced at 450°C for 0.5hrs) and their energy-dispersive X-ray spectroscopy (EDS) spectra*

Note: biochar manufactured by BESTEnergies Pty.
Source: Electron Microscope Unit, University of NSW using a Quanta SEM

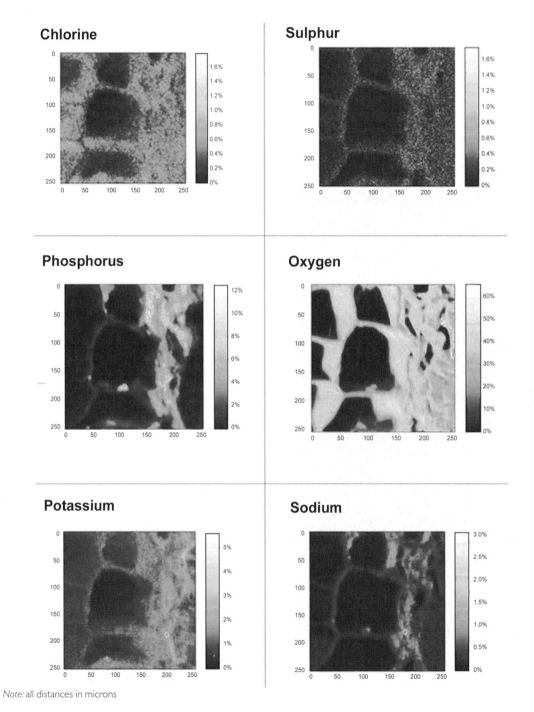

Note: all distances in microns

Figure 3.6 *Distribution of non-C elements on the surface of wood biochar (produced at 450°C for 0.5hrs) determined by microprobe analysis*

Note: biochar manufactured by BESTEnergies Pty.
Source: Electron Microscope Unit, University of NSW, Cameca, Japan

Surface chemistry

The surface chemistry of biochars, as expected from their heterogeneous compositions, is quite rich and varied. Biochar surfaces exhibit hydrophilic, hydrophobic, acidic and basic properties whose relative contributions to biochar reactivity depend upon the feedstock and on the thermal degra- dation process used to create the biochar. In this section we review the molecular properties that give rise to biochar surface chemistry and then discuss how these properties affect the ability of biochars to react with chemicals found in soil environments.

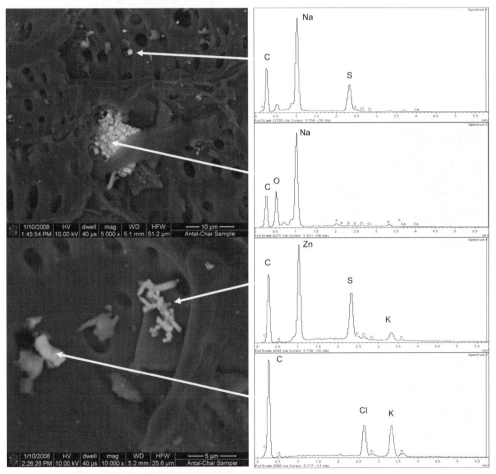

Figure 3.7 *SEM micrographs and associated EDS spectra for mineral phases in maize-cob biochar prepared by flash pyrolysis: probable minerals include (a) Na_2S; (b) Na_2O or Na_2CO_3; (c) ZnS; and (d) KCl*

Note: Operating conditions consisted of 2 to 20keV for SEM imaging and 20keV, 100 live seconds for the EDS analyses.

Source: Micrographs taken at the Environmental Molecular Sciences Laboratory, Richland, WA, using a Zeiss Leo 982 field emission-scanning electron microscope equipped with an Oxford INCA 300 EDS used for qualitative elemental analysis. Sample courtesy of Michael J. Antal, University of Hawaii.

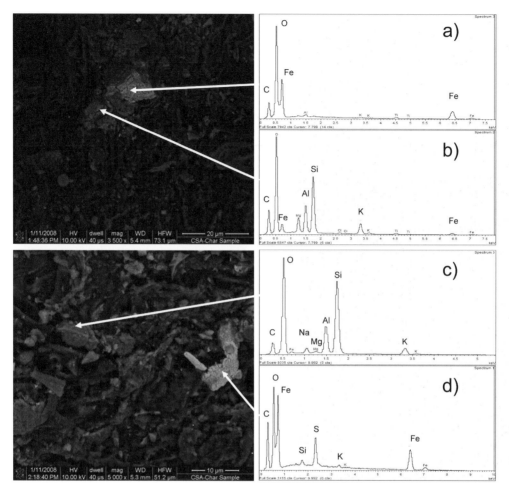

Figure 3.8 *SEM micrographs and associated EDS spectra for mineral phases in white oak biochar prepared by fast pyrolysis: probable minerals include*
(a) Fe_2O_3; (b) dehydroxylated layer silicate or a mixture of Si, Al, Mg and K oxides;
(c) dehydroxylated layer silicate or a mixture of Si, Al and K oxides; and (d) FeS, $FeCO_3$, S, Fe_2O_3

Source: Micrographs taken at the Environmental Molecular Sciences Laboratory, Richland, WA, as described in Figure 3.7. Sample courtesy of Stefan Czernik, National Renewable Energy Laboratory.

Carbon-based phases

Functional groups

Experimental evidence shows that a range of different functional groups exist on the surfaces of the graphene sheets (see Figure 3.10; Brennan et al, 2001). Hydrogen, O, N, P and S are incorporated in the aromatic rings as heteroatoms. Brennan et al (2001) state that the presence of heteroatoms results in surface chemical heterogeneity caused mainly by differences in the electronegativity of the heteroatoms relative to the C atoms. Groups such as OH, NH_2, OR or O(C=O)R are classified as electron donors (due to the presence of α or π electrons), whereas (C=O)OH, (C=O)H or NO_2 groups are classified as electron acceptors (due to the

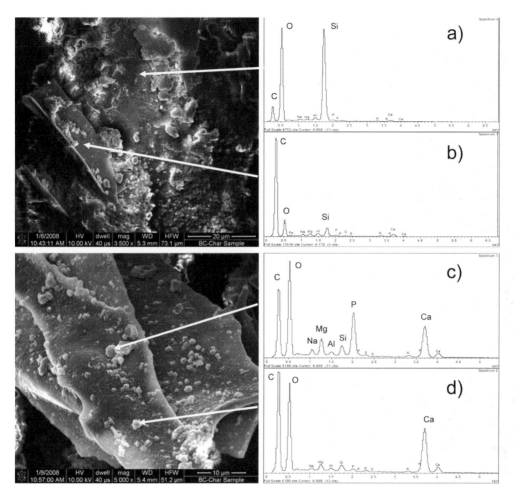

Figure 3.9 *SEM micrographs and associated EDS spectra for mineral phases in poplar wood biochar from a combustion facility: probable minerals include (a) amorphous SiO_2; (b) trace dehydroxylated silicates (mostly char); (c) $Ca_{10}(PO_4)_6(OH)_2$, $CaHPO_4$; and (d) CaO, $CaCO_3$*

Source: micrographs taken at the Environmental Molecular Sciences Laboratory, Richland, WA, as described in Figure 3.7

presence of empty orbitals). Carboxyl groups are strong Brønsted acids. Less acidic groups include phenols and carbonyls. Chromenes and pyrones are basic functional groups.

As demonstrated in Figures 3.7 to 3.9, there are very large differences in mineral matter content and composition on the surfaces of biochars. This difference is manifested at a level measured in micrometres. Thus, acidic and basic sites may coexist within micrometres of each other on the

outer surfaces and pores of the particle.

In high-mineral ash biochars, it is probable that some of the functional groups will contain metals. Schnitzer et al (2007a) and Koutcheiko et al (2007) detected a range of different N- and S-based functional groups in chicken manure biochar. Data from various studies (e.g. Elizalde-Gonzalez et al, 2007) indicate that the relative concentration of each of the functional groups depends upon initial composition of the biomass, final reaction temperature, composition of the gas surrounding the charring particle (at the final reaction temperature), rate of heating and any post-treatment.

Operational determination of acidic and basic functional groups on biochars can be performed by Boehm titrations (Boehm, 1994) in which the biochar is equilibrated in the presence of successively stronger bases (HCO_3^-, CO_3^{2-}, OH^-, ethoxide) or a strong acid, followed by titration of the extract with strong acid or base to determine the fraction that reacted. Differences in the amounts of acid or base needed are used to estimate the relative amounts of carboxylic, lactonic, phenolic and carbonylic functional groups (base equilibrations) or basic functionalities (acid equilibration). For characterization of biochars used as soil amendments, the ethoxide equilibration is commonly omitted as it measures functional groups that are dissociated only at very high pH.

The Boehm titration works well for hydrophilic biochars, but encounters difficulties when significant amounts of bio-oil or mineral surfaces are present. In these circumstances, analysis by spectroscopic means may be helpful. X-ray photoelectron spectroscopy (XPS) and electron energy loss spectroscopy (EELS) can both provide information about the types of functional groups present. For example, Cohen-Ofri et al (2007) used EELS to show the incorporation of O groups into ancient biochars as part of the aging process. Cheng et al (2008) used C1s XPS in a similar manner to follow oxidation of C in biochar from soils at charcoal production sites in eastern North America.

OXYGEN

Biochar reacts readily with atmospheric O_2 to yield O-containing functional groups at the surface (Shafizadeh, 1982; Bourke et al, 2007). Carbon-O groups are also formed from reaction with oxidizing gases such as ozone, nitric oxide and CO_2, as well as reactions with oxidizing solutions (Marsh et al, 1997). Swiatkowski et al (2004) note that pyrone sites may be the result of the adsorption of molecular O in the form of superoxide ions O_2^- and the dissociatively adsorbed O, such as O^- or O^{2-}.

NITROGEN AND SULPHUR

In biochars derived from manures, sewage sludge and rendering wastes, N and S functional groups will be more abundant than in lignocellulosic biochars. Areas of high N are

Table 3.2 *Summary of functional groups of S and N in a chicken-manure biochar (within the accuracy of XPS, pyridone-N cannot be distinguished from pyrrole-N)*

Sample	Peak	Functional groups	Binding energy (eV)	Content (percentage of total signal)
Raw biochar	N 1s	Pyridinic	398.4–398.8	31
		Pyrrolic or pyridonic, amine	399.4–400.5	69
		Quaternary N	⩾401.4	–
	S 2p	Thiophenic, sulphidic, pyrite	163.7–164.6	31
		Sulphonic and sulphates	⩾168.0	69
Activated carbon 800°C, CO_2	N 1s	Pyridinic	398.4–398.8	39
		Pyrrolic or or pyridonic[a]	399.8–400.3	24
		Quaternary N	⩾401.4	37
	S 2p	Thiophenic, sulphidic	164.3–165.5	100

Source: Koutcheiko et al (2007)

centres for high basicity. Koutcheiko et al (2007) prepared chicken manure biochar by heating to 360°C in a fast pyrolyis unit (no reaction time was reported). The biochar was then heated to 800°C and activated with CO_2. The main functional groups containing N for the low temperature biochar (as measured by XPS) were pyrrolic or pyridinic amines, whereas the high temperature biochars had nearly equal amounts of pyridinic and quaternary groups (see Table 3.2). Bagreev et al (2001) noted a similar trend when examining changes in sewage sludge biochars made at 450°C to 900°C in a fixed-bed reactor. At the lower temperatures, they detected amine functionalities by diffuse-reflectance infared spectroscopy, and at higher temperatures the same analysis suggested that the organic N was incorporated within the biochar as pyridine-like compounds.

Koutcheiko et al (2007) also identified S functional groups in their chicken manure biochar. In the low-temperature biochar, the main S functional groups were sulphonates and sulphates, whereas thiophene and sulphide groups predominated in the high-temperature biochar (see Table 3.2). Knudsen et al (2004) noted that in wheat straw biochar, the S remains as a sulphate until approximately 500°C, at which temperature it starts to transform to an insoluble sulphide (e.g. CaS, K_2S) in the biochar matrix, or from fixed to reactive biochar surfaces by either the addition of S to unsaturated sites or the substitution of O in surface oxides (Knudsen et al, 2004). These forms of S are expected to be water insoluble and biologically less available.

Mineral phases

A priori, one would expect that the functional groups on the surfaces of entrained mineral phases are similar to those of 'free' mineral phases not associated with biochar.

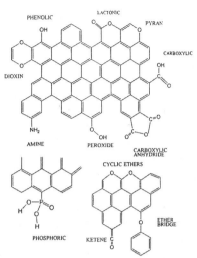

Figure 3.10 *Heteroatoms and functional groups commonly found in activated carbons*

Source: reprinted from Brennan et al (2001) with permission from Elsevier

Specifically, amphoteric sites (sites which react as both an acid and a base) exist on oxide surfaces whose surface charge varies with solution pH. Thus, under acidic conditions, the surfaces tend to be positively charged, and under alkaline conditions, negatively charged. The basal surfaces (and internal galleries) of layer silicates offer a permanently charged site that is negatively charged, in addition to edge sites that are amphoteric. However, many layer silicates that might have been present in the original biomass are irreversibly altered by dehydroxylation processes when thermal degradation temperatures exceed 500°C, and thus are transformed to oxides. The surfaces of carbonate minerals, in general, behave similarly to oxides due to the presence of O in the carbonate anion. Sulphide minerals, on the other hand, exhibit a significant range in behaviour when exposed to aqueous solutions, with the S atom at the surface eventually releasing seven electrons as the mineral surface is oxidized by water or other dissolved oxidants (Rimstidt and Vaughan, 2003). Thus, charge on the surface of the sulphide may range from negative to neutral to positive depending upon the oxidation state of S. With increasing oxidation, as one might expect, the surface properties of the sulphide mineral approach those of oxide minerals. An in-depth discussion of charge development on oxide and related mineral surfaces is beyond the scope of this chapter. The interested reader may wish to consult geochemical texts such as Stumm and Morgan (1996), Langmuir (1997) and Essington (2003).

Influence of surface properties on sorption

The various functional groups on the surfaces of biochar influence sorption by the nature of their surface charge and by the availability of π electrons. As with oxide surfaces, the charge on the functional groups may change depending upon the pH of the solution (i.e. the surface is amphoteric), thus affecting sorption behaviour. Examples of these changes and the associated functional groups are shown in Figure 3.11 and discussed in great detail by Radovic et al (2001). Not surprisingly, the nature of the sorbate also affects its ability to sorb. Non-transition metals, for example, are sorbed strictly by electrostatic forces, whereas transition metals with their exposed π-orbitals can bond with π electrons in the plane of the graphene sheets in addition to electrostatic bonding at oxidized sites on the edges of the graphene sheets. Many of these metals are also amphoteric, making a description of their sorption behaviour even more complicated. With transition metals, at least some sorption will occur simply by the π-electron mechanism if electrostatic repulsion forces

can be overcome. In their work on Pb^{2+} sorption, Swiatkowski et al (2004) listed the various ways in which metals can be adsorbed on biochar. We show them here for a generic divalent metal cation indicated as Me^{2+}:

Lewis base reaction:

$$\geqslant C{:}H_3O^+ + MeOH^+ \Leftrightarrow \geqslant C{:}MeOH^+ + H_3O^+$$

$C\pi$-cation interaction:

$$\geqslant C{:} + Me^{2+} \Leftrightarrow \geqslant C{:}Me^{2+}$$

For basic sites:

$$\geqslant C{-}OH + Me^{2+} + 3H_2O \Leftrightarrow \geqslant COMeOH + 2H_3O^+$$
$$\geqslant C{-}O^{-*} + Me^{2+} + 2H_2O \Leftrightarrow \geqslant C{-}O{-}MeOH + H_3O^+$$
$$\geqslant N{:} + Me^{2+} + 2H_2O \Leftrightarrow \geqslant N{-}MeOH^+ + H_3O^+.$$

For oxidized acidic sites:

$$\geqslant C{-}COOH + Me^{2+} + H_2O \Leftrightarrow \geqslant C{-}COOMe^+ + H_3O^+$$
$$(\geqslant C{-}COOH)_2 + Me^{2+} + 2H_2O \Leftrightarrow (\geqslant C{-}COO)_2Me + 2H_3O^+$$
$$\geqslant C{-}OH + Me^{2+} + H_2O \Leftrightarrow \geqslant C{-}OMe^+ + H_3O^+$$

Many organic sorbates, such as phenols, anilines and other functionalized aromatic molecules, also exhibit amphoteric behaviour and, like the amphoteric transition metals, must strike a balance between electrostatic and π-electron sorption mechanisms. In general, these molecules tend to sorb most strongly at solution pH values near their points of zero charge (Radovic et al, 2001). Recent work by Chen et al (2008), Nguyen et al (2007) and by Pignatello and co-workers (Braida et al, 2003; Sander and Pignatello, 2005, 2007; Zhu and Pignatello, 2005, Zhu et al, 2005, Pignatello et al, 2006) offers many insights into the sorption behaviour of aromatic molecules on biochar surfaces.

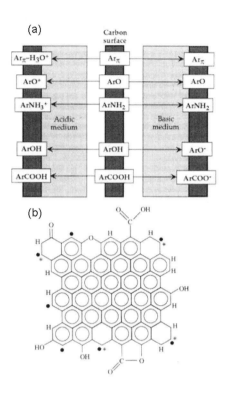

Figure 3.11 *(a) Macroscopic representation of the features of C surface chemistry thought to be sufficient for understanding aqueous-phase sorption phenomena; (b) microscopic representation of the functional groups thought to be sufficient for understanding aqueous-phase adsorption phenomena*

Notes: (a) Ar = aromatic. (b) • Represents an unpaired sigma electron; •* represents an in-plane sigma pair; * represents a localized π electron.

Source: reprinted from Radovic et al (2001) with permission from Elsevier

References

Akiyama, K. and Hayashi, H. (2006) 'Strigolactones: Chemical signals for fungal symbionts and parasitic weeds in plant roots', *Annals of Botany,* vol 97, pp925–931

Antal, M. J. Jr. and Grønli, M. (2003) 'The art, science, and technology of charcoal production', *Industrial and Engineering Chemistry Research,* vol 42, pp1619–1640

Antal, M. J. Jr., Allen, S. G., Dai, X.-F., Shimizu, B., Tam, M. S. and Grønli, M. (2000) 'Attainment of the theoretical yield of carbon from biomass', *Industrial and Engineering Chemistry Research,* vol 39, pp4024–4031

Bagreev, A., Bandosz, T. J. and Locke, D. C. (2001) 'Pore structure and surface chemistry of adsorbents obtained by pyrolysis of sewage sludge-derived fertilizer', *Carbon,* vol 39, pp1971–1977

Bergman, P. C. A. and Kiel, J. H. A. (2005) 'Torrefaction for biomass upgrading', www.ecn.nl/docs/library/report/2005/rx05180.pdf, accessed 1 August 2008

Boehm, H. P. (1994) 'Some aspects of the surface chemistry of carbon blacks and other carbons', *Carbon,* vol 32, pp759–769

Bourke, J. (2006) *Preparation and Properties of Natural, Demineralized, Pure, and Doped Carbons from Biomass; Model of the Chemical Structure of Carbonized Charcoal,* MS thesis, The University of Waikato, New Zealand

Bourke, J., Manley-Harris, M., Fushimi, C., Dowaki, K., Nunoura, T. and Antal, M. J. Jr., (2007) 'Do all carbonized charcoals have the same chemical structure? 2. A model of the chemical structure of carbonized charcoal', *Industrial and Engineering Chemistry Research,* vol 46, pp5954–5967

Bradbury, A. G. W. and Shafizadeh, F. (1980) 'Chemisorption of oxygen on cellulose char', *Carbon,* vol 18, pp109–116

Braida, W. J., Pignatello, J. J., Lu, Y., Ravikovitch, P., Neimark, A. V. and Xing, B. (2003) 'Sorption hysteresis of benzene in charcoal particles', *Environmental Science and Technology,* vol 37,

pp409–417

Brennan, J. K., Bandosz, T. J., Thomson, K. T. and Gubbins, K. E. (2001) 'Water in porous carbons', *Colloids and Surfaces A: Physicochemical and Engineering Aspects*, vol 187–188, pp539–568

Bridgwater, A. V. and Boocock, D. G. B. (eds) (1997) *Developments in Thermochemical Biomass Conversion*, Blackie Academic and Professional, London, UK

Bridgwater, A. and Boocock, D. G. B. (2006) *Science in Thermal and Chemical Biomass Conversion*, CPL Press, Newbury, UK

Chen, B., Zhou, D. and Zhu, L. Z. (2008) 'Transitional adsorption and partition of nonpolar and polar aromatic contaminants by biochars of pine needles with different pyrolytic temperatures', *Environmental Science and Technology*, vol 42, pp5137–5143

Cheng, C.-H., Lehmann, J. and Engelhard, M. H. (2008) 'Natural oxidation of black carbon in soils: Changes in molecular form and surface charge along a climosequence', *Geochimica et Cosmochimica Acta*, vol 72, pp1598–1610

Cohen-Ofri, I., Weiner, L., Boaretto, E., Mintz, G. and Weiner, S. (2006) 'Modern and fossil charcoal: Aspects of structure and diagenesis', *Journal of Archaeological Science*, vol 33, pp428–439

Cohen-Ofri, I., Popovitz-Biro, R. and Weiner, S. (2007) 'Structural characterization of modern and fossilized charcoal produced in natural fires as determined by using electron energy loss spectroscopy', *Chemistry, A European Journal*, vol 13, pp2306–2310

Cui, X. J., Antonietti, M. and Yu, S. H. (2006) 'Structural effects of iron oxide nanoparticles and iron ions on the hydrothermal carbonization of starch and rice carbohydrates', *Small*, vol 2, pp756–759

Degroot, W. F. and Shafizadeh, F. (1983) 'Influence of inorganic additives on oxygen chemisorption on cellulosic chars', *Carbon*, vol 21, pp61–67

Demirbas, A. (2001) 'Carbonization ranking of selected biomass for charcoal, liquid and gaseous products', *Energy Conversion and Management*, vol 42, pp1229–1238

Dixon, K. (1998) *Smoke Germination of Australian Plants*, RIRDC report (98/108, KPW–1A), Kings Park and Botanic Garden Plant Science

Division, Perth, Australia

Edye, L. A., Richards, G. N. and Zheng, G. (1993) 'Transition metals as catalysts for pyrolysis and gasification of biomass', in M. R. Khan (ed) *Clean Energy from Waste and Coal*, American Chemical Society Symposium Series 515, American Chemical Society, Washington, DC, pp90–103

Elizalde-Gonzalez, M. P., Mattusch, J., Pelaez-Cid, A. A. and Wennrich, R. (2007) 'Characterization of adsorbent materials prepared from avocado kernel seeds: Natural, activated and carbonized forms', *Journal of Analytical and Applied Pyrolysis*, vol 78, pp185–193

Essington, M. E. (2003) *Soil and Water Chemistry: An Integrative Approach*, CRC Press, Boca Raton, FL

Feng, J.-W., Zheng, S. and Maciel, G. E. (2004) 'EPR investigations of the effects of inorganic additives on the charring and char/air interactions of cellulose,' *Energy and Fuels*, vol 18, pp1049–1065

Figueiredo, J. L., Valenzuela, C., Bernalte, A. and Encinar, J. M. (1989) 'Pyrolysis of holm-oak wood: Influence of temperature and particle size', *Fuel*, vol 68, pp1012–1017

Franklin, R. E. (1951) 'Crystallite growth in graphitizing and non-graphitizing carbons', *Proceedings of the Royal Society of London, Series A, Mathematical and Physical Sciences*, vol 209, pp196–218

Guan, M. (2004) *Manual for Bamboo Charcoal Production and Utilization*, Bamboo Engineering Research Center, Nanjing Forestry University, China

Kercher, A. K. and Nagle, D. C. (2003) 'Microstructural evolution during charcoal carbonization by X-ray diffraction analysis', *Carbon*, vol 41, pp15–27

Knudsen, J. N., Jensen, P. A., Lin, W., Frandsen, F. J. and Dam-Johnson, K. (2004) 'Sulfur transformations during thermal conversion of herbaceous biomass', *Energy and Fuels*, vol 18, pp810–819

Koutcheiko, S., Monreal, C.M., Kodama, H., McCracken, T. and Kotlyar, L. (2007) 'Preparation and characterization of activated carbon derived from the thermo-chemical conversion of chicken manure', *Bioresource Technology*, vol 98, pp2459–2464

Krull, E. S., Skjemstad, J. O., Graetz, D., Grice, K., Dunning, W., Cook, G. D. and Parr, J. F. (2003) '^{13}C-depleted charcoal from C3 and C4 grasses and the role of occluded carbon in phytoliths', *Organic Geochemistry*, vol 34, pp1337–1352

Langmuir, D. (1997) *Aqueous Environmental Geochemistry*, Prentice-Hall, Upper Saddle River, NJ

Lima, I. M. and Marshall, W.E. (2005) 'Granular activated carbons from broiler manure: Physical, chemical and adsorptive properties', *Bioresource Technology*, vol 96, pp699–706

Maggi, R. and Delmon, B. (1994) 'Comparison between "slow" and "flash" pyrolysis oils from biomass', *Fuel*, vol 73, no 5, pp671–677

Marschner, H. (1995) *The Mineral Nutrition of Higher Plants*, Academic Press, San Diego, CA

Marsh, H., Heintz, E. A. and Rodriguez-Reinoso, F. (1997) *Introduction to Carbon Technologies*, University of Alicante, Alicante, Spain

Nguyen, T. H., Cho, H. H., Poster, D. L. and Ball, W. P. (2007) 'Evidence for a pore-filling mechanism in the adsorption of aromatic hydrocarbons to a natural wood char', *Environmental Science and Technology*, vol 41, pp1212–1217

Paris, O., Zollfrank, C. and Zickler, G. A. (2005) Decomposition and carbonisation of wood biopolymers – a microstructural study of softwood pyrolysis', *Carbon*, vol 43, pp53–66

Parr, J. F. (2006) 'Effect of fire on phytolith coloration', *Geoarchaelogy – An International Journal*, vol 21, pp171–185

Parr, J. F. and Sullivan, L. A. (2005) 'Soil carbon sequestration in phytoliths', *Soil Biology and Biochemistry*, vol 37, pp117–124

Pignatello, J. J., Kwon, S. and Lu, Y. (2006) 'Effect of natural organic substances on the surface adsorptive properties of environmental black carbon (char): Attenuation of surface activity by humic and fulvic acids', *Environmental Science and Technology*, vol 40, pp7757–7763

Purevsuren, B., Avida, B., Gerelmaa, T., Davaajava, Y., Morgan, T. J., Herod, A. A. and Kandiyoti, R. (2004) 'The characterisation of tar from the pyrolysis of animal bones', *Fuel*, vol 83, pp799–805

Radovic, L. R., Moreno-Castilla, C. and Rivera-Utrilla, J. (2001) 'Carbon materials as adsorbents in aqueous solutions', *Chemistry and Physics of Carbon: A Series of Advances*, vol 27, pp227–405

Raveendran, K., Ganesh, A. and Khilart, K. C. (1995) 'Influence of mineral matter on biomass pyrolysis characteristics', *Fuel*, vol 74, pp1812–1822

Rimstidt, J. D. and Vaughan, D. J. (2003) 'Pyrite oxidation: A state-of-the-art assessment of the reaction mechanism', *Geochimica et Cosmochimica Acta*, vol 67, pp873–880

Rothlein, B. (2006) 'Magic coal from the steam cooker', *Max Planck Research*, vol 3, pp20–25

Sander, M. and Pignatello, J. J. (2005) 'Characterization of charcoal adsorption sites for aromatic compounds: Insights drawn from single-solute and bi-solute competitive experiments', *Environmental Science and Technology*, vol 39, pp1606–1615

Sander, M. and Pignatello, J. J. (2007) 'On the reversibility of sorption to black carbon: Distinguishing true hysteresis from artificial hysteresis caused by dilution of a competing adsorbate', *Environmental Science and Technology*, vol 41, pp843–849

Schenkel, Y. (1999) *Modelisation des Flux Massiques et Energetiques dans la Carbonisation du Bois en Four Cornue*, PhD thesis, Université des Sciences Agronomiques de Gembloux, Gembloux, Belgium

Schnitzer, M. I., Monreal, C. M., Facey, G. A and Fransham, P. B. (2007a) 'The conversion of chicken manure to biooil by fast pyrolysis I. Analyses of chicken manure, biooils and char by C-13 and H-1 NMR and FTIR spectrophotometry', *Journal of Environmental Science and Health B*, vol 42, pp71–77

Schnitzer, M. I., Monreal, C. M., Jandl, G. and Leinweber, P. (2007b) 'The conversion of chicken manure to biooil by fast pyrolysis II. Analysis of chicken manure, biooils, and char by curie-point pyrolysis-gas chromatography/ mass spectrometry (Cp Py-GC/MS)', *Journal of Environmental Science and Health B*, vol 42, pp79–95

Scott, D. S., Piskorz, J., Bergougnou, M. A., Graham, R. and Overend, R. P. (1988) 'The role of temperature in the fast pyrolysis of cellulose and wood', *Industrial and Engineering Chemistry Research*, vol 27, pp8–15

Shafizadeh, F. (1982) 'Introduction to pyrolysis of biomass', *Journal of Analytical and Applied*

Pyrolysis, vol 3, pp283–305

Skodras, G., Grammelis, P., Basinas, P., Kakaras, E. and Sakellaropoulos, G. (2006) 'Pyrolysis and combustion characteristics of biomass and waste-derived feedstock', *Industrial and Engineering Chemistry Research*, vol 45, pp3791–3799

Smith, F. A. and White, J. W. C. (2004) 'Modern calibration of phytolith carbon isotope signatures for C3/C4 paleograssland reconstruction', *Palaeogeography, Palaeoclimatology, Palaeoecology*, vol 207, pp277–304

Stresov, V., Patterson, M., Zymla, V., Fisher, K., Evans, T. J. and Nelson, P. F. (2007) 'Fundamental aspects of biomass carbonisation', *Journal of Analytical and Applied Pyrolysis*, vol 79, pp91–100

Stumm, W. and Morgan, J. J. (1996) *Aquatic Chemistry: Chemical Equilibria and Rates in Natural Waters*, third edition, Wiley-Interscience, New York, NY

Swiatkowski, A., Pakula, B., Biniak, S. and Walczyk, M. (2004) 'Influence of the surface chemistry of modified activated carbon on its electrochemical behaviour in the presence of lead(II) ions', *Carbon*, vol 42, pp3057–3069

Titirici, M. M., Thomas, A., Yu, S. H., Muller, J. O. and Antonietti, M. (2007a) 'A direct synthesis of mesoporous carbons with bicontinuous pore morphology from crude plant material by hydrothermal carbonization', *Chemistry of Materials*, vol 19, pp4205–4212

Titirici, M. M., Thomas, A. and Antonietti, M. (2007b) 'Back in the black: Hydrothermal carbonization of plant material as an efficient chemical process to treat the CO_2 problem?', *New Journal of Chemistry*, vol 31, pp787–789

Tito Ferro, D., Torres, A., Beaton Soler, P. and Zanzi, R. (2004) 'Biomass torrefaction', in W. P. M. Van Swaaij, T. Fjällström, P. Helm and A. Grassi (eds) *2nd World Conference and Technology Exhibition on Biomass for Energy, Industry and Climate Protection*, 10–14 May 2004, Palazzo dei Congressi, Rome, Italy, ETA–Florence and WIP–Munich, pp859–862, http://hem.fyristorg.com/zanzi/paper/zanziV2A–17.pdf, accessed 1 August 2008

Varhegyi, G., Jakab, E. and Antal, M. J. (1994) 'Is the Broido–Shafizadeh model for cellulose pyrolysis true?', *Energy Fuels*, vol 8, p1345

Wilding, L. P., Brown, R. E. and Holowaychuk, N. (1967) 'Accessibility and properties of occluded carbon in biogenic opal', *Soil Science*, vol 103, pp56–61

Wornat, M. J., Hurt, R. H. and Yang, N. Y. C. (1995) 'Structural and compositional transformations of biomass chars during combustion', *Combustion Flame*, vol 100, pp131–143

Yu, C., Tang. Y., Fang, M., Luo, Z. and Cen, K. (2005) 'Experimental study on alkali emission during rice straw pyrolysis', *Journal of Zhejiang University (Engineering Science)*, vol 39, pp1435–1444

Zhu, D. and Pignatello, J. J. (2005) 'Characterization of aromatic compound sorptive interactions with black carbon (charcoal) assisted by graphite as a model', *Environmental Science and Technology*, vol 39, pp2033–2041

Zhu, D., Kwon, S. and Pignatello, J. J. (2005) 'Adsorption of single-ring organic compounds to wood charcoals prepared under different thermochemical conditions', *Environmental Science and Technology*, vol 39, pp3990–3998

4

Characteristics of Biochar: Organo-chemical Properties

Evelyn S. Krull, Jeff A. Baldock, Jan O. Skjemstad and Ronald J. Smernik

Introduction

In this chapter, we will focus on the discussion of the organo-chemical characteristics of biochar, based on information derived from the types of bonds and their configuration within biochars as well as elemental ratios and their associated changes with charring temperature. Specifically, we will explore the changes that occur during charring processes in the type and distribution of major biomolecules that constitute natural organic materials, based on information derived from ^{13}C solid state nuclear magnetic resonance (NMR) spectroscopy and elemental ratios. These changes are placed in context with regard to the specific combustion temperatures, the presence or absence of oxygen (O_2), as well as the influence of the type of original material on the biochar end product. We will discuss the chemical aspects of biochar types produced in the laboratory as well as char from natural vegetation fires.

As summarized in Schmidt and Noack (2000) and Schmidt et al (2001), 'char' is only one of several components of the 'Black Carbon (BC) continuum' that includes incomplete combustion residues from fossil fuels and vegetation fires. Biochar, as defined in this book (see Chapter 1), is the carbonaceous residue of biomass pyrolysis intended as a soil amendment. This chapter focuses on biochar types derived from natural biomass materials (e.g. wood, leaf, grass, etc.). In terms of its chemical structure, biochar is commonly considered to be highly aromatic and containing random stacks of graphitic layers (Schmidt and Noack, 2000). However, it was noted by Franklin in the 1950s that the structure of char depended not only upon the temperature, but also upon the nature of the starting material (Franklin, 1951). Furthermore, Schmidt and Noack (2000) noted that the exact chemical composition of biochar was a function of the conditions during combustion, such as temperature and moisture content of the fuel. For example, the temperature considered 'typical' for producing biochar through the carbonization of plant material is not well defined. Emrich (1985) described charcoal-like biochar as the residue, generated at temperatures above

300°C and in an O_2-restricted atmosphere. However, most studies that produce biochar in the laboratory choose a range of temperatures since charring is considered a process that does not occur at one specific temperature. As a result, chars produced from biomass burning in the environment are expected to vary in composition and uniformity, with the one common feature being the high content of aryl C, which tends to increase with the extent of thermal alteration.

Elemental ratios

The H/C ratio of unburned fuel materials, such as cellulose or lignin, is approximately 1.5, and Kuhlbusch and Crutzen (1996) used molar H/C ratios of ≤0.2 to define 'black carbon'. Graetz and Skjemstad (2003) concluded that temperatures during biomass burning are predominantly greater than 400°C (smouldering combustion) and that chars formed during these temperatures are likely to have H/C ratios of ≤0.5. Consequently, biochar production is often assessed through changes in the elemental concentrations of C, H, O and N and associated ratios. Specifically, H/C and O/C ratios are used to measure the degree of aromaticity and maturation, as is often illustrated in van Krevelen diagrams (e.g. Baldock and Smernik, 2002; Braadbaart et al, 2004, Hammes et al, 2006).

A review of the literature of natural and lab-produced biochars showed that the chemical composition of these combustion products varied greatly (see Figures 4.1 and 4.2 and Table 4.1). In fact, the data in Table 4.1 indicate that while some biochars do have H/C ratios of below 0.5, this number cannot be categorically applied to all biochars as many burning residues had significantly higher H/C ratios. This observation reflects the conclusion drawn by Schmidt and Noack (2000) on the characteristics of black C, which includes biochar: 'BC represents a continuum from partly charred material to graphite and soot particles with no general agreement on clear-cut boundaries.'

Consequently, this continuum of charring conditions can be extended to the compositional characteristics associated with these increasing degrees of oxidation. The data in Figure 4.1 and Table 4.1 show, for example, that H/C and O/C ratios tended to be highest in low-temperature biochars, partially charred plant materials and biochars produced during very short heating intervals. Lower ratios were observed in naturally produced wood char, vegetation fire residues, biochar produced in the laboratory under high temperatures, and/or prolonged heating. In general, H/C and O/C ratios in experimentally produced biochars decreased with increasing temperature (Shindo, 1991; Baldock and Smernik, 2002) and increased time of heating (Almendros et al, 2003) (see Figure 4.1). In addition, Knicker et al (2005) discussed the possibility of utilizing H/C ratios of organic materials to infer information about the bonding arrangements. For example, an H/C ratio of 1.3 for peat (see Table 4.1) is suggested to indicate that most C is either directly bonded to a proton or connected through an OH group. Knicker et al (2005) further concluded that an H/C ratio between 0.4 and 0.6 of the aromatic portion of chars indicates that every second to third C is connected to a proton. Soot and lignite, by comparison, often have H/C ratios of <0.1, indicating a more graphite-like structure.

Notably, Trompowsky et al (2005) observed that humic acids, extracted from biochars produced at different temperatures, had similar or slightly lower H/C ratios than the biochar itself. However, the O/C ratios were consistently higher compared with the equivalent biochar products, which the authors attributed to the extraction with nitric acid, introducing additional oxygen-containing functional groups. Thus, chemical treatment of biochars may alter their chemical characteristics, and care should be taken to distinguish between changes due to charring conditions and artefacts from chemical treatments or extractions.

Cheng et al (2008) found that artificial 'aging' of freshly produced biochar by incubation resulted in comparably lower organic C (OC) contents when aged at 70°C compared to 30°C (see Chapter 10). In contrast, experimental heating of wood, peas, cellulose and peat under O_2-reduced conditions showed an increase in percentage of OC as a function of increased temperature or length of heating time (see Table 4.1 and Figure 4.2). However, the OC content of grass material was comparably lower during all heating treatments (except for the starting temperatures of cellulose) and tended to decrease at or above 600°C.

These differences reflect not just variations in chemistry, but also differences in ash content. The ash content of fire residues depends upon the ash content of the vegetation. For example, the higher C content of wood biochar (68.2 per cent) compared to grass biochar (58.6 per cent) produced in the laboratory under identical conditions can be attributed to differences in ash content between the wood (<0.1 per cent) and grass (7.7 per cent) (Hammes et al, 2006). The efficiency of burning or charring also has an effect, as complete combustion to CO_2 increases the ash content of the residues.

Therefore residues from natural vegetation fire that are produced under natural

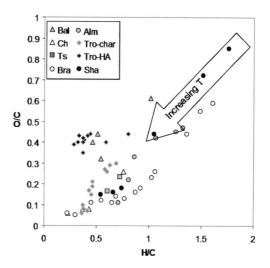

Figure 4.1 *Van Krevelen diagram of H/C and O/C ratios of biochars made under different temperature regimes (data taken from Table 4.1) between low-temperature biochars and those produced by high-temperature pyrolysis, as well as naturally occurring black C*

Source: Bal: Baldock and Smernik (2002); Ch: Cheng et al (2006); Ts: Tsai et al (2006); Bra: Braadbaart et al (2004); Alm: Almendros et al (2003); Tro (char and humic acids): Trompowsky et al (2005); and Sha: Shafizadeh and Sekiguchi (1983)

(oxygen-rich) conditions usually have lower OC contents than laboratory- or commercially produced biochars generated under higher temperatures and oxygen-poor pyrolytic conditions. This is an important observation as biochars are commonly regarded as OC-rich materials (i.e. $\gg$500mg g^{-1}); yet, grass chars produced by natural fires may contain less than 100mg g^{-1} OC (Krull et al, 2003; Graetz and Skjemstad, 2003). Similarly, biochars made from manures or grass species (such as rice husks) can contain much less than 500mg g^{-1} OC.

Table 4.1 *The data illustrate the chemical changes that occur during the charring process and the influence of charring temperature: hydrogen/carbon (H/C), oxygen/carbon (O/C) and hydrogen/oxygen (H/O) ratios are atomic ratios and carbon/nitrogen (C/N) and percentage organic carbon (OC) are based on mass*

Material	H/C	O/C	C/N	H/O	OC (mg g⁻¹)	Reference
200°C wood biochar	1.02	0.61	500	1.67	525	Baldock and Smernik (2002)
250°C wood biochar	0.51	0.44	370	1.15	610	Baldock and Smernik (2002)
300°C wood biochar	0.46	0.4	214	1.12	628	Baldock and Smernik (2002)
350°C wood biochar	0.54	0.32	269	1.7	673	Baldock and Smernik (2002)
Wood biochar	0.07		105		540	Fernandes et al (2003)
Pea-straw biochar	0.08		25		430	Fernandes et al (2003)
Vegetation fire residue	0.17		40		40	Fernandes et al (2003)
Rapeseed cake	0.5	0.3	11		550	Özçimen and Karaosmanoglu (2004)
350°C wood biochar		0.2	119		830	Cheng et al (2006)
Charred grass	0.6	0.2	20		180	Haumaier and Zech (1995)
Soot	0.59	0.3	19		650	Haumaier and Zech (1995)
Charred barley straw	0.73	0.2	76		680	Haumaier and Zech (1995)
Hardwood biochar	0.23	0.06			908	Cheng et al (2008)
Pyrolysed sewage sludge	0.06		7.3		470	Bridle and Pritchard (2004)
Rice straw biochar	0.726	0.2325	37.3	0.2	493	Tsai et al (2006)
Sugar cane bagasse biochar	0.605	0.165	40.3	0.2	714	Tsai et al (2006)
Coconut shell biochar	0.605	0.165	73.8	0.2	693	Tsai et al (2006)
Soybean cake biochar	0.605	0.39	7.52	0.1	588	Uzun et al (2006)
Peas 190°C	1.61	0.59	10.21	0.17	480	Braadbaart et al (2004)
Peas 220°C	1.49	0.55	20.80	0.17	520	Braadbaart et al (2004)
Peas 235°C	1.36	0.44	10.00	0.19	550	Braadbaart et al (2004)
Peas 250°C	1.06	0.26	9.85	0.25	640	Braadbaart et al (2004)
Peas 270°C	1.03	0.23	10.82	0.28	660	Braadbaart et al (2004)
Peas 290°C	0.92	0.18	10.94	0.31	700	Braadbaart et al (2004)
Peas 310°C	0.87	0.16	10.29	0.35	720	Braadbaart et al (2004)
Peas 340°C	0.77	0.13	11.21	0.36	740	Braadbaart et al (2004)
Peas 370°C	0.69	0.14	11.90	0.31	750	Braadbaart et al (2004)
Peas 400°C	0.65	0.11	11.69	0.37	760	Braadbaart et al (2004)
Peas 440°C	0.55	0.12	14.53	0.29	770	Braadbaart et al (2004)
Peas 500°C	0.45	0.11	17.02	0.25	800	Braadbaart et al (2004)
Peas 600°C	0.30	0.05	13.08	0.35	850	Braadbaart et al (2004)
Peas 700°C	0.22	0.06	20.71	0.23	870	Braadbaart et al (2004)
Cellulosic biochar 300°C	1.76	0.85		0.13	440	Shafizadeh and Sekiguchi (1983)
Cellulosic biochar 325°C	1.52	0.72		0.13	479	Shafizadeh and Sekiguchi (1983)
Cellulosic biochar 350°C	1.05	0.44		0.15	599	Shafizadeh and Sekiguchi (1983)
Cellulosic biochar 400°C	0.74	0.18		0.25	765	Shafizadeh and Sekiguchi (1983)

Material	H/C	O/C	C/N	H/O	OC (mg g^{-1})	Reference
Cellulosic biochar 450°C	0.66	0.16		0.25	788	Shafizadeh and Sekiguchi (1983)
Cellulosic biochar 500°C	0.54	0.15		0.23	804	Shafizadeh and Sekiguchi (1983)
Peat biochar at 350°C:						Almendros et al (2003) and
0 sec	1.32	0.47	35	0.18	420	Knicker et al (2005)
60 sec	1.26	0.45	36.00	0.17	576	
90 sec	1.07	0.42	33.22	0.16	598	
120 sec	0.86	0.33	34.21	0.16	650	
150 sec	0.81	0.22	32.59	0.23	717	
180 sec	0.71	0.11	29.81	0.39	805	
Barbecue char	0.48		343.0		823	
Wood biochar	0.7	0.3	690			Hammes et al (2006)
Grass biochar	0.7	0.3	49			Hammes et al (2006)
Themeda biochar:						Krull and Skjemstad (unpublished
250°C			97.60		488	data)
400°C			56.50		565	
600°C			69.13		553	
860°C			93.83		563	
Phalaris biochar:						
250°C			115.75		463	
400°C			66.22		596	
600°C			67.26		565	
860°C			65.36		549	
Cocksfoot biochar:						
250°C			32.44		519	
400°C			34.00		612	
600°C			49.57		694	
860°C			30.18		510	
Ryegrass biochar:						
250°C			12.29		467	
400°C			11.10		466	
600°C			13.87		484	
860°C			19.15		452	
Kikuyu grass biochar:						
250°C			22.00		462	
400°C			19.44		525	
600°C			18.15		530	
860°C			23.63		482	

Table 4.1 *continued*

Material	H/C	O/C	C/N	H/O	OC (mg g^{-1})	Reference
Eucalyptus saligna biochars						Trompowsky et al (2005)
300°C	0.69	0.30	479		688	
350°C	0.6	0.26	439		714	
400°C	0.46	0.19	582		769	
450°C	0.45	0.15	511		806	
500°C	0.41	0.07	631		883	
550°C	0.36	0.06	541		900	
E. grandis biochars						Trompowsky et al (2005)
300°C	0.63	0.29	705		692	
350°C	0.58	0.27	662		709	
400°C	0.46	0.21	630		759	
450°C	0.43	0.17	629		795	
500°C	0.38	0.08	777		876	
550°C	0.37	0.1	624		860	
E. saligna humic acids:						Trompowsky et al (2005)
300°C	0.80	0.44	21.8		585	
350°C	0.44	0.44	23.4		599	
400°C	0.38	0.41	26.5		618	
450°C	0.37	0.40	28.3		621	
500°C	0.37	0.35	28.6		649	
550°C	0.59	0.40	29.4		619	
E. grandis humic acids:						Trompowsky et al (2005)
350°C	0.41	0.43	22.6		601	
400°C	0.33	0.43	26.9		606	
450°C	0.28	0.39	27.9		631	
500°C	0.37	0.42	27.9		612	
550°C	0.32	0.40	27.7		624	

^{13}C-nuclear magnetic resonance (NMR) spectroscopy

Several studies have focused on determining the chemical structure and composition of natural and laboratory-produced biochars. For example, Baldock and Smernik (2002) investigated the chemical changes that occurred in wood, heated to temperatures of 150°C, 200°C, 250°C, 300°C and 350°C in a muffle furnace. While heating to 150°C did not alter C or N concentrations, at temperatures of >150°C, C concentrations increased progressively, while N concentrations were greatest at 300°C. They found that O/C ratios decreased at temperatures above 250°C, showing a progressive loss of H and O relative to C (see Table 4.1 and Figures 4.1 and 4.2). The decrease in H/C ratios was seen to be indicative of the formation of structures containing unsaturated C, such as aromatic rings. To investigate how these changes in elemental ratios were reflected in

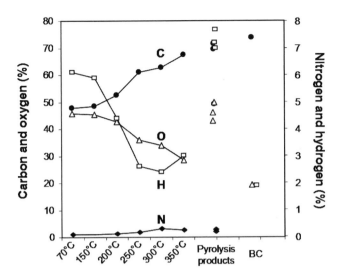

Figure 4.2 *Changes in elements with increasing temperature during the charring process of wood, as well as data from fast pyrolysis products and biochar: here, the differences are illustrated between low-temperature biochars and those produced by high-temperature fast pyrolysis as well as biochar (BC, black locust wood) produced at 350°C*

Source: Baldock and Smernik (2002): data from charring process of wood; Tsai et al (2006): data from fast pyrolysis products; Cheng et al (2006): data from biochar

the molecular composition of the biochars, they obtained ^{13}C-NMR spectra on each of the biochars, produced at different temperatures.

As expected, the changes in elemental ratios from the temperature treatments were accompanied by changes in the functional groups as identified by variations in the distribution of ^{13}C-NMR spectral intensity (see Figure 4.3). At 200°C, signal intensity associated with cellulose and hemicellulose structures (O-alkyl and di-O-alkyl C) declined, while the signal intensity of lignin (aryl and O-aryl C) increased. Further heating to 250°C increased the signal intensity of aryl C to 64 per cent, concomitant with a decrease in O-alkyl and di-O-alkyl C to <10 per cent, indicating a conversion of O-alkyl structures to aryl structures. In this context, it is important to point out that these chemical conversions occur concurrently with rapid changes in mass loss during the partial combustion process, which has to be taken into account when quantifying the chemical changes. Baldock and Smernik (2002) reported mass losses from 3 to 81 per cent (compared with the starting material) during a temperature increase from150°C to 300°C. Similarly, Czimczik et al (2002) reported

significant increases in mass loss with increased temperature, with 85 per cent total mass loss at 1000°C for softwood and 91 per cent for hardwood.

The increase in the proportion of aryl C found by Baldock and Smernik (2002) with increased heating temperatures is consistent with other studies investigating the effects of heating on wood (Solum et al, 2004; Czimczik et al, 2002), cellulose (Shafizadeh and Sekiguchi, 1983; Pastorova et al, 1994; Fonseca et al, 1996; Maroto-Valer et al, 1998), humic and fulvic acid (Almendros et al, 1990, 1992) and other lignocellulosic materials (Knicker et al, 1996; Maroto-Valer et al, 1996; Freitas et al, 1999, 2001).

Almendros et al (2003) specifically investigated the processes occurring during the charring of peat organic matter, using both ^{13}C- and ^{15}N-NMR. They found that, based on weight loss values and NMR data, both aromatic and heterocyclic N-containing structures were formed as a direct result of heating. They further suggested that it was these mechanisms – transformation of labile compounds into environmentally recalcitrant forms – that had important biochemical implications with regard to greater stability against decomposition.

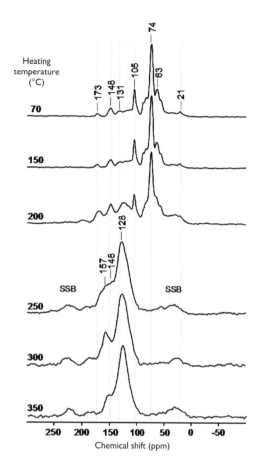

Figure 4.3 *Changes in functional group chemistry obtained by nuclear magnetic resonance (NMR) spectroscopy with increasing temperature: values above peaks are chemical shift positions; SSBs are spinning side bands*

Source: redrawn from Baldock and Smernik (2002)

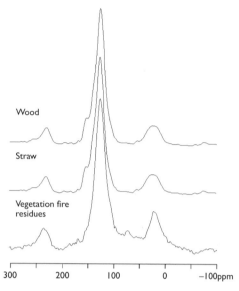

Figure 4.4 *Cross-polarization (CP) NMR spectra from biochar derived from wood (*Eucalyptus camaldulensis*) and pea straw (*Pisum sativum*) materials (biochar produced in the laboratory at 450°C in a muffle furnace for 1 hour) and vegetation fire residues from a natural fire*

Source: Fernandes et al (2003)

A direct comparison of the chemical composition of biochars derived from different materials by Fernandes et al (2003) showed that the chemical composition of the original material and the type of combustion process will affect the chemistry of the burned material. They analysed carbonaceous straw and wood biochar produced at 450°C in a muffle furnace and natural vegetation fire residues using cross-polarization (CP) ^{13}C-NMR (Figure 4.4).

The NMR spectra of the straw and wood biochar and char derived from vegetation fire residues are similar to the ones from the higher temperature experiments reported in Baldock and Smernik (2002) and shown in Figure 4.3, confirming that these biochars are dominated by highly aromatic (aryl-dominated) structures.

While many studies on the chemistry of biochar focus on wood-derived biochar, Krull and Skjemstad (unpublished data) investigated the changes occurring in different grasses (kikuyu, ryegrass, *Phalaris*, cocksfoot and *Themeda*), heated at a series of increasing temperatures. Plant materials were heated in a muffle furnace for one hour at 250°C, 400°C, 600°C and 800°C and CP-NMR spectra were obtained for all but the 800°C materials. Other studies have also reported difficulties in obtaining good NMR spectra for biochars produced at high temperatures. For example, Freitas et al (1999) reported tuning problems for peat samples heated to 1000°C and Bourke et al (2007) reported problems adjusting the tune and match on the probe for maize-cob biochar carbonized at 950°C. These problems occur in such high-temperature biochars due to the high electrical conductivity associated with the alignment of aromatic sheets (Freitas et al, 1999).

Increased heating also resulted in a significant peak shift in the aryl region from an average of 129ppm in plant materials to 127ppm for biochars produced at 400°C and 600°C. Similarly, Baldock and Smernik (2002) observed a shift in the aryl-C resonance from 131ppm to 127ppm during their heating experiments. Freitas et al (1999, 2001a, 2001b) observed such shifts in biochars produced from a number of different starting materials, with a maximum shift of 11ppm occurring during the charring process of peat. They attributed the effect to diamagnetic currents produced by delocalized π-electrons in extended aromatic structures or graphite-like microcrystallites, which produce an overall shielding effect or displacement to lower parts per million values (Freitas et al, 2001a). Peak shifts are also observed by near-edge X-ray absorption fine structure (NEXAFS) analysis, where aromatic C is shifted to lower energies below 285eV, as well as showing a characteristic peak at 286.1eV, hypothesized to indicate fused aromatic rings with low H and O substitutions (Lehmann et al, 2005).

In the study by Krull and Skjemstad, the original grass materials were all dominated by O-alkyl C; however, there were significant differences between the grasses with regard to the relative proportion of O-alkyl, alkyl C and carbonyl C present in the combustion products. For example, in decreasing order, ryegrass (22.4 per cent), cocksfoot (17.0 per cent) and kikuyu (15.4 per cent) had the highest proportion of alkyl C in their plant structure, whereas *Themeda* and *Phalaris* both had <10 per cent alkyl C. Alkyl C is representative of plant structures, such as lipids and cutans, which have been known to be biochemically resistant to degradation and can accumulate in recalcitrant soil organic matter (e.g. Poirier et al, 2000, 2006; Krull and Skjemstad, 2003). Biochars produced from ryegrass, cocksfoot and kikuyu at 250°C and 400°C retained a higher alkyl C content compared with other biochars (see Figure 4.5). These materials also had lower C/N ratios compared with the other grasses (both in the original plant material as well as in the biochars produced at 250°C and 400°C). Biochars produced at 600°C were all dominated by aryl C with minor contributions from O-aryl C and only small proportions from carbonyl, O-alkyl and alkyl C. These data suggest that the composition of the original plant materials will affect the composition of biochar produced at temperatures below 500°C to 600°C. This may have an effect on the types of C and N released during the weathering process and the resistance of biochar to weathering.

The NMR data from Baldock and Smernik (2002) and Krull and Skjemstad (unpublished data) show the progressive changes in composition with increasing temperature. These data may be used to infer the approximate temperature of biochars produced at an unknown temperature from similar materials and to make inferences about the stability of biochars.

Figure 4.6 shows the distribution of signal intensity of major functional groups from laboratory-produced biochars generated at an unknown temperature (wood and leaves from oil mallee and redwood gum) in comparison with biochars from the studies by Baldock and Smernik (2002) and Krull and Skjemstad (unpublished data). The oil mallee wood and the redgum biochar showed the most complete degree of conversion from biomass to biochar, consistent with the highly thermally altered material from the average grass materials produced at 600°C (see Figure 4.5). In comparison, the biochar from oil mallee leaves still showed the presence of other functional groups such as alkyl and O-alkyl, which has been shown to still be present in wood produced at 250°C and, to a lesser degree, 350°C (Baldock and Skjemstad, 2002).

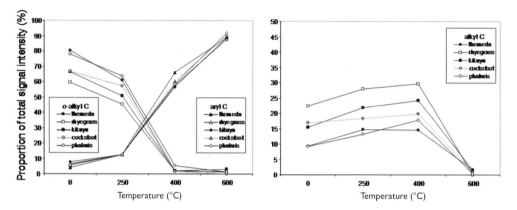

Figure 4.5 *Changes in the proportions of O-alkyl, aryl and alkyl C from grass biochars produced at different temperatures*

Source: Krull and Skjemstad (unpublished data); a more detailed description of the experimental set-up can be found in Krull et al (2003)

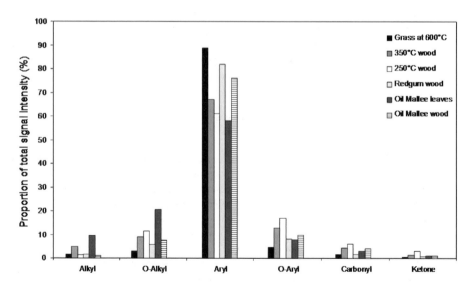

Figure 4.6 *Comparison of the proportion of total signal intensity from CP ^{13}C-NMR of biochars produced at unknown temperatures with those from known temperatures: Data for grass is the average composition of the biochars produced at 600°C from kikuyu, ryegrass,* Phalaris *and cocksfoot grasses (see Table 4.1); the wood biochars are produced from red pine (*Pinus resinosa*)*

Note: Oil mallee leaves and redgum wood are from Western Australia.

Source: Baldock and Smernik (2002); see Table 4.1 and Figure 4.3

Outlook

In summary, the data compiled here indicate that biochars produced above 350°C are dominated by aromatic (aryl) C with low H/C ratios. However, characteristics of the original plant material are still retained at these temperatures and greater heating at temperatures above 500°C tends to remove plant-characteristic functional group C structures observable by NMR. At these higher temperatures, the conversion of alkyl and O-alkyl C to aryl C is almost complete. Thus, particularly in biochars made at temperatures <500°C, the chemical characteristics can vary substantially; accordingly, its chemical stability is most likely influenced to a significant extent by the degree of aromaticity. In general, with higher temperatures, there is greater mass loss and the resulting biochar is dominated by aryl C and very low H/C ratios.

While the broad structural characterization of biochars by NMR and chemical analyses is well documented, future work is required to gain a better understanding of the specific differences of biochars from different materials and how they can be used as a soil amendment. [13]C- and ^{15}N-labelled biochars and advanced NMR spectroscopic techniques (e.g. dipolar de-phasing) can shed some light on how the original material may influence the product and at which temperatures the differences may vanish. Furthermore, Trompowsky et al (2005) attempted to distinguish between different components of biochar (humic and fulvic acids), and while they observed the potential of creating artefacts during chemical treatment, their approach is exemplary for future studies as it is the different components of biochar that are likely to be responsible for the differences in, for example, degradability or nutrient status. For example, the solvent-extractable component of biochar and subsequent analyses for biomarkers and compound-specific isotopic analyses has previously not been attempted and could aid in the further characterization of fresh as well as aged biochar, aiming to assess the weathering processes of biochar and the release of non-aromatic components.

References

Almendros, G., González-Vila, F. J. and Martin, F. (1990) 'Fire-induced transformation of soil organic matter from an oak forest: An experimental approach to the effects of fire on humic substances', *Soil Science*, vol 149, pp158–168

Almendros, G., Gonzalez-Vila, F. J., Martin, F., Frund, R. and Ludemann, H. D. (1992) 'Solid state NMR studies of fire-induced changes in the structure of humic substances', *The Science of the Total Environment*, vol 117–118, pp63–74

Almendros, G., Knicker, H. and González-Vila, F. J. (2003) 'Rearrangement of carbon and nitrogen forms in peat after progressive thermal oxidation as determined by solid–state ^{13}C- and ^{15}N-NMR spectroscopy', *Organic Geochemistry*, vol 34, pp1559–1568

Baldock, J. A. and Smernik, R. J. (2002) 'Chemical composition and bioavailability of thermally altered *Pinus resinosa* (red pine) wood', *Organic Geochemistry*, vol 33, pp1093–1109

Bourke, J., Manley-Harris, M., Fushimi, C., Dowaki, K., Nunoura, T. and Antal, M. J. (2007) 'Do all carbonized charcoals have the same chemical structure? 2. A model of the chemical structure of carbonized charcoal', *Industrial and Engineering Chemistry Research*, vol 46, pp5954–5967

Braadbaart, F., Boon, J. J., Veld, H., David, P. and Van Bergen, P. F. (2004) 'Laboratory simulations of the transformation of peas as a result of heat treatment: Changes of the physical and chemical properties', *Journal of*

Archaeological Science, vol 31, pp821–833

Bridle, T. R. and Pritchard, D. (2004) 'Energy and nutrient recovery from sewage sludge via pyrolysis', *Water Science and Technology*, vol 50, pp169–175

Cheng, C. H., Lehmann, J., Thies, J. E., Burton, S. D. and Engelhard, M. H. (2006) 'Oxidation of black carbon by biotic and abiotic processes', *Organic Geochemistry*, vol 37, pp1477–1488

Cheng, C. H., Lehmann, J. and Engelhard, M. (2008) 'Natural oxidation of black carbon in soils: Changes in molecular form and surface charge along a climosequence', *Geochimica et Cosmochimica Acta*, vol 72, pp1598–1610

Czimczik, C. I., Preston, C. M., Schmidt, M. W. I., Werner, R. A. and Schulze, E. D. (2002) 'Effects of charring on mass, organic carbon, and stable carbon isotope composition of wood', *Organic Geochemistry*, vol 33, pp1207–1223

Emrich, W. (1985) *Handbook of Charcoal Making: The Traditional and Industrial Methods*, Reidel Publishing Company, Dordrecht, The Netherlands

Fernandes, M. B., Skjemstad, J. O., Johnson, B. B., Wells, J. D. and Brooks, P. (2003) 'Characterization of carbonaceous combustion residues. I. Morphological, elemental and spectroscopic features', *Chemosphere*, vol 51, pp785–795

Fonseca, A., Zeuthen, P. and Nagy, J. B. (1996) '13C NMR quantitative analysis of catalyst carbon deposits', *Fuel*, vol 75, pp1363–1376

Franklin, R. E. (1951) 'Crystallite growth in graphitizing and non–graphitizing carbons', *Proceedings of the Royal Society London A*, vol 209, pp196–218

Freitas, J. C. C., Bonagamba, T. J. and Emmerich, F. G. (1999) '13C high-resolution solid-state NMR study of peat carbonization', *Energy and Fuels*, vol 13, pp53–59

Freitas, J. C. C., Bonagamba, T. J. and Emmerich, F. G. (2001a) 'Investigation of biomass- and polymer-based carbon materials using 13C high-resolution solid-state NMR', *Carbon*, vol 39, pp535–545

Freitas, J. C. C., Emmerich, F. G., Cernicchiaro, G. R. C., Sampaio, L. C. and Bonagamba, T. J. (2001b) 'Magnetic susceptibility effects on 13C MAS NMR spectra of carbon materials and

graphite', *Solid State Nuclear Magnetic Resonance*, vol 20, pp61–73

Graetz, R. D. and Skjemstad, J. O. (2003) 'The charcoal sink of biomass burning on the Australian continent', *CSIRO Atmospheric Research*, Aspendale

Hammes, K., Smernik, R. J., Skjemstad, J. O., Herzog, A., Vogt, U. F. and Schmidt, M. W. I. (2006) 'Synthesis and characterisation of laboratory-charred grass straw (*Oryza sativa*) and chestnut wood (*Castanea sativa*) as reference materials for black carbon quantification', *Organic Geochemistry*, vol 37, pp1629–1633

Haumaier, L. and Zech, W. (1995) 'Black carbon – possible source of highly aromatic components of soil humic acids', *Organic Geochemistry*, vol 23, pp191–196

Knicker, H., Almendros, G., González-Vila, F. J., Martin, F. and Lüdemann, H. D. (1996) '13C- and 15N-NMR Spectroscopic examination of the transformation of organic nitrogen in plant biomass during thermal treatment', *Soil Biology and Biochemistry*, vol 28, pp1053–1060

Knicker, H., Totsche, K. U., Almendros, G. and Gonzalez-Vila, F. J. (2005) 'Condensation degree of burnt peat and plant residues and the reliability of solid-state VACP MAS 13C NMR spectra obtained from pyrogenic humic material', *Organic Geochemistry*, vol 36, pp1359–1377

Krull, E. S. and Skjemstad, J. O. (2003) '13C and 15N profiles in 14C-dated Oxisol and Vertisols as a function of soil chemistry and mineralogy', *Geoderma*, vol 112, pp1–29

Krull, E. S., Skjemstad, J. O., Graetz, D., Grice, K., Dunning, W., Cook, G. and Parr, J. F. (2003) '13C-depleted charcoal from C4 grasses and the role of occluded carbon in phytoliths', *Organic Geochemistry*, vol 34, pp1337–1352

Kuhlbusch, T. A. J. and Crutzen, P. J. (1996) 'Black carbon, the global carbon cycle, and atmospheric carbon dioxide', in J. S. Levine (ed) *Biomass Burning and Global Change*, MIT Press, Cambridge, UK, pp161–169

Lehmann, J., Liang, B., Solomon, D., Lerotic, M., Luizão, F., Kinyangi, F., Schäfer, T., Wirick, S. and Jacobsen, C. (2005) 'Near-edge X-ray absorption fine structure (NEXAFS) spectroscopy for mapping nano-scale distribution of organic carbon forms in soil: Application to black carbon particles' *Global Biogeochemical Cycles*, vol 19, pGB1013

Maroto-Valer, M. M., Andrésen, J. M., Rocha, J. D. and Snape, C. E. (1996) 'Quantitative solid-state ^{13}C NMR measurements on cokes, chars and coal tar pitch fractions', *Fuel*, vol 75, pp1721–1726

Maroto-Valer, M. M., Atkinson, C. J., Willmers, R. R. and Snape, C. E. (1998) 'Characterization of partially carbonized coals by solid-state ^{13}C NMR and optical microscopy', *Energy and Fuels*, vol 12, pp833–842

Özçimen, D. and Karaosmanoglu, F. (2004) 'Production and characterization of bio-oil and biochar from rapeseed cake', *Renewable Energy*, vol 29, pp779–787

Pastorova, I., Botto, R. E., Arisz, P. W. and Boon, J. J. (1994) 'Cellulose char structure: A combined analytical Py-GC-MS, FTIR, and NMR study', *Carbohydrate Research*, vol 262, pp27–47

Poirier, N., Derenne, S., Rouzaud, J.-N., Largeau, C., Mariotti, A., Balesdent, J. and Maquet, J. (2000) 'Chemical structure and sources of the macromolecular, resistant, organic fraction isolated from a forest soil (Lacadée, south–west France)', *Organic Geochemistry*, vol 31, pp813–827

Poirier, N., Derenne, S., Balesdent, J., Chenu, C., Bardoux, G., Mariotti, A. and Largeau, C. (2006) 'Dynamics and origin of the non-hydrolysable organic fraction in a forest and a cultivated temperate soil, as determined by isotopic and microscopic studies', *European Journal of Soil Science*, vol 57, pp719–730

Schmidt, M. W. I. and Noack, A. G. (2000) 'Black carbon in soils and sediments: Analysis, distribution, implications, and current challenges', *Global Biogeochemical Cycles*, vol 14, pp777–793

Schmidt, M. W. I., Skjemstad, J. O., Czimczik, C. I., Glaser, B., Prentice, K. M., Gélinas, Y. and Kuhlbusch, T. A. J. (2001) 'Comparative analysis of black carbon in soils', *Global Biogeochemical Cycles*, vol 15, pp163–167

Shafizadeh, F. and Sekiguchi, Y. (1983) 'Development of aromaticity in cellulosic chars', *Carbon*, vol 21, pp511–516

Shindo, H. (1991) 'Elementary composition, humus composition, and decomposition in soil of charred grassland plants', *Soil Science and Plant Nutrition*, vol 37, pp651–657

Solum, M. S., Sarofim, A. F., Pugmire, R. J., Fletcher, T. H. and Zhang, H. (2001) '^{13}C NMR analysis of soot produced from model compounds and a coal', *Energy and Fuels*, vol 15, pp961–971

Trompowsky, P. M., Benites, V. D. M., Madari, B. E., Pimenta, A. S., Hockaday, W. C. and Hatcher, P. G. (2005) 'Characterization of humic like substances obtained by chemical oxidation of eucalyptus charcoal', *Organic Geochemistry*, vol 36, pp1480–1489

Tsai, W. T., Lee, M. K. and Chang, Y. M. (2006) 'Fast pyrolysis of rice husk: Product yields and compositions', *Bioresource Technology*, vol 98, pp22–28

Uzun, B. B., Pütün, A. E. and Pütün, E. (2006) 'Fast pyrolysis of soybean cake: Product yields and compositions', *Bioresource Technology*, vol 97, pp569–576

5

Biochar: Nutrient Properties and Their Enhancement

K. Yin Chan and Zhihong Xu

Introduction

Despite the recent interest in the use of biochar in agriculture, its current use is still limited. In terms of market development, if biochar can be used as a soil amendment to improve soil quality and to increase crop production, this will increase its appeal (Day et al, 2004). In this regard, an obvious positive attribute of biochar is its nutrient value, supplied either directly by providing nutrients to plants or indirectly by improving soil quality, with consequent improvement in the efficiency of fertilizer use. As a measure of the direct nutrient value of biochars, it is not the total content but, rather, the availability of the nutrient that is an important consideration. The total content of nutrients is not an appropriate indicator of the availability of nutrients as only a fraction of the total content is immediately available or is readily converted to available forms for uptake by plants (Keeney, 1982).

An example of the indirect nutrient value of biochar is its ability to retain nutrients in the soil and, therefore, to reduce leaching losses, resulting in increased nutrient uptake

by plants and higher production. According to Glaser et al (2001), one reason for the ability of Amazonian Terra Preta soils, which are characterized by their high content of biochar-like pyrogenic carbon (C), to maintain high fertility (compared to adjacent infertile soils) is their ability to retain nutrients. Another example of the indirect nutrient value of biochars is the removal of soil constraints limiting plant growth and production (e.g. the use of lime to overcome soil acidity, with resulting improvement in fertilizer-use efficiency and increases in plant production).

In this chapter, we review the existing information on the direct, as well as indirect, nutrient properties of biochars and their effect on crop yield and production. Factors controlling nutrient properties, both composition and the availability of nutrients during pyrolysis, are examined, and in the light of existing knowledge and information, research opportunities to improve the nutrient properties of biochars are identified.

Nutrient properties of biochars and crop production responses

Nutrient contents of biochars

Since biochars are manufactured from biomass, it is expected that they are high in C and contain a range of plant macro- and micro-nutrients. The composition of biochars depends upon the nature of the feedstocks and the operating conditions of pyrolysis. A review of the literature has revealed that only scant information is available on the nutrient properties of biochars. Most of the research on pyrolysis of biomass has focused on energy and fuel quality (Horne and Williams, 1996; Tsai et al, 2006) rather than on biochar as a soil amendment. Often, biochar is looked upon as a fuel for further energy production or as a by-product to be upgraded to activated carbon and used in purification processes (Horne and Williams, 1996). Furthermore, information on the nutrient content and properties of biochars used in agronomic studies has not always been included in the reporting of experimental results, making it difficult to assess the agronomic values of biochars used in previous research. Table 5.1 summarizes total elemental composition – C, nitrogen (N), phosphorus (P) and potassium (K), available P and mineral N – as well as the pH of biochars as recorded in the literature by various studies.

From this limited and, unfortunately, incomplete data set, the most striking feature is the high variability of all parameters, with the exception of pH. In the case of pH, the data show that biochars used as a soil amendment in prior research are usually alkaline in nature (pH>7.0). However, biochars can be produced at almost any pH between 4 and 12 (Lehmann, 2007) and can decrease to a pH value of 2.5 after short-term incubation of four months at 70°C (Cheng et al, 2006). Carbon contents range between 172g kg^{-1} and 905g kg^{-1} (coefficient of variation, CV =

106.5 per cent). The ranges are even larger in the case of total N (1.8g kg^{-1} to 56.4g kg^{-1}), total P (2.7g kg^{-1} to 480g kg^{-1}) and total K (1.0g kg^{-1} to 58g kg^{-1}), all with CV $\geqslant$ 100 per cent (see Table 5.1). The variability can be attributed to different feedstocks and different conditions under which the various biochars were manufactured. The influence of feedstocks is particularly evident in the case of total P where higher contents were found in biochars produced from feedstocks of animal origin – namely, sewage sludge and broiler litter – than those from plants (e.g. wood). Similarly, total N contents of biochars from sewage sludge (64g kg^{-1}; Bridle and Pritchard, 2004) and soybean cake (78.2g kg^{-1}; Uzun et al, 2006) were much higher than those from pure plant origins (e.g. green wastes) (1.7g kg^{-1}; Chan et al, 2007b). Compared to other forms of organic amendments commonly used in agriculture (see Table 5.2), both total N and P contents of biochars cover ranges that are wider than those reported for the whole spectrum of typical organic fertilizers. It is important to note that the same type of feedstock can produce very different biochars. For example, Chan et al (2007b) reported total N contents of 20g kg^{-1} for biochar produced from poultry litter compared to 7.5g kg^{-1} and 6.0g kg^{-1} for two biochars made from different poultry litter reported by Lima and Marshall (2005). Such large differences in total N are a result of either different poultry litter qualities or different pyrolysis conditions. This cannot be ascertained as information is typically not given to the extent that allows such conclusions to be drawn. A much higher temperature (700°C) was used by Lima and Marshall (2005) compared to the 450°C reported by Chan et al (2007b). This information may suggest that operating conditions during pyrolysis

Table 5.1 *Nutrient contents, pH and carbonate contents of biochars*

Biochar feedstocks	pH	C (g kg^{-1})	N (g kg^{-1})	C/N	P (g kg^{-1})	K (g kg^{-1})	P[a] (mg kg^{-1})	Nmin[b] (mg kg^{-1})	CO$_3$[c] (%)	Production conditions	References
Wood	–[d]	708	10.9	65	6.8	0.9	–	–	–	By local farmers	Lehmann et al (2003b)
Green wastes	6.2[e]	680	1.7	400	0.2	1.0	15	<2	<0.5	450°C	Chan et al (2007b)
Poultry litter	9.9[e]	380	20	19	25.2	22.1	11,600	2	15	450°C	Chan et al (2007b)
Sewage sludge	–	470	64	7	56	–	–	–	–	450°C	Bridle and Pritchard (2004)
Unknown	9.6[f]	905	56.4	16	2.7	51	–	–	–	Unknown	Topoliantz et al (2005)
Broiler litter	–	258	7.5	34	48	30	–	–	–	700°C and steam activated	Lima and Marshall (2005)
Broiler cake	–	172	6.0	29	73	58	–	–	–	700°C and steam activated	Lima and Marshall (2005)
Bark of *Acacia mangium*	7.4[f]	398	10.4	38	–	–	31	–	–	260°C–360°C	Yamato et al (2006)
Rice straw	–	490	13.2	37	–	–	–	–	–	500°C	Tsai et al (2006)
Sugar cane bagasse	–	710	17.7	40	–	–	–	–	–	500°C	Tsai et al (2006)
Coconut shell	–	690	9.4	73	–	–	–	–	–	500° C	Tsai et al (2006)
Oil mallee tree after oil extraction	8.4	340	12	28	1.2	7.0	–	–	–	'Moki' method	Blackwell et al (2007)
Soybean cake	–	590	78.2	7.5	–	–	–	–	–	550°C	Uzun et al (2006)
Eucalyptus deglupta	7.0[g]	824	5.73	144	0.6	–	49.5	–	–	350°C	Rondon et al (2007)
Range from	6.2	172	1.7	7	0.2	1.0	15	0	<0.5		
to	9.6	905	78.2	400	73	58	11,600	2	15		
Mean	8.1	543	22.3	67	23.7	24.3	–	–	–		
Percentage CV[h]	18	40	110	152	118	96	–	–	–		

Notes: a Plant available P.

b Mineral N (extractable nitrate plus ammonium).

c Carbonate content as a percentage of oven dry weight of biochar.

d Data not available.

e pH measured in 0.01 M CaCl$_2$.

f pH measured in 1 M KCl.

g pH measured in de-ionized water.

h CV = coefficient of variation

Table 5.2 *Typical N, P and K contents of common organic fertilizers*

Organic fertilizer/compost	N (%)	P (%)	K (%)	Nmin[1] (mg kg^{-1})	References
Poultry manure	3.1	2.5	1.6	–[2]	Burgess (1993)
Cow manure	1.5	0.5	1.2	–	Burgess (1993)
Blood and bone	5.3	5.2	1.6	–	Burgess (1993)
Green waste compost – unblended	1.0	0.16	–	16	Chan et al (2007a)
Green waste compost – blended	1.2	0.38	–	202	Chan et al (2007a)
Biosolids	2–8	1.5–3.0	0.1–0.6	–	Cogger et al (2006)

Notes: 1 Mineral N (extractable nitrate plus ammonium).
2 Data not available.

determine to a significant extent the N contents through greater N loss at higher pyrolysis temperatures, as will be discussed later in this chapter.

It is important to point out that the total elemental contents of many nutrients, especially organically bound nutrients such as N and sulphur (S), do not necessarily reflect the actual availability of these nutrients to plants. Very few data on the available nutrient contents of biochar are found in the literature. From the limited data available, mineral N is very low and available P is highly variable (see Table 5.1). Despite a high total N content of 6.4 per cent, biochar produced from sewage sludge was found to have negligible mineral N (ammonium-N + nitrate-N) even after 56 days of incubation (Bridle and Pritchard, 2004). Similarly, mineral N was found to be <2mg kg^{-1} for a green waste and poultry manure char with total N of 1.7g kg^{-1} and 20g kg^{-1}, respectively (see Table 5.1; Chan et al, 2007b). In contrast, available K in biochars are typically high and increased K uptake as a result of biochar application has been frequently reported (Lehmann et al, 2003b; Chan et al, 2007c).

The C/N ratios of biochars vary widely between 7 to 400, with a mean of 67 (see Table 5.1). This ratio is often used as an indicator of the ability of organic substrates to mineralize and release inorganic N when applied to soils. Generally, a C/N ratio of 20

of organic substrates is used as a critical limit above which immobilization of N by microorganisms occurs; therefore, the N applied with the substrate is not available to plants (Leeper and Uren, 1993). Sullivan and Miller (2001) suggested that composts with C/N ratios above 25 to 30 immobilize inorganic N. Based on these values, given their very high C/N ratios, most of the biochars are expected to cause N immobilization and possibly induce N deficiency of plants when applied to soils alone. However, there is a degree of uncertainty if the same criterion is directly applicable to biochars. C/N ratios of Terra Preta soils are usually higher than the adjacent Ferralsol; but they tend to have higher available N (Lehmann et al, 2003a). As the bulk of biochars is made up of biologically very recalcitrant organic C, which is not easily mineralized, it is expected that N immobilization is negligible or transient despite the high C/N ratios. Application of biochar may, indeed, lead to lower N uptake, as shown in several studies (e.g. Lehmann et al, 2003b; Rondon et al, 2007). It is likely that this is due to the presence of only a small portion of the freshly produced biochar that is relatively easily mineralizable, but may cause N immobilization because of its high C/N ratio. However, the bulk of the remaining organic C (with even higher C/N) does not cause mineralization–immobilization reactions because of its high degree of biological recalcitrance.

For 16 biochars made from different plant biomass as well as poultry litter, bicarbonate extractable available P (Colwell, 1963) was found to range between 15mg kg^{-1} and 11,600mg kg^{-1} (Chan et al, 2007b). Significantly higher levels of available P were found in biochars produced from poultry litter than those from plant biomass.

Few data are available on the content of trace elements in biochars. However, high contents of heavy metals have been reported in biochars produced from a range of feedstocks (e.g. sewage sludge and tannery wastes) (Muralidhara, 1982; Bridle and Pritchard, 2004). Bridle and Pritchard (2004) reported high concentrations of copper (Cu), zinc (Zn), chromium (Cr) and nickel (Ni) in a biochar produced from sewage sludge. Biochar produced from tannery wastes can be very high in Cr (Muralidhara, 1982) as this metal can make up 2 per cent of total dry weight of the wastes. The Cr was found to bind to the organic material in biochar in a trivalent complex form and can be recovered by leaching with dilute sulphuric acid (Muralidhar, 1982). Little is known about the availability of these potentially toxic metals.

Some of the biochars have fairly high concentrations of carbonates (see Table 5.1), which can be valuable as a liming material for overcoming soil acidity (Van Zweiten et al, 2007). Chan et al (2007b) reported carbonate contents of less than 0.5 to 33 per cent for a range of biochars produced from different feedstocks and conditions. There was no direct relationship between liming value and the pH of the biochars.

Biochars are therefore variable materials in terms of total nutrient content and availability, and given the very large variability in contents of different nutrients, we would expect varying plant and soil responses from direct nutrient additions of biochars. From the available data, no optimum rate of application for biochars can be obtained because of the stated large variability in biochar prop-

erties. In fact, both Glaser et al (2002) and FFTC (2007) concluded that the optimal application rate of biochars may have to be determined for each soil type and plant species.

Crop responses due to nutrient properties of biochars

Direct nutrient value of biochars

Positive and, to a lesser extent, negative yield responses as a result of biochar application to soils have been reported for a wide range of crops and plants in different parts of the world (see Table 5.3). Attempts to relate the crop responses to the nutrient contents of the biochar used in the experiments have been limited by the fact that in many of the studies, nutrient contents of the biochar or rate of application were often not provided. Amongst the studies in Table 5.3, only one attributed some of the positive crop response to nutrients supplied directly by the biochar (Lehmann et al, 2003b). The latter reported that using wood biochar at rates of 68t C ha^{-1} to 135t C ha^{-1} increased rice biomass by 17 per cent and cowpea by 43 per cent in a pot experiment (in the absence of leaching). The authors attributed the positive growth responses to improved P and K and, possibly, Cu nutrition provided by the biochar applied.

Indirect nutrient properties

A few studies attributed the positive plant responses to other effects of biochar on nutrient availability rather than simply as a direct supplier of nutrients (Iswaran et al, 1980; Wardle et al, 1998; Hoshi, 2001; Lehmann et al, 2003b; Chan et al, 2007c; Van Zwieten et al, 2007). The positive responses due to biochar application were attributed to either nutrient savings (in term of fertilizers) or improved fertilizer-use efficiency (higher yield per unit of fertilizer applied) and can therefore be regarded as an indirect nutrient value of biochars. Hoshi (2001), Yamato et al

Table 5.3 *Crop yield responses as related to relevant biochar properties*

Feedstock for biochar and rate of application	Crops/plants	Responses	Reasons for responses given by authors	References
Unknown wood (0.5t ha^{-1})	Soybean	Biomass increased by 51%	Water-holding capacity and black colour on temperature	Iswaran et al (1980)
Unknown wood (5t ha^{-1} and 15t ha^{-1})	Soybean	Yield reduced by 37 and 71%	pH-induced micro-nutrient deficiency	Kishimoto and Sugiura (1985)
Wood for charcoal production, unknown rates	Vegetation in charcoal hearth and non-hearth areas compared after 110 years	Tree density and basal area were reduced by 40%	Negative responses due to changes in soil properties	Mikan and Abrams (1995)
Wood for charcoal production (2t ha^{-1})	Trees (*Betula pendula* and *Pinus Sylvestris*)	Affected only *B. pendula* and only in substrates high in phenolics	Increased N uptake by countering the effect of phenolics	Wardle et al (1998)
Bamboo, unknown rate	Tea tree	Height and volume increased by 20 and 40%	Retained fertilizer and maintained pH	Hoshi (2001)
Secondary forest wood (68t C ha^{-1}–135t C ha^{-1})	Rice, cowpea and oats	Biomass of rice increased by 17%, cowpea by 43%	Improved P, K and possibly Cu nutrition	Lehmann et al (2003b), Glaser et al (2002)
Bark of *Acacia mangium* (37t ha^{-1})	Maize, cowpea and peanut at two sites	Response only at one site (less fertile) with 200% increase (fertilized)	Increase in P and N availability and reduction of exchangeable Al^{3+}; arbuscular mycorrhizal (AM) fungal colonization	Yamato et al (2006)
Secondary forest wood (11t ha^{-1})	Rice and sorghum	Little response with biochar alone, but with a combination of biochar and fertilizer yielded as much as 880% more than plots with fertilizer alone	Not stated	Steiner et al (2007)
Rice husk (10t ha^{-1})	Maize, soybean	10–40% yield increases	Not clearly understood, dependent upon soil, crop and other nutrients	FFTC (2007)
Green waste (0–100t ha^{-1})		No positive effect with biochar up to 100t ha^{-1}, but with added N fertilizer, 266% increase in dry matter	Indirect effect of improving physical properties of hard-setting soil	Chan et al (2007c)
Paper mill sludge (10t ha^{-1})	Wheat	Increase in wheat height by 30–40% in acid soil but not in alkaline soil	Mainly liming value	Van Zwieten et al (2007)

(2006), Rondon et al (2007), and Van Zwieten et al (2007) attributed the plant responses to the ability of the biochars applied in increasing or maintaining the pH of the soils. Hoshi (2001) suggested that the 20 per cent increase in height and 40 per cent increase in volume of tea trees were partly due to the ability of the biochar to maintain the pH of the soil. Such ability is related to the liming value of the biochar. In a pot experiment, Van Zwieten et al (2007) reported a nearly 30 to 40 per cent increase in wheat height when biochar produced from paper mill sludge was applied at a rate of 10t ha^{-1} to an acidic soil but not to a neutral soil. The lime (as carbonates) in the biochar promoted wheat growth by overcoming toxic effects of exchangeable aluminium (Al) of the acidic soils.

Other reasons offered for the observed positive responses due to biochar application that are not related to plant nutrition included toxin neutralization (Wardle et al, 1998); improved soil physical properties (e.g. increase in water-holding capacity) (Iswaran et al, 1980); or reduced soil strength (Chan et al, 2007c). The latter authors found no positive dry matter response of radish in a pot experiment when green waste biochar was applied alone at rates of up to 100t ha^{-1}. However, dry matter increased by up to 266 per cent when N fertilizer was also applied at 100kg N ha^{-1} compared to a control that received the same amount of N but no biochar (see Figure 5.1).

As a result, biochar application increased N fertilizer-use efficiency of radish and the authors attributed this to improved soil physical conditions – namely, reduced soil strength and higher field capacity – of the hard-setting soils. In addition, Lehmann et al (2003b) demonstrated the ability of biochar to retain applied fertilizer against leaching with resulting increase in fertilizer-use efficiency. This ability is related to the charge (see Chapter 10) and surface area properties of biochars (see Chapter 2). The above literature review highlights the potential benefits of the indirect nutrient value of biochars when compared to the limited direct nutrient value. In addition to the significant responses in plant productivity that have been reported, soil quality improvements and environmental benefits (e.g. reduced pollution due to reduced fertilizer losses via leaching) are likely to result (Lehmann, 2007).

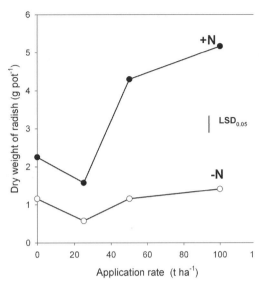

Figure 5.1 *Dry matter production of radish as a function of biochar application rate, either with (100kg ha^{-1}; solid symbol) or without (open symbol) N fertilizer application*

Note: LSD = least significant difference.
Source: Chan et al (2007c)

Negative yield responses to biochar applications

Kishimoto and Sugiura (1985) reported yield reductions of soybean by 37 and 71 per cent when biochar was applied at 5t ha^{-1} and 15t ha^{-1}, respectively, and they attributed this to micronutrient deficiency induced by the resulting pH increases. Such pH-induced adverse effect was also reported by Mikan and Abrams (1995), who observed significant retardation of calcifuge plant species in charcoal hearth areas even after 110 years and attributed this to the elevated pH and calcium (Ca) levels remaining from past charcoal production activities. Therefore, while the alkaline nature and liming value of the biochar might be beneficial for the amelioration of acid soils, with resulting increases in crop production, the same prop- erties might be deleterious to certain plant species. These observations highlight the specific nature of some of the soil amend- ment values of biochars, the limitation of the value of some biochars under certain soil conditions, and the importance of a better understanding of the properties of different biochars.

Factors controlling nutrient properties of biochar

Nutrient composition and availability of biochars depend upon both the nature of the feedstocks and the pyrolysis conditions under which they are produced.

Nature of feedstock

In addition to plant biomass, an entire range of organic materials, including waste materi- als such as poultry litter and sewage sludge, can be converted to biochars using pyrolysis. Recently, conversion of these other materials to biochars has been promoted as an alterna- tive way of managing a range of organic wastes (e.g. Bridle and Pritchard, 2004; Shinogi, 2004; Hospido et al, 2005; Lima and Marshall, 2005). Given the vast differences in the properties of the potential feedstocks, biochars can have very different nutrient contents and availability, as discussed earlier.

Biochar manufacturing process conditions: Temperature, heat- ing rate and heating time

For the same feedstock, biochar yield is highly dependent upon the conditions under which pyrolysis is carried out – namely, temperature, heating rate, heating time and particle size (Shafizadeh, 1982; Williams and Besler, 1996; Demirbas and Arin, 2002; Uzun et al, 2006; Tsai et al, 2007). While it is well documented that biochar yield decreases with increasing temperature and that the yield–temperature relationships are different with different feedstocks (Guha et al, 1986; Horne and Williams, 1996; Williams and Besler, 1996; Tsai et al, 2006), much less attention has been paid to the associated changes in biochar properties, particularly total nutrient contents as well as their avail- ability.

Pyrolysis is the degradation of biomass by heat in the absence of oxygen (O), which results in the production of solid (biochar), liquid and gaseous products (Demirbas and Arin, 2002). According to Shafizadeh (1982), pyrolysis of cellulose at <300°C involves reduction in molecular weight (decarboxylation and decarbonylation), evolution of water, carbon dioxide (CO_2) and carbon monoxide (CO), as well as formation of biochar. On heating to higher temperature (300°C to 500°C), molecules are rapidly depolymerized to anhydroglucose units that further react to provide a tarry pyrolysate. At even higher temperatures (>500°C), the anhydrosugar compounds undergo fission, dehydration, disproportionation and decar- boxylation reactions to provide a mixture of low molecular weight gaseous and volatile products, as well as the residual biochar (see Chapter 8).

Depending upon the operating condi- tions, the complex and varying changes of biomass during pyrolysis affect both the composition and chemical structure of the resulting biochar, with significant implications for nutrient contents and, especially, nutrient availability to plants. Changes in the composition of biochars during pyrolysis of organic matter using molecular techniques indicate a gradual decrease in the amounts of OH and CH_3 and an increase in C=C with increasing temperature (150°C to 550°C), suggesting a change from aliphatic to aromatic C structure of the biochar (see Chapter 4). By 550°C, most infrared (IR) bands, except those due to the aromatic CH and OH stretches, disappeared, resulting in mainly aromatic biochar. This transformation is confirmed by analyses which indicated that both H/C and O/C ratios of biochars decrease with increasing temperature (see Chapter 4). Furthermore, biochars prepared at higher temperature (500°C to 700°C) are well carbonized, as indicated by low H/C ratios and low O content (<10 per cent) (see Chapter 10), and also have a high surface area (see Chapter 2). In contrast, biochars formed at lower temperatures (300°C to 400°C) are only partially carbonized, with high H/C ratios and O contents, and have a lower surface area. As a consequence, low-temperature biochars are found to have higher amounts of acid–basic surface functional groups. Therefore, increasing temperature during pyrolysis results in changes in the molecular composition, as well as changes in biochar charge properties. Biochars containing large proportions of mineral matter (ash) produced at low temperatures also have a much greater concentration of sub-grain boundaries and defects on the surface than the same biochars produced at high temperatures. Mineral matter in low-temperature biochar is more likely to dissolve since these defects are centres for reactions with liquids and gases (see Chapter 3). These changes should have effects on the total nutrient content as well as their availability. The conversion of aliphatic C to aromatic C during pyrolysis is accompanied by a reduction in C mineralization rates (see Chapter 11). This reduction in mineral-

ization of organic C also suggests a reduction in the availability of nutrients in biochar that are bound in the organic structure, such as N, P and S.

Porosity of biochar significantly increases between 400°C and 600°C (see Chapter 2), and may be attributed to increases in water molecules released by dehydroxylation acting as pore-former and activation agent, thus creating very small (nanometre-size) pores in biochar (Bagreev et al, 2001). These increases in porosity result in significant increases in surface area by orders of magnitudes (see Chapter 2). Therefore, the differences in structural changes as a function of temperature have important consequences in terms of surface area and charge characteristics of the biochar produced under different conditions. These changes, in turn, should have important effects on the indirect nutrient value of biochars – for example, the nutrient retention ability of cations and anions of biochars are dependent upon their cation exchange capacity (CEC) and anion exchange capacity (AEC).

Indeed, CEC proved to be very low at low pyrolysis temperatures and to increase significantly at higher temperature (Lehmann, 2007), which would need to be tested more widely. So far, however, freshly produced biochars have proven minimal CEC compared to soil organic matter (Cheng et al, 2006, 2008; Lehmann, 2007). On the other hand, the AEC of freshly produced biochar is significant at low pH and biochars have a high point of zero net charge (Cheng et al, 2008). Biochars only possess variable charge. Strategies to enhance CEC by manufacturing processes are being explored. Once biochar is exposed to O_2 and water, spontaneous oxidation reactions occur that are most likely enhanced by microbial activity and result in very high CEC (Cheng et al, 2006, 2008; Liang et al, 2006). The changes in charge properties of biochar, once added to soil, are discussed in Chapter 10.

Table 5.4 *Effect of temperature and holding time on C and N composition and pH (measured in aqueous slurries) of sewage sludge biochar*

Temperature (°C)	Holding time (minutes)	C (mg g⁻¹)	H (mg g⁻¹)	N (mg g⁻¹)	pH
400	30	282	20.4	38.3	7.7
600	60	271	11.4	31.9	11.5
800	60	264	4.2	16.1	11.3
950	60	249	3.5	9.4	11.0

Source: adapted from Bagreev et al (2001)

Nitrogen

Lang et al (2005) monitored the changes in content of C, H, O, S and N of a range of organic materials – namely, four woody biomass, four herbaceous biomass and two coals under pyrolysis at 275°C to 1100°C. All of the biomass types lost at least half of their N as volatiles by 400°C. During pyrolysis of sewage sludge, total N contents decreased from 3.8 per cent at 400°C to 0.94 per cent at 950°C (see Table 5.4) because of loss of volatile organic matter (Bagreev et al, 2001). Similarly, Shinogi (2004) reported a reduction of total N in biochar from sewage sludge from 5.0 per cent at 400°C to 2.3 per cent at 800°C (see Figure 5.2).

The loss of total N at higher temperatures was also accompanied by a change in the chemical structure of the remaining N in the biochar. According to Bagreev et al (2001), organic N, probably present as amine functionalities in the material at low temperature, was gradually transformed into pyridine-like compounds with increased basicity of the surface at higher temperatures (>600°C). The change results in reduced availability of N present in the biochar. Significantly, this conversion occurred between 400°C and 600°C, which corresponded to a large increase in pH by 3.8 units as a result of dehydroxylation reactions (see Table 5.4). From the limited data available, N present in biochar products has very low availability. For biochar produced from sewage sludge, despite its relatively high total N content of 6.4 per cent, a laboratory incu-

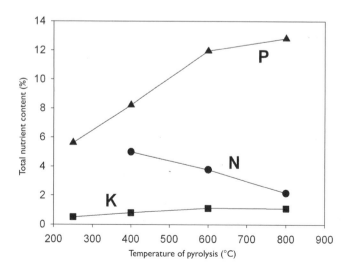

Figure 5.2 *Changes in total N, P and K concentrations in biochars produced from sewage sludge at different temperatures*

Source: adapted from Shinogi (2004)

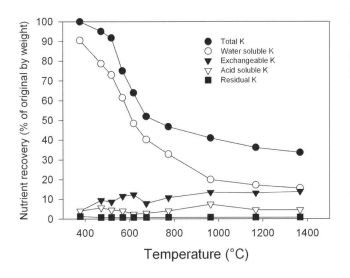

Figure 5.3 *Changes in K contents of rice straw biochar as a function of temperature during pyrolysis*

Source: Yu et al (2005)

bation study with soil at 25°C and field capacity indicated that negligible amounts of mineral N were detectable even after 56 days (Pritchard, 2003). This indicated that N in sewage sludge biochar was in forms that are very resistant to decomposition and mineralization.

Base cations

Yu et al (2005) studied the chemical forms and the release of K and Na during pyrolysis of rice straw between 400°C and 1373°C. Between 473°C and 673°C, about half of the total metal content (48 and 55 per cent, respectively, for K and Na) was lost by vaporization, and on further heating to 1373°C, loss was slower and totalled to ~70 per cent. About 90 per cent of total K in rice straw was in water-soluble form and was therefore plant available before pyrolysis: it was this form of K that was lost when heating up to 673°C (see Figure 5.3). With increasing temperature (>600°C), a greater proportion of the remaining K was found in exchangeable and acid extractable form. Wornat et al (1995) found that biochars from pine and switchgrass produced at 625°C contained 15 to 20 per cent O, and using energy dispersive X-ray spectroscopy (EDS), they concluded that

both K and Ca are well dispersed in the biochar matrices and may be bound to the O in biochars as ionic phenoxides (i.e. K phenoxides or as intercalated K). However, further heating to higher temperatures led to further losses by vaporization, as well as incorporation of K into the silicate structure, which is expected to be much less bioavailable. These results were supported by findings by Shinogi (2004), who reported a reduction of available K from 14 to <1 per cent during pyrolysis of sewage sludge, while total K concentrations doubled (0.51 per cent at 250°C to 1.12 per cent at 600°C) (see Figure 5.2).

Sulphur

Up to 50 per cent of total S from eight biomass types was lost during pyrolysis at 500°C (Lang et al, 2005). Knudsen et al (2004) studied S transformation during pyrolysis of typical Danish wheat straw. Before pyrolysis, S was found to be associated partly as inorganic sulphate (40 to 50 per cent of total S) and partly as proteins (50 to 60 per cent). Results indicated that 35 to 50 per cent of the total S was released to the gas phase during pyrolysis at 400°C as a result of thermal decomposition of organic S.

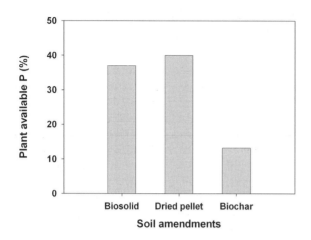

Figure 5.4 *Available P (bicarbonate extractable) as a percentage of total P of biochar as compared to biosolid and dried biosolid pellet*

Source: adapted from Pritchard (2003)

The latter commenced at 178°C to 283°C. At higher temperatures (500°C to 700°C), the residual S contents of biochar did not change significantly. However, the forms of S changed under the highly reducing conditions prevailing during pyrolysis, with a disappearance of inorganic sulphate (to 21.1 per cent at 500°C and to 3.1 per cent at 800°C) due to the conversion to insoluble sulphide (e.g. CaS, K_2S) in the biochar matrix, or from fixed to reactive biochar surfaces by either addition of S to unsaturated sites or by substitution of O in surface oxides (Knudsen et al, 2004). These forms of S are expected to be water insoluble and biological less available.

Phosphorus

Less information is available about the transformation of P during pyrolysis. For sewage sludge biochars, total P concentration increased with increasing temperature from 5.6 per cent at 250°C to 12.8 per cent at 800°C (see Figure 5.2). According to Bridle and Pritchard (2004), 100 per cent recovery of P was obtained in a biochar produced from sewage sludge at 450°C, in comparison to 45 per cent of N, which was lost during the same procedure. However, laboratory incubation studies indicated that the availability of P in the biochar is only 13 per cent of total P, much lower than those of the biosolid and dry-pelleted biosolid (30 to 40 per cent) (see Figure 5.4) (Pritchard, 2003). According to Bridle and Pritchard (2004), nearly half of the total P in biochar was in HCl-extractable form (i.e. as Ca-bound inorganic P) and was therefore less plant available, unlike the biosolid samples, which had most of the P in resin and extractable forms. Similarly, results of Shinogi (2004) indicated that available P (measured as citrate-extractable P) in biochar from sewage sludge decreased with increasing temperature, from 0.98 per cent at 250°C to 0.06 per cent at 800°C, despite an increase in total P.

Improving the nutrient value of biochars: Research opportunities and challenges

Optimal pyrolysis conditions and feedstock

Little research has been undertaken to identify the optimal pyrolysis conditions required for the production of biochars that are suitable as soil amendments. Identification of these conditions is also critical for the production of biochars with consistent quality, an essential requirement for market development. For composts produced from garden organics, a survey of commercially available products revealed high variability of nutrient composition, and this was identified as the major barrier for developing markets for this product in Australia (Chan et al, 2007a). From the discussion above, the most important conditions affecting nutrient composition and availability of biochars is the production temperature. But other factors such as the heating rate and particle size of the feedstocks may also be important. From a resource conservation point of view, it is important to retain as many nutrients of the feedstock as possible in the final biochar products. Typically, large amounts of nutrients such as N, K and S are lost via vaporization at higher temperature during pyrolysis. For instance, based on the literature reviewed earlier, up to 50 per cent of N, K and S are commonly lost when temperatures exceed 500°C. Furthermore, there is evidence suggesting that the remaining nutrient elements tend to become less available with further increases in temperature. For P, while total losses are minimal, available forms of P are also greatly reduced at higher temperature. For the purpose of maintaining high nutrient contents and availability, it is therefore preferable to keep the temperature low – for example, at or below 400°C to 500°C. However, the exact conditions for optimal production of biochars with improved nutrient properties may be different for different feedstocks, and these require further research and monitoring.

Opportunities also exist to produce biochars with a specific nutrient composition by co-pyrolysis of different feedstocks. For instance, blending of plant biomass with poultry litter as feedstock for pyrolysis may result in biochar with higher available P and liming value than the use of plant biomass alone.

Availability of nutrients and toxic metals

There is clearly a need to better understand the availability of the different nutrients, particularly N in biochars. While biochars are very low in mineral forms of N – namely, nitrate-N and ammonium-N – it is currently not clear if biochars with differing total N content produced from different feedstocks (see Table 5.1) are different in terms of N supply capacity when applied to the soil. Availability, including the rate of mineralization of the organic N present in biochar when applied to soil, will determine its value as a slow-release N fertilizer. This information is also needed for making a decision about the application rates of biochar, as well as in situations when N fertilizer application decisions have to be made. In general, mineralization rates of biochar are expected to be low since the stability of biochars is high (see Chapter 11); therefore, N release and N benefits from decomposition of stable biochar are likely to be minimal over time periods relevant to plant growth. Incubation studies, either in the field or in the laboratory, comparing their potential N mineralization potential (Drinkwater et al, 1996) will help to clarify this.

With the current interest in using organic wastes of different origin as feedstock in pyrolysis (Bridle and Pritchard, 2004; Shinogi, 2004), there is concern regarding the environmental impacts of potentially excessive levels of heavy metals in biochars – particularly, their availability. Some of these organic wastes (e.g. biosolids) can be high in heavy metal contents (such as Cd, Cu and Zn) (Hospido et al, 2005). The authors carried out a life-cycle assessment of different treatments of biosolids, including anaerobic digestion and pyrolysis, and identified heavy metals as having the most negative environmental impact. Of particular concern is the change in availability of the different heavy metals; however, currently, little research has been undertaken. Such research is needed to ensure the safe use of biochar as soil amendments in agriculture.

Enhancement of biochars

Recently, Day et al (2004, 2005) investigated the production of an N-enriched biochar. The novel system produces biochar and synthetic gas (mainly H_2 and CO_2) from biomass and NH_4HCO_3-biochar is then formed when the ammonia is combined with the biochar, H_2O and CO_2 at atmospheric pressure and ambient temperature. In the ammonium carbonation process (Li et al, 2003):

$$CO_2 + NH_3 + H_2O \rightarrow NH_4HCO_3 \qquad [1]$$

the biochar acts as a catalyst and the ammonia required for the process can be produced either from the hydrogen gas (H_2), a co-product of biochar formation or purchased from outside sources. The product is an N-enriched biochar fertilizer with fibrous deposits of ammonium carbonate permeating inside the fine pore structure of the biochar (Day et al, 2005). The effectiveness of such a product as a slow-release N fertilizer in terms of availability, crop production and reduction in leaching losses has not been tested in the field. However, the value of N-enriched lignin produced using chemical reactions between ammonia and lignocellulosic matrices as a slow-release N fertilizer has been demonstrated (Ramirez et al, 1997). Furthermore, Ramirez et al reported that the soil fertilized with N-functionalized lignin showed lower amounts of nitrate in percolating water than soil fertilized with inorganic fertilizer (ammonium sulphate). In the manufacture of the N-enriched biochar, Day et al (2004) suggested that biochar produced at a lower temperature of 400°C to 500°C is more effective in adsorbing ammonia than that produced at higher temperatures (700°C to 1000°C). Similarly, Asada et al (2002) compared adsorption properties of bamboo biochar prepared at 500°C, 700°C and 1000°C and found that only the biochar prepared at 500°C was effective in adsorbing ammonia. They attributed this to the presence of acidic functional groups, such as carboxyl, formed as a result of thermolysis of cellulose and lignin at temperatures of 400°C to 500°C. Acidic functional groups are effective in chemical adsorption of basic ammonia. Day et al (2004) also proposed using biochar to scrub fossil fuel exhausts from coal-fired power plants in combination with hydrated ammonia. In the process, CO_2, NO_x and SO_x emissions are directly captured at the smokestacks, which reduces air pollution and greenhouse gas emission. The biochar is converted in the process to valuable N and S fertilizers with C sequestration value. However, as pointed out by Asada et al (2002), the effectiveness of gas capture by biochar depends upon the pyrolysis temperature, which is different for varying nutrient elements.

Conclusions

Based on the information available, biochars are extremely variable in nutrient composition and availability depending upon feedstocks used and the pyrolysis conditions under which they were produced. Much of the positive crop responses from biochar application reported cannot be directly attributed to the nutrient content of the biochars, but instead to the indirect effect of increasing fertilizer-use efficiency. However, freshly produced biochars possess very little ability to retain cations. More research is needed to identify and quantify the indirect nutrient attributes of biochars made from different feedstocks and under different pyrolysis conditions, and how the ability of cation retention can be increased. Review of the pyrolysis conditions of biochar production highlights the importance of temperature in controlling the losses of essential plant nutrients such as N and K, as well as the conversion of nutrients to biologically unavailable forms. To promote the use of biochars, more consistent products with higher nutrient values and improved nutrient retention are desirable. Research is needed to identify these conditions for different feedstocks and blends of feedstocks. Research opportunities also exist to enhance the nutrient value of biochar by further reaction with nutrients and blending of different feedstocks to develop different products to suit different crops and soils.

References

Asada, T., Ishihar, S., Yamane, T., Toba, A., Yamada, A. and Oikawa, K. (2002) 'Science of bamboo charcoal: Study on carbonising temperature of bamboo charcoal and removal capability of harmful gases', *Journal of Health Science*, vol 48, pp473–479

Bagreev, A., Bandosz, T. J. and Locke, D. C. (2001) 'Pore structure and surface chemistry of adsorbents obtained by pyrolysis of sewage-derived fertiliser', *Carbon*, vol 39, pp1971–1979

Blackwell, P. S., Shea, S., Storier, P., Solaiman, Z., Kerkmans, M. and Stanley, I. (2007) 'Improving wheat production with deep banded oil mallee charcoal in Western Australia', in *Proceedings of the Conference of the International Agrichar Initiative*, 30 April–2 May 2007, Terrigal, NSW, Australia

Bridle, T. R. and Pritchard, D. (2004) 'Energy and nutrient recovery from sewage sludge via pyrolysis', *Water Science and Technology*, vol 50, pp169–175

Burgess, J. (1993) *Organic Fertiliser: An Introduction*, Agfact AC.20, NSW Agriculture, NSW, Australia

Chan, K. Y., Dorahy C. and Tyler S. (2007a) 'Determining the agronomic value of composts produced from garden organics from metropolitan areas of New South Wales, Australia', *Australian Journal of Experimental Agriculture*, vol 47, pp1377–1382

Chan, K. Y., Van Zwieten, L., Meszaros, I., Downie, A. and Joseph, S. (2007b) 'Assessing the agronomic values of contrasting char materials on Australian hardsetting soil', in *Proceedings of the Conference of the International Agrichar Initiative*, 30 April–2 May 2007, Terrigal, NSW, Australia

Chan, K. Y., Van Zwieten, L., Meszaros, I., Downie, A. and Joseph, S. (2007c) 'Agronomic values of green waste biochar as a soil amendment', *Australian Journal of Soil Research*, vol 45, pp629–634

Cheng, C. H., Lehmann, J., Thies, J. E., Burton, S. D. and Engelhard, M. H. (2006) 'Oxidation of black carbon through biotic and abiotic processes', *Organic Geochemistry*, vol 37, pp1477–1488

Cheng, C. H., Lehmann, J. and Engelhard, M. (2008) 'Natural oxidation of black carbon in soils: Changes in molecular form and surface charge along a climosequence', *Geochimica et Cosmochimica Acta*, vol 72, pp1598–1610

Cogger, S. G., Forge, T. A. and Neilsen, G. H. (2006) 'Biosolids recycling: Nitrogen management and soil ecology', *Canadian Journal of Soil Science*, vol 86, pp613–620

Colwell, J. D. (1963) 'The estimation of the phosphorus fertiliser requirements of wheat in southern New South Wales by soil analysis', *Australian Journal of Experimental Agriculture and Animal Husbandry*, vol 3, pp190–198

Day, D., Evans, R. J., Lee, J. W. and Reicosky, D. (2004) 'Valuable and stable co-product from fossil fuel exhaust scrubbing', *Prepr. Paper – American Chemical Society Div. Fuel Chemistry*, vol 49, pp352–355

Day, D., Evans, R. J., Lee, J. W. and Reicosky, D. (2005) 'Economical CO_2, SO_x and NO_x capture from fossil-fuel utilization with combined renewable hydrogen production and large-scale carbon sequestration', *Energy*, vol 30, pp2558–2579

Demirbas, A. and Arin, G. (2002) 'An overview of biomass pyrolysis', *Energy Sources*, vol 24, pp471–482

Drinkwater, L. E., Cambardella, C. A., Reder, J. D. and Rice, C. W. (1996) 'Potentially mineralisable nitrogen as an indicator of biological active soil nitrogen', in J. W. Doran and A. J. Jones (eds) *Methods for Assessing Soil Quality*, SSSA Special Publication 49, Soil Science Society of America, Madison, US, pp217–229

FFTC (Food and Fertilizer Technology Center) (2007) 'Application of rice husk charcoal', www.agnet.org/library/pt/2001004/, accessed 24 January 2008

Glaser, B., Haumaier, L., Guggenberger, G. and Zech, W. (2001) '"The Terra Preta" phenomenon: A model for sustainable agriculture in the humid tropics', *Naturwissenschaften*, vol 88, pp37–41

Glaser, B., Lehmann, J., Steiner, C., Nehls, T., Yousaf, M. and Zech, W. (2002) 'Potential of pyrolysed organic matter in soil amelioration', in *Proceedings of the 12th International Soil Conservation (ISCO) Conference*, Beijing, China

Guha, R., Grover, P. D. and Guha, B. (1986) 'Low temperature pyrolysis of pine needles', *Research and Industry*, vol 31, pp60–63

Horne, P. A. and Williams, P. T. (1996) 'Influence of temperature on the products from the flash pyrolysis of biomass', *Fuel*, vol 75, pp1051–1059

Hoshi, T. (2001) 'Growth promotion of tea trees by putting bamboo charcoal in soil', in *Proceedings of 2001 International Conference on O-cha (Tea) Culture and Science*, Tokyo, Japan, pp147–150

Hospido, A., Moreira, M. T., Martin, M., Rigola, M. and Feijoo, G. (2005) 'Environmental evaluation of different treatment processes for sludge from urban wastewater treatments: Anaerobic digestion versus thermal processes', *International Journal of Life Cycle Analysis*, vol 5, pp336–345

Iswaran, V., Jauhri, K. S. and Sen, A. (1980) 'Effect of charcoal, coal and peat on the yield of moog, soybean and pea', *Soil Biology and Biochemistry*, vol 12, pp191–192

Keeney, D. R. (1982) 'Nitrogen – availability indices', in A. L. Page (ed) *Methods of Soil Analysis Part 2: Chemical and Microbiological Properties*, American Society of Agronomy, Madison, WI, US, pp711–733

Kishimoto, S. and Sugiura, G. (1985) 'Charcoal as a soil conditioner', in *Symposium on Forest Products Research, International Achievements for the Future*, vol 5, pp12–23

Knudsen, J. N., Jensen, P. A., Lin, W., Frandsen, F. J. and Dam-Johnson, K. (2004) 'Sulfur transformations during thermal conversion of herbaceous biomass', *Energy and Fuels*, vol 18, pp810–819

Lang, T., Jensen, A. D. and Jensen, P. A. (2005) 'Retention of organic elements during solid fuel pyrolysis with emphasis on the peculiar behaviour of nitrogen', *Energy and Fuels*, vol 19, pp1631–1643

Leeper, G. W. and Uren, N. C. (1993) 'The nitrogen cycle', in *Soil Science: An Introduction*, Melbourne University Press, Melbourne, Australia, pp166–183

Lehmann, J. (2007) 'Bio-energy in the black', *Frontiers in Ecology and the Environment*, vol 5, pp381–387

Lehmann, J., Kern, D., German, L., McCann, J., Martins, G. and Moreira, A. (2003a) 'Soil fertility and production potential', in J. Lehmann, D. C. Kern, B. Glaser and W. I. Woods (eds.) *Amazonian Dark Earths: Origin,*

Properties, Management, Kluwer Academic Publishers, The Netherlands, pp105–124

Lehmann, J., da Silva, J. P., Steiner, C., Nehls, T., Zech, W. and Glaser, B (2003b) 'Nutrient availability and leaching in an archaeological Anthrosol and a Ferralsol of the Central Amazon basin: Fertiliser, manure and charcoal amendments', *Plant and Soils*, vol 249, pp343–357

Li, X., Hagaman, E., Tsouris, C. and Lee, J. W. (2003) 'Removal of carbon dioxide from flue gas by ammonia carbonation in the gas phase', *Energy and Fuel*, vol 17, pp69–74

Liang, B., Lehmann, J., Solomon, D., Kinyangi, J., Grossman, J., O'Neill, B., Skjemstad, J. O., Thies, J., Luizão, F. J., Petersen, J. and Neves, E. G. (2006) 'Black carbon increases cation exchange capacity in soils', *Soil Science Society of America Journal*, vol 70, pp1719–1730

Lima, I. M. and Marshall, W. E. (2005) 'Granular activated carbons from broiler manure: Physical, chemical and adsorptive properties', *Bioresource Technology*, vol 96, pp699–706

Mikan, C. J. and Abrams, M. D. (1995) 'Altered forest composition and soil properties of historic charcoal hearths in southeastern Pennsylvania', *Canadian Journal of Forest Research*, vol 25, pp687–696

Muralidhara, H. S. (1982) 'Conversion of tannery waste to useful products', *Resources and Conservation*, vol 8, pp43–59

Pritchard, D. (2003) *Nutrient Properties of Char*, Report prepared for ESI by Curtin University of Technology, Perth, Western Australia

Ramirez, F., Gonzalez, V., Crespo, M., Faix, O. and Zuniga, V. (1997) 'Ammoxidized kraft lignin as a slow-release fertilizer tested on *Sorghum vulgare*', *Bioresource Technology*, vol 61, pp43–46

Rondon, M. A., Lehmann J., Ramirez J. and Hurtado, M. (2007) 'Biological nitrogen fixation by common beans (*Phaseolus vulgaris* L.) increases with bio-char additions', *Biology and Fertility of Soils*, vol 43, pp699–708

Shafizadeh, F. (1982) 'Introduction to pyrolysis of biomass', *Journal of Analytical and Applied Pyrolysis*, vol 3, pp283–305

Shinogi, Y. (2004) 'Nutrient leaching from carbon products of sludge', ASAE/CSAE Annual International Meeting, Paper number 044063, Ottawa, Ontario, Canada

Steiner, G., Teixeira, W. G., Lehmann, J., Nehls, T., de Macedo, J., Blum, W. E. H. and Zech, W. (2007) 'Long term effect of manure, charcoal and mineral fertilisation on crop production and fertility on a highly weathered Central Amazonian upland soil', *Plant and Soil*, vol 291, pp275–290

Sullivan, D. M. and Miller, R. O. (2001) *Compost Quality Attributes, Measurements and Variability*, CRC Press, Bosca Baton, FL

Topoliantz, S., Pong, J. and Ballof, S. (2005) 'Manioc peel and charcoal: A potential organic amendment for sustainable soil fertility in the tropics', *Biology and Fertility of Soils*, vol 41, pp15–21

Tsai, W. T., Lee, M. K. and Chang, Y. M. (2006) 'Fast pyrolysis of rice straw, sugarcane bagasse and coconut shell in an induction-heating reactor', *Journal of Analytical and Applied Pyrolysis*, vol 76, pp230–237

Tsai, W. T., Lee, M. K. and Chang, Y. M. (2007) 'Fast pyrolysis of rice husk: Product yields and composition', *Bioresource Technology*, vol 98, pp22–28

Uzun, B. B., Putun, A. E. and Putun, E. (2006) 'Fast pyrolysis of soybean cake: Product yields and compositions', *Bioresource Technology*, vol 97, pp569–576

Van Zwieten, L., Kimber, S., Downie, A., Chan, K.Y., Cowie, A., Wainberg, R. and Morris, S. (2007) 'Papermill char: Benefits to soil health and plant production', in *Proceedings of the Conference of the International Agrichar Initiative*, 30 April–2 May 2007, Terrigal, NSW, Australia

Wardle, D. A., Zackrisson, O. and Nilsson, M. C. (1998) 'The charcoal effect in Boreal forests: Mechanisms and ecological consequences', *Oecologia*, vol 115, pp419–426

Williams, P. T. and Besler, S. (1996) 'The influence of temperature and heating rate on the slow pyrolysis of biomass', *Renewable Energy*, vol 7, pp233–250

Wornat, M. J., Hurt, R. H., Yang, N. C. and Headley, T. (1995) 'Structural and compositional transformations of biomass chars during combustion', *Combustion and Flame*, vol 100, pp131–143

Yamato, M., Okimori, Y., Wibowo, I. F., Anshori, S. and Ogawa, M. (2006) 'Effects of the application of charred bark of *Acacia mangium* on the yield of maize, cowpea and peanut and soil chemical properties in south Sumatra, Indonesia', *Soil Science and Plant Nutrition,* vol 52, pp489–495

Yu, C., Tang. Y., Fang, M., Luo, Z. and Cen, K. (2005) 'Experimental study on alkali emission during rice straw pyrolysis', *Journal of Zhejiang University (Engineering Science),* vol 39, pp1435–1444

6

Characteristics of Biochar: Biological Properties

Janice E. Thies and Matthias C. Rillig

Introduction

Decades of research in Japan and recent studies in the US have shown that biochar stimulates the activity of a variety of agriculturally important soil microorganisms and can greatly affect the microbiological properties of soils (Ogawa et al, 1983; Pietikäinen et al, 2000). The presence and size distribution of pores in biochar provides a suitable habitat for many microorganisms by protecting them from predation and desiccation and by providing many of their diverse carbon (C), energy and mineral nutrient needs (Saito and Muramoto, 2002; Warnock et al, 2007). With the interest in using biochar for promoting soil fertility, many scientific studies are being conducted to better understand how this affects the physical and chemical properties of soils and its suitability as a microbial habitat. Since soil organisms provide a myriad of ecosystem services, understanding how adding biochar to soil may affect soil ecology is critical for ensuring that soil quality and the integrity of the soil subsystem are maintained.

Among the ecosystem services that soil microorganisms provide are decomposing organic matter; cycling and immobilizing inorganic nutrients; filtering and bioremediating soil contaminants; suppressing and causing plant disease; producing and releasing greenhouse gases; and improving soil porosity, aggregation and water infiltration (Coleman, 1986; Thies and Grossman, 2006; Paul, 2007). As they interact with plants in the rhizosphere, bacteria, fungi, protozoa and nematodes strongly influence the ability of plants to acquire macro- and micro-nutrients. This may occur as a direct result of mutualistic associations between plant roots and microorganisms, such as with the arbuscular mycorrhizal (AM) fungi (*Glomeromycota*; Robson et al, 1994) or the nitrogen (N_2)-fixing rhizobia bacteria; or through trophic interactions resulting in nutrient excretion by secondary feeders, such as protozoa and nematodes (Brussaard et al, 1990). Clearly, soil microbial activity strongly affects soil function and, consequently, crop growth and yield. The physical and chemical environment of biochar may alter many of these biological activities, discussed in detail below.

The nature and function of soil microbial communities change in response to many edaphic, climatic and management factors, especially additions of organic matter (Thies and Grossman, 2006). Amending soils with biochar is no exception. However, the way in which biochar affects soil biota may be distinct from other types of added organic matter because the stability of biochar makes it unlikely to be a source of either energy or cell C after any initial bio-oils or condensates have been decomposed (see Chapter 11). Instead, biochar changes the physical (see Chapter 2) and chemical (see Chapters 3 to 5) environment of the soil, which will, in turn, affect the characteristics and behaviour of the soil biota.

The effects of biochar on the abundance, activity and diversity of soil organisms are the subjects of this chapter. This area of enquiry has lagged behind other areas of biochar research. Much of what is known about the biota in soils containing biochar results from the pioneering work of the Japanese researcher M. Ogawa and colleagues and from research on microbial communities in the Amazonian Dark Earths (ADE, also called 'Terra Preta de Indio') from Brazil. We include examples from these works here, with the aim of forecasting how both the soil flora and fauna populations may respond to biochar amendments and to suggest more fruitful avenues for future research.

Biochar as a habitat for soil microorganisms

The porous structure of biochar (see Chapter 2 and Figure 6.1), its high internal surface area and its ability to adsorb soluble organic matter (see Chapter 18), gases and inorganic nutrients (see Chapter 5) are likely to provide a highly suitable habitat for microbes to colonize, grow and reproduce, particularly for bacteria, actinomycetes and arbuscular mycorrhizal fungi (see Figure 6.2). Some members of these groups may preferentially colonize biochar surfaces depending upon the physical and chemical characteristics of different biochars, discussed below.

The pore space of pyrolysed biomass increases during charring by several thousand fold and is related to charring temperature and feedstock materials (see Chapter 2). Estimates of the resulting surface area of different biochars range from 10 to several hundred square metres per gram ($m^2 g^{-1}$) (see Chapter 2), which provides a significantly increased surface area for microbial colonization. Depending upon the size of a given pore, different microbes will or will not have access to internal spaces. Several authors have suggested that the biochar pores may act as a refuge site or microhabitat for colonizing microbes, where they are protected from being grazed upon by their

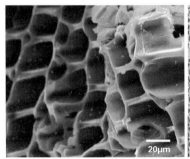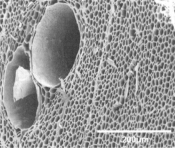

Figure 6.1 *The porous structure of biochar invites microbial colonization*

Source: (left photo) S. Joseph; (right photo) Yamamoto, with permission

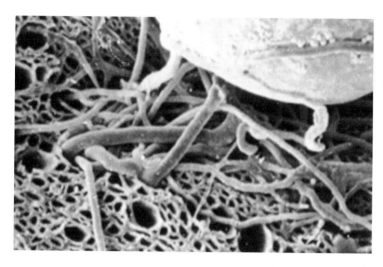

Figure 6.2 *Arbuscular mycorrhiza fungal hyphae growing into biochar pores from a germinating spore*

Source: Ogawa (1994)

natural predators (Saito and Muramoto, 2002; Warnock et al, 2007) or where microbes that are less competitive in the soil environment can become established (Ogawa, 1994). The pore size variation observed across biochar particles from different feedstocks and pyrolysis conditions is such that the microflora could, indeed, colonize and be protected from grazing, especially in the smaller pores (see Table 6.1).

The high porosity of biochar may also allow it to retain more moisture. Pietikäinen et al (2000) reported that two biochars, one prepared from humus and one from wood, had a higher water-holding capacity (WHC) (2.9mL g^{-1} dry matter) than activated carbon (1.5mL g^{-1} dry matter) or pumice

(1.0mL g^{-1} dry matter). An increase in the WHC of biochar may result in an overall increase in the WHC of the soils to which it is added (see Chapter 15). For biochars with a high mineral-ash content, the porosity will continue to increase as the ash is leached out over time; thus, the capacity of the biochar to retain water, provide surfaces for microbes to colonize, and for various elements and compounds to become adsorbed is also likely to increase over time. Smaller pores will attract and retain capillary soil water much longer than larger pores (larger than 10μm to 20μm) in both the biochar and the soil. Water is the universal biological solvent and its presence in biochar pores increases the 'habitability' of biochar substantially.

Table 6.1 *Pore diameters in wood and bamboo biochar compared to the ranges in the diameter of various soil microorganisms*

	Diameter (μm) Range	Mode
Bamboo biochar – pores[1]	0.001–1000	0.1
Wood biochar	10–3000	1495
Bacteria[2]	0.3–3	0.5
Fungi[2]	2–80	8.0
Protozoa[2]	7–30	20.0
Nematodes[2]	3–30	16.0

Notes: 1 See Chapter 2.
    2 See Swift et al (1979).

In addition to water, a variety of gases, including carbon dioxide (CO_2) and oxygen (O_2), will be dissolved in pore water, occupy the air-filled pore space or be chemisorbed onto biochar surfaces (Antal and Grønli, 2003); this latter is due to the defect structures present in the amorphous and micro-graphene lattices (see Chapter 3). Depending upon the ratio of air- to water-filled pore space, the relative concentrations of the gases, their diffusion rates and the extent of surface sorption, either aerobic or anaerobic conditions will predominate in the biochar pores. Where sufficient O_2 is available, aerobic respiration will be the dominant metabolic pathway for energy generation, resulting in water (H_2O) and CO_2 as the primary metabolic end products. As the O_2 concentration decreases, facultative aerobes will begin to use anaerobic respiratory pathways as long as suitable terminal electron acceptors are available. The end products of anaerobic respiration can be nitric oxide (NO), nitrous oxide (N_2O), nitrogen (N_2), hydrogen sulphide (H_2S) and methane (CH_4), among others. Thus, O_2 diffusion into biochar pores and the terminal electron acceptor used during microbial respiration will, in large part, determine what the remaining pore atmosphere will contain and how hospitable this environment is likely to be for its occupants. For further discussion of the evolution of N_2O and CH_4 from biochar amended soils, see Chapter 13.

Moisture, temperature and hydrogen ion concentration (pH) are the environmental factors that most strongly influence bacterial abundance, diversity and activity (Wardle, 1998). In a cross-continental study, Fierer and Jackson (2006) found that the diversity and richness of soil bacterial communities differed by ecosystem type, but that these differences were largely explained by soil pH, with bacterial diversity highest in neutral soils and lowest in acidic soils. The activity of bacterial populations is also strongly influenced by pH. Under both acidic and alkaline conditions, proteins become denatured and enzyme activity is inhibited, impairing most metabolic processes. Biochars vary considerably in their pH, depending upon feedstock and pyrolysis temperature (see Chapter 5) and, thus, will also vary in the microbial communities that develop on and around them. Under the extremes of pH, fungi will probably predominate due to their wide range of pH tolerance; most bacteria prefer circum-neutral pH. Adding biochar to soil, whether acid or alkaline, may lead to significant changes in the soil community composition by changing the overall ratio of bacteria to fungi, as well as the predominance of different genera within these populations. It may also significantly alter soil function by affecting enzyme activities and, thus, overall microbial activity. The influence of biochar pH on colonizing microbial communities and their metabolic processes will be an interesting area of future investigation.

Bacteria and fungi rely on their elaborated extracellular enzymes to degrade substrates in their environment into smaller molecules that can then be taken up into their cells and used for various metabolic activities (Thies and Grossman, 2006; Paul, 2007). Thus, they become highly 'invested' in remaining in close physical proximity to where they secrete extracellular enzymes into their environment. Surfaces become very important in this regard, whether these are the surfaces of a soil aggregate, a plant root, a particle of clay, soil organic matter or biochar. The activity of extracellular enzymes will depend upon the molecular location on these proteins that interacts with the biochar surface. If the enzyme active site is exposed, functional and free to interact with its milieu, then increased activity may occur. However, if the active site is obscured, reduced activity may result. It may be that certain classes of enzymes will be more active and others less so, based on their molecular composition and folding characteristics in relation to how (or whether) they become adsorbed to biochar surfaces. Very little is known currently about the functionality of microbial extracellular enzymes interacting with biochar of different compositions. This is an important area for future research.

Biochar as a substrate for the soil biota

Soil organic C plays a pivotal role in nutrient cycling and in improving plant-available water reserves, soil buffering capacity and soil structure (Horwath, 2007). Researchers used to regard biochar as a relatively inert substance that was altered very little by chemical or biochemical processes over time (Nichols et al, 2000). However, biochar surface properties do change with time (see Chapter 10) and it is slowly mineralized over long periods of time (see Chapter 11). Even though biochar is not strictly inert, decomposition rates are much slower than for uncharred organic matter (see Chapter 11). For example, in studies by Liang et al (2006) on black C from several Amazonian Dark Earths, near-edge X-ray absorption Fine structure (NEXAFS) spectroscopy was used to map the spatial distribution of C forms on black C particle thin sections with a resolution of up to 50nm. For all the black C particles, regardless of site age, the C forms in the centres of the particles were similar; however, each differed in the amount of surface oxidation according to its age, indicating some surface degradation, but over very long timescales. These data support the recalcitrance of black C and indicate that the stability of these particles ranges from hundreds to thousands of years. Hence, the biochar particles themselves do not appear to act as significant substrates for microbial metabolism. Instead, the residual bio-oils on the particles and the range of compounds adsorbed to the biochar surface appear to be the only substrates available – in the short term – to support microbial growth and metabolism.

Soil microbial populations can be affected by both the quality (see Chapters 2 to 5) and quantity of the biochar added to soil. The qualities of biochar depend largely upon the feedstock and pyrolysis conditions (see Chapter 2). Flash carbonizing (McClellan et al, 2007) and some low-temperature pyrolysis conditions leave residual bio-oils and other re-condensed derivatives on the biochar surfaces (see Chapter 8; Steiner et al, 2008). Depending upon the composition of these residual pyrolysis compounds, they may serve as substrates for microbial growth and metabolism, as proposed by Ogawa (1994) and Steiner et al (2008); but they may also be toxic to plants, as shown by McClellan et al (2007), and possibly to some microbes.

Populations that establish on the biochar surface will be those that are able to elaborate the enzymes necessary to metabolize the available substrates. The more complex and unusual a substrate is, the more restricted the population of organisms will be that can use it effectively as a source of energy, cell C and/or nutrients, and the longer it will take to be completely metabolized. It is likely that organisms colonizing fresh biochar that has post-pyrolysis condensates on its surfaces will differ substantially from those colonizing the biochar surfaces after these deposits have been metabolized. While some co-metabolism of the biochar itself has been shown to be likely over longer periods of time (Hamer et al, 2004; see Chapter 14), it is the C substrates and inorganic nutrients that become adsorbed to the biochar surfaces after the condensates and/or ash are gone that will be the dominant 'foodstuffs' of later colonizing organisms. The nature of other organic matter added, soil type and texture, plants cultivated and fire frequency (in forested systems – e.g. Zackrisson et al, 1996), among other factors, will also affect the nature of compounds adsorbed to biochar surfaces and the organisms that are able to successfully colonize them. Thus, there is likely to be a succession of organisms colonizing over time as the characteristics of the surface environment change.

Bio-oils, ash, pyroligneous acids (PAs) (Steiner et al, 2008) and volatile matter (VM) (McClellen et al, 2007), among others, are terms given by various researchers to the variety of residues remaining on biochar surfaces immediately following pyrolysis. Surface-adhering pyrolysis condensates can include water-soluble compounds such as acids, alcohols, aldehydes, ketones and sugars that are easily metabolized by soil microbes. However, depending upon feedstock and pyrolysis conditions, they may also contain compounds such as polycyclic aromatic hydrocarbons, cresols, xylenols, formaldehyde, acrolein and other toxic carbonyl compounds that can have bactericidal or fungicidal activity (Painter, 2001). Ogawa (1994) and Zackrisson et al (1996) have shown that these substances can, and do, serve as C and energy sources for selected microbes. The turnover time of these substrates is likely to be on the order of one to two seasons and, thus, will not determine community composition for any length of time.

Smith et al (1992) suggested that variability in the adsorption dynamics of nutrient- and C-containing substrates by biochar (see also Chapter 5) might alter the competitive interactions between microbes and change their overall community structure and dynamics. Pietikäinen et al (2000) explored the ability of biochar made from *Empetrum nigrum*, biochar made from humus, activated carbon and pumice to adsorb dissolved organic carbon (DOC) and to support microbial populations. These four materials were added to mesocosms in the laboratory. Non-heated humus was placed on top of each absorbent and the mesocosms were watered with leaf litter extract. The most DOC was removed by the activated carbon, whereas the least was removed by the pumice, with the two biochars intermediate between these two treatments. All of the adsorbents were colonized by microbes after one month; but the respiratory activity was highest in the two biochar-amended treatments. Phospholipid fatty acid (PLFA) profiles and substrate utilization patterns (i.e. Biolog Ecoplate®, Hayward, CA) demonstrated that different communities developed on the different adsorbents. Principal component analysis of the PLFA profiles showed that the communities in the two biochars were most similar to each other and that both harboured communities divergent from those on pumice and activated carbon. Communities colonizing pumice and activated carbon also diverged substantially from each other (Pietikäinen et al, 2000). Thus, the type and availability of substrates associated with the different adsorbents led to colonization by different microbial communities. Differences in these surface communities may, in turn, result in changes in the availability of nutrients to plants and nutrient cycling, in general, in the soils to which these adsorbents are added. More work is needed to better understand which organisms colonize biochar in its initial phases, how these communities change over time in different soils under varying management, and how such changes affect the agronomic outcomes in biochar-amended soils.

Methodological issues

The methodological issues that may arise when analysing biological communities in biochar-amended soils are many and varied. Most of these issues will be associated with the capacity of biochar to adsorb a wide range of organic and inorganic molecules. Most of the assays typically used to detect the abundance of soil biota in general (i.e. microbial biomass) and their activities (e.g. adenosine triphosphate (ATP) as a measure of soil energy charge and CO_2 evolution as a measure of soil respiratory activity) can be confounded by the strong sorption of the molecules being extracted or evolved and measured as surrogates for the specific processes involved. The sorption capacity of biochar is therefore likely to introduce significant biases into most methods used to assess the abundance, activity and diversity of the soil biota, including extraction of DNA from soil and follow-on molecular analyses. Since biochar can adsorb many inorganic nutrient elements (e.g. NH_4^+, HPO_4^{2-} and $H_2PO_4^-$ and DOC, as well as chemisorb CO_2 and O_2, our ability to fully extract these compounds (or measure gases released) is likely to be compromised; hence, we are likely to under-

estimate the values derived from most assays conducted on biochar-amended soils. Such sorption can affect an assay as straightforward as measuring inorganic N contents (typically a KCl or K_2SO_4 extraction) to more complex assays, such as using cell C contents liberated by fumigation to estimate microbial biomass and measuring CO_2 captured in the headspace of contained samples to calculate soil respiratory activity. We are studying the sorption capacity of a mineral soil from Auburn, New York, to which maize biochar was added at 12t ha^{-1}. The ability to extract DOC added to the soil was significantly reduced in the presence of biochar, indicating that the capacity of the amended soil to adsorb DOC was very high (see Figure 6.3).

These preliminary results illustrate that our estimates of microbial biomass derived from soil DOC extracts may be seriously underestimated as the proportion (and likely type) of biochar added to soil increases. Use of internal standards, such as spiking with specific marker molecules and assessing their recovery, will be necessary to improve estimates of microbial parameters that are based on extractions.

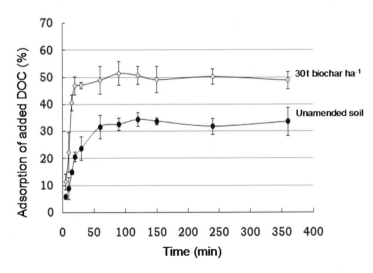

Figure 6.3 *Time course of dissolved organic carbon (DOC) adsorption in slurries of soil with 30t biochar ha^{-1} added compared to unamended soil*

Note: 10g soil shaken with 40mL of 0.05M K_2SO_4 containing 100mg DOC L^{-1} for either 5, 10, 15, 20, 30, 60, 90, 120, 150, 240 or 360 minutes; DOC measured by oxidation and infrared gas analysis (N = 3).

Source: Jin et al (2008)

In practical terms, this means that values derived from most microbial assays will be underestimated when these measured variables are derived from either soil extracts or headspace gas measurements. Thus, caution in interpreting data derived from these types of assays is clearly warranted.

Effects of biochar on the activity of the soil biota

In the Amazonian Dark Earths, which are rich in biochar, microbial community activity, biomass and composition are significantly different from those in adjacent unamended soils (Thies and Suzuki, 2003). In studies with ADE, different researchers have shown that these soils have a higher microbial biomass and abundance of culturable bacteria and fungi, but significantly lower respiratory activity and, thus, a higher metabolic efficiency (O'Neill, 2007; Liang, 2008). For example, Liang (2008) measured CO_2 evolved over a 532-day period from four ADE of varying ages and their adjacent background soils that were low in biochar. Regardless of site age, the microbial activity of the four ADE was similar and 61 to 80 per cent ($p < 0.05$) lower than any of the adjacent soils on a per unit C basis. However, microbial biomass was 43 to 125 per cent higher ($p < 0.05$) overall in the ADE than the adjacent soils. Thus, the metabolic quotient (the ratio of C evolved as CO_2 to

microbial biomass C) was significantly lower in the ADE, indicating a higher metabolic efficiency of the microbial community. It is this reduction in CO_2 evolved by a larger microbial biomass that is proposed to lead to the increased retention and stabilization of organic matter in the ADE over time, relative to the typically impoverished state of the highly weathered soils of the Amazon region.

In field studies in Aurora, New York, mineral soil was amended with varying rates (0, 1t ha^{-1}, 3t ha^{-1}, 12t ha^{-1} and 30t ha^{-1}) of maize-derived biochar. Soils were sampled at the end of the first cropping year and soil respiration was measured over an eight-week period (Jin et al, 2008). Total respiration and the respiratory rate decreased with increasing biochar added (see Figure 6.4) – just as observed by Liang (2008) with the ADE soils.

The decreased respiratory activity we observed in response to adding biochar could

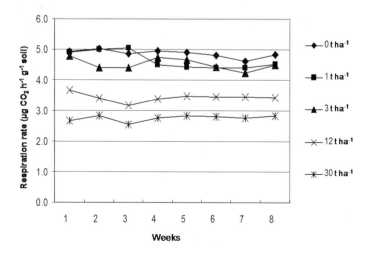

Figure 6.4 *Soil respiration rate decreases as the rate of biochar applied increases; incubations of 20g of soil at 50 per cent water-holding capacity, CO_2 captured in 0.5M NaOH and quantification of electrical conductivity as a measure of trapped CO_2 (N = 3)*

Source: Jin et al (2008)

indicate that the biochar is inhibiting the activity of biochar-colonizing microorganisms, changing bacterial to fungal ratios (or population structure), increasing C-use efficiency, and decreasing population abundance or some combination of these responses. Changes may also result from chemisorption of respired CO_2 to the biochar surface. If sorbed, CO_2 would not be recovered in the assay and, thus, artificially reduce the estimate of respiratory activity. Which of these scenarios is the primary driving mechanism for reduced CO_2 release from biochar amended soils is yet to be resolved. Evidence from the ADE soils (O'Neill, 2007; Liang, 2008) and our measurements of microbial biomass in the Aurora, New York, experiment suggest that microbial abundance increases in soils rich in biochar; thus, decreased abundance is not among the driving mechanisms. This is substantiated by the results of Zackrisson et al (1996), who investigated the effects of biochar on soil microbial properties at six sites. They found that microbial biomass was consistently enhanced in humus when it was placed adjacent to biochar particles.

Steiner et al (2008) studied the effect of adding different combinations of biochar, kaolin and PA on substrate-induced respiration (SIR) of the microbial community in a highly weathered Amazonian upland soil. In three separate mesocosm experiments, basal respiration was measured for 11 to 18 hours before adding glucose and measuring SIR. Basal respiration did not differ between treatments composed of:

• varying rates of wood biochar added;
• varying combinations of kaolin and wood biochar added; or
• varying combinations of biochar, water and PA (a potential microbial substrate) added to soil mesocosms.

When glucose was added, however, the substrate-induced respiratory activity of the soil biota as measured by the total CO_2 evolved over the following 34 hours increased with increasing amounts of biochar (0, 50g kg^{-1}, 100g kg^{-1} and 150g kg^{-1}) added to soil, with and without kaolin substitution. Adding only water to biochar did not increase microbial respiratory activity. However, when easily metabolizable organic matter (glucose) was added to the soil amended with biochar + water, soil microbial activity increased exponentially over the following 15-hour period. Amending soil with biochar, water and PA together increased microbial respiratory activity for a short period (10 hours) before it dropped back to the basal rate. When glucose was added to this treatment, an exponential increase in activity that was sustained over 15 hours was observed; but the respiratory rate was significantly higher than that of the biochar + water + glucose treatment. Thus, the PA added appeared to be a metabolizable substrate for the microbial community. Steiner et al (2008) used these SIR data to calculate microbial biomass and concluded that PA stimulated microbial growth above that of adding biochar alone; thus, PA must contain easily degradable substrates able to support microbial colonization, in general. SIR has been used as a means to calculate soil microbial biomass in many agricultural soils (Anderson and Domsch, 1978). However, the possibility that biochar may chemisorb CO_2 directly or that CO_2 may be fixed by chemolithotrophs associated with biochar particles has not been adequately explored; thus, the use of the exponential respiratory rate to calculate microbial biomass in experiments where biochar is added to soil must be done with caution.

Reduced respiratory activity in biochar-amended temperate soils (see Figure 6.4) and in the ADE soils of the tropics (Liang, 2008) contrasted with the respiratory response to added glucose observed by Steiner et al (2008) suggests that reduced respiratory activity in biochar-amended soils may, in part, be due to changes in substrate quality and/or availability.

Effects of chemisorption on soil biotic activity

The presence of biochar in soil enhances the adsorption of DOC (see Figure 6.3), inorganic nutrients and various gases, as well as potentially toxic compounds, such as pesticides, heavy metals and toxic secondary metabolites (see Chapters 14 and 16), all of which can influence the abundance, diversity and activity of soil organisms. For example, Wardle et al (1998) investigated the short-term effects on plant growth and microbial biomass of adding biochar to boreal forest soils in glasshouse studies. They found that adding biochar to humus collected from three forested systems differing in understorey vegetation increased soil microbial biomass and plant growth in the test system. They suggested that the biochar acted to adsorb secondary metabolites and phenolics that were produced by the decomposing ericaceous vegetation, with the net result of increasing soil nutrient availability. This is discussed in greater detail in Chapter 14.

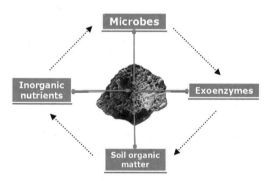

Figure 6.5 *Potential simultaneous adsorption of microbes, soil organic matter, extracellular enzymes and inorganic nutrients to biochar surfaces: availability of C, energy and nutrients for colonizing microorganisms will depend upon the nature and strength of these interactions and, in the case of enzymes, if adsorption affects access to the enzyme active site(s)*

Source: chapter authors

Whether an adsorbed chemical is bio-available or not, and, hence, whether its adsorption increases or decreases microbial activity, will depend upon the molecular structure of the chemical, the binding sites on the molecule and biochar surface, the type of biochar and the characteristics of the microorganisms in question (see Figure 6.5). The strength of binding will also vary in relation to the type of molecular surface interaction dominating (i.e. hydrophobic interactions, covalent bonding, van der Waals forces, cation or anion exchange, or ion substitution) (see Chapter 16).

Adsorption of both substrate and microorganisms to biochar surfaces may result in a higher concentration of substrate near the attached bacterial cells and, therefore, may increase substrate use (Ortega-Calvo and Saiz-Jimenez, 1998). Purines, amino acids and peptides that enter the interlayer region of expanding clays, such as montmorillonite, may not affect microbial metabolism because the cells cannot access the substrate. This may also be the case for these compounds in the porous structure of biochar.

It is still not clear if the adsorption of compounds to biochar inhibits microbes, increases nutrient immobilization, or simply provides microbes a protected site with adequate resources away from predation (Pietikäinen et al, 2000; Warnock et al, 2007). Considering the complexity of interactions among biochar, inorganic nutrients, minerals and microorganisms in soils, many questions still remain to be answered regarding the mechanisms governing the direct effects of biochar on soil organisms (e.g. surface interactions with microbial cell walls or capsular materials) and the indirect effects that may result from changes in adsorption of organic matter, nutrients and clays and other minerals (see Chapters 3, 10 and 11). Research on these topics will be critical for increasing our understanding of the potential benefits of biochar as a soil ameliorant.

Diversity of organisms interacting with biochar

Soil biological communities are complex assemblages of bacteria, archaea, fungi, algae, protozoa, nematodes, arthropods and a diversity of invertebrates. Interactions among the members of these populations and soil chemical and physical properties will determine overall ecosystem function and productivity. The chemical and physical characteristics of different biochars will add another layer of complexity to soil food web interactions by altering the availability of soluble and particulate organic matter (substrates), mineral nutrients, pH, soil aggregation and the activity of extracellular enzymes (see Figure 6.5), and, thus, will affect diversity, abundance and distribution of associated microbial communities.

Bacteria and Archaea

Work on characterizing bacteria and archaea populations associated with biochar is in its infancy. Pietikäinen et al (2000) showed that biochar-associated communities differed from those associated with pumice or activated carbon (see above) in terms of their phospholipid fatty acid (PLFA) and C substrate utilization profiles, but did not identify specific populations involved beyond the large groupings based on PLFAs predominating on the various substrate surfaces. Steiner et al (2008) examined respiratory activity and projected biomass estimates, but did not identify key groups colonizing biochar- or PA-amended Brazilian soils. Much of what we know about how the presence of biochar changes in bacterial and archaeal communities comes from work with the ADE soils in Brazil (Thies and Suzuki, 2003; Kim et al, 2007; Grossman et al, submitted). Grossman et al compared microbial community compositions between four anthrosols and adjacent background soils with the same mineralogy under four different land uses, using microbial community DNA fingerprinting followed by cloning and sequencing. Microbial communities from ADE were similar to each other regardless of site, and these communities were distinct from those in the adjacent soils. Archaeal communities in the adjacent soils diverged by over 90 per cent from those characterized from the ADE. Clearly, factors common to the ADE are stronger drivers of microbial community composition than factors associated with soil type, sampling depth or land use – factors that normally strongly influence microbial community composition in soils without biochar. Indeed, bacterial communities in the adjacent background soils separated primarily by soil type and/or land use. Sequencing of taxa unique to particular samples showed that both anthrosols and adjacent soils contained organisms that are taxonomically distinct from those found in sequence databases (i.e. GenBank). Most sequences obtained were novel and matched those in databases at less than 97 per cent similarity. Sequences obtained only from the ADE grouped at 93 per cent similarity with the *Verrucomicrobia*, a genus commonly found in rice paddies in the tropics and increasingly being shown to be present in agricultural soils. *Proteobacteria* and *Cyanobacteria* spp were found only in adjacent background soils, and *Pseudomonas*, *Acidobacteria*, and *Flexibacter* spp were common to both soil types. The predominant difference between the ADE and adjacent background soils was the presence of biochar in the ADE. The high similarity in bacterial and archaeal community composition in the ADE suggests that biochar-amended soils will also select for distinct microbial communities. Much work is needed to identify population differences arising from biochar amendments and what soil processes may be affected by changes in microbial community composition and dynamics.

Kim et al (2007) examined the gross diversity of bacterial populations extant in an ADE as compared to an undisturbed forest site in the western Amazon. They used oligonucleotide fingerprinting of 16S rRNA gene sequences amplified from soil DNA extracts, which indicated that, while there was considerable overlap in the broad groups of bacteria identified, the ADE soil bacterial population was 25 per cent more diverse than that in the undisturbed forest soil (see Figure 6.6).

In studies on the ADE, we used the BacLight™ fluorescent staining assay to visualize live and dead microbial cells on the surface of biochar particles picked out of the ADE. In Figure 6.7, live and dead bacteria, fungi and fine roots can be seen. This illustrates the capacity of biochar to support active microbial populations and retain dead organisms briefly on the biochar surfaces.

Nitrogen fixation by diazotrophs

The use of biochar as a soil ameliorant can potentially have many different effects on N_2-fixing bacteria (diazotrophs), root nodulation and N_2 fixation. Diazotrophs are a specialized group of bacteria with a diverse phylogeny, but the common functional capacity of sequentially reducing atmospheric N_2 to ammonia (NH_3), which is often used immediately to produce amino acids. Diazotrophs fix N_2 either as free-living soil bacteria (e.g. *Azotobacter* sp or *Azospirillum* sp) or as mutualists in association various plants, such as the rhizobia that form N_2-fixing nodules on legume roots and the actinorrhizal association of *Frankia* sp with the roots of various tree species. Only organisms in the domains Bacteria and Archaea have the genetic capacity to produce the enzyme nitrogenase, which is required to fix atmospheric N_2. Nitrogenase is, however, deactivated in the presence of O_2 and requires Fe and Mo to produce.

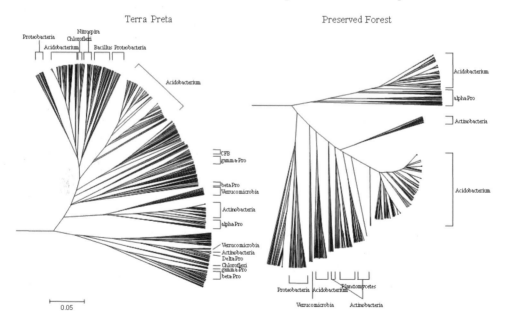

Figure 6.6 *Taxonomic cluster analysis of 16S rRNA gene sequences from Amazonian Dark Earths (ADE) and adjacent pristine forest soil based on oligonucleotide fingerprinting*

Source: Kim et al (2007), with permission from the publisher

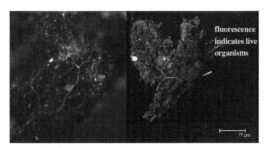

fluorescence
indicates live
organisms

75 μm

Figure 6.7 *Bacteria, fungi and fine roots*
readily colonize biochar surfaces

Source: Tsai et al (2008)

For free-living diazotrophs, the fine pores of biochar create a habitat where reduced O_2 tensions are likely. If Fe and Mo are available in sufficient supply, the fixation of atmospheric N_2 will increase an organism's competitiveness in the biochar environment and, thus, their proportional representation within the biochar and soil community.

For mutualists, such as rhizobia, availability of N will strongly influence nodulation and subsequent N_2 fixation because legumes will preferentially take up inorganic N from the soil solution. The low N content of most biochars and the exchange of NH_4^+ between the biochar surface and soil solution are likely to modify N availability to plant roots and may stimulate nodulation and N_2 fixation in legumes and actinorrhizal plants.

Matsuo Ogawa has worked with N_2-fixing bacteria and mycorrhizal fungi for over 30 years. In 1994, he summarized his work on the response of these organisms to adding biochar to soil. He reported that sprinkling biochar over field soils increased his ability to culture and isolate N_2-fixing bacteria from soil samples on to an N-free medium. He reported that *Azotobacter* sp was identified from among these isolates. He has tested the use of biochar as a carrier for N_2-fixing rhizobia inoculant and as a carrier material for mycorrhizal fungi. Inoculation of soybean

with biochar-based rhizobia preparations increased nodulation and N_2 fixation. Adding biochar to soil also appeared to stimulate the N_2-fixing activity of free-living diazotrophs. Ogawa (1994) proposed that these bacteria might be poorer competitors whose survival in soil may be enhanced by their ability to colonize the biochar pores. Most biochars are very low in inorganic N content, giving diazotrophs a competitive advantage for surface colonization. Increased N_2 fixation by rhizobia in association with plants may result, in part, from the transient adsorption of NH_4^+ on biochar surfaces that could lower the inorganic N concentration in the soil solution and improve root nodulation and subsequent nodule activity. Biochar may also sorb important signalling molecules, such as nod factors, increasing their longevity in soil and the likelihood that they will interact with compatible rhizobia bacteria and improve nodulation.

Rondon et al (2007) examined the effect of biochar additions on N_2 fixation by rhizobia-nodulating *Phaseolus vulgaris* in Colombia. Increasing rates of biochar (0, 30kg ha^{-1}, 60kg ha^{-1} and 90kg ha^{-1}) increased the proportion of nitrogen derived from fixation (percentage NdF) from 50 per cent in the control to 72 per cent in the 60kg ha^{-1} treatment and increased bean yields by 46 per cent. They attributed these findings to increased availability of molybdenum (Mo) and boron (B) (for nitrogenase function), increased soil pH and increased N immobilization. Rhizobia tend to prefer circum-neutral pH; thus, increasing pH in an otherwise strongly acidic soil may be a major factor in improving nodulation and N_2 fixation in these trials. These authors also examined whether arbuscular mycorrhizal fungi colonization was increased by adding biochar, but did not observe any significant effects.

Use of biochar as an inoculant carrier

Many microorganisms have been used to increase crop production through batch culturing, adding the inoculum to an appropriate carrier and either placing the inoculum in the planting furrow or adhering it to seeds immediately prior to planting. Both mutualistic and free-living N_2-fixing bacteria, other plant growth promoting rhizobacteria (PGPR), such as *Paenibacillus*, *Bacillus* and *Pseudomonas*, and saprophytic (e.g. *Trichoderma harzianum*) and mycorrhizal fungi have been used as inoculants applied to field soils. Ogawa (1994) has used biochar as a carrier substrate for both rhizobia and for arbuscular mycorrhizal (AM) over the past 20+ years with excellent success. Additional studies conducted in Japan (Takagi, 1990) and in Syria (Beck, 1991) have shown that biochar is a suitable carrier for the N_2-fixing root nodule bacteria *Rhizobium*, *Mesorhizobium* and *Bradyrhizobium*. It is not difficult to speculate on the variety of applications biochar inoculants may have in agriculture and environmental remediation. Biochar may prove a most efficient inoculant delivery system and may also improve outcomes of bioremediation efforts by increased sorption of organic pollutants onto biochar impregnated with bacteria selected for their capacity to degrade the target pollutants.

Fungi

Soil fungi are a heterogeneous group both functionally and phylogenetically (Thorn and Lynch, 2007), encompassing members of the phyla of the Eumycota, as well as non-Eumycotan phyla (notably the Oomycota). In terms of function, the fungi can be coarsely divided into saprophytes, plant pathogens and mycorrhizal fungi. Each one of these groups could exhibit very different responses to biochar application that need to be understood. While briefly addressing each of these groups, the main discussion is focused on mycorrhizal fungi, whose interaction with biochar has been studied the most.

Saprophytic fungi

Saprophytic fungi, as decomposers, are particularly important as they may influence the persistence and modification of biochar materials in soil. In contrast to bacteria, fungi have a hyphal, invasive growth habit (aptly likened to tunnelling machines; Wessels, 1999), which gives them access to the interior of solid materials. This means that saprophytic fungi could be effective colonizers of the interior of biochar particles. Fungi also have exceptional enzymatic capabilities, and this further highlights the need to study fungi as decomposers of biochar. For example, Laborda et al (1999) showed that fungi (*Trichoderma* and *Penicillium* spp) could contribute to depolymerization of coal (hard coal, sub-bituminous coal and lignite) via production of enzymes such as Mn-peroxidase and phenoloxidase. Hockaday (2006) reported degradation of biochar by fungal laccase.

To what extent do biochar particles serve as a habitat for soil fungi? Ogawa and Yamabe (1986) suggested that biochar may be an unsuitable habitat for saprophytic fungi, but not for mycorrhizal fungi. However, this will greatly depend upon the nature of the biochar, as well as upon the amount of labile organic molecules that sorb to biochar in soil, which may thus serve as a source of C and energy for soil microbes. For example, Pietikäinen et al (2000) found that naturally produced biochar from forest wildfires hosted microbial communities, but no specific emphasis was placed on colonizing fungi. More recently, in approximately 100-year-old biochar, Hockaday et al (2007) visualized filamentous growth of unidentified microbes inside of aged biochar particles by scanning electron microscopy. Given the scale in the figure, these filaments are about

4μm in diameter, and therefore likely to be fungi, rather than actinomycetes. Given that fungi can inhabit both the exterior and the interior of biochar particles, questions regarding the community composition and identity of these (presumably) saprophytic fungi arise. It is not clear whether they can modify the biochar material chemically through the secretion of extracellular enzymes, or whether the composition of fungal consortia and a suite of extracellular enzymes are important in this process.

Fungi, due to their mycelial nature, can also help to stabilize biochar in the soil matrix and within soil aggregates. Fungal filaments and metabolic products serve as binding agents at the level of meso- and macro-aggregates (Tisdall and Oades, 1982; Rillig and Mummey, 2006).

Pathogenic fungi

Fungal pathogens are widely recognized for their role in agro-ecosystems (Agrios, 1997) and increasingly also in natural ecosystems. Disease magnitude is a function of the interplay of host susceptibility, pathogen virulence and environmental conditions (the disease triangle), and some or all of these factors could be affected by biochar additions. Nevertheless, there are very few studies that have examined biochar effects on fungal root pathogens.

Matsubara et al (2002) provided the most detailed account of the interaction of biochar materials and pathogenic fungi using the *Fusarium oxysporum*–asparagus pathosystem. The authors also included inoculation with arbuscular mycorrhizal (AM) fungi as a treatment. They found that in AM pre-inoculated plants, disease indices were strongly reduced, and even further reduced when biochar was added. The results thus suggested that biochar may enhance the ability of AM fungi to help plants resist fungal pathogen infection. Steiner et al (2008) examined the role of smoke condensates from biochar production (PA) on soil microbes because previous

reports cited in this chapter had indicated a 'soil sterilizing' effect. Stimulated microbial populations and activity in response to PA addition were found (see discussion above); but the study did not include effects on potential pathogens. This may be a promising research avenue.

Given the scarcity of data, there are clear needs for research on the effects of biochar on pathogenic fungi: several selected pathosystems, especially those involving soil-borne phytopathogens, should be examined for how the interaction of pathogen and host could be affected, and what the specific mechanisms are. Additionally, it would be highly desirable to include monitoring of root lesions or other plant disease symptoms in fields where biochar is applied.

Mechanisms could, to some degree, be similar to the ones described for other biotrophic fungi-forming mycorrhizae (see the following sub-section). Biochar-mediated increases in water-holding capacity could also favour certain pathogens with zoospores, such as the *Pythium* or *Phytophthora* in the Oomycota. If biochar alters root architecture (e.g. through nutrient effects at the individual plant level, or increased abundance of fine-rooted plant species at the plant community level), this could also have consequences for host susceptibility since finer root systems may offer a greater surface area for attack by soil-borne pathogens (Newsham et al, 1995).

Mycorrhizal fungi

Mycorrhizae are common root-fungal mutualisms with key roles in terrestrial ecosystems (Rillig, 2004). There are several types of mycorrhizas, the most common of which are arbuscular mycorrhizae (AM) and ectomycorrhizae (EM) (Smith and Read, 1997). These two groups are distinct morphologically, physiologically and ecologically with respect to the plant hosts, and also in regard to phylogeny of the fungal partner. Thus, it is highly likely that they also respond differently to biochar additions.

There has been keen interest in the effects of biochar on mycorrhizae, with pioneering work coming primarily from Japanese researchers. The interest in mycorrhizae and biochar is probably due to three reasons. First, mycorrhizal fungi are ubiquitous key components in virtually all biomes (Treseder and Cross, 2006). Therefore, it is important to understand how any soil additive, including biochar, may affect their performance. AM fungi colonize most of the important crop species (maize, rice, wheat, etc.) so that they are also of interest from a perspective of agro-ecosystem productivity and sustainability. Second, mycorrhizae are sensitive to management interventions (Schwartz et al, 2006), such as adding biochar, and it is tempting to speculate on the possible synergistic effects of mycorrhizal inoculation and biochar application in enhancing soil quality and plant growth. Applying biochar to soil stimulated the colonization of crops by AM fungi. Nishio and Okano (1991) reported that root infection by AM fungi significantly increased alfalfa yield by 40 to 80 per cent when $1kg\ m^{-2}$ of biochar was added to an alfalfa field in a volcanic ash soil. Third, the majority of the studies reported in the literature show a strongly positive effect of biochar on mycorrhiza abundance (Warnock et al, 2007), which is intriguing from a mechanistic perspective.

Warnock et al (2007) summarized the literature on responses of mycorrhizae to biochar additions and provided several mechanisms for biochar effects on mycorrhizae. Some of these had been proposed previously, but very few have been thoroughly tested. Here, we regroup mechanisms of interaction into physical, chemical and biological; these are, of course, strongly interrelated and would be acting concurrently.

Physical effects

Saito (1989) reported that hyphae and spores of AM fungi were visible on extracted biochar particles following a field application of biochar in a C-rich soil, and that it appeared that AM fungi had colonized these particles. It was suggested that the porous nature of the biochar particles or the reduced competition from saprophytes (for which this habitat was presumed to be less suitable) could have contributed to this (Saito, 1989; Saito and Marumoto, 2002). Saito and Marumoto (2002) suggested that biochar particles act as a microhabitat for AM fungi and enable them to survive, and may also provide protection from predator grazing. Ezawa et al (2002) reported that AM fungal root colonization was increased in the presence of ground biochar as opposed to non-ground material, and also attributed this effect mainly to the porous nature of biochar; however, high application rates of 30 per cent volume per volume (v/v) were used. Apart from these observations, it seems that a quantitative or functional assessment of hyphal colonization of these particles remains lacking. Porous particles, such as expanded clay, are used often in AM inoculum production (as a carrier material) because of the documented association of AM fungi with these particles (e.g. Baltruschat, 1987). Therefore, it seems likely that surface phenomena and micropore habitats could play an important role in improving mycorrhizal interactions with plant roots; but the mechanisms are not yet understood.

Chemical effects

There is considerable evidence for the importance of chemical changes in the effects of biochar on mycorrhiza abundance (e.g. nutrient availability and pH changes; reviewed in Warnock et al, 2007). Biochar has frequently been documented to alter, and often increase, the availability of N and P in the rooting zone. Depending upon the generation temperature and feedstock properties, biochar itself may add nutrients (see Chapter 5). Mycorrhizal fungi and C supply from their hosts can react sensitively to these variables. A different chemical effect pertains to signalling in the rhizosphere, the soil information 'superhighway' (Bais et al, 2004). Adsorption of inhibitory compounds or their sequestration and the slow release of positive signalling molecules are examples of how biochar could interfere with root–fungus or other signal exchanges. AM fungi can respond to a number of chemical signals (such as flavonoids, sesquiterpenes and strigolactones), which alter growth or branching (e.g. Akiyama et al, 2005). While a likely mechanism, no direct evidence has been provided for biochar signal interference in the soil.

Biological effects

From the perspective of organism interactions, effects at the same, lower or higher trophic levels could influence organism abundance and functioning. Competition or facilitative interactions could be altered in the presence of biochar or as a consequence of effects on physico-chemical soil properties. Mycorrhizal fungi could, for example, compete with saprophytes (Gadgil and Gadgil, 1971), and this interaction could be altered by biochar. Alternatively, mycorrhization helper bacteria (Garbaye, 1994) could aid mycorrhizal fungi in colonizing roots, and this group of facilitative organisms could become stimulated. The trophic level below mycorrhizal fungi consists of roots, and fungi in the soil are hypothesized to be controlled mostly from the bottom up (Wardle, 2002). Carbon allocation to obligate biotrophic AM fungi and EM fungi (which do include species with saprophytic abilities) would be pivotal for mycorrhizal fungal abundance, and this allocation is regulated in numerous ways (Koide and Schreiner, 1992), including through delivery of fungal services, such as nutrient acquisition (Javot et al, 2007). Fungi, including mycorrhizal fungi, are subject to grazing by soil fauna. Altered grazing interactions – for example, through toxic effects on grazers or provision of refugia (enemy-free space) in biochar particles – could lead to changes in abundance.

There are pressing needs for research on the effects of biochar on mycorrhizal symbioses. It is important to explore the full parameter space (e.g. biochar feedstock, production temperature, application rate, soil nutrient status and ecosystem type) in terms of effects of biochar on this symbiosis. This also includes the reporting of negative or neutral effects; perhaps there has been biased reporting towards positive effects. In order to understand what effects biochar has on mycorrhiza, mycorrhizal response variables need to be examined in a more differentiated way. This entails measuring different phases of the fungus (e.g. for AM fungi the extra-radical and the intra-radical phases), the fungal community composition and the functioning of the fungal interaction with the host plant. Studies need to address specific mechanistic hypotheses, thus moving beyond mere phenomenological assessment of effects. Only in this way will causes of biochar effects be understood and, thus, can clear management recommendations be made.

Finally, the above discussion and that in Warnock et al (2007) has mostly centred on the mycorrhizae at the individual host plant level; but mycorrhizal effects in ecosystems manifest themselves in a hierarchical fashion (O'Neill et al, 1991). Thus, AM fungi are known to be important in mediating interactions among co-occurring plants, including weeds (e.g. Marler et al, 1999). It is therefore worth considering how biochar could – via affecting mycorrhizae – also alter the competitive balance among plant community members, such as weeds and crops. At the ecosystem level, effects on individual host plants are important, as well as plant community changes; but mycorrhizal fungi can also influence a variety of ecosystem-level processes in multiple ways (Rillig, 2004). One that may be of particular interest in the context of biochar and soil C storage is soil aggregation (Rillig and Mummey, 2006).

Mycorrhizal fungi, through various mechanisms, including physical, biological and biochemical pathways, can influence soil aggregation and, thus, the storage of C within these aggregates (Rillig and Mummey, 2006). One biochemical mechanism includes the production of the protein glomalin; concentrations of glomalin-related soil protein are often highly correlated with soil aggregate water stability (Wright and Upadhyaya, 1998). If biochar enhances the functionality of mycorrhizal fungi in this regard (e.g. by enhancing glomalin production), more C other than that contained in the biochar itself could be stored. This is a topic worthy of pursuit in future studies.

Soil fauna

Biochar could affect soil fauna directly or indirectly, but relatively little direct data are available yet. Indirectly, soil fauna could be affected by altered biotic resources. Energy and matter flow through soil food webs is, at a coarse level, organized into energy channels: the fungal-based and bacteria-based energy channels. Thus, if shifts between fungi and bacteria in response to biochar occur, these will probably ripple on to changes at the higher trophic levels within each energy channel. Directly, soil fauna could be influenced by ingesting biochar particles. This is the case for geophagous fauna, such as earthworms (Topoliantz and Ponge, 2003, 2005). Here, it may be an interesting question to examine how biochar may interfere with the intricate associations of earthworm gut microbes. Further direct effects include all documented physico-chemical changes caused by biochar additions.

Conclusions

Soil management strategies, such as amending soil with biochar, should aim to support and enable the soil biota to carry out the key ecosystem functions that they moderate in order to ensure long-term soil fertility and sustained crop production. Amending soil with biochar needs to involve a careful selection of the feedstock and pyrolysis conditions to find an optimal match of biochar type to the intended ecosystem goal(s). Among the many other aims of adding biochar to soil, it is important to ensure sustained functioning of the soil biota so that critical ecosystem functions are maintained. In future work, the effects of biochar on various soil biota groups, their diversity and functioning need to be carefully considered.

References

Agrios, G. N. (1997) *Plant Pathology*, fourth edition, Academic Press, San Diego, CA

Akiyama, K., Matsuzaki, K-I. and Hayashi, H. (2005) 'Plant sesquiterpenes induce hyphal branching in arbuscular mycorrhizal fungi', *Nature*, vol 435, pp824–827

Anderson, J. P. E. and Domsch, K. H. (1978) 'A physiological method for the quantitative measurement of microbial biomass in soils', *Soil Biology and Biochemistry*, vol 10, pp215–221

Antal, M. J. and Grønli, M. (2003) 'The art, science, and technology of charcoal production', *Industrial Engineering and Chemistry Research*, vol 42, pp1619–1640

Bais, H. P., Park, S. W., Weir, T. L., Callaway, R. M. and Vivanco, J. M. (2004) 'How plants communicate using the underground information superhighway', *Trends in Plant Science*, vol 9,

pp26–32

Baltruschat, H. (1987) 'Evaluation of the suitability of expanded clay as carrier material for VAM spores in field inoculation of maize', *Angewandte Botanik*, vol 61, pp163–169

Beck, D. P. (1991) 'Suitability of charcoal-amended mineral soil as a carrier for *Rhizobium* inoculants', *Soil Biology and Biochemistry*, vol 23, pp41–44

Brussaard, L., Bouwman, L. A., Geurs, M., Hassink, J. and Zwart, K. B. (1990) 'Biomass, composition and temporal dynamics of soil organisms of a silt loam soil under conventional and integrated management', *Netherlands Journal of Agricultural Science*, vol 38, pp282–302

Coleman, D. C. (1986) 'The role of microfloral and faunal interactions in affecting soil processes', in M. J. Mitchell and J. P. Naka (eds) *Microflora and Faunal Interactions in Natural and Agro-Ecosystems*, Martinus Nijhoff/Junk, Dordrecht, The Netherlands, pp317–348

Ezawa, T., Yamamoto, K. and Yoshida, S. (2002) 'Enhancement of the effectiveness of indigenous arbuscular mycorrhizal fungi by inorganic soil amendments', *Soil Science and Plant Nutrition,* vol 48, pp897–900

Fierer, N. and Jackson, R. B. (2006) 'The diversity and biogeography of soil bacterial communities', *Proceedings of the National Academy of Sciences*, vol 103, pp626–631

Gadgil, R. L. and Gadgil, P. D. (1971) 'Mycorrhiza and litter decomposition', *Nature*, vol 233, p133

Garbaye, J. (1994) 'Helper bacteria: A new dimension to the mycorrhizal symbiosis', *New Phytologist*, vol 128, pp197–210

Grossman, J. M., O'Neill, B. E., McPhillips, L., Tsai, S. M., Liang, B., Neves, E., Lehmann, J. and Thies, J. E. (2009) 'Amazonian anthrosols with high black carbon contents support microbial communities that differ distinctly from those extant in adjacent, background soils', *Microbial Ecology*, accepted pending minor revisions

Hamer, U., Marschner, B., Brodowski, S. and Amelung, W. (2004) 'Interactive priming of black carbon and glucose mineralisation', *Organic Geochemistry*, vol 35, pp823–830

Hockaday, W. C. (2006) *The Organic Geochemistry of Charcoal Black Carbon in the Soils of the University of Michigan Biological Station*, PhD thesis, Ohio State University, US

Hockaday, W. C., Grannas, A. M., Kim, S. and Hatcher, P. G. (2007) 'The transformation and mobility of charcoal in a fire-impacted watershed', *Geochimica et Cosmochimica Acta*, vol 71, pp3432–3445

Horwath, W. (2007) 'Carbon cycling and formation of soil organic matter', in E. A. Paul (ed) *Soil Microbiology, Ecology and Biochemistry*, third edition, Elsevier, Dordrecht, The Netherlands

Javot, H., Penmetsa, R. V., Terzaghi, N., Cook, D. R. and Harrison, M. J. (2007) 'A *Medicago truncatula* phosphate transporter indispensable for the arbuscular mycorrhizal symbiosis', in *Proceedings of the National Academy of Sciences*, vol 104, pp1720–1725

Jin, H., Lehmann, J. and Thies, J. E. (2008) 'Soil microbial community response to amending maize soils with maize stover charcoal', in *Proceedings of the 2008 Conference of International Biochar Initiative*, 8–10 September 2008, Newcastle, UK

Kim, J.-S., Sparovek, G., Longo, R. M., De Melo, W. J. and Crowley, D. (2007) 'Bacterial diversity of terra preta and pristine forest soil from the Western Amazon', *Soil Biology and Biochemistry*, vol 39, pp684–690

Koide, R. T. and Schreiner, R. P. (1992) 'Regulation of the vesicular-arbuscular mycorrhizal symbiosis', *Annual Review of Plant Physiology and Plant Molecular Biology*, vol 43, pp557–581

Laborda, F., Monistrol, I. F., Luna, N. and Fernandez, M. (1999) 'Processes of liquefaction/solubilization of Spanish coals by microorganisms', *Applied Microbiology and Biotechnology*, vol 52, pp49–56

Liang, B. (2008) *The Biogeochemistry of Black Carbon in Soils*, PhD thesis, Cornell University, Ithaca, NY

Liang, B., Lehmann, J., Solomon, D., Kinyangi, J., Grossman, J., O'Neill, B., Skjemstad, J. O., Thies, J. E., Luizão, F. J., Petersen, J. and Neves, E. G. (2006) 'Black carbon increases cation exchange capacity in soils', *Soil Science Society of America Journal*, vol 70, pp1719–1730

Marler, M. J., Zabinski, C. A. and Callaway, R. M. (1999) 'Mycorrhizae indirectly enhance competitive effects of an invasive forb on a native bunchgrass', *Ecology*, vol 80, pp1180–1186

Matsubara, Y.-I., Hasegawa, N. and Fukui, H. (2002) 'Incidence of *Fusarium* root rot in asparagus seedlings infected with arbuscular mycorrhizal fungus as affected by several soil amendments', *Journal of the Japanese Society of Horticultural Science*, vol 71, pp370–374

McClellan, A. T., Deenik, J., Uehara, G. and Antal, M. (2007) 'Effects of flash carbonized macadamia nutshell charcoal on plant growth and soil chemical properties', *American Society of Agronomy Abstracts*, 3–7 November, New Orleans, LA

Newsham, K. K., Fitter, A. H. and Watkinson, A. R. (1995) 'Multi-functionality and biodiversity in arbuscular mycorrhizas', *Trends in Ecology and Evolution*, vol 10, pp407–411

Nichols, G. J., Cripps, J. A., Collinson, M. E. and Scott, A. C. (2000) 'Experiments in waterlogging and sedimentology of charcoal: Results and implications', *Paleogeography, Paleoclimatology, Paleoecology*, vol 164, pp43–56

Nishio, M. and Okano, S. (1991) 'Stimulation of the growth of alfalfa and infection of mycorrhizal fungi by the application of charcoal', *Bulletin of the National Grassland Research Institute*, vol 45, pp61–71

Ogawa, M. (1994) 'Symbiosis of people and nature in the tropics', *Farming Japan*, vol 28, pp10–34

Ogawa, M. and Yamabe, Y. (1986) 'Effects of charcoal on VA mycorrhizae and nodule formation of soybeans', *Bulletin of the Green Energy Programme Group II*, no 8, Ministry of Agriculture, Forestry and Fisheries, Japan, pp108–133

Ogawa, M., Yamabe, Y. and Sugiura, G. (1983) 'Effects of charcoal on the root nodule formation and VA mycorrhiza formation of soy bean', *The Third International Mycological Congress (IMC3)*, Abstract 578

O'Neill, B. E. (2007) *Culture-Based and Molecular Approaches for Analyzing Microbial Communities in Amazonian Dark Earths*, MSc thesis, Cornell University, Ithaca, NY

O'Neill, E. G., O'Neill, R. V. and Norby, R. J. (1991) 'Hierarchy theory as a guide to mycorrhizal research on large-scale problems', *Environmental Pollution*, vol 73, pp271–284

Ortega-Calvo, J.-J. and Saiz-Jimenez, C. (1998) 'Effect of humic fractions and clay on biodegradation of phenanthrene by a *Pseudomonas fluorescens* strain isolated from soil', *Applied and Environmental Microbiology*, vol 64, pp3123–3126

Painter, T. J. (2001) 'Carbohydrate polymers in food preservation: An integrated view of the Maillard reaction with special reference to discoveries of preserved foods in *Sphagnum*-dominated peat bogs', *Carbohydrate Polymers*, vol 36, pp335–347

Paul, E. A. (ed) (2007) *Soil Microbiology, Ecology and Biochemistry*, third edition, Elsevier, Amsterdam, The Netherlands

Pietikäinen, J., Kiikkilä, O. and Fritze, H. (2000) 'Charcoal as a habitat for microbes and its effect on the microbial community of the underlying humus', *Oikos*, vol 89, pp231–242

Rillig, M. C. (2004) 'Arbuscular mycorrhizae and terrestrial ecosystem processes', *Ecology Letters*, vol 7, pp740–754

Rillig, M. C. and Mummey, D. L. (2006) 'Mycorrhizas and soil structure', *New Phytologist*, vol 171, pp41–53

Robson, A. D., Abbott, L. K. and Malajczuk, N. (1994) 'Management of mycorrhizas in agriculture, horticulture, and forestry', in *Proceedings of the International Symposium on Management of Mycorrhizas in Agriculture, Horticulture, and Forestry*, 28 September–2 October 1992, Perth, Australia

Rondon, M., Lehmann, J., Ramírez, J. and Hurtado, M. (2007) 'Biological nitrogen fixation by common beans (*Phaseolus vulgaris* L.) increases with bio-char additions', *Biology and Fertility of Soils*, vol 43, pp699–708

Saito, M. (1989) 'Charcoal as a micro-habitat for VA mycorrhizal fungi and its practical implication', *Agriculture, Ecosystems and Environment*, vol 29, pp341–344

Saito, M. and Marumoto, T. (2002) 'Inoculation with arbuscular mycorrhizal fungi: The status quo in Japan and the future prospects', *Plant and Soil*, vol 244, pp273–279

Schwartz, M. W., Hoeksema, J. D., Gehring, C. A., Johnson, N. C., Klironomos, J. N., Abbott, L. K. and Pringle, A. (2006) 'The promise and the potential consequences of the global transport of mycorrhizal fungal inoculum', *Ecology Letters*, vol 9, pp501–515

Smith, S. E. and Read, D. J. (1997) *Mycorrhizal Symbiosis*, second edition, Academic Press, San Diego, CA

Smith, S. C., Ainsworth, C. C., Traina, S. J. and Hicks, R. J. (1992) 'Effect of sorption on the biodegradation of quinoline', *Soil Science Society of America Journal*, vol 56, pp737–746

Steiner, C., Das, K. C., Garcia, M., Forster, B. and Zech, W. (2008) 'Charcoal and smoke extract stimulate the soil microbial community in a highly weathered xanthic Ferralsol', *Pedobiologia*, vol 51, pp359–366

Swift, M. J., Heal, O. W. and Anderson, J. M. (1979) *Decomposition in Terrestrial Ecosystems*, Studies in Ecology 5, Blackwell Scientific Publications, Oxford, UK

Takagi, S. (1990) 'Immobilization method of root nodule bacteria within charcoal and effective inoculation method to the legume', in *TRA Report*, pp229–248 (in Japanese)

Thies, J. E. and Grossman, J. M. (2006) 'The soil habitat and soil ecology', in N. Uphoff, A. S. Ball, E. Fernandes, H. Herren, O. Husson, M. Laing, C. Palm, J. Pretty, P. A. Sanchez, N. Sanginga and J. E. Thies (eds) *Biological Approaches to Sustainable Soil Systems*, CRC Press, Boca Raton, FL, pp59–78

Thies, J. E. and Suzuki, K. (2003) 'Amazonian Dark Earths – Biological measurements', in J. Lehmann, D. Kern, B. Glaser and W. I. Woods (eds) *Amazonian Dark Earths: Origin, Properties, Management*, Kluwer Academic Publishers, Dordrecht, The Netherlands, pp287–332

Thorn, R. G. and Lynch, M. D. J. (2007) 'Fungi and eukaryotic algae', in E. A. Paul (ed) *Soil Biology and Biochemistry*, third edition, Elsevier, Amsterdam, The Netherlands, pp145–162

Tisdall, J. M. and Oades, J. M. (1982) 'Organic matter and water-stable aggregates in soils', *Journal of Soil Science*, vol 33, pp141–163

Topoliantz, S. and Ponge, J.-F. (2003) 'Burrowing activity of the geophagous earthworm *Pontoscolex corethrurus* (Oligochaeta: Glossoscolecidae) in the presence of charcoal', *Applied Soil Ecology*, vol 23, pp267–271

Topoliantz, S. and Ponge, J.-F. (2005) 'Charcoal consumption and casting activity by *Pontoscolex corethrurus* (Glossoscolecidae)', *Applied Soil Ecology*, vol 28, pp217–224

Treseder, K. K. and Cross, A. (2006) 'Global distributions of arbuscular mycorrhizal fungi', *Ecosystems*, vol 9, pp305–316

Tsai, S. M., O'Neill, B., Cannavan, F. S., Saito, D., Falcão, N. P. S., Kern, D., Grossman, J. and Thies, J. E. (2008) 'The microbial world of terra preta', in W. I. Woods, W. Teixeira, J. Lehmann, C. Steiner and A. WinklerPrins (eds) *Terra Preta Nova: A Tribute to Wim Sombroek*, Springer, Berlin, Germany

Wardle, D. A. (1998) 'Controls of temporal variability of the soil microbial biomass: A global-scale synthesis', *Soil Biology and Biochemistry*, vol 30, pp1627–1637

Wardle, D. A. (2002) *Communities and Ecosystems*, Princeton University Press, Princeton, NJ, US

Wardle, D. A., Zackrisson, O. and Nilsson, M. C. (1998) 'The charcoal effect in Boreal forests: mechanisms and ecological consequences', *Oecologia*, vol 115, pp419–426

Warnock, D. D., Lehmann, J., Kuyper, T. W. and Rillig, M. C. (2007) 'Mycorrhizal responses to biochar in soil – concepts and mechanisms', *Plant and Soil*, vol 300, pp9–20

Wessels, J. G. H. (1999) 'Fungi in their own right', *Fungal Genetics and Biology*, vol 27, pp134–145

Wright, S. F. and Upadhyaya, A. (1998) 'A survey of soils for aggregate stability and glomalin, a glycoprotein produced by hyphae of arbuscular mycorrhizal fungi', *Plant and Soil*, vol 198, pp97–107

Zackrisson, O., Nilsson, M.-C. and Wardle, D. A. (1996) 'Key ecological function of charcoal from wildfire in the Boreal forest', *Oikos*, vol 77, pp10–19

7

Developing a Biochar Classification and Test Methods

Stephen Joseph, Cordner Peacocke, Johannes Lehmann and Paul Munroe

Why do we need a classification system?

Most products that are used in the agricultural and the industrial sector must conform to a standard (Tchobanoglous et al, 1993). Consumers will want to know the properties of the product that they are purchasing and what products are best suited to their specific application. They will want to know how to store and use the product safely. Not only consumers, but also scientists require categorization of products or substances with which they work.

Schaetzl and Anderson (2005) have noted that a classification system is established in order to define a name for an entity and then arrange elements in an orderly system and establish the interrelationships among them. Most importantly, it allows communication about the entities being classified.

Once a classification system is developed, a set of standards can be developed. These standards may or may not become formalized through either an international or a country standards association. For example,

there is now a range of standards worldwide for compost (as discussed below).

Most classification systems are open ended and are continually changing as more is learned about the particular entity being classified. As classification systems are refined, standards are altered to reflect the change in knowledge, generally in agreement with the industry manufacturing the product.

It is increasingly recognized that the properties of biochars can vary to a great extent in terms of their elemental composition; ash content (and composition); density; water adsorbance; pore size; toxicity; ion adsorption and release; recalcitrance to microbial or abiotic decay; surface chemical properties (such as pH or charge); or physical properties (such as surface area) (see Chapter 2 to 6, 10 and 11). The multitude of possible factors influencing biochar properties and the multitude of changes in relevant properties make a classification of biochars necessary.

The most important objectives that motivate a biochar management of soils are:

- improvement of water-holding capacity and other soil physical properties (see Chapters 2, 10, 12 and 15);
- increase in the stable pool of carbon (C) (see Chapters 11 and 18);
- adsorption/complexation of soil organic matter and toxic compounds (see Chapters 15 and 16);
- adsorption and reaction with gases within the soil (e.g. N_2O) (see Chapter 13);
- nutrient retention and addition (in the case of high mineral-ash biochars) (see Chapters 5 and 10);
- improvement in the growth of beneficial microorganisms (see Chapter 6).

Based on these desired effects of biochars on soil ecosystems (as outlined in the cited chapters), a provisional classification system will be detailed, along with a proposal for a range of both simple and more complicated test procedures.

Existing definitions and classification systems for charcoal, activated carbon and coal

Definition of terminology

Many researchers and practitioners use a range of terms when discussing biochar. There are a number of names applied to organic material that has been pyrolysed (carbonized) or gasified (partially oxidized) and used for agricultural and industrial purposes (e.g. amorphous carbon, char, charcoal, activated carbon, black carbon, biochar and Agrichar^{TM}). Fitzer et al (1995) have recommended the following terminology, as summarized in Table 7.1, for the description of some of these carbons as a solid, which are used in the science and technology of different forms of organic C. In this volume, we adopt a slightly different terminology (see Chapter 1). We use the term 'char' for the residue of natural fires, whereas 'charcoal' is used for fuel. The term 'biochar' is applied to the material that is or could be added to soil, as well as in situations where the information is relevant for environmental management.

The advisory committee of the International Biochar Initiative (IBI) has agreed on the following description of biochar:

Biochar is a fine-grained charcoal high in organic carbon and largely resistant to decomposition. It is produced from pyrolysis of plant and waste feedstocks. As a soil amendment, biochar creates a recalcitrant soil carbon pool that is carbon-negative, serving as a net withdrawal of atmospheric carbon dioxide stored in highly recalcitrant soil carbon stocks. The enhanced nutrient retention capacity of biochar-amended soil not only reduces the total fertilizer requirements, but also the climate and environmental impact of croplands.

Existing classification systems and standards for activated carbon, fuel charcoal, coal and compost

FAO (1983) and Clarke (2001) provide a very basic definition for charcoal when it is used as a fuel or a reductant (see Table 7.2), but no classification system for charcoals is available. Existing attempts to categorize not

Table 7.1 *Common classification of carbonized organic materials*

Term	Definition	Comments
Amorphous carbon	Carbon material without long-range crystalline order. Short-range order exists, but with deviations of the inter-atomic distances and/or inter-bonding angles with respect to the graphite lattice, as well as to the diamond lattice.	
Char	Solid decomposition product of a natural or synthetic organic material.	Precursor has not passed through a fluid stage; 'char' will retain the characteristic shape of the precursor (although becoming of smaller size).
Pseudo-morphous char	Solid decomposition product of a natural or synthetic organic material.	Precursor has passed through a fluid stage (e.g. sugar), has melted at an early stage of decomposition and then polymerized during 'carbonization' to produce 'chars'.
Charcoal	A 'char' obtained from the pyrolysis of wood and some related natural organic materials.	Note that 'charcoal' has highly reactive inner surfaces and a low sulphur content.
Activated carbon	A porous carbon material.	Activated carbon has a high surface area and relatively high concentration of functional groups at its surface.
Graphene layer	A single carbon layer of the graphite structure, describing its nature by analogy to a polycyclic aromatic hydrocarbon of quasi-infinite size.	Previously, descriptions such as graphite layers, carbon layers or carbon sheets have been used for the term 'graphene'.
Graphite	Allotropic form of the element carbon consisting of layers of hexagonally arranged carbon atoms in a planar condensed ring system ('graphene layers'). The layers are stacked parallel to each other in a three-dimensional crystalline long-range order. There are two allotropic forms with different stacking arrangements, hexagonal and rhombohedral. The chemical bonds within the layers are covalent with sp2 hybridization and with a C–C distance of 141.7pm. The weak bonds between the layers are metallic with strength comparable to van der Waals bonding only.	The term 'graphite' is also used often but incorrectly to describe graphite materials (i.e. materials consisting of graphitic carbon made from carbon materials by processing to temperatures greater than 2500K, even though no perfect graphite structure is present).

Source: adapted from Fitzer et al (1995)

only fuel charcoal but also other carbonaceous materials such as activated carbons use so-called volatile matter, fixed C and ash content. Volatile matter and fixed C are properties that give a relative measure of the stable (fixed carbon) and labile component of char at high temperatures. These were mainly developed for evaluating fuel value, but may be appropriate for evaluating general stability in soils as well. Ash content is the remaining solid after all of the organic elements – C, hydrogen (H) and nitrogen (N) – have been oxidized. These properties are measured according to the American Society for Testing Materials (ASTM) D1762-84 (ASTM, 2007) and the measurements are known as 'proximate analysis'. These test methods employ apparatus that is found in most laboratories and is adapted to routine analyses of a large number of samples.

In comparison, activated carbons from biomass and coal are also classified according to their surface area, average size and pore-size distribution, their adsorptive capacity (for different types of gases and liquids), crushing strength, moisture content and water-soluble component. The ASTM (2006) *D2652-94 Terminology Relating to Activated Carbon* provides a description of different types of activated carbon. There are a series of tests that are laid out by the ASTM that are followed to characterize a particular material. Manufacturers will tailor an activated carbon to a specific application.

The New South Wales Environment Protection Authority (NSW EPA, 1997) developed a classification system for biosolids that introduces five categories with associated contaminant and stabilization grades (see Table 7.3). Given that biochar will be made from wastes such as green waste and sewage sludge, a similar classification system may be required to meet regulatory guidelines related to the use of wastes from agriculture. 'Contaminant grade' is a category used to describe the quality of a biosolids product based on the concentration of a range of constituent contaminants (e.g. heavy metals and chlorinated hydrocarbons). Grades are assigned from A (high quality) to E (low quality). 'Stabilization grade' is a category used to describe the quality of a biosolids product based on its level of pathogen reduction, vector attraction reduction and odour reduction. Both contaminant and stabilization grades are used to assess the 'class' of biosolid, which in turn determines the

permitted uses and associated conditions (see Table 7.3).

More comprehensive classification systems have been developed for coal (Brame and King, 1961). These systems use the C and volatile content and calorific value as the primary characteristics to classify coal and employ a range of additional chemical and physical properties for further classification. Thus, a bituminous coal has a fixed C content (on an ash-free basis) ranging from 69 per cent to 78 per cent, a volatile content of 14 per cent to more than 31 per cent and a calorific value ranging from 10,700 to 14,400BTU lb^{-1}. These coals are then subdivided into strongly, medium, weakly or non-caking (Brame and King, 1961).

There a number of different classification systems that have been developed for organic matter that are used for agronomic purposes. From discussion with regulators, it is possible that biochar produced from waste may have to comply with all or part of the classifications related to compost and biosolids. Thus, a brief description of these standards is provided. The Australian Standard for Compost (Standards Australia, 2003) categorizes recycled organics (compost) as:

- soil conditioner;
- mulch;
- fine mulch; or
- vermicast.

The standard then details the properties of each of these categories in terms of its pH; electrical conductivity; soluble phosphorus (P); ammonium-N; nitrate-N; total ammonium-N + nitrate-N; total N; organic matter content; boron (B) content; sodium (Na) content; wettability; toxicity; particle size; $CaCO_3$ equivalent; chemical contaminants (heavy metals, organic contaminants and pathogens); glass, plastic, stone or clay admixtures; moisture content; the degree of self-heating; plant propagules; and vermicast sieve test.

Table 7.2 *Characterization of charcoal for fuel or as a reductant*

Application	Total C (%)	Volatile content (%)	Ash content (%)	Bulk density (kg m^{-3})
Industrial	60–80	15–20	3–5	180–20
Domestic	60–80	20–25	<5	N/A

Source: adapted from FAO (1983); Clarke (2001)

Table 7.3 *Classification of biosolids according to NSW EPA (1997)*

Categories	Allowable land application use		Minimum quality grades	
			Contaminant	Stabilization
Unrestricted use	1	Home lawns and garden	A	A
	2	Public contract stage		
	3	Urban landscaping		
	4	Agriculture		
	5	Forestry		
	6	Soil and site stabilization		
	7	Landfill disposal		
	8	Surface land disposal		
Restricted use 1	9	Agriculture	B	A
	10	Forestry		
	11	Soil and site stabilization		
	12	Landfill disposal		
	13	Surface land disposal		
Restricted use 2	14	Forestry	C	B
	15	Soil and site stabilization		
	16	Landfill disposal		
	17	Surface land disposal		
Restricted use 3	18	Forestry	D	C
	19	Soil and site stabilization		
	20	Landfill disposal		
	21	Surface land disposal		
Not suitable for use	22	Landfill disposal	E	D
	23	Surface land disposal		

Source: NSW EPA (1997)

Proposed classification system for biochar

From a users' perspective, an ideal classification system would be based on a table in which the desired agronomic properties are matched with the biomass type (e.g. high/low C, high/low porosity, high/low mineral content) and the type of production process (e.g. fast/medium/slow pyrolysis, high/medium/low temperature). However, there is insufficient data to develop a system based on feed properties and process conditions; thus, an outline of a system based on biochar properties has been developed. These properties are explored in the next section and an interim classification system is then proposed, as well as an outline of a research programme required to develop a system and standard analytical procedures.

Biochars are made from a range of biomass materials that have different chemical and physical properties. Appropriate feedstock types include, but are not restricted to, dedicated bioenergy crops (e.g. willow, miscanthus and switchgrass), crop and forest residues (e.g. sawdust, grain crops and nut shells) or organic wastes (e.g. green yard wastes and animal manures) (Bridgwater, 1999). Major differences in feedstock properties that are relevant to biochar properties as a soil amendment include:

- percentage of lignin, cellulose, hemicellulose and other minor organic compounds (Demirbas, 2001; Lehmann et al, 2006; see Chapters 3 to 5 and 8);
- percentage and composition of inorganics (Raveendran et al, 1995; Nik-Azar et al, 1997);
- percentage of materials other than biomass (plastic in the case of paper sludge waste) (HRL, 2005);
- bulk and true density (and, thus, the porosity and pore-size distribution) (see Chapter 2);

- particle size (average and distribution) (Bridgwater, 1999; Zanzi et al, 2002);
- compressive and tensile strength (see Chapter 8); and
- moisture content (Moghtaderi, 2006).

Biochars can be produced using different process conditions. These production conditions can, in many cases, be adjusted, but are often constrained by the pyrolysis technology chosen, such as slow or fast pyrolysis, high- or low-temperature pyrolysis, or gasification (see Chapter 8). The main production conditions that define the properties of the biochar include (Chapter 8):

- rate of heating of the feedstock;
- final temperature of the charring process and the time held at this temperature;
- pressure of the reactor;
- heat and mass transfer mechanisms taking place within the reactor vessel; and
- the amount of air and steam added to the kiln and the temperature of the biochar at the point of addition (steam and air can change the properties and structure of the surfaces and can also cause gasification if the temperature is sufficiently high).

The following references give a detailed review of the effect of production conditions on the properties of biochars (Di Blasi, 1996; Antal and Grønli, 2003; Demirbas, 2004; Moghtaderi, 2006) and are discussed in detail in Chapter 8.

Both the wide variations in feedstock properties and production conditions have significant effects on biochar properties (see Chapters 2 to 5). The high number of possible combinations of both feedstock and production types make it very difficult to predict biochar properties. Therefore, as a first step we propose a classification system

---

Box 7.1 Process parameters affecting yields and composition of the pyrolysis products the most

Note that it is not possible to isolate the effect of any single parameter since there are significant interactions between products as reactions develop.

Biomass related (controllable to a limited extent):
- biomass pre-treatment (additives/ash content, moisture, chemical composition);
- biomass density;
- biomass particle size;
- biomass particle shape;
- biomass properties (specific heat capacity, thermal conductivity and permeability); and
- intrinsic properties of the biomass.

Reactor operation (substantially controllable):
- reactor temperature (temperature at which pyrolysis occurs);
- vapour/gas product reactor residence time;
- vapour/gas product temperature;
- biomass heating rate and heat transfer;
- biomass decomposition temperature;
- pressure (hydrostatic and mechanical); and
- gaseous (reactor) environment.

Recovery of the final products (substantially controllable):
- rate of thermal quenching of the products; and
- time/temperature profile of the cooling.

Source: Peacocke (1994)

---

of the biochar properties themselves. These classes of biochars can then be related to the factors described above. It is recognized, however, that over the medium to long term, a classification of biochar properties will need to be related back to feedstock properties and production conditions, which are the variables that can be *a priori* adjusted. Further discussion of process parameters is given in Box 7.1.

Some of these properties of biochars have been amply proven to relate to effects relevant to soil functions with respect to plant growth and environmental health. Others are likely, while others are speculative. The properties of the biochars that are a function of

process conditions and initial biomass composition, loosely ordered in order of decreasing current experimental evidence, include:

- *Proportion of different C forms with respect to stability against abiotic and biotic oxidation/reduction and biological decomposition and mineralization to CO_2:* this has implications for both the recalcitrance of biochars (see Chapter 11) and, hence, the long-term effects in soil and value as a means of sequestering atmospheric CO_2 and reducing greenhouse gas emissions (see Chapter 18), as well as the surface properties of biochars with respect to adsorption (see Chapter 5) and transformation reactions (see Chapters 13 and 14).

- *Presence and concentration of potentially harmful organic C compounds:* all biochars contain some organic compounds on the surface that may exert negative effects on plant growth (Girard et al, 2006), but can also have a positive effect on microbial growth and activity (Bridgwater, 1999; Fischer and Bienkowski, 1999; Uvarov, 2000; Bridgwater and Boocock, 2006; Steiner et al, 2008; see Chapter 6).

- *Porosity, pore-size distribution and total surface area:* these properties have fundamental importance for a range of effects of biochar on soil properties. For example, a greater porosity increases the amount of water stored, whereas the pore sizes determine whether this water is mobile in soil, and available or unavailable to plants, as is amply illustrated in the standard soil science literature (e.g. Brady and Weil, 2002). But porosity and pore-size distribution may also be important for the way in which different soil microorganisms and fauna are able to explore soil pore space for the acquisition of resources such as nutrients or energy and for protection against predators (Ogawa, 1999; Warnock et al, 2007; see Chapter 6). Equally important is the amount of surface area for surface reactions with nutrient elements such as adsorptive reactions with ions (Liang et al, 2006; see Chapter 5) or element transformations (see Chapters 13 and 14). The greater the surface area, the more effective biochars will be in relation to affecting soil properties (although the nature of the surfaces plays an equally important role). However, trade-offs between maximizing surface areas, which increases with decreasing pore sizes of biochars (see Chapter 2), and the pore-size distribution has to be recognized; optimization for the differ-

ent objectives are discussed in the following sections.

- *Electrical conductivity and pH:* the amount of electrolytes added to soil affects its flocculation (Brady and Weil, 2002) – do all soils flocculate and why is it important? It can be expected that this has an effect on soil only at very high application rates, but may be a factor to consider with some crops that are sensitive to increased salt concentrations or soils with unstable soil structure. Little information is available to date. More important is the pH of biochar, which can be high or low depending upon feedstock and production conditions (see Chapter 5). A high pH can be a key feature of biochar in improving acid soils (Lehmann et al, 2003) but may be unwanted in naturally basic or even sodic soils.

- *Solubility of different mineral elements:* the solubility of mineral elements may have several effects:
  - the immediate fertilization effect of applied biochar with respect to the amount, type of element and rate of release (see Chapter 5);
  - mobilization of nutrient elements that cause detrimental environmental effects, as in the case of phosphate and eutrophication of surface waters (see Chapter 15); and
  - mobilization of elements that are detrimental to plant, soil and human health, such as heavy metals (e.g. copper (Cu), chromium (Cr) and arsenic (As) may derive from waste wood), excess amounts of Na that cause loss in soil structure, or K, which may induce deficiency of other base cations (Brady and Weil, 2002).

- *Bulk density:* bulk density is closely related to porosity and has significant effects on:
  - the transport properties of biochars and, therefore, costs and greenhouse

gas emissions associated with transportation; and

- the resulting bulk density of soils after biochar additions, which improves penetrability, drainage and aeration of soils that are essential for good plant growth (Brady and Weil, 2002).

• *Particle size:* particle-size distribution may exert influence on various handling and soil processes. Handling of coarse material above 15mm (the largest length of most pellets used for agricultural purposes) may be difficult for soil application if tubing for soil injection is involved (see Chapter 12). Blowing or broadcast applications also have size limits above which application is hampered or harmful (Chapter 12). Optimization for size may be specific to the method of application and equipment used, and will therefore not be considered in the classification scheme presented here. Limited information is available about the effects of biochar particle size on soil processes. On the one hand, one may justifiably argue that smaller particles increase efficiency due to greater contact area; on the other, the large porosity of a given biochar particle may make particle size a redundant parameter (see Chapter 2). Indeed, within the moderate variation of biochar particles (produced from wood) of less than 2mm and about 20mm investigated by Lehmann et al (2003), no relevant differences were found in terms of crop growth or nutrient availability. It is not clear whether size matters in terms of biochar stability and stabilization, recognizing that both decomposition and stabilizing interactions with soil minerals occur on biochar surfaces (see Chapter 11), or whether size has an influence on the mobility of the biochar itself (see Chapter 15). In conclusion, particle size will not be included in the proposed classification at the current stage of its development.

• *Compressive strength:* the physical stability of biochar particles may not only be important to its longevity and retention in soil (see Chapters 10 and 11), but also to its handling procedure, such as shipping and application to soil (see Chapter 12). However, compressive strength may be sufficiently related to stability measures or (similar to the discussion on particle size) may be a requirement of specific handling procedures so that it will not be included at this stage of the classification development.

• *Type and amount of functional groups:* the C functional group chemistry and molecular form of biochar may be expected to greatly differ between biochars, given the differences in feedstock types and production conditions. While charge properties and, hence, oxidized functional groups such as carboxyl groups differed significantly depending upon the production temperature (Lehmann, 2007), the values were low and differences were redundant compared to aged biochar (Liang et al, 2006; Cheng et al, 2008; see Chapter 10). However, the functional groups for high mineral-ash biochars are significantly different to wood and also vary with temperature (Schnitzer et al, 2007). Oxidation of all biochars placed in soil may progress rapidly (Cheng et al, 2006) and depends, for example, upon mean annual temperature of the site that it is applied to (Cheng et al, 2008). Conditions in soil may to a much larger extent control biochar charge properties in soil than properties of fresh biochar. Hence, gross differences such as mineral content and contents of non-aromatic tars and oils will be captured in this classification scheme; however, functional group chemistry with respect to charge and surface oxidation will be included after incubation.

- *Type and concentration of radicals:* it is likely but not proven that radicals have an effect on nutrient transformations on biochar surfaces (see Chapter 13). Future research should more rigorously investigate the extent to which radical formation in biochar modifies C and nutrient cycles in soil before this property is included in the classification scheme.
- *Oxidation and reduction potential:* the pH has a significant effect on oxidation or reduction reactions in soil (Brady and Weil, 2002), and pH of biochars can vary widely between 4 and 10 for the same feedstock (Lehmann, 2007) and even more for different feedstocks (see Chapter 5). Biochar oxidizes spontaneously (Cheng et al, 2006), and it is conceivable that reduction reactions occur on biochar surfaces. Little direct evidence is available, and further research is encouraged before including redox reactions in the classification.

It is not possible to develop a simple classification system and include all of the properties of feedstocks and biochars along with process conditions. Research findings that are detailed in Chapters 2 to 6 and 10 to 16 in this volume are used to outline a possible classification system. The justification for this classification system will be given in the following sections. The four main biochar properties that are used here to characterize biochars are:

1   Total C, H and O contents, and the labile and the stable fraction of total C. H and O contents are included as they are component atoms of the compounds that make up the labile fraction of biochar.
2   Elemental content other than C, H, O and their relative solubility and availability to plants and mobility. This will, for example, include all elements measured in a so-called 'ultimate analysis' (other

than C, H and O) and an ash constituent analysis described by ASTM D1762-84 (ASTM, 2007). It is noted that O is associated with the other minerals (as oxides) and H can be associated with both minerals (hydroxyapatite) and with anions (HCl and H_2S).
3   Surface area and pore-size distribution.
4   The ability to develop surface negative charge over time when placed in soils – as measured by change in potential cation exchange capacity (CEC) – and biochar pH.

In choosing the first three properties the system is similar to that used for classifying fuels and activated carbon (although the rationale is different). The fourth property tries to encapsulate differences in energy or charge-related properties of biochars. These include difference in defect concentrations (i.e. vacancies, dangling bonds and dislocations), radical concentration, type and concentration of functional groups, concentration of sites where redox reactions can take place, and concentration of O singlets. It is recognized that considerably more data is required to relate this property to beneficial effects of different biochars in soil. The goal is to determine these properties by using wet and dry chemical methods in laboratories that are not equipped with sophisticated equipment.

Percentage of total carbon and volatile content

Total carbon content

There are a number of reasons for using the total C content (dry basis) to classify biochars. These are summarized below:

- It provides a measure of the total amount of organic C that is added to the soil and is therefore relevant to the C balance and sequestration aspect of biochar management (see Chapter 18).

- It also provides a good indicator (along with knowing the ash composition) of the composition of the parent biomass and the process conditions under which the biochar is produced (Antal and Grønli, 2003; see Chapter 8). It is important to recognize that biochar can form at temperatures that are greater than 200°C if the biomass is held at this temperature for a sufficient period of time (Di Blasi, 1996).
- It supplies a baseline to determine the rate of removal of C from the biochar as a function of time in the environment.

Three categories for classification – high, medium and low – are proposed as they represent the range of composition that has been reported in the literature, as well as shown by our own results (see Figure 7.1). The review by Antal and Grønli (2003) of the data on C composition of biochar produced from wood shows that for produc-

tion temperatures greater than 500°C, the C composition exceeds 80 per cent, even though some biomass types may exceed 80 per cent already below 500°C, as shown for oak wood (see Figure 7.1). Thus, a high C content is set at >80 per cent. For wood biochar produced at a temperatures between 400°C and 500°C (Antal and Grønli, 2003) and for other biomass biochars, such as those made from maize stalks that have a slightly higher ash content than most woods (that are typically 2 to 8 per cent) and are produced at higher temperatures (Zabaniotou et al, 2008), the C content varies from 60 to 80 per cent. The third category covers biochars that have a C content ranging from 15 to 60 per cent. These include barks, grasses, husks, animal manures (Schnitzer et al, 2007), sludges (Shinogi, 2004), wood pyrolysed at very low temperatures (<350°C) or biochars made from the reaction of clay and biomass at low temperatures (240°C).

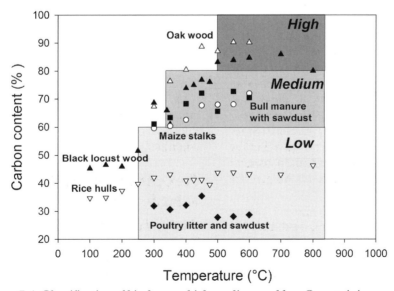

Figure 7.1 *Classification of biochars as high, medium and low C-containing as a function of temperature for different feedstocks: production of biochars from black locust and rice as described by Lehmann (2007); production of other biochars using a batch pyrolyser with a capacity of about 2kg of feedstock and 20-minute pyrolysis time (BEST Energies)*

Source: Lehmann, unpublished data; Lehmann (2007)

Labile carbon content

We define labile C in this study as the fraction of C in biochar that is mineralized abiotically or biotically to CO_2 within a short period of time. The mineralization of biochar typically shows a two-phased dynamic: a rapid mineralization followed by a slow mineralization (see Chapter 11). This initial rapid mineralization occurs within a few weeks to a few months for incubations at 20°C to 30°C used to quantify biochar decay (see Chapter 11). This labile fraction exists in a number of forms in biochar, such as:

- Mineral carbonates that are soluble in water. Some of these carbonates exist on the surface of the biochar or in cracks and pores that are connected with the surface. These will readily dissolve, whereas those that exist in the matrix of the biochar are unlikely to dissolve until the amorphous C matrix starts to break down (either due to physical, biological or chemical attack).
- Organic molecules (that contain H and O) that are readily dissolved in soil water (e.g. carbohydrates that have not been pyrolysed) and will therefore be rapidly mineralized by microorganisms, or aliphatic C forms such as oils that are less stable than the fused aromatic C structures presumed to form the more stable C fraction of biochar.
- Carbon that is part of the biochar's amorphous or microcrystalline structure and considered to be the stable portion of biochar, but is mineralized on particle surfaces. Surface oxidation is rapid (see Chapter 10). Although it is not clear to what extent this rapid surface oxidation (i.e. formation of oxidized functional groups or complexation with clays) is associated with mineralization (i.e. actual mass loss of C by evolution of CO_2), it is likely that it contributes, to a minor extent, to mineralization. Other forms include co-metabolism with the soluble

organic matter or oils (see Chapter 11), sites of dangling bonds and vacancies in the amorphous and crystalline lattice structure (Kercher et al, 2003; Bourke et al, 2007), or dislocations in high mineral-ash and low-temperature amorphous biochar (see Chapter 3) that offer opportunities for rapid oxidation due to low activation energy required.

There are a number of reasons for classifying C by the fraction of labile C:

- from a C accounting perspective, in order to have a measure of the rate of rapid decay of biochar (see Chapter 18);
- to determine the availability of organic C for use as a source of C for microorganisms (Chapter 6).
- as a potential source of toxic compounds that prevents germination or mature growth of certain plants (Girard et al, 2006); and
- as a source of compounds that facilitates germination (Flematti et al, 2004) and potentially provides energy for microorganism growth (Steiner et al, 2008).

Given the complex nature of the labile C in biochars, developing a classification system using distinct compound analyses or even molecular characteristics or functional group chemistry would be difficult. Tests using incubations as routinely done for research purposes are also time consuming, expensive and difficult to standardize. We therefore propose a classification system based on thermal and extraction properties that relate to experimentally determined mineralization, yet are more easily standardized and conducted. This classification system is based on three tests that capture properties of the labile fraction of biochar:

- *Test 1: fraction of C decomposed by heating the biochar in an atmosphere that excludes O_2 at relatively low temperature (350°C).*

This procedure will remove most of the organic molecules (bio-oils and tars) produced during pyrolysis that exist within the pores and on the surface chemically bonded water that remains in the biochar, as well as much of the carboxylic groups that are located on surfaces of biochars. Thermal degradability appears to be an appropriate integrated measure for mineralizability by microorganisms (Lopez-Capel et al, 2005).

- *Test 2: fraction of C decomposed by short heating in an inert atmosphere at a relatively high temperature (950°C).* This will result in the liberation of both the bio-oils and tars, as well as a percentage of the functional groups that are loosely held on the C matrix. This is the proximate analysis of different biochars. Bourke et al (2007) has noted that carboxylic groups thermally decompose to CO_2 at the lowest temperature region (100°C to 400°C), closely followed by carboxylic anhydrides and lactones (427°C to 657°C). The most thermally stable C–O groups are pyrone structures (900°C to 1200°C) followed by ethers, carbonylic, quinonic, phenolic and hydroquinonic groups that are not included in this fraction. This test is similar to the determination of the contents of volatiles as defined by ASTM D1762-84 (ASTM, 2007) with the modification that the fraction of C, as well as the total C, O and H removed, is reported.

- *Test 3: fraction dissolved in water, which will capture the soluble C.* Solubility of organic and inorganic C in soil is a key property that determines recalcitrance against both gaseous as well as dissolved export (Brady and Weil, 2002).

Mineral, nitrogen and sulphur (MNS) content

The MNS content of biomass and, thus, of biochars is highly variable. Most biochars derived from wood and nut shells contain less than 5 per cent total MNS content (Antal and Grønli, 2003); most biochars derived from green waste (Chan et al, 2007), maize stalks (Zabaniotou et al, 2008) and oat hulls (Fan et al, 2004) have a content of between 5 and 10 per cent; rice and wheat straw, bagasse and rice hulls have a content of between 10 and 20 per cent (Ioannidou and Zabaniotou, 2007); while sludges and animals manures have a range of between 20 and 70 per cent (Shinogi, 2004; see Chapter 5). Biochars that have high ash contents necessarily also have low C contents and vice versa.

Biochar contains both metallic (light and heavy) and non-metallic elements (e.g. P and S). ASTM D1762-84 (ASTM, 2007) for fuel charcoal gives a measure of the C, H, O, S and N contents (by dry combustion coupled to gas chromatography), and ash constituent analysis yields the composition of a range of metals and non-metals. It should be noted that total MNS does not give an indication of the availability of these minerals (see Chapter 5).

The understanding of the role of MNS in nutrient retention, improving crop yields, reducing greenhouse gas emissions from soils, changing the type and quantity of microorganisms, changing the water-holding capacity of the soil, and changing the rate at which biochar degrades or forms complexes with soil is not well understood. Chapter 5 shows that chicken manure biochar that has a high content of available P and K can significantly improve the yield of plants in the short term. Bagreev et al (2001) and Chapter 5 show that the pH and the electrical conductivity increase with increasing production temperature of high mineral-ash biochars (for biochars produced between 400°C and 600°C). They also report electrical conductivity (EC) of greater than $5dS\ m^{-1}$ and a pH greater than 7. Most wood biochars have a pH of less than 7 (Lehmann, 2007) and an EC of less than $1dS\ m^{-1}$.

However, there is no published data on the long-term effect of these high mineral-ash biochars on soil properties. It is known that certain minerals will promote the breakdown of humic and fulvic acids (Amonette et al, 2006), and other minerals (Fe, Si, Ca and S) are important for forming organo-clay minerals through either Ca-bridging, redox reactions or the formation of organo-mineral compounds (Basile-Doelsch et al, 2007). Shinogi (2004) has measured high rates of leaching of some of these high mineral-content biochars (K, Ca, P, S and Cl). Over time, these biochars may not be as effective in supplying nutrients as when they were first placed in the soil. Thus, it would appear that not only the quantity of the ash is important but also its resilience against leaching.

Total soluble MNS (which indicates both resilience against leaching, when used in comparison with total analyses, and availability of both cations and anions) is measured by EC (or total dissolved solids). Tests to evaluate plant-available nutrient contents are specific to different crops, and since the value of biochar arises from indirect effects on nutrient availability, these will not be used in classifying biochars.

Given the lack of data in the peer-reviewed literature on the short- and long-term effects of biochar mineral matter, it is currently difficult to develop a quantitative classification system.

Surface area and pore-size distribution

Surface area and pore-size distribution have been extensively covered in Chapter 2 (and are referred to in Chapters 3 and 15). Chapter 2 notes that macropores greater than 1μm play a significant role in the interaction with soil particles, microorganisms and root hairs. The pore structure, volume and surface area (which includes cracks) is dependent upon the biomass feedstock structure, as well as the process conditions under which the material is produced. Measuring surface area and volume and pore-size distribution accurately is difficult and expensive. The following preliminary conclusions have been drawn:

- There is a very large variation in surface area between different biochars produced at different temperatures and under varying process conditions. Chapter 2 summarizes a wide range of information (see Figure 2.3). The trend is for surface area to increase with temperature and for low mineral-ash biochar (wood) to have higher surface area than the high mineral-ash biochar, such as that produced from maize stalks and chicken litter. Between 400°C and 450°C, pine biochar, chicken litter and maize stover have a surface area of less than $50m^2 g^{-1}$, whereas alder wood biochar has surface areas of between $350m^2 g^{-1}$ and $400m^2 g^{-1}$ and nut biochar $>500m^2 g^{-1}$. At temperatures of between 450°C and 550°C, manures still have a surface below $50m^2 g^{-1}$, but other agricultural residues appear to have areas greater than $200m^2 g^{-1}$ and most wood-based biochars $>400m^2 g^{-1}$ (see Chapter 2).
- Data presented in Chapter 2 (see Figure 2.2) show that there is a linear relationship between surface area and pore volume. The chapter also notes that although the proportion of surface areas in micropores is significantly greater than the one in macropores, it is the reverse for volumes.
- Biochars produced using fast pyrolysis reactors have lower surface areas than those produced with slow pyrolysis (see Chapter 2). Chapter 2 also notes that pyrolysis carried out at high pressure can produce biochars with very high surface area (if the reaction time is long enough to allow volatiles to escape).
- Biochars with a high surface area and a high volume of macropores with diameters of greater than 50nm can have a high

water-holding capacity (with water available to plants residing in pores of about 10μm to 80μm; see Chapter 15 for discussion), are sites where clay, silt and silica particles are deposited, and provide a large number of microenvironments for microbes to grow in and root hairs to penetrate. Typical of this are wood biochars where the pores originate from the tracheids (micro-fibrils) in the parent material (see Chapter 2). These pores can have diameters greater than 100μm. At present, there is very little data on the relative percentage of these large pores in biochars and what process parameters are needed to optimize for the production of these macropores.

- Biochars that have a high surface area and a high volume of pores of less than 50nm also have a large capacity for adsorption of liquids and gases (Bagreev et al, 2001). Data is not yet available to determine, in detail, the role of these pores in gas–liquid–solid reactions in the soil. However, these pores could be sites for deposition of clay nanoparticles and for dissolved organic matter and nutrients such as N, P and K.

- Biochars with a high volume of pores of less than 10nm have a high adsorption capacity for gases. The interaction between water and biochar surfaces is also a function of pore size. Sugimoto et al (2007) was able to detect water in these nano-sized pores of biochars and suggested that water has an ice-like structure in the nanopores of biochar produced above 400°C. Water is probably in the super-cooled state when adsorbed into biochars produced above 450°C. Turov et al (2002) noted that the adsorption of water-insoluble organic compounds is a function of pore size and pore-size distribution, as well as surface functional groups. Thus, chloroform-*d* and benzene-*d6* replace adsorbed water in micropores (<50nm).

- In some biochars, the pore size may decrease as organic matter and dead microorganisms interact with their surfaces (Kwon and Pignatello, 2005).

The above summary and the details given in Chapter 2 indicate that classifying biochars just on the basis of surface area is not sufficient. It is important to know the difference in pore size distribution and, in particular, the percentage of pores above 1μm. Since there is little data on the pore-size distribution, it is, at present, not possible to give limits for classification. Based on the discussion in Chapter 2, we propose using the ratio of the volume of macropores to micropores to provide information on what could be the major benefits to soil processes.

CEC and functional groups

Chapters 5 and 10 have noted the increase in cation exchange capacity (CEC) of soil when biochars are added. CEC is a measure of the surface charge in soil or biochar. CEC increases as the biochar ages (Cheng et al, 2008) and this has been attributed to an increase in some of the oxygenated functional groups on the surface of the biochar (Cheng et al, 2006). Interactions between surfaces of the biochar and soil particles (Brodowski et al, 2006), dissolved organic matter (DOM) (Lehmann et al, 2005), gases (Chapter 13), microorganisms (Chapter 6) and water (Chapter 15) are also a function of the total surface charge and total concentration of functional groups.

At the surfaces of biochars, a range of functional groups exist that include pyranone, phenolic, carboxylic, lactone and amine groups (Brennan et al, 2001). Brennan et al (2001) have noted that carboxylic groups are classified as electron donors and strong Bronsted acids. Their effective strength as characterized using the acid dissociation constant pKa varies from 2 to 6. Phenols are electron acceptors and are of Lewis type,

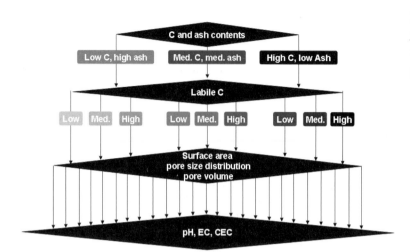

Figure 7.2 *Possible framework for classifying biochars*

Source: chapter authors

associated with p electron-rich regions found on the basal planes of the graphitic micro-crystals (Brennan et al, 2001). The basic functional groups (quinine and phenol) react with free radicals, and this reaction can be used for the grafting of functional molecules or polymers to the C surface (Brennan et al, 2001).

Biochar can show basic or acidic pH values in aqueous dispersions. The O contents of the functional groups are directly related to low pH (acidity) in dispersion (Lopez-Ramon, 1999). Such biochars with high O contents have high CEC (Cheng et al, 2008). Biochar with low O functional group contents show basic surface properties and anion exchange behaviour. This is mainly found in freshly produced biochars (Cheng et al, 2008). Bagreev et al (2001) notes that in high mineral-ash biochars, acid sites are also derived from metal oxides: silica (Si), iron (Fe) and aluminium (Al). The basic proper-ties are ascribed to the presence of basic surface oxides with a high concentration of π-electrons on the basal planes of biochars.

Lopez-Ramon (1999) has noted that these basic sites (especially quinine and phenolic groups) react with free radicals, and

this reaction can be used for the grafting of functional molecules or polymers to the biochar surface. Bagreev et al (2001) noted that basic N-containing functional groups (and Fe) located on micropores may be high-energy adsorption sites playing an important role in the oxidation of H_2S. Given the pres-ent research results, it is possible to conclude that biochars are more likely to assist in plant growth by cation retention if they have a higher concentration of surface functional groups (especially the carboxylic, but also phenolic, hydroxyl, carbonyl or quinone C forms), which relates to a higher CEC of the biochar.

Measuring concentrations of functional groups can be carried out using a Boehm titration method (Boehm, 1994). However Boehm titrations can be difficult to undertake and require experience to obtain repro-ducible results. Spectroscopy techniques (such as nuclear magnetic resonance, infrared and X-ray) can also give a measure of the relative concentration of different functional groups, but require specialized instrumentation.

We propose developing a classification based on the degree to which the CEC of biochar changes in soil (similar to the procedure described by Cheng et al, 2006). At this point in the development of the classification scheme, no values can be given to separate different categories of biochars according to CEC development. Detailed studies are required to determine the effect of change of CEC on plant growth as a function of type of soil and biochar.

Synthesis and classification system

In this chapter we show that biochars are complex multi-phased materials. Their properties depend upon the properties of the feedstock and the conditions of time, temperature and pressure under which they were processed. These properties change over time when exposed to the atmosphere and the soil.

There are major differences in the properties of biochars that have very low and very high C content and, conversely, very high and very low mineral matter. Some studies are beginning to indicate that high mineral-content biochars (Chan et al, 2007) have a greater short-term affect on plant growth than low mineral-content biochars. However, there are no data to indicate that high mineral-ash biochars have a greater long-term impact upon soil than low mineral-ash biochars.

Figure 7.2 provides a possible framework to classify biochars. More studies are required to fully characterize the range of biochars that may be applied to land. Furthermore, studies to determine the changes in biochars are required when applied to different soils in order to more accurately determine the most important parameters that affect stability, plant growth and soil health. Over the coming years, more rigorous greenhouse and field trials, in conjunction with detailed micro- and macro-analysis, will identify key properties of these chars that affect the impact upon different soils and plants/trees.

References

Amonette, J., Kim, J., Russell, C., Hendricks, M., Bashore, C. and Rieck, B. (2006) 'Soil charcoal – a potential humification catalyst', in *Annual Conference of ASA–CSA–SSSA*, Indianapolis, November 2006

Antal, M. J. and Grønli, M. (2003) 'The art, science, and technology of charcoal production', *Industrial Engineering and Chemical Research*, vol 42, pp1619–1640

ASTM (2006) *D2652-94 Terminology Relating to Activated Carbon*, ASTM International, West Conshohocken, PA, www.astm.org

ASTM (2007) *Standard Test Method for Chemical Analysis of Wood Charcoal ASTM D1762-84*, ASTM International, West Conshohocken, PA, www.astm.org

Bagreev, A., Bandosz, T. J. and Locke, D. C. (2001) 'Pore structure and surface chemistry of adsorbents obtained by pyrolysis of sewage-derived fertiliser', *Carbon*, vol 39, pp1971–1979

Basile-Doelsch, I., Amundson, R., Stone, W. E. E., Borschneck, D., Bottero, J.Y., Moustier, T., Masin, F. and Colin, F. (2007) 'Mineral control of carbon pools in a volcanic soil horizon', *Geoderma*, vol 137, pp477–489

Boehm, H. P. (1994) 'Some aspects of the surface chemistry of carbon blacks and other carbons', *Carbon*, vol 32, pp759–769

Bourke, J., Manley-Harris, M., Fushimi, C., Dowaki, K., Nunoura, T. and Antal, M. J. (2007) 'Do all carbonized charcoals have the same chemical structure? 2. A model of the chemical structure of carbonized charcoal', *Industrial Engineering and Chemical Research*, vol 46, pp5954–5967

Brady, N. C. and Weil, R. R. (2002) *The Nature and Properties of Soils*, 13th edition, Prentice Hall, Upper Saddle River, NJ

Brame, J. S. S. and King, J. G. (1961) *Fuel: Solid, Liquid and Gaseous*, Edward Arnold Publishing,

London, UK

Brennan, J. K., Bandosz, T. J., Thomson, K. and Gubbins, K. E. (2001) 'Water in porous carbons', *Colloids and Surfaces A: Physicochemical and Engineering Aspects*, vol 187–188, pp539–568

Bridgwater, A.V. (1999) 'An introduction to fast pyrolysis of biomass for fuels and chemicals', in A.V. Bridgwater (ed) *Fast Pyrolysis of Biomass: A Handbook*, CPL Scientific Publishing Services Ltd, Newbury, UK

Bridgwater, A. and Boocock, D.G.B. (2006) *Science in Thermal and Chemical Biomass Conversion*, CPL Press, Newbury, UK

Brodowski, S., John, B., Flessa, H. and Amelung, W. (2006) 'Aggregate-occluded black carbon in soil', *European Journal of Soil Science*, vol 57, pp539–546

Chan, K.Y., Van Zwieten, L., Meszaros, I., Downie, A. and Joseph, S. (2007) 'Agronomic values of green waste biochar as a soil amendment', *Australian Journal of Soil Research*, vol 45, pp629–634

Cheng, C. H., Lehmann, J., Thies, J. E., Burton, S. D. and Engelhard, M. H. (2006) 'Oxidation of black carbon by biotic and abiotic processes', *Organic Geochemistry*, vol 37, pp1477–1488

Cheng, C. H., Lehmann, J. and Engelhard, M. (2008) 'Natural oxidation of black carbon in soils: Changes in molecular form and surface charge along a climosequence', *Geochimica et Cosmochimica Acta*, vol 72, pp1598–1610

Clarke, K. (2001) *Alternative Reductants for Silicon Smelting*, Investigation report CET/IR289, CSIRO, Sydney, Australia

Di Blasi, C. (1996) 'Heat transfer mechanism and multistep kinetics in the ablative pyrolysis of cellulose', *Chemical Engineering Science*, vol 51, pp2211–2220

Demirbas, A. (2001) 'Carbonization ranking of selected biomass for charcoal, liquid and gaseous products', *Energy Conversion and Management*, vol 42, pp1229–1238

Demirbas, A. (2004) 'Determination of calorific values of bio-chars and pyro-oils from pyrolysis of beech trunkbarks', *Journal of Analytical and Applied Pyrolysis*, vol 72, pp215–219

Fan, M., Marshall, W., Daugaard, D. and Brown, R. C. (2004) 'Steam activation of chars produced from oat hulls and maize stover',

Bioresource Technology, vol 93, pp103–107

FAO (United Nations Food and Agriculture Organization) (1983) *Simple Technologies for Charcoal Making*, FAO Forestry Paper 41, FAO, Rome, Italy, www.fao.org/docrep/S5328e/x5328e00.htm, accessed 16 November 2007

Fischer, Z. and Bienkowski, P. (1999) 'Some remarks about the effect of smoke from charcoal kilns on soil degradation', *Environmental Monitoring and Assessment*, vol 58, pp349–358

Flematti, G. R., Ghisalberti, E. L., Dixon, K.W. and Trengove, R. D., (2004) 'A compound from smoke that promotes seed germination', *Science*, vol 305, p977

Fitzer, E., Kochling, K.-H., Boehm, H. P. and Marsh, H. (1995) 'Recommended terminology for the description of carbon as a solid', *Pure and Applied Chemistry*, vol 67, pp473–506

Girard, P., Blin, J., Bridgwater, A.V. and Meier, D. (2006), 'An assessment of bio-oil toxicity for safe handling and transportation: Toxicological and ecotoxicological tests', in A. V. Bridgwater and D. G. B. Boocook (eds) *Science in Thermal and Chemical Biomass Conversion*, CPL Press, Newbury, UK, p27

HRL (2005) *Char Production from Maryville Paper Sludge and Wood Waste Yards*, Technical Report HLC2002/039, Victoria, Australia

Ioannidou, O. and Zabaniotou, A. (2007) 'Agricultural residues as precursors for activated carbon production: A review', *Renewable and Sustainable Energy Reviews*, vol 11, pp1966–2005

Kercher, K., Dennis, C. and Nagle, D. (2003) 'Microstructural evolution during charcoal carbonization by X-ray diffraction analysis', *Carbon*, vol 41, pp15–27

Kwon, S. and Pignatello, J. J. (2005) 'Effect of natural organic substances on the surface and adsorptive properties of environmental black carbon (char): Pseudo pore blockage by model lipid components and its implications for N-2-probed surface properties of natural sorbents', *Environmental Science and Technology*, vol 39, pp7932–7939

Lehmann, J. (2007) 'Bio-energy in the black', *Frontiers in Ecology and the Environment*, vol 5, pp381–387

Lehmann, J., da Silva Jr, J. P., Steiner, C., Nehls, T., Zech, W. and Glaser, B. (2003) 'Nutrient availability and leaching in an archaeological Anthrosol and a Ferrasol of the Central Amazon basin: Fertilizer, manure, and charcoal amendments', *Plant and Soil*, vol 249, pp343–357

Lehmann, J., Liang, B., Solomon, D., Lerotic, M., Luizão, F., Kinyangi, J., Schäfer, T., Wirick, S., and Jacobsen, C. (2005) 'Near-edge X-ray absorption fine structure (NEXAFS) spectroscopy for mapping nano-scale distribution of organic carbon forms in soil: Application to black carbon particles', *Global Biogeochemical Cycles*, vol 19, pGB1013

Lehmann, J., Gaunt, J. and Rondon, M. (2006) 'Bio-char sequestration in terrestrial ecosystems – a review', *Mitigation and Adaptation Strategies for Global Change*, vol 11, pp403–427

Liang, B., Lehmann, J., Solomon, D., Kinyangi, J., Grossman, J., O'Neill, B., Skjemstad, J. O., Thies, J., Luizão, F. J., Petersen, J. and Neves, E. G. (2006) 'Black carbon increases cation exchange capacity in soils', *Soil Science Society of America Journal*, vol 70, pp1719–1730

Lopez-Capel, E., Sohi, S. P., Gaunt, J. L. and Manning, D. A. C. (2005) 'Use of thermogravimetry-differential scanning calorimetry to characterize modelable soil organic matter fractions', *Soil Science Society of America Journal*, vol 69, pp136–140

Lopez-Ramon, M. V., Stoeckli, F., Moreno-Castilla, C. and Carrasco-Marin, F. (1999) 'On the characterization of acidic and basic surface sites on carbons by various techniques', *Carbon*, vol 37, pp1215–1221

Moghtaderi, B. (2006) 'The state-of-the-art in pyrolysis modelling of lignocellulosic solid fuels', *Fire and Materials*, vol 30, pp1–34

Nik-Azar, M., Hajaligol, M. R., Sohrabi, M. and Dabir, B. (1997) 'Mineral matter effects in rapid pyrolysis of beech wood', *Fuel Processing Technology*, vol 51, pp7–17

NSW EPA (New South Wales Environment Protection Authority) (1997) *Environmental Guidelines: Use and Disposal of Biosolids Products*, Environment Protection Authority, Chatswood, NSW, Australia, www.epa.nsw.gov.au

Ogawa, M. (1999) 'Utilization of symbiotic microorganisms and charcoal in tropical agriculture and forestry and CO_2 fixation', *Soil Microorganisms*, vol 53, pp73–79

Peacocke, G. V. C. (1994) *Ablative Pyrolysis of Biomass*, PhD thesis, Aston University, UK

Raveendran, K., Ganesh, A. and Khilar, K. C. (1995) 'Influence of mineral matter on biomass pyrolysis characteristics', *Fuel*, vol 74, pp1812–1822

Schaetzl, R. and Anderson, A. (2005) *Soils: Genesis and Geomorphology*, Cambridge University Press, Cambridge, UK

Schnitzer, M. I., Monreal, C. M., Facey, G. A. and Fransham, P. B. (2007) 'The conversion of chicken manure to biooil by fast pyrolysis I. Analyses of chicken manure, biooils and char by C-13 and H-1 NMR and FTIR spectrophotometry', *Environmental Science and Health B.*, vol 42, pp71–77

Shinogi, Y. (2004) 'Nutrient leaching from carbon products of sludge', Paper presented to the ASAE/CSAE Annual International Meeting, no 044063, Ottawa, Ontario, Canada

Standards Australia (2003) *AS 3743 – Potting Mixes*, Standards Association of Australia, Homebush, NSW, Australia

Steiner, C., Das, K. C., Garcia, M., Forster, B. and Zech, W. (2008) 'Charcoal and smoke extract stimulate the soil microbial community in a highly weathered xanthic Ferralsol', *Pedobiologia*, vol 51, pp359–366

Sugimoto, H., Kanayama, K. and Norimoto, M. (2007) 'Dielectric relaxation of water adsorbed on wood and charcoal', *Holzforschung*, vol 61, pp89–94

Tchobanoglous, G., Theisen, H. and Vigil, S. A. (1993) *Integrated Solid Waste Management: Engineering Principles and Management Issues*, McGraw Hill Inc, NY

Turov, V. V., Gun'ko, V. M., Leboda, R., Bandosz, T. J. and Skubiszewska-Zieba, J. (2002) 'Influence of organics on the structure of water adsorbed on activated carbons', *Journal of Colloid and Interface Science*, vol 253, pp23–34

Uvarov, A. V. (2000) 'Effects of smoke emissions from a charcoal kiln on the functioning of forest soil systems: A microcosm study', *Environmental Monitoring and Assessment*, vol 60, pp337–357

Warnock, D. D., Lehmann, J., Kuyper, T. W. and Rillig, M. C. (2007) 'Mycorrhizal response to biochar in soil – concepts and mechanisms', *Plant and Soil*, vol 300, pp9–20

Zabaniotou, A., Stavropoulos, G. and Skoulou, V.

(2008) 'Activated carbon from olive kernels in a two-stage process: Industrial improvement', *Bioresource Technology*, vol 99, pp320–326

Zanzi, R., Sjöström, K. and Björnbom, E. (2002) 'Rapid pyrolysis of agricultural residues at high temperature', *Biomass and Bioenergy*, vol 23, pp357–366

8

Biochar Production Technology

Robert Brown

Introduction

Biochar production cannot be properly discussed without first distinguishing it from char and charcoal. All three forms of carbonaceous material are produced from pyrolysis, the process of heating carbon (C)-bearing solid material under oxygen (O_2)-starved conditions. Char is defined here as any carbonaceous residue from pyrolysis, including natural fires. Thus, char is the most general term to employ in scientific descriptions of the products of pyrolysis and fires, whether from biomass or other materials. Charcoal is char produced from pyrolysis of animal or vegetable matter in kilns for use in cooking or heating. Biochar is carbonaceous material produced specifically for application to soil as part of agronomic or environmental management (see Chapters 1 and 7). No standard currently prescribes the composition or preparation of biochar to distinguish it from charcoal produced as fuel. However, advances in our understanding of what makes for 'good' charcoal in agronomic and environmental management applications will inevitably encourage separate designations for charcoal and biochar.

Since most information on the preparation of carbonaceous material stems from charcoal production, this chapter will draw significantly from our understanding of charcoal. Although C is the major constituent of charcoal, its exact composition and physical properties depend upon the starting material and the conditions under which it is produced. Charcoal contains 65 to 90 per cent C with the balance being volatile matter and mineral matter (ash) (Antal and Grønli, 2003). Superficially, charcoal resembles coal, which is also derived from vegetable matter; indeed, the word charcoal may have originally meant 'the making of coal' (*Encyclopedia Britannica*, 1911). However, the geological processes from which coal is derived are quite different from charcoal-making, resulting in important differences in chemical composition, porosity and reactivity.

Charcoal is readily generated in open fires, whether forest fires or camp fires. Thus, it was available to early humankind whose first apparent use of it was in the creation of spectacular cave paintings during the last Ice Age (Bard, 2002). Charcoal eventually found application in other fields, including agronomy, medicine, metallurgy, pyrotechnics and chemical manufacture. However, its largest application has always been in the preparation of smokeless fuel for cooking, residential heating, smelting and steel-making. The process of charcoal-making removes most of the volatile matter responsible for smoke during burning. Charcoal is a relatively clean-burning fuel that represented an important

innovation in the controlled use of fire. Charcoal or, rather, biochar as a C sequestration agent and soil amendment, on the other hand, is still poorly understood.

This chapter is divided into three sections: historical production of charcoal in traditional kilns; mechanisms of char production from plant materials; and modern methods of pyrolysis appropriate to sustainable production of biochar. The carbonaceous residue of pyrolysis will be referred to variously as char, charcoal or biochar, depending upon the context of the discussion.

History of charcoal-making

The earliest charcoal kilns consisted of temporary pits or mounds, which have the virtue of simplicity and low cost. While these simple kilns are still widely employed in the developing world, various kinds of brick, metal and concrete kilns have been introduced to improve the yield of charcoal-making. All of these operate in batch mode, requiring the periodic charging and discharging of the kiln. A recent innovation in charcoal-making is the multiple hearth kiln, which operates continuously, offering energy efficiency and environmental performance advantages compared to batch kilns. Virtually all charcoal kilns employ wood as feedstock, although in principle any biomass could be used to produce charcoal. Traditional charcoal-making goes through three successive stages that can be characterized by the colour of smoke emitted: drying (white smoke), pyrolysis (yellow smoke) and process complete (blue smoke). Among the best sources of information on the construction and operation of charcoal kilns is the report by the United Nations Food and Agriculture Organization (FAO, 1983).

Pit kilns employ the simplest strategy for controlling access of air and reducing heat

loss during carbonization: burying a stack of smouldering wood in the ground (FAO, 1983). Small pit kilns may be only 1 cubic metre in volume. A small fire is started in the pit and additional wood is added to make a strong fire. At this point a canopy of branches and leaves is added to support a layer of earth of about 0.2m in depth. Carbonization may proceed for up to two days before the pit is uncovered and the charcoal is allowed to cool before unloading. Large pit kilns can be 30m^3 or larger and produce 6t or more of charcoal per load. As illustrated in Figure 8.1, burning in large pit kilns takes place progressively from one end to the other. Large pit kilns do not necessarily have higher yields than small pits, but they are more efficient in the use of labour. Pit kilns must be continuously tended, opening and closing vent holes in the soil layer, to ensure the correct balance between combustion and pyrolysis in the pile. The pit kiln is ideal where the soil is well drained, deep and loamy. Charcoal yields are generally very low and the charcoal is not uniform in quality. The venting of particulate matter and volatile organic compounds to the atmosphere are obvious disadvantages.

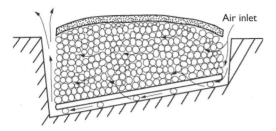

Figure 8.1 *Large pit kiln*

Source: adapted from FAO (1983)

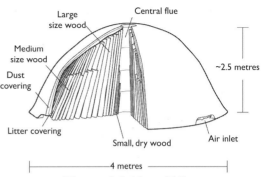

Figure 8.2 *Mound kiln*

Source: adapted from FAO (1983)

The mound kiln is essentially an above-ground version of the pit kiln, with earth mounded up over a stack of wood for the purpose of controlling air filtration and heat loss during carbonization (FAO, 1983). The mound is preferred to a pit when the water table is close to the surface or the soil is hard to work. It is also employed when a permanent site near an agricultural village (which has more scattered wood resources) is preferred to a temporary site located within a timber resource. A typical mound kiln is about 4m in diameter at the base and 1m to 1.5m high in the shape of a flattened hemisphere (see Figure 8.2). Long pieces of fuel wood are stacked vertically against a central post, while shorter logs are placed vertically towards the periphery. Gaps between logs are filled with small wood to make a dense pile. It is covered with straw or dry leaves and then a layer of loamy or sandy earth to seal the mound. The centre post is removed before lighting, the space serving as both the place to ignite the pile as well as the flue for the smoke to exhaust from the pile. About six to ten vents at the base of the mound allow for control of air filtration during carbonization. Similar to the pit kiln, the mound kiln has a relatively low charcoal yield and, as illustrated in Figure 8.3, is a source of significant atmospheric pollution.

The brick kiln is an important improvement over traditional pit and mound kilns, producing good-quality charcoal at relatively high yields (FAO, 1983). Capital cost is rela-tively low and labour costs are moderate. The kiln is constructed completely out of bricks, which provide good heat insulation, in a hemispherical or beehive shape of 5m to 7m in diameter, set into a brick foundation (see Figure 8.4). The kiln has two openings diametrically opposite one another and perpendicular to prevailing winds. One opening is used to charge the kiln, while the other is used to discharge the charcoal. These openings can either be closed with steel doors or simply bricked over and sealed with mud. Air infiltration is controlled by vents around the base of the kiln, while smoke is exhausted from an 'eye' hole at the top of the kiln. Carbonization may occur over the course of

Figure 8.3 *Operation of a mound kiln showing the heavy smoke emitted during the carbonization process*

Source: Weald and Downland Open Air Museum

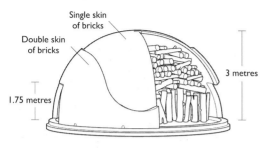

Figure 8.4 *Brick kiln*

Source: adapted from FAO (1983)

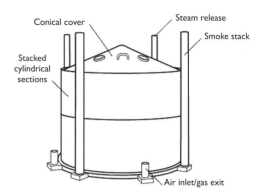

Figure 8.5 *Transportable metal kiln, Tropical Products Institute (TPI)*

Source: adapted from Whitehead (1980)

six to seven days, followed by a 'purging' stage of one to two days, during which the perimeter vents are sealed, and, finally, a cooling stage of three days in which the eye hole is also sealed.

Metal kilns originated in Europe during the 1930s and spread to the developing world in the 1960s. Although a number of variations exist, the transportable metal kiln developed by the Tropical Products Institute (TPI) (Whitehead, 1980) is illustrative of the main features of this type of kiln. As shown in Figure 8.5, the TPI kiln consists of two interlocking cylindrical sections and a conical cover with four steam release ports. The kiln is supported on eight channels projecting radially from the perimeter of the base section. These are designed to serve as air inlets or, when fitted with smoke stacks, to vent smoke out of the kiln. During carbonization, four of the channels are fitted with smoke stacks. The metal kiln has several advantages over traditional or brick kilns. The flow of air into, and smoke out of, the kiln is readily controlled, which improves charcoal yield and quality. Unskilled personnel can be quickly trained to operate the kiln and it does not require the constant attention of traditional kilns. Carbonization is complete in three days and all of the charcoal can be recovered from the kiln. The kiln can be operated in areas of high rainfall. The metal kiln does not, however, mitigate the air pollution associated with charcoal-making.

The concrete kiln, also known as the Missouri kiln, is a rectangular structure constructed of reinforced concrete or concrete block with steel doors (see Figure 8.6). The kiln is designed for mechanized loading and unloading of wood and charcoal. A typical kiln is about 7m wide and 11m long with a vault height of 4m. This gives it a capacity of about 180m^3 of wood, which is about three times greater than brick kilns. Concrete kilns typically produce 16t of charcoal during a three-week cycle. Yields are higher than for metal kilns because of better thermal insulation and larger volume-to-surface area ratios. Thermocouples within the kiln also contribute to better yields by allowing hot and cold spots to be identified and corrected by controlling airflow into the kiln. The Missouri kiln is fitted with eight 0.15m diameter pipes to serve as chimneys. These can be connected to a central flue and afterburner to mitigate atmospheric emissions of carbon monoxide (CO), volatile organic compounds (VOCs) and particulate matter (PM) (Yronwode, 2000). However, control of emissions from batch-type kilns is difficult because the emissions never reach a steady-state condition.

A multiple hearth kiln is a refractory-lined vertical steel shell containing a series of

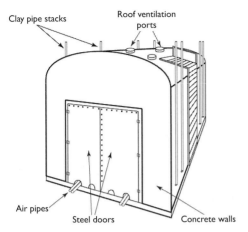

Figure 8.6 *The Missouri-type charcoal kiln*

Source: adapted from Maxwell (1976)

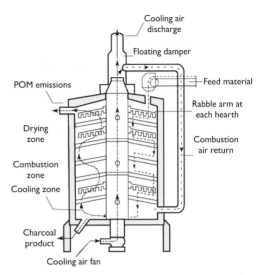

Figure 8.7 *The continuous multiple hearth kiln for charcoal production*

Note: POM = polycyclic organic matter
Source: adapted from Radian Corporation (1988)

shelves or hearths supported by the walls of the kiln (see Figure 8.7) (Radian Corporation, 1988). A rotating shaft fitted with rabble arms penetrates the centre of the shell. As the shaft rotates, the rabble arms sweep slowly across the hearths, moving carbonizing wood either radially inward or outward toward penetrations in the hearths where the material drops to the next lower hearth. Air flowing upward through the hollow shaft is admitted to the hearths. Gases and vapours released from the carbonizing wood travel counter-currently to the flow of biomass in the kiln. Continuous multiple hearth kilns produce an average of 2.5t hr^{-1} of charcoal. As a continuous flow reactor, the multiple hearth kiln offers superior control of carbonization time and gas flow, which is expected to improve charcoal yields and quality. Continuous processes are also more amenable to pollution control compared to batch processes. After-burning is estimated to reduce emissions of PM, CO and VOCs by at least 80 per cent (Rolke et al, 1972).

In addition to CO_2 and water (H_2O), smoke emitted from a charcoal kiln contains CO, methane (CH_4), VOCs and PM, which contribute to air pollution. Some of the VOCs are commercially valuable compounds,

which can be recovered by distillation. In fact, 'wood tar' and 'pyroligneous acid' were often the main reason to operate kilns before the development of petroleum-based chemicals. Destructive distillation of wood produced commercially significant quantities of acetic acid and methanol (wood alcohol) (Sjostrom, 1993). Emissions are usually characterized as CO, CH_4, non-methane hydrocarbons (NMHC), and total suspended particulates (TSP), although NMHC is a misnomer because it usually includes methanol, acetic acid and other oxygenated organic compounds. Table 8.1 lists ranges of emission levels for these pollutants from different kinds of charcoal kilns (Moscowitz, 1978). Clearly, dramatic improvements can be achieved using controlled continuous kilns compared to batch kilns.

The charcoal yield η_{char} from a kiln is given by:

$$\eta_{char} = (m_{char}/m_{bio}) \times 100 \qquad [1]$$

Table 8.1 *Air emissions per kilogram biomass from different kinds of charcoal kilns*

	CO (g kg^{-1})	CH4 (g kg^{-1})	NMHC[1] (g kg^{-1})	TSP[2] (g kg^{-1})
Uncontrolled batch	160–179	44–57	7–60	197–598
Low-control batch	24–27	6.6–8.6	1–9	27–89
Controlled continuous	8.0–8.9	2.2–2.9	0.4–3.0	9.1–30

Notes: 1 NMHC = non-methane hydrocarbons (includes recoverable methanol and acetic acid).
2 TSP = total suspended particulates.

Source: Moscowitz (1978)

Table 8.2 *Charcoal yields (dry weight basis) for different kinds of batch kilns*

Kiln type	Charcoal yield (%)
Pit	12.5–30
Mound	2–42
Brick	12.5–33
Portable steel (TPI)	18.9–31.4
Concrete (Missouri)	33

Source: Kammen and Lew (2005)

where m$_{char}$ is the dry mass of charcoal from the kiln and m$_{bio}$ is the dry mass of biomass loaded into the kiln. Table 8.2 shows the range of charcoal yields from different kinds of batch kilns, which all employ wood of unspecified species. Although reported yields range widely for a given type of kiln, in general, brick and steel kilns yield more charcoal than pit and mound kilns, and concrete kilns are expected to have highest yields among batch kilns. The effect of biomass composition and kiln operating conditions on charcoal yield and properties is virtually unexplored in the published literature.

Biochar is the product of pyrolysis, which is the decomposition of C-bearing compounds at elevated temperatures in the absence of O_2. This decomposition process is not perfectly understood, especially for complicated polymeric materials such as biomass from which charcoal is traditionally derived. In addition to biochar, other products of pyrolysis include condensable vapours (that yield insoluble tars and pyroligneous acid) and gas. The quantity of these products depends upon the composition of the biomass and the conditions under which pyrolysis occurs (Shafizadeh, 1982). An idea of the different yields of liquid, biochar and gas for various operating modes of pyrolysis is given in Table 8.3.

Table 8.3 *Typical product yields (dry basis) for different modes of pyrolysis*

Mode	Conditions	Liquid (%)	Char (%)	Gas (%)
Fast	Moderate temperature ~ 500°C short vapour residence time ~ 1sec	75	12	13
Moderate	Moderate temperature ~ 500°C Moderate vapour residence time ~ 10–20sec	50	20	30
Slow	Moderate temperature ~ 500°C Very long vapour residence time ~ 5–30min	30	35	35
Gasification	High temperature >750°C Moderate vapour residence time ~ 10–20sec	5	10	85

Source: Bridgwater (2007)

Mechanisms of biochar production from biomass substrates

The major constituents of fibrous biomass are cellulose, hemicellulose and lignin, with smaller quantities of organic extractives and inorganic minerals. These constituents can vary considerably among different kinds of biomass or even within a species depending upon soil type, climatic conditions and time of harvest. Examples of the variation in composition of different kinds of biomass are given in Table 8.4.

Cellulose is a linear condensation polymer of β-(1–4)-D-glucopyranose (O'Sullivan, 1997; see Figure 8.8). The repeating unit of the cellulose polymer is cellobiose, which consists of two anhydroglucose units. The number of glucose units in a cellulose chain is known as the degree of polymerization (DP). The average DP for native cellulose is on the order of 10,000. The coupling of adjacent cellulose molecules by hydrogen (H) bonds and van der Waal's forces results in a parallel alignment giving cellulose a crystalline structure. Cellulose exist as sheets of glucopyranose rings lying in a plane with successive sheets stacked on top

of each other to form three-dimensional particles that aggregate into elementary fibrils with a crystalline width of 4nm to 5nm. This crystalline micro-fibril arrangement makes cellulose more resistant to thermal decomposition than hemicellulose.

Hemicellulose is a large number of heteropolysaccharides built from hexoses (D-glucose, D-mannose and D-galactose), pentoses (D-xylose, L-arabinose and D-arabinose) and deoxyhexoses (L-rhamnose or 6-deoxy-L-mannose and rare L-fucose or 6-deoxy-L-galactose) (Sjostrom, 1993). Small amounts of uronic acids (4-O-methy-D-glucuronic acid, D-galacturonic acid and D-glucuronic acid) are also present. Hardwoods are rich in xylans such as O-acetyl-(4-O-methylglucurono) xylan and contain small amounts of gluco-mannan. Softwoods are rich in glucomannans such as O-acetyl-galactoglucomannan and smaller amounts of xylans such as arabino-(4-O-glucurono) xylan. Softwood hemicelluloses have more mannose and galactose units and less xylose units and acetylated hydroxyl

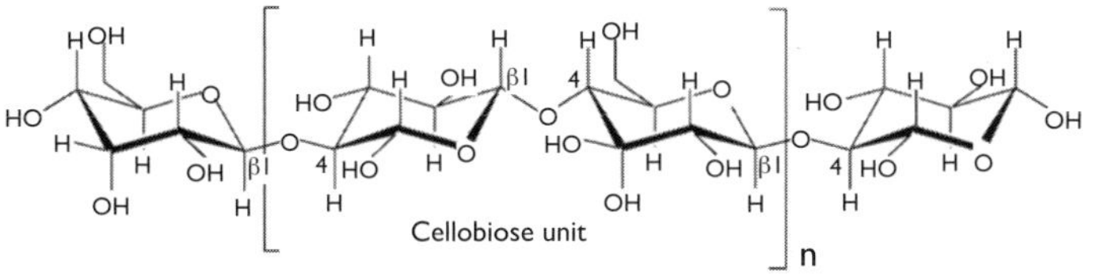

Figure 8.8 *Chemical structure of cellulose*

Source: adapted from Mohan et al (2006)

Table 8.4 *Typical content of several examples of biomass (dry basis)*

Feedstock	Cellulose (wt %)	Hemicellulose (wt %)	Lignin (wt %)	Extractives (wt %)	Ash (wt %)	Reference
Hybrid poplar	45	19	26	7	1.7	Hamelinck et al (2005)
Willow	43	21	26	–	1	Sassner et al (2006)
Switchgrass	32	25	18	17	6	Hamelinck et al (2005)
Miscanthus	38	24	25	5	2	de Vrije et al (2002)
Maize stover	39	19	15	–	4.6	Chandrakant and Bisaria (1998)
Wheat straw	38	25	14	–	10	Chandrakant and Bisaria (1998)

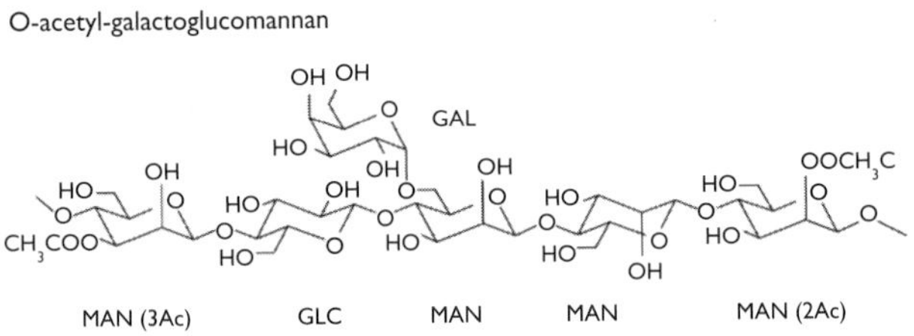

O-acetyl-galactoglucomannan

Figure 8.9 *Structural formula for a common hemicellulose found in softwoods*

Notes: Ac = acetyl group; GAL = galactose; GLC = glucose; MAN = mannose.

Source: adapted from Hartman (2006)

groups than do hardwood hemicelluloses.

Figure 8.9 gives the structural formula for a typical hemicellulose, illustrating the short side-chains that distinguish hemicellulose from cellulose. The chemical and thermal stability of hemicelluloses is lower than for cellulose due to its lack of crystallinity and lower degree of polymerization, which is only 100 to 200 (Sjostrom, 1993).

Lignin, a phenylpropane-based polymer, is the largest non-carbohydrate fraction of lignocellulose (Sjostrom, 1993). It is constructed of three monomers: coniferyl alcohol, sinapyl alcohol and coumaryl alcohol, each of which has an aromatic ring with different substituents (see Figure 8.10). Softwood lignin contains a higher fraction of coniferyl phenylpropane units (guaiacyl lignin), while hardwood lignin is a co-polymer of both coniferyl and sinapyl phenylpropane units (guaiacyl-syringyl lignin). Lignin has an amorphous structure, which leads to a large number of possible inter-linkages between individual units.

Ether bonds predominate between lignin units and covalent bonds exist between lignin and polysaccharides. Unlike cellulose, lignin cannot be depolymerized to its original monomers.

Bundles of elementary cellulose fibrils are embedded in a matrix of hemicellulose with a thickness of 7nm to 30nm. Lignin is located primarily on the exterior of microfibrils where it covalently bonds to hemicellulose (Klein and Snodgrass, 1993). Lignin impregnates the cell wall, reduces the pore sizes, shields the polysaccharides and contributes to the recalcitrance of lignocellulose (Saxena and Brown, 2005).

Plant materials also contain other organic compounds collectively known as 'extractives'. These include resins, fats and fatty acids, phenolics and phytosterols, among other chemical compounds. Extractives are classified as either hydrophilic or lipophilic, depending upon whether they are soluble in water or organic solvents, respectively. Resin is often used to describe the lipophilic extractives with the exception of phenolic substances. Extractives can influence gaseous emission profiles during pyrolysis, but they are not thought to substantially influence charcoal yield because of their low concentrations.

The inorganic content of biomass includes the major elemental nutrients nitrogen (N), phosphorus (P), and potassium (K), as well as smaller amounts of sulphur (S), chlorine (Cl), silicon (Si), alkaline earth metals, transition metals and various trace elements. That part of the inorganic content remaining after oxidation of the biomass at high temperature is known as ash.

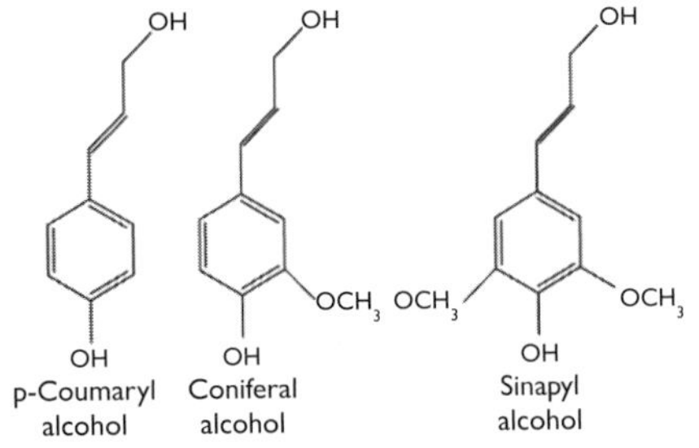

Figure 8.10 *Monomers from which lignin is assembled*

Source: adapted from Mohan et al (2006)

Table 8.5 *Influence of heating rate on pyrolysis of cellulose in a thermogravimetric analyser with nitrogen as sweep gas (flow rate unspecified)*

Heating rate ($°C min^{-1}$)	Enthalpy of pyrolysis ($J kg^{-1}$)	Onset temperature of pyrolysis ($°C$)	Temperature of maximum decomposition rate ($°C$)
5	+780	314	345
10	+498	337	360
30	+455	350	383
50	+440	362	396

Source: Gupta and Lilley (2003)

Cellulose, hemicellulose, and lignin have distinctive thermal decomposition behaviours that depend upon heating rates. As illustrated in Table 8.5, pyrolysis is initiated at higher temperatures as the heating rate is increased (Gupta and Lilley, 2003). At very low heating rates typical of muffle furnaces or traditional charcoal kilns, cellulose decomposition begins at temperatures as low as 250°C (William and Besler, 1996).

The temperature dependence of the decomposition of cellulose, hemicellulose (xylan) and lignin is illustrated in Figure 8.11 using data obtained by Yang et al (2007) from a thermogravimetric analyser (TGA) operated at a constant heating rate of 10°C min⁻¹ and swept with 120mL min⁻¹ of N_2. Hemicellulose is the first to decompose, beginning at 220°C and substantially completed by 315°C (see also Chapter 17). Cellulose does not start to decompose until about 315°C. In the swept gas environment of a TGA, essentially all of the cellulose is converted to non-condensable gas and condensable organic vapours and aerosols once 400°C is attained. As subsequently explained, cellulose can be the source of considerable biochar under different operating conditions. Although lignin begins to decompose at 160°C, it is a slow, steady process extending to 900°C and yielding a solid residue approaching 40 per cent by weight of the original sample.

Pyrolysis products of hemicellulose include non-condensable gases (primarily CO, CO_2, H_2 and CH_4), low molecular weight organic compounds (carboxylic acids, aldehydes, alkanes and ethers), and some water (Rutherford et al, 2004). Some of these compounds can be recovered in commercially significant quantities. For example, both acetic acid and furfural have been manufactured by thermal processing of hemicellulose-rich biomass. On the other hand, heavy molecular weight (tarry) compounds are produced in relatively small

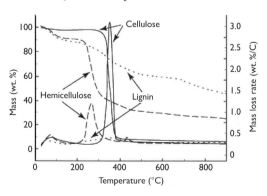

Figure 8.11 *Thermogravimetric analysis of the pyrolysis of cellulose, hemicellulose (xylan) and lignin at constant heating rate (10°C min⁻¹) with N_2 (99.9995 per cent) sweep gas at 120mL min⁻¹*

Source: adapted from Yang et al (2007)

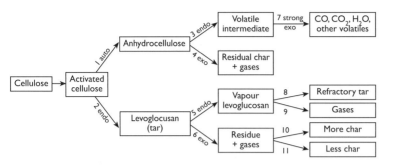

Figure 8.12 *Reaction pathways for cellulose decomposition*

Source: numbers refer to specific reactions described in Mok and Antal (1983)

amounts compared to pyrolysis of cellulose and lignin (Rutherford et al, 2004).

The products of cellulose decomposition can vary markedly depending upon reaction conditions. Figure 8.12 illustrates the detailed reaction mechanism proposed by Mok and Antal (1983). Cellulose decomposition includes both an exothermic pathway via anhydrocellulose and an endothermic pathway via levoglucosan. The anhydrocellulose pathway yields char and non-condensable gases in a process that is overall exothermic, but it occurs at extremely slow heating rates making this pathway of little practical importance. The levoglucosan (anhydroglucose) pathway is an endothermic devolatilization process that can lead to either predominately tarry vapours or char as the final product. A combination of temperature, residence time and naturally occurring catalysts in biomass determine the extent of secondary reactions, which yield a wide variety of organic compounds, including aldehydes, ketones, carboxylic acids, alcohols, and anhydrosugars from cellulose pyrolysis (Mohan et al, 2006).

Given sufficient time, the chemical equilibrium products of cellulose pyrolysis are mostly solid C (biochar), CO_2 and H_2O, and smaller quantities of CO and CH_4 (Antal and Grønli, 2003). As illustrated in Figure 8.13, pressure has little effect on equilibrium composition especially above 0.1MPa (atmospheric pressure), while increasing temperature slightly reduces biochar yield, which approaches an asymptotic limit of about 25 per cent by weight of the starting mass of cellulose.

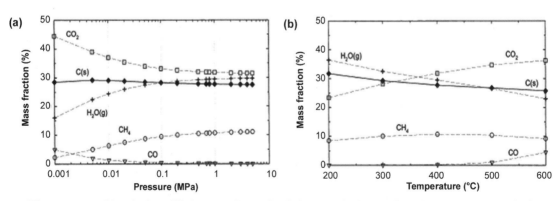

Figure 8.13 *Chemical equilibrium products of cellulose pyrolysis: (a) effect of pressure at 400°C; (b) effects of temperature at 1MPa*

Source: Robert Brown

Pyrolysis of lignin yields non-condensable gases, condensable vapours and liquid aerosols, and biochar (Mohan et al, 2006). The non-condensable gases, representing about 10 per cent by weight of the original lignin, consist of CO, CH_4 and ethane (C_2H_4). The condensable vapours and liquid aerosols are recovered as pyroligneous acid and insoluble tar. The pyroligneous acid is an aqueous phase of methanol, acetic acid, acetone and soluble tar. The insoluble tar contains homologous phenolic compounds derived from cleavage of ether and C–C bonds. Lignin is more difficult to dehydrate than cellulose or hemicelluloses and produces more residual biochar. For comparable temperatures and times, lignin weight loss is typically less than half that of cellulose.

From the previous discussions, carbonization efficiency is expected to be a function of both the composition of the biomass and the conditions under which biochar is produced. Although the biochar yield described by Equation 1 is of some practical application, it is not an exact measure of the amount of C produced from biomass since it does not account for the ash contents of the biomass feedstock and biochar product. A more meaningful measure of carbonization efficiency is the fixed C yield:

$$\eta_{fc} = \frac{m_{char}}{m_{bio}} \frac{c_{fc}}{1 - b_a} \qquad [2]$$

where c_{fc} is the fixed C content of biochar as measured by ASTM Standard 5142 (ASTM, 2004) and b_a is the ash content of the dry biomass. This represents the conversion of ash-free organic mass in the feedstock into ash-free C (Antal et al, 2000). A perfect kiln would have fixed C yield equal to the solid C yield predicted by thermodynamic equilibrium. For example, the pyrolysis of cellulose at 400°C and 1MPa should have a fixed C yield of 27.7 per cent, as illustrated in Figure 8.14 (calculated using the chemical equilibrium software package STANJAN; Bishnu et al, 1996).

In fact, biochar yields from biomass are considerably less than theoretical expectations. Traditional kilns can have efficiencies as low as 8 per cent (FAO, 1985). This can arise from the infiltration of O_2 with air into the kiln, which gasifies biochar to CO and CO_2 and greatly reduces equilibrium yields of C, as illustrated in Figure 8.14.

Even in the absence of O, however, low biochar yields can result if vapours and gases are removed from the reaction zone before thermodynamic equilibrium can be attained. Although it is often assumed that biochar is the result of solid-phase reactions in which devolatilized biomass leaves behind a carbonaceous residue (primary biochar), in fact, biochar is also formed by decomposition of organic vapours (tars) to form coke (secondary biochar). This secondary biochar is as chemically reactive as the primary

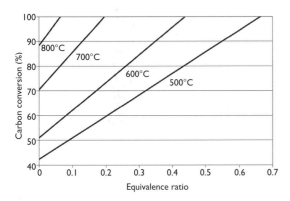

Figure 8.14 *Carbon conversion for gasification of cellulose as a function of equivalence ratio (fraction of stoichiometric O requirement for theoretical complete combustion) calculated with STANJAN chemical equilibrium software*

Source: Robert Brown

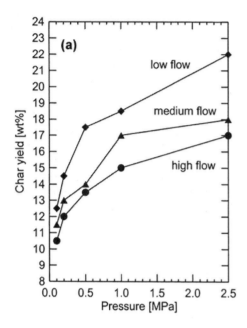

Figure 8.15 *Effect of pressure and purge gas flow rate on carbonization of cellulose*

Source: Mok and Antal (1983)

biochar despite differences in its formation (Chen et al, 1997). It is likely that decomposition of these vapours is catalysed by the primary biochar (Radovic and Sudhakar, 1997). At the very least, escape of pyrolytic vapours prevents the attainment of thermodynamic equilibrium by the original reactants, which favours high biochar yields. Varhegyi et al (1988) and later Suuberg et al (1996) were able to vary the biochar yield of pyrolysing cellulose from a few per cent to almost 20 per cent simply by controlling the venting of vapours during TGA experiments. Klason (1914) recognized the importance of primary and secondary reactions in biochar production almost 100 hundred years ago but this fact has yet to be fully exploited in biochar manufacture.

The existence of primary and secondary reactions in biochar-making helps to explain two phenomena that are otherwise difficult to understand. These are the effect of pressure on biochar yields and the report of both endotherms and exotherms during wood pyrolysis.

According to thermodynamic calculations, the pyrolysis of cellulose or wood should not be strongly influenced by pressure (see Figure 8.13). In fact, studies dating back as far as the pioneering research by Klason (1914) have claimed significant effects of pressure on biochar yields, although others have reported otherwise (Frolich et al, 1928). The question was taken up by Mok and Antal (1983) who demonstrated that, in tubular flow reactors, biochar yields increased from around 10 per cent by weight to over 20 per cent by weight as the pressure was increased from 0.1MPa to 2.5MPa. They also discovered that the effect was dependent upon the rate at which the reactor was purged with inert gas (see Figure 8.15). This later observation led them to suggest that pressure is a kinetic rather than a thermodynamic effect: high pressures prolong the intra-particle residence time of pyrolysing vapours, as well as increase the rate of decomposition reactions that allow a closer approach to the expectations of thermodynamic equilibrium. Sweep gas removes vapours before they have a chance to decompose and deposit secondary biochar.

Researchers have variously suggested enthalpies of pyrolysis that have ranged from endothermic (Kung and Kalelkar, 1973) to exothermic (Roberts, 1970) Mok and Antal (1983) used tubular flow reactors imbedded in a differential scanning calorimeter to measure the heat of pyrolysis as a function of pressure and purge gas flow (see Figure 8.16). They found the heat of pyrolysis was endothermic at low pressures and exothermic at high pressures. Furthermore, the pressure at which the process transitioned from endotherm to exotherm was dependent upon purge gas flow, with low flow rates moving the transition to lower pressures. They attrib-

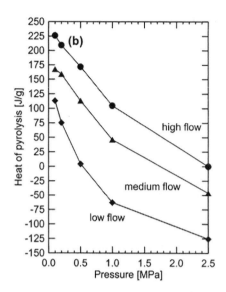

Figure 8.16 *Effect of pressure and purge gas flow rate on heat of pyrolysis for cellulose*

Source: Mok and Antal (1983)

uted the endotherm to the devolatilization of levoglucosan (reaction 5 in Figure 8.12) and the exotherm to *in-situ* carbonization of levoglucosan (reaction 6 in Figure 8.12). Taken together, Figure 8.15 and Figure 8.16 suggest the ability to control pyrolysis not only to improve biochar yields, but to improve the energy performance of biochar reactors.

Porosity is an important property of biochar. Although the vascular structure of plant materials contribute to large pores in biochar, most of biochar's high surface area derives from nanopores created during the heating process. Porosity is a complex function of heating temperatures, heating rates and heating times (see Chapter 2).

Under conditions of slow pyrolysis, Rutherford et al (2004) found evidence that aliphatic C in pyrolysing biomass must first be converted into fused-ring aromatic C before porosity can develop. For cellulose, this transformation of aliphatic C does not occur below 250°C, while for lignin, which already contains significant amounts of aromatic C, temperatures closer to 300°C are required to convert its aliphatic C. At higher temperatures, aromatic C was gradually lost and porosity began to develop. Thus, it would appear that the fused-ring structures of aromatic C provide a matrix in which micropores can be created.

Porous carbons are categorized as either graphitizable carbon or non-graphitizable carbon (Byrne and Marsh, 1995). In both cases, C atoms are arranged in fused hexagonal rings stacked as small crystallites. However, upon heating to high temperatures, the crystallites of graphitizable C reorient themselves into parallel sheets of C atoms, known as graphite, which destroys the porosity of the material. In non-graphitizable C, the crystallites are randomly oriented and strongly cross-linked to one another, which resists reorientation upon heating and preserves porosity. Carbon derived from pyrolysing biomass is non-graphitizable and is thought to be associated with the high oxygen content of the starting material (Franklin, 1951).

Opportunities for advanced biochar production

Traditional charcoal-making technologies are both energy inefficient and highly polluting. An examination of the physical and chemical processes associated with pyrolysis and carbonization of wood suggests that significant improvements can be made in both of these respects. It might also be possible to control the properties of biochar for agronomic and C sequestration applications. Finally, better utilization of the co-products of pyrolysis might improve the economic prospects of biochar production.

Some specific goals for advanced biochar manufacture include:

- continuous feed pyrolysers to improve energy efficiency and reduce pollution emissions associated with batch kilns;
- exothermic operation without air infiltration to improve energy efficiency and biochar yields;
- recovery of co-products to reduce pollution emissions and improve process economics;
- control of operating conditions to improve biochar properties and allow changes in co-product yields; and
- feedstock flexibility allowing both woody and herbaceous biomass (such as crop residues or grasses) to be converted to biochar.

Some technologies that hold promise for helping to achieve these goals include drum pyrolysers, rotary kilns, screw pyrolysers, the Flash Carbonizer, fast pyrolysis reactors, gasifiers, hydrothermal processing reactors, and wood-gas stoves, all of which produce varying quantities of gas and liquids along with biochar.

The drum pyrolyser moves biomass through an externally heated, horizontal cylindrical shell by the action of paddles. No air is intentionally admitted to the drum, although some air enters in the voids between feedstock particles. The process is characterized as 'slow pyrolysis', taking several minutes for the biomass to transit the drum, although the time is short compared to traditional batch carbonization. The residence time of vapours is long enough that most of it is cracked to non-condensable gases, even though some tar remains with the gas. Some of the gas is burned in a firebox below the drum to heat the biomass to pyrolysis temperatures. Biomass is first dried before entering the drum pyrolyser to ensure good

biochar and gas quality. The drum pyrolyser of BEST Energies (undated) is one of the few continuous pyrolysers that has been employed in production of biochar.

Rotary kilns should also be suitable as continuous pyrolysers (Arsenault et al, 1980; Bayer and Kutubuddin, 1988). They are similar to drum pyrolysers in the employment of an externally heated cylindrical shell except that the shell is oriented at an angle to the horizontal and rotated to allow gravity to move the biomass down the length of the kiln. They are expected to have similar solids residence times (5 to 30 minutes). The advantage over the drum pyrolyser is the absence of moving parts in the interior. Rotary kilns for biomass pyrolysis have been investigated at low temperatures (350°C) and moderately high temperatures (600°C to 900°C). Klose and Wiest (1999) showed that variations in biomass feed rate and operating temperatures for a rotary kiln pyrolyser allowed wide control on the relative yields of condensable vapours and non-condensable vapours, while biochar yield remained relatively constant in the range of 20 to 24 per cent. This lack of control over biochar yields suggests that the relatively large volume of a rotary (or drum) kiln does not encourage re-condensation of tarry vapours to produce secondary biochar.

Screw pyrolysers move biomass through a tubular reactor by the action of a rotating screw (see Figure 8.17). Some screw pyrolysers are externally heated while others use a heat carrier such as sand to heat the biomass as it is transported through the tube. The screw pyrolyser is attractive for its potential to operate at relatively small scales. One of the first such pyrolysers was the twin-screw Lurgi-Ruhrgas mixer reactor originally developed for producing town gas or olefins from coal using sand as a heat carrier. During recent years it has been successfully employed to convert biomass into bio-oil and biochar (Henrich, 2004). The Haloclean Pyrolysis Reactor is another screw reactor

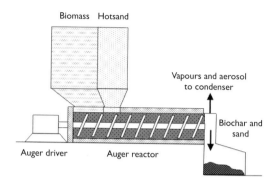

Figure 8.17 *Screw pyrolyser with heat carrier*

Source: Robert Brown

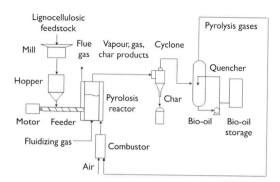

Figure 8.18 *Fluidized-bed fast pyrolysis reactor*

Source: Robert Brown

originally developed to treat electronic wastes, but finding applications in biomass pyrolysis (Haloclean, undated). It uses iron spheres as heat carrier. An example of an externally heated screw pyrolyser is the system developed by Advanced Biorefinery, Inc (ABRI, undated).

The Flash Carbonizer was developed by Antal et al (2003) at the University of Hawaii as a way of producing biochar through the ignition of a flash fire at elevated pressure in a packed bed of biomass. They report fixed C yields of up to 100 per cent of the theoretical limit in as little as 20 or 30 minutes, and observed a significant improvement in yields at elevated pressure and the preferential oxidation of combustible gases released during pyrolysis compared to biochar product.

Fast pyrolysis quickly heats biomass and extracts vapours for the preferential production of bio-oil compared to gas and biochar (Mohan et al, 2006). Although several kinds of reactors have been designed for fast pyrolysis, the high heat- and mass-transfer rates obtainable in fluidized beds make them ideal reactors for bio-oil production (see Figure 8.18). Typical yields are 60 to 70 per cent by weight bio-oil, 12 to 15 per cent by weight biochar, and 13 to 25 per cent by weight non-condensable gases for reactors operated at around 450°C to 500°C and for particles

comminuted to about 1mm to 2mm in diameter (for an extensive review of the subject, see Mohan et al, 2006). The distribution of products can be dramatically altered by changing particle size, reaction temperature and gas flow rate through the fluidized bed. The relatively high flow rates of gas and relatively low residence time of biochar in the bed might be expected to produce biochars with properties distinct from biochar produced by slow pyrolysis. However, whether this biochar has properties that are inferior or superior to biochar from more traditional charcoal kilns is not known.

Gasifiers would seem to be a poor choice for biochar production since they are designed to produce gaseous products (mostly CO, CO_2, H_2, and N_2) at the expense of oils and biochar (McKendry, 2002). In fact, the operation of traditional charcoal kilns more closely resembles the operation of gasifiers than pyrolysers and the amount of biochar produced can be as high as 10 per cent by weight of the biomass gasified (Reed, 1981). By definition, pyrolysis occurs in the complete absence of O_2, which requires an external heat source to reach operating temperatures. In contrast, a gasifier admits O_2 (or air) to burn part of the biomass in order to supply the heat needed to drive the endothermic biomass devolatilization processes that yield condensable vapours, flammable gases and biochar. Most traditional kilns are not externally heated but allow air infiltration to burn part of the kiln charge. Typical gasifiers operate at equivalence ratios close to 0.25 to provide sufficient heat to drive the gasification process. As Figure 8.14 illustrates, C conversion is a strong function of gasification temperature. Biochar yields could exceed 30 per cent in a gasifier operated at 500°C and an equivalence ratio of 0.25. Thus, modern gasifiers offer prospects for advanced biochar production with possible advantages in process control and reduction of pollution emissions.

Figure 8.19 illustrates three kinds of gasifiers suitable for co-production of producer gas and biochar: updraught, downdraught and fluidized bed (Brown, 2003). Updraught gasifiers are very similar to charcoal kilns except that more air is admitted in an effort to maximize gas production. Chipped fuel is admitted from above and insufficient air for complete combustion enters from below. The producer gas contains large quantities of tars, making them undesirable for many applications, but they have the virtue of relatively low cost. In contrast, downdraught gasifiers move fuel and gas in the same direction, which has the advantage of forcing tarry vapours released from the pyrolysing biomass through a zone of hot charcoal where it decomposes. Modern designs usually include tuyeres that admit air or O_2 directly into a region known as the throat where combustion forms a bed of hot biochar. The producer gas is relatively free of tar. Disadvantages include the need for tightly controlled fuel properties and a tendency for sintering of ash in the concentrated oxidation zone. In a fluidized-bed gasifier, the gas stream passes vertically upward through a bed of inert particulate material to form a turbulent mixture of gas and solid. Biomass injected into the bed is rapidly heated and pyrolysed. Fluidized beds can be scaled to a large size and are able to

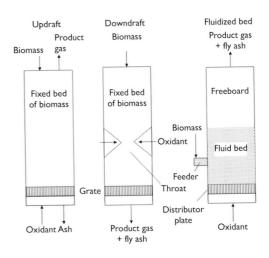

Figure 8.19 *Different kinds of gasifiers suitable for co-production of producer gas and biochar*

Source: Robert Brown

process a wide variety of fuels. Disadvantages include relatively high power for gas blowers and high particulate loadings in the gas exiting the fluidized bed.

Hydrothermal processing (HTP) describes the thermal treatment of wet biomass to produce primarily carbohydrate, liquid hydrocarbons or gaseous products, depending upon the reaction conditions, with biochar as a co-product (Elliot et al, 1991, 2004; Allen et al, 1996). As the reaction temperature increases, higher pressures are required to prevent boiling of the water in the wet biomass. Thus, processing conditions range from hot compressed water at 200°C to supercritical water above 374°C. Although systematic studies of biochar yields have not been performed for HTP, chemical equilibrium considerations would suggest that biochar yield decreases with increasing temperature.

Wood-gas stoves are designed for efficient domestic cooking with wood in the developing world (Kammen, 1996). As illustrated in Figure 8.20, they are essentially miniature batch-operated gasifiers with close-coupled combustion of the volatile

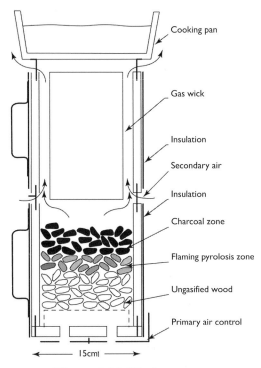

Cooking pan

Gas wick

Insulation

Secondary air

Insulation

Charcoal zone

Flaming pyrolosis zone

Ungasified wood

Primary air control

15cm

Figure 8.20 *Wood-gas stove*

Source: Robert Brown

gases to provide heat for cooking. The charcoal remaining at the end of devolatilization

of the biomass can be burned in the stove to supply additional heat, but it can also be recovered as biochar with yield of 20 to 25 per cent by weight (La Fontaine and Reed, 1993). Although the amount produced per batch is only about 150g, daily use by hundreds of thousands of households in a developing country might produce significant quantities of biochar for agronomic and environmental management (see Chapter 9).

Despite these several possibilities for producing biochar, very little work has been reported in the literature on the yields and properties of biochar relevant to agronomic or environmental management applications. As the discussion earlier in this chapter indicates, these yields and properties will be influenced by the composition of the biomass feedstock, but quantitative prediction is currently not possible. The possibility of controlling operating conditions to improve process efficiency and optimize co-product distribution has not been explored despite the theoretical possibilities. Advances in biochar production will require both basic research to understand the mechanisms of biochar formation and demonstration projects to prove the technical and economic feasibility of large-scale biochar production.

References

ABRI (undated) *50 DTPD Commercial/Industrial Systems*, www.advbiorefineryinc.ca/50ton.html, accessed 20 November 2007

Allen, S. G., Kam, L. C., Zemann, A. J. and Antal, M. J. (1996) 'Fractionation of sugar cane with hot, compressed, liquid water', *Industrial and Engineering Chemistry Research*, vol 35, pp2709–2715

Antal, M. J. and Grønli, M. (2003) 'The art, science and technology of charcoal production', *Industrial and Engineering Chemistry Research*, vol 42, pp1619–1640

Antal, M. J., Allen, S. G., Dai, X., Shimizu, B., Tam, M. S. and Grønli, M. G. (2000) 'Attainment of the theoretical yield of carbon from biomass', *Industrial and Engineering Chemistry Research*, vol 39, pp4024–4031

Antal, M. J., Mochidzuki, K. and Paredes, L. (2003) 'Flash carbonization of biomass', *Industrial and Engineering Chemistry Research*, vol 42, pp3690–3699

Arsenault, R. H., Grandbois, M. A., Chornet, E. and Timbers, G. E. (1980) 'Thermal conversion of solid wastes and biomass', *ACS Symposium Series*, vol 130, pp337–350

ASTM (2004) *Standard Test Methods for Proximate Analysis of the Analysis Sample of Coal and Coke by Instrumental Procedures*, ASTM D5142-04, ASTM International, West Conshohocken, PA, www.astm.org

Bard, E. (2002) 'Extending the calibrated radio-carbon record', *Science*, vol 292, pp2443–2444

Bayer, E. and Kutubuddin, M. (1988) 'Thermocatalytic conversion of lipid-rich biomass to oleochemical and fuel', in A. V. Bridgwater and J. L. Kuester (eds) *Research in Thermochemical Biomass Conversion*, Elsevier Applied Science, Amsterdam, The Netherlands, pp518–530

BEST Energies (undated) 'BEST Pyrolysis, Inc.', www.bestenergies.com/companies/ bestpyrolysis.html, accessed 5 January 2009

Bishnu, P. S., Hamiroune, D., Metghalchi, M. and Keck, J. C. (1996) 'Development of constrained equilibrium codes and their applications in non-equilibrium thermodynamics', *Advanced Energy Systems Division: Proceedings of the ASME Advanced Energy Systems Division*, vol 36, pp213–220

Bridgwater, A. (2007) 'IEA Bioenergy Update 27: Biomass Pyrolysis', *Biomass and Bioenergy*, vol 31, ppI–V

Brown, R. C. (2003) *Biorenewable Resources: Engineering New Products from Agriculture*, Blackwell Press, Ames, IA

Byrne, J. F. and Marsh, H. (1995) 'Introductory overview', in J. W. Patrick (ed) *Porosity in Carbons: Characterization and Applications*, Halsted Press, New York, NY, pp 2–48

Chandrakant P. and Bisaria, V. S. (1998) 'Simultaneous bioconversion of cellulose and hemicellulose to ethanol', *Critical Reviews in Biotechnology*, vol 18, pp295–331

Chen, G., Yu, Q. and Sjostrom, K. (1997) 'Reactivity of char from pyrolysis of birch wood', *Journal of Analytical and Applied Pyrolysis* vol 40–41, pp491–499

de Vrije, T., de Haas, G. G., Tan, G. B., Keijsers, E. R. P. and Claassen, P. A. M. (2002) 'Pretreatment of miscanthus for hydrogen production by *Thermotoga elfii*', *International Journal of Hydrogen Energy*, vol 27, pp1381–1390

Elliott, D. C., Beckman, D., Bridgwater, A. V., Diebold, J. P., Gevert, S. B. and Solantausta, Y. (1991) 'Developments in direct thermochemical liquefaction of biomass: 1983–1990', *Energy and Fuels*, vol 5, pp399–410

Elliott, D. C., Neuenschwander, G. G., Hart, T. R., Butner, R. S., Zacher, A. H., Engelhard, M. H., Young, J. S. and McCready, D. E. (2004)

'Chemical processing in high-pressure aqueous environments. 7. Process development for catalytic gasification of wet biomass feed-stocks', *Industrial and Engineering Chemistry Research*, vol 43, pp1999–2004

Encyclopedia Britannica (1911) 'Charcoal', *Encyclopedia Britannica*, vol 5, p856

FAO (United Nations Food and Agriculture Organization) (1983) *Simple Technologies for Charcoal Making*, FAO Forestry Paper 41, FAO, Rome, www.fao.org/docrep/S5328e/ x5328e00.htm, accessed 16 November 2007

FAO (1985) *Industrial Charcoal Making*, FAO Forestry Paper 63, FAO, Rome, Italy

Franklin, R. E. (1951) 'Crystallite growth in graphitizing and non-graphitizing carbons', *Proceedings of the Royal Society*, vol A209, pp196–218

Frolich, P. K., Spalding, H. B. and Bacon, T. S. (1928) 'Destructive distillation of wood and cellulose under pressure', *Industrial and Engineering Chemistry Research*, vol 20, p36–40

Gupta, A. K. and Lilley, D. G. (2003) 'Thermal destruction of wastes and plastics', in A. L. Andrady (ed) *Plastics and the Environment*, Wiley-Interscience, pp629–696

Haloclean (undated) *Haloclean Pyrolysis Reactor*, www.bioenergynoe.com/?_id=225, accessed 20 November 2007

Hamelinck, C. N., van Hooijdonk, G. and Faaij, A. (2005) 'Ethanol from lignocellulosic biomass: Techno-economic performance in short-, middle- and long-term', *Biomass and Bioenergy*, vol 28, pp384–410

Hartman, J. (2006) *Hemicellulose as Barrier Material*, Licentiate thesis, Royal Institute of Technology, Stockholm, Sweden

Henrich, E. (2004) 'Fast pyrolysis of biomass with a twin screw reactor: A first BTL step', *PyNe Newsletter*, vol 17, pp6–7

Kammen, D. M (1996) 'Cookstoves for the developing world', *Scientific American*, July, p72

Kammen, D. M. and Lew, D. J. (2005) *Review of Technologies for the Production and Use of Charcoal*, Renewable and Appropriate Energy Laboratory, Berkeley University, 1 March, http://rael.berkeley.edu/files/2005/ Kammen-Lew-Charcoal-2005.pdf, accessed 17 November 2007

Klason, P. (1914) 'Versuch einer Theorie der Trockendestillation von Holz', *Journal für*

Praktische Chemie, vol 90, pp413–447

Klein, G. L. and Snodgrass, W. R. (1993) 'Cellulose', in R. Macrae, R. K. Robinson and M. J. Saddler (eds) *Encyclopedia of Food Science, Food Technology and Nutrition*, Academic Press, London, UK, pp758–767

Klose, W. and Wiest, W. (1999) 'Experiments and mathematical modeling of maize pyrolysis in a rotary kiln', *Fuel*, vol 78, pp65–72

Kung, H. C. and Kalelkar, A. S. (1973) 'On the heat of reaction in wood pyrolysis', *Combustion and Flame*, vol 20, pp91–103

La Fontaine, H. and Reed, T. B. (1993) 'An inverted downdraft wood-gas stove and charcoal producer', in D. Klass (ed) *Energy from Biomass and Wastes XV*, Institute of Gas Technology, Washington, DC, pp1023–1049

Maxwell, W. H. (1976) *Stationary Source Testing of a Missouri-Type Charcoal Kiln*, EPA-907/9-76-0101, US Environmental Protection Agency, Research Triangle Park, NC, August 1972

McKendry, P. (2002) 'Energy production from biomass (part 3): Gasification technologies', *Bioresource Technology*, vol 83, pp55–63

Milosavljevic, I., Oja, V. and Suuberg, E. M. (1996) 'Thermal effects in cellulose pyrolysis: Relationship to char formation processes', *Industrial and Engineering Chemistry Research*, vol 35, pp653–662

Mohan, D., Pittman, Jr., C. U. and Steele, P. H. (2006) 'Pyrolysis of wood/biomass for bio-oil: A critical review', *Energy and Fuels*, vol 20, pp848–889

Mok, W. S. L. and Antal, M. J. (1983) 'Effects of pressure on biomass pyrolysis. II: Heats of reaction of cellulose pyrolysis', *Thermochimica Acta*, vol 68, pp165–186

Moscowitz, C. M. (1978) *Source Assessment: Charcoal Manufacturing – State of the Art*, EPA-600/2-78-004z, Cincinnati, OH

O'Sullivan, A. C. (1997) 'Cellulose: The structure slowly unravels', *Cellulose*, vol 4, pp173–207

Radian Corporation (1988) *Locating and Estimating Air Emissions from Sources of Polycyclic Organic Matter (POM)*, EPA-450/4-84-007p, US Environmental Protection Agency, Research Triangle Park, NC

Radovic, L. R. and Sudhakar, C. (1997) 'Carbon as a catalyst support: Production, properties, and applications', in H. Marsh, E. A. Heintz, and F. Rodriguez-Reinoso (eds) *Introduction to Carbon Technologies*, Universidad de Alicante, Alicante, Spain, pp103–165

Reed, T. B. (1981) *Biomass Gasification: Principles and Technology*, Noyes Data Corporation, Park Ridge, NJ

Roberts, A. F. (1970) 'A review of kinetics data for the pyrolysis of wood and related substances', *Combustion and Flame*, vol 14, pp261–272

Rolke, R. W., Hawthorne, R. D., Garbett, C. R. and Slater, T. T. (1972) *Afterburner Systems Study*, EPA-RZ-72-062, US Environmental Protection Agency, Research Triangle Park, NC

Rutherford, D. W., Wershaw, R. L. and Cox, L. G. (2004) *Changes in Composition and Porosity Occurring during the Thermal Degradation of Wood and Wood Components*, US Geological Survey, Scientific Investigation Report 2004-5292, Reston, VA

Sassner, P., Galbe, M. and Zacchi, G. (2006) 'Bioethanol production based on simultaneous saccharification and fermentation of steam-pretreated Salix at high dry-matter content', *Enzyme and Microbial Technology*, vol 39, pp756–762

Saxena, I. M. and Brown, Jr., R. M. (2005) 'Cellulose biosynthesis: Current views and evolving concepts', *Annals of Botany*, vol 96, pp9–21

Shafizadeh, F. (1982) 'Chemistry of pyrolysis and combustion of wood', *Progress in Biomass Conversion*, vol 3, pp51–76

Sjostrom, E. (1993) *Wood Chemistry: Fundamentals and Applications*, second edition, Academic Press, San Diego, CA

Suuberg, E. M., Milosavljevic, I. and Oja, V. (1996) 'Two-regime global kinetics of cellulose pyrolysis: The role of tar evaporation', Twenty-Sixth Symposium (International) on Combustion, The Combustion Institute, Pittsburgh, pp1515–1521

Varhegyi, G., Antal, M. J., Szekely, T., Till, F. and Jakab, E. (1988) 'Simultaneous thermogravi-metric–mass spectrometric studies of the thermal decomposition of biopolymers: 1. Avicel cellulose in the presence and absence of catalysts', *Energy and Fuels*, vol 2, pp267–272

Whitehead, W. (1980) *The Construction of a Transportable Charcoal Kiln*, Tropical Products Institute, London

Williams, P. T. and Besler, S. (1996) 'The influence of temperature and heating rate on the slow pyrolysis of biomass', *Renewable Energy*, vol 7, pp233–250

Yang, H., Yan, R., Chen, H., Lee, D. H. and Zheng, C. (2007) 'Characteristics of hemicellulose, cellulose and lignin pyrolysis', *Fuel*, vol 86, pp1781–1788

Yronwode, P. (2000) 'From the hills to the grills', *Missouri Resources Magazine*, spring issue, pp6–10

9

Biochar Systems

Johannes Lehmann and Stephen Joseph

Introduction

Biochar has the potential to deliver a variety of sustainability outcomes, including carbon (C) sequestration, improved soil fertility, mitigation of off-site effects from agrochemicals and renewable energy (Lehmann, 2007). However, the benefits of biochar need to be viewed from a systems perspective in order to fully capture the economic benefits and costs, environmental complexity and energy of the technology and to avoid or to minimize unacceptable trade-offs. For example, the clear-felling of tropical rainforests to provide biochar feedstock for C sequestration is clearly unsustainable (Lehmann, 2009). And transportation distances put limits to any biomass use from an economic (Caputo et al, 2005) and ecological point of view (Krotscheck et al, 2000). Biochar systems can be very different from each other. Choices are guided by the availability of biomass, the need for soil improvement or the demand for energy. In addition, biochar management is often not an alternative to best agricultural or energy management but improves upon advances previously made in practices.

This chapter outlines possible material flows and presents a variety of scenarios where biochar systems are used to deliver positive environmental outcomes based on appropriate matching of input materials, land-use practices and markets. The compilation of case studies presented in the second half of this chapter is not intended to provide a comprehensive overview of all possible biochar systems, nor is it able to provide in-depth analyses of individual systems because biochar systems are only emerging at present. It is a first step towards a survey that highlights very different systems in which biochar can be used for environmental management after discussing some fundamental system components of various biochar approaches.

Motivation for biochar soil management

Adding biochar to soil can be motivated by several aspects, such as:

- improvement of soils;
- mitigation of climate change;
- reduction of off-site pollution; and
- waste management on an economically viable basis (see Chapter 1).

Farmers may be mainly guided by the need to improve crop productivity if their soils respond positively to biochar additions. Positive plant growth responses to biochar additions have consistently been reported from regions that contain highly weathered soil minerals, such as oxides and 1:1 clay minerals (e.g. kaolinites), and are mainly linked to increases in cation retention or decreases in acidity (Lehmann and Rondon, 2006). Yield increases have also been reported from other regions (see Chapter 12) and may be related to processes such as changes in soil–water relationships (see Chapters 2 and 15) or microbial processes (see Chapter 6). Soils that are degraded by long-term continuous cultivation may benefit the most from biochar additions (Kimetu et al, 2008). In such cases when improvement of soil productivity is the main objective and creates the environmental as well as economic return, other aspects become secondary and biochar production is mainly optimized for its ability to improve soils. In specific cases, energy may not even be captured or the stability of biochar may be intentionally compromised for the ability of biochar to supply or retain nutrients or increase soil pH.

In other situations, mitigation of climate change may be the main incentive. In this scenario, energy capture during pyrolysis appears to be central, both from the viewpoint of reduction of greenhouse gas emissions, as well as economic viability (Gaunt and Lehmann, 2008; see Chapters 18 to 20). In the extreme scenario, optimization for the mitigation of climate change may prioritize biochar stability at the expense of its ability to improve soil properties and, some may even argue, to use biochar as a landfill for sequestration (Seyfritz, 1993) rather than as a soil amendment.

A major incentive for the production of biochar is both the upgrading and facilitation of transportation of low-grade wastes (see Chapter 21). For example, green waste is, in some cases, being converted into wet compost and transported long distances to find markets (Lundie and Peters, 2005). Transportation of composts increases the total energy required by 10 per cent for every 10km of transport (Diaz et al, 1986). In addition, large amounts of methane may be emitted during composting (see Chapter 18), which could render composting a net emitter of greenhouse gases. Converting some of this green waste into biochar and energy may be an option to improve product quality and reduce transportation costs.

In many cases, biochar management will probably attempt to make use of all four outcomes mentioned at the beginning of this section. The specific location may pose constraints with respect to soil type, crop, biomass availability and energy needs, as well as any regulatory or economic framework.

Components of biochar systems

Biochar systems can contain various components (see Figure 9.1) that may or may not be part of any particular system. These include the resource base; the existing agricultural and land-use base, and the capacity to expand or change this base; the local transportation system; the local industrial engineering and skills base; sales outlets and distribution network; energy infrastructure; and markets. Local economic, environmental, social, cultural and political factors can constrain the range of interventions that may, theoretically, be possible. A short description of the systems components will be given along with a general discussion of potential constraints on the system.

Resource base

There is a large difference in the resource base that exists between urban, industrial and rural areas and, to some extent, between developing and developed countries. Table 9.1 lists the most important resources that are likely feedstocks in many locations.

In developing countries, many areas are resource constrained in terms of biomass by-products for biochar production. Most of the urban residues are being recycled either as a fuel or for reuse in industry and rural opera-

tions. For example, 75 per cent of logging or mill residues may be recoverable in developed countries for bioenergy in comparison to 42 to 50 per cent in developing countries (Hoogwijk et al, 2003). Similarly in rural areas, by-products such as animal manures or crop residues are valuable resources as soil amendments, feed or construction material (Mueller et al, 2003; Mulugetta, 2006). On the other hand, dedicated biomass energy production per unit area is estimated to be greater in tropical areas due to greater productivity (Moreira, 2006). Therefore, the long-term potential in developing countries is large, but the short-term availability is generally limited.

Not only is the amount of biomass resource available important, but also its quality and availability over time. Contamination of agricultural and forest residues with soil and rocks decreases efficiency or damages equipment, and net energy gains therefore vary significantly between dedicated energy crops. For example, net energy gains were found to be higher for short-rotation forest and sugar beet ($160\mathrm{GJ}\ \mathrm{ha}^{-1}\ \mathrm{yr}^{-1}$ to $170\mathrm{GJ}\ \mathrm{ha}^{-1}\ \mathrm{yr}^{-1}$) than fallow crops such as clover-grass or lucerne ($110\ \mathrm{GJ}\ \mathrm{ha}^{-1}\ \mathrm{yr}^{-1}$ to $140\mathrm{GJ}\ \mathrm{ha}^{-1}\ \mathrm{yr}^{-1}$) or annual crops such as rape, wheat and pota-

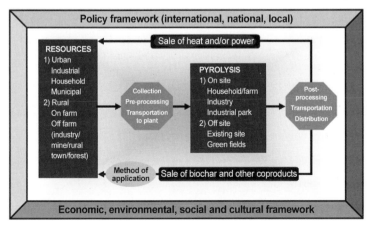

Figure 9.1 *Components of biochar systems*

Source: chapter authors

Table 9.1 *Availability, moisture and transportation requirements for different resource base options for biochar production*

Resource base	Location[1]	Global region[2]	Moisture[3]	Transportation[4]
Green waste from households, parks, gardens and from construction clearing	U, (R)[5]	DD	L–M	H
Source-separated organic waste (animal, grease-trap waste)	U	DD	H	L–H
Waste from wood- and paper-processing industries	I, R	(DG) DD	L–H	L–H
Source-separated commercial and industrial waste with low heavy-metal contents	U, I, (R)	DG, DD	L–H	L–H
Sewage sludge with low levels of contaminants	U, I	DG, DD	H	L
Residues from food crops	R	(DG) DD	L	L–H
Manures from confined animal operations	R	DD	H	L–H
Purpose-grown feedstock	R	DD	L	H
Forest thinnings and residues from timber production	R	(DG) DD	L	H
Residues from food- and crop-processing facilities	U, I, R	(DG) DD	L–H	L
Residues from the clearing of land at mines	R	DG, DD	L	L–H

Notes: 1 Location where the feedstock is most abundant: R = rural; I = industrial; U = urban.
　　　　2 Global region where the feedstock is most abundant: DG = developing; DD = developed countries.
　　　　3 H = high moisture content; L = low moisture content.
　　　　4 H = high transportation distances; L = low transportation distances, both with and without co-generation of energy.
　　　　5 Brackets indicate low importance.

Source: chapter authors

toes (50GJ ha^{-1} yr^{-1} to 90GJ ha^{-1} yr^{-1}) (Börjesson, 1996). Biomass delivery from field crop production has a distinct seasonality that poses significant challenges and may only be resolved through expensive storage. Diversification may offer a way forward in these cases.

Urban regions and, specifically, industrial regions have large feedstock options, but often problems with respect to quality. Many resources in these situations may have unacceptable amounts of heavy metals or contain non-biomass organic (such as plastics) or even metal wastes. Estimates of 75 per cent of organic materials in urban environments being available for bioenergy, in general (Hoogwijk et al, 2003), may need to be criti-cally examined as to whether they are suitable for biochar production.

Biochar production linked to the utilization of industrial by-products as feedstocks require specialized systems, but have, in a limited amount of cases, a high potential. For example, biomass from certain paper manufacturing processes may constitute a suitable, large, continuous and spatially concentrated resource. Most by-products from industrial processes have the advantage that they are available year round since the availability of the original biomass resource was already resolved for the manufacture of the primary product. With the declining availability of landfill and the imposition of C taxes these wastes may also have a negative value.

Apart from spatial and temporal availability of suitable feedstock, costs for these feedstocks play an important role in the accessibility of a specific resource. This aspect is discussed in more detail in Chapter 19.

Collection, pre-processing and transportation to plant

Different resources will require different methods of collection, pre-processing and transportation. The degree to which these steps are required increases the costs (see Chapter 19) as well as the potential emissions associated with them (see Chapter 18). This discussion can only be viewed as a starting point for analyses that will be critical for the development of biochar systems.

Urban waste sources will often require sorting and removal of metal and glass contamination. Some large companies (such as paper mills) may be able to process their waste on site. One of the largest obstacles of pre-processing for biochar production is the moisture content and need for pre-drying of the feedstock. Higher moisture contents result in increasing costs for transportation per unit of biochar and energy produced. If energy is captured from pyrolysis, keeping the moisture content below 10 per cent appears to be critical for several reasons:

- High moisture requires a larger feeding system to handle the increase in thermal loading (Knoef, 2005).
- This requires larger pipes and a larger gas clean-up system due to increased flow rates of the gases coming from the pyrolysing biomass.
- In turn, this can cause problems with temperature fluctuations that result in high drop-out of mixtures of biochar, bio-oil and water, creating materials handling issues and blocking of gas cleaning equipment, such as ceramic filters.

On the other hand, yields and quality of bio-oil may, for some biomass feedstocks, increase with increasing moisture content (Demirbas, 2004, 2005), showing an improved calorific value of bio-oil (Demirbas, 2008). Nevertheless, it is not clear that this is always the case, as decreasing yields of bio-oil have also been reported (Beaumont and Schwob, 1984).

In comparison, biochar yields typically increase with higher moisture. For example, change in the moisture of wood waste from dry conditions (dried at 105°C) to both 15 and 28 per cent water content increased the biochar yield by 5 per cent, irrespective of its mineral content (Gray et al, 1985). High moisture may also change the quality of biochar – for example, producing biochars that are less graphitic (Darmstadt et al, 2000) with currently unknown effects on biochar's suitability as a soil amendment.

Transportation distances are critical components of a biochar system and vary significantly between systems (see Table 9.1). Transportation of waste in urban areas will be carried out both by contractors and by the organizations, companies and households who generate the waste. Waste sources may need to be aggregated and source separated at transfer stations before going to a biochar processing plant. In general, waste streams in urban and industrial areas may provide opportunities to keep transportation needs low because they are already aggregated and, in many cases, close to energy consumption needs. In contrast, collection of distributed sources such as forest thinnings for fire prevention may be prohibitive in terms of the associated costs (Polagye et al, 2007). Transportation of biomass, in general, contributes significantly to overall costs (Caputo et al, 2005). Not only the distance, but also the type of transportation and the energy density of the transported material per unit mass or volume play a significant role. For example, energy efficiency of trains and coastal shipment is two and five times

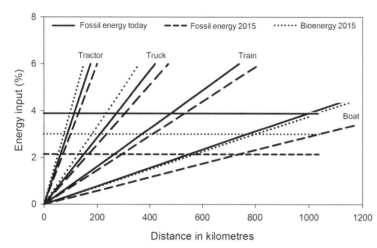

Figure 9.2 *Energy use in transportation of wood chips (*Salix*) as a percentage of energy delivered by the biomass; energy input in* Salix *production is given as horizontal lines*

Source: adapted from Börjesson (1996), with permission from the publisher

greater than truck transportation (see Figure 9.2).

In rural areas of developed countries, most of the on-farm resources can be collected using mechanized equipment. Low-density material such as straw may require bailing, while others may be harvested (such as coppiced willow or grasses) and taken directly to the biochar plant. Important differences with respect to emissions balances (Gaunt and Lehmann, 2008) and costs (Allen et al, 1998) exist between crop residue management in comparison to dedicated production of biochar feedstock. In most cases, the use of a by-product such as the straw of a grain crop has multiple advantages compared to growing a dedicated crop because all feedstock production costs (energy, emissions and financial) are covered through food production. While crop residues therefore have advantages over dedicated bioenergy crops, waste biomass such as yard wastes or animal manure are even more attractive since they currently still pose disposal issues and may even generate tipping fees. Manures that have been placed in ponds on farms require an initial dewatering and blending with biomass that has low moisture contents (such as sawdust).

Most of the collection and pre-processing in developing countries is carried out manually or with simple machines in both urban and rural areas, yet often with inefficient practices, leading to unacceptable social outcomes (Beede and Bloom, 1995). Significant improvements in the sorting process with respect to health concerns (Poulsen et al, 1995) may provide opportunities for low-cost and low-emission pre-processing. The same may apply to transportation if socially acceptable forms of moving biomass can be maintained. With increased mechanization, the presumed increasing costs of transportation fuels may make aggregation of biomass feedstock in developing countries even more challenging. The situation in developing countries is much more complex than in industrialized countries and requires considered policy intervention (UNEP, 1996).

Processing options

There are two main processing options. The first assumes that all of the waste has been aggregated at either an existing or new industrial area (or a specific industry), communal or co-operative site, central point at a forest operation, or at a waste-processing site (such as a landfill). A centralized plant will usually be larger and more expensive, but can typically operate at a lower cost per unit biochar, as shown for pyrolysis bioenergy (Dornburg and Faaij, 2001; Caputo et al, 2005; Polagye et al, 2007). Such a centralized operation will probably produce energy and, possibly, other co-products in addition to biochar, most likely in the framework of a bio-refinery (Ragauskas et al, 2006). It will be operated by skilled labour, which requires a full-time manager to organize the flow of materials in and out of the plant. In almost all cases, such processing will include the production and sale of energy. This will require biochar production units that are capable of large throughputs and production of various energy carriers that can be transported to the user. Some of the heat will be utilized internally for processing, but solutions for maximizing the energy use are necessary.

The second option is to process the resource at site, whether this is at a farm, forest or an industrial park that produces the biomass. Biochar may be the primary goal of such an operation and under certain circumstances no energy may be sold or even utilized externally at all. If no energy carrier is required, processing options can be very simple and inexpensive. It is possible that a transportable biochar unit will be developed so that waste can be processed at a number of sites throughout the year. Pure energy production with small transportable units from forest thinnings may currently not be viable from an economic point of view (Polagye et al, 2007). The question is whether biochar production could change the economic viability. Other processing options range from single household units, a small reactor at a co-operative or community enterprise where the unutilized heat is used for drying of food or building material processing, to a larger plant at a poultry production farm or for industrial waste management (see case studies). In most cases, the larger the operation, the greater is the likelihood that both biochar and energy are produced and sold. This requires different specifications for processing to meet market needs in terms of quantity and quality. Different units for a variety of biochar production options are described in Chapter 8.

Utilization of the biochar and energy

Once biochar and energy have been produced, there are a number of options for their utilization. In the simplest case, a house-

Table 9.2 *Categories of biochar systems*

Systems	Biochar use	Biochar buyer	Energy use	Category
Household, rural	Kitchen garden, sale	Collection system	Cooking, heating	Ia
Household, urban	Kitchen garden, sale	Collection system	Heating	Ib
Household farm	Kitchen garden, crop production	None, collection system	Heating, none	II
Commercial farm	Crop production, sale	Local distributors	Heating, none	III
Local commercial/ co-operative business	Sale	Local distributor	Drying, grinding, electricity	IV
Large commercial business	Sale	National–international distributor of certified biochar	Electricity, liquid fuel, heat	V

Source: chapter authors

hold, farm or a village co-operative will produce sufficient biochar for its own use (see Table 9.2). The heat may be used for grain drying or cooking. An agricultural enterprise such as a cotton-processing plant may use the biochar to improve crop production and employ the heat and the power to dry, clean and bale the product at the cotton gin. Similar approaches for combining biochar and energy use may be applied to vegetable- or fruit-producing operations.

A more complicated and yet to be tested case may be the utilization of the maize stover, local waste and distillers grain to produce biochar in the framework of a bioethanol plant. The biochar can be returned to soil to offset the C removed by the biomass harvest, could potentially reduce fertilizer needs (depending upon soil and crop type), and can contribute to the needs for heat and power required for the ethanol plant. This may lead to a more sustainable production of ethanol.

Centralized plants, farms growing trees and grasses, or large industrial plants (e.g. paper mills) will probably produce an excess of biochar, energy and other bio-products. These would be sold to markets (see Table 9.2), which demands certain requirements for both the biochar and energy product. The biochar will need to be processed to allow safe transportation and ease of application (see Chapter 12). Commercial sales of the biochar product may target either garden shops, fertilizer companies and their distribution systems, or specialized distributors for soil conditioners. The electricity or bio-oil will be sold either to a local industry or to an electricity retailer and distributor.

External factors that influence biochar systems

There are many factors that will affect the viability and sustainability of a biochar enterprise and, therefore, guide the development of biochar systems. Government policy on pricing of renewable energy and grants or subsidies for production of biomass for energy (fuels, electricity and heat) could be important in the early days of the industry. Government policy and regulations on land utilization, reforestation and protection of waterways could assist or restrict the production of biochar. National and international regulations for C trading will probably have a major impact upon biochar systems (see Chapter 18).

In developing countries, the need for a dual strategy of soil fertility management, conservation agriculture and C sequestration in soil has been recognized (Lal, 2004). In the framework of biochar management, C offset schemes to assist household or local enterprises to purchase a unit that produces both biochar and heat for food or crop processing could result in substantial adoption of the technology. Such schemes will probably need to be integrated within land management programmes to ensure that maximum benefits are achieved.

Many of these issues are reflected in the following case studies.

Biochar systems

The case studies that are presented here are not able to provide a comprehensive overview of all possible biochar systems. They may serve as a first step towards categorizing biochar systems and may demonstrate the significant differences existing between biochar systems.

Box 9.1 Large-scale bioenergy and biochar   *CASE STUDY 1*

Stephen Joseph and Phillip Watts

Generation of bioenergy is the main motivation for this biochar system, linked to large-scale production of biochar for sale through commercial distributors on regional or even international level (category V, Table 9.2). This case study discusses a scenario of linking pyrolysis energy production to cement kilns, which are major producers of CO_2 emissions. Typically, 800kg of CO_2 are released for every tonne of cement produced, half of which comes from the heating of limestone in an O_2-rich environment and half from the use of fossil fuels to heat the limestone and clay to 1400°C (van Oss and Padovani, 2002).

The cement kilns have a high flow rate of exhaust heat from both the clinker cooler system and from the exhaust stack at approximately 300°C. The waste heat can be used to dry the biomass to increase its calorific value. This case study explores the use of clean urban waste and sewage sludge to produce combustible gas and biochar.

There are a number of advantages in using a pyrolysis system where the gas is utilized directly in the cement kiln. First, there is very little unwanted contamination from the metallic elements in the cement kiln. Second, it is much easier to introduce a gas into an established cement kiln than a solid that requires complex material handling systems. If the pyrolysis kiln is operated at relatively low temperatures and the raw syngas has a high calorific value, then the flame temperature will not be to much lower (1200°C to 1250°C) than that from the combustion of the primary fuel (often coal, but also natural gas).

Approximately 170,000t of wet chipped green waste, clean commercial and demolition timber waste or wet sewage sludge are assumed to be transported to site from a major urban area located at a distance of approximately 50km. This timber waste material will be chipped and then delivered on site for approximately US$25 per tonne from a range of waste management sites. The composition of the biomass input will vary slightly due to seasonal factors; but it is probable that the calorific value of the combined feed will be 16MJ kg^{-1} to 18MJ kg^{-1} (oven dry basis) and the ash composition will vary from 3 to 10 per cent (Warnken, 2001). All of the biomass will be sieved to ensure oversized material does not enter the kiln and oversized material will be comminuted before going back into the sieve. Metals, rocks and glass will be removed before the biomass is dried in a kiln using waste heat from the cement plant and waste heat from the pyrolysis kiln. Blending will be undertaken to try and ensure that a uniform biochar is produced which complies with the relevant standards related to use of biosolids and green waste.

The input to the pyrolysis kiln is approximately 100,000t yr^{-1} (dry matter). It is expected that the output of this pyrolysis system will be approximately 35,000t of biochar with a C content of approximately 70 to 80 per cent and 65,000t of syngas. Approximately 19,000t to 24,000t of coal will be displaced, amounting to an approximate saving of US$1 million per year and a reduction in emissions of carbon dioxide (CO_2) of 46,000t yr^{-1}. For the purpose of this exercise, a C price of US$35 per tonne of CO_2e (equivalents, including greenhouse gases other than CO_2) was considered a reasonable estimate. It is expected that the biochar will be sold into the horticultural market at a price of approximately US120t^{-1}$ to US180t^{-1}$. The price will initially depend upon the mineral ash content. High calcium (Ca), potassium (K) and phosphorus (P) biochars are likely to have a higher market value. These prices are based on feedback from the Department of Primary Industries (New South Wales, Australia).

The capital cost of the materials handling equipment, dryer and pyrolysis kiln is estimated to lie between US$10 million and US$15 million. Annual operating and maintenance costs will depend on the quality of the waste and the specific configuration of the kiln but is expected to be in the order of US$500,000. A financial assessment over ten years using the above parameters shows an after-tax return exceeding 11 per cent. Importantly, this financial modelling also enabled an assessment of the financial sensitivity of input variables. Independently forcing the net present value (NPV) to zero by varying either capital cost, C price, biochar price or waste material resulted in the parameter limits of US$22 million, US$7 t^{-1}, US$83 t^{-1} and US$37 t^{-1}, respectively. The critical attribute of such an investment is to maximize the profitability of cash flows, especially the profitability of the biochar.

An important non-financial aspect identified by the modelling is the increased organizational complexity associated with the introduction of such a pyrolysis system. Compared with the traditional coal or natural gas fossil fuel systems, the site requires the management of the following additional inputs and risks:

- a US$15 million capital project using (currently) non-commercialized and somewhat specialized pyrolysis systems;
- the commercial agreements and supply management of a number of waste providers and their transport providers;
- on-site management of the new equipment and deliveries from multiple waste providers; and
- the financial risk management of future C and waste prices.

Box 9.2 Farm-scale bioenergy and biochar   CASE STUDY 2

Johannes Lehmann, Joshua Frye, Ken Davison and Stephen Joseph

Bioenergy production is the main motivation for this biochar system with on-farm feedstock production and off-farm or on-farm use of biochar (category II, Table 9.2). Frye Poultry Farm is located in Wardensville, West Virginia, and houses 99,000 chickens with seven breeding cycles per year, which generate annually about 125t to 600t of poultry litter (1.2t to 6t of litter per 1000 birds per year) (Pelletier et al, 2001; Flora and Riahi-Nezhad, 2006). The poultry litter is fed into a fixed-bed gasifier (see Figure 9.3) that has a capacity of 300kg dry litter hr^{-1} (operating temperature about 500°C) to produce heat for the three poultry houses. This heat offsets the need for 114,000L of propane gas to fuel the space heaters per year for the entire farm, which amounts to an annual saving of US$66,000 (April 2008 prices of US$2.2 per gallon). Some beneficial effects on bird weight and survival rate were noted as a result of the drier air from the heat exchanger used in conjunction with pyrolysis.

Depending upon the operating conditions, biochar has been produced with organic C contents ranging from 10 to 34 per cent. The 125t to 600t of poultry litter can be pyrolysed to generate an estimated 25t to 120t of biochar. This calculation assumes a 20 per cent recovery by total dry mass (a range of 15 to 30 per cent has been determined). Critical for the C recovery in the biochar and, hence, the total C balance and the amount of biochar is the moisture content of the poultry litter. With lower moisture contents, the C and biochar recovery increases.

The biochar is rich in P (1.7 to 3.2 per cent) and K (5.4 to 9.6 per cent) and has a fertilizer value in addition to its value as a soil conditioner. The biochar has been sold for US$480 per tonne at farm gate to be applied to soybean and hay production using a mounted spin spreader. Fertilizer savings in the amount of 20 per cent of total N applied and 100 per cent of both P and K are expected.

The combination of bioenergy production and biochar production from animal manures is a promising system that combines the needs for:

- energy for animal production;
- reduction of manure waste streams; and
- improvement of soil productivity.

The physical proximity of feedstock production and energy consumption on the same farm without creating surplus of either one is an ideal situation to keep transportation costs low. The high fertilizer value of biochar produced from poultry litter increases its monetary value; however, in this case study, this was not the primary incentive for soil application. Carbon trading has not been explored in this scenario.

Figure 9.3 *Pyrolysis unit and adjacent poultry house, Wardensville, West Virginia: biomass feedstock and energy demand are co-located with matching energy and manure disposal needs*

Source: Johannes Lehmann

Box 9.3 Household-scale bioenergy and biochar in developing countries   CASE STUDY 3

Dorisel Torres and Johannes Lehmann

Household-scale biochar systems to produce both energy and biochar as a soil amendment (category Ia, Table 9.2) address the need for energy to prepare food and restore or maintain soil fertility in resource-constrained smallholder agriculture in tropical regions. This case study presents the opportunities available to small-scale farmers to utilize on-farm residues in substitution or combination with wood as potential sources of energy and biochar production in a sustainable manner. Charles Mwoshi is a farmer in the village of Kamulembe, district of Vihiga, Tiriki, in western Kenya and has a total farm area of 2.65ha, including the homestead, which is large compared to the average of about 0.5ha in the area (Marenya and Barrett, 2007). The soils are Typic Hapludox, with a pH of 5.58, a C content of 15.1mg g^{-1} and the region has a high rainfall of about 2000mm per year (Kimetu et al, 2008). The area under agricultural production amounts to a total of 1.35ha, which consists of 0.62ha of maize and beans, 0.22ha of tea, 0.08ha of wood, 0.01ha of coffee, 0.04ha of banana trees and 0.05ha of collard greens. The remaining area is cropped with vegetables or remains fallow.

Fuel for cooking is typically harvested from the farm, which contains a tree standing biomass of 39.5t for the entire farm, or is collected from gazetted forests. The amount of wood allowed to be collected from the gazetted forest is around 34kg of wood per day (one head load). In addition, maize stalks are used as a source of fuel for cooking. Usually, maize cores are used after the harvest period and can last up to one month if used alone or three months if used in combination with wood. The production of maize cores amounted to 0.8t ha^{-1} and 0.4t ha^{-1} for long and short rain seasons, respectively (Kimetu et al, 2008). The maize stalk production for the two growing seasons is about 10t ha^{-1} with full fertilization (Kimetu et al, 2008), of which 25 per cent is used as construction materials and another 25 per cent is fed to the animals. Normally the remaining 50 per cent is left on the fields to decompose but could be source for fuel in the household if the biochar is returned to the same soil.

There is potential for the use of other sources of fuel within the farm. After harvesting, banana trees are left to decompose on the farm or are used as feed during the dry season. An estimated 75 per cent of the trees are employed as feed during this time. However, during rainy seasons with sufficient pasture production, banana trees are not used for animal feed. Instead, some of these banana stalks could be dried and used to make biochar during the process of cooking in combination with wood. The estimated biomass of banana trees on the farm is approximately 3.2t ha^{-1}. The potential use of stalks from collard green plants as fuel was acknowledged. Currently, the plants are allowed to grow until flowering and the stalks become dry and fibrous. These could serve as a source of fuel if allowed to dry fully and used in combination with other fuel resources. The amount of area planted to this crop is sufficient to produce 848kg of stalks per hectare.

The current cooking stove is the Three Stone Stove, typical of an African household. In addition, the kitchen contains an improved cooking stove called the Three Wood Stove, named for its reduced consumption of wood in comparison with the conventional stove. The household uses a total of 7.5kg of dry wood per day (2.7t yr^{-1}) to prepare typical daily meals. These biomass needs may be supplied with biomass residues available on farm (see Figure 9.4), especially if non-woody residues can be utilized, as is the case with pyrolysis. A pyrolysis unit for the delivery of the full required energy needs for food preparation would produce about 1.5kg of biochar per day (20 per cent of feedstock). As a result, the entire farm area under maize would be able to receive annually 0.5t biochar ha^{-1}. Compared with an approximate 25 to 67 per cent increase of maize grain yields achieved over three seasons, with approximately 8t biochar ha^{-1} per season on the same farm (Kimetu et al, 2008), a significant improvement in food production can be expected.

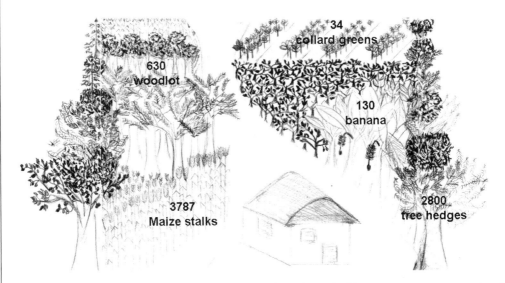

Figure 9.4 *Estimated annual production (kg yr^{-1}) of the main biomass resources appropriate for biochar and bioenergy production of a 2.7ha farm in western Kenya*

Note: Maize stalk (no N applied) from Kimetu et al (2008); greens from repeated plot sampling and destructive harvest (dried to constant weight); banana stems from allometric relationships (Hairiah et al, 2002); woody biomass from abundance and tabulated production determined for each species (Kassam et al, 1991)

Source: Torres and Lehmann, unpublished data

Box 9.4 Biochar and shifting cultivation

CASE STUDY 4

Johannes Lehmann and May Waddington

This case study illustrates the issues related to converting farming practices of slash-and-burn to slash-and-char (Lehmann et al, 2002; Lehmann and Rondon, 2006) and is motivated by the need to improve soil fertility without capturing energy (category II, Table 9.2). It also illustrates the potential issues of engaging traditional fuel charcoal producers in the production of biochar for agricultural use. This biochar system is therefore an alternative to land clearing solely by burning, but should not be understood as an alternative to forest use or forest preservation. The Fazenda Buriti Doce is a 395ha property in Maranhão, Brazil, close to the frontier with Piauí, with predominantly sandy Ultisols. This organically certified agro-ecological project is developing a role model of sustainable land use for the region. Farming in the Amazon Basin and in many other parts of the humid tropics is traditionally based on the slash-and-burn clearing method that faces significant challenges regarding the maintenance of soil productivity (Sanchez et al, 1982) and the occurrence of nutrient losses and greenhouse gas emissions during burning (Fearnside, 1997), as well as the uncontrolled spreading of fire, which all pose a significant threat to sustainable development (Nepstad et al, 2001). A local non-profit association (ASSEMA) developed improved burning methods, which results in maintenance of major trees, hauling of timber for construction, in lower and more thorough cutting of smaller branches and brush to reduce heat, in less biomass waste, and in lower risk of fire spreading. The key for the emerging biochar system lies in the hauling of wood from the area for charring prior to burning the small brush that is too small to be charred. Securing only the larger woody material from cut forest on 10ha of land required 10.5 man days per hectare (land clearing of an additional 6.5 man days per hectares was not accounted for as it would have occurred in the control scenario as well). The preparation of biochar using traditional buried kilns (so-called *caeiras*) required an additional 6.8 man days for building the kilns and 2.8 man days for unloading (per hectare). The total expenses amount to US$183 per hectare (exchange rate of US$0.608 per 1 Brazilian real in 2008) for the production of 1924kg biochar per hectare. The biochar production conditions in the buried kilns are not optimal and yields can be increased by about 60 per cent. In addition, improved kiln designs may be employed that increase biochar yields (see Chapter 8). Besides using the timber for farm buildings and fences, this biochar can be sold as charcoal at US$130 per hectare to the local fuel retail market, 30 per cent less than the actual cost of production. The costs would be covered if the biochar was directly sold to customers as fuel charcoal or even transported to the next market. However, this requires bagging, transport and licences, which the

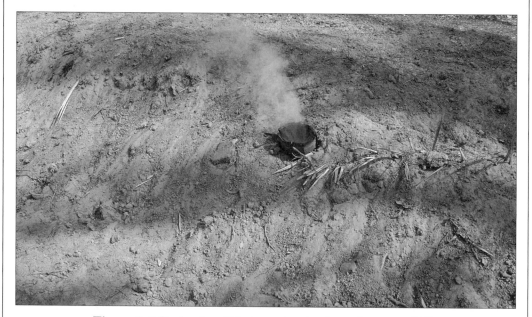

Figure 9.5 *Production of biochar using simple earthen mound kilns*

Source: M. Waddington

traditional farming families can usually not afford. The 1.9t ha^{-1} (estimated to 3t ha^{-1} to 5t ha^{-1} under optimum charring conditions in buried kilns and inclusion of all pyrolysable woody material that is not used as construction timber) applied to the same area where the feedstock was obtained is estimated to significantly increase crop production on these soils (Lehmann et al, 2003; Steiner et al, 2007). The Buriti Doce farm is currently planting an intercrop of annatto (*Bixa orellana* L.; 7000 trees per hectare) and pineapple (20,000 plants per hectare). With retail prices at farm gate of US$0.35 per pineapple (US$7000 per hectare) and of US$2.7 per kilogram of annatto (US$9675 per hectare for the first year), a 2 to 3 per cent increase in yield in either crop would offset biochar production costs already in the first year. Since crop yields on these soils are likely to increase significantly more in response to biochar additions and for multiple years (Steiner et al, 2007), biochar as a soil amendment is able to make a significant difference in farm revenue and may prove to be a sustainable alternative to the trading of biochar as charcoal fuel.

The success of a slash-and-char system will not only depend upon the financial viability but upon its sustainability with respect to environmental and social aspects, and upon the ability to integrate its practice within existing farming systems. One charcoal-maker stated that the Buriti Doce farm was 'wasting money' and 'did not know how to work'. According to his method, he would burn first and then produce biochar from the material that remained. This approach would save the labour for hauling the wood out of the area, but poses all the challenges discussed above with respect to conservation of biomass, nutrients and containment of fire. A slash-and-char system is able to address these issues. However, situating slash-and-char within an environmentally acceptable policy framework is crucial to its viability.

Box 9.5 Traditional biochar-based management of tropical soil in subsistence agriculture   *CASE STUDY 5*

Saran Sohi and Edward Yeboah

This case study from Ghana documents an example of traditional established use of biochar to maintain soil fertility in subsistence agriculture with no external inputs. The dual purpose is to maintain higher crop yield and attain sustainability of soil use (category II, Table 9.2). As for the case study in Box 9.4, the strategy is economic without any energy capture, and informal production methods are used. Unlike the case study in Box 9.4, the techniques practised in this example have evolved in the environment over the long term: the knowledge is indigenous and established. The barriers to its wider use are socio-economic, as is the barrier to technological development of the traditional practices. Asuano (7°35'N, 2°05'W) is a small village with a total population of about 760 (Adjei-Nsiah et al, 2004). It lies just 20km east of the Ivory Coast border at Sampa, and north to south halfway between Ghana's northern and southern margins. Farmers work here with scientists from Ghana's Soil Research Institute to test and evaluate soil management options. Despite lying on one of the few untarred roads connecting Ghana and Ivory Coast, the distance to the nearest town and the absence of motorized transport limits access to markets for farm products. The climate in this part of Ghana is characterized by a bimodal rainfall pattern (1271mm, mean annual temperature 26°C). The natural vegetation is 'transitional' forest contrasting with dense 'rain' forest to the south and savannah in the north. Satellite images reveal, however, a predominance of secondary forest that is heavily encroached by agriculture. A few tens of kilometres to the south the landscape is characterized by unbroken farmland and more organized agricultural activity. Soil texture is predominantly sandy and the topography undulating.

The village has a total of 270 farmers, all of whom participate in an organized democratic co-operative. According to the co-operative's leader, three-quarters of crop production is for domestic consumption – maize, plantain and coco-yam – with cashew and cocoa providing the main cash crops. Two crops are grown each year to coincide with the rainy seasons. Diminishing soil fertility and the land division are key challenges facing agriculture here. Outlying plots may be as far as 10km from habitation and extend to the ultimate boundaries in secondary forest that are defined (as is traditional) by local streams. The average landholding is 1ha and individual fragmented plots may be as small as 0.5ha. The use of chemical fertilizers is limited and, owing to tsetse-borne disease, livestock plays a minimum role in the farming systems.

Faustina Addai is among those with the largest landholding in the village, totalling 5ha; the following is based on her verbal information. Since all farming is performed with hand tools, continuous cultivation of such areas is not possible: at any point in time, half of Faustina's landholding is in cropping and the other half is undergoing short-term regeneration to secondary forest. Every five years, on average, the management is switched and regenerated vegetation 'partially burned' to enhance soil fertility for subsequent cropping. Her charring procedure is labour intensive: slashed vegetation is piled up, covered with soil and ignited. The charred product is then spread across entire plots. She emphasizes that she could farm the amended soils for as long as she wished; the switch between forest regeneration and agriculture is not a response to declining productivity, but due to the need to protect her extensive landholding from other farmers. The motive for repeated charring rather than simple one-off slash-and-char is not the maintenance of the benefits, but to gradually build them. Faustina has been practising her rotational slash-and-char regime for 20 years. She considers that her yields exceed those achieved on other farmers' land by 100 per cent. She augments these periodic inputs of biochar with annual charring of crop residues according to a similar protocol. Her perception is that the underlying mechanism for the effects she sees is entirely physical, citing two factors: enhanced rainwater infiltration and enhanced soil moisture retention. In drought-susceptible sandy soils – prevalent in most parts of Ghana – crop performance is considerably governed by the timing and extent of rainfall, and its effects on crop establishment and maturation. However, it is doubtful that productivity could be sustainably enhanced if there were not some benefit in terms of nutrient retention (see Chapter 5) – perhaps concomitant or perhaps resulting from control of nutrient release from other added organic matter to the growing crop.

With such a dramatic and demonstrable reported impact on crop productivity it is, on the face of it, surprising that Faustina's management practices have not been progressively adopted, and that the dominant land clearance practice remains open burning. Rather, the constraints to uptake are socio-economic. Previous conversations within the village suggest that farmer time horizons are diminished by the expectation that children will not continue in agriculture due to the very low cash income. More fundamentally, much land in the village is rented under informal and extremely short-term arrangements of one or two years. The land tenure situation makes investment in the soil unattractive. However, given the typical land rental rates of US$20 per hectare per year, the comparatively large returns available from engagement in the C offsetting market (see Chapter 18; Gaunt and Lehmann, 2008) should radically affect the uptake of biochar, given that there is no requirement to physically transport the commodity to market (though verification procedures would need to be defined; see Chapters 17 and 18).

The possibility of a formal village-wide engagement in the C offsetting market that would also enhance soil fertility is constrained by the size, accessibility, distribution and distance of farm plots from habitation. Specifically, moving feedstock – abundant elephant grass and *Leucaena* spp were identified in addition to crop residues – to some centralized, formal production facility, such as a kiln, and similarly the return of the biochar would demand scarce labour resources. However, concentrating on land closest to the village, where soil fertility has also declined the most, could ease this challenge.

Substituting slash-and-char for slash-and-burn in initial clearance of forest could provide baseline benefit and enduring improvement in crop production, although such additions would not be tradable.

Figure 9.6 *Highly diverse cropping system (maize, yam) with secondary forest in Ghana managed with rotational slash-and-char for 20 years*

Source: Saran Sohi

Box 9.6 Biochar production from dedicated plantations for sustainable agriculture

CASE STUDY 6

Stephen Joseph, Nikolaus Foidl and Johannes Lehmann

This biochar system is motivated mainly by the need for improving soil productivity with biochar and uses on-farm resources (category III, Table 9.2). The farm run by the agriculture company DESA is located in Santa Cruz in eastern Bolivia and has a total land holding of 24,500ha, with 14,000ha of cropland, 6000ha of forests and 3500ha of windbreaks. Crop products include lemon, soybean, maize, sunflower, sorghum, wheat, chia, beans, cotton and sesame. The soils are alluvial and silty Entisols with a pH of 6.5 to 8, low organic matter of 0.9 to 1.4 per cent and a cation exchange capacity of 170mmolc to 400mmolc kg^{-1} (0 to 0.25m). From forest and windbreak areas, 10,000m^3 of wood waste can be obtained annually that need to be removed, of which 2500m^3 are required for drying grain. The remaining biomass can be used to produce about 3000t biochar yr^{-1}. Biochar can be produced in a dedicated kiln (see Figure 9.7) at a capacity of 20t day^{-1}, operating at about 400°C, without energy capture. The costs of producing the biochar amount to about US$35 to US$40 per tonne of biochar without transportation costs, but including capital investment of US$180,000, calculated with a seven-year payback period. Since all operations of feedstock collection, biochar production and application to soil are on the same farm, transport distances are low, with an average of 20km for an entire operation. Biochar is applied at different rates of 20t ha^{-1}, 50t ha^{-1}, 100t ha^{-1} and 150t ha^{-1}. At current market prices (2008), a yield increase by 20 per cent in a sunflower and soybean rotation would increase the net earnings by US$128 and US$182 hectares per year. The business plan established by Desarollos Agrícolas SA (DESA) indicates that with an application rate of 25t ha^{-1} once, initial investments in the biochar application would be offset in six years.

Figure 9.7 *Batch kiln for production of biochar without energy capture*

Source: Nikolaus Foidl

Box 9.7 Biochar as a waste or bio-product management tool

Large biochar production systems using agricultural waste products are motivated by the opportunity to utilize by-products and the need for soil fertility maintenance and C sequestration (category IV, Table 9.2). This example presents a joint strategy of a pulp mill, a tree plantation company with an *Acacia mangium* stand of 200,000ha (with an eight- to nine-year rotation) and an energy company in Indonesia (Ogawa et al, 2006). Wood residues that cannot be used by the pulp mill with diameters of less than 80mm, or that are larger than 80mm but shorter than 1.4m, as well as twigs, leaves and dead trees amount to a total dry mass of 162,000t yr^{-1}. In addition, 14,500t of pre-processing waste accumulate per year, such as bark, tip dust or lignin waste, and can be used for biochar production. The entire biomass was calculated to produce biochar using simple drum or brick kilns, and half of the biochar from wood residues was used as a fuel. After discounting the C costs for operations, emission reductions from C sequestration alone were calculated to 15,500t C yr^{-1}. Energy capture, greater crop growth, lower fertilizer requirements or reduced emissions of greenhouse gases other than CO_2 were not part of this scenario and, if applied, would significantly decrease emissions that can be claimed (Gaunt and Lehmann, 2008).

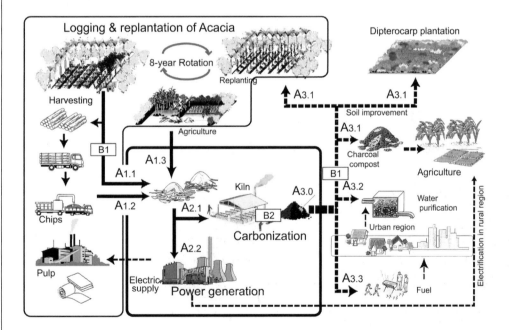

Figure 9.8 *Case study from Sumatra, Indonesia*

Note: (A1) Biomass residue: (A1.1) small stems, branches; (A1.2) bark, wood particles; (A1.3) rice husk, residue of oil palm and rubber. (A2) Resource for conversion: (A2.1) for carbonization; (A2.2) for power generation. (A3) Biochar production and utilization: (A3.1) for water purification; (A3.2) for fuel; (A3.3) for soil improvement. (B1) Fuel for transportation. (B2) Wood consumption for fuel wood.

Source: adapted from Ogawa et al (2006), with permission from the publisher

Outlook

The variety of biochar systems shown here are very different in terms of the resource base, conversion technology and product use and therefore require very different systems analyses. Critical elements are distribution of resources and biochar production and use, which are specific to a certain location. Where feedstock production, energy and biochar utilization are spatially close to each other, significant short-term opportunities for low emission exist at low investment. In addition to short transportation distances, continuity of an amount appropriate for a certain system and low moisture of the feedstock are central to a viable biochar system.

Energy production can but does not have to be part of a biochar system. In many cases, energy production is critical to the economic viability and always improves the emission balance. The opportunity to switch from biochar to energy production as a reaction to changing prices for each product may also offer advantages.

The biochar approach is scalable in a sense that biochar solutions can operate at small and large scales. However, a particular system can typically not be modified to operate at both small and large scales. In this respect, talking about 'the biochar approach' is misleading. Rather, multiple biochar approaches appear to emerge. As shown in this chapter, the solutions to biomass sourcing, pyrolysis design, energy and biochar utilization are very different for different systems. In the future, location-specific systems analyses have to be performed that are currently not available. Part of the reason for the lack of system-based assessments is the lack of sufficient information on process parameters at the scale of the operation as it will be deployed. Scale-appropriate process information will then enable meaningful system-level assessments.

References

Adjei-Nsiah, S., Leeuwis, C., Giller, K. E., Sakyi-Dawson, O., Cobbinah, J., Kuyper, T. W., Abekoe, M. and Van der Werf, W. (2004) 'Land tenure and differential soil fertility management practices among farmers in Wenchi, Ghana: Implications for interdisciplinary action research', *Wageningen Journal of Life Science*, vol 52, pp331–348

Allen, J., Browne, M., Hunter, A., Boyd, J. and Palmer, H. (1998) 'Logistics management and costs of biomass fuel supply', *International Journal of Physical Distribution and Logistics Management*, vol 28, pp463–477

Beaumont, O. and Schwob, Y. (1984) 'Influence of physical and chemical parameters on wood pyrolysis', *Industrial Engineering Chemical Research*, vol 23, p637

Beede, D. N. and Bloom, D. E. (1995) 'The economics of municipal solid waste', *The World Bank Research Observer*, vol 10, pp113–150

Börjesson, P. I. I. (1996) 'Energy analysis of biomass production and transportation', *Biomass and Bioenergy*, vol 11, pp305–318

Caputo, A. C., Palumbo, M., Pelagagge, P. M. and Scacchia, F. (2005) 'Economics of biomass energy utilization in combustion and gasification plants: Effects of logistic variables', *Biomass and Bioenergy*, vol 28, pp35–51

Darmstadt, H., Pantea, D., Sümmchen, L., Roland, U., Kaliaguine, S. and Roy, C. (2000) 'Surface and bulk chemistry of charcoal obtained by vacuum pyrolysis of bark: Influence of feedstock moisture content', *Journal of Analytical and Applied Pyrolysis*, vol 53, pp1–17

Demirbas, A. (2004) 'Effect of initial moisture content on the yields of oily products from pyrolysis of biomass', *Journal of Analytical and*

Applied Pyrolysis, vol 71, pp803–815

Demirbas, A. (2005) 'Relationship between initial moisture content and the liquid yield from pyrolysis of sawdust', *Energy Sources*, vol 27, pp823–830

Demirbas, A. (2008) 'Partial hydrogenation effect of moisture contents on the combustion oils from biomass pyrolysis', *Energy Sources*, vol 30, pp508–515

Diaz, L. F., Golueke, D. G. and Savage, G. M. (1986) 'Energy balance in compost production and use', in M. de Bertoldi, M. P. Ferranti, P. L'Hermite and F. Zucconi (eds) *Compost: Production, Quality and Use*, Proceedings of a symposium organized by the Commission of the European Communities, Udine, Italy, Elsevier, The Netherlands, pp6–19

Dornburg, V. and Faaij, A. P. C. (2001) 'Efficiency and economy of wood-fired biomass energy systems in relation to scale regarding heat and power generation using combustion and gasification technologies', *Biomass and Bioenergy*, vol 21, pp91–108

Fearnside, P. M. (1997) 'Greenhouse gases from deforestation in Brazilian Amazonia: Net committed emissions', *Climatic Change*, vol 35, pp321–360

Flora, J. R. V. and Riahi-Nezhad, C. (2006) *Availability of Poultry Manure as a [Potential] Bio-fuel Feedstock for Energy Production*, Final Report, South Caroline Energy Office, Columbia, SC, available at www.scbiomass.org/Publications/Poultry%20Litter%20Final%20Report.pdf, accessed 10 July 2008

Gaunt, J. and Lehmann, J. (2008) 'Energy balance and emissions associated with biochar sequestration and pyrolysis bioenergy production', *Environmental Science and Technology*, vol 42, pp4152–4158

Gray, M. R., Corcoran, W. H. and Gavalas, G. R. (1985) 'Pyrolysis of wood-derived material: Effects of moisture and ash content', *Industrial Engineering and Chemical Process Design Development*, vol 24, pp646–651

Hairiah, K., Arifin, J., Berlian, B., Prayogo, C. and van Noordwijk, M. (2002) 'Carbon stock assessment for a forest-to-coffee conversion landscape in Malang (East Java) and Sumber-Jaya (Lampung, Indonesia)', in *Proceedings of the International Symposium on Forest Carbon and Monitoring*, 11–15 November 2002,

Taiwan Forestry Research Institute, Taipei, Taiwan

Hoogwijk, M., Faaij, A., van den Broek, R., Berndes, G., Gielen, D. and Turkenburg, W. (2003) 'Exploration of the ranges of the global potential of biomass for energy', *Biomass and Bioenergy*, vol 25, pp119–133

Kassam, A. H., van Velthuizen, H. T., Fischer, G. W. and Shah, M. M. (1991) *Resources Data Base and Land Productivity. Agro-Ecological Land Resource Assessment for Agricultural Development Planning: A Case Study of Kenya*, Technical Annex 6: Fuelwood Productivity, World Soil Resources Report 71/6, FAO, IIASA, Rome, Italy

Kimetu, J., Lehmann, J., Ngoze, S., Mugendi, D., Kinyangi, J., Riha, S., Verchot, L., Recha, J. and Pell, A. (2008) 'Reversibility of soil productivity decline with organic matter of differing quality along a degradation gradient', *Ecosystems*, vol 11, pp726–739

Knoef, H. A. M. (2005) *Handbook Biomass Gasification*, BTG, The Netherlands

Krotscheck, C., König, F. and Obernberger, I. (2000) 'Ecological assessment of integrated bioenergy systems using the Sustainable Process Index', *Biomass and Bioenergy*, vol 18, pp341–368

Lal, R. (2004) 'Soil carbon sequestration impacts on global climate change and food security', *Science*, vol 304, pp1623–1627

Lehmann, J. (2007) 'Bio-energy in the black', *Frontiers in Ecology and the Environment*, vol 5, pp381–387

Lehmann, J. (2009) 'Terra Preta Nova – where to from here?' in W. I. Woods, W. Teixeira, J. Lehmann, C. Steiner, and A. WinklerPrins (eds) *Terra Preta Nova: A Tribute to Wim Sombroek*, Springer, Berlin, pp473–486

Lehmann, J. and Rondon, M. (2006) 'Bio-char soil management on highly weathered soils in the humid tropics', in N. Uphoff (ed) *Biological Approaches to Sustainable Soil Systems*, CRC Press, Boca Raton, pp517–530

Lehmann, J., da Silva Jr, J. P., Rondon, M., Cravo, M. S., Greenwood, J., Nehls, T., Steiner, C. and Glaser, B. (2002) 'Slash-and-char – a feasible alternative for soil fertility management in the central Amazon?' 17th World Congress of Soil Science, Bangkok, Thailand, CD–ROM Paper no, 449, pp1–12

Lehmann, J., da Silva Jr., J. P., Steiner, C., Nehls, T., Zech, W. and Glaser, B. (2003) 'Nutrient availability and leaching in an archaeological Anthrosol and a Ferralsol of the Central Amazon basin: Fertilizer, manure and charcoal amendments', *Plant and Soil*, vol 249, pp343–357

Lundie, S. and Peters, G. M. (2005) 'Life cycle assessment of food waste management options', *Journal of Cleaner Production*, vol 13, pp275–286

Marenya, P. M. and Barrett. C. B. (2007) 'Household-level determinants of adoption of improved natural resources management practices among smallholder farmers in western Kenya', *Food Policy*, vol 32, pp515–536

Moreira, R. (2006) 'Global biomass energy potential', *Mitigation and Adaptation for Global Change*, vol 11, pp313–333

Mueller, J. P., Pezo, D. A., Beintes, J. and Schlaepfer, N. P. (2003) 'Conflicts between conservation agriculture and livestock utilization of crop residues', in L. Garcia-Torres et al (eds) *Conservation Agriculture*, Kluwer Academic Publishers, Dordrecht, The Netherlands, pp221–234

Mulugetta, Y. (2006) 'Energy in rural Ethiopia: Consumption patterns, associated problems, and prospects for a sustainable energy strategy', *Energy Sources, Part A: Recovery, Utilization, and Environmental Effects*, vol 21, pp527–539

Nepstad, D. Carvalho, G., Barros, A. C., Alencar, A., Capobianco, J. P., Bishop, J., Moutinho, P., Lefebvre, P., Silva Jr., U. L. and Prins, E. (2001) 'Road paving, fire regime feedbacks, and the future of Amazon forests', *Forest Ecology and Management*, vol 154, pp395–407

Ogawa, M., Okimori, Y. and Takahashi, F. (2006) 'Carbon sequestration by carbonization of biomass and forestation: Three case studies', *Mitigation and Adaptation Strategies for Global Change*, vol 11, pp421–436

Pelletier, B. A., Pease, J. and Kenyon, D. (2001) 'Economic analysis of Virginia poultry litter transportation', *Virginia Agricultural Experiment Station Bulletin*, no 01-1, available at www.vaes.vt.edu/research/publications/index.html, accessed 15 July 2008

Polagye, B. L., Hodgson, K. T. and Malte, P. C. (2007) 'An economic analysis of bio-energy options using thinnings from overstocked forests', *Biomass and Bioenergy*, vol 31, pp105–125

Poulsen, O. M., Breum, N. O., Ebbehøj, N., Hansen, Å. M., Ivens, U. I., van Lelieveld, D., Malmros, P., Matthiasen, L., Nielsen, B. H., Møller Nielsen, E., Schibye, B., Skov, T., Stenbaek, E. I. and Wilkins, K. C. (1995) 'Sorting and recycling of domestic waste: Review of occupational health problems and their possible causes', *Science of the Total Environment*, vol 168, pp33–56

Ragauskas, A. J., Williams, C. K., Davison, B. H., Britovsek, G., Cairney, J., Eckert, C. A., Frederick Jr., W. J., Hallett, J. P., Leak, D. J., Liotta, C. L., Mielenz, J. R., Murphy, R., Templer, R. and Tschaplinski, T. (2006) 'The path forward for biofuels and biomaterials', *Science*, vol 311, pp484–489

Sanchez, P. A., Bandy, D. E., Villachica, J. H. and Nicholaides, J. J. (1982) 'Amazon basin soil: Management for continuous production', *Science*, vol 216, pp821–827

Seifritz, W. (1993) 'Should we store carbon in charcoal?', *International Journal of Hydrogen Energy*, vol 18, pp405–407

Steiner, C., Teixeira, W. G., Lehmann, J., Nehls, T., Macedo, J. L. V., Blum, W. E. H. and Zech, W. (2007) 'Long term effects of manure, charcoal and mineral fertilization on crop production and fertility on a highly weathered Central Amazonian upland soil', *Plant and Soil*, vol 291, pp275–290

UNEP (United Nations Environment Programme) (1996) *International Source Book on Environmentally Sound Technologies for Municipal Solid Waste Management*, UNEP Technical Publication 6, www.unep.or.jp/ietc/ESTdir/Pub/MSW/

van Oss, H. and Padovani, A. (2002) 'Cement manufacture and the environment, part I: Chemistry and technology', *Journal of Industrial Ecology*, vol 6, pp89–105

Warnken, M. (2001) *Utilisation Options for Wood Waste: A Review of European Technologies and Practices*, Gottstein Fellowship Report, Gottstein Trust, www.gottsteintrust.org/media/mwarnken.pdf

10

Changes of Biochar in Soil

Karen Hammes and Michael W. I. Schmidt

Introduction

Until recently, the paradigm has been that naturally occurring char (similar to certain forms of biochar) deposited in the soil is relatively inert and stable for millennia and can serve as a sink for atmospheric C (Schmidt and Noack, 2000; Forbes et al, 2006; Preston and Schmidt, 2006; Czimczik and Masiello, 2007). If char deposited by vegetation fires were inert, the Earth's carbon (C) reservoirs would be entirely converted to biochar in less than 100,000 years (Goldberg, 1985; Druffel, 2004). Although biochar pieces are still present in the dark-coloured, fertile Terra Preta soils of the Amazon thousands of years after slash-and-burn practices have ceased in the region, the majority of the highly aromatic biochar particles present in these soils are no longer recognizable as physical pieces (Glaser et al, 2001, 2002). The majority of the biochar applied and incorporated within the soil in this region of the Amazon over centuries underwent various changes and became macroscopically unrecognizable, while enriching the soil with nutrients and changing soil properties. Changes in soil properties have been recorded for different soils to which biochar was added and include increasing the cation exchange capacity and pH of the soil (Liang et al, 2006; Cheng et al, 2008), creating hydrophobic sites (Rumpel et al, 2006), and increasing adsorption sites for microbes (Baldock and Smernik, 2002; Hamer et al, 2004; Hockaday et al, 2006, 2007), minerals (Brodowski et al, 2005) or pesticides (Smernik et al, 2006).

Knowing the extent and implications of the changes that added biochar in the soil undergoes is vital for understanding the contribution that biochar can make to soil amelioration and sustainable soil management in the future. Ideally, biochar in the soil should be stable enough (i.e. change physically, chemically and biologically at a slow enough pace to provide long-term benefits to the environment, such as the biochar-rich Terra Preta soils). The topic of biochar stability is discussed extensively in Chapter 11.

The changes that biochar can undergo also depend upon its production conditions. These conditions are of great importance to achieve long-term soil enhancement – for example, its sorption properties are initially strongly influenced by the production temperature (Lehmann, 2007) and atmosphere, which determine the surface area of the particles (Brown et al, 2006). This is discussed in detail in Chapter 8. This chapter specifically looks at the mechanisms of change which biochar undergoes that are brought about by the environment to which it is added or in which it occurs. Many examples in this chapter relate to char from natural or anthropogenic burning, or char specifically produced for an experiment relating to changes in soil properties; but the changes that these char particles undergo can be applied to biochar in soil that is specifically produced and applied as a soil amendment.

Mechanisms of incorporation and movement of biochar in soil

As deliberate soil amendment (as apposed to char from vegetation fires), biochar is, in most cases, incorporated within the soil, rather than just being added on the surface where wind or water erosion can transport biochar particles (Glaser et al, 2002). Biochar has some unique properties that make it particularly susceptible to movement in the soil. Biochar can be mobilized at different scales in the landscape, ranging from fractions of metres in the soil profile that mainly involve tillage, turbation and dissolution, up to hundreds of metres through erosion of biochar from the soil.

Soil tillage

Little has been published about the application of biochar in soil (see Chapter 12). Specifically, the incorporation of biochar within the soil and its associated mobility in the soil profile is important to study since different locations in the soil's profile provide different environments for microbial activity, oxygen (O) supply and oxidation of biochar (Leifeld et al, 2007). We can gain some insight into how biochar can be incorporated and moves within the soil profile from studies where biochar, from natural or anthropogenic burning, already present in the soil was further incorporated in the soil profile. In soil that remained under sugar cane cultivation in Australia for more than 35 years, a large proportion of biochar was found in the subsoil (Skjemstad et al, 1999). There was evidence that some of this subsoil biochar had been relocated from shallower horizons via tillage. Most of this biochar pre-dated cane farming through a common historical practice to clear land under savannahs and open woodland in Australia and Southern Africa (Bird et al, 1999; Skjemstad et al, 1999). However, in some of the light-textured soils analysed in this study (Skjemstad et al, 1999), recent burning of cane could have contributed to the accumulation of biochar at depth, also by means of tillage.

Turbation

Physical mixing is not only restricted to management practices. Bioturbation is common in soils such as Alfisols and Mollisols, with high activity from earthworms and burrowing rodents, which can relocate biochar deeper in the soil (Eckmeier et al, 2007). In Vertisols, the extreme shrink–swell capacity of the soils physically mixes biochar to depth (Czimczik and Masiello, 2007).

Transport in solution (dissolution)

Over time, biochar particles can degrade to such a degree that dissolved organic carbon (DOC) of aromatic nature can be measured in soil pore water. One hundred years after char was deposited in a forest soil after a fire, Hockaday et al (2006, 2007) detected condensed aromatic ring structures with high functionality (O-containing functional groups), originating from the degradation of these char pieces, in soil pore waters. This type of finding has also been made in other places in North and South America: coastal waters off the East Coast of the US (Chesapeake Bay) (Mannino and Harvey, 2004), the Rio Negro or a black water stream from the New Jersey Pine Barrens (Kim et al, 2004). In drained peatland soils in Switzerland where wood and coal char residues were previously disposed, Leifeld et al (2007) found substantial amounts of biochar (up to 51g kg^{-1} soil) below 0.3m (ploughing depth of the soil). The large pore volume and water saturation of the soil could have led to the transport of soluble biochar down the profile (Leifeld et al, 2007). Hammes et al (2008) also found an increasing proportion of highly condensed black C (mellitic acid) in the subsoil (below 0.3m) of a recently sampled biochar-rich Chernozem soil compared to the same soil sampled 100 years earlier. Highly condensed biochar molecules are not easily degraded and are, instead, transported down the profile over time, whereas less condensed biochar is more easily broken down (Hammes et al, 2008). In another study, a mixture of biochar produced from two types of wood at 400°C was incubated with *Schizophyllum commune*, a typical wood-rotting fungus-producing exoenzyme. After 84 days, the transformation of biochar by the fungus was clearly demonstrated by the release of DOC that was rich in aromatic compounds (Wengel et al, 2006). In what way biochar-derived DOC differs in its adsorption to minerals (Kaiser and Guggenberger, 2000) is not known.

Erosion as a means of mobility in the landscape

On agricultural land subjected to slash-and-burn, with steep slopes that are prone to erosion, such as the tropical regions of northern Laos, biochar particles from burning of agricultural residues have been found to preferentially erode from the soil compared to bulk soil organic matter or mineral-bound C (Rumpel et al, 2006). Reasons for this include:

- the low density of biochar particles (Glaser et al, 2000), which even allows larger particles to float; and
- the small colloidal size of the smallest biochar particles compared to other soil components, allowing them to stay suspended for a longer period of time.

On the other hand, biochar particles bound to mineral matter are much harder to detach from the soil by splashing or to transport by discontinuous runoff (Rumpel et al, 2006). A similar set of rules apply in cold climate regions, such as northern Siberia, where permafrost stores large amounts of organic C, which includes biochar from biomass burning. The biochar in permafrost is usually protected from alteration and loss; but during snowmelt periods and concurrent surface water flow, biochar has been calculated at almost 4 per cent of the exported organic C in the stream water (Guggenberger et al, 2008). Similar to results from tropical regions, biochar was found to be mobilized in a dissolved and colloidal phase and exported from the soil. However, compared to the tropical soil and the permafrost, the mineral soil (with no permafrost) in the Siberian region did not store as much biochar as the mineral soil in the tropics, where biochar can be bound to minerals (Guggenberger et al, 2008). This could be due to a combination of unfavourable climatic conditions, reburning of biochar in organic layers and a different mineralogy in the cold climate mineral soil compared to the tropics.

Physical changes of biochar in soil

Particle fragmentation

When large biochar pieces are fragmented into smaller particles by physical means, they expose more surfaces that are accessible to further chemical and biological processes acting on these particles in the soil (Carcaillet, 2001; Cheng et al, 2006). Several processes have been identified to cause fragmentation of biochar particles in soil and are discussed below.

Freeze–thaw cycles
In places with steep temperature gradients and frequent freeze–thaw cycles (such as areas at high elevations), large biochar particles can be fragmented into smaller particles when water penetrates the pores and swell during freezing, forcing the bigger biochar particles to break (Carcaillet, 2001).

Rain and wind
Raindrops or wind may reduce the particle size of biochar from certain types of biomass (Skjemstad and Graetz, 2003). Biochar from grassland and understorey vegetation in savannahs and woodlands is more sensitive to physical impact than wood biochar (Skjemstad and Graetz, 2003). This type of fragmentation could be minimized by the incorporation of biochar amendments within the soil; but further research is needed to determine the extent of this type of fragmentation.

Penetration by plant roots and fungal hyphae
In an incubation study where biochar was mixed with soil and planted with cowpeas, biochar particles between 1mm and 20mm in size were covered with fine plant roots and sometimes even penetrated by plant roots after 45 days (Lehmann et al, 2003). This could be a possible mechanism whereby biochar particles are fragmented into smaller particles for further chemical and microbial reactions, while also directly delivering nutrients to the plant. Money (1995) describes the significant force that fungal hyphae can exert on solid materials to penetrate them, and ascribes it to increased cell turgor. Some fungi, such as *Magnaporthe*, can exert a pressure of up to 8.0MPa to penetrate a cell wall (Money, 1995, and references therein). This mechanism probably also occurs in soil when colonizing fungi penetrate and fragment biochar pieces.

Bioturbation
Small rodents and insects can actively incorporate biochar into the soil. In a slash-and-burn experiment, it was suggested that mice probably mixed biochar particles lying on the forest floor with the uppermost part of the soil (Eckmeier et al, 2007). Earthworms ingested these particles (>2mm) (but did not digest them) and redistributed them in the profile (concentrated at 0.8m depth) by excretion, as shown by thin sections of soil with small biochar particles present in earthworm casts (Eckmeier et al, 2007). In tropical organic-poor soils it was found that the earthworms do not ingest the particles, but push them aside as they burrow, or when they are ingested they are excreted in a muddy paste, transporting biochar deeper

into the soil (Glaser et al, 2000; Topoliantz and Ponge, 2003; Ponge et al, 2006). Bioturbation does not necessarily contribute to biotic transformation of biochar in soil, although it can be a first essential step, facilitating any further alteration of biochar, where particles are often ground to silt-size fractions (Ponge et al, 2006).

Pore size change with adsorption of organic matter

Biochar has a fine pore structure (depending upon the production temperature and atmosphere), which allows the trapping of different compounds physically within the pores (see Figure 10.1) (Nguyen et al, 2004; Yu et al, 2006). Biochar adsorbs organic C that is rich in functional groups (Kaiser and Guggenberger, 2000), a process which is made possible by the presence of oxidized functional groups (carboxylic and phenolic functionalities) on the surface of biochar particles (Glaser et al, 2002; Lehmann et al, 2005). Using nuclear magnetic resonance (NMR), Hockaday et al (2007) showed that biochar in soil originating from a forest fire over 100 years ago had acquired non-aromatic and O-containing functional groups during oxidation, compared to biochar from a recent fire.

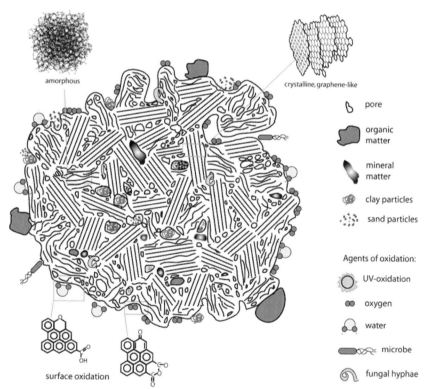

Figure 10.1 *A basic model of a complex biochar particle in the soil, containing two main distinguished structures of biochar: crystalline graphene-like sheets surrounded by randomly ordered amorphous aromatic structures and pores of various sizes*

Note: Biochar particles are subjected to surface oxidation by various agents and adsorption of non-biochar organic matter in the soil. The most important surface oxidation products, including phenol, carbonyl and carboxylic acid groups, are shown (amorphous carbon with permission under free document licence).

However, an aspect of this adsorption property that has not been investigated much is the fact that biochar pores may be blocked by the substances it is adsorbing, rendering inner pores inaccessible as further adsorption sites (Zackrisson et al, 1996; Kwon and Pignatello, 2005; Warnock et al, 2007). After 90 days of incubating maple biochar in a soil–water suspension, the total surface area reduced tenfold, probably due to the adsorption of organic matter (Kwon and Pignatello, 2005). In a complementary study, Pignatello et al (2006) determined that high molecular weight humic substances on the external surfaces of powdered wood biochar with pores smaller than 2nm blocked access to sorption sites deep within the pores and acted as competitive adsorbates. In a study on the ability of biochar to adsorb phenolic compounds, relatively fresh biochar (<100 years) could adsorb significantly more phenolic compounds than biochar from fires more than 100 years ago (Zackrisson et al, 1996). The authors suggest that, over time, biochar becomes deactivated as its pores become clogged and its sorption capacity decreases. Biochar pores from woody species are generally <20μm, which allows the entry of bacteria, fungi and certain nematodes that aid in the decomposition of the adsorbed phenols. This relationship leads to the reactivation of biochar particles (Zackrisson et al, 1996).

Another interesting phenomenon regarding polycyclic aromatic hydrocarbon (PAH) sorption to biochar was observed by Hockaday (2006). In soil rich with natural organic matter (NOM), the pyrene sorption capacity of biochar seems to decrease over a 100-year period in soil. The surface area of entire biochar particles produced in a fire in 1900 was at least half of that of recently produced biochar in 1998. However, this was not due to pore blockage by the NOM, but rather explained by the ability of NOM associated with the biochar surface to displace pyrene that would otherwise sorb to the biochar surface by multilayer stacking in the absence of NOM (Hockaday, 2006). How NOM interferes with PAH sorption to biochar particles has not been fully explained and this phenomenon requires further research.

Chemical changes of biochar in soil

An increasing number of long-term field studies give evidence that the chemical state of biochar is altered with residence time in the soil.

Non-aromatic functionality increases with residence time in soil

Fresh biochar mainly consists of a crystalline phase with graphene-like sheets and an amorphous phase of aromatic structures (see Figure 10.1 and Chapter 11; Lehmann et al, 2005; Cohen-Ofri et al, 2006). Already shortly after formation and definitely after incorporation in the soil, the outer surfaces of biochar particles undergo oxidation and interactions with various soil constituents (see Figure 10.1). These outer surfaces containing various functional groups (O- and H-containing) are exposed foremost to rapid surface oxidation (Lehmann, 2007). In a detailed study on biochar oxidation by Cheng et al (2006), results indicate that spontaneous abiotic oxidation of biochar particles takes place by chemisorption of O at high temperatures. When biochar was incubated at 70°C for four months, the acid functional groups significantly increased compared to biochar incubated at 30°C (Cheng et al, 2006). An increase in non-aromatic functionality was also recorded in biochar collected from historical charcoal blast furnaces in the US, and consisted mainly of OH bonds, carboxylic acid groups and phenolic acids (Cheng et al, 2008). Similar findings were made in Australian soils with varying biochar contents that were quantified using ultraviolet (UV) oxidation and NMR (Skjemstad et al, 1999). Apart from being rich in aryl C, these biochar samples also displayed relatively high carbonyl C peaks, which probably resulted from the partial oxidation of fine char particles. This would lead to the production of aryl carboxylic structures (Skjemstad et al, 1999). Additionally, with increasing acid functional groups, biochar can become more hydrophilic and enhance further physical, chemical, and biological weathering, such as fragmentation to smaller particles, leaching down the soil profile, forming DOC, or export from the soil profile (Shindo et al, 1986; Shindo, 1991; Haumaier and Zech, 1995; Bird et al, 1999; Kramer et al, 2004; Cheng et al, 2006).

Elemental composition change with oxidation in soil

Biochar often consists of >70% C, but also contains other elements (O, H, N, S, P, Si, base cations, heavy metals) to varying extents (see Chapter 5; Goldberg, 1985; Preston and Schmidt, 2006). The development of non-aromatic functionality initially takes place on the surface of the biochar with a resulting change in elemental composition of the biochar particles, with increasing proportions of mainly O and H (Cheng et al, 2006, 2008; Hammes et al, 2006; Hockaday et al, 2006, 2007). Apart from surface oxidation, sorption of organic matter to biochar particles can also lead to an increase in functionality, and the two mechanisms are difficult to discern. Figure 10.2 shows the H/C and O/C atomic ratios of different types of wood biochar in a van Krevelen diagram and how the biochar increases in functionality (acquires additional H and O atoms) when incubated for various lengths of time and at different temperatures compared to fresh biochar (Shindo, 1991; Baldock and Smernik, 2002; Cheng et al, 2006, 2008). The inset arrows show the main processes involved in the elemental composition change: oxidation, hydration and de-carboxylation (Hammes et al, 2006).

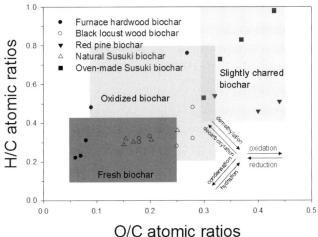

Figure 10.2 *Van Krevelen plot of the elemental composition change of five types of biochar with incubation and over time*

Note: 'Fresh biochar' implies biochar produced at around 450°C or higher. 'Oxidized biochar' implies biochar that has been subjected to oxidation conditions. 'Slightly charred biochar' implies biochar produced below 450°C. The arrows (lower right) indicate the processes involved in the change in elemental composition of biochar during its residence time in the soil under different circumstances (Hammes et al, 2006).

Source: furnace hardwood biochar: Cheng et al (2008); black locust wood biochar: Cheng et al (2006); natural Susuki plant biochar: Shindo (1991); oven-made Susuki biochar: Shindo (1991); red pine biochar: Baldock and Smernik (2002)

Changes in surface charge of biochar in soil

Cohen-Ofri et al (2006) compared the structures of modern and fossil biochar (3000 years' and 40,000 years old) and found that both types contained an inner crystalline phase composed of graphite-like microcrystals and a non-organized phase surrounding it (mainly consisting of aromatic groups). However, there were distinct differences between the modern and fossil biochar. The graphite-like phase of the fossil biochar had a higher electrical resistivity and a markedly altered surface electronic state compared to the modern biochar. This is a clear indication of the extent of surface oxidation that the fossil biochar particles had undergone. With time, the increase in functional groups (including mainly carboxyl groups, but also phenolic, hydroxyl, carbonyl or quinone C forms) leads to an evolution of surface negative charge by replacing the surface positive charge of the particles (Cheng et al, 2006, 2008). These negatively charged particles increase the charge density on the surfaces of biochar particles and are responsible for the high cation exchange capacity (CEC) in the pH range of soil (Liang et al, 2006).

Biochar interaction with different mineral phases

Mineral interactions (formation of 'organo-mineral complexes') can decrease oxidation and degradation of biochar particles (see Chapter 11; Brodowski et al, 2005) and contribute to the long mean-residence times of biochar in soil (Brodowski et al, 2006). Applying scanning electron microscopy and energy-dispersive X-ray spectrometry, Brodowski et al (2005) observed various associations of biochar particles with mineral particles in an agricultural soil in Germany (see Figure 10.3). Particle size fractionation revealed that the biochar particles occurred either as discrete particles unassociated with minerals, or as particles attached to minerals. Attachment was evident in mainly three forms:

1   free biochar particles with embedded and associated clay- and silt-sized minerals (see Figure 10.3);
2   small biochar particles bound to minerals; and
3   small mineral particles bound to large biochar particles.

In Amazonian Terra Preta soils, most biochar was found in the light soil fraction ($<2.0g$ cm^{-3}), indicating that it was not chemically stabilized, but intrinsically refractory. However, a large part of the biochar was found in the heavy soil fraction ($>2.4g$ cm^{-3}), where it was physically trapped in plaques of Fe or Al on the surface of mineral particles (Gu et al, 1995). The major part of the medium density fraction seemed to be associated with minerals (Glaser et al, 2000).

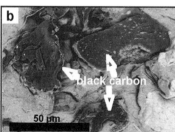

Figure 10.3 *Scanning electron micrographs of biochar particles (a) in the clay fraction and (b) in the density fraction $<2.0g$ cm^{-3}*

Source: adapted from Brodowski et al (2005), with permission from the authors and the publisher

Biotic changes of biochar in soil

Microorganisms in contact with biochar particles in the soil are able to change the amount and properties of biochar, but due to the long half-life of biochar, this effect is sometimes difficult to measure (Lehmann and Rondon, 2006). Indeed, in a short-term study (four months) of the oxidation of biochar, Cheng et al (2006) recorded significantly more abiotic oxidation on biochar than microbial (biotic) oxidation. The biochar with microbial inoculation showed no or little additional change in pH, CEC or elemental composition compared to the biochar incubated without an inoculum (Cheng et al, 2006). However, an increasing number of studies confirm that significant microbial-induced changes take place in biochar in the long term and that the initial abiotic oxidation could actually facilitate further microbial oxidation.

Fungal growth on biochar particles

Fungal hyphae growing on biochar particles in soil could be evidence that fungi may play a key role in changing biochar properties (Hockaday et al, 2007). The authors found filamentous microorganisms that infiltrated biochar particles, which were produced during a fire and deposited in the soil 100 years ago. As discussed above for pore sizes, this could influence the capacity and manner with which these overgrown particles can interact with other soil components such as minerals. The aged biochar also contained more functional groups and oxidized sites compared to fresh biochar in an adjacent soil where the forest was burned recently (Hockaday et al, 2007). On the other hand, Zackrisson et al (1996) propose that biochar particles in soil act as a foci for microbial activity, which decomposes soil organic matter that has adsorbed to the biochar surface, in this way cleaning and reactivating the surface, and effectively delaying the saturation of the biochar sorption capacity. Data from a boreal forest fire chronosequence suggests that saturation of biochar sorptive capacity for phenolic compounds requires approximately 200 years of residence time in the soil (Zackrisson et al, 1996).

Likely candidates for microbial alteration of biochar are wood-rotting and leaf litter-decaying basidiomycetes. Under oxic conditions, basidiomycetes can cleave C–C bonds in aromatic structures with extracellular enzymes (Mn-peroxidase, lignin-oxidase and laccase) in a co-metabolic process (Czimczik and Masiello, 2007, and references therein).

Other incubation studies also provide evidence for the degradation of biochar by microorganisms:

- a microbial inoculum isolated from a decomposing *Pinus resinosa* log, incubated with biochar for 120 days with partially charred material (Baldock and Smernik, 2002);
- an inoculum of coal-containing agricultural soil, incubated with biochar for 60 days (Hamer et al, 2004); and
- *Schizophyllum commune*, a typical wood-rotting fungus producing exoenzymes, incubated with biochar for 84 days (Wengel et al, 2006).

The authors of these studies did not indicate if microbes had, in fact, infiltrated the biochar particles or only mineralized them with enzymes on the outer surfaces. However, another study specifically looking at the habitation of biochar by microorganisms found that different types of biochar in soil could support various microbial communities (Pietikäinen et al, 2000).

Co-metabolism of biochar with nutrient-rich substrate

The addition of glucose has brought about positive priming effects on soil organic C under various circumstances (Hamer and Marschner, 2002) and changes to biochar properties occur to a greater extent under the addition of a nutrient-rich co-substrate. Biochar mineralization and most likely oxidation in incubated soil were increased with glucose addition by as much as 115 per cent relative to a control soil (Hamer et al, 2004). These observed positive priming effects were probably due to enhanced oxidation of the biochar materials themselves since the addi-tionally released CO_2-C largely exceeded the amount of microbial C and dissolved organic C introduced with the inoculum (Hamer et al, 2004). Biochar incubated at 30°C for four months with the addition of dairy manure showed a large change in elemental composi-tion (increase in O and decrease in C) compared to biochar incubated alone or with microorganisms (Cheng et al, 2006). In addi-tion, for biochar oxidized in a forest soil over 100 years, it is hypothesized that the oxida-tion of biochar to water-soluble condensed aromatic ring structures was accelerated by fungal co-metabolism (Hockaday et al, 2006).

Conclusions

Biochar is no longer viewed as an inert material that remains unaltered in the soil where it is deposited. Using the example of the fertile Amazonian Dark Earths, biochar is incorporated in soil with organic or inorganic fertilizer as a soil ameliorant to enhance certain soil properties such as pH, CEC and microbial proliferation. Other chapters in this book discuss the physical and structural properties (Chapter 2), microchemical prop-erties (Chapter 3), organo-chemistry (Chapter 4) and nutrient properties (Chapter 5) of biochar based on its formation conditions. These properties influence the changes that biochar can undergo in soil. After initial physical fragmentation, the most profound changes to biochar in the soil are chemical and microbial, with products including highly functionalized and nega-tively charged particles associated with clay particles or minerals (among others), as well as aromatic dissolved organic C. Due to the relative longevity of biochar in soil it is diffi-cult to estimate how long it can survive in one form or another (free particles, associated and dissolved) to serve soil fertility and act as a C sink before it is mineralized to CO_2.

Further studies on application rates, mixing and stability of biochar in the soil, under different climatic conditions, are necessary to understand its long-term role in soil fertility management. Moreover, it would be interesting to study whether it is more advantageous to add fresh biochar to the soil as an amendment compared to biochar that has been aged artificially. To this extent, the timescale of biochar change in an agronomic context is not clear yet.

References

Baldock, J. A. and Smernik, R. J. (2002) 'Chemical composition and bioavailability of thermally altered *Pinus resinosa* (red pine) wood', *Organic Geochemistry*, vol 33, pp1093–1109

Bird, M. I., Moyo, C., Veenedaal, E. M., Lloyd, J. and Frost, P. (1999) 'Stability of elemental carbon in a savanna soil'. *Global Biogeochemical Cycles*, vol 13, pp923–932

Brodowski, S., Amelung, W., Haumaier, L., Abetz, C. and Zech, W. (2005) 'Morphological and chemical properties of black carbon in physical soil fractions as revealed by scanning electron microscopy and energy-dispersive X-ray spectroscopy', *Geoderma*, vol 128, pp116–129

Brodowski, S., John, B., Flessa, H. and Amelung, W. (2006) 'Aggregate-occluded black carbon in soil', *European Journal of Soil Science*, vol 57, pp539–546

Brown, R. A., Kercher, A. K. Nguyen, T. H., Nagle, D. C. and Ball, W. B. (2006) 'Production and characterization of synthetic wood chars for use as surrogates for natural sorbents', *Organic Geochemistry*, vol 37, pp321–333

Carcaillet, C. (2001) 'Are Holocene wood-charcoal fragments stratified in alpine and subalpine soils? Evidence from the Alps based on AMS ^{14}C dates', *The Holocene*, vol 11, pp231–242

Cheng, C.-H., Lehmann, J., Thies, J. E., Burton, S. D. and Engelhard, M. H. (2006) 'Oxidation of black carbon through biotic and abiotic processes', *Organic Geochemistry*, vol 37, pp1477–1488

Cheng, C.-H., Lehmann, J. and Engelhard, M. (2008) 'Natural oxidation of black carbon in soils: Changes in molecular form and surface charge along a climosequence', *Geochimica et Cosmochimica Acta*, vol 72, pp1598–1610

Cohen-Ofri, I., Weiner, L., Boaretto, E., Mintz, G. and Weiner, S. (2006) 'Modern and fossil-charcoal: Aspects of structure and diagenesis', *Journal of Archaeological Science*, vol 33, pp428–439

Czimczik, C. I. and Masiello, C. A. (2007) 'Controls on black carbon storage in soils', *Global Biogeochemical Cycles*, vol 21, pGB3005

Druffel, E. R. M. (2004) 'Comments on the importance of black carbon in the global carbon cycle', *Marine Chemistry*, vol 92, pp197–200

Eckmeier, E., Gerlach, R., Skjemstad, J. O., Ehrmann, O. and Schmidt, M. W. I. (2007) 'Minor changes in soil organic carbon and charcoal concentrations detected in a temperate deciduous forest a year after an experimental slash-and-burn', *Biogeosciences*, vol 4, pp377–383

Forbes, M. S., Raison, R. J. and Skjemstad, J. O. (2006) 'Formation, transformation and transport of black carbon (charcoal) in terrestrial and aquatic ecosystems', *Science of the Total Environment*, vol 370, pp190–206

Glaser, B., Bashalov, E., Haumaier, L., Guggenberger, G. and Zech, W. (2000) 'Black carbon in density fractions of the Brazilian Amazon region', *Organic Geochemistry*, vol 31, pp669–678

Glaser, B., Haumeier, L., Guggenberger, G. and Zech, W. (2001) 'The "Terra Preta" Phenomenon: A model for sustainable agriculture in the humid tropics', *Naturwissenschaften*, vol 88, pp37–41

Glaser, B., Lehmann, J. and Zech, W. (2002) 'Ameliorating physical and chemical properties of highly weathered soils in the tropics with charcoal – a review', *Biology and Fertility of Soils*, vol 35, pp219–230

Goldberg, E. D. (1985) *Black Carbon in the Environment*, John Wiley and Sons, Inc, New York, NY

Gu, B., Schmitt, J., Chen, Z., Liang, L. and McCarthy, J. F. (1995) 'Adsorption and desorption of different organic matter fractions on iron oxide', *Geochimica et Cosmochimica Acta*, vol 59, pp219–229

Guggenberger, G., Rodionov, A., Shibistova, O., Grabe, M., Kasansky, O. A., Fuchs, H., Mikheyeva, N., Zhazhevskaya, G. and Flessa, H. (2008) 'Storage and mobility of black carbon in permafrost soils in the forest tundra ecotone in northern Siberia,' *Global Change Biology*, vol 14, pp1367–1381

Hamer, U. and Marschner, B. (2002) 'Priming effects of sugars, amino acids, organic acids and catechol on the mineralization of lignin and peat', *Journal of Plant Nutrition and Soil Science*, vol 165, pp261–268

Hamer, U., Marschner, B., Brodowski, S., and Amelung, W. (2004) 'Interactive priming of black carbon and glucose mineralization', *Organic Geochemistry*, vol 35, pp823–830

Hammes, K., Smernik, R. J., Skjemstad, J. O., Herzog, A., Vogt, U. F. and Schmidt, M. W. I. (2006) 'Synthesis and characterisation of laboratory-charred grass straw (*Oryza sativa*) and chestnut wood (*Castanea sativa*) as reference materials for black carbon quantification', *Organic Geochemistry*, vol 37, pp1629–1633

Hammes, K., Torn, M. S. Lapenas, A. P. and Schmidt, M. W. I. (2008) 'Centennial black carbon turnover observed in a Russian steppe soil', *Biogeosciences Discussion*, vol 5, pp661–683

Haumaier, L. and Zech, W. (1995) 'Black carbon – possible source of highly aromatic components of soil humic acids', *Organic Geochemistry*, vol 23, pp191–196

Hockaday, W. C. (2006) *The Organic Geochemistry of Charcoal Black Carbon in the Soils of the University of Michigan Biological Station*, PhD thesis, Ohio State University, US

Hockaday, W. C., Grannas, A. M., Kim, S. and Hatcher, P. G (2006) 'Direct molecular evidence for the degradation and mobility of black carbon in soils from ultrahigh-resolution mass spectral analysis of dissolved organic matter from a fire-impacted forest soil', *Organic Geochemistry*, vol 37, pp501–510

Hockaday, W. C., Grannas, A. M., Kim, S. and Hatcher, P. G. (2007) 'The transformation and mobility of charcoal in a fire-impacted watershed', *Geochimica et Cosmochimica Acta*, vol 71, pp3432–3445

Kaiser, K. and Guggenberger, G. (2000) 'The role of DOM sorption to mineral surfaces in the preservation of organic matter in soils', *Organic Geochemistry*, vol 31, pp711–725

Kim, S., Kaplan, L. A., Benner, R. and Hatcher, P. G. (2004) 'Hydrogen-deficient molecules in natural riverine water samples – evidence for the existence of black carbon in DOM', *Marine Chemistry*, vol 92, pp225–234

Kramer, R. W., Kujawinski, E. B. and Hatcher, P. G. (2004) 'Identification of black carbon derived structures in a volcanic ash soil humic acid by Fourier transform ion cyclotron resonance mass spectrometry', *Environmental Science and Technology*, vol 38, pp3387–3395

Kwon, S. and Pignatello, J. (2005) 'Effect of natural organic substances on the surface and adsorptive properties of environmental black carbon (char): Pseudo pore blockage by model lipid compounds and its implications for N_2-probed surface properties of natural sorbents', *Environmental Science and Technology*, vol 39, pp7932–7939

Lehmann, J. (2007) 'Bio-energy in the black', *Frontiers in Ecology and the Environment*, vol 5, pp381–387

Lehmann, J. and Rondon, M. (2006) 'Bio-char soil management on highly weathered soils in the humid tropics', in N. Uphoff, A. S. Ball, E. Fernandes, H. Herren, O. Husson, M. Laing, C. Palm, J. Pretty, P. Sanchez,, N. Sanginga and J. Thies (eds) *Biological Approaches to Sustainable Soil Systems*, CRC Press, Taylor and Francis Group, Boca Raton, FL, pp517–530

Lehmann, J., Pereira da Silva, (Jr), J., Steiner, C., Nehls, T., Zech, W. and Glaser, B. (2003) 'Nutrient availability and leaching in an archaeological Anthrosol and a Ferralsol of the Central Amazon basin: Fertilizer, manure and charcoal amendments', *Plant and Soil*, vol 249, pp343–357

Lehmann, J., Liang, B., Solomon, D., Lerotic, M., Luizão, F., Kinyangi, J., Schäfer, T., Wirick. S. and Jacobsen, C. (2005) 'Near-edge X-ray absorption fine structure (NEXAFS) spectroscopy for mapping nano-scale distribution of organic carbon forms in soil: Application to black carbon particles', *Global Biogeochemical Cycles*, vol 19, pGB1013

Leifeld, J., Fenner, S. and Müller, M. (2007) 'Mobility of black carbon in drained peatland soils', *Biogeosciences*, vol 4, pp425–432

Liang, B., Lehmann, J., Solomon, D., Kinyangi, J., Grossman, J., O'Neill, B. Skjemstad, J. O., Thies, J., Luizão, F. J., Petersen, J. and Neves, E. G. (2006) 'Black carbon increases cation exchange capacity in soils', *Soil Science Society of America Journal*, vol 70, pp1719–1730

Mannino, A. and Harvey, H. R. (2004) 'Black carbon in estuarine and coastal ocean dissolved organic matter', *Limnology and Oceanography*, vol 49, pp261–266

Money, N. P. (1995) 'Turgor pressure and the

mechanics of fungal penetration', *Canadian Journal of Botany*, vol 73 (Supplement 1), ppS96–S102

Nguyen, T. H., Brown, R. A. and Ball, W. P. (2004) 'An evaluation of thermal resistance as a measure of black carbon content in diesel soot, wood char, and sediment', *Organic Geochemistry*, vol 35, pp217–234

Pietikäinen J., Kiikkilä, O. and Fritze, H. (2000) 'Charcoal as a habitat for microbes and its effect on the microbial community of the underlying humus', *Oikos*, vol 89, pp231–242

Pignatello, J. J., Kwon, S. and Lu, Y. (2006) 'Effect of natural organic substances on the surface and adsorptive properties of environmental black carbon (char): Attenuation of surface activity by humic and fulvic acids', *Environmental Science and Technology*, vol 40, pp7757–7763

Ponge, J. F., Topliantz, S., Ballof, S., Rossi, J. P., Lavelle, P., Betsch, J. M. and Gaucher, P. (2006) 'Ingestion of charcoal by the Amazonian earthworm *Pontoscolex corethursus*: A potential for tropical soil fertility', *Soil Biology and Biochemistry*, vol 38, pp2008–2009

Preston, C. M. and Schmidt, M. W. I. (2006) 'Black (pyrogenic) carbon: A synthesis of current knowledge and uncertainties with special consideration of boreal regions', *Biogeosciences*, vol 3, pp397–420

Rumpel, C., Chaplot, V., Planchon, O., Bernadou, J., Valentin, C. and Mariotti, A. (2006) 'Preferential erosion of black carbon on steep slopes with slash and burn agriculture', *Catena*, vol 65, pp30–40

Schmidt, M. W. I. and Noack, A. G. (2000) 'Black carbon in soils and sediments: Analysis, distribution, implications, and current challenges', *Global Biogeochemical Cycles*, vol 14, pp777–794

Shindo, H. (1991) 'Elemental composition, humus composition, and decomposition in soil of charred grassland plants', *Soil Science and Plant Nutrition*, vol 37(4), pp651–657

Shindo, H., Matsui, Y. and Higashi, T. (1986)

'Humus composition of charred plant residues', *Soil Science and Plant Nutrition*, vol 32, pp475–478

Skjemstad, J. O. and Graetz, R. D. (2003) 'The impact of burning on the nature of soil organic matter in Australia', *Agronomia*, vol 37, pp85–90

Skjemstad, J. O., Taylor, J. A., Janik, L. J. and Marvanek, S. P. (1999) 'Soil organic carbon dynamics under long-term sugarcane monoculture', *Australian Journal of Soil Research*, vol 37, pp151–164

Smernik, R. J., Kookana, R. S. and Skjemstad, J. O. (2006) 'NMR characterization of ^{13}C-benzene sorbed to natural and prepared charcoals', *Environmental Science and Technology*, vol 40, pp1764–1769

Topoliantz, S. and Ponge, J. F. (2003) 'Burrowing activity of the geophagous earthworm *Pontoscolex corethrurus* (Oligochaeta: Glossoscolecidae) in the presence of charcoal', *Applied Soil Ecology*, vol 23, pp267–271

Warnock, D. D., Lehmann, J., Kuyper, T. W. and Rillig, M. C. (2007) 'Mycorrhizal responses to biochar in soil – concepts and mechanisms', *Plant and Soil*, vol 300, pp9–20

Wengel, M., Kothe, E., Schmidt, C. M., Heide, K. and Gleixner, G. (2006) 'Degradation of organic matter from black shales and charcoal by the wood-rotting fungus *Schizophyllum commune* and release of DOC and heavy metals in the aqueous phase', *Science of the Total Environment*, vol 367, pp383–393

Yu, X. Y., Ying, G. G. and Kookana, R. (2006) 'Sorption and desorption behaviors of diuron in soils amended with charcoal', *Journal of Agriculture and Food Chemistry*, vol 54, pp8545–8550

Zackrisson, O., Nilsson, M. C. and Wardle, D. A. (1996) 'Key ecological function of charcoal from wildfire in the boreal forest', *Oikos*, vol 77, pp10–19

11

Stability of Biochar in the Soil

Johannes Lehmann, Claudia Czimczik, David Laird and Saran Sohi

Introduction

The stability of biochar is of fundamental importance in the framework of biochar use for environmental management. There are two reasons why stability is important; first, stability determines how long C applied to soil as biochar will remain sequestered in soil and how long it may influence emissions of greenhouse gas from the pedosphere and contribute to the mitigation of climate change. Second, stability will determine how long biochar can provide benefits to soil and water quality.

Conversion of biomass to biochar followed by application of biochar to the soil increases the residence time of carbon (C) in the soil relative to the application of the same biomass directly to the soil, and therefore can be considered over particular timescales to result in a net withdrawal of atmospheric CO_2 (Lehmann, 2007a). In addition, biochar applied to soil may directly reduce emissions of other greenhouse gases, such as direct emissions of nitrous oxide or methane from soil (Yanai et al, 2007; see Chapter 13). Greenhouse gas emissions associated with

fertilizer or lime production may also be reduced through higher fertilizer-use efficiency and the liming effect of biochar (Lehmann et al, 2003; see Chapter 15). The long-term benefits of biochar additions to soil and water quality can be manifold and include improved nutrient retention and nutrient availability (see Chapter 5), reduced leaching of nutrients (see Chapter 15) and other contaminants (see Chapter 16), potentially increased water availability to plants, improved mycorrhizal activity (Warnock et al, 2007), and possible benefits to other groups of microorganisms and their function in soil (see Chapter 6).

If biochar decomposes rapidly, these benefits would be affected in extent and duration. Therefore, biochar must be of significantly greater stability in the environment than other organic matter in order to extend the duration of these benefits. This chapter explores the extent of biochar stability in soils, the mechanisms controlling its decay and stability, and implications of physical export for biochar stability.

Extent of biochar decay

Estimation of long-term stability of biochar

Ample evidence suggests that biochar is very stable in the environment. In soil, it typically has the greatest average age of any C fraction (Pessenda et al, 2001) but is not always the only form of very old C (Krull et al, 2006). Biochar as residues from forest fires is frequently found to be more than 10,000 years old in various soil ecosystems (reviewed by Preston and Schmidt, 2006). Biochar found in high proportions in the so-called 'Terra Preta' soils of the Amazon region (Glaser et al, 2001; Liang et al, 2008) have been radiocarbon dated and found to originate from 500 up to 7000 years BP (Neves et al, 2003). They provide a visually compelling proof for the longevity of biochar. Unfortunately, radiocarbon dates alone do not provide quantitative information about the decomposition rate of biochar, but rather establish the average time that has lapsed since photosynthesis formed the biomass that was pyrolysed to create the biochar currently remaining in the soil. In addition to the uncertainty around the time lag between carbon dioxide (CO_2) fixation into plant biomass, pyrolysis and deposition to soil – which can extend to a few hundred years and is already well acknowledged in research on the turnover of plant litter – decay of a one-time input of biochar cannot be quantified on the basis of its average age alone. A quantitative description of biochar decomposition can, in these cases, only be obtained if additional information about the amount of biochar at deposition is available. But since the period for which information is sought in most cases exceeds the availability of archived samples or historical records, very few opportunities may ever exist to conduct a straightforward mass balance (Hammes et al, 2008). However, the great age of biochar found in soil studies and many archaeological sites is proof of stability even with the mentioned constraints for obtaining decay rates.

Regional or global C budgeting of biochar (commonly referred to as biomass-derived black C in the scientific literature dealing with this aspect) suggests that biochar has a much greater average stability than plant litter. Global biochar production of only 0.05Gt C yr^{-1} to 0.3Gt C yr^{-1} (Forbes et al, 2006) is less than 0.5 per cent of the 60Gt C yr^{-1} estimated for global net primary productivity (Sabine et al, 2004), yet biochar concentrations are often above 10 per cent of total organic C in soils (Skjemstad et al, 1996, 2002). These data suggest a difference in decomposition rates of at least one order of magnitude. On the other hand, these global calculations also make clear that biochar is eventually mineralized to CO_2 (Schmidt, 2004), and microorganisms have been unmistakably shown to decompose biochar (Czimczik and Masiello, 2007). Future efforts in assessing the controls over sources and sinks of biochar, along with a broader effort to quantify biochar in soils on a regional to global scale, will enable calculation of decomposition rates in a more rigorous fashion.

On the spatial scale of individual sites, some estimates of turnover time of biochar is already possible if steady-state conditions of natural char production and disappearance occurred over long periods of time. By matching annual production of char by savannah fires to measured char stocks for various soils in Northern Australian woodlands, mean residence times of 718 to 9259 years were obtained (Lehmann et al, 2008). These estimates strongly depended upon the assumptions made for the proportion of char produced per unit biomass burned and the extent and frequency of biomass burning as

Box 11.1 Terminology for quantification of decay

Mineralization of soil organic carbon (SOC) to CO_2 is commonly modelled by assuming an exponential decay, with the resultant dynamic expressed as decay rate, mean residence time (equivalent to mean life time), half-life or turnover time, which can also be applied to biochar. These are not synonymous but are mathematically related. A decay rate is the exponent (k, as a function of environmental conditions) in the exponential decay function and has a unit of 1/time:

$$\text{biochar}_{(\text{at time } t)} = \text{biochar}_{(\text{at time } 0)} \, e^{-kt} \qquad\qquad [1]$$

Mean residence time (MRT) is then the inverse of the decay rate (1/k) and is the average time that biochar is present. The half-life is the time that elapses before half of the biochar decomposes and can be obtained by multiplying the mean residence time by the natural logarithm of 2. For computing the turnover time, information about the stock of biochar is required. It is calculated by dividing the stock at equilibrium by the loss per unit time.

Heterogeneous composite materials such as biochar and other natural organic matter are typically composed of a mixture of individual compounds or groups of compounds, here called 'fractions', each with different rates of decay. This may necessitate assigning multiple exponential functions to describe the overall decay process, using distinct (although usually conceptual) 'pools'. For biochar, since more recalcitrant fractions seem to predominate, simplification may be possible when considering long timescales. Such equations can be solved mathematically to yield an estimate for 'k', provided that the assumption of no interaction and no transfer of decomposition products to other pools can be made. Although this assumption cannot hold for all soil components, it may be argued for biochar. The alternate approach is multi-pool modelling typified by soil organic C models such as Century and RothC, in which material entering a pool as the product of one or more other pools is accounted for, and the status of each pool is reassessed at each successive calculation 'time step' (dynamic simulation). Thus, in this chapter 'mineralization' refers to the process by which CO_2 is emitted from a particular soil pool and which can be modelled relatively simply, and 'decomposition' refers to that which leads to both CO_2 emission and the transfers of organic by-products (such as microbial metabolites), and which demands pool-based modelling approaches.

well as biomass production. The most likely and conservative scenarios suggested mean residence times of 1300 to 2600 years under the dryland conditions of Northern Australia (Lehmann et al, 2008).

Measurements of biochar stocks in a time series or so-called chronosequence (set of sites with a common history of contrasting duration) from coastal temperate rainforest of western Vancouver suggest an average half-life of 6623 years (from Preston and Schmidt, 2006, calculated after Gavin et al,

2003). In contrast, Hammes et al (2008) calculated a turnover time of biochar from fires in a Russian steppe ecosystem of only 293 years. This study made use of an archived soil monolith taken in 1900 and proven fire suppression after 1900. In both types of studies, some uncertainty remained as to whether spatial variability affected the calculation.

Interpreting the difference of biochar stocks over time as decomposition or mineralization to CO_2, however, can lead to erroneous conclusions. Losses of biochar over time are potentially not only a result of mineralization, but also of leaching or erosion (see the following section), as well as reburning of biochar by subsequent fires (Czimczik et al, 2005). It is also conceivable that biochar is deposited by subsequent nearby fires or through sheet erosion, leading to an underestimate of decay. Losses other than mineralization may partly explain the rapid decrease in biochar stocks found after savannah burning in Zimbabwe, with calculated mean residence times of several decades (Bird et al, 1999) or after forest clearing by fire in Kenya with a calculated mean residence time of eight years (Nguyen et al, 2008).

Even during long-term decomposition, the remaining biochar still shows similar chemical characteristics and recalcitrance against microbial decay observed initially. Liang et al (2008) found no changes in aromaticity determined by X-ray techniques for biochar particles with ages ranging from 700 to 7000 years obtained from Amazonian Dark Earths. Concurrently, mineralization of biogenic organic matter in the biochar-rich dark earths (with generally more than 70 per cent biochar as a fraction of soil organic C) were identical irrespective of the age of the biochar (Liang et al, 2008). Similar results were reported over the first 100 years of biochar exposure to soil in Kenya (Nguyen et al, 2008). Surfaces of biochar particles oxidized rapidly within less than five years, while below an approximately 10nm thick surface layer the O/C ratio remained unchanged. It appears from these examples that although biochar certainly decomposes, the stability of the remaining biochar remains high over long periods of time, even though some indications exist that aging may decrease stability (Krull et al, 2006).

Short-term decomposition of biochar

Although information about short-term decay generally does not inform about long-term stability of biochar, quantification of the easily decomposable fraction of biochar is important for estimating the total amount of biochar ultimately remaining in soil, and to establish good estimates for mean residence time and prediction of long-term decay (see 'A biochar stability framework' at the end of the chapter).

In laboratory experiments, Hamer et al (2004) found a CO_2-C loss to the amount of 0.3 and 0.8 per cent of initial C for biochar produced from either oak wood or a maize/rye straw mixture at 800°C and 350°C, respectively, during a 60-day incubation at 20°C. Baldock and Smernik (2002) reported a C loss of less than 2 per cent from biochar made from *Pinus resinosa* Aiton sapwood (heated without restricting airflow at 250°C to 350°C) over 120 days (see Figure 11.1). Mineralization was even lower for aged biochars retrieved from various 130-year-old charcoal storage sites and amounted to 0.05 per cent to 0.4 per cent of initial C after 50 days (at 30°C) (Cheng et al, 2008). The average mean residence time of these biochars was estimated as 1335 years at a 10°C mean annual temperature (Cheng et al, 2008). Using a similar calculation approach with biochar from Amazonian Dark Earths (500–7000 years; Liang et al, 2008) results in a mean residence time of 4035 years for the stable pool of these very old biochars projected for a mean annual temperature of 10°C (using the Q_{10} of Cheng et al, 2008). Wardle et al (2008) found no mass loss at all after ten years of monitoring biochar decay in a boreal forest using buried mesh bags. These very low decomposition rates compared to uncharred organic matter (Baldock and Smernik, 2002) contrast with findings by Brodowski (2004), who reported 16 to 51 per cent loss of biochar (made from maize and rye residues at 350°C) during the first two years.

These differences may, to some extent, be explained by different feedstock proper-

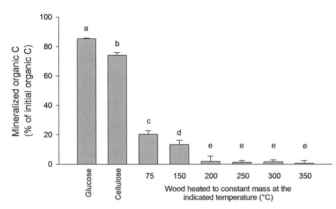

Figure 11.1 *Mineralization of organic C in glucose, cellulose and* Pinus resinosa *sapwood heated to equilibrium at increasing temperatures: bars with different letters are significantly different at P<0.05*

Source: Baldock and Smernik (2002), with permission from the publisher

ties and charring conditions used in the experiments. Another explanation may also be the different analytical approaches employed. For example, Hamer et al (2004) and Cheng et al (2008) determined the evolved CO_2-C, which should be equivalent to the C remaining in the incubation as measured by Baldock and Smernik (2002). These methods are not able to capture a decomposition of biochar if it did not lead to CO_2-C loss but only to the formation of non-biochar C such as microbial metabolites. The litterbag method used by Wardle et al (2008) may even have underestimated biochar decay due to adsorption of dissolved organic matter from the forest floor to biochar surfaces, which led to a slight increase in mass over time. On the other hand, the molecular marker method used by Brodowski (2004) would not only classify a transformation of biochar to microbial metabolites as a loss of biochar, but also surface oxidation. While surface oxidation may, indeed, initiate mineralization to CO_2 (see the following section) it may for the most part be an overestimate of C loss. Since surface oxidation of fresh biochar can be significant and very rapid (Cheng et al, 2006)

and since biochars can possess large surface areas (see Chapter 2), this overestimate of biochar decomposition could potentially be very high. One way of improving estimates of long-term stability by relatively short-term incubation experiments is to use aged biochars (Cheng et al, 2008; Liang et al, 2008). These differences have to be recognized in order to correctly interpret the results of such experiments. From a C accounting viewpoint as related to C sequestration and trading, it may be less relevant in what form the biochar is present in soil as long as it is not mineralized to CO_2.

It is also important to note that many of the incubation experiments reported in the literature were conducted in a sand medium (e.g. Baldock and Smernik, 2002; Hamer et al, 2004; some incubations from Brodowski, 2004). Exclusion of aggregation and clay–biochar interactions (see the following sections) may lead to significant overestimates of decay rates. Potentially important interactions between biochar properties and those of soil minerals are missed that could significantly affect biochar stabilization in soil, similar to uncharred organic matter.

Biochar properties and decay

The physical and chemical properties of biochar can, as outlined in detail in Chapters 2 to 5, vary considerably. Indeed, different biochar products decompose to greatly contrasting extents, as highlighted above (Brodowski, 2004; Hamer et al, 2004). In this respect, not only will the organic molecular structure differ between biochars (Czimczik et al, 2002; Bourke et al, 2007), but their mineral content and chemical composition will vary as well. Differences in mineral content and ramifications for biochar stability have rarely been assessed (and are therefore insufficiently captured in this chapter). Nevertheless, they deserve greater attention in future research. Since biochar properties may have differential effects on processes that control biochar decomposition, these properties are discussed in the individual sections below.

Mechanisms of biochar decay

Biological decomposition

The organo-chemical (see Chapter 4) and physical (Harris, 2005; Paris et al, 2005; Bourke et al, 2007; see Chapters 2 and 3) structure of biochar are the main reasons for the high stability of biochar (Schmidt and Noack, 2000) (see Figure 11.2). The diversity of cross-links in refractory macromolecules, in addition to steric protection, appears to be an important feature in the resistance of black C such as biochar to hydrolytic enzymes (Derenne and Largeau, 2001). However, biochar can be metabolized by microorganisms, and heterotrophic decomposition is the most important mechanism of biochar decay (Shneour, 1966; Baldock and Smernik, 2002; Brodowski, 2004), which is schematically presented in Figure 11.2. When microbial activity is suppressed, biochar mineralization does not occur to a significant extent (Schneour, 1966; Brodowski, 2004). The relative contribution of fungi or bacteria to the decomposition process is currently unknown (see Chapter 6). Both bacteria and fungi have been found to be located on surfaces and in the pores of biochar (see Chapter 6; Laird et al, 2008), but conclusions from mere presence to metabolization may not be valid. Fungi are more likely to metabolize biochar and the ability of, for example, white-rot fungi to metabolize coal and wood (Hofrichter et al, 1999) may suggest their importance in biochar decomposition. Extracellular enzymes such as laccase (abundant in white-rot fungi) have been shown to yield degradation products when added to biochar (Hockaday, 2006). Additions of inoculum consisting of the basidiomycete fungus *Schizophyllum commune* to biochar produced from a mixture of beech and oak wood also significantly increased decomposition, leading to an 11 per cent increase in dissolved organic C originating from biochar (Wengel et al, 2006).

Co-metabolism and priming

Numerous other organic compounds are present in soils apart from biochar and may influence its decomposition. Willmann and Fakoussa (1997) suggested that co-metabolism may be the major mechanism for the degradation of complex C forms such as brown coal. Therefore, microbial utilization of readily available sources of organic C may also promote concomitant decomposition of biochar. In laboratory experiments, additions of glucose (Hamer et al, 2004) or glucose

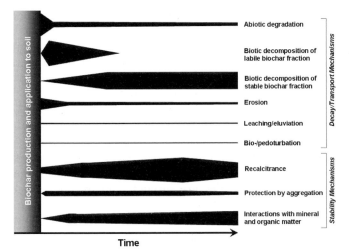

Figure 11.2

Schematic representation of the factors that may influence stability or decay and transport of biochar, and their proposed importance over time (as indicated by the thickness of the bars)

Source: chapter authors

together with nutrients (Brodowski, 2004) were, indeed, found to approximately double short-term decomposition of biochars made from oak wood, rye and maize residues. Whether the presence of easily degradable organic C is required for the decomposition of biochar is not proven but is possible.

This co-metabolism does not, however, necessarily mean that biochar decomposition is enhanced by the addition of labile organic matter, a process that is called 'priming' (Bingemann et al, 1953). Without direct evidence, it cannot be assumed that priming of biochar decay occurs to a significant extent in soils because:

- Added organic matter such as manures or crop residues are still much more recalcitrant and chemically complex than glucose and could have a different effect on biochar.
- A range of recalcitrant organic compounds beside biochar are present in soil and may be co-metabolized first if they are less resistant to decay than biochar.
- Aged biochar may behave very differently than fresh biochar, which may still have large amounts of aliphatic and aromatic surface groups.

- Interactions with both labile organic matter and mineral particles may change the behaviour of biochar in soils.

In fact, a greater increase in mineralization of uncharred soil organic matter (SOM) was found by additions of organic C (in this case, sugar cane residue) than mineralization of biochar over a period of 550 days (Liang, 2008). Nevertheless, priming of biochar decay by added labile C may exist, to some extent, in soils, and needs to be quantified. However, it may be small and possibly more important for the less aromatic fraction of biochar.

Labile compounds that cause co-metabolism may not only be found in soil but may also be intrinsic to the biochar. During pyrolysis, a range of different aliphatic materials remain in biochar (see Chapters 4 and 8). These compounds can be decomposed very rapidly within the first months of exposure to soil (Cheng et al, 2006) (see Figure 11.2). It is possible that this non-aromatic fraction of biochar accelerates the decomposition of the more aromatic fraction by co-metabolism. Proof of the existence and quantification of the extent of such a process appears to be difficult as changes in pyrolysis conditions to manipulate the quantity of the aliphatic fraction by, for example different, pyrolysis temperatures to test this hypothesis will also change the nature of the aromatic C.

Abiotic processes

Surfaces of fresh biochar are hydrophobic and have relatively low surface charge but can be rapidly transformed in soil environments (see Chapter 10). Hydrolysis and oxidation of biochar surfaces creates negatively charged carboxylate and phenolate groups after a few months of incubation (Cheng et al, 2006). During the initial stages of biochar aging in soil, this change is mainly abiotic (Cheng et al, 2006) (see Figure 11.2), although some enzymatic reactions may take place (Hockaday, 2006).

Degradation of biochar appears to also change the crystal structure of biochar (see the following section) first by oxidation of the ordered phases via a pathway to non-ordered

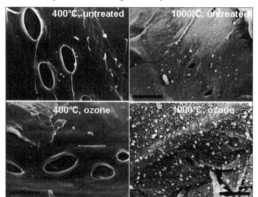

Figure 11.3 *Scanning electron micrographs of biochar samples produced from* Fagus crenata Blume *sawdust with and without ozone treatment for two hours*

Note: Biochars were produced at a heating rate of 5°C min⁻¹ either to 400°C (maintained for 24 hours) and treated with 7.3 per cent ozone or 1000°C (maintained at 500°C for 6 hours and at 1000°C for 6 hours) and treated with 3.8 per cent ozone. Bars are 5μm. Biochar produced at 1000°C showed signs of oxidation in the form of small carbonaceous deposits and pores as a result of ozone exposure.

Source: Kawamoto et al (2005), with permission from the publisher

phases (Cohen-Ofri et al, 2007). Abiotic oxidation may not be associated with a significant loss in C, but can result in the formation of polycarboxylic compounds (Decesari et al, 2002) and possibly even in a weight increase. However, such abiotic oxidation may facilitate the microbial metabolization of the otherwise highly recalcitrant aromatic ring structures and hydrophobic biochar surfaces. Abiotic oxidation tests using ozone revealed that the biochar with the greater polyaromatic structure (produced at higher temperature) oxidized on surfaces more vigorously than biochar with greater aliphatic C contents (produced at lower temperature), as shown by changes in surface morphology in Figure 11.3. It is plausible that abiotic oxidation is a necessary step towards microbial mineralization of highly aromatic biochar.

Physical breakdown of biochar

The size of biochar particles may have a significant effect on achieving microbial decay by increasing the accessible surface area and facilitating surface reactions necessary to initiate decomposition. Over time, biochar particles do become reduced in size, and 30 years after deposition to an Oxisol in Kenya, biochar particles larger than 50μm had disappeared (Nguyen et al, 2008). At the moment, it can only be speculated upon whether tillage accelerates the physical breakdown of biochar. Uncharred plant litter is typically broken down by litter transformers among the soil fauna (Brussaard, 1998), but similar observations have not been reported for biochar. In contrast, processing of biochar by soil fauna has, rather, been found to aid in its stabilization than promote its decay (see the following section).

In cold regions, seasonal freeze–thaw dynamics are conceivably of greater importance than faunal activity since biochar has a large proportion of fine pores and great internal pore space (see Chapter 2) that, once aged and hydrophilic, may be water filled.

Freezing would probably fragment biochars and render them more susceptible to transport and mineralization. In drylands, breakage during swell–shrinking dynamics of clay-rich Vertisols may occur (Gouveia and Pessenda, 2000). Whether these processes actually lead to a greater decomposition of biochar has not been demonstrated and will depend upon the extent to which stabilization mechanisms promoted by physical breakdown counteract the effect: several of the processes that stabilize organic matter and biochar rely on a small particle size and large exposed surface area (see following sections).

Stabilization of biochar in soil

Several principle mechanisms operate in soils through which organic matter entering the soil is stabilized and that significantly increase its residence time in soil. These involve its intrinsic recalcitrance, spatial separation of decomposers and substrate, and formation of interactions between mineral surfaces and organic matter (Sollins et al, 1996). The relatively stable nature of organic matter protected within aggregates or through the formation of organo-mineral interactions may also be of relevance to the stability and longevity of biochar in soil.

Recalcitrance

The conversion of organic matter to biochar by pyrolysis significantly increases the recalcitrance of C in the biomass. The composition changes through a complete destruction of cellulose and lignin and the appearance of aromatic structures (Paris et al, 2005) with furan-like compounds (Baldock and Smernik, 2002). Some differences in pyrolysis products are documented for thermal decomposition of different individual organic molecules (Knicker, 2007). Even though the clusters of condensed aromatic C remained relatively small with further heating of wood to 450°C (Czimczik et al, 2002), the mineralization rates of sapwood of *Pinus resinosa* decreased by one order of magnitude due to conversion to biochar (Baldock and Smernik, 2002). These changes in the composition of organic bonds by pyrolysis have a significant effect on the stability of biochar. Less information is available on the relevance of the crystal structure of biochar for its recalcitrance. Biochar is mainly characterized by amorphous structures and turbostratic crystallites (unordered graphene layers; see Figure 11.4b and c) that may contain defect structures in the graphene sheets with oxygen (O) groups and free radicals (Bourke et al, 2007). Ordered graphene sheets (see Figure 11.4a) were found to increase only at a carbonization temperature above 600°C (Kercher and Nagle, 2003). Carbonization temperatures for low-temperature pyrolysis would typically remain below such values (see Chapter 8). Because of their unordered structure, amorphous and turbostratic crystallites have a high stability (Paris et al, 2005), which could be one reason for the stability of biochar produced at relatively low temperatures of less than 600°C. In comparison, layers of graphene in graphite (see Figure 11.4a) are held together by comparatively weak van der Waals forces. Rounded structures may be even more stable than turbostratic structures in biochar (Cohen-Ofri et al, 2007). For cedar wood pyrolysed at 700°C, onion-like graphitic particles have been observed that are probably formed from lignin (Hata et al, 2000), but it is not clear whether these are a common feature in biochar (Shibuya et al, 1999). Round structures are known as fullerenes, molecular-scale spherical structures that include both hexagonal and pentagonal rings that have great stability

(Harris, 2005). Fullerene-related structures are probably present in biochars as folded or curved domains (see Figure 11.4d) that could contribute to its recalcitrance. Simulations of the development of fused aromatic ring structures during charring show the appearance of heptagons and, with increasing temperature, heptagons in conjunction with folding of the graphene sheets (Acharya et al, 1999; Kumar et al., 2005). Rounded features were also reported in biochars from German Chernozems with ages of 1160 to 5040 years using high-resolution transmission electron microscopy (Schmidt et al, 2002). The differences in crystal structures, their changes in soil and the importance for recalcitrance and reactions with soil material are not well documented and warrant further research.

Likewise, the effects of the mineral content on the stability of biochar have received little attention. Some biochars, such as those produced from poultry manure or rice husks, contain a large proportion of minerals. For example, poultry biochar was found to contain 45 per cent minerals (Koutcheiko et al, 2007). Knowledge about the interaction of high mineral contents with C structures in biochars is only evolving (see Chapter 3), and the implications on stability are not well understood at present.

Spatial separation

Biochar has been preferentially found in fractions of SOM that reside in aggregates rather than as free organic matter (Brodowski et al, 2006; Liang et al, 2008), which is considered to reduce its accessibility to decomposers. Biochar particles are, indeed, abundant within stable micro-aggregates (see Figure 11.5). However, Liang et al (2008) found no difference in mineralization between biochar-rich soils with 27, 10 and 0.3 per cent clay, suggesting that greater aggregation in the finer-textured soils had no influence on biochar mineralization. As shown in Chapter

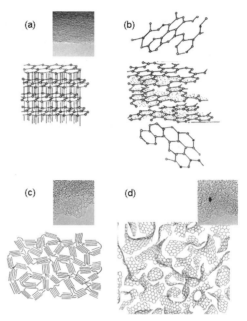

Figure 11.4 *Schematic of the structure of (a) crystalline graphite; (b) turbostratic C; (c) turbostratic crystallites (or non-graphitizing C); and (d) fullerene-type structures*

Source: Cahn and Harris (1969): turbostratic C; Franklin (1951): turbostratic crystallites; Harris (2005): fullerene-type structures. Insets are high-resolution electron micrographs from Harris et al (2000), which demonstrate the experimental evidence for the different schematics, with permission from the publishers

6 and by Laird et al (2008), microorganisms can be spatially associated with biochar in soils. Reducing accessibility by aggregation is therefore proposed to be significant in controlling biochar decomposition, but of less importance than chemical recalcitrance (see Figure 11.2).

In some soils, biochar may promote aggregation by initially forming a nucleus of biological activity and organic matter forms similar to the process described for plant litter (Tiessen and Stewart, 1988), which may lead to coatings of biochar particles with minerals (Lehmann, 2007b). If biochar, indeed, fosters proliferation of mycorrhizal fungi, as discussed by Warnock et al (2007),

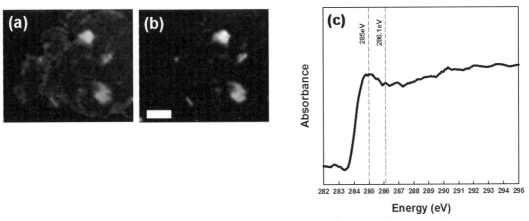

Figure 11.5 *Particulate and finely divided biochar embedded within micrometre-size aggregates from a biochar-rich Anthrosol of the central Amazon region: near-edge X-ray absorption fine structure (NEXAFS) spectroscopy coupled with scanning transmission X-ray microscopy (STXM) of (a) total C and (b) biochar-type C characterized by (c) dominance of aromatic C at 285eV and a characteristic peak at 286.1eV*

Note: Areas in white are regions rich in C. Bar is 6µm.

Source: for method see Lehmann et al (2005)

then aggregation may increase by greater abundance of fungal hyphae. The connection between mycorrhizal hyphae and aggregate abundance and stability is well established (Tisdall and Oades, 1982; Miller and Jastrow, 1990; Rillig et al, 2002). To what extent this process influences the stability of biochar is not known, and in the absence of experimental evidence, it may be considered limited (see Figure 11.2).

Ingestion and excretion of biochar by earthworms may be an important mechanism by which biochar is mixed with the soil and forms stable aggregates (Topoliantz et al, 2006). In some instances, earthworms may even preferentially ingest biochar (Topoliantz and Ponge, 2005). Such a process may prove to be useful for managing the stability of biochar. Similar information for other groups of soil fauna is not available.

The particulate form may have an important role in decreasing decomposition rates of biochar. Oxidation of biochar particles starts at its surfaces (Cheng et al, 2006) and typi-

cally remains restricted to the near-surface regions even for several millennia (Lehmann et al, 2005; Liang et al, 2006; Cohen-Ofri et al, 2007). Therefore, its particulate nature may lend stability to biochar, where the outer regions of a biochar particle protect the inner regions from access by microorganisms and their enzymes. This is considered a very important property that is responsible for much of the recalcitrance of biochar (see Figure 11.2).

Interactions with mineral surfaces

A significant portion of biochar was found in the organo-mineral fraction of soil (Brodowski et al, 2006; Laird et al, 2008; Liang et al, 2008), suggesting that biochar forms interactions with minerals. Direct spectroscopic evidence for large particles showed biochar to be embedded within the mineral matrix (Glaser et al, 2000; Brodowski et al, 2005), but can also be present as very

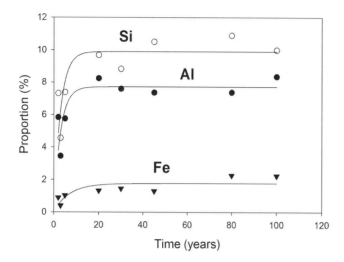

Figure 11.6 *Long-term dynamics of Si, Al and Fe on biochar surfaces originating from forest clearing in western Kenya: relative elemental proportions (percentage of total C, O, Si, Al and Fe) were obtained by wide-scan X-ray photoelectron spectroscopy (XPS) on intact particles, probing the surface properties to a depth of approximately 10nm*

Source: data from Nguyen et al (2008)

fine, yet distinguishably particulate, material within aggregates (see Figure 11.5). Therefore, finely divided biochar may indeed be able to form interactions with mineral surfaces, and vice versa.

Rapid association of biochar surfaces with Al and Si and, to a lesser extent, with Fe was found during the first decade after addition of biochar to soil (see Figure 11.6), which increased more slowly within biochar structures (Nguyen et al, 2008). It is not clear whether these associations are complexation with free Al^{3+} and Fe^{3+} or interaction with their oxides, and whether one or the other process is lending more stability to the biochar. Coating of biochar particles with mineral domains is frequently visible in soils (Lehmann, 2007b) and suggests interactions between negatively charged biochar surfaces and either positive charges of variable-charge oxides by ligand exchange and anion exchange, or positive charges of phyllosilicates by cation bridging. Concurrent increases of Si on biochar surfaces in the example shown in Figure 11.6 support the interpretation of interactions with phyllosilicates. Similarly, Ca was shown to increase biochar stability, most likely by enhancing interactions with mineral surfaces (reviewed by Czimczik and Masiello, 2007).

The relevance of electrochemical phenomena on biochar surfaces has not been sufficiently explored, but could be of importance for its interaction with mineral surfaces. Biochars carbonized at 1000°C have shown high electric conductivity (Bourke et al, 2007). The behaviour of high-mineral biochars in comparison to wood biochars that have been more commonly investigated is also a matter of ongoing research.

On the other hand, Laird et al (2008) found particulate biochar could be physically separated from an Iowa Mollisol in the coarse clay fraction (0.2 μm to 2 μm) along with quartz, feldspars, and discrete kaolinite and illite particles, whereas the finer fractions dominated by smectites were low in biochar, yet rich in biogenic organic matter (see Figure 11.7). Short-term mineralization normalized by organic C content was 48 to 78 per cent lower in coarse- than fine-clay fractions. This evidence suggests that either stabilization by the particulate nature or chemical recalcitrance of biochar is more important than by interaction with clay (as also concluded by Liang et al, 2008), or that there is a lower size limit of biochar for it to persist.

Large amounts of ionic Fe and Al were also found in biochar-type humic fractions (Nakamura et al, 2007), which may indicate that complexation between biochar surfaces and polyvalent metal ions could increase biochar stability. Decreases in mineralization rates by additions of free Al^{3+} to organic matter have been widely documented (Sollins et al, 1996). Adsorption of relatively large amounts of metals is a plausible mechanism for reducing bioavailability and, hence, stabilizing biochar.

In addition to interactions with mineral matter, biochar particles also interact with organic matter in soil, which may render biochar more stable. Surfaces of biochar were found to be coated by organic matter (Lehmann et al, 2005), mixed with biogenic organic material in soil fractions (Laird et al, 2008) and associated with microbial matter (Hockaday et al, 2007; Laird et al, 2008). Hydrophobic molecules produced from the microbial decomposition of plant cell walls may be involved in the protection of fresh biochar (Knicker and Skjemstad, 2000). In addition, 42 per cent of dissolved organic C from litter extracts were removed from solution by biochar produced from crowberry twigs (Pietikäinen et al, 2000). The reversibility of these adsorption processes and the quantitative significance for the soil C cycle is less clear, but must impact not only upon the stability of biochar but also upon that of the adsorbed organic matter (which is not the focus of this chapter).

Since aged biochar is highly oxidized and contains large amounts of negatively charged functional groups (Cheng et al, 2006; Liang et al, 2006), adsorption of hydrophilic organic matter by mechanisms similar to those applying to mineral matter would be the most likely process. Aged biochar was shown to be less prone to enzymatic degradation than relatively recently deposited biochar (Hockaday, 2006), which could be the result of either biochar–organic or biochar–mineral interactions. However, it is difficult to quantify the relative importance of such protection mechanisms in comparison to the effect of a relatively rapid decomposition of a

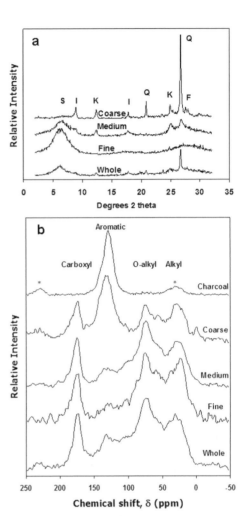

Figure 11.7 *(a) Mineralogy and (b) relative proportion of aromatic C forms as an indicator of biochar in coarse (0.2–2μm), medium (0.02–0.2μm) and fine (<0.02μm) clay fractions of a Typic Endoaquoll from Iowa, US*

Source: Laird et al (2008), with permission from the publisher

labile fraction of biochar that leaves more recalcitrant fractions characterized by lower mineralization rates (see Figure 11.1).

These interactions with mineral material and organic matter are most likely initiated soon after application to soil and gain importance over time (see Figure 11.2).

Environmental conditions affecting biochar stability and decay

Temperature sensitivity of biochar decomposition

Mineralization of organic matter generally increases with rising temperature, and biochar is no exception to this rule. Since one concern over future climate change is rising temperatures, the temperature sensitivity of biochar decay is an important question to resolve, specifically in the light of using biochar as a means of mitigating global warming (Lehmann et al, 2006). The increase in decomposition rate resulting from a 10°C rise in temperature is commonly referred to as the Q_{10}. This Q_{10} is expected to increase with greater chemical recalcitrance of an organic material (Davidson and Jannsens, 2006). Since biochar is a very recalcitrant form of organic matter, the Q_{10} may be significantly greater than for uncharred organic matter. Cheng et al (2008) calculated a Q_{10} of 3.4 between 5°C and 15°C, using a climosequence of sites in eastern North America where biochar accumulated during the 1800s as a result of the pig iron production process. This value is at the upper range of temperature sensitivity observed for different plant residues (Fierer et al, 2005). Given the much lower decomposition of biochar than uncharred litter, this calculated Q_{10} appears to be low. Litter decomposition may have very different and, most likely, greater temperature sensitivity than SOM that is in close contact and protected by mineral matter. If the mechanism of organic matter stability is physical inaccessibility to decomposition rather than chemical recalcitrance, as is often the case when organic matter is located within stable micro-aggregates or interacts with mineral surfaces, decomposition hardly increases with temperature (Davidson and Janssens, 2006). Therefore, some experimental evidence shows limited increase in mineralization of the more stable forms of SOM (Czimczik and Trumbore, 2007). If biochar shows strong interactions with the mineral matrix as described above, thereby decreasing its accessibility to enzymatic decay, temperature sensitivity may be less than what decomposition studies of isolated biochar suggest.

Transport and burial

In many field experiments, decreases in biochar content must not only be attributed to decomposition, but are, in most cases, also due to erosion, eluviation and leaching. Significant amounts of biochar at depth in various ecosystems (Skjemstad et al, 1999; Dai et al, 2005; Rodionov et al, 2006; Brodowski et al, 2007; Leifeld et al, 2007) suggest that biochar can be transported downwards in soil (Preston and Schmidt, 2006). In some cases, however, biochar distribution in a soil profile may not be the result of transport by water but of either deposition during times when the respective depth was at the surface, as in many anthropogenic soils, or of redistribution by soil faunal activity (Gouveia and Pessenda, 2000), mixing through root uplift during tree fall (Bormann et al, 1995) and through pedoturbation (Ping et al, 2005).

Direct evidence for leaching of biochar in the dissolved phase was provided by identification of aromatic structures in leachates from biochar particles, soil pore, and ground and river water (Kim et al, 2004; Hockaday et al, 2007). Direct quantification of the condensed aromatic portion of biochars derived from forest fires demonstrated a slightly preferential export of biochar from a Siberian watershed in comparison to other organic matter (Guggenberger et al, 2008). Initially, leachates from biochar appear to be aromatic and change towards a more aliphatic nature over the course of days (Bennett et al, 2004). After several years, intermediately oxidized biochar-type dissolved organic matter appears to be preferentially transported, with O/C ratios between 0.2 to 0.55, while both highly aromatic and highly oxidized biochar may be retained within the watershed (Hockaday et al, 2007). Oxidation of biochar may therefore not only be connected with gaseous losses of biochar as CO_2, but also with increases in transport by leaching and lateral export within stream networks.

Less information is available about transport of particulate biochar. Since subsoils are typically enriched in biochar (Czimczik et al, 2005; Dai et al, 2005; Brodowski et al, 2007), a likely mechanism is a transport in dissolved form. In peatlands with very large porosity of up to 91 per cent, a very rapid transport of at least 6mm yr^{-1} to 12mm yr^{-1} was estimated over 50 years for both dissolved and particulate black C of various sources, including biochar and coal char or soot (Leifeld et al, 2007).

Erosion of biochar can be a significant pathway of export from a watershed (Rumpel et al, 2006). Erosion is probably more important than leaching, especially initially after application to soil (see Figure 11.2), but direct evidence is still sparse. Biochar is then either accumulating in depressions (Bassini and Becker, 1990) or transported within aqueous systems (Guggenberger et al, 2008) and eventually deposited in fluvial or oceanic sediments (Masiello and Druffel, 1998). The extent of mineralization of biochar during transport in water is not known. However, the contribution of biochar to total C along the transport pathway from soils to sediments appears to increase rather than decrease, suggesting a decreasing turnover rate. Using a quantification method that only captures the most aromatic portion in the black C continuum, Mitra et al (2002) found up to 28 per cent of

the C transported in the Mississippi River to be composed of combustion-derived C. Using a method that fully includes biochar will most likely result in a much greater proportion. In estuary sediments in Eastern Australia, biochar made up a large proportion of the total organic C (Golding et al, 2004), underpinning the slow turnover and enrichment in sediments.

The oldest black C that invariably contains biochar was found in ocean sediments up to 13,900 years older than the age of other organic C (Masiello and Druffel, 1998), and it has been identified in sediments that are several million years old with little trend in sizes with age, indicating low decomposition over time (Herring, 1985). Black C makes up a significant portion of 15 to 31 per cent of total organic C in these sediments (Masiello and Druffel, 1998; Middelburg et al, 1999). With an increase of O_2, decomposition of uncharred organic matter in ocean sediments was found to be 83 per cent over a period of 10,000 to 20,000 years in comparison to only 64 per cent for black C (Middelburg et al, 1999). Without O_2, the biochar probably remains virtually unchanged in deep ocean sediments over geological timescales.

These results indicate that once biochar is buried in sediments under low O_2 or even anoxic conditions, the turnover time probably significantly increases compared to terrestrial environments, even though the biochar will be of less use for soil improvement. It is not clear to what degree transport within the water column of fluvial or marine environments affects overall losses of biochar.

Soil cultivation and biochar stability

Even though cultivation typically increases decomposition of SOM, this has not been found to significantly increase biochar decay. In fact, long-term cultivation of two Australian Vertisols was shown to leave the size of the UV-unoxidizable fraction of SOM, which mainly consists of biochar, largely unaffected (Skjemstad et al, 2001). As a result, the proportion of this biochar-dominated C as a fraction of total SOM increased from native savannah at 33 and 7 per cent during 50 and 45 years of cropping mainly wheat and sorghum to 53 and 27 per cent. The chemical composition of this fraction that was isolated by UV oxidation gradually changed towards a greater proportion of aryl C determined by nuclear magnetic resonance (NMR) spectroscopy, indicative of biochar (Skjemstad et al, 2001). This observation suggests that biochar was the most refractory portion of the stable C fraction during cultivation.

High proportions of biochar in SOM after long-term cultivation were also observed in the US (Skjemstad et al, 2002), Germany (Schmidt et al, 2001), Russia (Rodionov et al, 2006) and Kenya (Nguyen et al, 2008).

Nutrient management during cultivation may also affect biochar stability. Application of nutrients that limit decomposition, such as nitrogen (N) added to organic material with a high C/N ratio, typically increase its mineralization (Hobbie, 2003). Since biochar shows high C/N ratios (see Chapter 5), N fertilization could conceivably increase decomposition of applied biochar. Experimental evidence does, at present, not support this mechanism. On the contrary, an application of commercial fertilizers was not found to affect the contents of biochar-type organic matter (Brodowski et al, 2007).

A biochar stability framework

The available scientific evidence clearly demonstrates that biochar is the most stable form of organic matter that can be added to soil, even though residues of uncharred plant biopolymers also show great ages in some instances (Krull et al, 2006). However, some types of biochar can be mineralized to a significant extent in the short term and all types of biochar eventually decompose, with a complex interplay of stabilization, destabilization and transport processes that change over time (see Figure 11.2). It is therefore important to quantify the extent of short-term decomposition both for the calculation of C credits as well as for its effects on soil.

Assessing biochar decay in soil

The generally slow decay of biochar poses challenges to quantifying its longevity. Decomposition rates of plant litter have often been established experimentally by adding litter to soil and measuring its disappearance (Melillo et al, 1982). Since the turnover time of litter ranges between weeks and years, the organizational and financial commitment to such efforts is feasible. In contrast, direct measures of turnover times for biochar may require centuries to millennia, and are therefore not experimentally accessible by such an approach. For example, Wardle et al (2008) used a litterbag experiment for assessing biochar decay in the organic horizon of a boreal forest and found no mass loss after ten years.

Some studies (Baldock and Smernik, 2002; Brodowski, 2004; Hamer et al, 2004) have determined biochar decay over timescales of months to two years using incubation experiments. However, extrapolations from such short-term incubations to long-term decay are problematic because of the heterogeneity of fresh biochar and its particulate nature, as discussed by Lehmann (2007b). For example, decomposition of biochar produced from rye and maize was found to be 48 per cent of the initial biochar

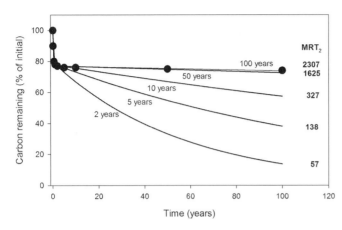

Figure 11.8 *Double-exponential model ($C_{remaining} = C_1 e^{-k_1 t} + C_2 e^{-k_2 t}$, with 1 and 2 being a labile and stable pool, respectively) fitted to hypothetical data of biochar decay after 0.1, 0.5, 2, 5, 10, 50 or 100 years, assuming data availability for either the first 2, 5, 10, 50 or 100 years*

Note: MRT_2 is the mean residence time (see Box 11.1) of the stable pool 2, calculated from the rate k_2, and is given in years.

Source: chapter authors

during the first six months of a laboratory incubation; but was only 3 per cent of initial mass greater during the following 18 months (Brodowski, 2004).

Schematically, this challenge is depicted for a hypothetical data set in Figure 11.8. The calculated MRT increases if data are available for longer periods of time. If data were only available for two years, the MRT obtained by a double-exponential model is merely 57 years for the data shown in Figure 11.8. In this hypothetical example, the MRT of the stable pool of the modelled decay (MRT_2) continued to increase significantly depending upon whether 50 or 100 years of data were available, from 1625 to 2307 years (see Figure 11.8). This example illustrates that long-term decomposition data are necessary to predict biochar decay and that extrapolations from short-term decomposition experiments are likely to fail in many instances. Considering the strongly bi-phasal dynamics of a rapid decay of the labile fraction of biochar (Brodowski, 2004), disregarding the initial mineralization may, in some cases, be a viable strategy. Omitting the first two data points and only using the data between one and ten years in Figure 11.8 resulted in a calculated MRT_2 of 2306 years – similar to the results obtained by using all data for 100 years of observation. This calculation is certainly a simplistic way of handling a complicated decay process of a mixture of compounds, but illustrates the challenges with respect to extrapolation of short-term decay data. Future modelling efforts should recognize the stabilization of decomposition products from biochar and, thus, the transfer of C from biochar to other pools of soil C.

The long-term decay rates of the more stable fractions of SOM are typically quantified *in situ* by using information about either input or output and stocks. This approach is only valid under equilibrium conditions of C input and output. However, biochar additions to soil under anthropogenic and even natural conditions are rarely continuous over the timescales of thousands of years necessary to perform such simulations as mentioned before. Exceptions may be those savannah grassland and woodland ecosystems that burn almost annually (Lehmann et al, 2008).

Monitoring biochar stability: The way forward

Notwithstanding any significant initial decomposition of biochar, the long-term stability of most biochars appears to be by at least one order of magnitude greater than that of other organic additions under the same environmental conditions (Baldock and Smernik, 2002; Cheng et al, 2008; Liang et al, 2008) and the stable fraction of biochar

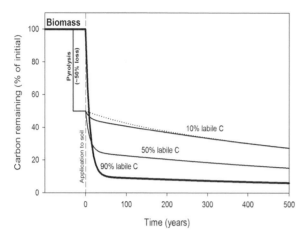

Figure 11.9 *Conceptual model of C remaining from biomass using a double-exponential decay model with a mean residence time of 10 years for the labile C pool and 1000 years for the stable C pool, but different proportions of labile C*

Note: Thin lines represent of conversion of biomass into biochar; thick line represents decomposition of uncharred biomass. Dotted line shows decomposition with 10 per cent labile C using 100 years as a mean residence time of the labile pool. Carbon losses by pyrolysis average approximately 50 per cent (Lehmann et al, 2003), but can vary significantly depending upon feedstock and production conditions (see Chapter 8).

Source: chapter authors

probably has a mean residence time of greater than 1000 years (see discussion above and Cheng et al, 2008; Lehmann et al, 2008; Liang et al, 2008). In terms of pure C accounting, this greater long-term stability compensates for the C losses during conversion of biomass to biochar by pyrolysis (see Figure 11.9). The MRT of the easily decomposable fraction is of little consequence to the difference in remaining C between a scenario where biomass was pyrolysed before adding it to soil (dashed line in Figure 11.9). For obtaining values for the emission reduction after adding biochar to soil, the decomposition of the stable fraction of biochar has to be estimated. The mean residence time of this stable fraction is estimated to be about several hundred to a few thousand years, given the available information discussed earlier in this chapter. Once this has been established, an assessment of the short-term decay and, specifically, the proportion of the relatively labile fraction may be sufficient and can be used to quantify the proportion of stable C in biochar. Better constraint to the mean residence time of the stable fraction of biochar is therefore desirable, but is of lower importance than an accurate assessment of its proportion (see Figure 11.9). Quantification schemes of the labile fraction then become the basis for classifying the stability of biochars (see Chapter 7).

Even short-term decay will most likely not be part of a routine procedure for quantifying the labile fraction of biochar. Therefore, a more comprehensive approach has to be explored that predicts long-term decay based on easily obtainable characteristics which can be assessed by rapid test methods:

• Establish relationships between biochar properties or rapid stability tests and the proportion of the labile fraction of biochar that will decompose in annual to decadal timescales. This may be achieved by incubation experiments over a few years.
• Establish the decomposition rate of the stable fraction of biochar by a combination of long-term incubation experiments with fresh and aged biochar under elevated temperature, and field experiments that either exclude physical losses or allow their quantification.
• Develop a mechanistic understanding of long-term biochar decay as a function of biochar properties and environmental conditions such as climate and soil.
• Apply the modelling framework recognizing stable and labile fractions of biochar, including decomposition products of biochar, and validate these with long-term field experiments.

References

Acharya, M., Strano, R. F., Mathews, J. P., Billinge, J. L., Petkov, V., Subramoney, S. and Foley, H. C. (1999) 'Simulation of nanoporous carbons: A chemically constraint structure', *Philosophical Magazine B*, vol 79, pp1499–1518

Baldock, J. A. and Smernik, R. J. (2002) 'Chemical composition and bioavailability of thermally altered *Pinus resinosa* (red pine) wood', *Organic Geochemistry*, vol 33, pp1093–1109

Bassini, F. and Becker, P. (1990) 'Charcoal's occurrence in soil depends on topography in *terra firme* forest near Manaus', Brazil. *Biotropica*, vol 22, pp420–422

Bennett, D., Angove, M. J., Wells, J. D., Johnson, B. B. and Baldwin, D. (2004) 'Characterisation of bushfire residues and their leachates', *SuperSoil 2004: Third Australian New Zealand Soils Conference*, 5–9 December 2004, University of Sydney, Australia, Paper 1549

Bingemann, C. W., Varner, J. E. and Martin, W. P. (1953) 'The effect of the addition of organic materials on the decomposition of an organic soil', *Soil Science Society of America Proceedings*, vol 17, pp34–38

Bird, M. I., Moyo, C., Veendaal, E. M., Lloyd, J. and Frost, P. (1999) 'Stability of elemental carbon in a savanna soil', *Global Biogeochemical Cycles*, vol 13, pp923–932

Bormann, B. T., Spaltenstein, H., McClellan, M. H., Ugolini, F. C., Cromack, K. J. and Nay, S. M. (1995) 'Rapid soil development after windthrow disturbance in pristine forests', *Journal of Ecology*, vol 83, pp747–757

Bourke, J., Manley-Harris, M,. Fushimi, C., Dowaki, K., Nonoura, T. and Antal, M. J. (2007) 'Do all carbonized charcoals have the same chemical structure? 2. A model of the chemical structure of carbonized charcoal', *Industrial and Engineering Chemistry Research*, vol 46, pp5954–5967

Brodowski, S. B. (2004) *Origin, Function, and Reactivity of Black Carbon in the Arable Soil Environment*, PhD thesis, University of Bayreuth, Bayreuth, Germany

Brodowski, S., Amelung, W., Haumeier, L., Abetz, C. and Zech, W. (2005) 'Morphological and chemical properties of black carbon in physical soil fractions as revealed by scanning electron microscopy and energy-dispersive X-ray spectroscopy', *Geoderma*, vol 128, pp116–129

Brodowski, S., John, B., Flessa, H. and Amelung, W. (2006) 'Aggregate-occluded black carbon in soil', *European Journal of Soil Science*, vol 57, pp539–546

Brodowski, S., Amelung, W., Haumaier, L. and Zech, W. (2007) 'Black carbon contribution to stable humus in German arable soils', *Geoderma*, vol 138, pp220–228

Brussaard, L. (1998) 'Soil fauna, guilds, functional groups and ecosystem processes', *Applied Soil Ecology*, vol 9, pp123–135

Cahn, R. W. and Harris, B. (1969) 'Newer forms of carbon and their uses', *Nature*, vol 221, pp132–141

Cheng, C. H., Lehmann, J., Thies, J. E., Burton, S. D. and Engelhard, M. H. (2006) 'Oxidation of black carbon by biotic and abiotic processes', *Organic Geochemistry*, vol 37, pp1477–1488

Cheng, C. H., Lehmann, J., Thies, J. E. and Burton, S. D. (2008) 'Stability of black carbon in soils across a climatic gradient', *Journal of Geophysical Research*, vol 113, pG02027

Cohen-Ofri, I., Popovitz-Niro, R. and Weiner, S. (2007) 'Structural characterization of modern and fossilized charcoal produced in natural fires as determined by using electron energy loss spectroscopy', *Chemistry – A European Journal*, vol 13, pp2306–2310

Czimczik, C. I. and Masiello, C. A. (2007) 'Controls on black carbon storage in soils', *Global Biogeochemical Cycles*, vol 21, pGB3005

Czimczik, C. I., and Trumbore, S. E. (2007) 'Short-term controls on the age of microbial carbon sources in boreal forest soils', *Journal of Geophysical Research*, vol 112, pG03001

Czimczik, C. I., Preston, C. M., Schmidt, M. W. I., Werner, R. A. and Schulze, E.-D. (2002) 'Effects of charring on mass, organic carbon, and stable carbon isotope composition of wood', *Organic Geochemistry*, vol 33, pp1207–1223

Czimczik, C. I., Schmidt, M. W. I., and Schulze, E.-D. (2005) 'Effects of increasing fire frequency on black carbon and organic matter in Podzols of Siberian Scots pine forests', *European Journal of Soil Science*, vol 56, pp417–428

Dai, X., Boutton, T. W., Glaser, B., Ansley, R. J. and Zech, W. (2005) 'Black carbon in a temperate mixed-grass savanna', *Soil Biology and Biochemistry*, vol 37, pp1879–1881

Davidson, E. A. and Jannsens, I. A. (2006) 'Temperature sensitivity of soil carbon decomposition and feedbacks to climate change', *Nature*, vol 440, pp165–173

Decesari, S., Facchinia, M.C., Mattaa, E., Mirceaa, M., Fuzzia, S., Chughtaib, A. R. and Smith, D. M. (2002) 'Water soluble organic compounds formed by oxidation of soot', *Atmospheric Environment*, vol 36, pp1827–1832

Derenne, S. and Largeau, C. (2001) 'A review of some important families of refractory macromolecules: Composition, origin, and fate in soils and sediments', *Soil Science*, vol 166, pp833–847

Fierer, N., Craine, J. M., McLauchlan, K. and Schimel, J. P. (2005) 'Litter quality and the temperature sensitivity of decomposition', *Ecology*, vol 86, pp320–326

Forbes, M. S., Raison, R. J. and Skjemstad, J. O. (2006) 'Formation, transformation and transport of black carbon (charcoal) in terrestrial and aquatic ecosystems', *Science of the Total Environment*, vol 370, pp190–206

Franklin, R. E. (1951) 'Crystallite growth in graphitizing and non-graphitizing carbons', *Proceedings of the Royal Society of London, Series A, Mathematical and Physical Sciences*, vol 209, pp196–218

Gavin, D. G., Brubaker, L. B. and Lertzman, K. P. (2003) 'Holocene fire history of a coastal temperate rain forest based on soil charcoal radiocarbon dates', *Ecology*, vol 84, pp186–201

Glaser, B., Balashov, E., Haumaier, L., Guggenberger, G. and Zech, W. (2000) 'Black carbon in density fractions of anthropogenic soils of the Brazilian Amazon region', *Organic Geochemistry*, vol 31, pp669–678

Glaser, B., Haumaier, L., Guggenberger, G. and Zech, W. (2001) 'The "Terra Preta" phenomenon: A model for sustainable agriculture in the humid tropics', *Naturwissenschaften*, vol 88, pp37–41

Golding, C. J., Smernik, R. J. and Birch, G. F. (2004) 'Characterisation of sedimentary organic matter from three south-eastern Australian estuaries using solid-state ^{13}C-NMR techniques', *Marine and Freshwater Research*, vol 55, pp285–293

Gouveia, S. E. M. and Pessenda, L. C. R. (2000) 'Datation par le ^{14}C de charbons inclus dans le sol pour l'etude du role de la remontee biologique de matiere et du colluvionnement dans la formation de latosols de l'etat de Sao Paulo, Bresil', *C. R. Acad. Sci. [Sciences de la Terre e des Planetes]*, vol 330, pp133–138

Guggenberger, G., Rodionov, A., Shibistova, O., Grabe, M., Kasansky, O. A., Fuchs, H., Mikheyeva, N., Zhazhevskaya, G. and Flessa, H. (2008) 'Storage and mobility of black carbon in permafrost soils in the forest tundra ecotone in northern Siberia', *Global Change Biology*, vol 14, pp1367–1381

Hamer, U., Marschner, B., Brodowski, S. and Amelung, W. (2004) 'Interactive priming of black carbon and glucose mineralization', *Organic Geochemistry*, vol 35, pp823–830

Hammes, K., Torn, M. S., Lapenas, A. G. and Schmidt, M. W. I. (2008) 'Centennial black carbon turnover observed in a Russian steppe soil', *Biogeosciences Discussion*, vol 5, pp661–683

Harris, P. J. F. (2005) 'New perspectives on the structure of graphitic carbons', *Critical Reviews in Solid State and Materials Sciences*, vol 30, pp235–253

Harris, P. J. F., Burian, A. and Duber, S. (2000) 'High-resolution electron microscopy of a microporous carbon', *Philosophical Magazine Letters*, vol 80, pp381–386

Hata, T., Imamura, Y., Kobayashi, E., Yamane, K. and Kikuchi, K. (2000) 'Onion-like graphitic particles observed in wood charcoal', *Journal of Wood Science*, vol 46, pp89–92

Herring, J. R., (1985) 'Charcoal fluxes into sediments of the North Pacific Ocean: The Cenozoic record of burning', in E. T. Sundquist and W. S. Broecker (eds) *The Carbon Cycle and Atmospheric CO₂: Natural Variations Archean to Present*, Proceedings of the Chapman Conference on Natural Variations in Carbon Dioxide and the Carbon Cycle, Tarpon Springs, FL, 9–13 January 1984 (A86-39426 18-46), AGU, Washington, DC, pp419–442

Hobbie, S. E. (2003) 'Interactions between litter lignin and soil nitrogen availability during leaf litter decomposition in a Hawaiian montane forest', *Ecosystems*, vol 3, pp484–494

Hockaday, W. (2006) *The Organic Geochemistry of Charcoal Black Carbon in Soils of the University of Michigan Biological Station*, PhD thesis, Ohio State University, Columbus, US

Hockaday, W. C., Grannas, A. M., Kim, S. and Hatcher, P. G. (2007) 'The transformation and mobility of charcoal in a fire-impacted watershed', *Geochimica et Cosmochimica Acta*, vol 71, pp3432–3445

Hofrichter, M., Ziegenhagen, D., Sorge, S., Ullrich, R., Bublitz, F. and Fritsche, W. (1999) 'Degradation of lignite (low-rank coal) by lignolytic basidiomycetes and their peroxidase system', *Applied Microbiology and Biotechnology*, vol 52, pp78–84

Kawamoto, K., Ishimaru, K. and Imamura, Y. (2005) 'Reactivity of wood charcoal with ozone', *Journal of Wood Science*, vol 51, pp66–72

Kercher, A. K. and Nagle, D. C. (2003) 'Microstructural evolution during charcoal carbonization by X-ray diffraction analysis', *Carbon*, vol 41, pp15–27

Kim, S., Kaplan, L. A., Benner, R. and Hatcher, P. G. (2004) 'Hydrogen-deficient molecules in natural riverine water samples: Evidence for the existence of black carbon in DOM', *Marine Chemistry*, vol 92, pp225–234

Knicker, H. (2007) 'How does fire affect the nature and stability of soil organic nitrogen and carbon?', *Biogeochemistry*, vol 85, pp91–118

Knicker, H. and Skjemstad, J. O. (2000) 'Nature of organic carbon and nitrogen in physically protected organic matter of some Australian soils as revealed by solid-state ^{13}C and ^{15}N NMR spectroscopy', *Australian Journal of Soil Research*, vol 38, pp113–127

Koutcheiko, S., Monreal, C. M., Kodama, H., McCracken, T. and Kotlyar, L. (2007) 'Preparation and characterization of activated carbon derived from the thermo-chemical conversion of chicken manure', *Bioresource Technology*, vol 98, pp2459–2464

Krull, E. S., Swanston, C. W., Skjemstad, J. O. and McGowan, J. A. (2006) 'Importance of charcoal in determining the age and chemistry of organic carbon in surface soils', *Journal of Geophysical Research*, vol 111, pG04001

Kumar, A., Lobo, R. F. and Wagner, N. J. (2005) 'Porous amorphous carbon models from periodic Gaussian chains of amorphous polymers', *Carbon*, vol 43, pp3099–3111

Laird, D. A., Chappell, M. A., Martens, D. A., Wershaw, R. L. and Thompson, M. (2008) 'Distinguishing black carbon from biogenic humic substances in soil clay fractions', *Geoderma*, vol 143, pp115–122

Lehmann, J. (2007a) 'A handful of carbon', *Nature*, vol 447, pp143–144

Lehmann, J. (2007b) 'Bio-energy in the black', *Frontiers in Ecology and the Environment*, vol 5, pp381–387

Lehmann, J., da Silva Jr., J. P., Steiner, C., Nehls, T., Zech, W. and Glaser, B. (2003) 'Nutrient availability and leaching in an archaeological Anthrosol and a Ferralsol of the Central Amazon basin: Fertilizer, manure and charcoal amendments', *Plant and Soil*, vol 249, pp343–357

Lehmann, J., Liang, B., Solomon, D., Lerotic, M., Luizão, F., Kinyangi, J., Schäfer, T., Wirick, S., and Jacobsen, C. (2005) 'Near-edge X-ray absorption fine structure (NEXAFS) spectroscopy for mapping nano-scale distribution of organic carbon forms in soil: Application to black carbon particles', *Global Biogeochemical Cycles*, vol 19, pGB1013

Lehmann, J., Gaunt, J. and Rondon, M. (2006) 'Bio-char sequestration in terrestrial ecosystems – a review', *Mitigation and Adaptation Strategies for Global Change*, vol 11, pp403–427

Lehmann, J., Skjemstad, J. O., Sohi, S., Carter, J., Barson, M., Falloon, P., Coleman, K., Woodbury, P. and Krull, E. (2008) 'Australian climate-carbon cycle feedback reduced by soil black carbon'; *Nature Geoscience*, vol 1, pp832–835

Leifeld, J., Fenner, S. and Müller, M. (2007) 'Mobility of black carbon in drained peatland soils', *Biogeosciences*, vol 4, pp425–432

Liang, B. (2008) *Black Carbon Biogeochemistry in Soils*, PhD thesis, Cornell University, Ithaca, NY

Liang, B., Lehmann, J., Solomon, D., Kinyangi, J., Grossman, J., O'Neill, B., Skjemstad, J. O., Thies, J., Luizão, F. J., Petersen, J. and Neves, E. G. (2006) 'Black carbon increases cation exchange capacity in soils', *Soil Science Society of America Journal*, vol 70, pp1719–1730

Liang, B., Lehmann, J., Solomon, D., Sohi, S., Thies, J. E., Skjemstad, J. O., Luizão, F. J., Engelhard, M. H., Neves, E. G. and Wirick, S. (2008) 'Stability of biomass-derived black carbon in soils'; *Geochimica et Cosmochimica Acta*, vol 72, pp6078–6096

Masiello, C. A. and Druffel, E. R. M. (1998) 'Black carbon in deep-sea sediments', *Science*, vol 280, pp1911–1913

Melillo, J. M., Aber, J. D. and Muratore, J. F. (1982) 'Nitrogen and lignin control of hardwood leaf litter decomposition dynamics', *Ecology*, vol 63, pp621–626

Middelburg, J. J., Nieuwenhuize, J. and Breugel, P. V. (1999) 'Black carbon in marine sediments', *Marine Chemistry*, vol 65, pp245–252

Miller, R. M. and Jastrow, J. D. (1990) 'Hierarchy of root and mycorrhizal fungal interactions with soil aggregation', *Soil Biology and Biochemistry*, vol 22, pp579–584

Mitra, A., Bianchi, T. S., McKee, B. A. and Sutula, M. (2002) 'Black carbon from the Mississippi River: Quantities, sources, and potential implications for the global carbon cycle', *Environmental Science and Technology*, vol 36, pp2296–2302

Nakamura, S., Hiraoka, M., Matsumoto, E., Tamura, K. and Higashi, T. (2007) 'Humus composition of Amazonian Dark Earths in the Middle Amazon, Brazil', *Soil Science and Plant Nutrition*, vol 53, pp229–235

Neves, E. G., Petersen, J. B., Bartone, R. N. and Silva, C. A. D. (2003) 'Historical and socio-cultural origins of Amazonian Dark Earths', in J. Lehmann, D.C. Kern, B. Glaser and W. I. Woods (eds) *Amazonian Dark Earths: Origin, Properties, Management*, Kluwer Academic Publishers, Dordrecht, The Netherlands, pp29–50

Nguyen, B., Lehmann, J., Kinyangi, J., Smernik, R. and Engelhard, M. H. (2008) 'Long-term black carbon dynamics in cultivated soil', *Biogeochemistry*, vol 89, pp295–308

Paris, O., Zollfrank, C. and Zickler, G. A. (2005) 'Decomposition and carbonisation of wood biopolymers – a microstructural study of softwood pyrolysis', *Carbon*, vol 43, pp53–66

Pessenda, L. C. R., Boulet, R., Aravena, R., Rosolen, V., Gouveia, S. E. M., Ribeiro, A. S. and Lamotte, M. (2001) 'Origin and dynamics of soil organic matter and vegetation changes during the Holocene in a forest-savanna transition zone, Brazilian Amazon region', *Holocene*, vol 11, pp250–254

Pietikäinen, J., Kiikkila, O. and Fritze, H. (2000) 'Charcoal as a habitat for microbes and its effect on the microbial community of the underlying humus', *Oikos*, vol 89, pp231–242

Ping, C. L., Michaelson, G. J., Packee, E. C., Stiles, C. A., Swanson, D. K. and Yoshikawa, K. (2005) 'Soil catena sequences and fire ecology in the Boreal forest of Alaska', *Soil Science Society of America Journal*, vol 69, pp1761–1772

Preston, C. M. and Schmidt, M. W. I. (2006) 'Black (pyrogenic) carbon: A synthesis of current knowledge and uncertainties with special consideration of boreal regions', *Biogeosciences*, vol 3, pp397–420

Rillig, M. C., Wright, S. F. and Eviner, V. T. (2002) 'The role of arbuscular mycorrhizal fungi and glomalin in soil aggregation: Comparing effects of five plant species', *Plant and Soil*, vol 238, pp325–333

Rodionov, A., Amelung, W., Haumaier, L., Urusevskaja, I. and Zech, W. (2006) 'Black carbon in the zonal steppe soils of Russia', *Journal of Plant Nutrition and Soil Science*, vol 169, pp363–369

Rumpel, C., Chaplot, V., Planchon, O., Bernadou, J., Valentin, C. and Mariotti, A. (2006) 'Preferential erosion of black carbon on steep slopes with slash and burn agriculture', *Catena*, vol 54, pp30–40

Sabine, C. L., Heimann, M., Artaxo, P., Bakker, D. C. E., Chen, C. T. A., Field, C. B., Gruber, N., Quéré, C. le, Prinn, R. G., Richey, J. E., Lankao, P. R., Sathaye, J. A. and Valentini, R. (2004) 'Current status and past trends of the global carbon cycle', in C. B. Field and M. R. Raupach, (eds) *SCOPE 62, The Global Carbon Cycle: Integrating Humans, Climate, and the Natural World*, Island Press, Washington, DC, Chapter 2, pp17–44

Schmidt, M. W. I. (2004) 'Carbon budget in the black', *Nature*, vol 427, pp305–306

Schmidt, M. W. I. and Noack, A. G. (2000) 'Black carbon in soils and sediments: Analysis, distribution, implications, and current challenges', *Global Biogeochemical Cycles*, vol 14, pp777–793

Schmidt, M. W. I., Skjemstad, J. O., Czimczik,

C. I., Glaser, B., Prentice, K. M., Gelinas, Y. and Kuhlbusch, T. A. J. (2001) 'Comparative analysis of black carbon in soils', *Global Biogeochemical Cycles*, vol 15, pp777–794

Schmidt, M. W. I., Skjemstad, J. O. and Jäger, C. (2002) 'Carbon isotope geochemistry and nanomorphology of soil black carbon: Black chernozemic soils in central Europe originate from ancient biomass burning', *Global Biogeochemical Cycles*, vol 16, pGB1123

Shibuya, M., Kato, M., Ozawa, M., Fang, P. H. and Osawa, E. (1999) 'Detection of buckminsterfullerene in usual soots and commercial charcoals', *Fullerene Science and Technology*, vol 7, pp181–193

Shneour, E. A. (1966) 'Oxidation of graphite carbon in certain soils', *Science*, vol 151, pp991–992

Skjemstad, J. O., Clarke, P., Taylor, J. A., Oades, J. M. and McClure, S. G. (1996) 'The chemistry and nature of protected carbon in soil', *Australian Journal of Soil Research*, vol 34, pp251–271

Skjemstad, J. O., Taylor, J. A., Janik, L. J. and Marvanek, S. P. (1999) 'Soil organic carbon dynamics under long-term sugarcane monoculture', *Australian Journal of Soil Research*, vol 37, pp151–164

Skjemstad, J. O., Dalal, R. C., Janik, L. J. and McGowan, J. A. (2001) 'Changes in chemical nature of soil organic carbon in Vertisols under wheat in southeastern Queensland', *Australian Journal of Soil Research*, vol 39, pp343–359

Skjemstad, J. O., Reicosky, D. C., Wilts, A. R. and McGowan, J. A. (2002) 'Charcoal carbon in US agricultural soils', *Soil Science Society of America Journal*, vol 66, pp1249–1255

Sollins, P., Homann, P. and Caldwell, B. A. (1996) 'Stabilization and destabilization of soil organic matter: Mechanisms and controls', *Geoderma*, vol 74, pp65–105

Tiessen, H. and Stewart, J. W. B. (1988) 'Light microscopy of stained microaggregates: The role of organic matter and microbes in soil aggregation', *Biogeochemistry*, vol 5, pp312–322

Tisdall, J. M. and Oades, J. M. (1982) 'Organic matter and water-stable aggregates in soils', *Journal of Soil Science*, vol 33, pp141–163

Topoliantz, S. and Ponge, J. F. (2005) 'Charcoal consumption and casting activity by *Pontoscolex corethrurus* (Glossoscolecidae)', *Applied Soil Ecology*, vol 28, pp217–224

Topoliantz, S., Ponge, J. F. and Lavelle, P. (2006) 'Humus components and biogenic structures under tropical slash-and-burn agriculture', *European Journal of Soil Science*, vol 57, pp269–278

Wardle, D. A., Nilsson, M. C. and Zackrisson, O. (2008) 'Fire-derived charcoal causes loss of forest humus', *Science*, vol 320, p629

Warnock, D. D., Lehmann, J., Kuyper, T. W. and Rillig, M. C. (2007) 'Mycorrhizal responses to biochar in soil – concepts and mechanisms', *Plant and Soil*, vol 300, pp9–20

Wengel, M., Kothe, E., Schmidt, C. M., Heide, K. and Gleixner, G. (2006) 'Degradation of organic matter from black shales and charcoal by the wood-rotting fungus *Schizophyllum commune* and release of DOC and heavy metals in the aqueous phase', *Science of the Total Environment*, vol 367, pp383–393

Willmann, G. and Fakoussa, R. M. (1997) 'Extracellular oxidative enzymes of coal-attacking fungi', *Fuel Processing Technology*, vol 52, pp27–41

Yanai, Y., Toyota, K. and Okazaki, M. (2007) 'Effects of charcoal addition on N_2O emissions from soil resulting from rewetting air-dried soil in short-term laboratory experiments', *Soil Science and Plant Nutrition*, vol 53, pp181–188

12

Biochar Application to Soil

Paul Blackwell, Glen Riethmuller and Mike Collins

Introduction

The application of biochar techniques to soil has rarely been investigated to date. The effectiveness of applications of composts, animal manures or mineral fertilizers are known to vary significantly whether they are incorporated or surface applied, banded or broadcast (Jarvis and Bolland, 1991; Gherardi and Rengel, 2003), and similar responses can be expected to the method of biochar application. The biophysical responses to the way in which biochar is applied have to be considered, as well as technical feasibility, economic constraints and safety. For example, the properties of fineness ('dustiness'), spontaneous combustion risk, occasional health risks and very low packing density of biochar may provide specific challenges for safe and cost-effective application to soil.

In this chapter some of the known yield and productivity responses to biochar applications to soil are summarized. Agricultural productivity is often reported to increase with biochar application to soil, but variability is high and it is not yet clear under what soil and climatic conditions and plant species high or low yields can be expected (Lehmann and Rondon, 2006). The type of biochar also plays an important role in its effectiveness, and is itself a function of the type of feedstock and production conditions (see Chapter 8). Therefore, yield responses are currently difficult to predict, and global patterns need to be identified to move towards an understanding of the crop production potential using biochar.

We outline the principles behind a range of techniques of applying biochar to soil. We also provide the context for these techniques in relation to application, biochar properties influencing application methods, and the farming system or environment concerned. Some practical safety issues are considered and suggestions are also made for aspects of biochar application worth further investigation and evaluation.

Purpose of biochar application

The methods and success of biochar application depend predominantly upon the purposes of applying biochar to soil. During recent years, this has been assisted by considerable information and science-based understanding of the role that biochar plays in plant–soil processes which drive the management of agriculture and the environment. During earlier times in such places as the Amazon Basin and the islands of Japan, the choice of methods was perhaps based more on observations and anecdotes of the effects of disposed charred materials on wild plants and crops. Ogawa (1994) describes early Japanese farmers using a unique manure called 'haigoe' prepared by adding human waste to rice husk biochar or biochar powder and leaving it for some time before planting wheat or other crops. Sombroek et al (2002) describe that the pre-Columbian Amerindian tribes of the Amazon Basin may have intentionally added biochar or ashes together with human and animal waste, green manure, hunting and fishing remains, and calcium (Ca) from pounded mollusc shells and root accretions, thus forming so-called Terra Mulata. These observations suggest that soil improvement may have also originated from other materials and not just biochar, which requires some scrutiny in interpreting results obtained from studies on traditional soil management, such as Terra Preta soils.

In many contemporary farming systems worldwide, the overriding influence on the choice of application method is the availability or necessity of powered machinery, compared to the use of manual labour and livestock power. The largest influence on the choice of techniques for applying materials such as fertilizers, minerals and organic waste to soil in industrialized agriculture has been the emergence of commercially available centrifugal, pneumatic and liquid spreading and conveying equipment. However, the opportunity and, perhaps, obligation to employ manual labour and animal power can provide options for biochar application that are difficult to achieve mechanically (e.g. precise application to tree plantations within the root zone of specific trees).

The purpose of applying biochar to soil mainly falls into four broad categories:

1 agricultural profitability;
2 management of pollution and eutrophication risk to the environment;
3 restoration of degraded land; and
4 sequestration of C from the atmosphere.

Agricultural profitability

Reduction of soil acidity, improvements to soil cation exchange capacity (CEC) and pH (see Chapter 5), water-holding capacity (see Chapter 2), and improved habitat for beneficial soil microbes (see Chapter 6) are most likely the primary causes of productivity improvements. While some information exists about increases in productivity (see the following section), very little information is available on profitability. Improved profitability requires costs of improvement to be sufficiently lower than the value of the improved productivity. The technology of biochar use is generally at too early a stage to accurately obtain costs of application. The production effects are better known and are discussed in more detail below.

Effects of biochar application on crop productivity

A limited amount of published information currently exists about the effects of biochar on agricultural productivity and most research derives from tropical climates. Table 12.1 summarizes much of the current information, specifically on field trials, that is

Table 12.1 *List of published field experiments regarding the application of biochar to soil for growing agricultural crops*

Location (reference)	Soil (as described in the literature)	Crop	Biochar type and production method	Treatments	Responses (compared to recommended practice)	Comments
Tropical forest soil, Indonesia (Igarashi, 1996)	Volcanic ash soil Loam	Soybean and maize	Rice husk (carbonizer)	Biochar with magnesium phosphate and lime; rates unknown	Biochar increased root nodule formation, plant growth and yield	Residual effects in the second crop and up to the tenth rotation, especially for maize
Semi-tropical woodland soil, Thailand (Oka et al, 1993)	Sandy soil, low fertility	Soybean	Rice husk (carbonizer)	Rates up to 10t ha^{-1}	Increase of N fixation, soybean growth and yield; response at lower fertilizer application rate is higher than at normal rates	Residual effects to the second and third season (sorghum, soybean)
Tropical forest soil, Indonesia (Ogawa and Yamabe, 1986)	Volcanic ash soil Loam	Soybean	Bark biochar (flat kiln)	Bark biochar of a broad-leafed tree with 1% (w/w) of inorganic fertilizer (NPK ratio of 8: 8: 8), urea, super lime phosphate, ammonium sulphate and oilcake powder; mixed in the topsoil at 5t ha^{-1} and 15t ha^{-1}	Soybean yields that were harvested from the plots with biochar additions of 500g m^{-2} were mostly equal to those from the plots with 100g and 200g of chemical fertilizer. Through this method the amount of chemicals could be saved by 1/20. Root nodule formation and mycorrhizal infection rates and the spore numbers increased with biochar application	
Tropical montane savannah soil, Colombia (Rondon et al, 2004)	Andosol	Carrots and beans	Wood	30t ha^{-1}	Increase of biomass between 100% and 30% of fully fertilized controls	

Table 12.1 *continued*

Location (reference)	Soil (as described in the literature)	Crop	Biochar type and production method	Treatments	Responses (compared to recommended practice)	Comments
Tropical forest soil, Indonesia (Yamato et al, 2006)	Acid soil	Maize	Bark biochar at 260°C to 360°C in flat kilns	At 15t ha⁻¹ alone or with 500kg ha⁻¹ fertilizer	Higher yields (~50% greater) than fertilizer alone	Large increase in colonization of roots by mycorrhizal fungi; biochar reduced exchangeable Al
Tropical forest soil, Brazil (Steiner et al, 2007)	Zanthic Ferralsol	Sorghum and rice over four seasons	Wood biochar from local kilns	At 11t ha⁻¹ with or without mineral fertilizer; compost, manure or leaf litter	Biochar increased yields with mineral fertilizer, especially with manure	Reduced exchangeable Al; yield and nutrient uptake more than anticipated; no measurements of beneficial microbial activity
Tropical savannah soil, Colombia (Rondon et al, 2006)	Typic Haplustox	Maize and *Brachiaria* pasture over three seasons	Wood biochar from local kilns	0, 8t ha⁻¹ and 20t ha⁻¹ all with full fertilization	Biochar increased yields by up to 30%	
Tropical savannah soil, Colombia (Rondon et al, 2007)	Typic Haplustox	Beans over one season	From *Eucalyptus* sp at 350°C in controlled kiln	0, 30g kg⁻¹, 60g kg⁻¹ or 90g kg⁻¹, all with full fertilization	Bean yield increased by 46% at 90g kg⁻¹ biochar and biomass production by 39% at 60g kg⁻¹ biochar	30g kg⁻¹ gave intermediary yield increases; biomass yields were similar to the control with the 90g kg⁻¹ addition rate, but bean yields continued to increase with the highest application rate
Tropical forest soil, Brazil (Steiner, 2006)	Xanthic Ferralsol	Bananas	Wood biochar from local kilns	11t ha⁻¹	Soil acidity reduced and K uptake increased	No effect on fruit production in the first season

Location (reference)	Soil type	Crop	Biochar	Application rate	Results	Notes
Semi-tropical montane savannah soil, Kenya (Kimetu et al, 2008)	Ultisol	Maize	Wood biochar from local kilns	6t C ha⁻¹	Up to 100% more productivity when used in soil with >30 years of cultivation; some production decline in soils cultivated for ten years	Biochar added to mineral fertilizers
Tropical forest soil, Brazil (Nehls, 2002)	Oxisol	Rice	Wood biochar from local kilns	7.9t C ha⁻¹	115–320% increase in biomass	
Semi-tropical soil, Australia (Van Zwieten et al, 2008)	Ferrosol	Maize (sweetcorn) Faba beans	Poultry litter and paper mill waste; slow pyrolysis at 450°C	Maize: 0.5–50t ha⁻¹ poultry litter (PL) biochar; Beans: 10t ha⁻¹ PL biochar and paper mill waste biochar; compared to lime (3t ha⁻¹) – a commercial compost	Maize: PL biochar at 10t ha⁻¹ 51% yield increase, at 50t ha⁻¹ 109% increase over nil. Beans: highest yields were observed where biochars were added with fertilizer. PL biochar alone outperformed luxury fertilizer treatment, lime amendment and compost	
Semi-tropical soil, Australia (Sinclair et al, 2008)	Ferrosol	Pasture legume and rye grass	Cattle feedlot or municipal green waste; slow pyrolysis at 450°C	Either biochar at 10t ha⁻¹ with or without NPK fertilizer at 46 (N):28 (P):50 (K)	7.6% increase in pasture production from the PL biochar with fertilizer compared to fertilizer alone; no benefit from the green waste biochar	
Dry Mediterranean savannah soil, Australia (Blackwell et al, 2007)	Haplic Xerosol (sandy loam)	Wheat	Leaf and stem (low C; open-pan method)	Deep banded with two rates of soluble fertilizer or mineral fertilizer and 0–6t ha⁻¹ in band	3–400kg yield increase for half soluble fertilizer rate at 6t ha⁻¹ banded biochar and mineral fertilizer at 1.5t ha⁻¹ banded biochar	A dry season and mycorrhiza may have assisted mid-season water supply from wide inter-rows

pertinent to the discussion of biochar application methods in this chapter (for summaries that include greenhouse trials, see Glaser et al, 2002, and Lehmann and Rondon, 2006). This brief summary is not intended to provide a synopsis of the current state of research on yield responses, but rather to highlight some of the central issues of biochar functioning in soils to guide decisions for biochar application techniques to soil.

Of the currently published research using field trials (see Table 12.1), there is little or no information on the effects of biochar on pasture, fodder shrubs or trees, including semi-perennial fruit trees such as banana or papaya. These are important components of many agriculture, agroforestry and forestry systems and should benefit from biochar in the same way as some field crops have been able to. The possible beneficial effects of biochar on the production of woody biomass may also be very important to the potential biomass supply for renewable energy and biochar production itself.

Current information is also limited for dry and temperate climates. Most of the published research on field responses of crops to biochar application comes from tropical forest and savannah climates in South America and South-East Asia. The largest effect on productivity is documented for tropical and irrigated systems on highly weathered and acid soils with low-activity clays (see Table 12.1). This may mainly stem from the immediate yield responses to the alleviation of acid soil conditions and aluminium (Al) toxicity in highly weathered soils through the application of biochar (see Chapter 5). It is important to note that crop yields on different soils will respond to biochar differently. Depending upon the particular soil constraints, biochar may or may not increase crop yields. On some fertile soils or with sufficient amounts of fertilizers, an addition of biochar may not significantly improve yields. Under these conditions,

biochar may be an approach to reduce fertilizer application rates while maintaining crop yields due to its effects on nutrient leaching (see Chapter 15) and nitrous oxide emissions (see Chapter 13), and may fulfil non-agronomic purposes, such as reduction of greenhouse gas emissions or reduction of eutrophication, as detailed below.

There is a common observation in tropical climates from soils in Brazil, Colombia and Indonesia that wood or rice husk biochar increases soil pH and reduces available Al (Oka et al, 1993; Lehmann et al, 2003; Rondon et al, 2004, 2007; Yamato et al, 2006; Steiner et al, 2007). Recent research on Ferrosols in the sub-tropics in Australia has shown similar effects (Sinclair et al, 2008; Van Zwieten et al, 2008). The toxic effects of available Al on root growth can explain why crop root systems may be able to better explore acid soils after biochar application to take up nutrients and water, regardless of other influences on soil nutrient retention (CEC), water-holding capacity or soil microorganisms. Research from Brazilian Oxisols in central Amazon (e.g. Smyth and Cravo, 1992; Fahrenhorst et al, 2000) shows that the benefits of liming may not always be a result of reduced Al toxicity, but of correcting Ca deficiency since yields increased when gypsum ($CaSO_4$) was added without a pH change.

Additions of biochar together with mineral fertilizer were shown to improve yield by more than the nutrient supply value of the biochar. This may be explained by an increase in soil CEC through biochar additions (see Chapter 5), which reduces nutrient losses through leaching in high rainfall climates (see Chapter 15).

Research from Indonesia (Yamato et al, 2006) has shown that beneficial symbiotic soil fungi may help to explain part of such yield increases, especially at sites with low levels of available phosphorus (P). The lack of response to inoculation and infection by mycorrhizal fungi in soils with high levels of soluble P may be explained by the crops preferring P supply from the soil solution, rather than the symbiotic pathway through the fungus, which is more energy demanding.

The role of beneficial soil microorganisms may also help to explain a greater observed response to biochar at lower rates of applied fertilizer – for example, those observed by Oka et al (1993). Symbiotic fungal hyphal networks may enable interception of leachable nutrients in high-rainfall environments, resulting in a more efficient use of applied nutrients, as observed in more arid environments (Allen, 2007).

These very different effects of biochar additions to soil emphasize the need for recognizing the soil and plant mechanisms influenced by biochar in each soil and in each environment. Site-specific understanding of the processes involved will significantly guide decisions about the method of biochar application.

For biochar to improve soil reaction, nutrient supply, CEC and microbial population or function effectively, it needs to be present at depths commonly used by roots. This requires forms of mechanical incorporation to place biochar into the active plant root zone. However, even small quantities of biochar added to seed coatings may, in some cases, be sufficient for a beneficial effect (Hill et al, 2007). In this respect, a smaller particle size of biochar could be expected to result in greater positive effects on nutrient availability and crop yields. However, within the size limits studied by Lehmann et al (2003), biochar with a particle size of about 20mm showed identical effects on crop yield and nutrient uptake as biochar sieved to sizes of less than 2mm. Therefore, particle sizes of biochar may not play an overriding role for soil fertility enhancement and may, rather, be chosen as a function of ease of application and cost.

Profitability of increased production by biochar additions will not only depend upon the costs of biochar production or purchase, but also upon the cost of application per unit area or length of tree row. Thus, the choice of application method can have a strong influence on profitability. Agricultural products with narrow gross margins may need to maximize biochar benefits to minimize the costs of application. An example of a suitable operational analysis methodology to assess the benefits of biochar application for agronomic profitability is shown in Sorensen et al (2005). The situation is different for C sequestration, where it is not the minimum amount of biochar that is applied to provide the maximum return on investment, but where the application rate is probably being maximized. Tschakert (2004) demonstrates C sequestration economics for small-scale farming, which may be adapted to biochar soil management.

Biochar and composting

Biochar may be applied to organic wastes and is reported to accelerate composting (Yoshizawa et al, 2007) and deodorize manures (Ogawa, 1994). This may be explained by greater reproduction rates of microorganisms in the presence of biochar (Steiner et al, 2004) and by higher retention of microorganisms (Pietikäinen et al, 2000). This significantly adds to the value of biochar in organic agriculture. Application techniques may vary considerably between organic and conventional agriculture due to the amounts applied, the need for organic fertilization and soil tillage methods.

Managing pollution and eutrophication risk

From an environmental point of view, it is important to intercept leachable nutrients and pesticides from soil to reduce eutrophication and pollution risks in adjacent water bodies, as well as to reduce the need for fertilizer application that would be required to compensate for such nutrient losses. Biochar shows good evidence for adsorbing nutrients such as phosphate and ammonium (Lehmann et al, 2003; Lehmann, 2007) that may cause eutrophication, as well as adsorbing pesticides before they enter local water sources (Takagi and Yoshida, 2003; see Chapter 18). Location of the biochar within the root zone is required for the interception of nutrients leached to lower soil depths (see Chapter 15), and deeper application may be desirable. However, nutrients transported by overland flow may require biochar application close to the surface in buffer zones around water bodies at risk in order to maximize contact between runoff and biochar. Therefore, different environmental management techniques require different application methods.

Re-vegetation of degraded land

Re-vegetation efforts for degraded lands may use biochar as a carrier for beneficial soil microorganisms, for improved CEC, and possibly for soil aggregation and water-holding capacity. Since re-vegetation includes reclamation of denuded landscapes, biochar application offers the ability to enhance soil functions in advance of accumulation of plant litter that would otherwise provide the source of soil organic matter under climax vegetation. The scale of re-vegetation and the availability of labour will influence the methods of application. In some instances, such as during the reclamation of mine spoils, it may be necessary to rebuild the entire soil through thorough mixing.

Sequestration of carbon

Biochar application to soil places C originating from atmospheric CO_2 into the soil to protect it from surface combustion by fires and to maintain it in relatively stable forms for a long period of time (see Chapter 11), with opportunities for C trading (see Chapter 16). A better contact with soil minerals enhances biochar stability and increases its mean residence time (see Chapter 11). Sequestration in subsoils may be an especially effective way to increase stability. A deeper application method may therefore be useful for increasing the C trading value of biochar.

Biochar properties and application methods

In addition to the purpose of biochar application discussed above, the choice of application methods also depends upon physical and chemical properties. Highly soluble salts, for example, that are intended for rapid uptake by plants, are often applied onto the surface for dissolution in subsequent rains and transfer to the root–soil interface by unsaturated flow of water. In contrast, relatively insoluble materials (e.g. lime or biochar) are often mechanically incorporated into the topsoil to encourage a sufficiently intimate mixture for beneficial reactions to occur. The most important physical properties of biochar influencing the application method may be density, fineness ('dustiness'), and fire hazard and health risk.

Density

Of a wide range of solid materials applied to soil, biochar probably has the lowest density. Packing densities of 0.17t m^{-3} are quoted for bamboo biochar (Yoshizawa et al, 2007) and 0.37t m^{-3} for bark biochar (Yamato et al, 2006). Bulk transportation costs in Western Australia are about US$0.14 t^{-1} km^{-1} for sand at 1.8t m^{-3} (2008 figures). This can increase about sixfold up to US$0.9 t^{-1} km^{-1} for leaf and stem biochar at 0.3t m^{-3}

(Blackwell et al, 2007). Increasing the packing density of biochar, for example, by pelleting may reduce transport costs. Conti et al (2002) report a low energy-cost pelleting system for biomass achieving densities of 1.4t m^{-3} to 1.8t m^{-3}. Such a process may also be cost effective for pelleting biochar (Demirbas, 1999; Abakr and Abasaeed, 2006) to reduce transportation costs.

Since pelleting uses pressure, it will be important to verify that the porosity in the biochar is maintained, which is a valuable feature in enhancing interaction between solutes, soil water, microorganisms and biochar (see Chapters 2, 5 and 6). Care will also be needed to avoid increasing risks of spontaneous combustion by pelleting of biochar. Pellets of biochar may require a binding agent in order to retain pellet integrity during transport and application as is often applied in the production of charcoal briquettes (Van der Klashorst and Gore, 1988). Whether or not binding agents are needed will also depend upon the feedstock and charring temperature that will probably produce greater variability in biochar properties than is currently considered for charcoal briquettes, which are mainly produced from materials with low mineral contents. There is also an energy cost to be considered that will affect economic viability. Pelleting of sawdust (not including grinding or drying) may cost US\$4 per tonne to US\$6 per tonne in Austria and Sweden, and the binding agent constitutes a significant proportion of total costs (Thek and Obernberger, 2004). Pelleting is not only a financial but also an energy cost, which translates into CO_2 emissions that need to be accounted for when using biochar as a way of mitigating climate change and monetizing emission reductions through C trading.

Pelleting can also assist mechanical application of biochar to soil, especially for pneumatic systems, which are well designed for granular materials such as seed (e.g.,

Kiliçkan and Güner, 2006) and granular fertilizer (Solie et al, 1994). Biochar pellets with a similar density to seed and fertilizer will flow relatively easily through pneumatic delivery systems such as air seeders designed for cotton with target lengths of 10mm. Spinning disc spreaders are also designed for granular materials (Fulton et al, 2005); thus, pellets of biochar should be easier to spread with such spreaders.

Dust fraction

Dustiness is a negative property during the transport and application of biochar to soil. Dustiness of the very light fraction of biochar is most likely to occur with a median aerodynamic diameter of about 10µm, as determined for other dusts (US Bureau of Mines, 2008). The light fraction can be suspended in the air and easily moved by light winds. Losses can occur during transport and from storage heaps, as well as during loading and spreading with methods such as spinning disc spreaders. Distribution characteristics with spinning disc spreaders will be poor with biochar containing a large dust fraction, and direction of discs will have a strong influence on the uniformity of spreading. Problems may also occur where biochar dust poses unacceptable pollution in neighbouring residential zones.

Covering biochar heaps with sheets or spraying solutions to stabilize the surface may be required to minimize the risk of dust formation during storage. On-site application of water to assist spreading may be a feasible solution. In contrast, if a combination of liquid manure and application by injection is appropriate, a fine biochar material may even be preferred. A positive aspect of the fineness of biochar may also be its ability to be spread into existing forests and orchards using systems already employed for applying fungicidal dusts to orchards and vineyards (Holownicki et al, 2000).

Fire hazard

The fire hazard of charcoals through spontaneous combustion has been recognized for a long period of time (Anonymous, 1912; Naujokas, 1985). Dustiness may exacerbate the fire hazard if the dust accumulates in an enclosed space, as shown with flour dust in mills and stores and coal dust in mines (Giby et al, 2007). Densification through pelleting may decrease the hazard of spontaneous combustion, as shown for biomass (Werther et al, 2000). Fire hazard can also develop from the content of volatiles in the biochar that ignite first (Werther et al, 2000), which is related to biomass characteristics, temperature of biochar production and duration of pyrolysis, among other parameters. Wood biochar pyrolysed at about 600°C or higher often has low volatility levels (see Chapter 8), which may decrease the risk of spontaneous combustion during storage and handling. Suitable care is required to minimize fire and spontaneous combustion risks, which are typically regulated by national agencies. Fire retardants such as boric acid or ferrous sulphate can be added and have shown to significantly delay spontaneous combustion of biochar made from rice husks (Maiti et al, 2006). Water is often used to reduce combustion risks, even though its effectiveness is not conclusive unless the biochar is completely saturated; but it is effective in cooling (Naujokas, 1985). The most reliable method for eliminating combustion reactions is the exclusion of atmospheric oxygen by inert gases (Naujokas, 1985). Current handling of biochar in Australia is classified under United Nations Hazardous Goods Class 4.2, which is spontaneously combustible, and packing group III, relating to minor danger (see Box 12.1).

Health risk

Rice husk biochar made at temperatures above 550°C can contain crystalline material (cristobalite and tridymite) that is toxic (Ibrahim and Helmy, 1981; Stowell and Tubb 2003). Thus, the manufacture of rice husk biochar must ensure quality control, and the use of such biochar must employ suitable health and safety precautions during handling and application to soil. The UK Health and Safety Executive (HSE) has assigned a maximum exposure limit of $0.3mg\ m^{-3}$ for crystalline silica, expressed as an eight-hour time-weighted average. The US permissible exposure limit (PEL) is $10mg\ m^{-3}$ divided by the percentage of SiO_2. This level is considered as being too high and lower levels of $0.1mg\ m^{-3}$ for crystalline

---

Box 12.1 Safe handling of biochar in Australia

Storage and transport: store in cool, dry conditions in well-sealed containers. Keep from contact with oxidizing agent.

United Nations 1362, Hazard class: 4.2, packing group: III.
Proper shipping name: charcoal.

Spills and disposal: wear protective equipment. Ensure adequate ventilation. Small amounts: sweep material onto paper and place in fibre carton. Large amounts: make into small packages with paper or other flammable material for incineration. Wash area well with soap and water.

Dispose by incineration according to local, state and federal laws. *Do not* allow substance to be released into the environment without proper governmental permits.

Source: United Nations Hazardous Goods Class 4.2, www.usyd.edu.au/ohs/ohs_manual/haz-subs/DngGoods.shtml

silica, 0.05mg m^{-3} for cristobalite and 0.05mg m^{-3} for tridymite, are recommended (Stowell and Tubb, 2003).

Safety recommendations can only be very general because of the unique variations in biochar properties according to biomass source and processing procedures. Each biochar must be assessed for its own properties and environment for handling and storage. Research and development of procedures specific to biochars for soil application are needed.

Methods of application and incorporation: Specific examples

Uniform topsoil mixing

Biochar can be applied to an entire area mechanically, by spreaders, by hand (see Figure 12.1) or with the assistance of draught animals. Incorporation can be achieved by hand hoe, animal draught during primary and secondary tillage (see Figure 12.2), or by mechanical ploughing or discing and incorporation to a suitable depth. The goals of uniform topsoil mixing of biochar range from improvement of soil fertility, especially improvements to CEC, water-holding capacity and beneficial soil biology, to adsorption of leachable herbicides and reduction of greenhouse gas emissions. During uniform topsoil mixing, a significant proportion of biochar may be lost as dust due to its low density, with possible negative effects on human health. Risks may be reduced by dust control techniques during transport and storage, as described above. Inversion mouldboard ploughing may create deep layers of biochar and may fail to mix the biochar evenly throughout the topsoil. Offset disc ploughs will generally provide better mixing. The influence of deep tillage on the soil structure varies according to the type of tillage, the soil water content at tillage and the soil type (Coulouma et al, 2006). Risk of poor mixing will be reduced if the tillage system is checked for uniformity and suitability of mixing using test runs.

Erosion risks from wind may exist for biochar applied to sandy soils and from water in clayey and compacted soils, but no quantitative information is available. Conservation agriculture methods, which help to maintain a protective soil surface cover, will help to reduce erosion risk. Knowler and Bradshaw (2007) describe these methods and their adoption for many climatic regions. For example, leaving crop residues on the soil surface or growing cover crops and applying green manures maintain surface cover that decrease concerns about wind or water erosion of biochar. Risk of erosion will also be minimized if sufficient anchored ground cover (approximately 50 per cent) is retained

Figure 12.1 *Spreading biochar into planting holes for banana near Manaus, Brazil*

Source: C. Steiner, with permission

by using conservation tillage systems. Schuller et al (2007) provide evidence of a 43 per cent reduction of cropping area prone to erosion on a 10 per cent slope in Chile by the adoption of no-tillage instead of regular cultivation. A compromise between the need for mixing the topsoil and cover retention may be achieved by employing partial incorporation with disc cultivators set at a shallow angle and working through a standing crop residue. The use of disc methods instead of tines causes less disturbance and improves coverage of the biochar, as shown for manures (Rahman and Chen, 2001), and may therefore also reduce risk of biochar dust formation.

Incorporation with composts and manures

Composts and manures are commonly used in organic agriculture, and biochar can be applied to composting biomass to accelerate the composting process (Yoshizawa et al, 2007). The biochar also reduces possible odour from organic nutrient sources (Kleegberg et al, 2005). Reduction of odour may be achieved by intimate mixing of compost and manure with biochar or even by pelleting together with a suitable fixing agent for easier handling. O'Grady Rural (www.smartbugs.com.au) reports mixing 25 per cent wood biochar with a commercial manure fertilizer (Dynamic Lifter®), followed by mixing with a paste made from boiling flour and water (flour at 10 per cent w/w of the manure and biochar mixture), before pelleting with a mincing machine and drying the pellets.

The compost or manure mixed with biochar can be applied by uniform topsoil mixing, as described above, or can also be top-dressed between rows of trees and vines without incorporation (see Figure 12.3). Deep banding of compost and biochar mixtures in the soil may be achieved by top-dressing the mix into suitable trenches or

Figure 12.2 *Rotary hoeing to mix biochar uniformly in field plots in Bolivia*

Source: N. Foidl, with permission

holes prepared by tillage machinery, livestock-drawn ploughs or hand hoes. When the biochar is incorporated, the soil is levelled and the mixture covered. This procedure will ensure that the biochar is concentrated in the rhizosphere.

Limitations and their solutions are similar, as described for uniform incorporation above. However, organic farming methods

Figure 12.3 *Side dressing compost into rows of trees in an organic orchard within Okura Plantations, Kerikeri, New Zealand*

Source: Mike Collins

often maintain better soil cover than other farming methods through either crop residues or application of organic matter such as composts. Therefore, risks of erosion of biochar by both wind and water may be lower than in conventional systems.

Incorporation with liquid manures and slurries

Biochar may be applied to the soil surface in a uniform layer or in bands after suitable combination with liquid manures or slurries; however, there is currently no published evidence of this being successful. Incorporation is similar to the one described for uniform topsoil application above, as well as for possible localized incorporation in or between rows with strip tillage using tines or discs. The main motivation for this type of application includes the reduction of odour from manures (Kleegberg et al, 2005), retention of P in liquid manures (Lehmann, 2007) and reduction of dust formation.

Concerns exist regarding possible blockages of flow if the biochar particles are too large or the concentration of biochar is too high in the liquid or slurry. Careful testing of the viscosity and flow characteristics of mixtures of biochar and slurry to avoid blockages in the field should minimize risks of poor flow characteristics. Scotford et al (2001) suggest an improved method for applying slurries because, traditionally, the coefficient of variation (CV) across the spreader width can be over 35 per cent. They used novel fluidic diodes to effectively reduce the CV to less than 9 per cent. The fluidic diodes allow increased pressure in the manifold to achieve a more uniform pressure across the spreader without restricting the outlet nozzle diameter, which would normally cause blockages. Viscosity reduction may additionally require suspension agents and viscosity improvers. There will be a need to verify that such additives do not adversely affect the beneficial properties of biochar in the soil.

Test runs should minimize the risk of poor mixing during application. It may be advisable to avoid application to bare soil, especially on sloping land with risk of surface erosion following heavy rain. Use of disc openers with injectors will minimize water erosion risks. At the correct concentration, biochar may reduce odour; otherwise, safe distances and wind directions may have to be observed as operating guidelines. Odour of the mixture during handling and application may cause environmental concerns if the biochar is insufficient to reduce odours.

Deep-banded application in rows

Deep banding is very compatible with the layout of many crop and tree plantings and may also be a useful method for pastures. The main motivation for applying biochar by such deep-banding methods include the placement of the biochar into the rhizosphere for improved efficiency to increase crop growth, as well as reducing the risk of erosion.

Biochar is applied in bands of about 50mm to 100mm wide, with a spacing of approximately 200mm to 600mm and at a suitable depth that is compatible with the particular cropping system (see Figure 12.4; Blackwell et al, 2007). In certain cases it is possible to deep band the biochar alongside established plants, especially perennial crops, where plant disturbance may be a problem and ploughing is not possible.

For such deep banding, pneumatic systems are commonly used in industrialized agriculture, often with belt-driven feeds from supply hoppers at rates of greater than 500kg ha^{-1} applied to the whole area. If biochar is applied at 1t ha^{-1} calculated for the entire field in bands 100mm wide using 300mm row spacing, the effective application rate in the bands themselves is 3t ha^{-1}. Dustiness may induce blockages in pneumatic systems. The mechanisms and processes involved in methods such as air-

Figure 12.4 *Deep banding of biochar into soil before planting a crop, Western Australia*

Source: P. Blackwell

stream delivery systems are discussed by Fielke and Slattery (2002) and Srivastava et al (2007). The air volume must be increased and air speed decreased for lower particle density. This requires larger pipe sizes to reduce air speed that will decrease the pressure drop and increase the air volume (decreasing the back pressure on the fan).

As an alternative to expensive pneumatic systems, low-cost methods are possible by pre-cultivating furrows or trenches to top-dress the biochar into the furrow or trench manually or mechanically. The trench or furrow is then levelled, often in the same operation as planting.

Addition of water at the application site may minimize dust risks during spreading and incorporation. Kernebone et al (1986) used suspension agents to keep lime and gypsum in suspension for deep liquid injec-

tion on a paraplough. These authors had to add viscosity improvers, such as fine clays, to allow unabated flow through injection pipes for particles <300μm. The same principles may be appropriate to handle and deliver biochar in suspension for injection into soil. Investigations are required to avoid negative effects on biochar from suspension agents for liquid delivery.

Top-dressing

Some environments and agricultural systems make mechanical access or soil movement difficult or undesirable, such as in no-till cropping systems, established pasture systems, forests or perennial cropping systems. In such cases, biochar may be applied to the surface manually or by disc or rotating hammer spreaders. Dust blowers may be tested for application to well-established forests with dense understorey. Subsequent leaf fall, macro-faunal activity and 'illuviation' by rain and water infiltration may incorporate the biochar into the topsoil. It is not clear how rapidly biochar moves into subsoils; but the fact that large proportions of biochar are found at depth suggests a significant vertical transport (see Chapter 11).

Especially with top-dressing, protection against wind and water erosion is required, including managing risks for human health through dustiness. These may be addressed by appropriate pre-treatment of biochars, such as pelleting and ground cover management, as discussed above.

Specific application to remedy ailing trees

Biochar can be used to establish and remedy tree plantings. Ogawa (1992) investigated remedial effects of biochar on established pine trees, in combination with the cultivation of mushrooms (see Figure 12.5). Urea, ammonium sulphate, super lime phosphate and

Figure 12.5 *(left) Trenching method to incorporate biochar and correct wilting of a pine tree; (right) addition of biochar to holes around mature orchard trees near Wollongbar, New South Wales, Australia*

Source: (left) M. Ogawa, with permission; (right) L. Van Zwieten, with permission

synthetic chemical fertilizer were added to bark biochar powder at a concentration of 0.1 to 1.0 per cent (w/w). The mixture was applied to circular trenches with a depth and width of 0.3m around trees after cutting the roots, which was then covered by sand. The regenerating fresh roots grew vigorously inside the biochar layers after three months. Mushrooms also appeared abundantly along the trenches nine months later. After one year, the abundance of roots and mycorrhiza considerably increased in the biochar layers and the growth of the tree shoots improved. This was accompanied by the disappearance of deficiency symptoms of the pine needles, indicating that plant nutrition was improved (Ogawa, 1992). In addition, the gravimetric water content in the biochar-treated soil was higher than in the surrounding soil (Ogawa, 1992). These improvements in plant nutrient and water uptake probably resulted from the regeneration of roots and the formation of mycorrhiza.

A similar method, probably less destructive to an established tree root system, has been developed by Van Zwieten (pers comm, 2008) in New South Wales Australia (see Figure 12.5). Four holes with a diameter of about 300mm and a depth of 500mm are made around an existing tree and biochar is applied to the base of the hole before refilling the hole with the remaining soil. As described for the application in a ring around trees, this method may also be able to improve water and nutrient uptake of established trees.

Ecological delivery via animal feed

This is a concept which is, to our knowledge, untested, but may occur in nature when animals browse on the charred bases of plants after fire. The benefits may be mainly in animal health and nutrition, as biochars are known de-tannifiers. Van et al (2006) have shown production benefits of goats from small amounts of bamboo biochar added to tannin-rich feed from *Acacia* sp. No adverse health effects were detected (Van et al, 2006). Similar observations were made for both goats and sheep when mixing activated carbons with diets of native shrubs from the Mediterranean (Rogosic et al, 2006). Activated carbons have been widely utilized for gastrointestinal decontamination of both animals and humans (Decker and Corby, 1970; Bond, 2002), and the relevant research can provide insights into desirable properties of biochars that may be used for animal feed. Ingestion and excretion by animals may then be a way to apply biochar to soil, albeit in very low amounts. Similar to dispersal mechanisms of plant seeds by wild animals (such as the Woylie: Christensen, 1980; but many others as described by, e.g., Schupp, 1993, or Bartuszevige and Endress, 2008), biochar in feed may be delivered to soil.

Comparison of methods and outlook

The list of methods and their characteristics in Table 12.2 show that some methods are relatively well understood, such as mechanical incorporation into topsoil, because they have been part of agricultural technology for a long time to include other soil amendments, such as manures or composts. Other methods are mainly at the concept stage (e.g. blowing biochar into established forests). Depending upon the objectives of a particular biochar system, the appropriate application technique should be chosen. Table 12.2 also provides a roadmap for further development of application methods. Development should target those techniques that can be rapidly brought to commercial application, whereas research may be primarily aimed at testing the feasibility of the less-developed techniques.

Table 12.2 *Summary of methods of incorporating biochar within soil, their characteristics and current need for information*

Method	Purpose[1]	Biochar limitations[2]	Solutions[3]	Farming system limitations[4]	CO_2 emission risk[5]	Solutions	Inadequate knowledge
Uniform topsoil mixing	A, P, S	D, DU, H	P?, SHS, DC	E, poor mixing, EC	High	Check tillage Maintain cover Check gross margins	Pelleting Long-term effects Health and safety
Forming deep layers	A, P, S	D, DU, H	P?, SHS, DC	E, over-mixing, EC	High	Check tillage Maintain cover Check gross margins	Pelleting Long-term effects Health and safety
Addition to composts and manures	A, P, S	D, DU, H	DC, SHS	E, O, L (?)	High?	Maintain cover Odour control systems	Biochar/ composting interactions
Adding to slurries or liquid manures	A, P, S	D, H	SHS	E, O, EC	Low	Check mixing risks Odour control systems	Mixing effects on flow Mixing and suspension agent effects on beneficial biochar properties
Deep banding	A, P, S	D, DU, blockages H	P, DC, SHS Correct design and suspension agents	E, EC, D	Low, more with pelleting	Check design of carrier system, maintain cover/use disc systems for tillage	Pelleting Mixing and suspension agent effects on beneficial biochar properties
Top dressing	A, P, S	D, DU, H	P, DC, SHS	D	Low, more with pelleting	Develop safe handling systems for the environment	Pelleting Air-blowing systems
Remediation of mature trees	R, S	D, DU, H	P, DC, SHS	L?	High		Understanding the processes and health risks
Ecological delivery	A, S	?	?	?	Low	?	Understanding the processes

Notes: 1 Purpose: A = agricultural profitability; P = pollution control; R = re-vegetation; S = sequestration.
2 Biochar limitations: D = density; DU = dustiness; H = health hazard.
3 Physical solutions: DC = dust control; P= pelleting; SHS = safe handing systems.
4 Farming system limitations: EC = economic cost; L = availability of labour; E = erosion; O = odour; (?) and () indicate uncertainty and partial application.
5 CO_2e emission risk is also compared between the methods to help clarify total sequestration potential in a full carbon life-cycle analysis.

References

Abakr, Y. A. and Abasaeed, A. E. (2006) 'Experimental evaluation of a conical-screw briquetting machine for the briquetting of carbonized cotton stalks in Sudan', *Journal of Engineering Science and Technology*, vol 1, pp212–220

Allen, M. F. (2007) 'Mycorrhizal fungi: Highways for water and nutrient movement in arid soils', *Vadose Zone Journal*, vol 6, 291–297

Anonymous (1912) 'The spontaneous combustion of charcoal', *The Journal of Industrial and Engineering Chemistry*, vol 4, pp541–542

Bartuszevige, A. M. and Endress, B. A. (2008) 'Do ungulates facilitate native and exotic plant spread? Seed dispersal by cattle, elk and deer in northeastern Oregon', *Journal of Arid Environments*, vol 72, pp904–913

Blackwell, P., Shea, S., Storer, P. Solaiman, Z., Kerkmans, M. and Stanley, I. (2007) 'Improving wheat production with deep banded oil mallee charcoal in Western Australia', in *Proceedings of the International Agrichar Conference*, Terrigal, NSW Australia, May 2007

Bond, R. (2002) 'The role of activated charcoal and gastric emptying in gastrointestinal decontamination: A state-of-the-art-review', *Annals of Emergency Medicine*, vol 39, pp273–286

Christensen, P. E. S. (1980) 'The biology of *Bettongia penicillata* (Gray, 1837) and *Macropus eugenii* (Desmarest, 1817) in relation to fire', *Bulletin no 91*, Forests Department of Western Australia, Perth, Western Australia

Conti, L., Mascia, S. and Scano, G. (2002) 'Commercial process for low cost production of charcoal, activated carbon, bio-hydrogen from low value biomass', in *12th European Conference on Biomass Energy, Industry and Climate Protection*, Amsterdam, The Netherlands, pp1339–1441

Coulouma, G., Boizard, H., Trotoux, G., Lagacherie, P. and Richard, G. (2006) 'Effect of deep tillage for vineyard establishment on soil structure: A case study in southern France', *Soil and Tillage Research*, vol 88, pp132–143

Decker, W. A. and Corby, D. G. (1970) 'Activated charcoal as a gastrointestinal decontaminant: Experiences with experimental animals and human subjects', *Clinical Toxicology*, vol 3, pp1–4

Demirbas, A. (1999) 'Properties of charcoal derived from hazelnut shell and the production of briquettes using pyrolytic oil', *Energy*, vol 24, pp141–150

Fahrenhorst, C., Botschek, J., Skowronek, A. and Ferraz, J. (2000) 'Application of gypsum and lime to increase cation adsorption of a Geric Ferralsol in the Brazilian Amazon region', *Journal of Plant Nutrition and Soil Science*, vol 162, pp41–49

Fielke, J. M. and Slattery, M. G. (2002) 'Pneumatic conveying principles applied to an air seeder', in *Proceedings of the Australian Conference on Engineering in Agriculture*, Charles Sturt University, Wagga Wagga, NSW, 26–29 September 2002, pp1–8

Fulton, J. P., Shearer, S. A., Higgins, S. F., Hancock, D. W. and Stombaugh T. S. (2005) 'Distribution pattern variability of granular VRI applicator', *Transactions of the ASAE*, vol 48, pp2053–2064

Gherardi, M. J. and Rengel, Z. (2003) 'Deep banding improves residual effectiveness of manganese fertiliser for bauxite residue revegetation', *Australian Journal of Soil Research*, vol 41, pp1273–1282

Giby, J., Blair, A., Barab, J., Kaszniak, M. and MacKenzie, C. (2007) 'Combustible dusts: A serious industrial hazard', *Journal of Hazardous Materials*, vol 142, pp589–591

Glaser, B., Lehmann, J. and Zech, W. (2002) 'Ameliorating physical and chemical properties of highly weathered soils in the tropics with charcoal – a review', *Biology and Fertility of Soils*, vol 35, pp219–230

Hill, R. A., Harris, A., Stewart, A., Bolstridge, N., McLean, K. L. and Blakeley, R. (2007) 'Charcoal and selected beneficial microorganisms: Plant trials and SEM observations', in *Proceedings of the International Agrichar Conference*, Terrigal, NSW, Australia, May 2007

Holownicki, R., Doruchowski, G., Godyn, A. and Swiechowski, W. (2000) 'PA – Precision agriculture variation of spray deposit and loss with air-jet directions applied in orchards', *Journal of Agricultural Engineering Research*, vol 77,

pp129–136

Ibrahim, D. M. and Helmy, M. (1981) 'Crystallite growth of rice husk ash silica', *Thermochimica Acta*, vol 45, pp79–85

Igarashi, T. (1996) *Soil Improvement Effect of FMP and CRH in Indonesia*, JICA pamphlet, p30

Jarvis, R. J. and Bolland, M. D. A. (1991) 'Lupin grain yields and fertiliser effectiveness are increased by banding superphosphate below the seed', *Australian Journal of Experimental Agriculture*, vol 31, pp357–366

Kernebone, F. E., Osborne, G. J. and Poile, G. J. (1986) 'Subsoil amelioration with suspensions of lime and gypsum', in *Proceedings of the Conference on Agricultural Engineering*, Adelaide 24–28 August 1986, pp191–195

Kiliçkan, A. and Güner, M. (2006) 'Pneumatic conveying characteristics of cotton seeds', *Biosystems Engineering*, vol 95, pp537–546

Kimetu, J. M., Lehmann, J., Ngoze, S., Mugendi, D. N., Kinyangi, J., Riha, S., Verchot, L., Recha, J. W. and Pell, A. (2008) 'Reversibility of productivity decline with organic matter of differing quality along a degradation gradient', *Ecosystems*, vol 11, pp726–739

Kleegberg, K. K., Schlegelmilch, M., Strees, J., Steinhart, H. and Stegmann, R. (2005) 'Odour abatement strategy for a sustainable odour management', in *Proceedings of the Tenth International Waste Management and Landfill Symposium*, Sardinia, 3–7 October 2005

Knowler, D. and Bradshaw, B. (2007) 'Farmer's adoption of conservation agriculture: A review and synthesis of recent research', *Food Policy*, vol 32, pp25–48

Lehmann, J. (2007) 'Bio-energy in the black', *Frontiers in Ecology and the Environment*, vol 5, pp381–387

Lehmann, J. and Rondon, M. (2006) 'Bio-char soil management on highly weathered soils in the humid tropics', in N. Uphoff (ed) *Biological Approaches to Sustainable Soil Systems*, CRC Press, Boca Raton, FL, pp517–530

Lehmann, J., da Silva Jr., J. P., Steiner, C., Nehls, T., Zech, W. and Glaser, B. (2003) 'Nutrient availability and leaching in an archaeological Anthrosol and a Ferralsol of the Central Amazon basin: Fertilizer, manure and charcoal amendments', *Plant and Soil*, vol 249, pp343–357

Maiti, S., Dey, S., Purakayastha, S. and Ghosh, B.

(2006) 'Physical and thermochemical characterization of rice husk char as a potential biomass energy source', *Bioresource Technology*, vol 97, pp2065–2070

Naujokas, A. A. (1985) 'Spontaneous combustion of carbon beds', *Plant/Operations Progress*, vol 4, pp120–126

Nehls, T. (2002) *Fertility Improvement of a Terra Firme Oxisol in Central Amazonia by Charcoal Applications*, MSc thesis, University of Bayreuth, Germany

Ogawa, M. (1992) *Cultivation of Wild Mushroom*, Ringyo Kairyo Fukyu Sousho 110, Zenkoku Ringyo Fukyu Kyokai, Tokyo (in Japanese)

Ogawa, M. (1994) 'Symbiosis of people and nature in the tropics', *Farming Japan*, vol 28, pp10–34

Ogawa, M. and Yamabe, Y. (1986) *Effects of Charcoal on VA Mycorrhiza and Nodule Formations of Soy Bean*, Studies on Nodule Formation and Nitrogen Fixation in Legume Crops, Bulletin of Green Energy Program Group II no 8, MAFF (with English summary), pp108–134

Oka, H., Rungattanakasin, W., Arroratana, U. and Idthipong, S. (1993) 'Improvement of sandy soil in the northeast by using carbonized rice husks', *JICA Technical Report*, vol 13, pp42–40 (in Japanese, with translation)

Pietikäinen, J., Kiikkila, O. and Fritze, H. (2000) 'Charcoal as a habitat for microbes and its effect on the microbial community of the underlying humus', *Oikos*, vol 89, pp231–242

Rahman, S. and Chen, Y. (2001) 'Laboratory investigation of cutting forces and soil disturbance resulting from different manure incorporation tools in a loamy sand soil', *Soil and Tillage Research*, vol 58, pp19–29

Rogosic, J., Pfister, J., Provenza, F. and Grbesa, D. (2006) 'The effect of activated charcoal and number of species offered on intake of Mediterranean shrubs by sheep and goats', *Applied Animal Behaviour Science*, vol 101, pp305–317

Rondon, M., Ramirez, A. and Hurtado, M. (2004) *Charcoal Additions to High Fertility Ditches Enhance Yields and Quality of Cash Crops in Andean Hillsides of Columbia*, CIAT Annual Report Cali, Colombia

Rondon, M., Molina, D., Ramirez, J., Amezquita, E., Major, J. and Lehmann, J. (2006)

'Enhancing the productivity of crops and grasses while reducing greenhouse gas emissions through bio-char amendments to unfertile tropical soils', Poster presented at the World Congress of Soil Science, Philadelphia, PA, 9–15 July 2006

Rondon, M., Lehmann, J., Ramirez, J. and Hurtado, M. (2007) 'Biological nitrogen fixation by common beans (*Phaseolus vulgaris* L.) increases with bio-char additions', *Biology and Fertility of Soils*, vol 43, pp699–708

Schuller, P., Walling, D. E., Sepulveda, A., Castillo, A. and Pino, I. (2007) 'Changes in soil erosion associated with a shift from conventional tillage to a no-tillage system, documented using ^{137}Cs measurements', *Soil and Tillage Research*, vol 94, pp183–192

Schupp, E. W. (1993) 'Quantity, quality and the effectiveness of seed dispersal by animals', *Vegetation*, vol 107/108, pp15–29

Scotford, I. M., Cumby, T. R. and Inskip, P. F. (2001) 'Improving the control and accuracy of slurry spreaders', *Journal of Agricultural Engineering Research*, vol 79, pp139–149

Sinclair, K., Slavich, P., Van Zwieten, L. and Downie, A. (2008) 'Productivity and nutrient availability on a Ferrosol: Biochar, lime and fertiliser', in *Proceedings of the Australian Society of Agronomy Conference*, 21–25 September 2008, Adelaide Australia

Smyth, T. J. and Cravo, M. S. (1992) 'Aluminum and calcium constraints to continuous crop production in a Brazilian Amazon oxisol', *Agronomy Journal*, vol 84, pp843–850

Solie, J. B., Whitney, R. W. and Broder, M. F. (1994) 'Dynamic pattern analysis of two pneumatic granular fertilizer applicators', *Applied Engineering in Agriculture*, vol 10, pp335–340

Sombroek, W., Kern, D., Rodriques, T., Cravo, M. da S., Jarbas, T. C., Woods, W. and Glaser, B. (2002) 'Terra Preta and Terra Mulata: Pre-Columbian Amazon kitchen middens and agricultural fields, their sustainability and their replication', in *Proceedings of the 17th World Congress of Soil Science*, Thailand, Paper no 1935

Sorensen, C. G., Madsen, N. A. and Jacobsen, B. H. (2005) 'Organic farming scenarios: Operational analysis and costs of implementing innovative technologies', *Biosystems Engineering*, vol 91, pp127–137

Srivastava, A. K., Goering, C. E., Rohrbach, R. P. and Buckmaster, D. R. (2007) 'Conveying of agricultural materials', in A. K. Srivastava (ed) *Engineering Principles of Agricultural Machines*, second edition, ASAE, no 6, pp491–524, Chapter 14

Steiner, C. (2006) *Slash and Char as Alternative to Slash and Burn*, PhD thesis, University of Bayreuth, Bayreuth, Germany

Steiner, C., Teixeira, W. G., Lehmann, J. and Zech, W. (2004) 'Microbial response to charcoal amendments of highly weathered soils and Amazonian Dark Earths in Central Amazonia – preliminary results', in B. Glaser and W. I. Woods (eds) *Amazonian Dark Earths: Explorations in Time and Space*, Springer, Berlin, Germany, pp195–212

Steiner, C., Teixeira, W. G., Lehmann, J., Nehls, T., Luis, J., de Macedo, L. V., Blum, W. E. H. and Zech, W. (2007) 'Long term effects of manure, charcoal and mineral fertilization on crop production and fertility on a highly weathered central Amazonian upland soil', *Plant and Soil*, vol 291, pp275–290

Stowell, G. and Tubb, V. (2003) *Rice Husk Ash Market Study*, ETSU U/00/00061/REP, DTI/Pub URN 03/668, available at www.berr.gov.uk/files/file15138.pdf, accessed 15 August 2008

Takagi, K. and Yoshida, Y. (2003) '*In situ* bio-remediation of herbicides simazine-polluted soils in a golf course using degrading bacteria-enriched charcoal', in *Proceedings of the International Workshop on Material Circulation through Agro Ecosystems in East Asia and Assessment of its Environmental Impact*, Tsukuba, Japan, pp58–60

Thek, G. and Obernberger, I. (2004) 'Wood pellet production costs under Austrian and in comparison to Swedish framework conditions', *Biomass and Bioenergy*, vol 7, pp671–693

Tschakert, P. (2004) 'Costs of carbon sequestration: An economic analysis for small scale farming systems in Senegal', *Agricultural Systems*, vol 81, pp227–253

US Bureau of Mines (2008) 'Dust and its control', in *Dust Control Handbook for Mineral Processing*, US Department of the Interior, Chapter 1, www.osha.gov/SLTC/silicacrystalline/dust/chapter_1.html, accessed 16 August 2008

Van, D. T. T., Mui, N. T. and Ledin, I. (2006) 'Effect of method of processing foliage of *Acacia mangium* and inclusion of bamboo charcoal in the diet on performance of growing goats', *Animal Feed Science and Technology*, vol 130, pp242–256

Van der Klashorst, G. H. and Gore, W. T. (1988) 'The utilization of bagasse hemicellulose. III: A binder for charcoal and coal briquettes', *APPITA*, vol 41, pp304–307

Van Zwieten, L., Kimber, S., Sinclair, K., Chan, K. Y. and Downie, A. (2008) 'Biochar: Potential for climate change mitigation, improved yield and soil health', in *Proceedings of the New South Wales Grassland Conference, 2008*, NSW, Australia

Werther, J., Saenger, M., Hartge, E.-U., Ogada, T.

and Siagi, Z. (2000) 'Combustion of agricultural residues', *Progress in Energy and Combustion Science*, vol 26, pp1–27

Yamato, M., Okimori, Y., Wibowo, I. F., Anshori, S. and Ogawa, M. (2006) 'Effects of the application of charred bark of *Acacia mangium* on the yield of maize, cowpea, peanut and soil chemical properties in south Sumatra, Indonesia', *Soil Science and Plant Nutrition*, vol 52, pp489–495

Yoshizawa, S., Tanaka, S. and Ohata, M. (2007) 'Proliferation effect of aerobic micro-organisms during composting of rice bran by addition of biomass charcoal', in *Proceedings of the International Agrichar Conference*, Terrigal NSW, Australia, May 2007, p26

13

Biochar and Emissions of Non-CO$_2$ Greenhouse Gases from Soil

Lukas Van Zwieten, Bhupinderpal Singh, Stephen Joseph, Stephen Kimber, Annette Cowie and K. Yin Chan

Introduction

Climate change caused by an increase in atmospheric concentrations of greenhouse gases (GHGs) is predicted to cause catastrophic impacts on our planet (IPCC, 2006). This provides the impetus to take action to reduce emissions and increase removal of GHGs from the atmosphere. The soil is both a significant source and sink for the greenhouse gases carbon dioxide (CO$_2$), methane (CH$_4$) and nitrous oxide (N$_2$O). As the global warming potential of N$_2$O and CH$_4$ is 298 and 25 times greater, respectively, than the equivalent mass of CO$_2$ in the atmosphere (Forster et al, 2007), small reductions in their emissions could potentially provide significant benefits for the environment.

Biochar application to soil has been shown to affect carbon (C) and nitrogen (N) transformation and retention processes in soil (see Chapters 6 and 14). These processes, along with other mechanisms influenced by biochar, can play a significant role in reducing emissions and increasing sink capacity for GHGs. In this chapter we focus on the role that biochar could play in mitigating soil emissions of two significant non-CO$_2$ GHGs, N$_2$O and CH$_4$.

Factors controlling N$_2$O and CH$_4$ emissions from soil

Anthropogenic sources of N$_2$O contributed 3 giga tonnes (Gt) CO$_2$e (carbon dioxide equivalents), around 8 per cent of global emissions, in 2004; importantly, agriculture was responsible for 42 per cent of this total (Denman et al, 2007). Nitrogen fertilizers, biological N fixation by associative, free-living and mutualistic bacteria, organic N and the excreta of grazing animals are all sources of N that can lead to N$_2$O emissions from soil. The factors that significantly influence agricultural and forestry emissions of N$_2$O are N application rate, crop type, fertilizer type, soil organic C content, soil pH and texture (see review by Dalal et al, 2003).

Methane constituted around 14 per cent of global GHG emissions (CO$_2$e) in 2004

(Forster et al, 2007, Summary for Policy-Makers, SPM Topic 2.1). Aerobic well-drained soils are usually a sink for CH_4, due to the high rate of CH_4 diffusion into such soils and subsequent oxidation by methanotrophic microorganisms (Dalal et al, 2008). Globally, soils are a net sink for CH_4 and are estimated to have consumed 30Tg CH_4 yr^{-1} during 2000 to 2004, equivalent to 5 per cent of the annual load of CH_4 to the atmosphere (Denman et al, 2007). The CH_4 uptake capacity of soil varies with land use, management practices (Liebig et al, 2005; Saggar et al, 2007) and soil conditions (Schutz et al, 1990). In contrast, large emissions of CH_4 are common where anaerobic conditions (e.g. wetlands, rice paddies and landfills), coupled with warm temperatures and the presence of soluble C, provide ideal conditions for the generation of CO_2 and incompletely oxidized substrates, thus supporting high activity of methanogenic microorganisms (Dalal et al, 2008).

Potential for greenhouse gas mitigation using biochar as a soil ameliorant

Recent studies have indicated that incorporating biochar within soil reduces N_2O emissions and increases CH_4 uptake from soil, which could contribute to mitigating greenhouse gas emissions (Rondon et al, 2006; Yanai et al, 2007). However, there is currently very limited understanding of the mechanisms through which biochar impacts upon fluxes of CH_4 and N_2O. It is important to understand these mechanisms, both to determine the potential role of biochar in decreasing net GHG emissions and to ensure that there are no negative environmental consequences associated with adding biochar to soils.

In this chapter, we present new data as well as published material demonstrating the potential for biochar to reduce emissions of N_2O and CH_4 from soil. Although the mechanisms for these reductions are not fully understood, it is likely that a combination of biotic and abiotic factors are involved, and these factors will vary according to soil type, land use, climate and the characteristics of the biochar.

Evidence for reduced soil greenhouse gas (GHG) emissions using biochar

Evidence for reduced N_2O emissions

Yanai et al (2007) used biochars (called charcoal) derived from municipal biowaste (pH 9.3 [H_2O] and total C circa 38 per cent) and showed a decrease in emissions of N_2O in laboratory chambers when soil (Typic Hapludand) was re-wetted to 73 per cent water-filled pore space. Reductions from 105µg N_2O-N m^{-2} in an unamended control to only 11µg N_2O-N m^{-2} in a biochar-treated

soil over a seven-day incubation were noted. Large amendments of biochar (10 per cent by weight) were used (estimated from the evidence available in the manuscript to be approximately 150t ha^{-1}). Maximum emission rate of 2620µg N_2O-N m^{-2} was found in the control soil (see Figure 13.1), while the maximum emission rate in the biochar-amended soil was 383µg N_2O-N m^{-2} hr^{-1}. In parallel trials, Yanai et al (2007) compared biochar derived from municipal biowaste and ash derived from the same feedstock (pH

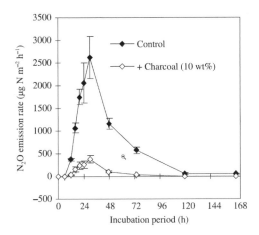

Figure 13.1 *Municipal waste biochar decreased emission of N$_2$O in an incubation study*

Source: Yanai et al (2007), reproduced with permission by Blackwell Publishing

11.6). Results demonstrated that the reduced N$_2$O emissions were not linked to the acid-neutralizing capacity of the biochar or ash, as emissions from ash-amended soil were equivalent to the control.

Work conducted by Rondon et al (2006) in unfertile tropical soils has also shown reduced N$_2$O emissions. Biochar produced from the wood of mango trees was applied to experimental plots (20m^2) at a rate of 8t and 20t biochar ha^{-1}. The biochar was ground to <2mm, broadcast on the soil surface and then incorporated by discing to 50mm depth. After four months these plots were sown to maize and a number of other crops and native pasture. Periodically, the grass and the native vegetation (mostly native grasses) was cut to a height of 10cm, simulating grazing, and the biomass produced in each interval was recorded. Gas exchange between the soil and the atmosphere was monitored monthly over a three-year period using a closed chamber method. During the initial year of this experiment, N$_2$O emissions were reduced, on average, by 15mg N$_2$O m^{-2} for the higher-rate biochar plots. Rondon et al (2006) noted increases in soil pH, cation exchange capacity (CEC), potassium (K) availability, and possibly higher water retention in the soil.

In laboratory incubation studies conducted by the authors, glass jars (5L) with air-tight lids were filled with 1.5kg dry weight equivalent soil (Ferrosol, 2mm sieved). No fertilizer was added to the soil. Low and high temperature biochars derived from both green waste and poultry litter waste were applied at an equivalent of 10t dry biochar ha^{-1} (0–0.05m profile), and thoroughly mixed into the soil. Acid-washed sand was added to the control treatment at an equivalent rate to the biochar.

Soil moisture was increased to 70 per cent water-holding capacity and maintained (by mass) for the duration of the incubation. Mesocosms were maintained in the dark at 23°C in a controlled temperature chamber. Results clearly demonstrate that there is potential to reduce N$_2$O emissions using biochars, although what is clearly evident is that biochars differ in their capacity to reduce emissions (see Figure 13.2). For example, soil amended with poultry litter biochar and high temperature green-waste biochar emitted almost no N$_2$O during the incubation, while low-temperature green-waste biochar increased N$_2$O emissions by over 100 per cent that of the control.

The soil analyses following the incubation showed that the initial nitrate concentrations were similar among the biochar-amended and control treatments, and increased up to 3.5-fold over the incubation period in all but one of the treatments (see Table 13.2); N$_2$O emissions were concomitantly reduced, especially from the poultry biochar-amended soils (see Figure 13.2). However, in soil amended with the low temperature green-waste biochar, the nitrate concentration decreased by 20 per cent over 47 days of incubation concomitant with the increased N$_2$O produced in this treatment

Table 13.1 *Source, pyrolysis conditions and biochar characteristics*

Biochar	Feedstock	Pyrolysis conditions	C (%)	N (%)	Colwell P (mg kg^{-1})	Acid-neutralizing capacity (% CO$_3^{2-}$)
Litter 1	Poultry litter[1]	Activated[2] 550°C	27	0.8	1700	33
Litter 2	Poultry litter	Non-activated 450°C	35	2.2	11,000	14
Green waste 1	Green waste	Activated 550°C	32	0.06	26	<0.5
Green waste 2	Green waste	Non-activated 450°C	36	0.12	14	<0.5

Notes: 1 Poultry litter consists of manure and sawdust bedding.
2 Activation was achieved by cooling the biochars in the presence of steam. Pyrolysis residence time was 45 minutes undertaken by BEST Energies, Australia.

Source: chapter authors

(see Table 13.2 and Figure 13.2). The initial NH_4^+-N concentration in the biochar-amended treatments was considerably lower than the control. The reason for the decrease in extractable NH_4^+-N in biochar-amended soils is not clear; but this suggests that biochar application did not add significant amounts of NH_4^+-N to support high nitrifier activity. The NH_4^+-N concentration did not significantly increase during incubation in any treatment except for the poultry litter 1 biochar treatment (see Table 13.2).

The data presented in Table 13.2 and Figure 13.2 suggest that nitrification would have been either enhanced (in the poultry-litter biochar-amended soils) or remained the same (in the high-temperature green-waste biochar-amended soils). The reduction in N_2O emissions from the poultry biochar-amended soil suggests that poultry biochar may have contained certain compounds that suppressed the activity of denitrifying enzymes involved in conversion of NO_3^--N to N_2O (and this reaction may have also contributed to build up of NO_3^--N in these soils), and/or enhanced the activity of denitrifying enzymes involved in conversion of N_2O to N_2, especially in anaerobic micro-sites rich in bioavailable organic C. On the other hand, denitrification activity seems to have been enhanced in the low-temperature green-waste biochar-amended soil.

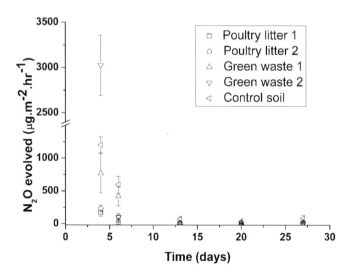

Figure 13.2 N_2O *generated from a Ferrosol amended with biochar in laboratory mesocosms*

Notes: 1.5kg of soil was amended with 10g kg^{-1} biochar (described in Table 13.1) (a rate equivalent to 10t ha^{-1} incorporated to 100mm). Acid-washed sand was added to controls in lieu of biochar. Soils were incubated in triplicate in 5L glass jars, maintained at 70 per cent water-holding capacity. Jars were sealed for 24 hours prior to headspace gas sampling. Mesocosms were maintained at 23°C in the dark.

Source: chapter authors

The effect of these biochars on microbial biomass was also determined by incubating soil for 72 hours and then performing a chloroform fumigation extraction (Vance et al, 1987). The microbial biomass C was decreased by about 40 per cent (from 1.08 ± 0.12mg C g^{-1} dry weight soil to 0.64 ± 0.32 mg C g^{-1} dry weight soil) in the low-temperature green-waste biochar. In contrast, poultry litter biochars did not affect the soil microbial biomass C concentrations during this incubation study (data not shown). The data suggest that although there were components in the low-temperature green-waste biochar that suppressed microbial biomass growth, the activity of denitrifying enzymes was enhanced, especially those that are involved in conversion of NO_3^--N to N_2O.

Thus, it appears that, while biochar application can lead to significant reductions in N_2O emission, this is not universally true for all biochars. It is likely that characteristics of specific biochars affect the activity of microorganisms responsible for N transformations. More research is required to clearly understand the effect of biochar and its associated components (such as contents of mineral oxides, hydroxides and carbonates in ash; the presence of chemicals – e.g. phenolics, inorganic salts, cations, anions, etc.) that could potentially affect the activity of microbes carrying out N-cycling processes in soil (Gundale and DeLuca, 2006; Yanai et al, 2007), and to distinguish their effects on soil N_2O production as well as reduction, using a range of different biochar types produced from different feedstocks and under different processing conditions.

Evidence of reduced CH₄ emissions

Evidence that biochar increases methane oxidation in soil exists (Rondon et al, 2006); however, only very limited literature is available to support this phenomenon. Rondon et al (2005) found a complete suppression of CH₄ emissions when biochar was applied:

- at 15g kg^{-1} soil in a grass stand (*Brachiaria humidicola*); and
- at 30g kg^{-1} soil in soybean.

The biochar feedstock was *Calliandra callothyrsus*. The biochar was ground to <1mm and mixed into the soil prior to sowing. In other work, Rondon et al (2006) demonstrated that applications of 20t ha^{-1} of wood-derived biochar into a non-fertile tropical soil increased the annual methane sinks in soil by around 200mg CH₄ m^{-2} relative to controls.

Table 13.2 *Nitrate and ammonium concentration in soils following incubation with various biochars for 47 days (mean values of three incubation chambers)*

	KCl-extractable Nitrate-N (mg kg^{-1})		KCl-extractable Ammonium-N (mg kg^{-1})	
	Initial	Final	Initial	Final
Control soil	26.3	67.3	3.9	4.0
Poultry litter 1[1]	27.7	92.7	2.7	4.4
Poultry litter 2	28.3	91.0	2.5	3.5
Green waste 1	21.0	67.3	2.1	2.6
Green waste 2	25.7	20.2	2.6	3.0
Least significant difference	15.3		1.2	
Average standard error of the mean	5.4		0.44	

Note: 1 Biochars are described in Table 13.1.

Source: chapter authors

Biological mechanisms for reduced GHG emissions following biochar application

Nitrous oxide gas is produced in soil through three biological processes (Wrage et al, 2005):

1 *Nitrification:* in the first stage of nitrification, N_2O is produced as a by-product during the oxidation of ammonium to nitrite.
2 *Nitrifier denitrification:* in the second stage of nitrification, nitrite is converted to nitrate; however, under low oxygen (O) conditions, specialized nitrifying bacteria (denitrifying nitrifiers) use nitrite as an alternative electron acceptor, in this way producing N_2O.
3 *Denitrification:* here, heterotrophic denitrifying aerobic bacteria cause respiratory reduction of nitrate or nitrite to N_2O and N_2 under anoxic conditions.

These processes are thought to occur simultaneously in soil, with process 1 taking place in aerobic micro-sites and the latter two processes confined to sub-oxic and anoxic micro-sites. Many studies have proposed denitrification as the major contributor to soil N_2O emissions, especially when O is limited in soil – for example, when water-filled porosity exceeds 60 to 70 per cent (Dalal et al, 2003). However, under aerobic conditions (e.g. at water-filled porosity of 50 per cent or less), nitrification can be a major source of soil N_2O emissions. Some research has shown that nitrifier denitrification can contribute over 40 per cent of the N_2O released from a silt loam soil at 50 per cent water-filled pore space (Wrage et al, 2005). Further research (Bateman and Baggs, 2005) has indicated that even under the so-called highly aerobic conditions in soil (20 to 50 per cent water-filled porosity), there may be pockets of anaerobic micro-sites that would allow high rates of denitrification, which may

give rise to N_2O release, or that aerobic denitrification (and/or heterotrophic nitrification) can occur at this water-filled porosity.

During denitrification, NO_3^- is sequentially reduced to N_2 via a set of four enzymes: nitrate reductase (*Nar*), nitrite reductase (*Nir*), nitric oxide reductase (*Nor*) and nitrous oxide reductase (*Nos*), which are usually induced under increasingly high anaerobic conditions (Robertson and Groffman, 2007). These enzymes sequentially convert nitrate to nitrite (*Nar*), nitrite to NO (*Nir*), NO to N_2O (*Nor*) and N_2O to N_2 (*Nos*), respectively:

$$NO_3^- \xrightarrow{Nar} NO_2^- \xrightarrow{Nir} NO \xrightarrow{Nor} N_2O \xrightarrow{Nos} N_2$$

N_2O production through the denitrification process is a balance between N_2O-producing mechanisms, involving *Nar*, *Nir*, *Nor* enzymes and N_2O-reducing mechanisms, involving *Nos* enzyme.

The observed reduction in N_2O emission resulting from application of biochar could therefore be a result of inhibition of either stage of nitrification and/or inhibition of denitrification, or promotion of the reduction of N_2O, and these impacts could occur simultaneously in a soil. The evidence for each of these possibilities is discussed below.

Rather than reducing nitrification, studies using biochar from forest wildfire (DeLuca et al, 2006), commercially produced activated carbon (Berglund et al, 2004) or biochar produced in a laboratory from timber products at 350°C or 800°C (Gundale and DeLuca, 2006) found increases in gross and net nitrification rates in soils from boreal and temperate forests. The forest soils studied by these authors had exceptionally low rates of nitrification, with actual rates of nitrifier activity ranging from negative to 0.02mg kg^{-1} d^{-1}. The observed enhancement of nitrification following biochar application could be explained by several indirect processes and effects, such as:

- through removal of nitrifier inhibitory compounds (e.g. phenolics) from soil solution, which are then adsorbed onto activated carbon surfaces on biochar (Berglund et al, 2004; Gundale and DeLuca, 2006);
- by formation of a biofilm of nitrifiers around biochar particles, promoted by adsorption and increased availability of labile organic substrates to microbes on or around biochar surfaces (Berglund et al, 2004);
- by suppressing the activity of substrate (NH$_4^+$-N)-competing microorganisms (heterotrophs) (e.g. through low-quality organic matter input), thus increasing the availability of NH$_4^+$-N for better proliferation of nitrifiers; and
- by bringing positive changes to soil pH (e.g. through additions of alkalinity through ash and alkaline biochar, which encourages N mineralization and, subsequently, nitrification) (Alexander, 1991).

In contrast to these observations, DeLuca et al (2006) clearly demonstrated that when biochar was added to a soil with high nitrification (three different grassland soils), there was no effect of biochar on nitrification. The results presented in Table 13.2 indicate that nitrifier activity was not limited in this Ferrosol soil, nor that nitrification was reduced in those treatments that showed reduced N$_2$O emission. Thus, there is no evidence that biochar reduces N$_2$O release through inhibition of nitrification.

As suggested above, applying biochar may decrease soil N$_2$O emissions by affecting the denitrification process (i.e. by encouraging the activity of enzymes involved in reduction of N$_2$O to N$_2$) (Yanai et al, 2007). For example, increases in soil pH due to the addition of alkalinity through ash in biochar

could potentially encourage the activity of N$_2$O-reducing organisms (Yanai et al, 2007). Alternatively, NO$_2^-$, NO and N$_2$O formed in soil through the denitrification process could be chemically adsorbed on biochar surfaces and electrochemically reduced to N$_2$ (see abiotic mechanisms below).

The influence of biochars on nitrification is complex to interpret from measurement of soil NO$_3^-$-N as there are likely to be interacting influences on both nitrifiers and denitrifiers. For example, the increase in NO$_3^-$-N in poultry biochar-amended soil may have resulted from increased nitrification; alternatively, nitrification may have been unaffected, and NO$_3^-$-N accumulated due to decreased rates of denitrification. The high N$_2$O emissions from the low-temperature green-waste biochar treatment indicate that the decline in NO$_3^-$-N observed in this treatment was probably a result of enhanced activity of denitrifiers causing rapid conversion and loss of NO$_3^-$-N in soil through N$_2$O emissions rather than an inhibition of nitrification.

Note that if nitrification activity increases while the activity of enzymes producing N$_2$O from NO$_3^-$ decreases due to biochar application (such as apparently occurred when biochar from poultry litter was added), there is potential for accumulated nitrate to leach from the soil profile, which may have detrimental off-site impacts.

Besides direct effects of biochar on nitrifying organisms, it is possible that biochar (since it is an organic material with a high C-to-N ratio) could induce strong N immobilization, especially during initial decomposition of N-poor, but labile components of biochar; consequently, biochar application could decrease ammonification and nitrification in the short term (Lehmann et al, 2006; Warnock et al, 2007). However, the increases in nitrate and ammonium during incubation reported in Table 13.2 suggest that there was no inhibition of ammonification or nitrification due to microbial immobilization of organic and inorganic N decreasing supply of N to ammonifiers and nitrifiers in this case.

It is important to understand which component(s) of the N cycles and associated enzymes within N-cycling processes (i.e. mineralization, nitrification, denitrification) are most affected by biochar applications, so that biochar is better managed for mitigation of soil N_2O emissions and reduction of nitrate leaching.

Methane flux measured at the soil–atmosphere interface is the net effect of two processes: methane production by methanogens and methane uptake by methanotrophs (Knowles, 1993). Both methanogens and methanotrophs are ubiquitous in soils, can prevail under unfavourable conditions, and may occur in close proximity to each other (Dalal et al, 2008). A negative CH_4 flux (i.e. uptake or consumption) of CH_4 by soil, occurs when the magnitude of the CH_4 uptake process is larger than its production (Chan and Parkin, 2000). Methane production in soil occurs mainly under anaerobic conditions. Neue et al (1997) suggested that redox potentials below $-150mV$ are generally needed for significant methane production in the presence of easily degradable organic matter and a pH of 6 to 8. Other estimates for critical soil redox values range from $-150mV$ to $-215mV$ (Yu et al, 2001). Substrates for methane production are usually acetate, formate, CO_2 and H_2 produced during anaerobic decomposition of organic matter in soil. Methanotrophs require O_2, which is the main limiting factor for the oxidation of CH_4 in soil (Dalal et al, 2008).

Biochar applications are expected to make soil conditions favourable for methanotrophs and unfavourable for methanogens, thereby increasing the CH_4 sink capacity of soil. Some of the likely mechanisms for biochar action in soil are explained below.

Improved soil physical conditions

Soil is a porous medium; its porosity, pore-size distribution and pore continuity together control important physical and chemical functions in soil ecosystems. Soil moisture retention characteristics, gas and water movement, and aeration (redox potential) are all factors that are controlled by soil structure, which can, in turn, be influenced through application of biochar.

It is well established that soil bulk density (BD) decreases with increases in organic matter content (Adams, 1973) following the relationship:

$$BD = 100/((x/K_1) + (100 - x/K_2))$$

where:
x = percentage by weight of organic matter;
K_1 = bulk density of organic matter (t m^{-3});
K_2 = bulk density of mineral matter (t m^{-3}).

Therefore, adding organic matter to soil can reduce bulk density and increase soil total porosity. Adams (1973) reported that BD decreased from 1.25t m^{-3} to 0.80t m^{-3} as a result of an increase in soil organic matter from 0 to 10 per cent. Applications of compost to soil can significantly reduce BD and increase the number of pores in the ranges of 30μm to 50μm and 50μm to 500μm (Dick and McCoy, 1993). Pores of these sizes (i.e. macroporosity) are usually air-filled under field conditions (drier than field capacity) and are important in maintaining aerobic conditions in the soil (Kay and Angers, 2000).

Given that biochars have a very porous nature and improve soil aggregation (Brodowski et al, 2006, Liang et al, 2006), their application to soils should improve soil aeration. Furthermore, improved water-holding capacity and reduced tensile strength (Chan et al, 2007) have been demonstrated. Improved aeration will be partly due to increases in macroporosity with resulting higher air-filled porosity and improved supply of oxygen to soil under a wide range of soil water conditions. However, the extent of changes will depend upon the porosity characteristics of different biochars and application rates. Pore-size distribution of biochars depends upon the anatomical structure of parent feedstock and process conditions during pyrolysis, such as charring temperature and activation (see Chapter 2).

The porosity of biochar particles in soil could decrease over time due to the adsorption of 'native' organic molecules onto biochar surfaces, blocking pores (Kwon and Pignatello, 2005). Conversely, biochar, clay and soil organic matter interactions may lead to the formation of micro-aggregates over time (Brodowski et al, 2006; Cheng et al, 2006; Liang et al, 2006), which will improve soil porosity. Overall, biochar addition to soil should increase soil aeration and decrease anaerobic micro-sites per unit volume of soil (Yanai et al, 2007).

By improving the soil physical properties and thereby increasing O$_2$ diffusion, application of biochar will reduce the incidence of anaerobic conditions required for CH$_4$ production. Concurrently, these physical changes in soil properties will also favour diffusion of atmospheric CH$_4$ into the soil atmosphere, which is considered a major limitation to the rate of CH$_4$ oxidation in soil (Templeton et al, 2006; Tate et al, 2007; Werner et al, 2007) and, thus, may stimulate CH$_4$ uptake.

Since anoxic or sub-oxic conditions are required for N$_2$O to be produced through denitrification or nitrifier denitrification, reduction of anoxic or sub-oxic sites in soil is important to mitigate N$_2$O emissions through these two processes. However, the N$_2$O-reductase enzyme, which catalyses the reduction of N$_2$O to N$_2$ in highly anaerobic conditions in soil, seems to be more sensitive to O$_2$ than the enzymes involved in the production of N$_2$O during denitrification

(Tiedje, 1988). This may mean that improved soil aeration caused by biochar application could potentially suppress the reduction of N$_2$O to N$_2$ due to inhibition of the *Nos* enzyme. Cavigelli and Robertson (2001) have shown that there is physiological diversity among denitrifiers in terms of O$_2$ sensitivity of their *Nos* enzyme; thus, changes in denitrifier community composition can also potentially influence the magnitude of *in-situ* soil N$_2$O fluxes. Biochar applications may bring about changes in functionality and diversity of denitrifiers simply by improving soil aeration.

pH effects on biological mechanisms

It is well documented that biochar applications can significantly alter soil pH (see Chapter 5). Similar to burned plant residues, biochars can contain varying concentrations of ash alkalinity that is directly added into the soil as Ca, Mg, K and Na oxides, hydroxides and carbonates (see Chapter 5). This soluble form of ash alkalinity in biochar can be rapidly released into soil and then leaches down the soil profile to ameliorate soil acidity (Raison, 1979; Brennan et al, 2004).

There is evidence that when pH of a soil is increased (e.g. by liming), denitrification liberates less N$_2$O and the ratio of N$_2$O/N$_2$ is decreased. In other words, alkalinity through biochar addition could potentially encourage the activity of N$_2$O reductase enzymes of denitrifying microorganisms (Yanai et al, 2007). We could expect similar observations when high-ash biochar (e.g. poultry litter biochar) is applied to soil, compared to low-ash biochar (green-waste biochar). This is reflected in the data presented in Figure 13.2, which show greater decreases in N$_2$O liberated from soil when poultry litter biochar rather than green-waste biochar was added. In this work, poultry litter biochar 1 increased soil pH from 4.8 (CaCl$_2$ method) to 6.0, while the low-temperature (lower-ash) poultry litter biochar increased soil pH to 5.8. Green-waste biochars did not increase soil pH.

However, oxidation of biochar could lower the pH of soil around the vicinity of biochar particles (Cheng et al, 2006). Thus, one could speculate as to whether the effect of adding alkaline biochar on decreasing N_2O product ratio (N_2O/N_2) during denitrification would be sustained over the longer term.

Both methanogenic and methanotrophic communities can be active under a wide range of soil pH conditions. Studies have shown that soil CH_4 production can increase with an increase in soil pH from 5 to 7.5 (Inubushi et al, 2005), whereas increased soil acidity can reduce CH_4 consumption (Hutsch, 1998) and production (Neue et al, 1997) rates in soil. However, whether biochar application would increase the activity of methanogens or methanotrophs through changes in soil pH will depend upon soil moisture and aeration conditions, as well as the influence of biochars on these conditions.

Biochar application alters quality and availability of substrates

The macro-molecular structure of biochar is dominated by aromatic C, thus making biochar more recalcitrant to microbial decomposition than the parent organic materials (Baldock and Smernik, 2002). Biochar is believed to possess a turnover time of hundreds to thousands of years (see Chapter 11). As a result, biochar will be unlikely to decompose to produce simpler organic molecules (monomers) in significant quantities.

Biochar may, however, contain some proportion of labile organic components (Bird et al, 1999; Hamer et al, 2004), which may serve as energy sources for heterotrophs during the initial stages of decomposition of N-poor biochars and, hence, could potentially induce N immobilization in soil in the short term (Lehmann et al, 2006).

Overall, increases in microbial biomass and growth, and subsequent reduction in available N in soil through microbial immobilization, following biochar application to soil, can potentially occur in three ways:

1 Biochar could serve as a source of energy for microorganisms (heterotrophs) (see above).
2 Biochar may provide protection from grazing for microorganisms colonizing the pore spaces (Pietikäinen et al, 2000; Samonin and Elikova, 2004).
3 By adsorbing labile C substrates and nutrients in soil, biochar could increase metabolic efficiency and growth of microbes proliferating on or around biochar surfaces (Berglund et al, 2004).

Using 11 different biochars, Bhupinderpal-Singh and Cowie (2008) did not find significant interactive effects of biochar type and time (since the start of incubation) on microbial biomass C. When averaged over 196 days (across four different times – i.e. 0, 9, 63 and 196 days after incubation), compared with unamended soil, microbial biomass C (determined according to Vance et al, 1987) was:

• significantly higher at $P<0.05$ in soil amended with poultry litter biochar (400°C, non-activated), paper sludge biochar (550°C, activated) and leaf litter biochar (400°C, activated);
• significantly higher only at $P<0.1$ in soil amended with leaf litter biochar (550°C, activated), poultry litter biochar (550°C, activated), cow manure biochar (400°C, non-activated); and
• not significantly different in soil amended with four different wood-waste biochars (400°C/550°C, activated/non-activated) and one cow manure biochar (550°C, non-activated).

Generally, the quantity of microbial biomass C was high for those biochars that decomposed to a greater extent in soil, indicating that microbial growth could be affected by the form of C present in biochar-amended soils (Bhupinderpal-Singh and Cowie, 2008). Moreover, on day 196 of the laboratory incubation, total bacterial and fungal counts determined by the viable plate count method were significantly higher in most of the biochar-amended soils than in the unamended soil (Bhupinderpal-Singh and Cowie, 2008).

As mentioned above, porous biochar particles may provide a safe habitat for microbes colonizing them (Pietikäinen et al, 2000; Samonin and Elikova, 2004; Warnock et al, 2007). Due to differences in body sizes of soil micro-, meso- and macro-organisms, with the sizes of bacteria and fungal hyphae more comparable to the sizes of pores in biochar particles, it is likely that biochar particles will accommodate microorganisms (bacteria and many fungi), but will exclude their larger predators (Warnock et al, 2007). Thus, in the absence of predation, micro-organisms in biochar would proliferate, which may induce soil N immobilization and, consequently, reduction of soil N$_2$O emissions.

Although the ratio of N$_2$O/N$_2$ production through denitrification (governed by the activity of the *Nos* enzyme) decreases with the supply of water-soluble, readily decomposable organic matter (Burford and Bremner, 1975; Dalal et al, 2003), high amounts of readily available C tend to result in increased N$_2$O production in soils, particularly following N fertilizer application (Zebarth et al, 2008). NO$_3^-$ was not shown to affect denitrification, but was positively correlated with N$_2$O production, especially where available C was high (Gillam et al, 2008). As biochar is capable of adsorbing 'native' organic matter in soil (Gundale and DeLuca, 2006), the reduced emissions of N$_2$O via denitrification from biochar-

amended soils could partially be due to decreased availability of readily decomposable organic matter in whole soil (due to adsorption on biochar surfaces) that is required for supporting the activity of heterotrophic denitrifiers. Alternatively, adsorption of simpler organic molecules on biochar surfaces could enhance their accessibility to microorganisms that flourish on or around biochar (Berglund et al, 2004). Hence, even under optimum soil moisture conditions, biochar particles could create localized anaerobic micro-sites in soil by lowering redox potential in those sites (due to depletion of O$_2$ around biochar caused by enhanced microbial respiration using adsorbed labile C substrates). This situation will probably support an efficient nitrous oxide reductase activity for conversion of N$_2$O produced in soil to N$_2$ (see above).

On the other hand, it is also possible that biochar in soil may serve as a favourable habitat for autotrophic nitrifiers (e.g. by concentrating the supply of labile C substrates in soil on biochar surfaces and by creating high pH micro-sites within its porous structure) (Berglund et al, 2004; Gundale and DeLuca, 2006). Thus, biochar application would enhance nitrification processes and thereby produce greater N$_2$O during conversion of NH$_4^+$-N into NO$_3^-$-N and subsequent loss of NO$_3^-$-N through denitrification unless a highly reduced (low-O$_2$) condition is created around biochar particles, as discussed above.

Recent research has shown that biochar applications to soil, particularly when N is limiting, may reduce total microbial activity in soil. Chan et al (2007) observed significant declines in activity, measured by using fluorescein diacetate hydrolysis, in pot trials on a hard-setting Alfisol in the absence of N fertilizer, while slight increases in microbial activity were seen with higher rates of biochar (50t ha^{-1} and 100t ha^{-1}) when N fertilizer was applied. Gundale and DeLuca (2006) found low quantities of total and soluble phenols in high-temperature Douglas-fir and ponderosa pine wood and bark biochar (800°C) relative to low-temperature biochar (350°C) from the same materials. High concentration of phenols in low-temperature biochar may be toxic to plant roots, and autotrophic and heterotrophic microorganisms (Fritze et al, 1998; Villar et al, 1998; Berglund et al, 2004; DeLuca et al, 2006; Gundale and DeLuca, 2006).

It is frequently reported that NH_4^+ produced in soil or added through ammoniacal fertilizers competitively inhibits CH_4 oxidation because some methanotrophs are also autotrophic ammonium-oxidizers and can potentially use NH_4^+ as an energy source instead of CH_4, while using O_2 as an electron acceptor (Bedard and Knowles, 1989; Powlson et al, 1997; Bykova et al, 2007). Biochar application could possibly regulate the supply of NH_4^+-N in soil for use by methanotrophs – for example:

- through increases in redox potential and CEC, consequently resulting in increased fixation of NH_4^+-N in 2:1 clay lattices (Schneiders and Scherer, 1998); or
- by inducing microbial N immobilization in soil due to its high C:N ratio (Lehmann et al, 2006).

However, conflicting or no effects of NH_4^+-N on CH_4 consumption in soil are also reported (e.g. Tate et al, 2006; Jacinthe and Lal, 2006). Differential responses of methanotrophic communities in soil to N fertilization may be responsible for any conflicting effects (e.g. the activity of type I methanotrophs generally increases and type II decreases following application of N fertilizers) (Mohanty et al, 2006). It remains to be seen how biochar will interact with N fertilizer or NH_4^+ availability and the activity of methanotrophic communities in soil to influence CH_4 consumption in soil under different vegetation systems. Concurrently, biochar application may increase the diffusion of atmospheric CH_4 into soil through improved aeration, in this way increasing its availability to soil methanotrophs.

Biochar application alters supply of electron acceptors and redox potential in soil

The order in which electron acceptors are used by microbial populations decreases as follows: $O_2 > NO_3^- > SO_4^{2-} > PO_4^{3-} > CO_2$. The mineralization of organic N in soil can be controlled by the availability of inorganic electron acceptors, including NO_3^- and SO_4^{2-} (White and Reddy, 2001). Availability of O_2, NO_3^-, SO_4^2, PO_4^{3-} and CO_2 (as electron acceptors) and also NH_4^+ and dissolved organic substrates (as electron donors) can be directly or indirectly regulated through the incorporation of biochar. For example, Gundale and DeLuca (2006) have shown that there could be significant differences in the amount of NO_3^-, PO_4^{3-}, NH_4^+ and dissolved organic substrates added through biochar in soil depending upon feedstock type and biochar production temperature. The nitrifiers obtain their energy from oxidation of NH_4^+, obtain C from soil CO_2 or simpler organic compounds (which may be affected by biochar presence in soil), and use O_2 as the electron acceptor, the supply of which can be enhanced via biochar addition to soil (see above). During the heterotrophic denitrification process, however, denitrifers use nitrate as the electron acceptor and use C from complex organic compounds and prefer low to zero dissolved O_2 (low redox potential). Thus, biochar application may affect the magnitude of soil N_2O production (occurring via nitrification and denitrification) by directly or indirectly affecting the availability of electron acceptors and donors, with consequent changes in soil redox conditions.

Methane production in soil occurs under anaerobic conditions; but the extent of CH_4 production is further controlled by:

- a supply of intermediate organic substrates (such as acetate) and CO$_2$ produced during anaerobic decomposition of soil organic matter; and
- the level of redox potential changes brought about by organic matter inputs (Dalal et al, 2008).

For example, after four years of rice-straw incorporation versus burned straw treatments, Bossio et al (1999) found that the redox potential was lower (–275mV versus –225mV) and CH$_4$ emissions were fivefold higher in soil with rice straw incorporated than in the burned straw treatment over the rice-growing period. Where the C input was from char in burned straw, compared to the uncharred straw input, the reduced CH$_4$ emissions could have been due to:

- a lower quantity of available, easily decomposable organic matter in soil (Bossio et al, 1999); or
- a lower CH$_4$/CO$_2$ ratio of decomposition

products at relatively higher redox potential.

We could expect similar processes (i.e. higher redox potential, reduced rate of C cycling) in soil amended with biochar in comparison to uncharred organic matter.

Biochars can contain significant quantities of available K (see Chapter 5), which is well known to decrease reduction reactions and increase the redox status of flooded soil (Chen et al, 1997). There is evidence that K addition to soil can stimulate methanotrophs and inhibit methanogens (Babu et al, 2006). When soil redox potential increases, CH$_4$ emissions were found to decrease (Babu et al, 2006). Therefore, by increasing soil redox potential through the supply of K in biochar, as well as via increasing soil aeration and the relative proportion of low-quality (recalcitrant) organic matter in soil following biochar application (see above), one may expect low CH$_4$ emissions in biochar-amended soil.

Abiotic mechanisms influencing GHG emissions using biochar

Biochar surfaces are heterogeneous, with a complex defect structure and a significant quantity of organic and metallic compounds (see Chapters 3 and 4). The highly porous surfaces of biochars have been shown to adsorb N$_2$O, CO$_2$ and CH$_4$, as well as substrates for N$_2$O production, including NH$_4^+$ and NO$_3^-$ (Bagreev et al, 2001; Hitoshi et al, 2002). Once biochar is added in substantial quantities to soil, it is likely that changes to the quantity and composition of the mass and energy flows of gases, absorbed photons from the sun, transfer of heat from water, and movement of electrons and ions will occur at the surface and within biochar. On the soil surface, biochar is likely to absorb more radiant energy than soils and have a higher temperature than the surrounding

environment (Keijzer and Hermann, 1966), possibly increasing reaction rates. It is also possible that metals in biochar, such as TiO$_2$, can act as catalysts reducing N$_2$O and oxidizing CH$_4$ (Oviedo and Sanz, 2005). Abiotic mechanisms are explored below.

Structural interactions between biochar surfaces

Biochar has a very complex chemical and physical structure. It consists of regions of microcrystalline graphene sheets that are surrounded by an amorphous carbon phase. As the temperature of pyrolysis increases above 450°C, microcrystalline graphene sheet formation occurs. Kercher et al (2003) has hypothesized that as the temperature increases the disordered C decomposes and becomes incorporated within the graphene sheets of the turbostratic C. The rigid covalent structure of the disordered C cannot rearrange during decomposition to allow the non-uniform growth of turbostratic crystallites. Instead, some graphene sheets grow extensively, and other sheets become terminated and pinned by structural defects (these are a source of micro-pores). Based on these observations, it is possible that a reduction of N_2O could take place at active defect sites at the end of the graphene sheets, especially in the presence of metal ions (Kapteijn et al, 1996).

It is also well documented that many biochars have surfaces that can adsorb a range of gases (LeLeuch and Bandosz, 2007), and these gases can then interact with the water or cations in the water and on the surface of the biochar. In addition, a wide range of highly oxygenated volatile compounds (e.g. levoglucosan, hydroxy-acetaldehyde, furfurals, methoxyphenols and carboxylic compounds) are retained on the surface of the pores of biochar pyrolysed at temperatures below 500°C. Some of these compounds have the potential to react with N_2O (Milne et al, 1998).

Biochar surfaces are complex (see Chapter 3) and there will be areas where there are concentrations of dangling bonds, dislocations and vacancies in the lattice struc-ture, which will be preferential sites for adsorption and reduction of N_2O. Mineral phases in biochar may also have surfaces with a range of broken edges, steps and related defects that would minimize the energy required to reduce N_2O. Many fresh biochars have both acidic and basic sites on their surfaces (Cheng et al, 2008). Oxidized biochars and high mineral-ash biochars that have a highly variable composition of cations and anions on their surfaces (see Chapter 5) will, when placed in soil, probably interact with clay and water. N_2O is more likely to be electro-catalytically reduced on metallic

surfaces where the pH>7 (Wang and Li, 1998).

Metallic and metal oxide catalytic reactions on biochar surfaces

Considerable research has shown that some mineral elements, such as TiO_2, will reduce N oxides in the presence of ultraviolet light (Oviedo and Sanz, 2005, 2007). Thus, it is possible that N_2O will react with biochars that have high concentrations of this mineral at the soil surface. Plane-wave pseudo-poten-tial density-functional theory calculations undertaken by Oviedo and Sanz (2007) indi-cate that the following is a probable mechanism for N_2O reduction on TiO_2 surfaces. The O atom of the N_2O molecule is adsorbed onto the surface site that has an O vacancy in the TiO_2 lattice. The molecule bends and feels the force of an adjacent Ti atom. A bridge molecule is then formed and the NO bond breaks, leading to an N_2 molecule and an O atom. It is yet to be deter-mined whether TiO_2 with or without light will catalyse the reduction of N_2O on biochar surfaces and whether there is sufficient residence time for the gas in the pores for the reactions to go to completion.

Sang et al (2005) have noted that the oxidation–reduction properties of Fe cations exchanged into zeolites have been known for some time, and zeolites that contain ion-exchanged Fe are now known to be catalytically active for the decomposition of N_2O. The active Fe is believed to exist as isolated ion-exchanged ferric cations that have no other Fe species in close proximity. High mineral-ash biochars appear to have similar properties to zeolites; thus, a similar reaction scheme could be partly responsible for the reduction of N_2O. Sang et al (2005) proposed the following reaction mechanism as being the most likely to fit their experi-mental data for the reduction of N_2O:

$$N_2O + FeO \leftrightarrow N_2O\text{-}FeO$$
$$N_2O\text{-}FeO \leftrightarrow OFeO + N_2$$
$$N_2O + OFeO \leftrightarrow N_2O\text{-}OFeO$$
$$N_2O\text{-}OFeO \leftrightarrow O_2\text{-}FeO + N_2$$
$$O_2\text{-}FeO \leftrightarrow FeO + O_2$$

Sang et al (2005) also note that in the presence of nitrate and NO species around the biochar particle, it is possible that a further mechanism could be involved in the reactions on the biochar surface. The authors proposed the following nitrite-nitrate redox cycle as replacing the oxide-oxo cycle in the presence of NO:

$$2NO + O_2 \leftrightarrow 2NO_2$$
$$NO_2 + FeO \leftrightarrow NO_2\text{-}FeO$$
$$N_2O + NO_2\text{-}FeO \leftrightarrow N_2O\text{-}NO_2\text{-}FeO$$
$$N_2O\text{-}NO_2\text{-}FeO \leftrightarrow NO_3\text{-}FeO + N_2$$
$$N_2O\text{-}NO_3\text{-}FeO \leftrightarrow N_2O\text{-}NO_3\text{-}FeO$$
$$N_2O\text{-}NO_3\text{-}FeO \leftrightarrow O_2\text{-}NO_2\text{-}FeO + N_2$$
$$O_2\text{-}NO_2\text{-}FeO \leftrightarrow N_2O\text{-}FeO + O_2$$

N_2O is commonly employed in radiation chemistry in aqueous media as a scavenger for hydrated electrons. Wang and Li (1998) have noted that N_2O can be reduced electrocatalytically on C electrodes that have a deposit of palladium (Pd) catalyst in alkali conditions. The mechanism proposed by Wang and Li (1998) for the electrolytic reduction of N_2O is given below:

$$Pd\star + N_2O \leftrightarrow Pd\text{-}N_2O \text{ (dominant}$$
$$\text{reaction when pH>7.0)}$$
$$Pd\star + H^+ + e^- \leftrightarrow Pd\text{-}H \text{ (dominant}$$
$$\text{reaction when pH<7.0)}$$
$$Pd\text{-}N_2O + 2e^- \rightarrow Pd\text{-}O^{2-} + N_2 \text{ (slow)}$$
$$Pd\text{-}O^{2-} + 2H^+ \rightarrow Pd\star + H_2O \text{ (fast)}$$
$$Pd\star + H^+ + e^- \leftrightarrow Pd\text{-}H$$

Biochar produced from the pyrolysis of coal has been used to reduce N_2O and NO in power station applications (Bueno-López et al, 2006). Experimental work has been carried out at temperatures ranging from 100°C to 600°C using a range of catalysts at relatively high rates of NO and N_2O concentrations in the gas stream (higher than is measured from soil). Bueno-López et al (2006) found that pyrolysed coal (containing approximately 13 per cent ash) impregnated with 15 per cent by weight of K reduced NO and N_2O by approximately 60 per cent at temperatures of 400°C in a gas stream containing 5 per cent O and 0.2 per cent NO$_x$. Higher results were achieved using biochar doped with copper (Cu) and rubidium (Rb). Soriano-Mora et al (2007) reported that pellets manufactured with K-doped coke could operate at even lower temperatures. Kim et al (2006) reported that activated carbon impregnated with K could adsorb NO and O at 150°C. The NO reacted with the O to form NO_2, which is then further oxidized to produce N_2. Given the differences in concentration of N_2O in the aqueous soil environment and the much higher concentrations in gaseous combustion, it is not possible to determine whether these mechanisms are significant.

Hayhurst and Lawrence (1992) demonstrated that heterogeneous reactions between N_2O with CaO and biochar surfaces are a significant process for N_2O destruction during coal combustion. This is particularly relevant for biochars with high concentrations of Ca^{2+}, such as those derived from poultry litter or paper mill wastes. These authors have characterized the decomposition of N_2O by the following consecutive reactions:

- the adsorption of N_2O on biochar surfaces;
- decomposition of the adsorbed molecule with N_2 formation to leave surface O; and
- desorption of O_2 by combination with another surface O atom or by direct reaction with another N_2O molecule.

In these circumstances, the dissociative adsorption of N_2O on vacant lattice sites leads to a progressive development of an O

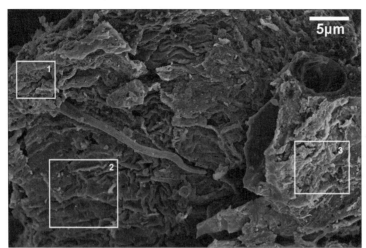

Figure 13.3 *Scanning electron microscopy (SEM) of aged (six months in a Ferrosol) poultry litter biochar with regions of energy dispersive spectroscopy (EDS) analysis (UNSW Electron Microscope Unit)*

Note: Clay platelets are bonded to the biochar. Regions 1 and 3 are described in the text. Biochar manufactured by BESTEnergies Pty.

Source: chapter authors

layer that inhibits the adsorption and consequent reaction of more N_2O. In the presence of H_2 (and H radicals), CO, carboxylic acid and CH_4, the reductant regenerates the reduced active sites by removing the adsorbed O atoms. The reactions take place preferentially at sites that have K^+ and Ca^{2+} atoms or oxides of Fe, Mg and Ti (Parmon et al, 2005).

There are significant interactions between clays and biochars that influence their aging and reactivity in soil. Figure 13.3 demonstrates clay/mineral coatings over chicken manure biochar using scanning electron microscopy (SEM). Energy dispersive spectroscopy (EDS) analysis of region 1 had high C and Ca contents, typical of the analysis of poultry biochars (see Chapter 5), while region 3 had significant contents of minerals, especially Si, Al, Fe, K and Ti. These interactions between the clay and biochar may

influence not only abiotic mechanisms for N_2O reduction, but possibly also the CEC of the biochar (see Chapter 5).

Interactions with organic molecules in biochar

Most biochars produced below 550°C initially contain a range of non-aromatic organic compounds on their internal and external surfaces. These organic compounds are not particularly stable (Bridgwater et al, 1999). Biochars can also adsorb a range of soil organic compounds (see Chapter 18). Avdeev at al (2005) report that a range of aromatic and aliphatic compounds have been oxidized by N_2O. Calculations indicate that an O atom is transferred through the 1,3-dipolar cyclo-addition of N_2O to the C=C bond (see Figure 13.4). Next, the resulting intermediate decomposes, yielding a ketone

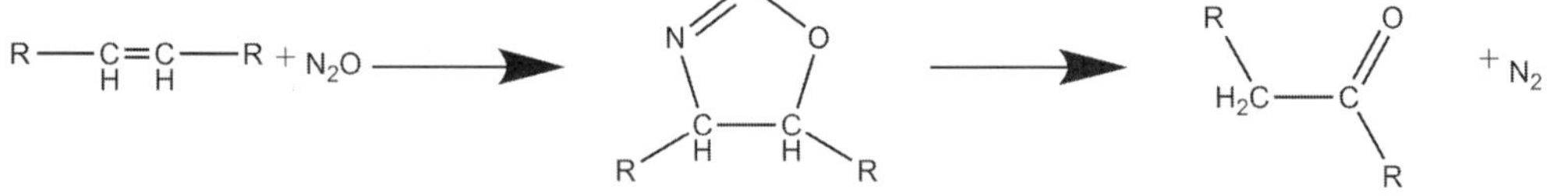

Figure 13.4 *Proposed oxidation of aromatic C by N_2O*

Source: adapted from Avdeev at al (2005)

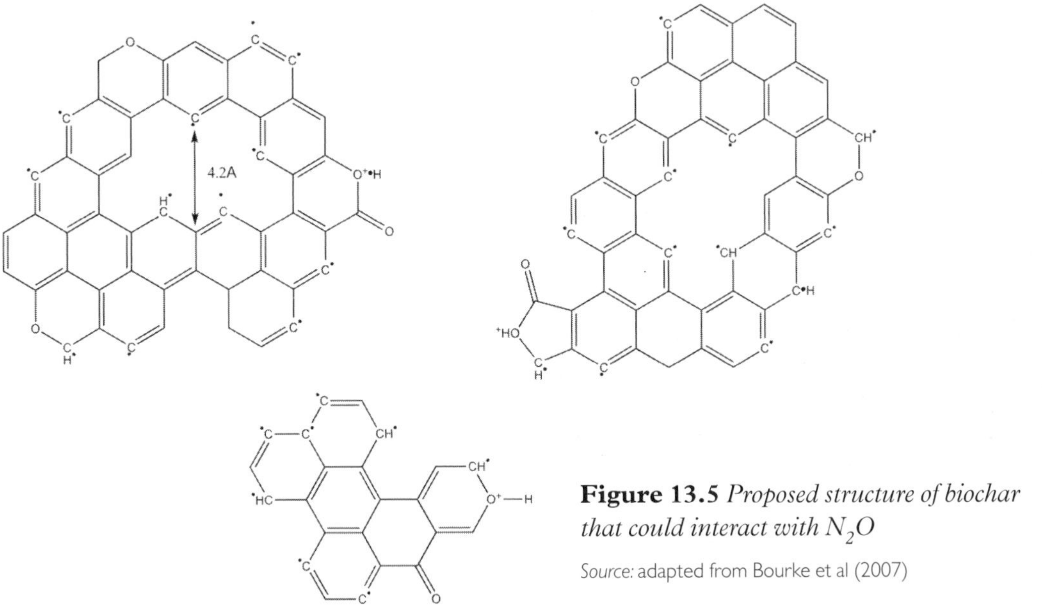

Figure 13.5 *Proposed structure of biochar that could interact with N_2O*

Source: adapted from Bourke et al (2007)

and releasing N_2 to the gas phase. Therefore, given that biochar surfaces adsorb aromatic and aliphatic compounds as mentioned above, it would seem possible that these compounds may be partly responsible for the reduction in N_2O emissions observed in biochar-amended soils.

Using electron spin resonance (ESR), Bourke et al (2007) measured a high concentration of free radicals associated with C aromatic rings. The concentration of these radicals decreases as the temperature of pyrolysis increases. Bourke et al (2007) also found that there are micropores of 0.3nm to 1nm, which he attributed to voids within the hexagonal C planes. These voids will have concentrations of radicals and dangling bonds that could contribute to the chemi-absorption properties of biochars (see Figure 13.5). It is probable that there is a significant concentration of O singlets that could react with CH_4 to produce CO_2. Bourke et al (2007) attributed the propensity of fresh biochars to combust at temperatures below 100°C to the high concentration of free radicals.

Conclusions

In this chapter, we have shown that biochar can, under certain conditions, reduce soil N_2O and CH_4 emissions. A range of both biotic and abiotic mechanisms for this reduction were discussed. The development of biochar as a tool to reduce GHG emissions from soil will require detailed understanding of the interactions between biochar and site-specific soil and climate conditions, and management practices that alter the greenhouse source sink capacity of soils. We need to explore how the key non-CO₂ GHG emission control mechanisms (e.g. soil aeration, moisture, pH, microbial processes, soil structure, nutrient levels and easily mineralizable C pools) interact with biochar to influence

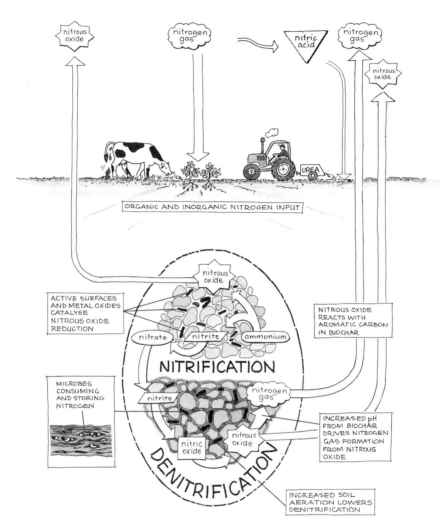

Figure 13.6 *Summary schematic for reduced emissions of N$_2$O from soil*

Source: chapter authors

soil GHG emissions. Figure 13.6 summarizes some of the key mechanisms for both the production of N$_2$O in soil, as well as its reduction through the application of biochar.

Variations in these controlling factors can play a significant role in altering soil microsite conditions, which will probably alter diurnal dynamics of soil non-CO$_2$ GHG emission and uptake. Seasonal and inter-annual variations in rainfall patterns, temperature, land-use change, and plant growth behaviour can also alter dynamics of soil N$_2$O emissions and CH$_4$ uptake; but the processes through which biochar interacts with these long-term controls to influence soil GHG fluxes are still unclear. An improved understanding of the role of biochar in reducing non-CO$_2$ GHG emissions will promote its incorporation within climate change mitigation strategies and, ultimately, its commercial availability and application.

References

Adams, W. A. (1973) 'The effect of organic matter on the bulk and true densities of some uncultivated podsolic soils', *Journal of Soil Science*, vol 24, pp11–17

Alexander, M. (1991) *Introduction to Soil Microbiology*, Krieger Publishing Co, FL, US

Avdeev, V. I., Ruzankin, S. F. and Zhidomirov, G. M. (2005) 'Molecular mechanism of direct alkene oxidation with nitrous oxide: DFT Analysis', *Kinetics and Catalysis*, vol 46, pp177–188

Babu, J. Y., Nayak, D. R. and Adhya, T. K. (2006) 'Potassium application reduces methane emission from a flooded field planted to rice', *Biology and Fertility of Soils*, vol 42, pp532–541

Bagreev, A., Bandosz, T. J. and Locke, D. C. (2001) 'Pore structure and surface chemistry of adsorbents obtained by pyrolysis of sewage sludge-derived fertilizer', *Carbon*, vol 39, pp1971–1977

Baldock, J. A. and Smernik, R. J. (2002) 'Chemical composition and bioavailability of thermally altered *Pinus resinosa* (red pine) wood', *Organic Geochemistry*, vol 34 pp1093–1109

Bateman, E. J. and Baggs, E. M. (2005) 'Contributions of nitrification and denitrification to N$_2$O emissions from soils at different water-filled pore space', *Biology and Fertility, of Soils,* vol 41, pp379–388

Bedard, C. and Knowles, R. (1989) 'Physiology, biochemistry, and specific inhibitors of CH$_4$, NH$_4^+$, and CO oxidation by methanotrophs and nitrifiers', *Microbiology Reviews*, vol 53, pp68–84

Berglund, L. M., DeLuca, T. H. and Zackrisson, O. (2004) 'Activated carbon amendments to soil alters nitrification rates in Scots pine forests', *Soil Biology and Biochemistry*, vol 36, pp2067–2073

Bhupinderpal-Singh and Cowie, A. L. (2008) 'A novel approach, using ^{13}C natural abundance, for measuring decomposition of biochars in soil', in L. D. Currie and J. A. Hanly (eds) *Carbon and Nutrient Management in Agriculture: Proceedings of a Fertilizer and Lime Research Centre Workshop*, Massey University, Palmerston North, New Zealand, Occasional Report no 21, p4

Bird, M. I., Moyo, C., Veenendaal, E. M., Lloyd, J. and Frost, P. (1999) 'Stability of elemental carbon in savanna soil', *Global Biogeochemical Cycles*, vol 13, pp923–932

Bossio, D. A., Horwath, W. R., Mutters, R. G. and Van Kessel, C. (1999) 'Methane pool and flux dynamics in a rice field following straw incorporation', *Soil Biology and Biochemistry*, vol 31, pp1313–1322

Bourke, J., Manley-Harris, M., Fushimi, C., Dowaki, K., Nunoura, T. and Antal, M. J. Jr. (2007) 'Do all carbonized charcoals have the same chemical structure? 2. A model of the chemical structure of carbonized charcoal', *Industrial and Engineering Chemistry Research*, vol 46, pp5954–5967

Brennan, R. F., Bolland, M. D. A. and Bowden, J. W. (2004) 'Potassium deficiency, and molybdenum deficiency and aluminium toxicity due to soil acidification, have become problems for cropping sandy soils in south-western Australia', *Australian Journal Experimental Agriculture*, vol 44, pp1031–1039

Bridgwater, A. V., Meier, D. and Radlein, D. (1999) 'An overview of fast pyrolysis of biomass', *Organic Geochemistry*, vol 30 pp1479–1493

Brodowski, S., John, B., Flessa, H. and Amelung, W. (2006) 'Aggregate-occluded black carbon in soil', *European Journal of Soil Science*, vol 57, pp539–546

Bueno-López, A., Soriano-Mora, J. M. and García-García, A. (2006) 'Study of the temperature window for the selective reduction of NO$_x$ in O$_2$-rich gas mixtures by metal-loaded carbon', *Catalysis Communications*, vol 7, pp678–684

Burford, J. R. and Bremner, J. M. (1975) 'Relationships between denitrification capacities of soils and total, water-soluble and readily decomposable soil organic matter', *Soil Biology and Biochemistry,* vol 7, pp389–394

Bykova, S., Boeckx, P., Kravchenko, I., Galchenko, V. and Van Cleemput, O. (2007) 'Response of CH$_4$ oxidation and methanotrophic diversity to NH$_4^+$ and CH$_4$ mixing ratios', *Biology and*

Fertility of Soils, vol 43, pp341–348

Cavigelli, M. A. and Robertson, G. P. (2001) 'Role of denitrifier diversity in rates of nitrous oxide consumption in a terrestrial ecosystem', *Soil Biology and Biochemistry*, vol 33, pp297–310

Chan, A. S. K. and Parkin, T. B. (2000) 'Evaluation of potential inhibitors of methanogenesis and methane oxidation in a landfill cover soil', *Soil Biological and Biochemistry*, vol 32, pp1581–1590

Chan, K. Y., Van Zwieten, L., Meszaros, I., Downie, A. and Joseph, S. (2007) 'Agronomic values of greenwaste biochar as a soil amendment', *Australian Journal of Soil Research*, vol 45, pp629–634

Chen, J., Xuan, J., Du, C. and Xie, J. (1997) 'Effect of potassium nutrition of rice on rhizosphere redox status', *Plant and Soil*, vol 188, pp131–137

Cheng, C. H., Lehmann, J., Thies, J. E., Burton, S. D. and Engelhard, M. H. (2006) 'Oxidation of black carbon by biotic and abiotic processes', *Organic Geochemistry*, vol 37, pp1477–1488

Cheng, C. H., Lehmann, J. and Engelhard, M. H. (2008) 'Natural oxidation of black carbon in soils: Changes in molecular form and surface charge along a climosequence', *Geochimica et Cosmochimica Acta*, vol 72, pp1598–1610

Dalal, R. C., Wang, W. J., Robertson, G. P. and Parton, W. J. (2003) 'Nitrous oxide emission from Australian agricultural lands and mitigation options: A review', *Australian Journal of Soil Research*, vol 41, pp165–195

Dalal, R. C., Allen, D. E., Livesley, S. J. and Richards, G. (2008) 'Magnitude and biophysical regulators of methane emission and consumption in the Australian agricultural, forest, and submerged landscapes: A review', *Plant and Soil*, vol 309, pp43–76

DeLuca, T. H., MacKenzie, M. D., Gundale, M. J. and Holben, W. E. (2006) 'Wildfire-produced charcoal directly influences nitrogen cycling in ponderosa pine forests', *Soil Science Society of America Journal*, vol 70, pp448–453

Denman, K. L., Brasseur, G., Chidthaisong, A., Ciais, P., Cox, P. M., Dickinson, R. E., Hauglustaine, D., Heinze, C., Holland, E., Jacob, D., Lohmann, U., Ramachandran, S., da Silva Dias, P. L., Wofsy, S. C. and Zhang, X. (2007) 'Coupling between changes in the climate system and biogeochemistry', in S. Solomon, D. Qin, M. Manning, Z. Chen, M. Marquis, K. B. Averyt, M. Tignor and H. L. Miller (eds) *Climate Change 2007: The Physical Science Basis. Contribution of Working Group I to the Fourth Assessment Report of the Intergovernmental Panel on Climate Change*, Cambridge University Press, Cambridge, UK, pp499–587

Dick, W. A. and McCoy, E. L. (1993) 'Enhancing soil fertility by addition of compost', in H. A. J. Hoitink and H. M. Keener (eds) *Science and Engineering of Composting*, Renaissance Publication, OH, US, pp 622–643

Forster, P., Ramaswamy, V., Artaxo, P., Berntsen, T., Betts, R., Fahey, D. W., Haywood, J., Lean, J., Lowe, D. C., Myhre, G., Nganga, J., Prinn, R., Raga, G., Schulz, M. and Van Dorland, R. (2007) 'Changes in atmospheric constituents and radiative forcing', in S. Solomon, D. Qin, M. Manning, Z. Chen, M. Marquis, K. B. Averyt, M. Tignor and H. L. Miller (eds) *Climate Change 2007: The Physical Science Basis. Contribution of Working Group I to the Fourth Assessment Report of the Intergovernmental Panel on Climate Change*, Cambridge University Press, Cambridge, UK, pp129–234

Fritze, H., Pennanen, T. and Kitunen, V. (1998) 'Characterization of dissolved organic carbon from burned humus and its effects on microbial activity and community structure', *Soil Biology and Biochemistry*, vol 30, pp687–693

Gillam, K. M., Zebarth, B. J. and Burton, D. L. (2008) 'Nitrous oxide emissions from denitrification and the partitioning of gaseous losses as affected by nitrate and carbon addition and soil aeration', *Canadian Journal of Soil Science*, vol 88, pp133–143

Gundale, M. J. and DeLuca, T. H. (2006) 'Temperature and source material influence ecological attributes of ponderosa pine and Douglas fir charcoal', *Forest Ecological and Management*, vol 231, pp86–93

Hamer, U., Marschner, B., Brodowski, S. and Amelung, W. (2004) 'Interactive priming of black carbon and glucose mineralisation', *Organic Geochemistry*, vol 35 pp823–830

Hayhurst, A. N. and Lawrence, A. D. (1992) 'Emissions of nitrous oxide from combustion sources', *Progress in Energy and Combustion*

Science, vol 18, pp529–552

Hitoshi, T., Ai, F. and Haruo, H. (2002) 'Development of advanced utilization technologies for organic waste: (Part 1) Greenhouse gas and nutrient salt adsorption properties of wood–based charcoal', *Denryoku Chuo Kenkyujo Abiko Kenkyujo Hokoku*, Research Report of Abiko Research Laboratory, no U02010

Hutsch, B. W. (1998) 'Methane oxidation in arable soil as inhibited by ammonium, nitrite, and organic manure with respect to soil pH', *Biology and Fertility of Soils*, vol 28, pp27–35

Inubushi, K., Otake, S., Furukawa, Y., Shibasaki, N., Ali, M., Itang, A. M. and Tsuruta, H. (2005) 'Factors influencing methane emission from peat soils, comparison of tropical and temperate wetlands', *Nutrient Cycling in Agroecosystems*, vol 71, pp93–99

IPCC (Intergovernmental Panel on Climate Change) (2006) *2006 IPCC Guidelines for National Greenhouse Gas Inventories*, National Greenhouse Gas Inventories Programme, Hayama, Japan, www.ipcc-nggip.iges.or.jp/public/2006gl/index.html

Jacinthe, P. A. and Lal, R. (2006) 'Methane oxidation potential of reclaimed grassland soils as affected by management', *Soil Science*, vol 171, pp772–783

Kapteijn, F., Rodriguez-Mirasol, J. and Moulijn, J. (1996) 'Heterogeneous catalytic decomposition of nitrous oxide', *Applied Catalysis B: Environmental*, vol 9, pp25–64

Kay, B. D. and Angers, D. A. (2000) 'Soil structure', in M. E. Sumner (ed) *Handbook of Soil Science*, CRC Press, Boca Raton, FL, ppA229–A276

Keijzer, S. D. and Hermann, R. K. (1966) 'Effect of charcoal on germination of Douglas fir seed', *Northwest Science*, vol 40, pp155–163

Kercher, K., Dennis, C. and Nagle, D. (2003) 'Microstructural evolution during charcoal carbonization by X-ray diffraction analysis', *Carbon*, vol 41, pp15–27

Kim, B., Kim, J. and Park, J. (2006) 'Characteristics in NO reduction by a powder type impregnated activated carbon on the filter support system', *Fourth International Conference on Combustion, Incineration/Pyrolysis and Emission Control*, Kyoto, Japan

Knowles, R. (1993) 'Methane: Process of production and consumption', in G. A. Peterson, P. S. Baenzinger and R. J. Luxmoore, (eds) *Agricultural Ecosystem Effects on Trace Gases and Global Climate Change: Proceedings of a Symposium*, American Society of Agronomy, Madison, WI, pp145–178

Kwon, S. and Pignatello, J. J. (2005) 'Effect of natural organic substances on the surface and adsorptive properties of environmental black carbon (char): Pseudo pore blockage by model lipid components and its implications for N$_2$-probed surface properties of natural sorbents', *Environmental Science and Technology*, vol 39, pp7932–7939

Lehmann, J., Gaunt, J. and Rondon, M. (2006) 'Bio-char sequestration in terrestrial ecosystems – a review', *Mitigation and Adaptation Strategies for Global Change*, vol 11, pp403–427

LeLeuch, L. M. and Bandosz, T. J. (2007) 'The reactive adsorption of ammonia on modified activated carbons', *Carbon*, vol 45, pp568–578

Liang, B., Lehmann, J., Solomon, D., Kinyangi, J., Grossman, J., O'Neill, B., Skjemstad, J. O., Thies, J., Luizão, F. J., Petersen, J. and Neves, E. G. (2006) 'Black carbon increases cation exchange capacity in soils', *Soil Science Society of America Journal*, vol 70, pp1719–1730

Liebig, M. A., Morgan, J. A., Reeder, S. J., Ellert, B. H., Gollany, H. and Schuman, G. E. (2005) 'Greenhouse gas contributions and mitigation potential of agricultural practices in northwestern USA and western Canada', *Soil and Tillage Research*, vol 83, pp25–52

Milne, T. A., Evans, R. J. and Abatzoglou, N. (1998) *Biomass Gasifier 'Tars': Their Nature, Formation, and Conversion*, Report no NREL/TP-570-25357, National Renewable Energy Laboratory, Colorado, www.nrel.gov/docs/fy99osti/25357.pdf, accessed July 2008

Mohanty, S. R., Bodelier, P. L. E., Floris, V. and Conrad, R. (2006) 'Differential effects of nitrogenous fertilizers on methane-consuming microbes in rice field and forest soils', *Applied and Environmental Microbiology*, vol 72, pp1346–1354

Neue, H. U., Wassmann, R., Kludze, H. K., Wang, B. and Lantin, R. S. (1997) 'Factors and processes controlling methane emissions from rice fields', *Nutrient Cycling in Agroecosystems*, vol 49, pp111–117

Oviedo, J. and Sanz, J. F. (2005) 'TiO$_2$ (110) from dynamic first principles calculations', *Journal of Physical Chemistry B*, vol 109, pp16,223–16,226

Oviedo, J. and Sanz, J. F. (2007) 'Influence of temperature on the interaction between Pd clusters and the TiO$_2$ (110)', *Physical Review Letters*, vol 99, article number 066102

Parmon, V. N., Panov, G. I., Uriarte, A. and Noskov, A. S. (2005) 'Nitrous oxide in oxidation chemistry and catalysis: Application and production', *Catalyst Today*, vol 100, pp115–131

Pietikäinen, J., Kiikkilä, O. and Fritze, H. (2000) 'Charcoal as a habitat for microbes and its effect on the microbial community of the underlying humus', *Oikos*, vol 89, pp231–242

Powlson, D. S., Goulding, K. W. T., Willison, T. W., Webster, C. P. and Hütsch, B. W. (1997) 'The effect of agriculture on methane oxidation in soil', *Nutrient Cycling in Agroecosystems*, vol 49, pp59–70

Raison, R. J. (1979) 'Modification of the soil environment by vegetation fires, with particular reference to nitrogen transformations: A review', *Plant and Soil*, vol 51, pp73–108

Robertson, G. P. and Groffman, P. M. (2007) 'Nitrogen transformations', in E. A. Paul (ed) *Soil Microbiology and Biochemistry*, Elsevier Academic Press, Oxford, UK, pp341–362

Rondon, M., Ramirez, J. A. and Lehmann, J. (2005) 'Greenhouse gas emissions decrease with charcoal additions to tropical soils', in *Proceedings of the Third USDA Symposium on Greenhouse Gases and Carbon Sequestration*, Soil Carbon Center, Kansas State University, United States Department of Agriculture, Baltimore, p208, http://soilcarboncenter. k-state.edu/conference/USDA%20Abstracts% 20html/Abstract%20Rondon.htm, accessed June 2008

Rondon, M. A., Molina, D., Hurtado, M., Ramirez, J., Lehmann, J., Major, J. and Amezquita, E. (2006) 'Enhancing the productivity of crops and grasses while reducing greenhouse gas emissions through bio-char amendments to unfertile tropical soils', in *18th World Congress of Soil Science*, 9–15 July, Philadelphia, PA, http://crops.confex.com/ crops/wc2006/techprogram/P16849.HTM, accessed June 2008

Saggar, S., Tate, K. R., Giltrap, D. L. and Singh, J. (2007) 'Soil–atmosphere exchange of nitrous oxide and methane in New Zealand terrestrial ecosystems and their mitigation options: A review', *Plant and Soil*, vol 309, pp25–42

Samonin, V. V. and Elikova, E. E. (2004) 'A study of the adsorption of bacterial cells on porous materials', *Microbiology*, vol 73, pp810–816

Sang, C., Kim, B. H. and Lund, R. F. H. (2005) 'Effect of NO upon N$_2$O decomposition over Fe/ZSM-5 with low iron loading', *Journal of Physical Chemistry B*, vol 109, pp2295–2301

Schneiders, M. and Scherer, H. W. (1998) 'Fixation and release of ammonium in flooded rice soils as affected by redox potential', *European Journal of Agronomy*, vol 8, pp181–189

Schutz, H., Seiler, W. and Rennenberg, H. (1990) 'Soil and land use related sources and sinks of methane (CH$_4$) in the context of the global methane budget', in A. F. Bouwman (ed) *Soils and the Greenhouse Effect*, Wiley, Chichester, NY, US, pp269–285

Soriano-Mora, J. M., Bueno-López, A., García-García, A., Perry, R. E. and Snape, C. E. (2007) 'NO$_x$ removal by low-cost char pellets: Factors influencing the activity and selectivity towards NO$_x$ reduction', *Fuel*, vol 86, pp949–956

Tate, K. R., Ross, D. J., Scott, N. A., Rodda, N. J., Townsend, J. A. and Arnold, G. C. (2006) 'Post-harvest patterns of carbon dioxide production, methane uptake and nitrous oxide production in a *Pinus radiata* D. Don plantation', *Forest Ecology and Management*, vol 228, pp40–50

Tate, K. R., Ross, D. J., Saggar, S., Hedley, C. B., Dando, J., Singh, B. K. and Lamb, S. J. (2007) 'Methane uptake in soils from *Pinus radiata* plantations, a reverting shrubland and adjacent pastures: Effects of land-use change, and soil texture, water and mineral nitrogen', *Soil Biology and Biochemistry*, vol 39, pp1437–1449

Templeton, A. S., Chu, K. H., Alvarez-Cohen, L. and Conrad, M. E. (2006) 'Variable carbon isotope fractionation expressed by aerobic CH$_4$-oxidizing bacteria', *Geochimica et Cosmochimica Acta*, vol 70, pp1739–1752

Tiedje, J. M. (1988) 'Ecology of denitrification and dissimilatory nitrate reduction to ammonium', in A. J. B. Zehnder (ed) *Biology of Anaerobic Microorganisms*, Wiley, Chichester, UK, pp179–244

Vance, E. D., Brookes, P. C. and Jenkinson, D. S. (1987) 'An extraction method for measuring soil microbial biomass C', *Soil Biology and Biochemistry*, vol 19, pp703–707

Villar, M. C., González-Prieto, S. J. and Carballas, T. (1998) 'Evaluation of three organic wastes for reclaiming burnt soils: Improvement in the recovery of vegetation cover and soil fertility in pot experiments', *Biology and Fertility of Soils*, vol 26, pp122–129

Wang, B. and Li, X.-Y. (1998) 'Electrocatalytic properties of nitrous oxide and its voltametric detection at palladium electrodeposited on a glassy carbon electrode', *Analytical Chemistry*, vol 70, pp2181–2187

Warnock, D. D., Lehmann, J., Kuyper, T. W. and Rillig, M. C. (2007) 'Mycorrhizal responses to biochar in soil – concepts and mechanisms', *Plant and Soil*, vol 300, pp9–20

Werner, C., Kiese, R. and Butterbach-Bahl, K. (2007) 'Soil–atmosphere exchange of N_2O, CH_4 and CO_2 and controlling environmental factors for tropical rain forest sites in western Kenya', *Journal of Geophysical Research*, vol 112, pp1–15

White, J. R. and Reddy, K. R. (2001) 'Influence of selected inorganic electron acceptors on organic nitrogen mineralization in Everglades soil', *Soil Science Society of America Journal*, vol 65, pp941–948

Wrage, N., van Groeningen, J. W., Oenema, O. and Baggs, E. M. (2005) 'Distinguishing between soil sources of N_2O using a new [15]N- and ^{18}O-enrichment method', *Rapid Communications in Mass Spectrometry*, vol 19, pp3298–3306

Yanai, Y., Toyota, K. and Okazaki, M. (2007) 'Effects of charcoal addition on N_2O emissions from soil resulting from rewetting air-dried soil in short-term laboratory experiments', *Soil Science and Plant Nutrition*, vol 53, pp181–188

Yu, K., Wang, Z., Vermoesen, A., Patrick, Jr. W. and Van Cleemput, O. (2001) 'Nitrous oxide and methane emissions from different soil suspensions: Effect of soil redox status', *Biology and Fertility of Soils*, vol 34, pp25–30

Zebarth, B. J., Rochette, O. and Burton, D. L. (2008) 'N_2O emissions from spring barley production as influenced by fertilizer nitrogen rate', *Canadian Journal of Soil Science*, vol 88, pp197–205

14

Biochar Effects on Soil Nutrient Transformations

Thomas H. DeLuca, M. Derek MacKenzie and Michael J. Gundale

Introduction

Nutrient transformations are influenced by a myriad of biotic and abiotic factors. However, to date, there have been no attempts to synthesize the literature regarding the influence of biochar on soil nutrient transformations. Although the major focus of this book is to review biochar as a soil amendment in agro-ecosystems, the majority of the literature that addresses the effects of biochar on nutrient transformations has originated from studies in natural forest ecosystems. The addition of biochar to forest soils has been found to directly influence nitrogen (N) transformations in phenol-rich acidic forest soils of both temperate (DeLuca et al, 2006; Gundale and DeLuca, 2006; MacKenzie and DeLuca, 2006) and boreal (DeLuca et al, 2002; Berglund et al, 2004) forest ecosystems. Applying biochar to forest soils along with natural or synthetic fertilizers has been found to increase the bioavailability and plant uptake of phosphorus (P), alkaline metals and some trace metals (Glaser et al, 2002; Lehmann et al, 2003; Steiner et al, 2007), but the mechanisms for these increases are still a matter of speculation. Biochar additions to soil have been found to stimulate mycorrhizal infection (Saito, 1990; Ishii and Kadoya, 1994) and influence P solubility in forest soils (Gundale and DeLuca, 2007), which may be responsible for observed increases in P uptake. The influence of biochar on sulphur (S) transformations has received little or no attention and has not stood out as a dominant effect of adding biochar to natural soil environments. However, biochar applications to mineral soils may have a noted effect on P and S transformations in manure-enriched agro-ecosystems. The mediation of nutrient turnover by biochar has significant implications for organic agricultural systems where biochar may increase stabilization of organic nutrient sources (Glaser et al, 2001) and reduce nutrient leaching losses (Lehmann et al, 2003).

The purpose of this chapter is to provide a state-of-knowledge review of the influences of biochar on N, P and S transformations in soil ecosystems and to provide an overview of the known and potential mechanisms driving these processes. This chapter provides a discussion of the nutrient content of biochar; the potential mechanisms by which biochar modifies nutrient transformations; and the direct and indirect influences of biochar on soil nutrient transformations.

Nutrient content of biochar

Prior to considering the influence of biochar on nutrient transformations, the nutrient capital associated with biochar additions must be considered. In other words, does biochar serve as a significant source of nutrients irrespective of other inputs? The nutrient content of biochar is discussed in depth in Chapter 5. It is important to note that biochar is somewhat depleted in N and slightly depleted in S relative to more thermally stable nutrients. During the pyrolysis or oxidation process that generates biochar, heating causes some nutrients to volatilize, especially at the surface of the material, while other nutrients become concentrated in the remaining biochar (see Chapter 5).

Temperature, the time a material is held at a given temperature and the heating rate directly influence the chemical properties of biochar. Individual elements are potentially lost to the atmosphere, fixed into recalcitrant forms or liberated as soluble oxides during the heating process. In the case of wood-based biochar formed under natural conditions, carbon (C) begins to volatilize around 100°C, N above 200°C, S above 375°C, and potassium (K) and P between 700°C and 800°C. The volatilization of magnesium (Mg), calcium (Ca) and manganese (Mn) occurs at temperatures above 1000°C (Neary et al, 1999; Knoepp et al, 2005). Biochar produced from sewage sludge pyrolysed (heated in the absence of oxygen) at 450°C contains over 50 per cent of the original N (although not in a readily bioavailable form) and all of the original P (Bridle and Pritchard, 2004). The relative concentration and molecular speciation of these elements during heating generates substantial variability in the chemical composition of the resulting biochar and is discussed in greater detail in Chapter 5.

Nitrogen is the most sensitive of all macronutrients to heating; thus, the N content of high-temperature biochar is extremely low (Tyron, 1948). Pyrolysis conditions during the production of wheat straw biochar resulted in the loss of about 50 per cent of the S at temperatures of 500°C and about 85 per cent of the S was lost in 950°C pyrolysis (Knudsen et al, 2004), greatly reducing the S content of the resulting biochar. Accordingly, extractable concentrations of NH_4^+ and PO_4^{3-} generally decrease with increasing pyrolysis temperature during biochar generation, with a portion of NH_4^+ being oxidized to a small exchangeable NO_3^- pool at higher temperatures (Gundale and DeLuca, 2006).

Gundale and DeLuca (2006) evaluated the effect of temperature on biochar formation from several woody substrates collected from a Montana ponderosa pine/Douglas-fir forest. High-temperature (800°C) biochar demonstrated higher pH, electrical conductivity (EC) and extractable NO_3^- relative to low-temperature (350°C) biochar (see Figure 14.1). In contrast, density, extractable PO_4^{3-}, NH_4^+ and soluble and total phenols were lower in high-temperature biochars relative to low-temperature biochars (see Figure 14.2). These data suggest that substantial variation can occur in the chemical properties of biochar due to the temperature that the plant material reaches during charring.

Biochar additions to soil provide a modest contribution of nutrients depending, in part, upon the nature of the feedstock

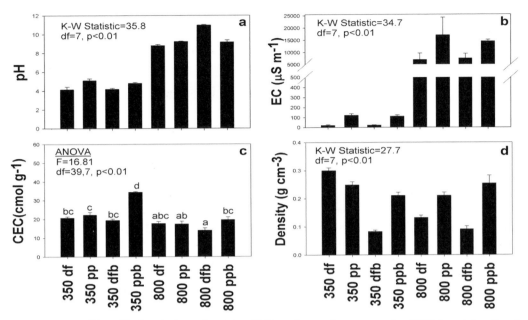

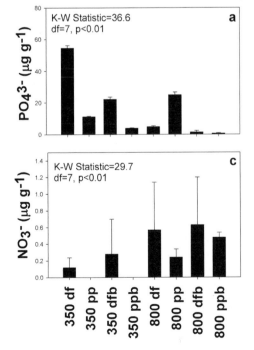

Figure 14.1 *The pH, electrical conductivity (EC), cation exchange capacity (CEC) and density of biochar produced from Douglas-fir or ponderosa pine wood or bark at 350°C or 800°C*

Notes: Data meeting the assumptions of normality were compared with one-way ANOVA followed by the Student-Neuman-Kuels post-hoc procedure where letters indicate pair-wise differences. Non-normal data were compared using the Kruskal–Wallis (K–W) statistic. df = Douglas-fir wood; dfb = Douglas-fir bark; pp = ponderosa pine wood; ppb = ponderosa pine bark; numbers before abbreviations indicate temperature.

Source: adapted from Gundale and DeLuca (2006)

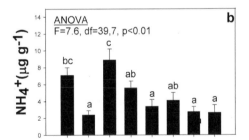

Figure 14.2 *The soluble PO_4^{3-}, NH_4^+ and NO_3^- concentration in biochar produced from Douglas-fir or ponderosa pine wood or bark at 350°C or 800°C*

Notes: Data meeting the assumptions of normality were compared with one-way ANOVA followed by the Student-Neuman-Kuels post-hoc procedure where letters indicate pair-wise differences. Non-normal data were compared using the Kruskal–Wallis statistic. df = Douglas-fir wood; dfb = Douglas-fir bark; pp = ponderosa pine wood; ppb = ponderosa pine bark; numbers before abbreviations indicate temperature.

Source: adapted from Gundale and DeLuca (2006)

(wood versus manure) and upon the temperature under which the material is formed (Bridle and Pritchard, 2004; Gundale and DeLuca, 2006). However, biochar is probably more important as a soil conditioner and driver of nutrient transformations and less so as a primary source of nutrients (Glaser et al, 2002; Lehmann et al, 2003). Therefore, the following discussion is focused on biochar as a modifier of N, P and S transformations in mineral soils.

Potential mechanisms for how biochar modifies nutrient transformations

Biochar is a high surface-area, highly porous, variable-charge organic material that has the potential to increase soil water-holding capacity, cation exchange capacity (CEC), surface sorption capacity and base saturation when added to soil (Glaser et al, 2002; Bélanger et al, 2004; Keech et al, 2005; Liang et al, 2006). The surface area, porosity, nutrient content and charge density all change in relation to the temperature of biochar formation (Gundale and DeLuca, 2006; Bornermann et al, 2007). Biochar additions to soil also have the potential to alter soil microbial populations and to shift functional groups (Pietikäinen et al, 2000) and have the potential to reduce soil bulk density (Gundale and DeLuca, 2006). The broad array of beneficial properties associated with biochar additions to soil may function alone or in combination in order to influence nutrient transformations, described below. The physical characteristics of biochar are discussed in Chapter 2, pH and nutrient contents in Chapter 5, and biotic influences in Chapter 6. Here, we extend this discussion by exploring the known and potential effects of these bio-physico-chemical changes on nutrient transformations.

It is well understood that autotrophic nitrifying bacteria are favoured by less acidic soil conditions (Stevenson and Cole, 1999). Thus, biochar additions to mineral soil that increase soil pH are likely to favourably influence nitrification. However, activated biochar and glycine added to acid boreal forest soils was found to have no influence on pH, but significantly increased net nitrification (Berglund et al, 2004). Furthermore, the addition of natural field-collected biochar – a soil-neutral phosphate buffer slurry – immediately stimulated nitrification potential with no shift in the pH of the suspension (DeLuca et al, 2006). This puts into question the assumption that pH is the major driver of the nitrification response to biochar additions to soil. It is possible that archaeal ammonia oxidizers (*Crenarchaeota*), which have the capacity to nitrify under low pH conditions (Leininger et al, 2006), are the primary drivers of nitrification in coniferous forest soils.

Bioavailable C may be adsorbed to biochar surfaces, thereby reducing the potential for immobilization of nitrate formed under biochar stimulation of nitrification. Biochar added to soil with an organic N source yielded an increase in net nitrification; however, the addition of organic N with or without biochar resulted in high rates of NH_4^+ production that were not immobilized (DeLuca et al, 2006), reducing the likelihood of this explanation.

Biochar may act as a habitat or safe site for soil microorganisms (Pietikäinen et al, 2000) involved in N, P or S transformations. Biochar certainly has the capacity to support the presence of adsorbed bacteria (Pietikäinen et al, 2000; Rivera-Utrilla et al, 2001) from which the organisms may influence soil processes. Both saprophytic and mycorrhizal fungi have been observed to colonize soil biochar; but the significance of their presence has not been clarified (Saito,

1990; Zackrisson et al, 1996). Some researchers have suggested that the small pore sizes of biochar might exclude grazing protozoa and nematodes, allowing for the proliferation of fungi and bacteria (Warnock et al, 2007). However, recent studies suggest that bacteria and fungi primarily colonize the surface of biochar, but that limited oxygen availability may limit growth inside the small internal pores (Yoshizawa et al, 2005).

The high surface area, porous and often hydrophobic nature of biochar makes it an ideal surface for the sorption of hydrophobic organic compounds (Cornelissen et al, 2004; Bornermann et al, 2007). Numerous papers have reported a reduction in soluble or free phenolic compounds when activated carbon is added to soils (DeLuca et al, 2002; Wallstedt et al, 2002; Berglund et al, 2004; Gundale and DeLuca, 2006). Additional studies have demonstrated that biochar formed during wildfires or agricultural residue burning also functions to adsorb phenolic and various aromatic and hydrophobic organic compounds (Yaning and Sheng, 2003; Brimmer, 2006; DeLuca et al, 2006; Gundale and DeLuca, 2006; MacKenzie and DeLuca, 2006; Bornermann et al, 2007). Through these sorption reactions, biochar may reduce the activity of compounds that may be either inhibitory to nutrient transformation specialists, such as nitrifying bacteria (White, 1991; Ward et al, 1997; Paavolainen et al, 1998), or reduce the concentration of phenolic compounds in the soil solution that would otherwise enhance the immobilization of inorganic N, P or S (Schimel et al, 1996; Stevenson and Cole, 1999).

Direct and indirect influences of biochar on soil nutrient transformations

Nitrogen

Nitrogen is the single most limiting plant nutrient in most cold or temperate terrestrial ecosystems (Vitousek and Howarth, 1991). In soils, the majority of N exists in complex organic forms that must be ammonified to NH_4^+ and then nitrified to NO_3^- prior to uptake by most agricultural plants (Stevenson and Cole, 1999). Recent studies have demonstrated that the addition of biochar to surface mineral soils may directly influence N transformations. Here we review the evidence for the direct and indirect influences of biochar on ammonification, nitrification, denitrification and N_2 fixation, and provide potential mechanisms that may be driving these relationships.

Ammonification and nitrification

Nitrogen mineralization is the process whereby organic N is converted to inorganic N through the methods of ammonification (where NH_4^+ is formed) and nitrification (where NO_3^- is formed). Ammonification is a biotic process driven primarily by heterotrophic bacteria and a variety of fungi (Stevenson and Cole, 1999). Nitrification is considered to be a strictly biotic process that is most commonly mediated by autotrophic organisms, including bacteria and archaea, in agricultural, grassland and forest soils (Stevenson and Cole, 1999; Grenon et al, 2004; Leininger et al, 2006; Islam et al, 2007). Biochar has been found to increase net nitrification rates in temperate and boreal forest soils that otherwise demonstrate no net nitrification (Berglund et al, 2004; DeLuca et al, 2006). There is no evidence for such an effect in grassland (DeLuca et al, 2006) or agricultural soils (Lehmann et al, 2003; Rondon et al, 2007), which may already accommodate an active nitrifying community. Results from the studies cited above are

Table 14.1 *Effect of biochar (natural biochar, lab-generated biochar or activated carbon) on nitrogen mineralization and nitrification from studies performed in different forest ecosystems*

Ecosystem	Biochar type	Nutrient source and incubation	Control NH$_4^+$-N	Control NO$_3^-$-N	Biochar addition NH$_4^+$-N	Biochar addition NO$_3^-$-N	Statistical difference	Reference
Ponderosa pine, western Montana	Wildfire biochar, ponderosa pine wood	Glycine in greenhouse, resin collected, 30 days	150 ± 200 (µg N cap⁻¹)[1]	200 ± 100 (µg N cap⁻¹)	700 ± 400 (µg N cap⁻¹)	1200 ± 500 (µg N cap⁻¹)	No NH$_4^+$ Yes NO$_3^-$	MacKenzie and DeLuca (2006)
Ponderosa pine, western Montana	Lab biochar, ponderosa pine wood	(NH$_4$)SO$_4$ and KH$_2$PO$_4$ in lab, aerobic incubation, 15 days	NA (µg N g soil⁻¹)	40 ± 5 (µg N g soil⁻¹)	NA	70 ± 3 (µg N g soil⁻¹)	Yes NO$_3^-$	DeLuca et al (2006)
Ponderosa pine, western Montana	Lab biochar, ponderosa pine (wood and bark), Douglas-fir (wood and bark)	Glycine in lab, aerobic incubation, 14 days	47 ± 4 (µg N g soil⁻¹)	5 ± 1 (µg N g soil⁻¹)	ppw² 20 ± 5 ppb 25 ± 6 dfw 32 ± 8 dfb 27 ± 3	ppw 21 ± 4 ppb 20 ± 8 dfw 11 ± 8 dfb 16 ± 4	Yes NH$_4^+$ Yes NO$_3^-$ Yes NH$_4^+$ Yes NO$_3^-$ No NH$_4^+$ No NO$_3^-$ No NH$_4^+$ Yes NO$_3^-$	Gundale and DeLuca (2006)
Scots pine, Sweden	Activated carbon	Glycine in field, resin collected, 30 days	20 ± 13 (µg N cap⁻¹)	0.06 ± 0.02 (µg N cap⁻¹)	low³ 410 ± 99 high 780 ± 302 (µg N cap⁻¹)	low 0.12 ± 0.03 high 1.89 ± 1.1 (µg N cap⁻¹)	Yes NH$_4^+$ No NO$_3^-$ Yes NH$_4^+$ Yes NO$_3^-$	DeLuca et al (2002)
Scots pine, Sweden	Activated carbon	Glycine in lab, aerobic incubation, 60 days	46 ± 6 (µg N g soil⁻¹)	2.8 ± 0.4 (µg N g soil⁻¹)	1350 ± 50 (µg N g soil⁻¹)	5.5 ± 0.6 (µg N g soil⁻¹)	Yes NH$_4^+$ Yes NO$_3^-$	Berglund et al (2004)
Scots pine, Sweden	Activated carbon	Glycine in field, resin collected, 75 days	20 ± 3 (µg N cap⁻¹)	0.20 ± 0.20 (µg N cap⁻¹)	146 ± 42 (µg N cap⁻¹)	0.6 ± 0.1 (µg N cap⁻¹)	Yes NH$_4^+$ No NO$_3^-$	Berglund et al (2004)

Notes: 1 Ionic resin analysis used approximately 1g mixed bed resin in nylon mesh capsules approximately 25.4mm in diameter.
2 ppw = ponderosa pine wood; ppb = ponderosa pine bark; dfw = Douglas-fir wood; dfb = Douglas-fir bark biochar produced at 350°C.
3 Low biochar application rate of 1000kg ha⁻¹; high application rate was 10,000kg ha⁻¹.
NA = not available.

summarized in Table 14.1, specifically focusing on ammonification and nitrification in biochar or activated carbon-amended soil samples, field plots or mesocosms in comparison to unamended controls. Both activated carbon (DeLuca et al, 2002; Berglund et al, 2004) and biochar collected from recently burned forests (DeLuca et al, 2006; MacKenzie and DeLuca, 2006) or generated in laboratories by heating biomass in a muffle furnace (Gundale and DeLuca, 2006) were found to stimulate net nitrification in forest soils.

Nitrification was found to be below the detection limit in the acidic phenol-rich, late succession forest soils of northern Sweden, whereas forest sites recently exposed to fire were found to have measurable levels of nitrification (DeLuca et al, 2002). The injection of glycine (a labile organic N source) into these late succession soils readily stimulated ammonification, but failed to stimulate any nitrification. The injection of activated carbon into the humus layer induced a slight stimulation of nitrification (see Table 14.1), but the injection of glycine with activated carbon consistently stimulated nitrification, demonstrating that ammonification in these soils was substrate limited, whereas nitrification was being inhibited by a factor that could be mitigated by adding activated carbon (DeLuca et al, 2002; Berglund et al, 2004). In all soils treated with activated carbon, a significant reduction in soluble phenols was recorded (DeLuca et al, 2002; Berglund et al, 2004). It is possible that the activated carbon adsorbed organic compounds that either inhibited net nitrification (White, 1991; Ward et al, 1997; Paavolainen et al, 1998) or caused immobilization of the accumulated NO_3^- (McCarty and Bremner, 1986; Schimel et al, 1996).

Biochar collected from forests that had been exposed to recent forest fires was found to stimulate net nitrification in soils from low-elevation ponderosa pine forests that otherwise demonstrated little or no nitrifica-

tion (DeLuca et al, 2006). Nitrifier activity, as measured using an aerated slurry method (Hart et al, 1994), was found to be extremely low in soils collected from sites that had not been exposed to fire for approximately 100 years and relatively high in soils exposed to recurrent fire (DeLuca and Sala, 2006). The addition of field-collected biochar to soils expressing no net nitrification readily stimulated nitrifier activity in a 24-hour aerated soil slurry assay (DeLuca and Sala, 2006; DeLuca et al, 2006). The addition of biochar to grassland soils that already demonstrated relatively high levels of nitrification had no measurable effect on nitrifier activity (DeLuca et al, 2006). A small increase in nitrification was observed in sterile control samples amended with sterile biochar, suggesting that the oxide surfaces on biochar may stimulate some quantity of auto-oxidation of NH_4^+ (DeLuca et al, 2006). Wood ash commonly contains high concentrations of metal oxides, including CaO, MgO, Fe_2O_3, TiO_2, and CrO (Koukouzas et al, 2007). Exposure of biochar to solubilized ash may result in the retention of these potentially catalytic oxides on active surfaces of the biochar (Le Leuch and Bandosz, 2007). These oxide surfaces may, in turn, effectively adsorb NH_4^+ or NH_3 and potentially catalyse the photo-oxidation of NH_4^+ (Lee et al, 2005).

The rapid response of the nitrifier community to biochar additions in soils with low nitrification activity and the lack of a stimulatory effect on actively nitrifying communities suggest that biochar may be adsorbing inhibitory compounds in the soil environment (Zackrisson et al, 1996), which then allows nitrification to proceed. Fire induces a short-term influence on N availability; but biochar may act to maintain that effect for years to decades after a fire (see Figure 14.3).

The temperature of biochar formation and the type of plant material from which the biochar is generated also potentially influence

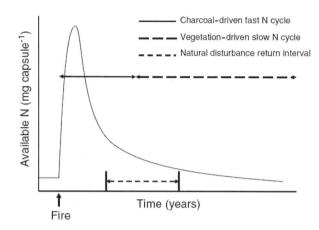

Figure 14.3 *Hypothetical change in N availability with time since the last fire, where biochar induces a fast turnover of N for years after a fire event*

Source: adapted from MacKenzie and DeLuca (2006)

ammonification and nitrification (Gundale and DeLuca, 2006). Gundale and DeLuca (2006) evaluated how biochar produced at two different temperatures (350°C and 800°C) from the bark and wood of two different tree species common to western North America (ponderosa pine and Douglas-fir) influences N mineralization and nitrification. All biochar treatments increased nitrification, except for Douglas-fir wood, which suggests that for some species, bark may create a more effective biochar than wood. In these experiments, biochar addition to soil also caused reduced ammonification compared to the control (Gundale and DeLuca, 2006). This is possibly due to NH_4^+ adsorption to biochar (Berglund et al, 2004). Results were similar for biochar created at 800°C, except for ponderosa pine bark, which did not significantly increase nitrification. It is clear that the temperature of formation and type of organic material pyrolysed are important factors to consider when assessing the effects of biochar on nutrient-cycling processes in soil, and ones not easily dealt with given the multiplicity of combinations that these two factors represent.

In a study of forest floor/mineral soil mesocosms collected intact from a site not exposed to fire for over 100 years in western Montana, biochar was found to stimulate

nitrification under the ericaceous shrub community, but not under the sedge community (see Table 14.1; MacKenzie and DeLuca, 2006). The shrub mesocosm was found to have high concentrations of free phenolic compounds whose recovery was greatly reduced by adding biochar. The sedge mesocosm had low concentrations of free phenols and measurable levels of net nitrification prior to biochar additions. Nitrification in the sedge mesocosm was stimulated by glycine addition to soil without biochar, suggesting that nitrification under sedge was substrate limited (not inhibited) and thus not affected by adding biochar. In this study, charred material was scraped off of the outside of burned trees, making it similar to the charred bark material described above. It is possible that the wildfire biochar functioned as an inoculant, introducing nitrifying bacteria into the soil system; however, nitrifying bacteria are found in most forest soils, but often induce little net nitrification due to rapid N immobilization rates (Stark and Hart, 1997) or inhibition, as described above.

Biochar additions to agricultural soils of the tropics have been reported to either reduce N availability (Lehmann et al, 2003) or to increase N uptake and export in crops (Steiner et al, 2007). Reduced N availability may be a result of the high C/N ratio of biochar and, thus, greater potential for N immobilization (see below) or due to biochar adsorption of NH_4^+ (described above), which in turn reduces the potential for N leaching losses and sustained higher N fertility over time in surface soils (Steiner et al, 2007). It should be noted, however, that immobilization potential associated with biochar additions to soil would be greatly limited by the recalcitrant nature of biochar (DeLuca and Aplet, 2007).

To summarize, biochar additions to acid phenol-rich soils that lack net nitrification have the potential to stimulate nitrification. Biochar additions to agricultural and grassland soils that already demonstrate net nitrification will probably have no effect on nitrification and may express a slight decline in net ammonification due to NH_4^+ adsorption or enhanced immobilization. Whether adsorption is sustained after biochar weathering in soil or decreases as shown for adsorption of polyaromatic hydrocarbons to biochar (Chapter 18) remains to be investigated.

Immobilization, volatilization and denitrification

Little direct evidence exists to demonstrate the effect of biochar on N immobilization, volatilization or denitrification. The latter is discussed in greater detail in Chapter 13. A few studies have suggested that biochar can adsorb both NH_4^+ and NH_3^- from the soil solution (Lehmann et al, 2006), thus reducing solution inorganic N at least temporarily, but perhaps concentrating it for microbial use. Because biochar residing in soil becomes occluded with organic matter (Zackrisson et al, 1996; Wardle et al, 1998), or aggregates both mineral and organic matter fractions together into physically protected pools (Brodowski et al, 2006), the N in those organic matter pools may remain unavailable for some period of time.

As discussed above, biochar is an N-depleted material having a uniquely high C/N ratio. Some decomposition occurs when fresh

biochar is added to soil (Schneour, 1966; Liang et al, 2006), which could induce net immobilization of inorganic N already present in the soil solution or applied as fertilizer. Low-temperature biochar, in particular, would probably induce net immobilization when applied to mineral soils as microbes degrade residual bio-oils (Steiner et al, 2007) or surface functional groups (Liang et al, 2006). This immobilization process could create a temporary reservoir of organic N, which would reduce the potential for leaching of inorganic N in highly leached soils (Steiner et al, 2007).

There have been no studies that have directly evaluated the influence of biochar on NH_3 volatilization. Ammonia volatilization in agricultural soils is favoured at alkaline pH and when high concentrations of NH_4^+ are present (Stevenson and Cole, 1999). Biochar and biochar mixed with ash have the potential to raise the pH of acid soils (Glaser et al, 2002), but not to a level that would increase volatilization (Stevenson and Cole, 1999). Biochar additions to agricultural soils, as well as acid forest soils, have been found to reduce NH_4^+ concentrations, which could be a result of volatilization; but it is more likely that surface adsorption of NH_4^+ (Le Leuch and Bandosz, 2007) reduces soil NH_4^+ concentrations and reduces the potential for NH_3 volatilization.

Denitrification is a biotic dissimilatory process in which NO_3^- is reduced to N_2 (g) in the absence of O_2. Several intermediates (including NO and N_2O) are formed during this reductive process and are potentially released into the soil atmosphere when conditions are not favourable for complete reduction of NO_3^- to N_2. The influence of biochar on denitrification is partially covered in Chapter 13, where it is demonstrated that biochar has the potential to catalyse the reduction of N_2O to N_2, potentially reducing the emission of this important greenhouse gas to the atmosphere.

To date, there have been few studies that directly address the influence of biochar on denitrification. Our evaluation of the fire effects literature suggests that biochar could directly or indirectly influence denitrification. The process of denitrification requires the presence of substrate (available C) and a terminal electron acceptor, such as NO_3^- (Stevenson and Cole, 1999). An increase in net nitrification in acid forest soils when biochar is added (e.g. DeLuca et al, 2006) would increase the potential for denitrification under anaerobic conditions where available C is high. Adding manure with biochar (e.g. Lehmann et al, 2003; Steiner et al, 2007) would potentially increase bioavailable C in the soil solution. The combination of these two factors could increase denitrification potential in mineral soils amended with a mixture of biochar and manure.

Drawing from the fire effects literature, Castaldi and Aragosa (2002) found that fire treatments caused co-variation between moisture content, NH_4^+ concentrations and denitrification enzyme activity (DEA); but the trends were only evident during the wettest time of the year, which was September to November in the studied Mediterranean climate. In a 'light fire treatment', DEA varied with NH_4^+ concentration, and in the 'intense fire treatment', DEA varied with soil moisture content (Castaldi and Aragosa, 2002). It is not clear whether the high-intensity fire treatment yielded a greater amount of biochar or not, as higher-intensity fires generally result in greater volatilization of C and a greater potential to deposit ash rather than biochar (Neary et al, 1999). However, the fact that DEA varied with moisture content and not pH suggests that ash production was minimal (Castaldi and Aragosa, 2002).

Biological nitrogen fixation

Biological N_2 fixation is uniquely important in low-input agro-ecosystems where external N inputs are minimal. Therefore, it is important to know whether biochar applications have the capacity to alter symbiotic or free-living N_2-fixing organisms. Rondon et al (2007) tested the effect of adding different amounts of biochar to nodulating and non-nodulating varieties of the common bean, *Phaseolus vulgaris*, inoculated with *Rhizobium* strains, and measured changes in N uptake using an isotope pool dilution technique. Biochar significantly increased N_2 fixation compared to a control; but the highest application rate, 90g biochar kg^{-1} soil, did not produce the highest soil N concentration or plant biomass (Rondon et al, 2007). The study further indicates that biochar may stimulate N_2 fixation as the result of increased availability of trace metals such as nickel (Ni), iron (Fe), boron (B), titanium (Ti) and molybdenum (Mo). The highest rates of biochar application decreased the magnitude of the effect and, if taken to the extreme, might interfere with N_2 fixation. Legume nodulation might also be affected if added biochar interfered with signalling compounds in the soil environment (Warnock et al, 2007). The formation of root nodules in leguminous plants is initiated by their release of flavonoids, which are polyphenolic signalling compounds (Jain and Nainawatee, 2002). Biochar is highly effective in the sorption of phenolic compounds, including flavonoids (Gundale and DeLuca, 2006). Therefore, high biochar applications may interfere with signal reception and initiation of the legume root infection process.

Free-living N_2-fixing bacteria are ubiquitous in the soil environment. Agro-ecosystems that enhance the presence of these organisms may reduce the need for external inputs. Unfortunately, to date, there are no studies that directly demonstrate an influence of biochar on free-living N_2-fixing bacteria. In forest restoration studies involving prescribed fire, Burgoyne (2007) found no effect of fire treatments on the activity of free-living N-fixing bacteria, although these same plots revealed a significant increase in biochar in both the forest floor and surface mineral soil (DeLuca, unpublished data). It is well understood that excess soluble N in the soil solution reduces N_2-fixation rates in free-living N_2-fixing bacteria (Kitoh and Shiomi, 1991; DeLuca et al, 1996) and available soil P stimulates N_2 fixation (Vitousek et al, 2002). Therefore, it is possible that the activity of these N_2-fixing bacteria could be increased in an environment where applied biochar functions to increase P solubility (Lehmann et al, 2003; Steiner et al, 2007) and reduce soluble soil N concentrations (due to immobilization or surface adsorption of NH_4^+). Conversely, biochar additions to forest soils that stimulate nitrification (e.g. DeLuca et al, 2006) may ultimately down-regulate N_2 fixation by free-living N_2-fixing bacteria.

Phosphorus

Similar to N cycling, microbial turnover and decomposition regulate P mineralization and, thus, influence how much P is available for plant uptake. In contrast to N cycling, however, P availability is also greatly affected by a series of pH-dependent abiotic reactions that influence the ratio of soluble-to-insoluble P pools in the soil. Several studies have demonstrated enhanced P uptake in the presence of biochar; but very little work has focused on the variety of mechanisms through which biochar may directly or indirectly influence the biotic and abiotic components of the P cycle. In this section we discuss a few of these mechanisms, including:

- biochar as a direct source of soluble P salts and exchangeable P;
- biochar as a modifier of soil pH and ameliorator of P complexing metals (Al^{3+}, Fe^{3+2+}, Ca^{2+}); and
- biochar as a promoter of microbial activity and P mineralization.

Soluble P salts and exchangeable P
Altered P availability associated with biochar is probably due, in part, to:

- the release of P salts from woody tissues during charring;
- biochar interference with P sorption to Al and Fe oxides;
- biochar-induced changes in the soil ion exchange capacity; and
- biochar sorption of plant and microbial chelates.

The release of P from biochar has long been recognized (Tyron, 1948), and the mechanism for direct P release from biochar is not complex. The concentration of P in plant tissues is small relative to the large concentration of C, and a significant portion of plant P is incorporated within organic molecules through ester or pyrophosphate bonds (Stevenson and Cole, 1999). This organic P in dead plant tissues is not available for plant uptake without microbial cleavage of these bonds. When plant tissue is heated, organic C begins to volatilize at approximately 100°C, whereas P does not volatilize until approximately 700°C (Knoepp et al, 2005). Combustion or charring of organic materials can greatly enhance P availability from plant tissue by disproportionately volatilizing C and by cleaving organic P bonds, resulting in a residue of soluble P salts associated with the charred material. Gundale and DeLuca (2006) demonstrated this as an increased extractable PO_4^{3-} from biochar made from bark and bole samples of Douglas-fir and ponderosa pine trees from a Montana pine forest. Furthermore, it was found that charring at both low and high temperatures (350°C and 800°C) resulted in a significant extractable PO_4^{3-} pool from all substrates, but that extractable P declined in biochar produced at high relative to low temperatures, where the volatilization threshold for P had been reached. Increased extractable P in soils amended with a variety of charred materials has also been observed for tropical soils (Glaser et al, 2002; Lehmann et al, 2003).

In addition to directly releasing soluble P, biochar can have a high ion exchange capacity (Liang et al, 2006), and may alter P availability by providing anion exchange capacity or by influencing the activity of cations that interact with P. It has been demonstrated that fresh biochar has an abundance of anion exchange capacity in the acid pH range (Cheng et al, 2008), which can initially be in excess of the total cation exchange capacity of the biochar. It is possible that these positive exchange sites compete with Al and Fe oxides (e.g. gibbsite and goethite) for sorption of soluble P, similar to that observed for humic and fulvic acids (Sibanda and Young, 1986; Hunt et al, 2007). To date, however, there is a noted lack of studies evaluating the effect of short-term anion exchange capacity on P cycling and availability.

As biochar ages, the positive exchange sites on biochar surfaces decline and negative charge sites develop (Cheng et al, 2008). The biochemical basis for the high CEC is not fully understood, but is probably due to the presence of oxidized functional groups (such as carboxyl groups), whose presence is indicated by high O/C ratios on the surface of charred materials following microbial degradation (Liang et al, 2006; Preston and Schmidt 2006) and is further influenced by the large surface area (Gundale and DeLuca, 2006) and high charge density of biochar (Liang et al, 2006). Phosphorus availability and recycling may be influenced by the biochar CEC over long timescales and in soils that have inherently low exchange capacities. By reducing the presence of free Al^{3+} and Fe^{3+} near root surfaces, biochar may promote the formation and recycling of labile P fractions. This is also an area of research that deserves greater attention.

Complexation

A significant component of the P cycle consists of a series of precipitation reactions that influence the solubility of P, ultimately influencing the quantity of P that is available for uptake and actively recycled between plants and microbes. The degree to which these precipitation reactions occur is strongly influenced by soil pH due to the pH-dependent activities of the ions responsible for precipitation (Al^{3+}, Fe^{2+3+} and Ca^{2+}) (Stevenson and Cole, 1999). In alkaline soils, P solubility is primarily regulated by its interaction with Ca^{2+}, where a cascading apatite mineral pathway develops. In acid soils, P availability is primarily regulated by its interaction with Al^{3+} and Fe^{2+3+} ions, where highly insoluble Al- and Fe-phosphates form. Biochar may influence precipitation of P into these insoluble pools by altering the pH and, thus, the strength of ionic P interactions with Al^{3+}, Fe^{2+3+} and Ca^{2+} (Lehmann et al, 2003; Topoliantz et al, 2005) or by sorbing organic molecules that act as chelates of metal ions that otherwise precipitate P (DeLuca, unpublished data; see below).

Numerous studies have demonstrated that biochar can modify soil pH, normally by increasing pH in acidic soils (Mbagwu 1989; Matsubara et al, 2002; Lehmann et al, 2003). There are few, if any, studies that have demonstrated a reduction in pH with biochar addition in alkaline soils, however, the addition of acid biochar to acidic soils has been observed to reduce soil pH (Cheng et al, 2006). An increase in pH associated with adding biochar to acid soils is due to an increased concentration of alkaline metal (Ca^{2+}, Mg^{2+} and K^+) oxides in the biochar and a reduced concentration of soluble soil Al^{3+} (Steiner et al, 2007). Adding these alkaline metals, both as soluble salts and associated with biochar exchange sites, is probably the single most significant effect of biochar on P solubility, particularly in acidic soils where subtle changes in pH can result in substantially reduced P precipitation with Al^{3+} and Fe^{3+}. In contrast, adding biochar (and associated ash residue) to neutral or alkaline soils may have a limited effect on P availability because adding alkaline metals would only exacerbate Ca-driven P limitations. In support of this, Gundale and DeLuca (2007) found reduced concentra-

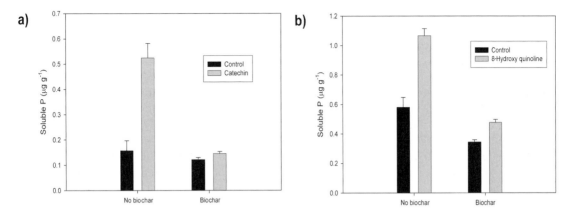

Figure 14.4 *Soluble P leached from columns filled with (a) calcareous soil (pH = 8) amended with catechin alone or with biochar; or (b) acid and Al-rich soil (pH = 6) amended with 8-hydroxy quinoline alone or with biochar*

Notes: Studies were conducted by placing 30g of soil amended with 50mg P kg^{-1} soil as rock phosphate into replicated 50mL leaching tubes (n = 3). Soils were then treated with chelate, or chelate plus biochar (1 per cent w/w) in comparison to an unamended control, allowed to incubate for 16 hours moist and then leached with three successive rinsings of 0.01M CaCl$_2$. Leachates were then analysed for orthophosphate on a segmented flow Auto Analyser III. Data were subject to ANOVA by using SPSS.

Source: DeLuca, unpublished data

tions of resin-sorbed PO_4^{3-} in a neutral (pH 6.8) forest soil when the soil was amended with a biochar generated by wildfire containing a high concentration of soluble salts (including Ca^{2+}). However, these biochar amendments did not appear to inhibit the growth of grass seedlings (Gundale and DeLuca, 2007).

In addition to its effect on soil pH, biochar may also influence the bioavailability of P through several other mechanisms associated with P precipitation, such as biochar-induced surface sorption of chelating organic molecules. Biochar is an exceptionally good surface for sorbing polar or non-polar organic molecules across a wide range of molecular mass (Sudhakar and Dikshit, 1999; Schmidt and Noack, 2000; Preston and Schmidt, 2006; Bornermann et al, 2007). Organic molecules involved in chelation of Al^{3+}, Fe^{3+} and Ca^{2+} ions will potentially be sorbed to hydrophobic or charged biochar surfaces. Examples of such chelates include simple organic acids, phenolic acids, amino acids, and complex proteins or carbohydrates (Stevenson and Cole, 1999).

The sorption of chelates may have a positive or negative influence on P solubility. A clear example of this type of interaction is provided in Figure 14.4. Here, two compounds that have been reported as possible allelopathic compounds released as root exudates (catechin and 8-hydroxy quinoline) (Vivanco et al, 2004; Callaway and Vivanco, 2007) have also been reported to function as potent metal chelates (Stevenson and Cole, 1999; Shen et al, 2001) that may indirectly increase P solubility. Catechin effectively increased P solubility in an alkaline (pH 8.0) calcareous soil and the 8-hydroxy quinoline increased P solubility when added to an acidic (pH 5.0) and Al-rich soil (see Figure 14.4). The addition of biochar to these soils eliminated the presence of soluble chelate in the soil system and, in turn, eliminated the effect of the chelate on P solubility (DeLuca, unpublished data). This interaction may explain the observed reduction in P sorption by ionic resins with increasing biochar application rates in the presence of actively growing *Koeleria macrantha* (Gundale and DeLuca, 2007). Such indirect effects of biochar on P solubility would vary with soil type and vegetative cover and underscores the complexity of plant–soil interactions.

Microorganisms

Biochar may have an indirect effect on P availability and uptake by providing a beneficial environment for microorganisms that, in turn:

- provide greater access to P from organic and insoluble inorganic pools;
- produce and recycle a highly labile pool of organic P; and
- improve plants' direct access to P through improved mycorrhizal activity.

Several studies have demonstrated shifts in microbial activity or community composition with biochar additions to soil (Wardle et al, 1998; Pietikäinen et al, 2000; DeLuca et al, 2006). The mechanisms for increased microbial activity remain unclear because very little research has focused on factors such as how the microbial community size, community structure or specific interactions within soil microbial communities and soil food web change in the presence of biochar (see Chapter 6).

Warnock et al (2007) reviewed several mechanisms through which biochar might affect soil microorganisms, including its effect on sorption of microbial signalling compounds (described above) and the physical structure of biochar, which provides a habitat for microbes within the porous structure of charred material. The physical structure of biochar is inherited from the plant tissue from which it is formed and, thus, can have an extremely high pore density, such as that found in woody xylem tissue. Substantial variability in pore density

and pore size can occur, and this can influence the size of organisms able to enter biochar (Pietikäinen et al, 2000) and the total surface area of biochar that could sorb compounds (Keech et al, 2005). The pore size of wood-derived biochar may range from approximately $10\mu m^2$ to approximately $3000\mu m^2$, depending upon the species from which it is derived (Keech et al, 2005). Thus, some biochars may create pore spaces for bacteria and fungi that are safe from even the smallest soil grazers, such as protozoa, whereas, other biochars may only restrict very large soil grazers, such as mites and collembola. The ability of biochar to exclude soil grazers might allow soil microbes to mediate nutrient transformations more efficiently. However, it is possible that microbes primarily colonize the surface of biochar and not the internal pore surface (Yoshizawa et al, 2005).

Very little work has focused on the role of biochar pore spaces within the context of soil food webs. Warnock et al (2007) speculated that the safe pore environment of biochars might enhance activity of mycorrhizal fungi or stimulate mycorrhization helper bacteria. These potential mechanisms may help to explain several studies that have demonstrated higher mycorrhizal colonization in the presence of biochar (Saito, 1990; Ishii and Kadoya, 1994; Ezawa et al, 2002; Matsubara et al, 2002; Yamato et al, 2006).

Sulphur

Given the similarities between the S and N cycles (Stevenson and Cole, 1999), there is a significant potential for biochar to influence S mineralization and oxidation activity in the soil. Although the majority of soil S originates from the geologic parent material, most soil S exists in an organic state and must be mineralized prior to plant uptake (Stevenson and Cole, 1999). Organic S exists as either ester sulphate or as C-bonded S, the latter having to be oxidized to SO_4^{2-} prior to plant uptake.

To date, no studies have directly assessed the influence of biochar on S transformations or S availability in agricultural or forest soils. However, numerous studies involving biochar or biochar additions to soils have recorded changes in the soil environment that suggest that biochar additions could increase soil S bioavailability. Biochar additions to acid agricultural soils have been observed to yield a net increase in soil pH (see Chapter 5), potentially as a function of the alkaline oxides applied along with the biochar or potentially as a result of the influence on free Al/Ca ratios in soils amended with biochar (Glaser et al, 2002; Topoliantz et al, 2005). Sulphur mineralization is favoured at slightly acid to neutral pH. Sulphur mineralization rates have been found to increase following fire in pine forest ecosystems (Binkley et al, 1992), much the same as that observed for N (Smithwick et al, 2005). Separating the effect of fire from the effect of the natural addition of biochar is difficult; but this effect is most likely due to the release of soluble S from litter following partial combustion during fire or heating events at temperatures in excess of 200°C (Gray and Dighton, 2006).

Sulphur oxidation is carried out by both autotrophic (e.g. *Thiobacillus* spp) and heterotrophic organisms. Sulphur oxidation by acidophilic *Thiobacillus* spp would not be favoured by pH increases induced by the presence of biochar. However, these autotrophic organisms have uniquely high requirements for certain trace elements that are in relatively high concentrations in biochar (see Chapter 5) and are increased in soil when biochar is added (Rondon et al, 2007). Biochar additions to soil that ultimately reduce the surface albedo of mineral soils and result in faster warming of soils in springtime may, in turn, increase S oxidation or mineralization rates (Stevenson and Cole, 1999).

Biochar additions to mineral soils may also directly or indirectly affect S sorption reactions and S reduction. As noted in Chapters 2 and 15, biochar improves soil physical properties through increased specific surface area, increased water-holding capacity and improved surface drainage. Improved soil aeration through these improvements in soil physical condition would, in turn, reduce the potential for dissimilatory S reduction (Stevenson and Cole, 1999). Sulphur is readily adsorbed to mineral surfaces in the soil environment and particularly to exposed Fe and Al oxides. Organic matter additions to soil are known to reduce the extent of SO_4^{2-} sorption in acid forest soils (Johnson, 1984); therefore, biochar amendments may act to increase solution concentrations of S in acid iron-rich soils.

Conclusions

The application of biochar to agricultural soils has the potential to greatly improve soil physical, chemical and biological conditions. In this chapter we reviewed biochar as a modifier of soil nutrient transformations and discussed the known and potential mechanisms that drive these modifications. Biochar clearly has the potential to increase net nitrification in acid forest soils that otherwise demonstrate little or no nitrification. The mechanisms behind this stimulation of nitrification remains the subject of ongoing debate; however, it is probably due to the sorption of compounds that otherwise lead to the inhibition of nitrification or immobilization of inorganic N. In contrast, biochar has not been found to increase ammonification, and although biochar applications have been found to increase plant uptake of N, there is no evidence for an increase in N availability following harvest of the crop. This may be a result of the capacity of biochar to adsorb NH_4^+ once it is formed, thereby leading to no measurable increases in net ammonification.

There is a distinct need for studies directed at explaining mechanisms for increased P uptake with biochar additions to agricultural soils. Although plant P uptake has been found to increase with increasing biochar added in some agro-ecosystems, this has not been directly observed in natural forest soils amended with biochar. It is possible that biochar additions to soils stimulate mycorrhizal colonization, which may increase P uptake; but when applied with P-rich materials, this effect may be lost.

The effect of biochar on soil nutrient transformations has not been adequately studied. Some key areas that require attention include:

- By what mechanisms does biochar affect N mineralization and immobilization in different ecosystems?
- Does NH_4^+ adsorption by biochar greatly reduce N availability or does it concentrate N for plant and microbial use?
- By what mechanism do biochar additions to mineral soils stimulate P availability?
- How do different plant materials and different temperatures affect the physical character and biochemical potential of biochar?
- How do biochar additions affect S availability and by what mechanism(s)?

The answers to these questions can only be obtained through rigorous investigation of biochar as a natural component of grassland and forest soils, and as a soil conditioner and amendment added to agricultural soils.

References

Bélanger, N. I., Côté, B., Fyles, J. W., Chourchesne, F. and Hendershot, W. H. (2004) 'Forest regrowth as the controlling factor of soil nutrient availability 75 years after fire in a deciduous forest of southern Quebec', *Plant Soil*, vol 262, pp363–372

Berglund, L. M., DeLuca, T. H. and Zackrisson, T. H. (2004) 'Activated carbon amendments of soil alters nitrification rates in Scots pine forests', *Soil Biology and Biochemistry*, vol 36, pp2067–2073

Binkley, D., Richter, J., David, M. B. and Caldwell, B. (1992) 'Soil chemistry in a loblolly/longleaf pine forest with interval burning', *Ecological Applications*, vol 2, pp157–164

Bornermann, L., Kookana, R. S. and Welp, G. (2007) 'Differential sorption behavior of aromatic hydrocarbons on charcoals prepared at different temperatures from grass and wood', *Chemosphere*, vol 67, pp1033–1042

Bridle, T. R. and Pritchard D. (2004) 'Energy and nutrient recovery from sewage sludge via pyrolysis', *Water Science and Technology*, vol 50, pp169–175

Brimmer, R. J. (2006) *Sorption Potential of Naturally Occurring Charcoal in Ponderosa Pine Forests of Western Montana*, MS thesis, University of Montana, Missoula, US

Brodowski, S., John, B. Flessa H. and Amelung, W. (2006) 'Aggregate-occluded black carbon in soil', *European Journal of Soil Science*, vol 57, pp539–546

Burgoyne, T. (2007) *Free Living Nitrogen-Fixation in Ponderosa Pine/Douglas-Fir Forests in Western Montana*, MS thesis, University of Montana, Missoula, US

Callaway, R. M. and Vivanco J. M. (2007) 'Invasion of plants into native communities using the underground information superhighway', *Allelopathy Journal*, vol 19, pp143–151

Castaldi, S. and Aragosa, D. (2002) 'Factors influencing nitrification and denitrification variables in a natural and fire-disturbed Mediterranean shrubland', *Biology and Fertility of Soils*, vol 36, pp418–425

Cheng, C. H., Lehmann J., Thies J. E., Burton

S. D. and Engelhard M. H. (2006) 'Oxidation of black carbon by biotic and abiotic processes', *Organic Geochemistry*, vol 37, pp1477–1488

Cheng, C. H., Lehmann J. and Engelhard, M. H. (2008) 'Natural oxidation of black carbon in soils: Changes in molecular form and surface charge along a climosequence', *Geochimica et Cosmochimica Acta*, vol 72, pp1598–1610

Cornelissen, G., Elmquist, M., Groth, I. and Gustafsson, Ö. (2004) 'Effect of sorbate planarity on environmental black carbon sorption', *Environmental Science and Technology*, vol 38, pp3574–3580

DeLuca, T. H. and Aplet, G. H. (2007) 'Charcoal and carbon storage in forest soils of the Rocky Mountain West', *Frontiers in Ecology and the Environment*, vol 6, pp1–7

DeLuca, T. H. and Sala, A. (2006) 'Frequent fire alters nitrogen transformations in ponderosa pine stands of the inland northwest', *Ecology*, vol 87, pp2511–2522

DeLuca, T. H., Drinkwater, L. E., Wiefling, B. A. and DeNicola, D. (1996) 'Free-living nitrogen-fixing bacteria in temperate cropping systems: Influence of nitrogen source', *Biology and Fertility of Soils*, vol 23, pp140–144

DeLuca, T. H., Nilsson, M.-C. and Zackrisson, O. (2002) 'Nitrogen mineralization and phenol accumulation along a fire chronosequence in northern Sweden', *Oecologia*, vol 133, pp206–214

DeLuca, T. H., MacKenzie, M. D., Gundale, M. J. and Holben, W. E. (2006) 'Wildfire-produced charcoal directly influences nitrogen cycling in forest ecosystems', *Soil Science Society America Journal*, vol 70, pp448–453

Ezawa, T., Yamamoto, K. and Yoshida, S. (2002) 'Enhancement of the effectiveness of indigenous arbuscular mycorrhizal fungi by inorganic soil amendments', *Soil Science and Plant Nutrition*, vol 48, pp897–900

Glaser, B., Haumaier, L., Guggenberger, G. and Zech, W. (2001) 'The "Terra Preta" phenomenon: A model for sustainable agriculture in the humid tropics', *Naturwissenschaften*, vol 88, pp37–41

Glaser, B., Lehmann, J. and Zech, W. (2002) 'Ameliorating physical and chemical properties of highly weathered soils in the tropics with charcoal – a review', *Biology and Fertility of Soils*, vol 35, pp219–230

Gray, D. M. and Dighton, J. (2006) 'Mineralization of forest litter nutrients by heat and combustion', *Soil Biology and Biochemistry*, vol 38, pp1469–1477

Grenon, F., Bradley, R. L. and Titus, B. D. (2004) 'Temperature sensitivity of mineral N transformation rates, and heterotrophic nitrification: Possible factors controlling the post-disturbance mineral N flush in forest floors', *Soil Biology and Biochemistry*, vol 36, pp1465–474

Gundale, M. J., and DeLuca, T. H. (2006) 'Temperature and substrate influence the chemical properties of charcoal in the ponderosa pine/Douglas-fir ecosystem', *Forest Ecology and Management*, vol 231, pp86–93

Gundale, M. J. and DeLuca, T. H. (2007) 'Charcoal effects on soil solution chemistry and growth of *Koeleria macrantha* in the ponderosa pine/Douglas-fir ecosystem', *Biology and Fertility of Soils*, vol 43, pp303–311

Hart, S. C., Stark, J. M., Davidson, E. A. and Firestone, M. K. (1994) 'Nitrogen mineralization, immobilization, and nitrification', in R. W. Weaver et al (eds) *Methods of Soil Analysis. Part 2: Microbiological and Biochemical Properties*, Soil Science Society of America, Madison, WI, pp985–1018

Hunt, J. F., Ohno, T., He, Z., Honeycutt, C. W. and Dail, D. B. (2007) 'Inhibition of phosphorus sorption to goethite, gibbsite, and kaolin by fresh and decomposed organic matter', *Biology and Fertility of Soils*, vol 44, pp277–288

Ishii, T. and Kadoya, K. (1994) 'Effects of charcoal as a soil conditioner on citrus and vesicular-arbuscular mycorrhizal development', *Journal of the Japanese Society of Horticultural Science*, vol 63, pp529–535

Islam, A., Chen, D. and White, R. E. (2007) 'Heterotrophic and autotrophic nitrification in two acid pasture soils', *Soil Biology and Biochemistry*, vol 39, pp972–975

Jain, V. and Nainawatee, H. S. (2002) 'Plant flavonoids: Signals to legume nodulation and soil microorganisms', *Journal of Plant Biochemistry and Biotechnology*, vol 11, pp1–10

Johnson, D. W. (1984), 'Sulfur cycling in forests', *Biogeochemistry*, vol 1, pp29–43

Keech, O., Carcaillet, C. and Nilsson, M. C. (2005) 'Adsorption of allelopathic compounds by wood-derived charcoal: The role of wood porosity', *Plant and Soil*, vol 272, pp291–300

Kitoh, S. and Shiomi, N. (1991) 'Effect of mineral nutrients and combined nitrogen sources in the medium on growth and nitrogen fixation of the Azolla–Anabaena association', *Journal of Soil Science and Plant Nutrition*, vol 37, pp419–426

Knoepp, J. D., DeBano, L. F. and Neary, D. G. (2005) *Soil Chemistry*, RMRS-GTR 42-4, US Department of Agriculture, Forest Service, Rocky Mountain Research Station, Ogden, UT

Knudsen, J. N., Jensen, P. A., Lin, W. G. Frandsen, F. J. and Dam-Johansen, K. (2004) 'Sulfur transformations during thermal conversion of herbaceous biomass', *Energy and Fuels*, vol 18, pp810–819

Koukouzas, N., Hämäläinen, J., Papanikolaou, D., Tourunen, A. and Jäntti, T. (2007) 'Mineralogical and elemental composition of fly ash from pilot scale fluidised bed combustion of lignite, bituminous coal, wood chips and their blends', *Fuel*, vol 86, pp2186–2193

Lee, D. K., Cho, J. S. and Yoon, W. L. (2005) 'Catalytic wet oxidation of ammonia: Why is N_2 formed preferentially against NO_3^-?', *Chemosphere*, vol 61, pp573–578

Lehmann, J., da Silva Jr., J. P., Steiner, C., Nehls, T., Zech, W. and Glaser, B. (2003) 'Nutrient availability and leaching in an archaeological Anthrosol and a Ferrasol of the Central Amazon basin: Fertilizer, manure, and charcoal amendments', *Plant and Soil*, vol 249, pp343–357

Lehmann, J., Gaunt, J. and Rondon, M. (2006) 'Bio-char sequestration in terrestrial ecosystems – a review', *Mitigation and Adaptation Strategies for Global Change*, vol 11, pp403–427

Leininger, S., Urich, T. Schloter, M. Schwark, L., Qi, J., Nicol, G. W., Prosser, J. I., Schuster, S. C. and Schleper, C. (2006) 'Archaea predominate among ammonia-oxidizing prokaryotes in soils', *Nature*, vol 442, pp806–809

Le Leuch, L. M. and Bandosz, T. J. (2007) 'The role of water and surface acidity on the reactive adsorption of ammonia on modified activated carbons' *Carbon*, vol 45, pp568–578

Liang, B., Lehmann, J., Solomon, D., Kinyangi, J., Grossman, J., O'Neill, B., Skjemstad, J. O., Thies, J., Luizao, F. J., Petersen, J. and Neves, E. G. (2006) 'Black carbon increases cation exchange capacity in soils', *Soil Science Society America Journal*, vol 70, pp1719–1730

MacKenzie, M. D. and DeLuca, T. H. (2006) 'Charcoal and shrubs modify soil processes in ponderosa pine forests of western Montana', *Plant and Soil*, vol 287, pp257–267

Matsubara, Y.-I., Hasegawa, N. and Fukui, H. (2002) 'Incidence of *Fusarium* root rot in asparagus seedlings infected with arbuscular mycorrhizal fungus as affected by several soil amendments', *Journal of the Japanese Society of Horticultural Science*, vol 71, pp370–374

Mbagwu, J. S. C. (1989) 'Effects of organic amendments on some physical properties of a tropical Ultisol', *Biological Wastes*, vol 28, pp1–13

McCarty, G. W. and Bremner, J. M. (1986) 'Inhibition of nitrification in soil by acetylenic compounds', *Soil Science Society of America*, vol 50, pp1198–1201

Neary, D. G., Klopatek, C. C., DeBano, L. F. and Folliott, P. F. (1999) 'Fire effects on belowground sustainability: A review and synthesis', *Forest Ecology and Management*, vol 122, pp51–71

Paavolainen, L., Kitunen, V. and Smolander, A. (1998) 'Inhibition of nitrification in forest soil by monoterpenes', *Plant and Soil*, vol 205, pp147–154

Pietikäinen, J., Kiikkila, O. and Fritze, H. (2000) 'Charcoal as a habitat for microbes and its effect on the microbial community of the underlying humus', *Oikos*, vol 89, pp231–242

Preston, C. M. and Schmidt, M. W. I. (2006) 'Black (pyrogenic) carbon: A synthesis of current knowledge and uncertainties with special consideration of boreal regions', *Biogeosciences*, vol 3, pp397–420

Rivera-Utrilla, J., Bautilsta-Toledo, I., Ferro-Carcia, M. A. and Moreno-Catilla, C. (2001) 'Activated carbon surface modifcations by adsoption of bacteria and their effect on aqueous lead adsorption', *Journal of Chemical Technology and Biotechnology*, vol 76, pp1209–1215

Rondon, M., Lehmann, J., Ramirez, J. and Hurtado, M. (2007) 'Biological nitrogen fixation by common beans (*Phaseolus vulgaris* L.) increases with bio-char additions', *Biology and Fertility of Soils*, vol 43, pp699–708

Saito, M. (1990) 'Charcoal as a micro habitat for VA mycorrhizal fungi, and its practical application', *Agriculture, Ecosystems, and the Environment*, vol 29, pp341–344

Schimel, J. P., Van Cleve, K., Cates, R. G.,
Clausen, T. P. and Reichardt, P. B. (1996)
'Effects of balsam polar (*Populus balsamifera*)
tannin and low molecular weight phenolics on
microbial activity in taiga floodplain soil:
Implications for changes in N cycling during
succession', *Canadian Journal of Botany*, vol
74, pp84–90

Schmidt, M. W. I. and Noack, A. G. (2000) 'Black
carbon in soils and sediments: Analysis, distribution, implications, and current challenges',
Global Biogeochemical Cycles, vol 14,
pp777–793

Schneour, E. A. (1966) 'Oxidation of graphite
carbon in certain soils', *Science*, vol 151,
991–992

Shen, C., Kahn, A. and Schwartz, J. (2001)
'Chemical and electrical properties of inter-
faces between magnesium and aluminum and
tris-(8-hydroxy quinoline) aluminum', *Journal
of Applied Physics*, vol 89, pp449–459

Sibanda, H. M. and Young, S. D. (1986)
'Competitive adsorption of humus acids and
phosphate on goethite, gibbsite and two tropical soils', *European Journal of Soil Science*, vol
37, pp197–204

Smithwick, E. A., Turner, H. M., Mack, M. C. and
Chapin, C. F. S. III (2005) 'Post fire soil N
cycling in northern conifer forests affected by
severe, stand replacing wildfires', *Ecosystems*,
vol 8, pp163–181

Stark, J. M. and Hart, S. C. (1997) 'High rates of
nitrification and nitrate turnover in undisturbed coniferous forests', *Nature*, vol 385,
pp61–64

Steiner, C., Teixeira, W. G., Lehmann, J., Nehls, T.,
de Macedo, J. L. V., Blum, W. E. H. and Zech,
W. (2007) 'Long term effects of manure, charcoal, and mineral fertilization on crop
production and fertility on a highly weathered
Central Amazonian upland soil', *Plant and Soil*,
vol 291, pp275–290

Stevenson, F. J., and Cole, M. A. (1999) *Cycles of
the Soil*, second edition, John Wiley and Sons,
Inc, New York, NY

Sudhakar, Y. and Dikshit, A. K. (1999) 'Kinetics of
endosulfan sorption onto wood charcoal',
Journal of Environmental Science and Health B,
vol 34, pp587–615

Topoliantz, S., Pong, J.-F. and Ballof, S. (2005)
'Manioc peel and charcoal: A potential organic

amendment for sustainable soil fertility in the
tropics', *Biology and Fertility of Soils*, vol 41,
pp15–21

Tyron, E. H. (1948) 'Effect of charcoal on certain
physical, chemical, and biological properties of
forest soils', *Ecological Monographs*, vol 18, pp
82–115

Vitousek, P. M. and Howarth, R. W. (1991)
'Nitrogen limitation on land and in the sea:
How can it occur?' *Biogeochemistry*, vol 13,
pp87–115

Vitousek, P. M., Cassman, K., Cleveland, C.,
Crews, T., Field, C. B., Grimm, N. B.,
Howarth, R. W., Marino, R., Martinelli, L.,
Rastetter, E. B. and Sprent, J. I. (2002)
'Towards an ecological understanding of
biological nitrogen-fixation', *Biogeochemistry*,
vol 57/58, pp1–45

Vivanco, J. M., Bais, H. P., Stermitz, F. R., Thelen,
G. C. and Callaway, R. M. (2004)
'Biogeographical variation in community
response to root allelochemistry: Novel
weapons and exotic invasion', *Ecology Letters*,
vol 7, pp285–292

Wallstedt, A., Coughlan, A., Munson, A. D.,
Nilsson, M.-C. and Margolis, H. A. (2002)
'Mechanisms of interaction between *Kalmia
angustifulia* cover and *Picea mariana* seedlings',
Canadian Journal of Forest Research, vol 32,
pp2022–2031

Ward, B. B., Courtney, K. J. and Langenheim, J. H.
(1997) 'Inhibition of *Nitrosmonas europea* by
monoterpenes from coastal redwood (*Sequoia
sempervirens*) in whole-cell studies', *Journal of
Chemical Ecology*, vol 23, pp2583–2599

Wardle, D. A., Zackrisson, O. and Nilsson, M.-C.
(1998) 'The charcoal effect in boreal forests:
Mechanisms and ecological consequences',
Oecologia, vol 115, pp419–426

Warnock, D. D., Lehmann, J., Kuyper, T. W. and
Rillig, M. C. (2007) 'Mycorrhizal response to
biochar in soil – concepts and mechanisms',
Plant and Soil, vol 300, pp9–20

White, C. (1991) 'The role of monoterpenes in
soil nitrogen cycling processes in ponderosa
pine', *Biogeochemistry*, vol 12, pp43–68

Yamato, M., Okimori, Y., Wibowo, I. F., Anshiori,
S. and Ogawa, M. (2006) 'Effects of the application of charred bark of *Acacia mangium* on
the yield of maize, cowpea and peanut, and soil
chemical properties in South Sumatra,

Indonesia', *Soil Science and Plant Nutrition*, vol 52, pp489–495

Yaning, Y. and Sheng, G. (2003) 'Enhanced pesticide sorption by soils containing particulate matter from crop residue burning', *Environmental Science and Technology*, vol 37, pp3635–3639

Yoshizawa, S., Tanaka, S., Ohata, M., Mineki, S., Goto, S., Fujioka, K. and Kokubun, T. (2005) 'Composting of food garbage and livestock waste containing biomass charcoal', *Proceedings of the International Conference and Natural Resources and Environmental Management 2005*, Kuching, Sarawak

Zackrisson, O., Nilsson, M.-C. and Wardle, D. A. (1996) 'Key ecological function of charcoal from wildfire in the Boreal forest', *Oikos*, vol 77, pp10–19

15

Biochar Effects on Nutrient Leaching

Julie Major, Christoph Steiner, Adriana Downie and Johannes Lehmann

Introduction

Leaching is often an important aspect of nutrient cycling in agriculture (Brady and Weil, 2008). It occurs when mobile nutrients in the soil solution are displaced by percolating water to an area outside the rooting zone where plants cannot utilize them. Nutrients adsorbed to small mobile particles or colloids can also be leached to deeper soil horizons through facilitated transport. For nutrients dissolved in the soil solution, a migration of anions must be accompanied by an equivalent migration of cations for the maintenance of electro-neutrality. As such, the loss of highly mobile nitrate molecules after nitrogen (N) fertilization or organic matter mineralization must occur along with the loss of cations such as calcium (Ca), potassium (K), magnesium (Mg), etc. The amounts of plant-essential nutrients lost from the rooting zone by leaching can be considerable: losses up to 80 per cent of applied N (Lehmann et al, 2004), 172 per cent of applied Ca (Omoti et al, 1983) and 136 per cent of applied Mg (Cahn et al, 1993) have been reported in the field. Values greater than 100 per cent indi-

cate that nutrients other than those added were also mobilized (e.g. by the process of desorption). Leaching, like most soil properties and processes, can be spatially and temporally highly variable.

While large proportions of nutrient losses certainly imply economic impacts with fertilizer-use efficiency and soil nutrient stock depletion, the environmental impacts brought about by nutrient leaching can be considerable. Phosphorus (P) and other nutrients cause eutrophication when they leach or run off from agricultural land into water bodies. This is currently one of the most common causes of unacceptable water quality levels in the developed world (Daniel et al, 1998; Sharpley et al, 2001). In 1992, as much as 26 per cent of water wells in intensive agricultural areas of the US were found to have nitrate levels above the maximum contaminant level (MCL) set by the Environmental Protection Agency (EPA) (Mueller et al, 1995). British water supply companies have made costly investments in blending and other technology to reduce nitrate levels to European Union (EU) limits (through the UK Department for Environment, Food and Rural Affairs, or Defra).

Biochar has been found to decrease nutrient leaching on its own (Downie et al, 2007; Dünisch et al, 2007), as well as after incorporation within soil (Lehmann et al, 2003). In this chapter we review empirical evidence on the magnitude and dynamics of biochar's effect on nutrient leaching, and discuss possible mechanisms and processes by which this effect is observed.

General factors that influence nutrient leaching

Before considering the effect of biochar application on soil nutrient leaching, the contributory factors to the leaching process must be examined. Indeed, factors other than biochar application, such as rainfall patterns, will probably be stronger determinants of leaching losses. Biochar application represents a controllable production factor and has the potential to help manage such losses.

Management of vegetation and fertilization

Nutrient leaching is generally greatest under fertilized row crops such as maize or horticultural crops, and targeting these cropping systems may yield the best results for reducing leaching. Roots exert suction on the soil, and the horizontal and vertical distribution of roots that are intercepting and taking up nutrients influences leaching. Deep-rooted plants such as trees can act as 'safety nets' and recycle leached nutrients that have migrated to deeper soil horizons (Rowe et al, 1998; Allen et al, 2004). Nutrient-use efficiency also varies among crop species and varieties, as well as if other stress factors are present, such as drought and pest pressure. Lower efficiencies should lead to greater losses of unutilized nutrients through leaching. The amounts, chemical form, timing and

placement of fertilizers, synthetic and organic, also greatly affect nutrient leaching patterns (Melgar et al, 1992; Cahn et al, 1993; van Es et al, 2002). Ideally, these should match crop requirements in both time and space; but practical considerations often prevent this. With greater nutrient retention by biochar additions to soil, timing of nutrient applications will become less critical with respect to nutrient leaching.

Soil structure and texture

Surface soil porosity is critical in determining the rate at which rain can infiltrate into soil and carry nutrients with it away from the rooting zone. There, small pores retain soil solution by capillarity, reducing leaching and crop water stress. Amounts of leached nitrate are greater on coarser-textured soil, or when hydraulic conductivity and infiltration rates are higher (Melgar et al, 1992; van Es et al, 2002, 2006). This suggests that biochar should have the greatest value for reducing nutrient leaching in sandy soils. However, in certain cases, differences between soil textures could be linked to changes in denitrification rates and the loss of N gases, and not to changes in water percolation (van Es et al, 2002). The flow of nutrient-carrying water through soil is also greatly influenced by the soil's macropore structure, which allows water to avoid permeating the soil matrix and can cause rapid flow down the profile (Ghodrati and Jury, 1990; Flury et al, 1994; Renck and Lehmann, 2004), even through paddy rice soil where surface structure is periodically destroyed (Sander and Gerke, 2007). The physical characteristics of biochar (see Chapter 2) suggest that it can change the pore-size distribution of the soil and possibly alter percolation patterns, residence times of soil solution and flow paths.

Rainfall patterns

As expected, a linear relation exists between depth of movement of nitrate, which is highly mobile in soil, and cumulative rainfall

(Melgar et al, 1992). Biochar may therefore be most effective in reducing leaching losses in regions of high rainfall. Rainfall patterns, through their effect on N mineralization as well as leaching, influence surface soil N availability, at times more so than soil drainage class (Sogbedji et al, 2001; van Es et al, 2006). Year-to-year variability in weather – most importantly, rainfall patterns – have often been observed as explaining the most variability in leaching patterns at single sites.

Soil and soil solution chemistry

The chemistry of clays, soil minerals (e.g. metal oxides and carbonates) and organic matter, as well as the chemistry of elements in the soil solution, affect leaching. For example, whether a nutrient is organic or inorganic, the size of the molecule it is a part of and its charge properties will dictate how it will interact with charges on constituents of the soil matrix. Positively charged ions or molecules can be adsorbed to negatively charged clays and soil organic matter (Brady and Weil, 2008), which is quantified as cation exchange capacity (CEC). Biochar displays a high CEC, and its application to soil will contribute negative charge (see Chapter 5). In a pot experiment, soil-applied biochar increased soil pH by 0.36 and 0.75 units with and without fertilizer, respectively, in acid soil (Lehmann et al, 2003).

Soil biology and nutrient cycles

Leaching of nutrients must be considered in the context of the general cycling of nutrients, where fluxes are partitioned among denitrification and other gaseous losses (in the case of N), fixation, precipitation, immobilization, mineralization and leaching. Biochar has been found to reduce N_2O gaseous losses by more than half under maize (Rondon et al, 2006; see also Chapter 13). Biochar application to soil alongside labile organic N amendments led to increased net rates of nitrification in laboratory experiments using forest soils (Berglund et al, 2004; Gundale et al, 2007), most likely due to the sorption of nitrification-inhibiting phenolic compounds by biochar (see Chapter 14). However, the implications of these processes for N leaching are unclear.

Evidence for relevant characteristics of biochar

Biochar produced from different feedstocks and under different conditions exhibits a range of physical and chemical properties (Treusch et al, 2004; Mermoud et al, 2006; Krzesinska and Zachariasz, 2007) (see Chapters 2 to 5), which will have impacts upon nutrient leaching, once it is applied to soil.

Physical properties

Water-holding capacity in soils is partly determined by organic matter contents, and organic matter amendments generally increase the water-holding capacity of soil. Humic substances derived from coal have been found to increase the water-holding capacity, as well as the aggregate stability of degraded soil (Piccolo et al, 1996). Empirical evidence suggests that sandy soils amended with biochar will experience an increase in water content, while the effect could be opposite in clay soil (Tryon, 1948). Lysimeter work using a biochar-amended clay soil from the Amazon showed that water percolation was related to crop growth: less water percolated from soil/biochar mixtures than pure soil, in accordance with increased crop growth when biochar had been added (Lehmann et al, 2003). This indicates that in clay soils, biochar can indirectly reduce water mobility through increased plant biomass and evaporative surfaces, while in sandy soils this mechanism can be complemented by the direct retention of water by biochar.

The bulk density of biochar is lower than that of mineral soils (see Chapter 2). This suggests that its application to soil will modify soil hydrology in line with application rates because of changes in porosity and, in the long term, aggregation. While fresh biochar alone may not influence the aggregation of 2:1 clays (Watts et al, 2005), it is possible that aggregation will be favoured by interactions with soil organic matter and microorganisms (Warnock et al, 2007) or by additions of biochar and labile organic matter in combination since organic molecules sorb to appropriate biochar domains (Pietikäinen et al, 2000; Smernik, 2005; Tseng and Tseng, 2006; Yu et al, 2006; see Chapter 16). Biochar effects on soil aggregation will, among others, be linked to its surface charge characteristics, which develop gradually by weathering and are affected by overall soil pH (Cheng et al, 2006). Improved soil aggregation promotes water infiltration; thus, the amount of water moving through the soil as opposed to running off could be increased. This may result in increased leaching for soluble and mobile ions such as nitrate.

The total porosity of biochar is high and varies with production method and feedstock (see Chapter 2). For soil, no universal pore-size categorization system is widely accepted (Hayashi et al, 2006); however, proposed classifications are expressed in the micrometre range (Luxmoore, 1981; Soil Science Society of America, 1997; Lal and Shukla, 2004). Water is usually considered mobile when present in pores of sizes in the order of a few tens of micrometres (e.g. 30μm) (Brady and Weil, 2008). According to the definition of the Soil Science Society of America (1997), macropores (>80μm) can contribute to the rapid flow of water through soil by gravity, and after heavy rainfall can lead to pronounced leaching events (Flury et al, 1994; Renck and Lehmann, 2004). Meso-

pores (30 μm to 80μm) will allow water to move in response to matric potential differences (i.e. from 'wetter' to 'drier' areas), while micropores (<30μm) hold water in place. Pore sizes for biochar are usually reported according to standard IUPAC value ranges (i.e. micropores are $<2 \times 10^{-3}$μm diameter, mesopores $2–50 \times 10^{-3}$μm, and macropores $>50 \times 10^{-3}$μm) (see Bornemann et al, 2007; Chapter 2). Pore-size classification systems make comparisons between biochar and soil difficult, and pore sizes within biochar depend upon the parent material and the charring conditions. However, activated biochar has been found to contain a large proportion (over 95 per cent) of micropores ($<2 \times 10^{-3}$μm) (Tseng and Tseng, 2006), and biochar porosity probably contributes to nutrient adsorption by the trapping of nutrient-containing water held by capillary forces as in soil micropores. If 95 per cent of biochar pores are $<2 \times 10^{-3}$μm in diameter, the mobility of soil water through the matrix after biochar application will be reduced. In sandy soil where the volumetric amount of water held decreases sharply as matric potential increases (i.e. as the soil dries), biochar particles may act similarly to clay and hold large volumes of immobile water even at elevated matric potentials. Nutrients dissolved in this water would thus be retained near the soil surface if water is immobile or moves slowly. Plants can access part of the nutrients in this retained soil solution as they transpire and elevate soil matric potential.

Evidence suggests that biochar porosity contributes to nutrient adsorption directly through charge or covalent interaction on a large surface area. The high porosity of biochar is accompanied by high surface areas (see Figure 15.1), to which both hydrophobic and hydrophilic molecules can sorb depending upon the functional groups displayed by the biochar (see Chapters 5 and 16). Surface area generally increases with charring temperature, and activation processes can drastically increase surface area further (see

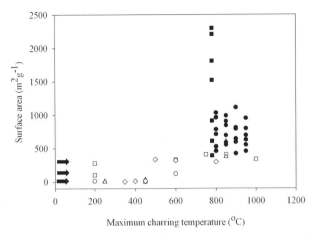

Figure 15.1 *Surface area of activated and non-activated biochar produced at varying temperatures*

Source: chapter authors, from data specified in notes below

Notes: Non-activated hardwood biochar: ᐃ Bornemann et al (2007); ◇ Lehmann (2007); ▢ Nguyen et al (2004); ○ Macias-Garcia et al (2004). Activated: ● hardwood, Macias-Garcia et al (2004); ■ sugar cane pith, Tseng and Tseng (2006). Points above $1500m^2 g^{-1}$ were obtained by activation using KOH/biochar weight ratios >3:1 at 780°C. Arrows indicate, for comparison, the surface area of a 72 per cent clay (top), 90 per cent sand (bottom) soil, which were textural extremes and the average (middle) for 33 US soils studied by Cihacek and Bremner (1979). Surface area for all biochars was measured by N_2 absorption and the Brunauer, Emmett and Teller (BET) equation. Since the surface area of soils increases with increasing moisture content and the N_2-BET method uses dry soil, surface area data for soils were obtained using the ethylene glycol monoethylene ether (EGME) method on moist samples.

Chapter 2). It is clear from Figure 15.1 that biochar must be produced at temperatures at or above 500°C or be activated if its application to soil is to immediately result in increased surface area for the direct sorption of nutrients.

Apart from impacts upon the movement of the soil solution and direct interactions with nutrients dissolved in it, the size of biochar particles may also influence leaching potential. Leaching of organic and inorganic nutrients sorbed to larger biochar particles may be either reduced or facilitated by colloidal transport with small particles as they themselves travel through the soil profile. Negatively charged colloids were shown to facilitate the downward migration of metals and organic pollutants through soil (Karathanasis, 1999; Sen and Khilar, 2006). Particle sizes of biochar produced for soil application can be controlled to some extent. Very small particles (e.g. <2μm: the size of clay particles) will most likely be present in

the material after pyrolysis or created during transportation and application (see Figure 15.2). After soil application, rain impact, chemical weathering and physical disturbance from biota will also result in fine biochar particles. Soil porosity varies widely among soils, and particles of up to 10μm were found to move through a structured sandy loam in the laboratory (Jacobsen et al, 1997), particles with a median size of 2μm to 5μm moved from topsoil through a sandy loam in the field (Laubel et al, 1999), and natural colloids of up to 200μm were mobilized through a coarse disturbed soil (Totsche et al, 2007), also in the field. The data compiled in Figure 15.2 show that fine biochar particles smaller than values mentioned above can represent a large proportion, and these particles are subject to movement through the soil profile and can act as agents of facilitated transport of nutrients.

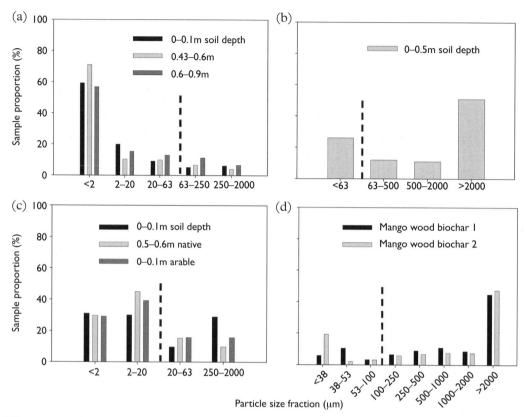

Figure 15.2 *Particle-size distribution of naturally occurring chars (a) in fertilized intensive crop soil, Germany; (b) in burned savannah soil, Zimbabwe; (c) in a Russian steppe Mollisol; and (d) hardwood biochar produced traditionally in mounds for soil application, hand ground to pass through a 0.9mm sieve*

Note: Bars to the left of vertical dashed lines (<200µm) represent the proportion of sample particles which may be translocated through soil profiles.

Source: Brodowski et al (2007): fertilized intensive crop soil, Germany; Bird et al (1999): burned savannah soil, Zimbabwe; Rodionov et al (2006): Russian steppe Mollisol; Major et al (unpublished): hardwood biochar

Chemical properties

Aged biochar has a high CEC, as shown by high concentrations of negative charges on biochar surfaces, as well as the adsorption of charged organic matter to biochar surfaces (Liang et al, 2006). As is the case with clays, this high CEC may promote soil aggregation where organic matter and minerals bind to each other and to biochar. Abiotic processes are more significant in driving the oxidation of fresh biochar surfaces than are biotic

processes in the short term (i.e. months), with higher temperatures leading to the oxidation and creation of negative charge on deeper layers of biochar particles (Cheng et al, 2006); thus, variation occurs between different climate regimes (Cheng et al, 2008). Fresh biochar may also sorb anions, and the CEC and anion exchange capacity (AEC) vary with overall soil pH, and age and weathering environment of biochar (Cheng et al, 2008). The intrinsic pH of biochar materials can be acidic or basic (see Chapter 5).

Fresh biochar, with low surface oxidation, is hydrophobic and sorbs hydrophobic molecules, such as organic contaminants (Lebo et al, 2003; Bornemann et al, 2007) (see Chapter 16). Organic hydrophobic forms of nutrients (e.g. N, P and S) could also become sorbed to biochar particles; in fact, this might effectively reduce their surface area at the molecular scale by steric hindrance, and block the subsequent direct adsorption of organic and inorganic nutrients directly to biochar particles. This effect will depend upon the size and composition of the macro-molecules and the temperature (Kwon and Pignatello, 2005; Pignatello et al, 2006). Since molecules of various sizes and chemical characteristics could sorb onto biochar particles, adsorption is likely whereby inorganic molecules sorb directly to biochar surfaces, to minerals or organic matter attached to biochar, or precipitate on biochar surfaces (e.g. Ca-phosphates). As mentioned above, soil aggregation could be modified in this way; but it is not clear to what extent and how rapidly this process occurs.

Dünisch et al (2007) noticed a larger mass of N, P and K sorbed to wood biochar/ash samples after these materials were dipped in a commercial inorganic fertilizer solution compared to 'fresh' wood feedstock (see Figure 15.3). However, the amount of water absorbed by these materials was not taken into account and, thus, the greater nutrient sorption might result partly from greater amounts of solution and dissolved nutrients held in the porous biochar before drying and analysis. Still, given different proportional increases for each nutrient, it seems that water absorption alone did not explain observed differences. Smaller-sized particles generally sorbed more nutrients than larger ones, suggesting an effect of surface area. In addition, up to 52 per cent of the P in dairy farm effluent was removed by chicken litter biochar (made at 500°C, activated) in a 100:1 effluent/biochar mixture at 50°C (Downie et al, 2007). Phosphorus

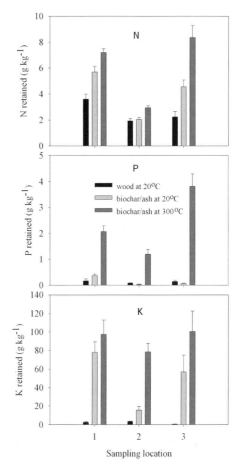

Figure 15.3 *Compilation of results obtained by Dünisch et al (2007) for wood feedstocks and biochar–ash mixtures obtained after pyrolysis: a given weight of substrates at 20°C or 300°C in mesh bags was submerged in a nutrient solution for 30 minutes*

Note: Data are for particles <5mm, the smallest size class in the report.

Source: adapted from Dünisch et al (2007)

probably precipitated, along with Ca, on the alkaline biochar matrix. Importantly, 70 per cent of this removed P could subsequently be extracted from the biochar using $CaCl_2$, suggesting that it would, nevertheless, remain available to plants (Neri et al, 2005). While reducing nutrient leaching losses is valuable,

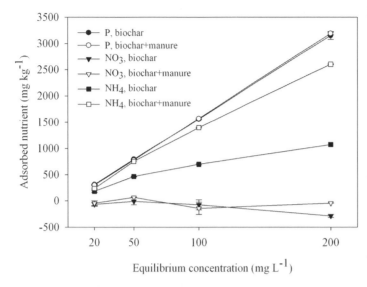

Figure 15.4 *Adsorption isotherms for biochar from the tree* Robinia pseudoacacia *L., with and without manure*

Notes: Adsorption isotherms were obtained by equilibrating 3g soil in a 20mL centrifuge tube with 10mL solution containing 0, 20, 50, 100 or 200mg L^{-1} of KH_2PO_4, KNO_3 or NH_4Cl. A 10 per cent azide solution was added to each tube to suppress microbial activity. The tubes were agitated on a horizontal shaker at room temperature (about 20°C) for one day. Samples were centrifuged at 5000rpm (relative centrifugal force of 2988g) for ten minutes and the supernatant was analysed for phosphate using the molybdate ascorbic acid method, and for nitrate and ammonium by segmented flow analysis.

Source: Lehmann et al (2002)

retained nutrients should equally remain available for plant growth. This is not the case when P in bulk soil is irreversibly adsorbed by amorphous metal oxides in acid soils (Brady and Weil, 2008). In this experiment, the sorption of NH_4-N to biochar was not found to be significant or to follow any trends.

Lehmann et al (2002) produced adsorption isotherms for P, NH_4 and NO_3 on fresh laboratory-produced biochar and biochar/manure mixtures (see Figure 15.4). This work clearly shows that phosphate was adsorbed readily by both the biochar and biochar/manure mixture, while nitrate was not adsorbed at all. Ammonium had an intermediate behaviour, with the biochar/manure mixture adsorbing more than pure biochar. Phosphorus was also shown to adsorb vigorously to biochar made from pine and surface litter at 561°C to 700°C (Beaton et al, 1960).

Biochar interactions with soil biota

Soil-applied biochar particles harbour microorganisms (see Chapter 6), including bacteria (Pietikäinen et al, 2000) and mycorrhizal fungi (Ezawa et al, 2002; Saito and Marumoto, 2002). Such organisms often have a great impact on plant nutrition – for example, through the mineralization of organic N into forms available to plants or susceptible to volatilization, and through improved P and Mg nutrition via extensive fungal hyphal systems. Current data (reviewed by Warnock et al, 2007) indicate that biochar application is often followed by an enhancement of mycorrhizal communities in the rhizosphere, coinciding with improved nutrient uptake by associated plants, thereby potentially reducing leaching. While reductions in gaseous N emissions have been observed in biochar-amended soil (Rondon et al, 2006), it is possible that N leaching and gaseous losses could also be favoured in certain cases where mineralization by bacteria occurs beyond the plants' N requirements, and if anaerobic conditions prevail around microorganisms because of changes in water retention. Nitrogen immobilization is not likely to be directly increased by biochar application since the bulk of biochar carbon

(C) is recalcitrant and not expected to immediately enter the C cycle – hence, the C sequestration properties of biochar (see Chapter 11). Still, if present, easily mineraliz-able labile biochar domains could cause N immobilization in the short term (Gundale and DeLuca, 2007; see Chapters 5 and 14).

Magnitude and temporal dynamics of biochar effects on nutrient leaching

Currently, experimental work that assesses the impact of biochar on nutrient leaching is scarce. Some work has been carried out using biochar alone under laboratory conditions and biochar/soil mixtures in the greenhouse, as well as in the field. However, results on nutrient leaching *per se* have not yet been reported for field experiments.

Direct nutrient leaching measurement in biochar/soil mixtures were undertaken only by Lehmann et al (2003), using pot lysimeters in the greenhouse (see Figure 15.5). Biochar made locally near Manaus in the central Brazilian Amazon was mixed with a typic Hapludox, rice was seeded and fertilizer applied. Leaching of applied ammonium was generally reduced by more than 60 per cent over 40 days of cropping rice, compared to treatments not receiving biochar (Lehmann et al, 2003). Fertilization reduced the efficiency of biochar for nutrient retention, perhaps due to high amounts of nutrients being present. Leaching of Ca and Mg was also reduced during the first week, although absolute amounts were low. Leaching of K was not reduced since fresh biochar typically contains large amounts of K. Aged biochar with much greater CEC (Cheng et al, 2008) may have much greater retention capacity. Lehmann et al (2003) showed that in Amazonian Dark Earths (ADE) that contain large proportions of aged biochar, leaching of Ca was approximately 20 per cent lower than in Oxisols with low biochar contents. At the same time, Ca availability on the exchange sites of ADE was more than double. It appears that aged ADE biochar resulted in greater nutrient availability, while simultane-ously exhibiting significantly reduced leaching losses.

Dünisch et al (2007) found that biochar/ash mixtures impregnated with fertilizer in the laboratory 'leached' proportionally lower amounts of nutrients back into de-ionized water when compared to equal weights of wood feedstock (see Figures 15.5 and 15.6). Since amounts of nutrients retained by the biochar mixtures during impregnation were greater than for wood (see Figure 15.3), actual amounts leached were similar for both material types. While smaller particles (<5mm) retained greater amounts of nutrients, they also released proportionally more nutrients than large particles. The kinetics of sorption on outer surfaces versus internal pores might explain this, where smaller particles with greater outer surface areas released more nutrients than larger particles where more nutrients were retained inside pores.

Comparable data were obtained in preliminary laboratory work carried out by Downie et al (2007) on nutrient leaching through columns of fresh biochar without soil (see Figure 15.5). However, biochars in this experiment did not retain any nutrients beyond 20 pore volumes (816mm water applied), which suggests that weak surface processes or water trapping in small pores were probably responsible for the nutrient retention. This mechanism alone would therefore not lead to long-term effects of biochar on nutrient leaching. In addition, bases such as Ca, K and Mg were more abundant in leachate from biochar than acid-washed sand. This is expected since biochar

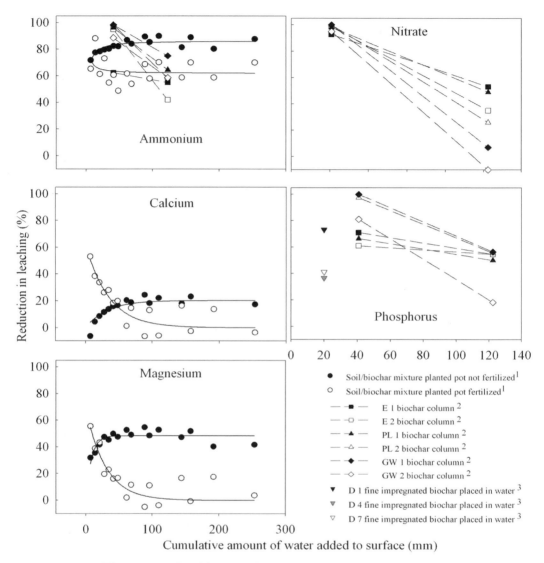

Figure 15.5 *Leaching reduction data compiled from the literature*

Notes: 1 Rice grown in lysimeters filled with Oxisol alone or a mixture of soil and wood biochar, with and without fertilization with NPK (Lehmann et al, 2003).

2 Reduction is for NPK fertilizer granules placed on top of columns packed with biochar, compared to a control column packed with acid-washed sand; E 1: garden waste (GW) biochar made at 550°C, activated, enriched with N; E2 : GW biochar, same as previous with additional minerals; PL 1: poultry litter (PL) biochar made at 550°C, activated; PL 2: PL biochar made at 450°C, non-activated; GW 1: GW biochar made at 550°C, activated; GW 2: GW biochar made at 450°C, non-activated (Downie et al, 2007).

3 Reduction is for biochar–ash mixtures compared to original wood feedstock. D 1: *Pinus sylvestris* L. charred in a flash-pyrolysis plant for bio-oil production, Germany; D 4: *Pinus taeda* L. combusted to heat kiln dryers, Brazil; D 7: *Cordia goeldiana* Huber (same as previous), for particles <5mm. Substrates in mesh bags were impregnated in an NPK solution, dried and placed in de-ionized water for 120 minutes to assess nutrient desorption (Dünisch et al, 2007). Points on P graph for Dünisch et al (2007) were placed at an approximate value on the X-axis since calculating actual volume was not possible.

Source: Lehmann et al (2003); Downie et al (2007); Dünisch et al (2007)

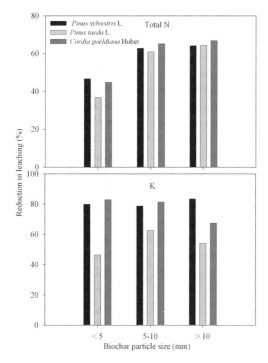

Figure 15.6 *Reduction in leaching for nutrient-impregnated biochar particles of different sizes*

Note: See notes on methodology in Figure 15.5.

Source: Dünisch et al (2007)

contains large amounts of these elements compared to sand, which were probably displaced due to their solubility and to maintain the electro-neutrality of the leachate. For these freshly made biochars, oxidation is most likely not sufficiently advanced to create the negative surface charge observed in incubated or aged biochars (Cheng et al, 2006, 2008). Despite this, short-term retention of nutrients even by fresh biochars could still prove to be highly beneficial – for example, during annual crop establishment, when fertilizer application is facilitated in the field but seedlings are still exclusively using nutrients available in the seed.

In the field, the recovery of fertilizer N in soil (0 to 0.1m depth), harvested material and crop residue was enhanced by the application of both biochar and compost. However, the enhanced N retention in compost-amended plots was mainly a result of higher crop production (retention in plant biomass), whereas on the biochar plots more N remained in the soil especially after the second growing season (see Figure 15.7). These data only provide an assessment of total N losses since the 80 to 90 per cent of fertilizer-N that was not recovered could have left the system through both gaseous losses and leaching below 0.1m, which was not directly measured. Still, deep N leaching in this specific soil was found to be highly significant (Renck and Lehmann, 2004), suggesting that biochar has the potential to reduce leaching in the longer term through more complex mechanisms involving interactions with the soil matrix.

Based on the data presented here, biochar is effective in reducing the leaching of all nutrients tested, at least in the short term. Several studies show that leaching of P, ammonium- and nitrate-N, which are usually most limiting to crop growth, was reduced by over 50 per cent initially, and in one case after 250mm of water were applied to the surface (Lehmann et al, 2003). Ca and Mg were also retained after biochar addition without fertilizer (20 and 40 per cent leaching reduction after 250mm water applied, respectively). When NPK fertilizer was applied, biochar addition significantly reduced Ca and Mg leaching during the first week only. Potassium retention was also high with impregnated biochar reported by Dünisch et al (2007). However, Lehmann et al (2003) found that K in leachate increased after the addition of biochar to soil, and attributed this to the high K content of the biochar itself.

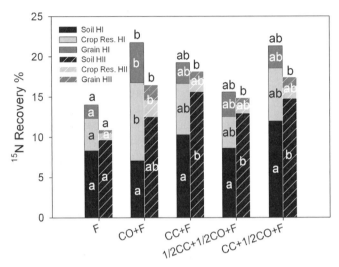

Figure 15.7 *Recovery of ^{15}N-labelled fertilizer applied to an Oxisol in the Brazilian Amazon during two growing seasons (HI, HII)*

Notes: Crop was *Sorghum* sp; F: synthetic fertilizer; CO: compost; CC: biochar. Organic amendments were applied and soil was sampled to 0.1m depth. Rate of biochar application was 11t ha^{-1}, and compost was applied at the same C-based rate. The last treatment received 1.5 times the C applied to others. Different letters represent significant differences (p<0.05; n = 5) between treatments. In HII, letters for crop residue and grain recovery were the same and are only shown once.

Source: data from Steiner et al (2008)

Conclusions and research needs

We reviewed data which suggest that biochar application to soil will affect nutrient leaching through several mechanisms – for example, by increasing the retention of water in the rooting zone, by directly binding or sorbing nutrients or by interacting with other soil constituents, and by facilitating the movement of attached nutrients when fine biochar particles are transported in percolating water. These mechanisms may either increase or decrease leaching. However, data available, to date, suggest that biochar does sorb organic and inorganic molecules and, in the case of inorganic nutrients, retains them against leaching losses. Table 15.1 summarizes biochar characteristics relevant to nutrient leaching and associated leaching reduction mechanisms, and indicates the extent to which each has been demonstrated. Figure 15.8 illustrates these mechanisms schematically. Long-term leaching reduction has not been shown directly, and some experiments presented here focused on pure biochar systems and inorganic nutrients, where microbes were excluded or not a study factor.

Research on biochar effects on leaching in agronomic settings must be carried out in soil–biochar and soil–biochar–plant systems, in the laboratory as well as in the field and, ultimately, on a watershed scale using an ecosystem approach. Clearly, biochar interacts with other soil constituents, and biochar–soil mixtures will behave differently than pure biochar, especially over long periods of time. Increased plant productivity also needs to be part of leaching assessments because this alone can translate into reduced nutrient leaching through increased uptake. Both fresh and aged biochar should be tested, since the oxidation of these materials varies. The effect of various application methods for biochar as well as for nutrients should also be tested.

The mechanisms that explain nutrient retention by biochar require investigation since this information will probably allow the production of specific biochar for particular uses (e.g. for nutrient management in acid or degraded soil). As mentioned, interactions between biochar and soil are probably significant, complex and can drastically modify the chemical and physical characteristics of biochar surfaces and, thus, its interaction with nutrients. These interactions require

Table 15.1 *Proposed biochar characteristics affecting nutrient leaching, related mechanisms and degree of certainty associated with each process*

Mechanism	Impact upon leaching	Biochar characteristic[1]	Leaching impact mechanism[2]	Source(s)
Biochar's negative surface charge directly retains positively charged nutrients	Decrease for positively charged ions and domains of nutrient-containing organic matter	Proven	Strong evidence	Liang et al (2006); Downie et al (2007)
Biochar increases the soil's water-holding capacity	Decrease (extent will vary with soil texture)	Strong evidence	Not proven	Tryon (1948)
Biochar leads to increased soil aggregation	Increase or decrease	Not proven	Not proven	NA
Biochar increases microbial biomass and nutrient cycling	Increase or decrease	Proven	Strong evidence	Reviewed by Warnock et al (2007); Steiner et al (2008)
Sorbed nutrients are preferentially transported by biochar particles	Increase	Not proven	Not proven	NA
Fresh biochar sorbs nutrients in hydrophobic organic matter	Decrease	Strong evidence	Not proven	Lebo et al (2003); Smernik (2005); Bornemann et al (2007)

Notes: 1 Degree of certainty for this characteristic of biochar when applied to soil.
2 Degree of certainty in attributing this mechanism to changes in leaching by biochar.
NA = not available.

further study. The beneficial effect of biochar on leaching should also be related to other factors that impact upon leaching in the field, such as rainfall or crop management.

We consider that biochar could become a useful tool for the complex task of managing crop nutrition and its environmental impacts. Managing soils with biochar to reduce nutrient leaching would bring a dual benefit of decreasing applied fertilizer requirements, as well as mitigating the environmental effects of nutrient loss. Reduced fertilizer applications not only decrease environmental concerns of non-point source pollution by agriculture, but also translate into reduced C emissions from the production and transport of synthetic fertilizers (see Chapter 18).

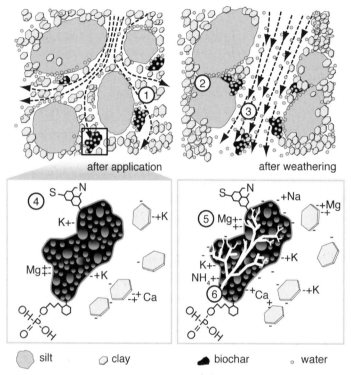

after application   after weathering

silt   clay   biochar   water

Figure 15.8 *Schematic representation of proposed biochar effects on nutrient leaching: (1) Upon biochar application to soil, water retention increases because porous biochar particles retain water and reduce its mobility; (2) after weathering, soil aggregation is improved as biochar binds to other soil constituents, and preferential flow of water occurs as well as the facilitated transport of biochar particles (3); (4) at a smaller scale, newly applied biochar sorbs hydrophobic organic forms of nutrients; (5) after weathering, the surface charge of biochar increases, thus improving cation exchange capacity, and soil biota is enhanced (6)*

Note: This illustration is not strictly to scale, and water is not shown in the bottom panels.
Source: chapter authors

References

Allen, S. C., Jose, S., Nair, P. K. R., Brecke, B. J., Nkedi-Kizza, P. and Ramsey, C. L. (2004) 'Safety-net role of tree roots: Evidence from a pecan (*Cary illinoensis* K. Kroch)-cotton (*Gossypium hirsutum* L.) alley cropping system in the southern United States', *Forest Ecology and Management*, vol 192, pp395–407

Beaton, J. D., Peterson, H. B. and Bauer, N. (1960) 'Some aspects of phosphate adsorption to charcoal', *Soil Science Society of America Proceedings*, vol 24, pp340–346

Berglund, L. M., DeLuca, T. H. and Zackrisson, O. (2004) 'Activated carbon amendments to soil alters nitrification rates in Scots pine forests', *Soil Biology and Biochemistry*, vol 36, pp2067–2073

Bird, M. I., Moyo, C., Veendaal, E. M., Lloyd, J. and Frost, P. (1999) 'Stability of elemental carbon in a savanna soil', *Global Biogeochemical Cycles*, vol 13, pp923–932

Bornemann, L. C., Kookana, R. S. and Welp, G. (2007) 'Differential sorption behaviour of aromatic hydrocarbons on charcoals prepared at different temperatures from grass and wood', *Chemosphere*, vol 67, pp1033–1042

Brady, N. C. and Weil, R. R. (2008) *The Nature and Properties of Soils*, 14th edition, Prentice Hall, Upper Saddle River, NJ

Brodowski, S., Amelung, W., Haumaier, L. and Zech, W. (2007) 'Black carbon contribution to stable humus in German arable soils', *Geoderma*, vol 139, pp220–228

Cahn, M. D., Bouldin, D. R., Cravo, M. S. and Bowen, W. T. (1993) 'Cation and nitrate leaching in an Oxisol of the Brazilian Amazon', *Agronomy Journal*, vol 85, pp334–340

Cheng, C. H., Lehmann, J., Thies, J. E., Burton, S. D. and Engelhard, M. H. (2006) 'Oxidation of black carbon by biotic and abiotic processes', *Organic Geochemistry*, vol 37,

pp1477–1488

Cheng C. H., Lehmann, J. and Engelhard, M. (2008) 'Natural oxidation of black carbon in soils: Changes in molecular form and surface charge along a climosequence', *Geochimica et Cosmochimica Acta*, vol 72, pp1598–1610

Cihacek, L. J. and Bremner, J. M. (1979) 'A simplified ethylene glycol monoethyl ether procedure for assessment of soil surface area', *Soil Science Society of America Journal*, vol 43, pp821–822

Daniel, T. C., Sharpley, A. N. and Lemunyon, J. L. (1998) 'Agricultural phosphorus and eutrophication: A symposium overview', *Journal of Environmental Quality*, vol 27, pp251–257

Defra (UK Department for Environment, Food and Rural Affairs), 'Nitrogen', www.defra.gov.uk/ENVIRONMENT/water/quality/nitrate/nitrogen.htm, accessed 26 March 2008

Downie, A., Van Zwieten, L., Chan, K. Y., Dougherty, W. and Joseph, S. (2007) 'Nutrient retention characteristics of agrichar and the agronomic implications', Poster presented at the International Agrichar Initiative Conference, April 2007, Terrigal, NSW, Australia

Dünisch, O., Lima, V. C., Seehann, G., Donath, J., Montoia, V. R. and Schwarz, T. (2007) 'Retention properties of wood residues and their potential for soil amelioration', *Wood Science and Technology*, vol 41, pp169–189

Ezawa, T., Yamamoto, K. and Yoshida, S. (2002) 'Enhancement of the effectiveness of indigenous arbuscular mycorrhizal fungi by inorganic soil amendments', *Soil Science and Plant Nutrition*, vol 48, pp897–900

Flury, M., Flühler, H., Jury, W. A. and Leuenberger, J. (1994) 'Susceptibility of soils to preferential flow of water – A field-study', *Water Resources Research*, vol 30, pp1945–1954

Ghodrati, M. and Jury, W. A. (1990) 'A field-study using dyes to characterize preferential flow of water', *Soil Science Society of America Journal*, vol 54, pp1558–1563

Gundale, M. J. and DeLuca, T. H. (2007) 'Charcoal effects on soil solution chemistry and growth of *Koeleria macrantha* in the ponderosa pine/Douglas-fir ecosystem', *Biology and Fertility of Soils*, vol 43, pp303–311

Hayashi, Y., Ken'ichirou, K. and Mizuyama, T.

(2006) 'Changes in pore size distribution and hydraulic properties of forest soil resulting from structural development', *Journal of Hydrology*, vol 331, pp85–102

Jacobsen, O. H., Moldrup, P., Larsen, C., Konnerup, L. and Petersen, L. W. (1997) 'Particle transport in macropores of undisturbed soil columns', *Journal of Hydrology*, vol 196, pp185–203

Karathanasis, A. D. (1999) 'Subsurface migration of copper and zinc mediated by soil colloids', *Soil Science Society of America Journal*, vol 63, pp830–838

Krzesinska, M. and Zachariasz, J. (2007) 'The effect of pyrolysis temperature on the physical properties of monolithic carbons derived from solid iron bamboo', *Journal of Analytical and Applied Pyrolysis*, vol 80, pp209–215

Kwon, S. and Pignatello, J. J. (2005) 'Effect of natural organic substances on the surface and adsorptive properties of environmental black carbon (char): Pseudo pore blockage by model lipid components and its implications for N_2-probed surface properties of natural sorbents', *Environmental Science and Technology*, vol 39, pp7932–7939

Lal, R. and Shukla, M. K. (2004) *Principles of Soil Physics*, Marcel Dekker, New York, NY

Laubel, A., Jacobsen, O. H., Kronvang, B., Grant, R. and Andersen, H. E. (1999) 'Subsurface drainage loss of particles and phosphorus from field plot experiments and a tile-drained catchment', *Journal of Environmental Quality*, vol 28, pp576–584

Lebo, J. A., Huckins, J. N., Petty, J. D., Cranor, W. L. and Ho, K. T. (2003) 'Comparisons of coarse and fine versions of two carbons for reducing the bioavailabilities of sediment-bound hydrophobic organic contaminants', *Chemosphere*, vol 50, pp1309–1317

Lehmann, J. (2007) 'Bio-energy in the black', *Frontiers in Ecology and the Environment*, vol 5, pp381–387

Lehmann, J., da Silva Jr., J. P., Rondon, M., Cravo, M. S., Greenwood, J., Nehls, T., Steiner, C. and Glaser, B. (2002) 'Slash-and-char – a feasible alternative for soil fertility management in the central Amazon?', in *Proceedings of the 17th World Congress of Soil Science*, Bangkok, Thailand, Paper no 449

Lehmann, J., da Silva Jr., J. P., Steiner, C., Nehls,

T., Zech, W. and Glaser, B. (2003) 'Nutrient availability and leaching in an archaeological Anthrosol and a Ferralsol of the Central Amazon basin: Fertilizer, manure and charcoal amendments', *Plant and Soil*, vol 249, pp343–357

Lehmann, J., Lilienfein, J., Rebel, K., do Carmo Lima, S. and Wilcke, W. (2004) 'Subsoil retention of organic and inorganic nitrogen in a Brazilian savanna Oxisol', *Soil Use and Management*, vol 20, pp163–172

Liang, B., Lehmann, J., Solomon, D., Kinyangi, J., Grossman, J., O'Neill, B., Skjemstad, J. O., Thies, J., Luizão, F. J., Petersen, J. and Neves, E. G. (2006) 'Black carbon increases cation exchange capacity in soils', *Soil Science Society of America Journal*, vol 70, pp1719–1730

Luxmoore, R. J. (1981) 'Microporosity, meso-porosity, and macroporosity of soil', *Soil Science Society of America Journal*, vol 45, pp671–672

Macias-Garcia, A., Garcia, M. J. B., Diaz-Diez, M. A. and Jimenez, A. H. (2004) 'Preparation of active carbons from a commercial holm-oak charcoal: Study of micro- and meso-porosity', *Wood Science and Technology*, vol 37, pp385–394

Melgar, R. J., Smyth, T. J., Sanchez, P. A. and Cravo, M. S. (1992) 'Fertilizer nitrogen movement in a Central Amazon Oxisol and Entisol cropped to maize', *Fertilizer Research*, vol 31, pp241–252

Mermoud, F., Salvador, S., de Steene, L. V. and Golfier, F. (2006) 'Influence of the pyrolysis heating rate on the steam gasification rate of large wood char particles', *Fuel*, vol 85, pp1473–1482

Mueller, D. K., Hamilton, P. A., Helsel, D. R., Hitt, K. J. and Ruddy, B. C. (1995) 'Nutrients in ground water and surface water of the United States – an analysis of data through 1992', US Department of the Interior, Geological Survey, Washington, DC

Neri, U., Diana, G. and Indiati, R. (2005) 'Change point in phosphorus release from variously managed soils with contrasting properties', *Communications in Soil Science and Plant Analysis*, vol 36, pp2227–2237

Nguyen, T. H., Brown, R. A. and Ball, W. P. (2004) 'An evaluation of thermal resistance as a measure of black carbon content in diesel soot, wood char, and sediment', *Organic Geochemistry*, vol 35, p217–234

Omoti, U., Ataga, D. O. and Isenmila, A. E. (1983) 'Leaching losses of nutrients in oil palm plantations determined by tension lysimeters', *Plant and Soil*, vol 73, pp365–376

Piccolo, A., Pietramellara, G. and Mbagwu, J. S. C. (1996) 'Effects of coal-derived humic substances on water retention and structural stability of Mediterranean soils', *Soil Use and Management*, vol 12, pp209–213

Pietikäinen, J., Kiikkila, O. and Fritze, H. (2000) 'Charcoal as a habitat for microbes and its effect on the microbial community of the underlying humus', *Oikos*, vol 89, pp231–242

Pignatello, J. J., Kwon, S. and Lu, Y. F. (2006) 'Effect of natural organic substances on the surface and adsorptive properties of environmental black carbon (char): Attenuation of surface activity by humic and fulvic acids', *Environmental Science and Technology*, vol 40, pp7757–7763

Renck, A. and Lehmann, J. (2004) 'Rapid water flow and transport of inorganic and organic nitrogen in a highly aggregated tropical soil', *Soil Science*, vol 169, pp330–341

Rodionov, A., Amelung, W., Haumaier, L., Urusevskaja, I. and Zech, W. (2006) 'Black carbon in the Zonal steppe soils of Russia', *Journal of Plant Nutrition and Soil Science*, vol 169, pp363–369

Rondon, M., Molina, D., Ramirez, J., Amezquita, E., Major, J. and Lehmann, J. (2006) 'Enhancing the productivity of crops and grasses while reducing greenhouse gas emissions through bio-char amendments to unfertile tropical soils', Poster presented at the World Congress of Soil Science, Philadelphia, PA, 9–15 July 2006

Rowe, E. C., Hairiah, K., Giller, K. E., Van Noordwijk, M. and Cadisch, G. (1998) 'Testing the safety-net role of hedgerow tree roots by N-15 placement at different soil depths', *Agroforestry Systems*, vol 43, pp81–93

Saito, M. and Marumoto, T. (2002) 'Inoculation with arbuscular mycorrhizal fungi: The status quo in Japan and the future prospects', *Plant and Soil*, vol 244, pp273–279

Sander, T. and Gerke, H. H. (2007) 'Preferential flow patterns in paddy fields using a dye tracer', *Vadose Zone Journal*, vol 6, pp105–115

Sen, T. K. and Khilar, K. C. (2006) 'Review on

subsurface colloids and colloid-associated contaminant transport in saturated porous media', *Advances in Colloid and Interface Science*, vol 119, pp71–96

Sharpley, A. N., McDowell, R. W. and Kleinman, P. J. A. (2001) 'Phosphorus loss from land to water: Integrating agricultural and environmental management', *Plant and Soil*, vol 237, pp287–307

Smernik, R. J. (2005) 'A new way to use solid-state carbon-13 nuclear magnetic resonance spectroscopy to study the sorption of organic compounds to soil organic matter', *Journal of Environmental Quality*, vol 34, pp1194–1204

Sogbedji, J. M., van Es, H. M., Klausner, S. D., Bouldin, D. R. and Cox, W. J. (2001) 'Spatial and temporal processes affecting nitrogen availability at the landscape scale', *Soil and Tillage Research*, vol 58, pp233–244

Soil Science Society of America (1997) *Glossary of Soil Science Terms*, Madison, WI

Steiner, C., Glaser, B., Teixeira W. G., Lehmann, J., Blum, W. E. H. and Zech, W. (2008) 'Nitrogen retention and plant uptake on a highly weathered central Amazonian Ferralsol amended with compost and charcoal', *Journal of Plant Nutrition and Soil Science*, vol 171, pp893–899

Totsche, K. U., Jann, S. and Kögel–Knabner, I. (2007) 'Single event-driven export of polycyclic aromatic hydrocarbons and suspended matter from coal tar-contaminated soil', *Vadose Zone Journal*, vol 6, pp233–243

Treusch, O., Hofenauer, A., Troger, F., Fromm, J. and Wegener, G. (2004) 'Basic properties of specific wood–based materials carbonised in a nitrogen atmosphere', *Wood Science and Technology*, vol 38, pp323–333

Tryon, E. H. (1948) 'Effect of charcoal on certain physical, chemical, and biological properties of soils', *Ecological Monographs*, vol 18, pp81–115

Tseng, R. L. and Tseng, S. K. (2006) 'Characterization and use of high surface area activated carbons prepared from cane pith for liquid-phase adsorption', *Journal of Hazardous Materials*, vol B136, pp671–680

van Es, H., Czymmek, K. J. and Ketterings, Q. M. (2002) 'Management effects on nitrogen leaching and guidelines for a nitrogen leaching index in New York', *Journal of Soil and Water Conservation*, vol 57, pp499–504

van Es, H., Sogbedji, J. M. and Schindelbeck, R. R. (2006) 'Effect of manure application timing, crop, and soil type on nitrate leaching', *Journal of Environmental Quality*, vol 35, pp670–679

Warnock, D. D., Lehmann, J., Kuyper, T. W. and Rillig, M. C. (2007) 'Mycorrhizal responses to biochar in soil – concepts and mechanisms', *Plant and Soil*, vol 300, pp9–20

Watts, C. W., Whalley, W. R., Brookes, P. C., Devonshire, B. J. and Whitmore, A. P. (2005) 'Biological and physical processes that mediate micro-aggregation of clays', *Soil Science*, vol 170, pp573–583

Yu, X. Y., Ying, G. G. and Kookana, R. S. (2006) 'Sorption and desorption behaviors of diuron in soils amended with charcoal', *Journal of Agricultural and Food Chemistry*, vol 54, pp8545–8550

16

Biochar and Sorption of Organic Compounds

Ronald J. Smernik

Introduction

Sorption to organic matter is the key process that controls the toxicity, transport, fate and behaviour of non-polar organic compounds in soils. This class of compounds includes many important environmental pollutants, including polyaromatic hydrocarbons, poly-chlorinated biphenyls (PCBs), and many herbicides and pesticides.

An important property of biochar, one that sets it apart from other types of organic matter, is its very high affinity and capacity for sorbing organic compounds. This property of biochar is the reason why activated carbon – a form of high-temperature biochar that has been treated with steam or CO_2 to remove tars and maximize porosity – has long been used to remove or 'strip' organic compounds from polluted air and water (Dias et al, 2007). The past decade has seen a growing awareness of the importance of natural chars, which are ubiquitous in the environment (Schmidt and Noack, 2000), in controlling the fate and behaviour of organic pollutants (Cornelissen et al, 2005; Koelmans et al, 2006). The addition of biochar to soil would therefore be expected to enhance the sorption properties of the soil and, hence, have a strong influence on the fate and behaviour of non-polar organic compounds present in, or added to, that soil.

This chapter discusses the sorption prop-erties of biochars themselves (in particular, how these are affected by parent material and production temperature), and the sorption properties of soils that contain biochar (mainly produced by fires). Finally, it discusses the potential for using the measure-ment of sorption properties to assess biochar properties and to follow changes to biochar added to soil over time.

Sorption properties of 'pure' biochars

The sorption properties of biochars and related materials have been studied extensively during the past decade in response to the growing awareness of the importance of biochar to the overall sorption properties of soils and sediments. Sorption studies of activated carbon significantly pre-date this (e.g. Walters and Luthy, 1984; Luehrs et al, 1996), and relate to the use of activated carbon in water purification. All of these studies emphasize differences in sorption properties between 'normal' organic matter and 'pyrogenic' organic matter (e.g. biochar, charcoal, soot and activated carbon). The most obvious of these differences is the higher sorption affinity of pyrogenic organic matter, often of the order of 1 to 3 orders of magnitude (Bucheli and Gustafsson, 2000; Allen-King et al, 2002; Baring et al, 2002; Kleineidam et al, 2002; Bucheli and Gustafsson, 2003; Huang et al, 2003; Yang and Sheng, 2003; Nguyen et al, 2004). There are also important differences between pyrogenic and non-pyrogenic organic matter in the concentration dependence of sorption, the mechanism of sorption and sorption reversibility.

Sorption affinity of non-pyrogenic components usually shows little or no concentration dependence. In other words, sorption isotherms that plot sorbed versus solution concentrations are linear (the slope of which is K_d, the sorption distribution coefficient). This behaviour is often described as *ab*sorption or partitioning. On the other hand, the sorption affinity of biochar materials usually shows a distinct decrease with increasing concentration.

Figure 16.1 (from Yang and Sheng, 2003) illustrates the distinctiveness of biochar sorption when compared with sorption to fresh plant material or soil. Clearly, the biochar has much higher affinity and exhibits non-linear sorption isotherms, whereas the fresh plant material and soil both exhibit linear sorption isotherms.

The non-linear sorption behaviour of biochar is indicative of *ad*sorption to external or internal surfaces and has been approximated using a number of different equations, including the Freundlich (Bucheli and Gustafsson, 2000; Nguyen et al, 2004; James et al, 2005; Wang and Xing, 2007) and Langmuir (Walters and Luthy, 1984; Yang

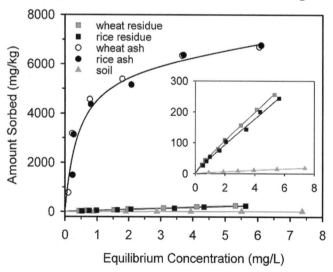

Figure 16.1 *Comparison of sorption properties of biochar (ash containing char), plant residues and soil for the pesticide diuron*

Source: reprinted with permission from Yang and Sheng (2003), copyright 2003 American Chemical Society

and Sheng, 2003; van Noort et al, 2004) equations. More recently, equations based on pore-filling models have been shown to provide better fits (Kleineidam et al, 2002; Nguyen et al, 2004; Nguyen and Ball 2006; Bornemann et al, 2007).

A number of studies have reported that certain classes of compound, especially poly-cyclic aromatic hydrocarbons (PAHs) are sorbed particularly strongly to biochar surfaces. This has been attributed to specific $\pi-\pi$ interactions between the aromatic rings of the PAH molecules and those of the biochar (Sander and Pignatello, 2005), and also to the planar nature of PAHs, which allows access to small and narrow pores (Baring et al, 2002; Jonker and Koelmans, 2002; Bucheli and Gustafsson, 2003; van Noort et al, 2004).

Sorption to biochar has also been reported to be less reversible than for other types of organic matter. Braida et al (2003) reported that sorption of benzene to biochar was strongly hysteretic (exhibiting very different sorption and desorption isotherms), especially at low benzene concentrations. Sander and Pignatello (2007) confirmed that sorption can be hysteretic in some cases, although in other cases apparent hysteresis is an artefact.

It is important to note that while the studied biochars and related (pyrogenic) materials appear to have high sorption affinity for neutral organic compounds, there is substantial variation of sorption affinity amongst these materials. Jonker and Koelmans (2002) and van Noort et al (2004) compared sorption properties of a series of soots (condensation products of fossil fuel combustion), charcoal (for the most part identical to biochar) and activated carbon (made for filtration purposes), and found that both sorption affinity and sorption capacity generally reflected the order of increasing surface area of the materials they studied. A number of recent studies have compared the sorption properties of different biochars. Yang and Sheng (2003) found that char produced from the uncontrolled burning of wheat and rice residues had similar sorption properties. On the other hand, James et al (2005) reported variations in organic C-normalized sorption affinity (K_{OC}) of 1 to 2 orders of magnitude amongst both biochars collected from the field and biochars produced in the laboratory. Amongst the latter, both temperature and starting material affected sorption properties. Sorption affinity (for phenanthrene) increased with increasing temperature, as did sorption non-linearity. Sorption affinity for biochars produced at the same temperature from wood of different species also showed considerable variation. Some of this variation was explained by differences in surface area; but the correlation of K_{OC} with surface area across all of the biochars was fairly weak. Similar findings were reported by Bornemann et al (2007) in a study of the sorption properties of biochars produced at three temperatures (250°C, 450°C and 850°C) from two starting materials (a wood and a grass). Wang and Xing (2007) also reported an increase in sorption affinity for biochars produced from chitin and cellulose with increasing treatment temperature. Finally, Nguyen and Ball (2006) reported differences in sorption properties amongst three different soots – one produced from hexane and the other two from diesel engine exhaust.

It is worth noting that most sorption studies, to date, have used low-mineral biochars produced from relatively pure plant residues. Although some of these contain considerable ash (e.g. grass biochars that contain substantial silica in the form of phytoliths), the sorption properties of the ash component have not generally been considered. For sorption of neutral organic molecules, it is reasonable to assume that the hydrophobic organic (char) component would still dominate the sorption of mineral-rich biochars. However, the presence of minerals is likely to have at least a secondary influence (e.g. by affecting the formation of aromatic structures during pyrolysis). Research is needed into the sorption of high-mineral biochars, such as those produced from animal manure and industrial by-products.

Influence of biochar on the sorption properties of soils

Given that biochar is a much stronger sorbent for neutral organic compounds than other forms of organic matter present in most soils, and that biochar is ubiquitous in the environment (Schmidt and Noack, 2000), it should be expected that biochar naturally present in soil would play an influential role in overall soil sorption properties. The influence of biochar on the sorption properties of soil was first suggested by Chiou (1995) to explain why some soils exhibited non-linear sorption at very low sorbate concentrations. In the same year, McGroddy and Farrington (1995) attributed anomalously low PAH concentrations in highly polluted Boston Harbor pore waters to effectively irreversible sorption of PAHs to soot particles. Gustafsson et al (1997), having developed a method for quantifying soot carbon (C) in sediments, reported that the low PAH concentrations in Boston Harbor pore waters could be explained simply by (reversible) sorption to soot, assuming that the soot had similar sorption properties as activated carbon. Numerous subsequent studies attributed strong and/or non-linear sorption of soils and sediments to the presence of biochar or similar materials (Chiou and Kile, 1998; Kleineidam et al, 1999; Xia and Ball, 1999; Chiou et al, 2000; Jonker and Smedes, 2000; Karapanagioti et al, 2000, 2001; Karapanagioti and Sabatini, 2000; Accardi-Dey and Gschwend, 2002, 2003). Accardi-Dey and Gschwend (2002) took the Gustafsson et al (1997) methodology one step further by using the measured sorption properties of the isolated soot fraction in fitting the sorption isotherms of sediments. However, Cornelissen and Gustafsson

(2004) showed that this can overestimate the sorption of the soot component in natural sediments, possibly because the soot surfaces get covered with organic matter and/or sorbed molecular species, which are removed by the oxidative treatment before the sorption experiment.

Two recent reviews (Cornelissen et al, 2005; Koelmans et al, 2006) provide a distillation of the many studies that have led to the view that sorption of neutral organic compounds to soils and sediments is best understood as two separate processes – relatively weak and linear *ab*sorption into amorphous organic matter and relatively strong and non-linear *ad*sorption onto the surfaces of biochar (or similar materials, including coal and kerogen). The relative importance of each process then depends upon the relative proportions of each type of organic matter, but also upon the concentration of sorbate molecules. At low concentrations, the biochar phase is more important due to its strong affinity; but at high sorbate concentrations, biochar sorption sites may become saturated, after which the amorphous organic matter phase, which usually constitutes the bulk of total organic matter, may become dominant. The nature of the sorbate also has an influence, with biochar being a relatively more important sorbent for small and planar aromatic molecules.

Despite the weight of evidence for this 'dual-mode' sorption theory, our ability to quantitatively predict or, indeed, identify the proportion of a given sorbate molecule that is sorbed to a biochar phase in a given soil or sediment remains limited. The main problem is that, as yet, there is no way to directly differentiate molecules sorbed to each phase. Rather, the proportions of molecules sorbed to each phase are determined by fitting the bulk sorption properties to a two-component model. This fit is sensitive to the assumed sorption properties of the biochar phase, and, as discussed above, the sorption properties may vary widely between biochars and soots and also within both of these classes. The situation is further complicated by the finding that sorption properties of biochars within soils and sediments appear to be substantially lower than those of isolated biochars (Jonker and Smedes, 2000; Cornelissen and Gustafsson, 2004;

Cornelissen et al, 2004; Ran et al, 2007a, b; Rhodes et al, 2008). Even the determination of naturally occurring char contents of soils (similar to biochar) and sediments is very uncertain, as demonstrated in the recent 'black carbon ring trial' (Hammes et al, 2007). Crucially, the 'CTO-375' technique most commonly used to quantify char in sorption studies actually identified virtually none of the C in wood and grass biochars as being char. Finally, it should be noted that non-linear sorption behaviour has been attributed to organic matter components other than char, including glassy domains in humic acid and kerogen (Huang et al, 2003; Ran et al, 2007a, b).

Effects on sorption of adding biochar to soil

Based on the above discussion, it appears clear that the addition of biochar to soil will have a profound influence on the sorption properties of the soil towards neutral organic compounds. As early as 1948, it was shown that the addition of activated carbon to soil decreased the bioavailability of 2,4-dichlorophenoxyacetic acid (2,4-D) to sweet potatoes (Arle et al, 1948), presumably due its strong sorption to this biochar-like material. Activated carbon amendment to soil has also been shown to decrease the bioavailability of organochlorine insecticides (Lichtenstein et al, 1968), polychlorinated biphenyls (Strek et al, 1981), 2,4,6-trinitro-toluene (Vasilyeva et al, 2001) and phenanthrene (Rhodes et al, 2008). Yang and Sheng (2003) investigated the effect of adding charred crop (wheat and rice) residues to soil. They found that the addition of 0.1 per cent charred wheat residues resulted in the added biochar dominating sorption of diuron – this equates to the addition of around 100kg ha^{-1} of biochar C. Addition of biochar has also been found to increase sorption of anionic (Sheng et al,

2005; Hiller et al, 2007) and cationic (Sheng et al, 2005) organic compounds.

From these results, it would appear that there is some potential for amendment of soils with biochar to control the toxicity and movement of organic chemicals. Applications to highly contaminated sites and for use in riparian 'filter-strips' to prevent contamination of waterways would appear possible. However, the practicality of such treatments would depend upon the longevity of the effect of biochar, particularly considering the potential for sorption sites to become 'blocked'. Indeed, Rhodes et al (2008) reported that although there were initially decreases in the mineralization rate of phenanthrene with increasing contact time (presumably due to slow movement of phenanthrene to high-affinity sites), for some soils, mineralization increased again at incubation times of 50 to 100 days, and this was attributed to blocking of biochar sorption sites by organic matter or competition for sorption sites by native organic compounds.

Direct identification of organic molecules sorbed to biochar

Our understanding of the influence of biochar on the sorption properties of soils (and sediments) is limited by the lack of techniques that can directly differentiate and quantify organic molecules sorbed to different organic matter phases within a single sample. In most studies reporting an influence of biochar on sorption, the evidence is indirect – bulk sorption and biochar (or soot) contents are determined separately, and higher sorption affinity for biochar-rich samples is taken as evidence that biochar is providing the additional sorption sites. As discussed above, attempts to isolate and measure the sorption affinity of the biochar itself (Accardi-Dey and Gschwend, 2002) can overestimate its sorption (Cornelissen and Gustafsson, 2004). Biochar-like particles have been isolated from aquifer sediments using gentle fractionation, and these particles were shown to be strongly sorptive (Karapanagioti et al, 2000). However, this procedure is not applicable to surface soils and sediments, where biochar becomes so intimately associated with other organic matter that the two components cannot easily be separated.

Two recently developed NMR-based techniques do have the potential to directly differentiate and quantify organic molecules sorbed to different organic matter phases within a single sample. However, they cannot be used for 'natively sorbed' contaminants, since both require the use of ^{13}C-labelled compounds.

The first technique is proton spin relaxation editing (PSRE). PSRE can generate nuclear magnetic resonance (NMR) sub-spectra of different organic matter 'domains' within a single sample and has been described as 'virtual fractionation' (Smernik et al, 2000). These domains are differentiated on the basis of their different T1H relaxation rates, a property that is dependent mainly upon molecular mobility and the concentration of unpaired electron spins. A process called 'spin diffusion' homogenizes T1H relaxation rates, but is only efficient on the scale of 10nm to 100nm. Therefore, organic matter domains that are spatially and chemically distinct at scales greater than this can have different T1H relaxation rates and can be identified by PSRE. Fortunately, biochar usually has a distinctly shorter T1H relaxation rate than other types of organic matter. This has been attributed to the stabilization of organic free radicals by the condensed aromatic systems in biochar. Biochar domains have been identified in both soils (Smernik et al, 2000) and sediments (Golding et al, 2004) using PSRE.

What makes PSRE such a useful technique in sorption studies is that sorbed molecules inherit the 'T1H signature' of the organic matter phase to which they are sorbed (Smernik, 2005). For example, the T1H relaxation rate of molecules sorbed to biochar is the same as that of the biochar itself. Therefore, so long as an NMR signal for the sorbate molecules can be detected, one can determine the relative quantities sorbed to the different types of organic matter present. Sensitivity of detection can be greatly enhanced by using ^{13}C-labelled sorbate molecules. The PSRE technique has been used to show directly that phenanthrene preferentially sorbs to char-rich organic domains in sediments (Golding et al, 2005). It was also used to show that a range of organic molecules preferentially sorbed to biochar-rich domains in soil – this preference was especially strong for more hydrophobic molecules (Smernik, 2005).

The second new NMR-based technique that can identify molecules sorbed to biochar is even more direct. Close proximity of a molecule to an aromatic ring system affects its chemical shift (i.e. its peak position or

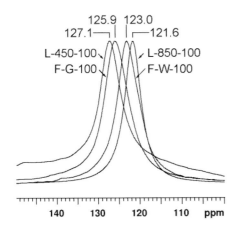

Figure 16.2 ^{13}C *cross-polarization (CP) nuclear magnetic resonance (NMR) spectra of ^{13}C-benzene sorbed to four different biochars exposed to 100mg L^{-1} of ^{13}C-benzene: L-450 and L-850 are laboratory-synthesized biochars produced at 450°C and 850°C, respectively; F-G and F-W are chars collected from the field and are charred residues of grass and wood fires, respectively*

Note: It would appear that the wood biochar is more condensed than the grass biochar and that both are intermediate between the two laboratory-produced biochars.

Source: reprinted with permission from Smernik et al (2006), copyright 2006 American Chemical Society

resonant frequency) through 'ring current effects' (Freitas et al, 2001a, b; Sander and Pignatello, 2005; Smernik et al, 2006). The cause is diamagnetic currents in aromatic ring systems which produce magnetic fields that are felt by nearby nuclei. Sander and Pignatello (2005) used this effect to show that nitrobenzene has a stronger affinity than benzene or toluene for model graphene units (naphthalene, phenanthrene and pyrene). The displacements in chemical shift reported in this study were <1ppm. Larger aromatic ring systems, such as those of graphite-like microcrystallites found in biochars, produce larger chemical shift displacements (Freitas et al, 1999, 2001a, b). It has been shown that the chemical shift of ^{13}C-benzene sorbed to

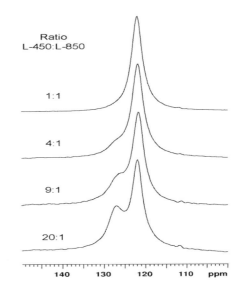

Figure 16.3 ^{13}C *CP-NMR spectra of mixtures of biochar L-450 and biochar L-850 (more information in Figure 16.2) exposed to 100mg L^{-1} of ^{13}C-benzene*

Source: reprinted with permission from Smernik et al (2006), copyright 2006 American Chemical Society

char is similarly affected, being shifted several parts per million up-field (Smernik et al, 2006). Furthermore, the magnitude of the shift was shown to be sensitive to the degree of aromatic condensation of the biochar and, therefore, is larger for biochars produced at higher temperatures (see Figure 16.2).

The effect on chemical shift is localized – only molecules very close to the aromatic surfaces are affected. This is demonstrated in Figure 16.3, which shows that when two biochars are mixed, separate resonances are observed for molecules sorbed to each biochar. Integration of the spectra in Figure 16.3 enables direct measurement of the relative affinities of each biochar within the mixture – in this case, the sorption affinity of biochars produced at 850°C is around 20 times that of biochars produced at 450°C.

It would appear that this technique should be ideally suited to differentiating and quantifying molecules sorbed to biochar and non-biochar organic matter in soils and sediments. However, the chemical shift of ^{13}C-labelled molecules sorbed to soil and sediments naturally rich in char is not significantly shifted up-field (unpublished results). There are a number of possible explanations. It may be that the surfaces of natural char particles in soils and sediments become oxidized (see Chapter 10; Smernik et al, 2000); hence, the surfaces of aged biochars are not that aromatic. A second possibility is that biochar surfaces become 'blocked' or 'fouled' with other sorbed molecules or organic matter (Jonker and Smedes, 2000; Cornelissen and Gustafsson, 2004; Cornelissen et al, 2004; Ran et al, 2007a, b; Rhodes et al, 2008) or, indeed, through interactions with clay minerals, and so the newly added ^{13}C molecules do not get close enough to the aromatic surfaces for their chemical shift to be affected. Further studies are needed to differentiate between these possibilities.

Conclusions and directions for future research

The addition of biochar to soil is expected to have a profound effect on the affinity of the soil for neutral organic compounds because fresh biochars are strong sorbents of these molecules. There are several implications of this. Addition of biochar should decrease the bioavailability, toxicity and mobility of organic pollutants. This has the potential to be beneficial for soil contaminated with high concentrations of these molecules. However, the addition of biochar also has the potential to reduce the efficacy of pesticides and herbicides that are deliberately applied to the soil to control pest species. On the other hand, aged biochar in soil has limited sorption capacity for pesticides and herbicides, not affecting their efficacy in the long term.

Perhaps of most interest is the potential for sorption properties to be used to gauge changes in the chemistry of biochar over time. Understanding these changes is vital to assessing the potential benefits of biochar amendments. Once added to the soil, biochar is expected to slowly oxidize and become intimately associated with other soil components (see Chapter 10), although the timescale of these processes is currently unknown. Partial oxidation of biochar produces carboxyl groups, which contribute cation exchange capacity (CEC) to the soil. The production of CEC sites is seen as one of the most important long-term benefits of biochar in soil (see Chapter 5), so it is important to understand how quickly these sites are produced. Association of biochar with organic matter and mineral soil components is an important process that is likely to affect the turnover of both the biochar C and the natural organic matter C, in this way affecting the C storage benefit of biochar amendment.

Since these processes will influence the sorption properties of the biochar and the sorption properties of the soil overall (because biochar is such a strong sorbent), it may be possible to use sorption measurements to detect and follow the changes. For example, while it has been shown that freshly added biochar greatly increases overall sorption affinity of a soil, it has also been shown that the sorption affinity of soils that naturally contain large amounts of char is not as high as would be expected based on the sorption properties of fresh char. Measurement of changes in sorption properties of biochar-amended soils would be an easy and sensitive way to follow these changes, especially in the short term (days, months and years). Combination of bulk sorption measurements with the novel ^{13}C-NMR techniques described here would provide an even more sensitive gauge of these changes.

References

Accardi-Dey, A. and Gschwend, P. M. (2002) 'Assessing the combined roles of natural organic matter and black carbon as sorbents in sediments', *Environmental Science and Technology*, vol 36, pp21–29

Accardi-Dey, A. and Gschwend, P. M. (2003) 'Reinterpreting literature sorption data considering both absorption into organic carbon and adsorption onto black carbon', *Environmental Science and Technology*, vol 37, pp99–106

Allen-King, R. M., Grathwohl, P. and Ball, W. P. (2002) 'New modelling paradigms for the sorption of hydrophobic organic chemicals to heterogeneous carbonaceous matter in soils, sediments, and rocks', *Advances in Water Resources*, vol 25, pp985–1016

Arle, H. F., Leonard, O. A. and Harris, V. C. (1948) 'Inactivation of 2,4-D on sweet-potato slips with activated carbon', *Science*, vol 107, pp247–248

Baring, H., Bucheli, T. D., Broman, D. and Gustafsson, Ö. (2002) 'Soot-water distribution coefficients for polychlorinated dibenzo-p-dioxins, polychlorinated dibenzofurans and polybrominated diphenylethers determined with the soot cosolvency-column method', *Chemosphere*, vol 49, pp515–523

Bornemann, L. C., Kookana, R. S. and Welp, G. (2007) 'Differential sorption behaviour of aromatic hydrocarbons on charcoals prepared at different temperatures from grass and wood', *Chemosphere*, vol 67, pp1033–1042

Braida, W. J., Pignatello, J. J., Lu, Y., Ravikovitch, P. I., Neimark, A. V. and Xing, B. (2003) 'Sorption hysteresis of benzene in charcoal particles', *Environmental Science and Technology*, vol 37, pp409–417

Bucheli, T. D. and Gustafsson, Ö. (2000) 'Quantification of the soot-water distribution coefficient of PAHs provides mechanistic basis for enhanced sorption observations', *Environmental Science and Technology*, vol 34, pp5144–5151

Bucheli, T. D. and Gustafsson, Ö. (2003) 'Soot sorption of non-ortho and ortho substituted PCBs', *Chemosphere*, vol 53, pp515–522

Chiou, C. T. (1995) 'Comment on "thermodynamics of organic chemical partition in soils"', *Environmental Science and Technology*, vol 29, pp1421–1422

Chiou, C. T. and Kile, D. E. (1998) 'Deviations from sorption linearity on soils of polar and nonpolar organic compounds at low relative concentrations', *Environmental Science and Technology*, vol 32, pp338–343

Chiou, C. T., Kile, D. E. and Rutherford, D. W. (2000) 'Sorption of selected organic compounds from water to a peat soil and its humic-acid and humin fractions: Potential sources of the sorption nonlinearity', *Environmental Science and Technology*, vol 34, pp1254–1258

Cornelissen, G. and Gustafsson, Ö. (2004) 'Sorption of phenanthrene to environmental black carbon in sediment with and without organic matter and native sorbates', *Environmental Science and Technology*, vol 38, pp148–155

Cornelissen, G., Kukulska, Z., Kalaitzidis, S., Christanis, K. and Gustafsson, Ö. (2004) 'Relations between environmental black carbon sorption and geochemical sorbent characteristics', *Environmental Science and Technology*, vol 38, pp3632–3640

Cornelissen, G., Gustafsson, Ö., Bucheli, T. D., Jonker, M. T. O., Koelmans, A. A. and van Noort, P. C. M. (2005) 'Extensive sorption of organic compounds to black carbon, coal, and kerogen in sediments and soils: Mechanisms and consequences for distribution, bioaccumulation, and biodegradation', *Environmental Science and Technology*, vol 39, pp6881–6895

Dias, J. M., Alvim-Ferraz, M. C. M., Almeida, M. F., Rivera-Utrilla, J. and Sanchez-Polo, M. (2007) 'Waste materials for activated carbon preparation and its use in aqueous-phase treatment: A review', *Journal of Environmental Management*, vol 85, pp833–846

Freitas, J. C. C., Bonagamba, T. J. and Emmerich, F. G. (1999) '13C high-resolution solid-state NMR study of peat carbonization', *Energy and Fuels*, vol 13, pp53–59

Freitas, J. C. C., Bonagamba, T. J. and Emmerich, F. G. (2001a) 'Investigation of biomass- and polymer-based carbon materials using 13C high-resolution solid-state NMR', *Carbon*, vol

39, pp535–545

Freitas, J. C. C., Emmerich, F. G., Cernicchiaro, G. R. C., Sampaio, L. C. and Bonagamba, T. J. (2001b) 'Magnetic susceptibility effects on ^{13}C MAS NMR spectra of carbon materials and graphite', *Solid State Nuclear Magnetic Resonance*, vol 20, pp61–73

Golding, C. J., Smernik, R. J. and Birch, G. F. (2004) 'Characterisation of sedimentary organic matter from three south-eastern Australian estuaries using solid-state ^{13}C-NMR techniques', *Marine and Freshwater Research*, vol 55, pp1–9

Golding, C. J., Smernik, R. J. and Birch, G. F. (2005) 'Investigation of the role of structural domains identified in sedimentary organic matter in the sorption of hydrophobic organic compounds', *Environmental Science and Technology*, vol 39, pp3925–3932

Gustafsson, Ö., Haghseta, F., Chan, C., MacFarlane, J. and Gschwend, P. M. (1997) 'Quantification of the dilute sedimentary soot phase: Implications for PAH speciation and bioavailability', *Environmental Science and Technology*, vol 31, pp203–209

Hammes, K., Schmidt, M. W. I., Smernik, R. J., Currie, L. A., Ball, W. P., Fukudome, M., Nguyen, T. H., Louchouarn, P., Houel, S., Gustafsson, Ö., Elmquist, M., Cornelissen, G., Skjemstad, J. O., Masiello, C. A., Song, J., Peng, P., Mitra, S., Dunn, J. C., Hatcher, P. G., Hockaday, W. C., Smith, D. M., Hartkopf-Fröder, C., Böhmer, A., Lüer, B., Huebert, B. J., Amelung, W., Brodowski, S., Huang, L., Zhang, W., Gschwend, P. M., Flores-Cervantes, D. X., Largeau, C., Rouzaud, J.-N., Rumpel, C., Guggenberger, G., Kaiser, K., Rodionov, A., Gonzalez-Vila, F. J., Gonzalez-Perez, J. A., de la Rosa, J. M., López-Capél, E., Manning, D. A. C. and Ding, L. (2007) 'Comparison of quantification methods to measure fire-derived (black/elemental) carbon in soils and sediments using reference materials from soil, water, sediment and the atmosphere', *Global Biogeochemical Cycles*, vol 21, pB3016

Hiller, E., Fargasova, A., Zemanova, L. and Bartal, M. (2007) 'Influence of wheat ash on the MCPA immobilization in agricultural soils', *Bulletin of Environmental Contamination and Toxicology*, vol 78, pp345–348

Huang, W., Peng, P., Yu, Z. and Fu, J. (2003)

'Effects of organic matter heterogeneity on sorption and desorption of organic contaminants by soils and sediments', *Applied Geochemistry*, vol 18, pp955–972

James, G., Sabatini, D. A., Chiou, C. T., Rutherford, D., Scott, A. C. and Karapanagioti, H. K. (2005) 'Evaluating phenanthrene sorption on various wood chars', *Water Research*, vol 39, pp549–558

Jonker, M. T. O. and Koelmans, A. A. (2002) 'Sorption of polycyclic aromatic hydrocarbons and polychlorinated biphenyls to soot and soot-like materials in the aqueous environment: Mechanistic considerations', *Environmental Science and Technology*, vol 36, pp3725–3734

Jonker, M. T. O. and Smedes, F. (2000) 'Preferential sorption of planar contaminants in sediments from Lake Ketelmeer, The Netherlands', *Environmental Science and Technology*, vol 34, pp1620–1626

Karapanagioti, H. K. and Sabatini, D. A. (2000) 'Impacts of heterogeneous organic matter on phenanthrene sorption', *Environmental Science and Technology*, vol 34, pp2453–2460

Karapanagioti, H. K., Kleineidam, S., Sabatini, D. A., Grathwohl, P. and Ligouis, B. (2000) 'Impacts of heterogeneous organic matter on phenanthrene sorption: Equilibrium and kinetic studies with aquifer material', *Environmental Science and Technology*, vol 34, pp406–414

Karapanagioti, H. K., Childs, J. and Sabatini, D. A. (2001) 'Impacts of heterogeneous organic matter on phenanthrene sorption: Different soil and sediment samples', *Environmental Science and Technology*, vol 35, pp4684–4690

Kleineidam, S., Rugner, H., Ligouis, B. and Grathwohl, P. (1999) 'Organic matter facies and equilibrium sorption of phenanthrene', *Environmental Science and Technology*, vol 33, pp1637–1644

Kleineidam, S., Schuth, C. and Grathwohl, P. (2002) 'Solubility-normalized combined adsorption-partitioning sorption isotherms for organic pollutants', *Environmental Science and Technology*, vol 36, pp4689–4697

Koelmans, A. A., Jonker, M. T. O., Cornelissen, G., Bucheli, T. D., van Noort, P. C. M. and Gustafsson, Ö. (2006) 'Black carbon: The reverse of its dark side', *Chemosphere*, vol 63, pp365–377

Lichtenstein, E. P., Fuhremann, T. W. and Schulz, K. R. (1968) 'Use of carbon to reduce the uptake of insecticidal soil residues by crop plants', *Journal of Agricultural and Food Chemistry*, vol 16, pp348–355

Luehrs, D. C., Hickey, J. P., Nilsen, P. E., Godbole, K. A. and Rogers, T. N. (1996) 'Linear solvation energy relationship of the limiting partition coefficient of organic solutes between water and activated carbon', *Environmental Science and Technology*, vol 30, pp143–152

McGroddy, S. E. and Farrington, J. W. (1995) 'Sediment porewater partitioning of polycyclic aromatic hydrocarbons in three cores from Boston Harbor, Massachusetts', *Environmental Science and Technology*, vol 29, pp1542–1550

Nguyen, T. H. and Ball, W. P. (2006) 'Absorption and adsorption of hydrophobic organic contaminants to diesel and hexane soot', *Environmental Science and Technology*, vol 40, pp2958–2964

Nguyen, T. H., Sabbah, I. and Ball, W. P. (2004) 'Sorption nonlinearity for organic contaminants with diesel soot: Method development and isotherm interpretation', *Environmental Science and Technology*, vol 38, pp3595–3603

Ran, Y., Sun, K., Ma, X., Wang, G., Grathwohl, P. and Zeng, E. (2007a) 'Effect of condensed organic matter on solvent extraction and aqueous leaching of polycyclic aromatic hydrocarbons in soils and sediments', *Environmental Pollution*, vol 148, pp529–538

Ran, Y., Sun, K., Yang, Y., Xing, B. and Zeng, E. (2007b) 'Strong sorption of phenanthrene by condensed organic matter in soils and sediments', *Environmental Science and Technology*, vol 41, pp3952–3958

Rhodes, A. H., Carlin, A. and Semple, K. T. (2008) 'Impact of black carbon in the extraction and mineralization of phenanthrene in soil', *Environmental Science and Technology*, vol 42, pp740–745

Sander, M. and Pignatello, J. J. (2005) 'Characterization of charcoal adsorption sites for aromatic compounds: Insights drawn from single-solute and bi-solute competitive experiments', *Environmental Science and Technology*, vol 39, pp1606–1615

Sander, M. and Pignatello, J. J. (2007) 'On the reversibility of sorption to black carbon: Distinguishing true hysteresis from artificial hysteresis caused by dilution of a competing adsorbate', *Environmental Science and Technology*, vol 41, pp843–849

Schmidt, M. W. I. and Noack, A. G. (2000) 'Black carbon in soils and sediments: Analysis, distribution, implications, and current challenges', *Global Biogeochemical Cycles*, vol 14, pp777–793

Sheng, G., Yang, Y., Huang, M. and Yang, K. (2005) 'Influence of pH on pesticide sorption by soil containing wheat residue-derived char', *Environmental Pollution*, vol 134, pp457–63

Smernik, R. J. (2005) 'A new way to use solid-state carbon-13 nuclear magnetic resonance spectroscopy to study the sorption of organic compounds to organic matter', *Journal of Environmental Quality*, vol 34, pp1194–1204

Smernik, R. J., Skjemstad, J. O. and Oades, J. M. (2000) 'Virtual fractionation of charcoal from soil organic matter using solid state ^{13}C NMR spectral editing', *Australian Journal of Soil Research*, vol 38, pp665–683

Smernik, R. J., Kookana, R. S. and Skjemstad, J. O. (2006) 'NMR characterization of ^{13}C-benzene sorbed to natural and prepared charcoals', *Environmental Science and Technology*, vol 40, pp1764–1769

Strek, H. J., Weber, J. B., Shea, P. J., Mrozej Jr, E. and Overcash, M. R. (1981) 'Reduction of polychlorinated biphenyl toxicity and uptake of carbon-14 activity by plants through the use of activated carbon', *Journal of Agricultural and Food Chemistry*, vol 29, pp288–293

van Noort, P. C. M., Jonker, M. T. O. and Koelmans, A. A. (2004) 'Modeling maximum adsorption capacities of soot and soot-like materials for PAHs and PCBs', *Environmental Science and Technology*, vol 38, pp3305–3309

Vasilyeva, G. K., Kreslavski, V. D., Oh, B.–T. and Shea, P. J. (2001) 'Potential of activated carbon to decrease 2,4,6-trinitrotoluene toxicity and accelerate soil decontamination', *Environmental Toxicology and Chemistry*, vol 20, pp965–971

Walters, R. W. and Luthy, R. G. (1984) 'Equilibrium adsorption of polycyclic aromatic hydrocarbons from water onto activated carbon', *Environmental Science and Technology*, vol 18, pp395–403

Wang, X. and Xing, B. (2007) 'Sorption of organic contaminants by biopolymer-derived chars', *Environmental Science and Technology*, vol 41, pp8342–8348

Xia, G. and Ball, W. P. (1999) 'Adsorption-partitioning uptake of nine low-polarity organic chemicals on a natural sorbent', *Environmental Science and Technology*, vol 33, pp262–269

Yang, Y. and Sheng, G. (2003) 'Enhanced pesticide sorption by soils containing particulate matter from crop residue burns', *Environmental Science and Technology*, vol 37, pp3635–3639

17

Test Procedures for Determining the Quantity of Biochar within Soils

David A. C. Manning and Elisa Lopez-Capel

Introduction

This chapter briefly reviews the methods that are available for assessing whether or not biochar is present in a soil and, if so, how much biochar there is. Quantification of biochar in soil is important for several reasons. First, for carbon (C) accounting purposes (e.g. Mathews, 2008; see Chapter 18), it is essential that the amount of biochar which remains in soil over the long term is known. Second, it is important for verification purposes that the biochar determined within a soil can be recognized and distinguished from other forms of black C that might be present, through natural processes, such as soot or coal. Third, it is important in research to be able to quantify biochar within soils so that its longevity, reactions and impact upon the soil system are understood. Finally, it is important from a practical point of view to determine the quantities of biochar using methods that are sufficiently rapid and inexpensive that their widespread use becomes possible. This chapter does not attempt to examine quantification methods for all forms of black C such as soot or graphitic black C (Masiello, 2004), but specifically addresses biochar in the context of a soil amendment. It also focuses on applicability of quantification methods as tests that can be employed to achieve the objectives mentioned above, rather than on research methods that are covered elsewhere (Schmidt et al, 2001; Hammes et al, 2007).

Even if separated from soil, the quantitative investigation of biochar presents many analytical challenges in view of its heterogeneity, chemical complexity and the inherently non-reactive nature of C compounds that remain after pyrolysis. As described in earlier chapters, the characteristics of biochar are complex and varied (e.g. see Figure 17.1). Importantly, Figure 17.1 shows how the organic components of biochar are intimately mixed with biological materials and mineral matter derived either from the charring process or inherited from the soil, or newly formed within the soil. Reliable determination of the C content of this refractory and heterogeneous material is a major challenge for the analyst.

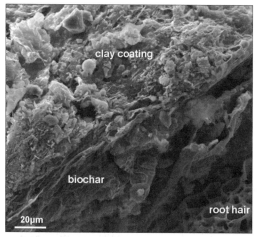

Figure 17.1 *Secondary electron image of biochar produced from poultry litter (450°C for 20 minutes using slow pyrolysis without activation) after 12 months in soil*

Notes: Biochar was washed in a water bath for 30 minutes before mounting for measurement. A root hair (bottom right) has bonded with the biochar, with clay minerals adhering to the surface (top left).

Source: courtesy of Stephen Joseph

Paying particular attention to the practicalities of soil analysis for the determination of biochar *quantity*, we will now briefly review six methods proposed for the determination of black C in the context of their suitability for biochar:

1   determination of solvent-extractable aromatic compounds as benzene poly-carboxylic acids (Brodowski et al, 2005) or other biomarkers (e.g. Elias et al, 2001);
2   chemo-thermal oxidation at 375°C followed by elemental analysis of the residue (Gustafsson et al, 1997; Gélinas et al, 2001; Gustafsson et al, 2001);
3   chemical oxidation using acid dichromate (Song et al, 2002) or sodium hypochlorite, followed by elemental analysis of the residue by ^{13}C nuclear magnetic resonance (NMR) analysis (Simpson and Hatcher, 2004a, 2004b);

4   thermal/optical laser transmittance or reflectance (a method used for airborne particulates; Huang et al, 2006);
5   ultraviolet (UV) photo-oxidation of the sample followed by ^{13}C-NMR analysis of the residue (Skjemstad et al, 1996, 1999);
6   thermogravimetric analysis of the sample under flowing $He_{80}O_{20}$ (Lopez-Capel et al, 2005; Manning et al, 2008).

Most of these methods were not designed originally for the determination of biochar in soils. They represent analytical techniques that are intended to determine the black C content of a range of environmental matrices. The term 'black C' can include soot, kerogen and coal, as well as char, and all of these materials have different properties and functions within soil. The UV photo-oxidation method has been used specifically to investigate char in soils (Skjemstad et al, 1996, 1999), and this research group has extended their approach by developing a rapid method for the estimation of char using mid-infrared spectroscopic analysis calibrated against a reference sample set determined using UV photo-oxidation and ^{13}C-NMR analysis (Janik et al, 2007).

Other techniques, such as pyrolysis gas chromatography–mass spectrometry (GC-MS) and other sophisticated mass spectrometric methods, allow changes in biochar *character* to be described, but at this stage have a less significant role in quantifying the *amount* of C that has been sequestered in soil as a consequence of applying biochar. For further information on the techniques referred to in this chapter, some of which are long established for other applications within organic geochemistry, other reviews should be consulted (e.g. Whelan and Thompson-Rizer, 1993).

A key issue that limits the value of almost all methods for determining biochar within soils concerns possible interferences from other materials that are present, both in the biochar itself (see Figure 17.1) and also in the soil (Hammes et al, 2007). Within the biochar, possible interferences arise from mineral inclusions, such as clays and carbonates (which can affect weight loss or evolved gas analytical methods), or other forms of soil C that become incorporated within the biochar structure (such as degraded fungal hyphae). It is important to be aware of the other possible sources of black C that could interfere with quantification of biochar that was applied to soil, such as coal, which, in some cases, is a natural fossil biochar (Scott and Glasspool, 2007). Fragments of bituminous coals occur widely within soils developed on Carboniferous sediments and glacial till derived from those sediments, and thus are likely to occur in soils in large areas of the eastern US, parts of the Rocky Mountains and much of northern mainland Europe. Coal of this type is a highly variable material, with differing proportions of the coal macerals, first described by Stopes (1935). These include lipid-rich liptinite, which is much more reactive in soils than, for example, inertinite. Because of its unreactive status and relic plant cell structure (Senftle et al, 1993), inertinite may be mistaken for biochar. Of all coal macerals, the inertinite subgroup of fusinites most closely match biochar and are regarded as fossil charcoals (Scott et al, 2000; Scott and Glasspool, 2007).

A particular challenge is to distinguish the applied biochar from any biochar-type material that soils may already contain. Biochar-type materials such as char from vegetation fires are ubiquitous in the environment, and soils worldwide invariably contain some biochar (Krull et al, 2008).

For quantification purposes, analytical methods and protocols need to be able to cope with the possible presence of background or natural inputs of black C that are similar to biochar or included in quantification of biochar that could mistakenly be determined as biochar derived from deliberate application. As with many environmental analytical protocols, the key to success is likely to lie in:

- careful determination of baseline conditions prior to biochar application to soil; and
- very careful sample preparation in order to ensure that potential interferences are removed prior to analysis.

These matters will now be considered for selected methods currently used for the much wider range of black C material determination in soils; their relevance to biochar test methods in the context of biochar soil management is also discussed.

Biochar quantification methods

A summary of the methods for black C determination that are described below and their specific relevance to biochar is given in Table 17.1.

Figure 17.2 compares the methods for black C determination listed in Table 17.1 for analysing grass biochar and wood biochar, using results published by Hammes et al (2007). It shows that the results obtained can vary greatly according to the method used. If

we assume that grass char and wood char are biochars typical of those that we want to quantify, the individual methods vary significantly in their ability to report biochar quantity. For wood biochar, thermal oxidation (TOT/R), thermogravimetry and UV oxidation all report almost 90 per cent or more of the biochar as black C, suggesting that these methods will reliably report biochar contents in soils. Dichromate oxida-

Table 17.1 *Summary of key methods for determining black C in environmental samples and their relevance to biochar determination*

Method	Principle	Relevance to biochar determination
Biomarker analysis (Brodowski et al, 2005)	After removal of cations with trifluoroacetic acid, the sample is oxidized using nitric acid, converting aromatic C to benzene polycarboxylic acids, which are then determined using gas chromatography.	All aromatic C within a sample is determined, so this method does not distinguish biochar specifically.
Chemo-thermal oxidation (Gustafsson et al, 1997)	Sample oxidized at 375°C for 18 hours after acid pre-treatment, followed by elemental analysis of residual C.	Labile organic matter may be charred during this process, leading to overestimation of the original biochar content. Conversely, some biochar may be destroyed. The method is not specific to biochar.
Chemical oxidation: dichromate method (Song et al, 2002) or sodium hypochlorite method (Simpson and Hatcher, 2004a, 2004b)	In these methods, organic matter other than black C is oxidized, and the C content of the residue is determined using elemental analysis.	The dichromate oxidation method determines aromatic C and therefore may overestimate biochar contents if other sources of aromatic C are present. The hypochlorite oxidation method appears to destroy biochar and thus underestimates biochar contents.
Thermal/optical transmittance and reflectance (Chow et al, 2004)	Particulate samples on a filter membrane are heated, and the evolved CO_2 is determined following reduction to CH_4, coupled with measurement of optical transmittance and reflectance of the residual solid.	Designed originally to analyse airborne particulates, this method has been extended (Han et al, 2007) to determine biochar in soils. Regulatory authorities may find it useful to determine the impact of biochar applications to soil on air quality.
UV oxidation (Skjemstad et al, 1996).	Sample is oxidized in oxygenated water using UV light; residual C is determined using elemental analysis and ^{13}C-NMR.	Expressly designed for the determination of char and other black C components in soils, this method may overestimate biochar as other aromatic C may interfere.
Thermal analysis (Lopez-Capel et al, 2005; Manning et al, 2008)	Sample heated under a controlled atmosphere; individual C constituents determined by: 1 evolved gas analysis; 2 differential scanning calorimetry; and/or 3 weight loss.	Sample pre-treatment is essential to remove clay minerals, which contribute to weight loss. Biochar is not distinguished from other black C.

Source: based on Hammes et al (2008)

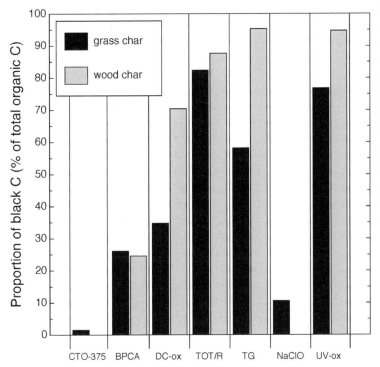

Figure 17.2 *Comparison of analytical methods used to determine black C contents of biochar and soils*

Note: CTO-375 refers to chemo-thermal oxidation at 375°C; BPCA to benzene polycarboxylic acid determination; DC-ox to dichromate oxidation; TOT/R to thermal/optical laser transmittance and reflectance methods; TG to thermogravimetry; NaClO to sodium hypochlorite oxidation; and UV-ox to oxidation using ultraviolet light.

Source: data from Hammes et al (2007)

tion reports 70 per cent of the wood char as black C. For grass char, the reported proportions as black C are lower. Thermal oxidation (TOT/R) reports over 80 per cent of the biochar C as black C, and UV oxidation reports 75 per cent as black C. These methods are being extended to soils (Han et al, 2007), and evidently have substantial scope for use in biochar determination (although the extraction process is highly laborious, meaning that they may not become routine).

Individual methods, and their relevance specifically for the determination of the amounts of biochar within a soil, are discussed below.

Molecular marker methods

Chemically, a defining characteristic of biochar is that it contains aromatic ring compounds, some of which can be extracted as benzene polycarboxylic acids (BPCAs) (Glaser et al, 1998; Brodowski et al, 2005;

method b of Hammes et al, 2007). These compounds have a single benzene ring, which carries a variable number of carboxyl groups (examples are shown in Figure 17.3). The method uses the assumption that the proportion of BPCAs determined can be directly related to the total bulk biochar content by reference to a standard. Glaser et al (1998) analysed commercially produced biochars and proposed a correction factor of 2.27 to multiply the total BPCA content to give the biochar content. In a critical review of the procedure, Brodowski et al (2005) found that the correction factor varies from 2.27 to 4.5. These authors concluded that the correction factor of 2.27 should be retained, and that the BPCA method should be regarded as an indicator of the minimum content of all black C forms, including biochar, within a sample.

The determination of BPCAs involves a complex chemical extraction process. First, trifluoroacetic acid is used to remove mineral

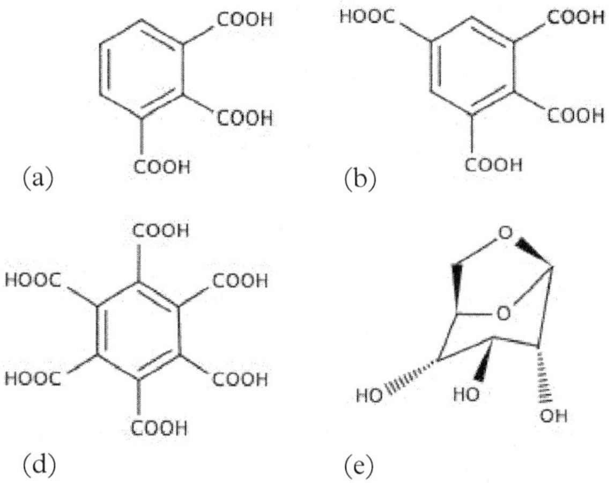

Figure 17.3 *Structures of selected benzene polycarboxylic acids used in the determination of black C: (a) hemimellitic acid; (b) mellophanic acid; (c) benzene pentacarboxylic acid; (d) mellitic acid; and (e) levoglucosan*

Source: redrawn from Brodowski et al (2005); levoglucosan redrawn from Elias et al (2001)

matter (Glaser et al, 1998, Brodowski et al, 2005). Subsequently, the residual solid (which contains the biochar) is oxidized using concentrated nitric acid at high pressure at 170°C. After further treatments to remove possible remaining cations, the sample is derivatized (addition of trimethylsilyl functional groups) to allow determination using gas chromatography.

In the ring trial reported by Hammes et al (2007), the BPCA method had the advantages of being able to report black C in solution and of being able to fingerprint different materials, as characteristic BPCA profiles can be obtained. For materials that are assumed not to contain biochar, in this case shale and coal, the method overestimated the amount of black C present by up to 20 per cent, suggesting that for these materials additional components of the organic constituents are reported as biochar. For wood and grass biochars, 24 to 26 per cent of the total C were captured in the analysis as black C. This appears to be a low proportion considering that approximately 75 per cent of C was aromatic C (Hammes et al, 2007, 2008).

When applied to biochar, this method has to be used with care. It employs the benzene polycarboxylic acids (which are just

one component of biochar) as a marker that indicates biochar quantity, and so it needs to be calibrated, ideally for each specific biochar that is being investigated. Although the method can then be used to determine, for example, how soil biochar content might vary as it ages, this assumes that the proportion of BPCAs within a specific biochar remains constant, which may not necessarily be so.

Other molecular markers used to specifically identify biochar include levoglucosan (see Figure 17.3; Elias et al, 2001). In some circumstances, this compound is produced from cellulose during pyrolysis and may be trapped in the resulting biochar. It has been used to track aerosols derived from forest fires and to determine the origin of char within soils and sediments. Like the BPCAs, assumptions concerning the proportion of levoglucosan within biochar would have to be made in order to use the levoglucosan concentration as a proxy for the biochar content of a soil.

Chemo-thermal oxidation

Gustafsson et al (1997) reported a method for determining black C, mainly in sediments, that exploited an initial oxidation step by heating a sediment sample at 375°C in oxygen-saturated air. This method of preparation operationally defines black C as the proportion of the organic matter that is not destroyed by this process. Gélinas et al (2001) developed the method further, with the following steps. Prior to thermal oxidation, the sample is freeze dried, demineralized using a combination of hydrochloric and hydrofluoric acids, and then hydrolysable organic matter is removed using a succession of treatments with trifluoroacetic acid and hydrochloric acid. The residues after oxidation at 375°C are then analysed using an elemental analyser to determine their C and N contents. Additional analysis of the residues can be carried out to characterize the material obtained using the sample preparation scheme: Gélinas et al (2001) used ^{13}C-NMR to determine the extent to which alkyl and unsaturated C carried over, and found this proportion negligible. They do report, however, that graphitic C is not destroyed in the preparation process. Other refractory forms of C (graphene and turbostratic) may behave similarly, leading to under-determination of black C of ultimately biological origin.

According to Hammes et al (2007), this method distinguished soot and biochars. It gave low results for the biochars (near zero), suggesting that biochars may be 'invisible' to this method, although biochars produced commercially may differ from those reported by Hammes et al (2007). The method gave the lowest reported proportions of black C (relative to total organic C) for the geological (coal and shale) samples, indicating that after the chemical treatment and oxidation steps the residue contained very little C. This is consistent with what is known about the ashing behaviour of coals under strongly oxidizing conditions (Senftle et al, 1993). For the two soils, this method again determined that residual C levels were very low. The cited detection limit is 10mg kg^{-1}, with 85 per cent recovery (Gélinas et al, 2001), which suggests that this method could be useful for determining soot or geological C within soils; but so far it appears to be unable to detect low-temperature biochar.

Chemical oxidation

Acid dichromate $(Cr_2O_7^{2-})$

As an alternative approach to oxidation by heating in air, a method using chemical oxidation using acid dichromate $(Cr_2O_7^{2-})$ has been described by a number of authors (e.g. Wolbach and Anders, 1989; Lim and Cachier, 1996; Song et al, 2002; method c in Hammes et al, 2007). Again, sample pre-treatment involves removal of minerals and labile organic matter using hydrochloric and hydrofluoric acids to give a residue that contains humic acids, kerogen (geological C) and black C. After treatment to remove humic acids using sodium hydroxide solution, the residual solid is oxidized using potassium dichromate in sulphuric acid, heated at 55°C for 60 hours. This aggressive oxidation stage removes kerogen, leaving black C 'fairly unchanged' (Song et al, 2002). In their method development, Song et al (2002) used X-ray diffraction to determine which mineral phases survived the extraction process, and organic petrography to determine the loss of kerogen. Scanning electron microscopy and ^{13}C-NMR were used to investigate the final product of the extraction process. Under normal operational conditions, the black C content is determined by elemental analysis of the residue. Wolbach and Anders (1989) distinguish different C forms on the basis of difference in reaction rates, with a short half-life during dichromate oxidation for labile organic matter (50 hours).

According to Hammes et al (2007), this method gave high proportions of black C for the biochars and the geological materials, suggesting that chemical oxidation captures most of the biochar. It gave similar or lower proportions of black C for the soil samples.

Sodium hypochlorite (NaClO)

In an alternative method using chemical oxidation, repeated treatment by sodium hypochlorite is used to oxidize C, leaving a black C residue (Simpson and Hatcher, 2004a, 2004b). After oxidation, the residue (which contains mineral matter) is analysed by elemental analysis to determine the C (and N) contents. Method development has again used ^{13}C-NMR to characterize the residue and to determine the C content by measurement of the relative amount of aromatic C. Within the ring trial (Hammes et al, 2007), only one laboratory used the method, and it was deemed to have promise but to require further development. The method did not detect black C in the geological (shale and coal) samples, and gave similar results for the soils to the BPCA method. It gave very low values for wood and grass biochar, probably due to the harsh chemical oxidation that destroys most C, suggesting that it is not suitable specifically for biochar studies.

Thermal/optical laser transmittance and reflectance (TOT/R)

Hammes et al (2007) report the use of thermal/optical laser transmittance and/or reflectance (TOT/R) as a method to determine black C within suspended matter (in water or air) that has been collected on filters (Chow et al, 2004). This is a specialist application that, as initially described, is distant from the purpose of determining biochar in soils. There is no doubt that it could be vital in determining wind-blown dust or suspended solids in water, arising from field applications of biochar. It thus may have an important role in the environmental monitoring of biochar use. The method has been applied to soils by Han et al (2007), who demineralized the soil using a succession of treatments culminating in hydrofluoric acid, collecting the remaining organic fraction on a filter paper and then proceeding as for suspended solids.

In this method, solid particulates of C are collected on quartz fibre filters. Sub-samples of the filter are then heated under helium or helium with 2 per cent O_2, and the evolved gases collected, oxidized to give CO_2 and then reduced to give methane, which is determined using a flame ionization detector (Chow et al, 2004). The method reports the amount of C evolved at different temperatures, which can then be related to the optical reflectance and transmittance of the sample, which effectively measure the 'blackness' of the filter. Compared with the previous methods described here, sample preparation for airborne or water-borne particulates is negligible.

Although the method appears to be very reproducible (Hammes et al, 2007; Han et al, 2007), it did overestimate the amount of black C for the coal and (to a lesser extent) soil samples. This reflects, in part, the experimental difficulties inherent in presenting the solids for analysis; the method is most suitable for samples that can be collected on a filter with the minimum amount of processing. Both the original method (Hammes et al, 2007) and that developed for analysis of soils and sediments (Han et al, 2007) yield the highest black C contents (85 to 90 per cent and 74 to 80 per cent, respectively, for the two approaches) for the grass and wood biochar, suggesting that it is well suited to biochar analysis (see Figure 17.2).

UV oxidation

Oxidation of organic matter by exposure to UV light as a biochar quantification method was developed by Skjemsted et al (1996). In this method, an aqueous suspension of the fine-grained fraction from a soil (clay or silt) or pure biochar is exposed to ultraviolet light for up to eight hours. After washing and centrifuging, the residual solid is analysed using elemental analysis, again employing

^{13}C-NMR to characterize and quantify the relative proportions of different black C components (Skjemsted et al, 1996, 2001). This method avoids chemical oxidation of the sample.

According to Hammes et al (2007), the method was found to detect black C consistently for different sample types. It appears to overestimate the amount of black C in coal samples, but agrees with other oxidative methods on determining proportions of black C in shale and soil samples. Hammes et al (2007) comment that the method is not widely used, and that commercial equipment for UV oxidation is not available, requiring 'home-built' oxidation apparatus. Although far from being a routine method, UV oxidation appears to have considerable promise for biochar analysis. In the ring trial, it gave the highest black C content reported for wood biochar (approximately 95 per cent) and the second highest black C content (exceeded by thermal oxidation) for grass biochar (approximately 75 per cent).

Thermal analysis in combination with calorimetry and isotope analyses (TG-DSC)

Thermal analysis has been used for decades for the characterizing and quantifying of carbonaceous materials in the context of fuels (e.g. Grimshaw and Roberts, 1957). In the oil industry, early use of thermal analysis (e.g. Whelan et al, 1990) led to the development of the Rock-Eval instrument (Espitalié et al, 1977; Delvaux et al, 1990), which is routinely used for the analysis of rocks to assess their petroleum source potential or for the characterization of coals (e.g. Bostick and Dawes, 1994). More recently, the Rock-Eval instrument has been used in characterizing soils (Disnar et al, 2003; Sebag et al, 2006), demonstrating both its value in determining proportions of labile and refractory C pools and its potential for analysing relatively large numbers of samples on an automated basis. This track record of development shows that it is possible to take thermal analysis from a research environment to a commercial and routine end use (initially in the petroleum industry).

Consideration of thermal analysis allows for a greater understanding of the analytical procedures that involve a heating process. We have used thermal analysis to investigate a number of biochars, and we now use these results in the context of other analytical methods to illustrate the character of biochar and how this might influence analytical procedures (especially those using thermal oxidation in analysis or sample preparation).

The technique of thermal analysis involves heating a sample under controlled conditions and measuring its response as temperature increases. Typically, mass is measured continuously (through thermogravimetric analysis, or TG), and weight losses occur at temperatures that are characteristic of the thermal decomposition behaviour of specific materials. These measurements are made under a controlled atmosphere to enhance, inhibit or prevent reaction. For organic matter, it is common to use an oxidizing atmosphere to ensure oxidation of the material. Typically, cellulose decomposes at 350°C to 400°C, and lignin between 450°C and 500°C, corresponding to labile and recalcitrant pools within a soil system (Lopez-Capel et al, 2005; de la Rosa et al, 2008). More refractory C, a major component of biochar, decomposes at higher temperatures (500°C to 550°C) and can therefore be separated analytically for quantification. The residual mass at the end of a thermal analysis experiment indicates the ash content of the sample, reflecting the presence and quantity of mineral matter.

In addition to mass, continuous recording of the energy flux into and out of the sample is recorded using differential scanning calorimetry (DSC). This indicates

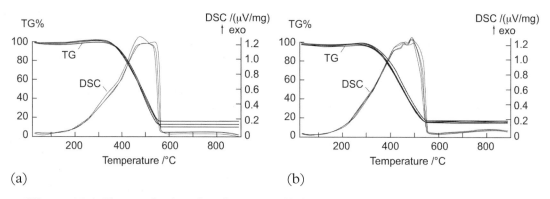

(a)   (b)

Figure 17.4 *Characterization of a reference set of industrial biochars by thermogravimetry and differential scanning calorimetry (TG-DSC)*

Notes: TG-DSC traces for (a) pine and (b) peanut husk biochar produced under different process conditions. The six different peanut biochars were produced at reactor temperatures of 473°C to 501°C; the three different pines biochars at reactor temperatures of 466°C to 500°C, both with either steam or N_2 as sweep gas and 0.4–6.0psi pressure. Apparatus used was a Netzsch STA 449C Jupiter thermal analyser (type S) and a $PtRh_{10}$-Pt thermocouple connected to a Netzsch Aeolus QMS system (Netzsch Instruments, Aldridge, UK). Samples supplied by Eprida Inc. (www.eprida.com).

Source: chapter authors

whether or not a reaction (with an associated weight loss) at a particular temperature is endothermic or exothermic. Dehydration and decarbonation reactions involving clay and carbonate minerals are endothermic, and (in an oxidizing atmosphere) reactions involving the combustion of organic matter are exothermic. When combined with observed weight losses, the relative contributions of inorganic and organic impurities to observed reactions can be determined. Figure 17.4 shows typical weight-loss and DSC curves for pine and peanut husk biochars. Despite different production conditions and feedstocks of the biochars, both give very similar results. Importantly, oxidation begins (as indicated by the DSC curve) at as low as 200°C, with weight losses complete by 550°C. Thus, a method that involves thermal oxidation by heating at 375°C may, in this case, lead to thermal decomposition of some components of the biochar, meaning that use of this method may underestimate the biochar content of soil to which this specific biochar has been applied.

As well as estimating the proportions of biochar using the observed weight losses, the DSC curves alone can be decomposed to resolve individual peaks that correspond to different components, and then to quantify these from peak height or peak area measurements (Leifeld, 2007). At present, these two approaches have not been compared.

Although on its own TG-DSC has much to offer, its potential as a technique is greatly enhanced by coupling to online analysis of evolved gas compositions using quadrupole mass spectrometry (QMS) or isotope ratio mass spectrometry (IRMS). QMS monitors the masses of different molecular species in the evolved gas, enabling specific weight losses to be attributed to the loss of, for example, water in the case of clays, CO_2 in the case of carbonates or organic matter, and nitrogen (N) or sulphur (S) species if present in the biochar. Typically, the evolution of these occurs at specific temperatures that are characteristic of the material (Lopez-Capel et al, 2006). The use of QMS can allow detection of residual oils within a biochar. IRMS enables the determination of C isotope ratios for discrete organic components within a sample (Manning et al, 2008). The method has yet to be used with biochar samples other than natural char from forest fires, where it allows the origin of the biochar component to be identified as C3 or C4 vegetation (de la Rosa et al, 2008).

Comparison of thermal analysis with the other methods described here was reported by Hammes et al (2007), who highlighted the possibility that interferences from mineral matter can lead to overestimation (based on weight loss measurements) of black C contents. Clay minerals, in particular, decompose (losing water) at temperatures that are characteristic of specific mineral species. For example, kaolinite decomposes at approximately 500°C, while illites and smectites lose water slowly from 250°C to 600°C. Since

these reactions coincide with decomposition of organic components, the measurement of weight loss alone will overestimate organic matter if clay reactions are ignored. The most common carbonate minerals, calcite and dolomite, decompose at higher temperatures than biochar and need not interfere. Thus, for quantitative analysis, either sample preparation has to be used to separate the organic matter prior to analysis (Sohi et al, 2001; Lopez-Capel et al, 2005) or evolved CO_2 must be determined and quantified using methods like those of Leifeld (2007). Interpretation of DSC curves is less subject to interference by clay mineral reactions, although since these are endothermic they reduce the magnitude of the DSC signal and will cause underestimation of organic components (which show exothermic reactions).

Routine quantification of biochar in soils

The methods described above vary in their complexity and the time taken to process individual samples. If ^{13}C-NMR is involved, each sample may require several hours to collect a spectrum. It is important to consider how biochar quantification can be developed to provide robust methods that adequately quantify the biochar content of soils routinely and sufficiently rapidly to assess large numbers of samples at a reasonable cost. As already stated, the development of the Rock-Eval instrument from thermal analysis systems shows that it is feasible to do this.

One approach that has considerable promise is infrared spectroscopy (Janik et al, 2007). This method demonstrated by Janik et al (2007) uses the mid-infrared region ($4000cm^{-1}$ to $500cm^{-1}$), which is where peaks attributable to key diagnostic functional groups relevant to organic C are

observed. Thus, different C pools can be quantified, interpreting the spectra using a partial least-square method that allows correlation with a set of reference soils that have been analysed using other techniques. Once the method has been set up and calibrated, it can be used rapidly and cheaply for large numbers of samples.

In this method, ground soil samples are scanned in diffuse reflectance mode (collecting the IR spectrum from the surface of a powder). Janik et al (2007) used samples to which known amounts of biochar had been added as a way of testing the method, and compared the results obtained with results from ^{13}C-NMR analysis. A good correlation was obtained for biochar-bearing soils (see Figure 17.5), with much better correlations for total C determined by IR spectrometry and dry combustion elemental analysis.

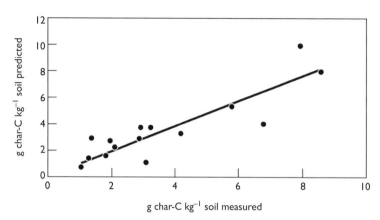

Figure 17.5 *Determination of biochar in soil samples, measured using infrared spectroscopy*

Source: adapted from Janik et al (2007), reproduced with permission from the *Australian Journal of Agricultural Research,* copyright CSIRO Publishing, Melbourne Australia

Conclusions

Quantification of biochar depends upon a thorough understanding of the qualities of biochar. Some methods appear to be poorly suited to the determination of biochar, especially those that were unable to quantify wood biochar in the ring trial (Hammes et al, 2007). This is partly because they quantify operationally defined parameters that are assumed to relate directly to biochar – for example, by empirical correlation (as in the BPCA method). In soil systems, biochar changes in its overall chemical composition with time (Solomon et al, 2007), perhaps invalidating assumptions used for correlation.

So far, comparative analytical studies have focused on characterization of biochar produced under laboratory conditions. There appears to be a need for substantial work to investigate biochars produced under industrial or field conditions, to establish the extent to which they vary qualitatively (i.e. to determine unambiguous chemical fingerprints for biochars of different origins), to ascertain

how homogeneous individual biochars are, and to determine how such variation influences the response of different analytical procedures.

Finally, in order to gain wide acceptance, analytical methods need to achieve a compromise between price and reliability. The use of mid-infrared spectroscopy is robust in that it is specific to chemical moieties within biochar, and as long as it is calibrated against a relevant (i.e. appropriate matrix, etc.) sample set with known biochar content, this method offers great promise for routine analysis of large numbers of samples. Other methods, such as thermal analysis, can provide substantial insight into determining the qualities of biochar and offer scope for understanding its role in soils, as well as specifying its possible origin. But methods such as thermal analysis are not cheap and are likely to remain more useful for research or forensic/audit applications than for quantification of bulk biochar contents of soil.

References

Bostick, N. H. and Daws, T. A. (1994) 'Relationships between data from Rock-Eval pyrolysis and proximate, ultimate, petrographic and physical analyses of 142 diverse United States coal samples', *Organic Geochemistry*, vol 21, pp35–49

Brodowski, S., Rodionov, A., Haumaier, L., Glaser, B. and Amelung, W. (2005) 'Revised black carbon assessment using benzene polycarboxylic acids', *Organic Geochemistry*, vol 36, pp1299–1310

Chow, J. C., Watson, J. G., Chen, L.-W. A., Arnott, W. P. and Moosmüller, H. (2004) 'Equivalence of elemental carbon by thermal/optical reflectance and transmittance with different temperature protocols', *Environmental Science and Technology*, vol 38, pp4414–4422

de la Rosa, J. M., Knicker, H., Lopez-Capel, E., Manning, D. A. C., Gonzalez-Perez, J. A. and Gonzalez-Vila, F. J. (2008) 'Direct detection of black carbon in soils by Py-GC/MS, carbon-13 NMR spectroscopy and thermogravimetric techniques', *Soil Science Society of America Journal*, vol 72, pp258–267

Delvaux, D., Martin, H., Leplat, P. and Paulet, J. (1990) 'Comparative Rock-Eval pyrolysis as an improved method for sedimentary organic matter analysis', *Organic Geochemistry*, vol 16, pp1221–1229

Disnar, J. R., Guillet, B., Keravis, D., Di-Giovanni, C. and Sebag, D. (2003) 'Soil organic matter (SOM) characterization by Rock-Eval pyrolysis: Scope and limitations', *Organic Geochemistry*, vol 34, pp327–343

Elias, V. O., Simoneit, B. R. T., Cordeiro, R. C. and Turcq, B. (2001) 'Evaluating levoglucosan as an indicator of biomass burning in Carajás, Amazônia: A comparison to the charcoal record', *Geochimica et Cosmochimica Acta*, vol 65, pp267–272

Espitalié, J., Laporte, J. L., Madec, M., Marquis, F., Leplat, P., Paulet, J. and Boutefeu, A. (1977) 'Méthode rapide de caractérisation des roches mères, de leur potential pétrolier et de leur degré d'evolution', *Revue de l'Institut Français du Pétrole*, vol 32, pp23–42

Gélinas, Y., Prentice, K. M., Baldock, J. A. and Hedges, J. I. (2001), 'An improved thermal oxidation method for the quantification of soot/graphitic black carbon in sediments and soils', *Environmental Science and Technology*, vol 35, pp3519–3525

Glaser, B., Haumaier, L., Guggenberger, G. and Zech, W. (1998) 'Black carbon in soils: The use of benzenecarboxylic acids as specific markers', *Organic Geochemistry*, vol 29, pp811–819

Grimshaw, R. W. and Roberts, A. L. (1957) 'Carbonaceous materials', in R. C. McKenzie (ed) *The Differential Thermal Investigation of Clays*, Mineralogical Society, London, UK, pp 404–417

Gustafsson, Ö., Haghseta, F., Chan, C., Macfarlane, J. and Gschwend, P. M. (1997) 'Quantification of the dilute sedimentary soot phase: Implications for PAH speciation and bioavailability', *Environmental Science and Technology*, vol 31, pp203–209

Gustafsson, Ö., Bucheli, T. D., Kukulska, Z., Andersson, M., Largeau, C., Rouzaud, J.-N., Reddy, C. M. and Eglinton, T. I. (2001) 'Evaluation of a protocol for the quantification of black carbon in sediments', *Global Biogeochemical Cycles*, vol 15, pp881–890

Hammes, K., Schmidt, M. W. I., Smernik, R. J., Lloyd, A., Currie, W. P., Nguyen, H., Louchouarn, P., Houel, S., Gustafsson, Ö., Elmquist, M., Cornelissen, G., Skjemstad, J. O., Masiello, C. A., Song, J., Peng, P., Mitra, S., Dunn, J. C., Hatcher, P. G., Hockaday, W. C., Smith, D. M., Hartkopf-Fröder, C., Böhmer, A., Lüer, B., Huebert, B. J., Amelung, W., Brodowski, S., Huang, L., Zhang, W., Gschwend, P. M., Flores-Cervantes, D. X., Largeau, C. R. J. N., Rumpel, C., Guggenberger, G., Kaiser, K., Rodionov, A., Gonzalez-Vila, F. J., Gonzalez-Perez, J. A., de la Rosa, J. M., Manning, D. A. C., López-Capél, E. and Ding, L. (2007) 'Comparison of quantification methods to measure fire-derived (black/elemental) carbon in soils and sediments using reference materials from soil, water, sediment and the atmosphere', *Global Biogeochemical Cycles*, vol 21, pGB3016

Hammes, K., Smernik, R. J., Skjemstad, J. O. and Schmidt, M. W. I. (2008) 'Characterisation and evaluation of reference materials for black carbon analysis using elemental composition, colour, BET surface area and ^{13}C NMR spectroscopy', *Applied Geochemistry*, vol 23, pp2113–2122

Han, Y., Cao, J., An, Z., Chow, J. C., Wilson, J. G., Jin, Z., Fung, K. and Liu, S. (2007) 'Evaluation of the thermal/optical reflectance method for quantification of elemental carbon in sediments', *Chemosphere*, vol 69, pp526–533

Huang, L., Brook, J. R., Zhang, W., Li, S.M., Graham, L., Ernst, D., Chivulescu, A. and Lu, G. (2006) 'Stable isotope measurements of carbon fractions (OC/EC) in airborne particulate: A new dimension for source characterization and apportionment', *Atmospheric Environment*, vol 40, pp2690–2705

Janik, L. J., Skjemstad, J. O., Shepherd, K. D. and Spouncer, L. R. (2007) 'The prediction of soil carbon fractions using mid-infrared-partial least square analysis', *Australian Journal of Soil Research*, vol 45, pp73–81

Krull, E., Lehmann, J., Skjemstad, J. O., Baldock, J. and Spouncer, L. (2008) 'The global extent of black C in soils: Is it everywhere?', in H. G. Schröder (ed) *Grasslands: Ecology, Management and Restoration*, Nova Science Publishers, Inc, Hauppauge, NY

Leifeld, J. (2007) 'Thermal stability of black carbon characterised by oxidative differential scanning calorimetry', *Organic Geochemistry*, vol 38, pp112–127

Lim, B. and Cachier, H. (1996) 'Determination of black carbon by chemical oxidation and thermal treatment in recent marine and lake sediments and Cretaceous–Tertiary clays', *Chemical Geology*, vol 131, pp143–154

Lopez-Capel, E., Sohi, S. P., Gaunt, J. L. and Manning, D. A. C. (2005) 'Use of thermogravimetry-differential scanning calorimetry to characterize modelable soil organic matter fractions', *Soil Science Society of America Journal*, vol 69, pp136–140

Lopez-Capel, E., Abbott, G. D., Thomas, K. M. and Manning, D. A. C. (2006) 'Coupling of thermal analysis with quadrupole mass spectrometry and isotope ratio mass spectrometry for simultaneous determination of evolved gases and their carbon isotopic composition', *Journal of Analytical and Applied Pyrolysis*, vol 75, pp82–89

Manning, D. A. C., Lopez-Capel, E., White, M. L. and Barker, S. (2008) 'Carbon isotope determination for separate components of heterogenous materials using coupled thermogravimetric analysis/isotope ratio mass spectrometry', *Rapid Communications in Mass Spectrometry*, vol 22, pp1187–1195

Masiello, C. A. (2004) 'New directions in black carbon organic geochemistry', *Marine Chemistry*, vol 92, pp201–213

Mathews, J. A. (2008) 'Carbon-negative biofuels', *Energy Policy*, vol 36, pp940–945

Schmidt, M. W. I., Skjemstad, J. O., Czimczik, C. I., Glaser, B., Prentice, K. M., Gélinas, Y. and Kuhlbusch, T. A. J. (2001) 'Comparative analysis of black carbon in soils', *Global Biogeochemical Cycles*, vol 15, pp163–167

Scott, A. C. and Glasspool, I. J. (2007) 'Observations and experiments on the origin and formation of inertinite group macerals', *International Journal of Coal Geology*, vol 70, pp53–66

Scott, A. C., Cripps, J. A., Collinson, M. E. and Nichols, G. J. (2000) 'The taphonomy of charcoal following a recent heathland fire and some implications for the interpretation of fossil charcoal deposits', *Palaeogeography, Palaeoclimatology and Palaeoecology*, vol 164, pp1–31

Sebag, D., Disnar, J. R., Guillet, B., Di Giovanni, C., Verrecchia, E. P. and Durand, A. (2006) 'Monitoring organic matter dynamics in soil profiles by "Rock-Eval pyrolysis": Bulk characterisation and quantification of degradation', *European Journal of Soil Science*, vol 57, pp344–355

Senftle, J. T., Landis, C. R. and McLaughlin, R. L. (1993) 'Organic petrographic approach to kerogen characterization', in M. H. Engel and S. A. Macko (eds) *Organic Geochemistry*, Plenum Press, New York, NY, pp355–374

Simpson, M. J. and Hatcher, P. G. (2004a) 'Determination of black carbon in natural organic matter by chemical oxidation and solid-state ^{13}C nuclear magnetic resonance spectroscopy', *Organic Geochemistry*, vol 356, pp923–935

Simpson, M. J. and Hatcher, P. G. (2004b) 'Overestimations of black carbon in soils and sediments', *Naturwissenschaften*, vol 91, pp436–440

Skjemstad, J. O., Clarke, P., Taylor, J. A., Oades,

J. M. and McClure, S. G. (1996) 'The chemistry and nature of protected carbon in soil', *Australian Journal of Soil Research*, vol 34, pp251–271

Skjemstad, J. O., Taylor, J. A. and Smernik, R. J. (1999) 'Estimation of charcoal (char) in soils', *Communications in Soil Science and Plant Analysis*, vol 30, pp2283–2298

Skemstad, J. O., Dalal, R. C., Janik, L. J. and McGowan, J. A. (2001) 'Changes in chemical nature of soil organic carbon in Vertisols under wheat in south-eastern Queensland', *Australian Journal of Soil Research*, vol 39, pp343–359

Sohi, S. P., Mahieu, N., Arah, J. R. M., Powlson, D. S., Madari B. and Gaunt J. L. (2001) 'A procedure for isolating soil organic matter fractions suitable for modeling', *Soil Science Society of America Journal*, vol 65, pp1121–1128

Solomon, D., Lehmann, J., Thies, J., Schäfer, T., Liang, B., Kinyangi, J., Neves, E., Petersen, J., Luizão, F. and Skjemstad, J. (2007) 'Molecular signature and sources of biochemical recalcitrance of organic C in Amazonian Dark Earths', *Geochimica et Cosmochimica Acta*, vol 71, pp2285–2298

Song, J., Peng, P. and Huang, W. (2002) 'Black carbon and kerogen in soils and sediments. 1. Quantification and characterization', *Environmental Science and Technology*, vol 36, pp3960–3967

Stopes, M. C., (1935) 'On the petrology of banded bituminous coals', *Fuel*, vol 14, pp4–13

Whelan, J. K. and Thompson-Rizer, C. L. (1993) 'Chemical methods for assessing kerogen and protokerogen types and maturity', in M. H. Engel and S. A. Macko (eds) *Organic Geochemistry*, Plenum Press, New York, NY, pp289–353

Whelan, J. K., Carangelo, R., Solomon, P. R. and Dow, W. G. (1990) 'TG/plus – a pyrolysis method for following maturation of oil and gas generation zones using T_{max} of methane', *Organic Geochemistry*, vol 16, pp1187–1201

Wolbach, W. S. and Anders, E. (1989) 'Elemental carbon in sediments: Determination and isotopic analysis in the presence of kerogen', *Geochimica et Cosmochimica Acta*, vol 53, pp1637–1647

Biochar, Greenhouse Gas Accounting and Emissions Trading

John Gaunt and Annette Cowie

The climate change context

The concentrations of greenhouse gases (GHGs) in the atmosphere have reached unprecedentedly high levels and climate change is no longer a threat, but a reality. Atmospheric carbon dioxide (CO_2) concentration has risen from 280ppm prior to the industrial revolution to 379ppm in 2005 (Forster et al, 2007). The rate of increase between 2000 and 2005 was 3.3 per cent per annum, attributed to expansion of economic activity, increased GHG intensity of economic activity, and declining strength of the oceanic and terrestrial C sinks (Canadell et al, 2007).

The Intergovernmental Panel on Climate Change's *Fourth Assessment Report* (IPCC, 2007) clearly outlines the projected impacts of climate change, which are anticipated to be catastrophic unless the atmospheric CO_2 level is stabilized at or below 550ppm. The Kyoto Protocol, adopted by the parties to the 1992 United Nations Framework Convention on Climate Change (UNFCCC) in December 1997, committed industrialized countries (those listed under the Kyoto Protocol's Annex 1) to legally binding targets for the period 2008 to 2012, aimed to deliver a 5 per cent reduction in emissions compared with 1990. However, it is estimated that stabilization at 550ppm will require developed countries to reduce their emissions by 60 per cent below 2000 levels by 2050 (Defra, 2003).

Given the potentially catastrophic impacts of climate change, particularly the evidence of non-linear and non-reversible changes or 'tipping points', some argue that a reduction in emissions is not sufficient to address the risk of impacts due to elevated CO_2 levels, and propose strategies to withdraw CO_2 from the atmosphere to stabilize atmospheric CO_2 levels more rapidly (see Chapter 22).

The scope of the challenge that faces us is significant. The Vattenfall report (Vattenfall, 2007), for example, estimates that stabilizing CO_2 at 450ppm requires approximately 27Gt CO_2e (all greenhouse gases on the basis of CO_2 equivalents) to be withdrawn from the atmosphere by 2030.

The need for Annex I countries to encourage emissions mitigation so that they may reach their targets under the Kyoto Protocol has spawned the emergence of mandatory emissions trading schemes, while voluntary schemes have emerged to satisfy the growing demand from individuals and business seeking to offset their GHG emissions. Pyrolysis of biomass to produce renewable energy and biochar, and the use of biochar as a soil amendment, can contribute to mitigating GHG emissions through several routes explained in the section on 'How biochar contributes to climate change mitigation', and thus could constitute an offset activity within emissions trading schemes.

Greenhouse gas emissions trading

The policy options available to governments to reduce greenhouse gas emissions range from voluntary measures and incentive schemes through to C taxes, such as implemented in the fuel sector in Sweden (Johansson, 2000), or emissions trading.

The objective of emissions trading is to create a market-based incentive to reduce emissions: an emissions trading scheme imposes a cost on those who release a polluting substance, and rewards those who implement abatement measures. It allows those emitters who can reduce their emissions at low cost to trade emissions rights with others who can only do so at a higher cost, and thus it allows the market to identify and implement practices that achieve mitigation at least overall cost (e.g. Gehring and Streck, 2005).

Emissions taxes and emissions trading each have their merits (e.g. Productivity Commission, 2007). In a 'capped' emissions trading scheme (see below), the quantity of emissions is fixed; but the emissions price and, thus, the costs to society are uncertain. In contrast, with an emissions tax, the tax rate and the costs to the economy are fixed. For this reason, emissions taxes are favoured over trading mechanisms by many economists (Productivity Commission, 2007). And yet emissions taxes have virtually no political support due largely to the unpopularity of 'taxes' (Thomas, 2008) other than in countries such as Sweden where the community has strong trust in their government (Hammar and Jagers, 2006). Furthermore, and of most significance to this debate, an emissions tax cannot be guaranteed to deliver a specific emissions-reduction target (Productivity Commission, 2007).

The concept of emissions trading is not new; it has been successfully used, for example, to control sulphur dioxide (SO_2) and nitrous oxides (NO_x) emissions in the US (Gehring and Streck, 2005; EPA, 2007). GHG emissions trading has gained traction and C offset markets have developed under both *compliance schemes* and as *voluntary programmes*.

The Kyoto Protocol (http://unfccc.int/kyoto_protocol/items/2830.php) and the European Union's Emissions Trading Scheme (ETS: http://ec.europa.eu/environment/climat/emission/index_en.htm) or the Regional Greenhouse Gas Initiative (RGGI: www.rggi.org) of the US north-eastern states are examples of compliance schemes. The compliance markets are created and regulated by mandatory regional, national or international emissions reduction regimes. Mandatory schemes often utilize a 'cap-and-trade' approach: the governing authority issues tradable permits, or allowances, that allow the permit holder to emit a specified volume of greenhouse gases. The cap constitutes a finite supply of permits, set by regulation and political negotiation. These permits are neither created nor removed, but merely traded among participants. This finite supply creates a scarcity and drives the demand and price for permits (Kollmus et al, 2008). The sum of all permits issued equates to the total greenhouse gases that may be emitted to the atmosphere under the agreed cap. For example, the cap under the Kyoto Protocol is the commitment to a 5 per cent reduction against 1990 levels. Those parties who are able to reduce their emissions below their target can sell their excess permits to those who exceed their target.

Alternatively, a scheme may operate through a 'baseline-and-credit' approach, such as that used in the New South Wales Greenhouse Gas Reduction Scheme (NSW GGAS: www.greenhousegas.nsw.gov.au) and the Chicago Climate Exchange (CCX: www.chicagoclimatex.com). In baseline-and-credit schemes, the emissions entitlement for each liable party is determined from a baseline, which may be centred on historical emissions or an emissions intensity benchmark; liable parties that exceed their emissions entitlement must purchase permits to offset emissions above their baseline; those who emit less than their entitlement under the baseline are able to create tradable permits. In a baseline-and-credit scheme there is no target aggregate cap on emissions; however, the sum of individual baselines of liable parties is an implicit cap.

Either type of scheme may include an 'offsets' market. Offsets are a financial instrument representing a reduction in greenhouse gas emissions; sectors not covered by the scheme can participate by creating offsets that can be sold to liable parties within the scheme. Scheme regulations determine how much of the reduction needs to be achieved within the country or targeted industry and what proportion can be achieved through reductions elsewhere.

Voluntary offset markets exist and function outside of the compliance markets and enable companies and individuals to purchase C offsets on a voluntary basis. Hamilton et al (2008) divide the voluntary market into the CCX and a more disaggregated over-the-counter market (OTC). Through market survey, they estimate the total voluntary market in 2006 at 25Mt CO_2e, while the regulated markets represented 1702Mt CO_2e, with rapid growth to 65Mt CO_2e and 2918Mt CO_2e, respectively, in 2007. Currently, in the voluntary market the OTC dominates CCX. In 2007, OTC traded 42Mt CO_2e, while the CCX traded 23Mt CO_2e. Given the influence of the Kyoto Protocol on both the compliance and voluntary market, we examine it further below.

Kyoto Protocol

The Kyoto Protocol established a market for emissions reductions and removals through 'sink activities' by allowing emissions trading between liable parties, and defining project-based mechanisms, the Clean Development Mechanism (CDM) and Joint Implementation (JI) (see details below) that allow parties to implement emissions reduction projects in other countries which have ratified the Protocol (at the time of writing, this includes 181 countries and excludes the US; UNFCCC, 2008). Aspects of the Kyoto Protocol that are relevant to biochar production and application include:

• Article 3.3, which allows certain forestry activities – afforestation and reforestation since 1990 on land that was cleared prior to 31 December 1989 – to be considered towards a party's emissions reduction commitment. The growth increment of eligible forests during the commitment period (2008–2012) creates 'removal units' that can offset an equivalent amount of fossil fuel emissions. Carbon stock change in soil, as well as biomass, is counted.

Box 18.1 Concepts of relevance for emissions trading with biochar

Permanence. For how long and by what mechanism will the offset be secured? Under C sequestration strategies such as reforestation or grazing management, sequestered C is vulnerable to future loss through disturbance due to planned (e.g. harvest, grazing management, cultivation) or unintentional events (e.g. fire, disease or pest attack). This potential non-permanence must be managed either through maintenance of a particular management regime or a regulatory mechanism ensuring that future losses are compensated.

Coverage. Different standards and C emissions trading schemes target different economic sectors, different C pools and different greenhouse gases (GHGs).

Uncertainty. There will always be uncertainty in the estimation of abatement attributable to an offset project. Some schemes require offset providers to meet a specified level of precision, while others (e.g. NSW GGAS) discount the credits generated according to the uncertainty of the estimate. Alternatively, market mechanisms may be used to manage the risk associated with uncertainty. For example, the value of credits may be reduced if they are considered uncertain; insurance policies have been used to guarantee that delivery and payments may be staged as the offsets predicted are realized. For example, the Voluntary Carbon Standard (VCS) proposes staged payment for C stored in soil as its stability over time is proven.

Additionality and baselines. A credible offset project must demonstrate that it will achieve mitigation that would not otherwise have occurred (i.e. that the project is 'additional'). Some schemes require that the project demonstrate 'financial additionality' (i.e. that it would not have been financially viable in the absence of emissions trading). Project-based mitigation is calculated based on emission reductions measured against a 'baseline'. This baseline may be the previous land use at the time of project initiation. Some schemes, however, require measurement against a counterfactual 'without project' scenario that estimates the emissions that would have occurred over the life of the project if the market for offsets did not exist. This hypothetical reality cannot be proven and is always, to some extent, subjective. It may be based on historical practices or, more validly, on anticipated future developments in practice in that locality. For example, the appropriate baseline practice for waste management would be covered landfill with methane collection and flaring if that is the locally recommended best practice, whether or not methane flaring is currently widely practised. Similarly, the displaced emissions from electricity generation should be based on the type of plant (i.e. the fuel used and conversion efficiency) that would be built today to provide that capacity (the 'build margin'), rather than the current average plant.

Leakage. Emissions that are indirectly attributable to the project and occur outside the project boundary should be considered. For example, if organic matter in the form of mulch is applied to soil it will increase soil C at that site. But the C stock will be reduced at the site from which the mulch was obtained. This reduction in C stock is leakage that should be taken into consideration in calculating the impacts of the activity.

- Article 3.4, which allows parties the option of including in their accounting additional sequestration in plants and soil through management of cropland, grazing land and existing forests, as well as revegetation.
- Article 6, which allows an Annex 1 party to implement emissions reduction proj-

ects in another Annex 1 country and count the resulting 'emission reduction units' against its own target. This is known as the Joint Implementation (JI) mechanism.

- Article 12, which defines the Clean Development Mechanism (CDM), through which parties to the Protocol can obtain 'certified emission reductions' from emissions reduction projects implemented in non-Annex 1 (developing) countries.
- Article 17, which allows for emission trading between parties that have ratified the Protocol.

The features of the Kyoto Protocol – including the accounting framework and rules governing the inclusion of sequestration activities and methods for estimation of emissions and removals – have had, and will continue to have, a strong influence over national emission trading schemes emerging in many countries around the world.

Trading emissions offsets

There are a growing number of schemes that seek to market C offsets, and a corresponding development of standards designed to bring quality control to the offsets market. The review by Kollmus et al (2008) contrasts CDM rules with a range of other standards or accounting protocols, including the Gold Standard (Gold Standard, 2008), Voluntary Carbon Standard (VCS, 2007), Chicago Climate Exchange (CCX, 2007a), the Climate, Community and Biodiversity Standards (CCBA, 2005), International Organization for Standardization standards for greenhouse gas reporting and verification (ISO 14064; ISO, 2006) and GHG Protocol for Project Accounting (WRI WBCSD, 2005).

It is beyond the scope of this chapter to review these programmes, protocols and certification schemes. However, some important concepts of particular relevance to mitigation through pyrolysis for biochar and bioenergy production are listed in Box 18.1. Emissions trading schemes must address these issues through the rules devised for eligibility, and in the monitoring, reporting and verification of emissions abatement.

How biochar contributes to climate change mitigation

Avoided emissions from conventional use of feedstock biomass

The conventional management of biomass often leads to release of methane (CH_4) or nitrous oxide (N_2O) as the biomass decomposes under anoxic conditions. For example, urban green waste (tree trimmings and garden waste) deposited in landfill releases significant quantities of CH_4, while animal manures rich in both C and N often break down to release CH_4 and N_2O. CH_4 and N_2O are GHGs with global warming poten-

tial 25 and 298 times greater than CO_2 (Forster et al, 2007). Management strategies that avoid these emissions can therefore contribute significantly to mitigation of climate change.

Many biomass wastes are suitable feedstocks for production of biochar. The quantity of emissions avoided through use of wastes for biochar would depend both upon the nature of the biomass resource and the management change involved, as is illustrated further below.

Stabilization of biomass C

Discussions of soil C sequestration typically focus on the issue of permanence (i.e. whether the change in soil C levels is reversible). However, a more fundamental issue is whether or not an increase in soil C reflects a change in management that has added to the total terrestrial C stocks, either by increasing biomass and, therefore, organic matter input to the soil C pool, or by reducing the decomposition of soil organic matter. If an increase in soil C results from increased inputs of organic matter, then unless the increased input is the result of increased production of organic matter (e.g. due to enhanced productivity), then the net release of C to the atmosphere may not have been reduced: the apparent increase in soil C results simply from the transfer of organic matter from one location to another. This is an example of 'leakage', as discussed above.

Soil C is derived from plant matter, such as leaf and, particularly, fine root litter, and plays a fundamental role in the C cycle. The soil C pool is large: globally, it is estimated to hold 2500Gt of C, including 1550Gt soil organic C, compared with 560Gt C in vegetation (Lal, 2008). Annually, 120Gt of C is captured through photosynthesis, of which 50 per cent is retained in plant biomass and 50 per cent is released as CO_2 through autotrophic respiration. It is estimated that global C release from soil as litter breaks down approximately matches C inputs. Thus, the annual flux of C from soil is estimated at 55Gt (Prentice et al, 2001).

Biomass C added to soil decomposes through the actions of soil fauna and microorganisms. In this mineralization process, soil microbes digest organic matter, respiring C to the atmosphere and simultaneously releasing plant nutrients. The pattern of breakdown of organic matter in soil and associated release of CO_2 is well understood: the labile fractions decompose rapidly over one to five years; the more stable organic matter fractions break down over decades to centuries; while the most recalcitrant fractions turn over in several hundred to a few thousand years (Davidson and Janssens, 2006). The net result is that the bulk of C added as biomass is rapidly released back to the atmosphere as CO_2. For example, Jenkinson and Ayanaba (1977) found that, in a tropical environment, 80 to 90 per cent (depending upon soil type) of C added to soil as ryegrass or maize biomass was lost after five to ten years.

If, through a change of management, we are able to increase the proportion of the organic matter that is resistant to decay and radically slow the rate of release of CO_2, this delay in release of CO_2 can be considered as an avoided emission of CO_2. One strategy that has been proposed by some is composting to stabilize the organic matter in forms resistant to breakdown. However, evidence that the C contained in compost decomposes within 10 years (Gerzabek et al, 1997) and 20 years (Lynch et al, 2005) suggests that the turnover of C stabilized in compost is similar to that of un-composted organic matter added to soil.

In contrast to composting, pyrolysis of biomass creates a real increase in terrestrial C stocks because it stabilizes biomass C and significantly delays decomposition (see Chapter 11). Conversion of biomass to biochar fundamentally alters the transformation dynamics of plant-derived material in soil. Pyrolysis releases a portion of the C contained in the biomass immediately, and the energy associated with this release of C can be used for the production of bioenergy (see Chapters 8 and 9). This initial release is more rapid than would occur during natural decomposition; however, the majority of the remaining portion is likely to be stable for at least hundreds of years when added to soil (see Chapter 11).

Lehmann (2007) estimates that where biomass is converted to biochar, the potential net C storage is 20 per cent of the C captured through photosynthesis (gross primary productivity, or GPP). At the global GPP flux of 120Gt C (Prentice et al, 2001), this would equate to a theoretical annual potential of 24Gt C (88Gt CO_2e), though much of this biomass is not available for conversion to biochar. The actual potential will depend upon our ability to access biomass feedstocks in an economically viable and environmentally responsible manner. Lehmann et al (2006) estimated that conversion of current 'slash-and-burn' practices to 'slash-and-char' – that is, pyrolysis of slash that would otherwise have been burned in the forest – could stabilize 0.2Gt C, equivalent to 0.7Gt CO_2e, globally, and biochar from agricultural and forestry wastes such as forest residues, mill residues, field crop residues and urban wastes could, conservatively, stabilize 0.16Gt C (0.6Gt CO_2e) annually. At a national level, Evelein (2008) estimated for the UK that between 0.5Mt C and 1.0Mt C (1.8Mt CO_2e to 3.7Mt CO_2e) could be stabilized annually as biochar utilizing forest and waste resources. Lehmann (2007) estimated that 4.5Mt C (16Mt CO_2e) could be stabilized as biochar in the US using existing forest residues and crop wastes, and fast growing biomass crops established on idle cropland.

Avoided emissions of N_2O and CH_4 from soil

Because CH_4 and N_2O are potent greenhouse gases, reduction in these emissions from soil through application of biochar could significantly contribute to mitigating GHG emissions, particularly in situations where N_2O emissions are greatest, such as in intensively fertilized, irrigated agriculture. Nitrogen (N) fertilizers, biological N fixation by legume species, and the urine and dung of grazing animals are all potential sources of N_2O emissions. Nitrous oxide is produced in soil during nitrification (i.e. conversion of NH_4^+-N to NO_3^--N), and through denitrification, where heterotrophic denitrifying

aerobic bacteria cause respiratory reduction of nitrate or nitrite to N_2O and N_2 under anoxic conditions (Wrage et al, 2005; see also Chapter 13).

Recent research suggests that N_2O and CH_4 emissions from soil may be significantly reduced by biochar application. Rondon et al (2005) found that CH_4 emissions were completely suppressed and N_2O emissions were reduced by 50 per cent when biochar was applied to soil. Yanai et al (2007) also found suppression of N_2O when biochar was added to soil. The possible explanations for these impacts of biochar are discussed in Chapter 13.

Displaced fertilizer and agricultural inputs

The use of biochar may displace fertilizer use in two ways:

- by substituting directly for other sources of fertilizer (e.g. where biochar is produced from nutrient-rich feedstock); and
- by increasing the efficiency with which fertilizer is used because biochar increases the soils' nutrient retention capacity (see Chapters 5 and 15).

Manufacture of nitrogenous fertilizer is an emissions-intensive process due to the consumption of natural gas as a hydrogen and energy source. Emissions range from 3kg CO_2e kg^{-1} N to 10kg CO_2e kg^{-1} N, depending upon processing technologies, energy sources and utilization of co-products (Wood and Cowie, 2004). Therefore, to the extent that use of biochar reduces the requirement for fertilizer, biochar displaces the emissions associated with the manufacture of fertilizer.

Our understanding of the influence of biochar on soil physical properties is still incomplete. However, recent evidence shows that biochar can influence soil structural properties affecting soil strength, soil moisture-holding capacity and infiltration. Chan et al (2007) reported that the incorporation of biochar at 50t ha^{-1} improved soil moisture-holding capacity and reduced soil strength (see Chapter 5).

Tractor fuel used in cultivation is directly related to soil strength (e.g. McKenzie and So, 1989); therefore, in situations where biochar application leads to a reduction in soil strength, this will result in a reduction in fuel use and associated emissions.

Biochar enhances soil moisture-holding capacity and infiltration in some soils (see Chapter 15), which may lead to a reduction in the frequency and duration of irrigation. Therefore, application of biochar to irrigated crops and pastures may reduce the emissions associated with energy use in irrigation.

Enhancement of agronomic efficiency and yield

Biochar has been shown to enhance agronomic efficiency – that is, yield of harvested product per unit of fertilizer input (see Chapters 5 and 12). In high-productivity situations, this benefit may be manifest as

fertilizer savings, whereas in low-yield situations, crop yields may be increased.

In situations where greater plant growth results from biochar application, there will be greater C sequestration in growing biomass. This may result in increased returns of organic matter to soil. Given that this represents an enhanced capture of CO_2 from the atmosphere, the resulting increase in soil C reflects a genuine sequestration of C, as discussed above.

Fossil fuel displacement

The net energy output from pyrolysis will depend upon the feedstock properties and pyrolysis process deployed. Energy streams can include syngas, bio-oils and heat (see Chapter 8). These renewable energy sources can be used to displace fossil energy sources.

The mitigation benefit will depend upon the application (heat and electricity) that determines the efficiency of conversion and emissions intensity of the fossil fuel source displaced (e.g. there is greater benefit from displacing coal than natural gas due to the lower emissions intensity of natural gas).

What mitigation benefits are tradable in a pyrolysis for biochar and bioenergy project?

The mitigation benefits of biochar can be accounted for in several ways. First, the renewable energy output would be counted as a reduction in GHG emissions from the energy sector in national-level emissions accounting. At the project scale, if implemented outside a capped sector, it could generate a credit for avoided GHG emissions, calculated from the displacement of fossil fuel energy. Recognition of reduced fossil fuel use, such as resulting from increased use of renewable energy, is a common feature of mandatory and voluntary emissions trading schemes.

Credit could also be claimed for avoided emissions from a change in the management of biomass, where the conventional management leads to emissions of CH_4 or N_2O. Several schemes recognize the benefit of avoided CH_4 emissions where waste is diverted from landfill (e.g. by NSW GGAS), or management of manure is improved (e.g. by RGGI).

Increase in soil C stock through biochar application could be recognized as an eligible sequestration activity. Theoretically, it could be claimed under Kyoto Protocol Articles 3.3, 6 (JI) and 12 (CDM), if applied to forest, or Article 3.4, if applied to agricultural land. However, modification of the standard methodology of estimating soil C (IPCC, 2006) would be required. Due to concerns about permanence and additionality, sequestration projects are often subject to strict criteria governing eligibility, estimation and reporting, which can escalate transaction costs and restrict participation. Difficulties in accurate monitoring of soil C due to spatial and temporal variation have been raised as barriers to including agricultural soil management in emissions trading. The VCS, for example, proposes a method requiring monitoring that involves sampling to prove the permanence of C stored in soil over time (VCS, 2007). However, in contrast, the CCX has successfully monetized soil C sequestration using conservative defaults to estimate sequestration based on implementing eligible management practices rather than monitoring soil C change (CCX, 2007b). Estimating soil C change due to biochar application could be based on an estimate of the quantity of C applied and the turnover rate, which should be much less uncertain than estimating impacts of tillage or grazing practices on soil C (Ogle et al, 2003).

An alternative approach involves claiming credit for C captured and stored in biochar: rather than focusing on the increase in soil C stock, credit could be based on the avoided C emissions due to stabilizing organic matter. However, this approach would not readily fit within the offset rules of schemes currently operating as most schemes do not recognize avoidance of CO_2 from biomass decomposition. One possible exception is the California Climate Action Registry (www.climateregistry.org), which recognizes ongoing storage of C in wood products. Under this scheme, a claim for credit for ongoing storage of C in biochar as a component of the wood products pool may be accepted (this has not been tested and would be applicable only where biochar is created from wood obtained from eligible forests).

The reduction in agricultural emissions resulting from application of biochar to agricultural land is also tradable. Under Article 3.4 of the Kyoto Protocol, increased sequestration in plants and soil resulting from biochar-induced enhancement of productivity could be credited.

In conclusion, our assessment of the various schemes indicates that pyrolysis of biomass for bioenergy and biochar could be claimed through various routes: credit for bioenergy is widely recognized; credit for increasing C stocks in the soil, if biochar is applied to an eligible forest, is recognized by several schemes; avoided landfill emissions and avoided emissions from manure could be claimed under a few schemes; one scheme recognizes agricultural management of soil C and one recognizes long-term storage in wood products, either of which could provide an avenue to crediting the benefit of pyrolysis in stabilizing organic matter. In the following section we quantify the emission GHG mitigation by pyrolysis for biochar and bioenergy using concrete case studies.

Greenhouse gas balance of example biochar systems

In the previous sections, we outlined the sources of GHG mitigation associated with pyrolysis of biomass for biochar and bioenergy. In summary, the following sources were identified:

- changes in the emissions associated with baseline management of feedstock;
- avoided emissions associated with the substitution of fossil fuel by bioenergy;
- stabilization and storage of C in biochar;

- the reduction in agricultural emissions of N_2O;
- savings in fertilizer and other agricultural inputs when biochar was applied to agricultural land; and
- enhanced C storage in growing crops.

In this section we explore the avoided emissions associated with each of these through examples of typical potential feedstocks processed by slow pyrolysis technology suited to a range of bioenergy crops and waste materials.

We first calculate the avoided emissions associated with biochar production – that is, due to the changes in management of typical potential feedstocks, stabilization of C as biochar and fossil fuel substitution. Second, we calculate the reduction in emissions due to application of biochar as a soil amendment.

Emissions avoided through change in feedstock management, bioenergy and C stabilization

We consider three feedstocks that have been demonstrated as suitable for slow pyrolysis – namely, green waste (largely comprised of stem and branch wood in the example given) diverted either from landfill or composting, cattle stall manure (typically stored as solid waste prior to field spreading) and cereal straw. Calculation methods are described briefly below and assumptions are summarized in Table 18.1.

Avoided landfill emissions

We calculate emissions for green waste in landfill, managed with and without gas flaring to reduce CH_4 emissions, using a mass balance method based on the *Revised 1996 IPCC Guidelines for National Greenhouse Gas Inventories* (Houghton et al, 1997) and the *Good Practice Guidance and Uncertainty Management in National Greenhouse Gas*

Inventories (IPCC, 2000) 'tier 1' method. We acknowledge that the first-order decay model (Forster et al, 2007) produces a time-dependent profile that better matches the actual pattern of degradation over time. However, for the purpose of calculating emissions avoided by diverting waste from landfill, the mass balance approach is 'fit for purpose'. We use the following equation:

$$CH_4 \text{ emissions (t t}^{-1} \text{ dry biomass)} = MGP \times (1 - R) \times (1 - OX) \quad [1]$$

where R is the recovered CH_4 (fraction), OX is the oxidation factor (fraction) and MGP is the CH_4 generation potential, defined as:

$$MGP = MCF \times DOC \times DOC_f \times F \times 16/12 \quad [2]$$

where MCF is the CH_4 correction factor (fraction), DOC is the degradable organic C, DOC_f is the fraction of DOC that is dissimilated, and F is the fraction by volume of CH_4 in landfill gas. This gives an estimate of $0.147t$ CH_4 t^{-1} dry green waste, equivalent to $3.7t$ CO_2e t^{-1} feedstock for waste facilities where no flaring of CH_4 occurs (R = 0), and $0.044t$ CH_4 t^{-1} dry green waste, or $1.1t$ CO_2e t^{-1} feedstock with methane recovery and flaring (R = 0.7).

Nitrous oxide and CH_4 emissions from composting are estimated as $0.2kg$ CO_2e kg^{-1} and $1.5kg$ CO_2e kg^{-1} dry matetr (DM) based on the findings of Beck-Friis et al (2000).

Manure emissions

Emissions from livestock waste are highly dependent upon the animals in question, their diet and how their waste is managed. For the purpose of this study, we consider the emissions from dairy manure in temperate regions of the US (emissions are greater in the tropics and lower in cool climates). We have selected a solid storage system in which manure is stored typically for a period of several months in unconfined piles or stacks

Table 18.1 *Assumptions for the calculation of avoided emissions from feedstock management and pyrolysis (see Table 18.2)*

Global warming potential			Source
CH_4		25	5
N_2O		298	5
Feedstock characteristics	*Energy density*	*Moisture content*	
Feedstock	*(GJ t DM)*	*(% FW)*	
Green waste	18	35	1
Cattle manure	17	38	1
Wheat straw	18	10	1
Pyrolysis process	*Biochar yield (% DM)*	*Energy yield (GJ t^{-1} DM)*	
Green waste	35	3.7	1
Cattle manure	42	2.5	1
Wheat straw	38	4.5	1
Emission factors			
Natural gas small-scale combustion	66	(kg CO_2e GJ^{-1})	2
Natural gas-fired electricity	590	(g CO_2e kW_e h^{-1})	2
Black coal-fired electricity	981	(g CO_2e kW_e h^{-1})	2
Emissions from landfill			
Degradable organic C (green waste)	0.49		3
Fraction of DOC that is dissimilated	0.5		3
Fraction of landfill gas that is CH_4	0.5		4
CH_4 correction factor (managed landfill)	1.0		4
CH_4 oxidation factor	0.1		4
Emissions from compost			
Methane emitted	1.47	(kg CO_2e kg^{-1} DM)	7
Nitrous oxide emitted	0.20	(kg CO_2e kg^{-1} DM)	7
Emissions from wheat straw			
Nitrous oxide emitted	0.03	(kg CO_2e kg^{-1} DM)	3
Emissions from manure management system			
CH_4 conversion factor (solid storage, dairy cattle, temperate climate)	0.04		3
CH_4-producing capacity (solid storage, dairy cattle, North America and Europe)	0.16	(kg CH_4 kg^{-1} volatile solids)	3
Nitrogen excretion rate (dairy cattle, North America)	0.05	(kg N kg^{-1} volatile solids)	3
Direct N_2O emission factor (solid storage)	0.005	(kg N_2O-N kg^{-1} N excreted)	3
Indirect N loss, volatilization (dairy cattle, solid storage manure management)	0.3	(kg N kg^{-1} N excreted)	3
Indirect N_2O emission factor, volatilization	0.01	(kg N_2O-N kg^{-1} N excreted)	3
Indirect N loss, runoff and leaching	0.2	(kg N kg^{-1} N excreted)	6
Indirect N_2O emission factor, runoff and leaching	0.0075	(kg N_2O-N kg^{-1} N excreted)	3
Emissions from manure application			
Direct N_2O emission factor (manure application)	0.01	(kg N_2O-N kg^{-1} N applied)	3
Indirect N loss, volatilization	0.2	(kg N kg^{-1} N applied)	3
Indirect N_2O emission factor, volatilization	0.01	(kg N_2O-N kg^{-1} N applied)	3
Indirect N loss, runoff and leaching	0.3	(kg N kg^{-1} N applied)	6
Indirect N_2O emission factor, runoff and leaching	0.0075	(kg N_2O-N kg^{-1} N applied)	3

Source: 1 In confidence, 2008

2 Department of Climate Change (Australia) (2008)   5 Forster et al (2007)

3 IPCC (2006)   6 EPA (2006)

4 IPCC (2000)   7 Beck-Friis et al (2000)

(EPA, 2006). This storage system is representative of the management used for a significant portion of dairy waste in the US (IPCC, 2006). We base our methodology on the approach developed for the US national greenhouse gas inventory (EPA, 2006), based on the IPCC methodology for calculating CH_4 emissions, as well as direct and indirect N_2O emissions (IPCC, 2006).

The IPCC and EPA use numbers of animals as the basis for their calculations. The IPCC methods relate emissions to volatile solid (VS) production. We use a conversion factor of 1.087 to convert VS to dry matter based on Pattey et al (2005).

Biochar and energy production from slow pyrolysis

We assume that the proportion of biochar produced from feedstock and the C contained in the biochar varies with feedstock (see Table 18.1). We also assume that 75 per cent of the C contained in biochar is stable over a ten-year period. Furthermore, the energy yield from the pyrolysis process is assumed to vary with feedstock (see Table 18.1). These estimates are based on the operational experiences of the pyrolysis sector.

Total avoided emissions associated with change in feedstock management, C stabilization and fossil fuel substitution range from 0.9t CO_2e t^{-1} to 3.8t CO_2e t^{-1} feedstock (see Table 18.2a), which is equivalent to 2.5t

CO_2e t^{-1} to 10.9t CO_2e t^{-1} biochar. The major factor contributing to this variation is the emissions related to the current conventional feedstock management (0.03t CO_2e t^{-1} to 3.7t CO_2e t^{-1} feedstock), which varies widely between alternative waste management practices depending upon the degree of anaerobicity and the extent of CH_4 capture.

Given that a modest commercial biochar production facility is likely to process between 2t feedstock per hour and to operate up to 8000 hours annually, this suggests that a single 2t facility would generate emissions reduction in the order of 14,400t CO_2e to 68,000t CO_2e in one year and that over the ten-year operating life a 2t facility would avoid 0.14Mt CO_2e to 0.68Mt CO_2e emissions.

The actual figures will depend somewhat upon location as this will affect the emissions attributed to conventional feedstock management and fossil fuel substitution (which depend upon energy source and technology displaced), as well as other life-cycle emissions such as transportation and plant construction. However, the studies of Gaunt and Lehmann (2008) and Cowie (2008), which both take a more complete life-cycle approach, show that the factors considered above dominate the C balance for an individual facility (inclusion of these components reduces emissions mitigation by 4 to 8 per cent)

Table 18.2 *Net emissions associated with the use of a range of feedstocks for slow pyrolysis expressed either (a) relative to mass of feedstock used or (b) mass of biochar produced (positive values indicate emissions; negative values indicate avoided emissions or removals)*

(a) Emissions (t CO_2e t^{-1} feedstock)

Feedstock	Conventional management	Conventional feedstock management				Feedstocks pyrolysed for biochar and energy			Net emissions (biochar–conventional feedstock management)	
		Emissions			C stored in biomass	Net emissions from electricity: fossil fuel substitution		C stabilized as biochar	Replacing gas	Replacing coal
		CH_4	N_2O	Total		Replacing gas	Replacing coal			
Green waste	Landfill – no CH_4 recovery	3.68	0	3.68	−0.90	−0.17	−0.30	−0.72	−3.67	−3.80
Green waste	Landfill – CH_4 recovery	1.10	0	1.10	−0.90	−0.17	−0.30	−0.72	−1.09	−1.23
Green waste	Compost	1.47	0.20	1.67	0.00	−0.17	−0.30	−0.72	−2.56	−2.70
Cattle manure	Solid storage, land spread	0.00	0.37	0.37	0.00	−0.09	−0.18	−0.58	−1.04	−1.13
Wheat straw	Decompose in field	0.00	0.03	0.03	0.00	−0.21	−0.37	−0.65	−0.90	−1.06

(b) Emissions (t CO_2e t^{-1} biochar produced)

Feedstock	Conventional management	Conventional feedstock management				Feedstocks pyrolysed for biochar and energy			Net emissions (biochar–conventional feedstock management)	
		Emissions			C stored in biomass	Net emissions from electricity: fossil fuel substitution		C stabilized as biochar	Replacing gas	Replacing coal
		CH_4	N_2O	Total		Replacing gas	Replacing coal			
Green waste	Landfill – CH_4 recovery	3.15	0	3.15	−2.57	−0.48	−0.86	−2.06	−3.12	−3.51
Green waste	Compost	4.20	0.58	4.78	0.00	−0.48	−0.86	−2.06	−7.32	−7.71
Cattle manure	Solid storage, land spread	0.00	0.88	0.88	0.00	−0.22	−0.43	−1.38	−2.47	−2.69
Wheat straw	Decompose in field	0.00	0.10	0.10	0.00	−0.58	−1.04	−1.82	−2.49	−2.95

Emissions from the application of biochar to agricultural soils

The influence of biochar on emissions from agriculture is uncertain as field data are currently limited and benefits vary depending upon the agricultural situation. Basing assumptions on the limited data available, we undertake a preliminary sensitivity analysis of the potential reduction in emissions associated with the use of biochar as an agricultural amendment. For each of the factors considered we have a low, medium and high scenario, where medium corresponds with the 'best guess', and low and high are the least and greatest emissions reduction, respectively, regarded as likely for each process considered. These assumptions are applied for a range of crops that have contrasting land preparation needs, input requirements and yield. The assumptions used to calculate emissions reduction are shown in Table 18.3.

Rate of biochar application and duration of benefits

The optimal rate for biochar application to soil and, thus, the area of land that can be treated is not yet established. Application rates typically range from 5t to 50t biochar ha^{-1} (see Chapters 5 and 12), and optimal rates will vary between biochar types, soil type and target species. It is likely that benefits in terms of improved agronomic performance and reduced nutrient losses will last over a number of years. We assume an application rate of 5t biochar ha^{-1} for our analysis, and that the benefits continue for ten years.

Reduced soil nitrous oxide emissions

Nitrous oxide emissions from added fertilizer and manure occur directly from the site of application and indirectly through translocation of N by volatilization, leaching and runoff. IPCC (2006) provides a default method for calculation of these losses. The literature suggests that N$_2$O losses may be reduced by biochar application. Rondon et al (2005) found that N$_2$O emissions were reduced by up to 50 per cent when 20g biochar kg^{-1} soil was applied to soybean and by 80 per cent in grass stands. Thus, we test the sensitivity at 10, 50 and 75 per cent reduction in direct and indirect emissions of N$_2$O from applied fertilizer.

Improved agronomic efficiency

It is most likely that biochar will reduce the rates of N, potassium (K) and phosphorus (P) fertilizer required due to a greater N-use efficiency (Steiner et al, in press). Given that manufacture of N fertilizer is emissions intensive compared with manufacture of K and P fertilizers (Wood and Cowie, 2004), we consider only the impact on N fertilizer requirement. We assume a 10, 20 or 30 per cent reduction in N fertilizer use and estimate the avoided emissions associated with its manufacture.

Savings in energy use for field operations

It is widely recognized that there is an interaction between soil physical properties and energy used in cultivation. For example, seedbeds are easier to prepare, requiring fewer cultivations to ready the soil for planting and therefore using less fuel. However, research evidence is difficult to obtain for the relationship between soil organic matter levels and energy use in field operations. Beer et al (2007) report that incorporation of maize stubble, in contrast with stubble-burning, led to a significant increase in soil C and a 30 per cent reduction in engine power required for ripping. Because similar field-scale studies of fuel use have not been undertaken with biochar, no farm level data are available. Chan et al (2007) found 50 per cent reduction in tensile strength with 50t ha^{-1}, but, confusingly, a small, non-significant increase at 10t ha^{-1}. Our analysis assumes a 5, 15 and 30 per cent reduction in energy use for primary land preparation.

Table 18.3 *Assumptions used in calculating emissions reduction from the application of biochar to crops*

	Value	Unit	Source
Emission factor N fertilizer manufacture (urea, MAP)	5	(kg CO_2e kg^{-1} N applied)	1
Direct N_2O emission factor (winter wheat – UK – maize)	0.01	(kg N_2O-N kg^{-1} N applied)	2
Direct N_2O emission factor (canola, wheat – Australia)	0.003	(kg N_2O-N kg^{-1} N applied)	3
Direct N_2O emission factor (broccoli)	0.021	(kg N_2O-N kg^{-1} N applied)	3
Indirect N loss, volatilization	0.1	(kg N kg^{-1} N applied)	2
Indirect N_2O emission factor, volatilization	0.01	(kg N_2O-N kg^{-1} N applied)	2
Indirect N loss, runoff and leaching (broccoli, wheat – UK – maize)	0.3	(kg N kg^{-1} N applied)	2
Indirect N loss, runoff and leaching (canola, wheat – Australia)	0.0	(kg N kg^{-1} N applied)	2
Indirect N_2O emission factor, runoff and leaching	0.0075	(kg N_2O-N kg^{-1} N applied)	2
Fuel use in cultivation			
Canola	7	(L diesel ha^{-1})	4, 5
Broccoli	29	(L diesel ha^{-1})	4, 5
Winter wheat (UK)	46	(L diesel ha^{-1})	5
Maize	35	(L diesel ha^{-1})	5
Wheat (Australia)	3	(L diesel ha^{-1})	5
Nitrogen fertilizer application rate			
Canola	62	(kg N ha^{-1})	4
Broccoli	259	(kg N ha^{-1})	4
Winter wheat (UK)	180	(kg N ha^{-1})	6
Maize	120	(kg N ha^{-1})	6
Wheat (Australia)	67	(kg N ha^{-1})	4
Crop yield (fresh weight harvested product)			
Canola	2000	(kg ha^{-1})	4
Broccoli (two crops annually)	16,000	(kg ha^{-1})	4
Winter wheat (UK)	7800	(kg ha^{-1})	7
Maize (New York State, US)	7965	(kg ha^{-1})	8
Wheat (Australia)	3050	(kg ha^{-1})	4
Harvest index			
Canola (Australia)	0.33		9
Broccoli (Australia)	0.85		9
Winter wheat (UK)	0.50		10
Maize (New York State, US)	0.50		8
Wheat (Australia)	0.43		10
Moisture content			
Canola	10.0	(%)	9
Broccoli (two crops annually)	85.0	(%)	9
Winter wheat (UK)	14.5	(%)	7
Maize (New York State, US)	16.0	(%)	8
Wheat (Australia)	6.0	(%)	9

Note: MAP = monoammonium phosphate.

Source: 1 Wood and Cowie (2004); 2 IPCC (2006); 3 Department of Climate Change (Australia) (2008); 4 NSW Department of Primary Industries (undated); 5 Hunt (1983); 6 Gaunt and Lehmann (2008); 7 Defra (2008); 8 USDA (2007); 9 J. Ekman (NSW DPI, pers comm, 2008); 10 Hay (1995)

Table 18.4 *Net emissions (t CO_2e ha^{-1} yr^{-1}) for biochar applied to agricultural crops at a rate of 5t biochar ha^{-1} once (positive values indicate emissions; negative values indicate avoided emissions, or removals)*

Crop	Avoided emissions (t CO_2e ha^{-1} yr^{-1})														
	N_2O emissions from soil			Field operations			Fertilizer savings			Carbon capture			Total		
	Low	Medium	High	Low	Medium	High	Low	Medium	High	Low	Medium	High	Low	Medium	High
Canola	−0.02	−0.04	−0.06	0.00	0.00	−0.01	−0.03	−0.06	−0.09	0.00	−0.11	−0.23	−0.05	−0.22	−0.39
Broccoli	−0.52	−1.10	−1.77	0.00	−0.01	−0.02	−0.13	−0.26	−0.39	0.00	−0.19	−0.38	−0.66	−1.56	−2.57
Wheat (UK)	−0.19	−0.39	−0.63	−0.01	−0.02	−0.04	−0.09	−0.18	−0.27	0.00	−0.28	−0.55	−0.28	−0.87	−1.49
Maize	−0.13	−0.26	−0.42	0.00	−0.01	−0.03	−0.06	−0.12	−0.18	0.00	−0.28	−0.55	−0.19	−0.67	−1.18
Wheat (Australia)	−0.03	−0.04	−0.07	0.00	0.00	0.00	−0.03	−0.07	−0.10	0.00	−0.14	−0.28	−0.06	−0.25	−0.45

Carbon stored in biomass

Biochar has been shown to result in enhanced plant productivity expressed either as an increase in agronomic efficiency (i.e. unit of harvested product per unit of fertilizer input) due to reductions in fertilizer use in high-yield situations or increases of yield in low-yield situations (see Chapters 5 and 12). Our analysis assumes a yield enhancement of 0, 25 and 50 per cent.

In situations where greater plant growth results from biochar application, this may result in increased returns of organic matter both as above- and below-ground inputs. Given that this represents an enhanced capture of CO_2 from the atmosphere, the resulting increase in soil C reflects a genuine sequestration of C, as discussed above.

In this analysis we consider the above-ground C pool only, using harvest index (the ratio of harvest yield to shoot biomass) to calculate above-ground biomass at harvest. Carbon capture is estimated as the difference in average C stock in above-ground biomass between the biochar-amended fields and un-amended fields. This difference is averaged over the typical life of a C-offsetting project, assumed to be ten years.

Our calculations of avoided emissions are intended to describe the likely envelope in which the actual avoided emissions will fall for each of the crops under consideration. The range is large, from 0.05 to 2.57t CO_2e t^{-1} yr^{-1} ha^{-1} when biochar was applied to soil at a rate of 5t biochar ha^{-1} (see Table 18.4).

Of these avoided emissions, the reduction in N_2O emissions and the C capture by biomass are the largest components. As described above, the C capture represents the difference in average C stock between the baseline and biochar-amended crop and is spread over ten years.

Table 18.5 *Total avoided emissions (t CO_2e) over a ten-year period, per tonne of biochar applied, at an application rate of 5t biochar ha^{-1} once, assuming a constant influence of biochar*

	Avoided emissions (t CO_2e t^{-1} biochar)		
	Low	Medium	High
Dryland rotation[1]	0.12	0.48	0.86
Broccoli	1.31	3.12	5.13
Winter wheat	0.57	1.73	2.97
Maize	0.38	1.34	2.36

Note: 1 Three-year rotation: wheat, wheat, canola, wheat, wheat, canola, etc.

Expressed relative to 1t of biochar, the emissions abatement over a ten-year period through application of biochar as a soil amendment ranges from 0.1t CO_2e t^{-1} to 5.1t CO_2e t^{-1} biochar (see Table 18.5). When combined with the emissions abated due to pyrolysis of biomass to produce biochar (2.5t CO_2e t^{-1} to 10.9t CO_2e t^{-1} biochar; Table 18.2b) the total emissions abatement ranges from 2.6t CO_2e t^{-1} to 16t CO_2e t^{-1} biochar produced.

We have presented evidence to show how the operation of a slow pyrolysis facility processing a range of feedstocks at a rate of 2t DM hr^{-1} will deliver a potential of 0.14Mt to 0.68Mt CO_2e avoided emissions over a ten-year operating period. A facility that processes 2t DM hr^{-1} would produce in the order of 64,000t of biochar over a ten-year operating life (assuming 40 per cent of feedstock DM is converted to biochar). Utilization of this quantity of biochar as a soil amendment will deliver an estimated emissions abatement of 0.008Mt to 0.3Mt CO_2e. Therefore, the total abatement achieved is estimated at 0.15Mt to 0.98Mt CO_2e for a single plant over the ten-year operating period.

Issues for emissions trading based on pyrolysis for bioenergy and biochar

In Box 18.1 we outlined key concepts, relevant to offsets, which must be addressed in an emissions trading scheme. Here we examine the application of these principles to biochar projects. The issue of *permanence* is less significant for biochar projects than for projects that sequester C in biomass or soil through management of plant productivity because biochar represents a stabilized form of C that is resistant to further breakdown in soil. Nevertheless, until the stability of biochar is better understood, there may be a requirement to monitor its stability in soil (see below).

With respect to *coverage* of gases and sectors, pyrolysis for biochar and bioenergy contributes across the possible range, avoiding CO_2 emissions in the energy sector, enhancing soil and biomass C pools in the agriculture sector, and reducing emissions of non-CO_2 GHGs both from the waste and agriculture sectors.

In relation to bioenergy from pyrolysis, once a facility design is established, *uncertainty* in estimation of avoided emissions is low provided the plant is operated as designed, and with the feedstocks specified in the design, because the processes are well understood. Greater uncertainty applies to the estimation of avoided emissions from landfill or manure management due to the immaturity of scientific understanding of these processes and the variability associated with feedstocks, management systems and climate (IPCC, 2006). The reduction of emissions when biochar is applied to agricultural crops is particularly uncertain due to the scarcity of experimental data, limited understanding of the biological and chemical processes involved, and inherent variability in N_2O emissions, both temporally and spatially, due to the influence of variable edaphic and climatic factors (see Chapter 13).

Leakage refers to emissions that are indirectly attributable to the project and occur outside the project boundary and should be reported. For example, if cropland is converted to short-rotation forest to produce biomass for biochar, then indirect land-use change may occur: native forest may be cleared to provide new cropland. The loss of C stock in the forest would represent leakage that should be factored into the calculation of the offset benefit.

The current mechanisms for monetizing GHG offset activities are typically designed for individual projects that are tightly bounded. In some situations, pyrolysis and biochar products may be designed to fit within this conventional bounded project approach. In this approach, feedstock is used to produce biochar that is utilized within the boundary of the project or in a well-defined location remote from the pyrolysis facility. This is the case, for example, in the restoration of a wetland or a degraded site.

A key issue becomes how to realize the C offset value in situations where biochar is distributed as a product. At least two approaches are possible: the first is to allow the user to develop a project and claim the offsets that accrue to their use of biochar. This will require information on the provenance of biochar to ensure that no double-counting or leakage occurs. However, the major limiting factor is likely to be economic viability. For example, based on the analysis above, a broccoli grower using biochar may generate 7.5t to 25.5t CO_2e ha^{-1} avoided emissions over a ten-year period. This amounts to US$750 to US$2500 of revenue at projected CO_2 market prices of US$100 t^{-1} CO_2e (Stern, 2007) However, even at such levels, the costs of project development and reporting are likely to outweigh the income, and the scale is incompatible with the market.

Possible mechanisms to realize its mitigation include incorporating the GHG offset value into the price of the biochar product or providing mechanisms to aggregate across locations. In the first case, the farmer forgoes C credits and the distributor aggregates the credits to a volume that are appropriate for C markets. In return, the farm gains the implied or forgone value of the C credits in the form of a discount for the biochar product. Under this model, the challenge then becomes for the supplier to demonstrate that the use of their product corresponds with the assumptions made in claiming the GHG offset.

Aggregation may be possible in vertically integrated businesses (e.g. a food manufac-turer, retailer, contracting farming models or certification scheme). The parties responsible for the integration would be in a position to track the application of biochar to specific crops and areas of land and the value could be reflected in the price paid for the agricultural produce.

Monitoring and verification

Robust protocols will be required to justify a claim for an avoided emission under each category of avoided emission. For the components associated with the operation of a pyrolysis facility (i.e. avoided emissions associated with feedstock source, fossil fuel offsets and biochar production and deployment), this is a relatively straightforward accounting exercise. There are potential concerns that the use of IPCC defaults, while straightforward, may lead to inaccurate estimates (e.g. Crutzen et al, 2008; Ximenes et al, 2008) or at least be subject to significant uncertainty (IPCC, 2006).

Depending upon the market in which the offset is being monetized, existing methods for monitoring and verification can be used. As described above, defining the project boundaries and baseline are critical first steps in monitoring and verification. Some schemes require a 'life-cycle' approach, in which the project boundary encompasses all sources of emissions and removals attributable to the project, while others allow a narrower definition. The former approach is appropriate in a situation, such as the Clean Development Mechanism, where emissions that are indirectly attributable, or beyond the control of the project proponent, will not be reported by another party.

The baseline, as described earlier, represents the 'without project' scenario and may be determined from land-use history and neighbouring developments. The project then needs to implement appropriate record keeping. For example, weighbridge and truck manifests could be used to demonstrate that feedstock from a specified source was delivered to a facility. Records of energy use and energy exported, based on calibrated metering systems, may be required.

As was described above, with respect to biochar, the key aspects to be verified are:

- biochar production;
- end use of biochar; and
- the impacts of this biochar on agricultural emissions.

The monitoring systems used will be tailored to different situations. For example, the monitoring needs will be different for a project where biochar was applied to a nearby plantation and one where biochar entered a retail market as a soil-enhancing product.

In addition to monitoring (and providing a means of verifying) the end use of the biochar, given the current lack of long-term evidence of biochar stability, protocols will need to be put in place to demonstrate the stability of the biochar over time in the environments where it is deployed (see Chapter 17).

The most complex area for monitoring and verification of biochar-based offsets will arise where a project seeks to claim credit for avoided emissions associated with biochar use in agricultural situations. Currently, the evidence base to substantiate claims is weak and very situation specific, as already seen for yield increases (Lehmann and Rondon, 2006). Sufficient evidence does not yet exist to propose credible defaults. Once these defaults are established, it will be relatively easy to calculate and validate claims of abatement using primary data (e.g. farm records of fertilizer purchase and use, crops grown and records of sales) for monitoring purposes.

These difficulties should not deter efforts to monetize the GHG offsets derived from pyrolysis and biochar production. The bulk of the emissions trading value in most situations is likely to be realized from avoided emissions associated with changes in feedstock management, fossil fuel substitution and C stabilization. Once the defaults for agricultural N_2O emissions are established, these can potentially be claimed retrospectively where appropriate records have been kept.

The emissions trading market is expanding rapidly and is likely to continue to grow as more countries introduce mandatory schemes, and as targets are tightened in response to increased urgency to curb emissions. The parties to the Kyoto Protocol have agreed that a second commitment period should commence after 2012 (UNFCCC, 2005). It is likely that the rules for inclusion of agricultural offsets will be revised for the new commitment period. Details of targets and the accounting framework for the second commitment period will be negotiated over the next few years. Future implementation of climate change policy may involve large-scale programmes monitored and credited at the national scale in order to minimize transaction costs and leakage. The same drivers to deliver economies of scale for monitoring, verification and registration of abatement exist in the voluntary market.

Future implementation of climate change policy may involve large-scale programmes monitored and credited at the national scale in order to minimize transaction costs and leakage. These developments may assist in reducing transaction costs and, thus, increase the incentive that participation in emissions trading could provide for biochar-based projects.

Conclusions

Currently, there is no term that captures well the process of C sequestration through the use of biochar. The term soil C sequestration typically refers to C that is stored in soil as a result of a change in management that increases returns of biomass to soil or slows its decomposition. However, such sequestration is often debated, as was described above, due to issues of permanence and leakage. By contrast, pyrolysis transforms biomass and stabilizes C in biochar in a form that is largely resistant to further decomposition when added to soil. Thus, we argue that it is important to differentiate the use of pyrolysis for C stabilization from discussion of C sequestration.

We have presented evidence to show how the operation of a single slow pyrolysis facility processing a range of feedstocks at a rate of 2t DM hr^{-1} will deliver a potential of 0.1Mt to 1.0Mt CO_2e emissions abatement over a ten-year period. This range reflects the influence of feedstock source and biochar use, illustrating the importance of selecting appropriate combinations of feedstock and biochar application if the goal is to maximize the mitigation of climate change. This illustrates the importance of project design (both in terms of feedstock source and biochar use) if the goal is to maximize the mitigation of climate change. This analysis also reveals the exciting prospect that with sufficient deployment of pyrolysis facilities for biochar production, biochar can offer a significant contribution to mitigation of climate change at the gigatonne scale.

There is a need to develop a body of experience based on well-designed laboratory and field studies undertaken at scales that enable the agricultural and environmental benefits and risks of using biochar to be explored and demonstrated. These studies will need to be designed to capture all dimensions of the avoided emissions described above (i.e. from feedstock to agricultural emissions). Such studies should also cover a range of situations representative of feedstocks, pyrolysis installation, environments and agricultural systems, and will require deployment of biochar at levels that have not been possible, to date, due to the lack of pyrolysis facilities with an appropriate level of process control and capacity to produce biochar in the necessary quantities. This is likely to remain a constraint until commercial-scale pilot pyrolysis facilities are established.

Of at least equal importance to establishing effective mechanisms for trading C offsets generated from pyrolysis installations is to establish a value for biochar as an agricultural amendment to develop a market demand for biochar (see Chapter 21). Demonstration of the agricultural and environmental benefits will be crucial to the creation of demand for biochar.

While this discussion focused on the mitigation of GHG emissions, other environmental benefits of biochar, such as water quality management, could also be monetized in an environmental services market once these benefits are proven. Environmental objectives can more efficiently and effectively be pursued by multi-attribute policies (Cowie et al, 2007). Integration of climate change policy within broader measures for sustainable land management would allow the multiple benefits of biochar to be recognized and rewarded.

Pyrolysis and biochar projects are likely to be complex and to require mechanisms to aggregate the C offsets produced across a network of pyrolysis installations and from biochar use in agriculture or environmental management. This will require innovative project design and business models underpinned by cost-effective approaches in monitoring and verification.

References

Beck-Friis, B., Pell, M., Sonesson, U., Jönsson, H. and Kirchmann, H. (2000) 'Formation and emission of N_2O and CH_4 from compost heaps of organic household waste', *Environmental Monitoring and Assessment*, vol 62, pp317–331

Beer, T., Meyer, M., Grant, T., Russell, K., Kirkby, C., Chen, D., Edis, R., Lawson, S., Weeks, I., Galbally, I., Fattore, A., Smith, D., Li, Y., Wang, G., Park, K., Turner, D. and Thacker, J. (2007) *Life-Cycle Assessment of Greenhouse Gas Emissions from Agriculture in Relation to Marketing and Regional Development – Irrigated Maize: From Maize Field to Grocery Store*, Report HQ06A/6/F3.5Z, Commonwealth Scientific and Industrial Research Organisation, Australia

Canadell, J., Le Quéré, C., Raupach, M., Field, C., Buitehuis, T., Ciais, P., Conway, T., Gillett, N., Houghton, R. and Marland, G. (2007) 'Contributions to accelerating atmospheric CO_2 growth from economic activity, carbon intensity, and efficiency of natural sinks', *Proceedings of the National Academy of Sciences*, vol 104, pp18866–18870

CCBA (2005) *Climate, Community and Biodiversity Project Design Standards*, first edition, CCBA, Washington, DC, www.climate-standards.org/images/pdf/CCBStandards.pdf

CCX (Chicago Climate Exchange) (2007a) *CCX Exchange Offsets and Exchange Early Action Credits*, CCX, Chicago, IL, Chapter 9, www.chicagoclimatex.com/docs/offsets/CCX_Rulebook_Chapter09_OffsetsAndEarlyActionCredits.pdf, accessed 18 August 2008

CCX (2007b) *Rangeland Soil Carbon Management Offsets*, CCX, Chicago, IL, http://carboncredit.ndfu.org/pdfs/Rangeland/RangelandProtocol.pdf accessed 18/08/2008

Chan, K. Y., Van Zwieten, L., Meszaros, I., Downie, A. and Joseph, S. (2007) 'Agronomic values of greenwaste biochar as a soil amendment', *Australian Journal of Soil Research*, vol 45, pp629–634

Cowie, A. L. (2008) *Impact on GHG Balance of Utilising Biochar as a Soil Amendment*, IEA Bioenergy Task 38, www.ieabioenergy-task38.org/projects/

Cowie, A. L., Schneider, U. A. and Montanarella, L. (2007) 'Potential synergies between existing multilateral environmental agreements in the implementation of land use, land-use change and forestry activities', *Environmental Science and Policy*, vol 10, pp335–352

Crutzen, P. J., Mosier, A. R., Smith, K. A. and Winiwarter, W. (2008) 'N_2O release from agro-biofuel production negates global warming reduction by replacing fossil fuels', *Atmospheric Chemistry and Physics*, vol 8, pp389–395

Davidson, E. A. and Janssens, I. A. (2006) 'Temperature sensitivity of soil carbon decomposition and feedbacks to climate change', *Nature*, vol 440, pp165–173

Defra (UK Department for Environment, Food and Rural Affairs) (2003) *The Scientific Case for Setting a Long-Term Emission Reduction Target*, Defra, www.defra.gov.uk/Environment/climatechange/pubs/pdf/ewp_targetscience.pdf accessed 14 August 2008

Defra (2008) *Agricultural Survey*, Defra, www.defra.gov.uk/esg/work_htm/publications/cs/farmstats_web/default.htm, accessed 16 August 2008

Department of Climate Change (Australia) (2008) *National Inventory Report 2006 Australian Government Submission to the UN Framework Convention on Climate Change June 2008*, Commonwealth of Australia, Canberra, Australia, www.climatechange.gov.au/inventory/2006/pubs/inventory2006-national-reportv1.pdf, accessed 15 August 2008

EPA (US Environmental Protection Agency) (2006) *Inventory of US Greenhouse Gas Emissions and Sinks: 1990–2006*, US EPA, Washington, DC, www.epa.gov/climatechange/emissions/usinventoryreport.html, accessed 16 August 2008

EPA (2007) *NOx Budget Program 2006 Progress Report*, EPA-430-R-07-009, www.epa.gov/airmarkt/progress/docs/2006-NBP-Report.pdf, accessed 18 August 2008

Evelein, M. (2008) *The Potential for Reducing Atmospheric Concentrations of CO_2 through Biochar in the UK*, MSc thesis, University of East London, UK

Forster, P., Ramaswamy, V., Artaxo, P., Berntsen, T., Betts, R., Fahey, D. W., Haywood, J., Lean, J., Lowe, D. C., Myhre, G., Nganga, J., Prinn, R., Raga, G., Schulz, M. and Van Dorland, R. (2007) 'Changes in atmospheric constituents and in radiative forcing' in S. Solomon, D. Qin, M. Manning, Z. Chen, M., Marquis, K. B. Averyt, M. Tignor and H. L. Miller (eds) *Climate Change 2007: The Physical Science Basis. Contribution of Working Group I to the Fourth Assessment Report of the Intergovernmental Panel on Climate Change*, Cambridge University Press, Cambridge, UK

Gaunt, J. and Lehmann, J. (2008) 'Energy balance and emissions associated with biochar sequestration and pyrolysis bioenergy production', *Environmental Science and Technology* vol 42, pp4152–4158

Gehring, M. W. and Streck, C. (2005) 'Emissions trading: Lessons from SOx and NOx emissions allowance and credit systems: Legal nature, title, transfer, and taxation of emission allowances and credits', *The Environmental Law Reporter News and Analysis Journal*, www.climatefocus.com/downloads/publications/ELR_gehring_streck.pdf, accessed 18 August 2008

Gerzabek, M., Pichlmayer, F., Kirchmann, H. and Haberhauer, G. (1997) 'The response of soil organic matter to manure amendments in a long-term experiment at Ultuna, Sweden', *European Journal of Soil Science*, vol 48, pp273–282

Gold Standard (2008) *Introducing Gold Standard Version 2*, www.cdmgoldstandard.org/materials.php?PHPSESSID=0a2738b8e7a60b2bba8339735cc17af6

Hamilton, K., Sjardin, M., Marcello, T. and Xu, G. (2008) *Forging a Frontier: State of the Voluntary Carbon Markets 2008*, Ecosystem Marketplace and New Carbon Finance, www.newcarbonfinance.com/, accessed 16 August 2008

Hammar, H. and Jagers, S. C. (2006) 'Can trust in politicians explain individuals' support for climate policy? The case of CO_2 tax', *Climate Policy*, vol 5, pp613–625

Hay, R. K. M. (1995) 'Harvest index: A review of its use in plant breeding and crop physiology', *Annals of Applied Biology*, vol 126, pp197–216

Houghton, J. T., Meira Filho, L. G., Lim, B.,

Tréanton, K., Mamaty, I., Bonduki, Y., Griggs, D. J. and Callander, B. A. (eds) (1997) *Revised 1996 IPCC Guidelines for National Greenhouse Gas Inventories; Volume 1: Greenhouse Gas Inventory Reporting Instructions; Volume 2: Greenhouse Gas Inventory Workbook; Volume 3: Greenhouse Gas Inventory Reference Manual*, Intergovernmental Panel on Climate Change, Meteorological Office, Bracknell, UK, www.ipcc-nggip.iges.or.jp/public/gl/invs1.htm, accessed 12 August 2008

Hunt, D. (1983) *Farm Power and Machinery Management*, Iowa State University Press, Ames, IA

IPCC (Intergovernmental Panel on Climate Change) (2000) *Good Practice Guidance and Uncertainty Management in National Greenhouse Gas Inventories*, Intergovernmental Panel on Climate Change, IGES, Japan

IPCC (2006) *2006 IPCC Guidelines for National Greenhouse Gas Inventories*, Eggleston, H. S., Buendia, L., Miwa, K., Ngara, T. and Tanabe, K. (eds) Prepared by the National Greenhouse Gas Inventories Programme, Intergovernmental Panel on Climate Change, IGES, Japan

IPCC (2007) *IPCC Fourth Assessment Report, Climate Change*, Cambridge University Press, Cambridge

ISO (International Organization for Standardization) (2006) *ISO 14064 Greenhouse Gases – Part 1: Specification with Guidance at the Organization Level for Quantification and Reporting of Greenhouse Gas Emissions and Removals; Part 2: Specification with Guidance at the Project Level for Quantification and Reporting of Greenhouse Gas Emission Reductions and Removal Enhancements; Part 3: Specification with Guidance for the Validation and Verification of Greenhouse Gas Assertions*, International Organization for Standardization, Geneva, Switzerland

Jenkinson, D. S. and Ayabana, A. (1977) 'Decomposition of carbon-14 labelled plant material under tropical conditions', *Soil Science Society of America Journal* vol 41, pp912–915

Johansson, B. (2000) *Economic Instruments in Practice 1: Carbon Tax in Sweden Workshop on Innovation and the Environment*, OECD, www.oecd.org/dataoecd/25/0/2108273.pdf, accessed 13 August 2008

Kollmuss, A., Zink, H. and Polycarp, C. (2008) *Making Sense of the Voluntary Carbon Market: A Comparison of Carbon Offset Standards*, WWF, Germany

Lal, R. (2008) 'Carbon sequestration', *Philosophical Transactions of the Royal Society B*, vol 363, pp815–830

Lehmann, J. (2007) 'A handful of carbon', *Nature*, vol 447, pp143–144

Lehmann, J. and Rondon, M. (2006) 'Bio-char soil management on highly weathered soils in the humid tropics', in N. Uphoff (ed) *Biological Approaches to Sustainable Soil Systems*, CRC Press, Boca Raton, FL, pp517–530

Lehmann, J., Gaunt, J. and Rondon, M. (2006) 'Bio-char sequestration in terrestrial ecosystems – a review', *Mitigation and Adaptation Strategies for Global Change*, vol 11, pp403–427

Lynch, D., Voroney, R. and Warman, P. (2005) 'Soil physical properties and organic matter fractions under forages receiving composts, manure or fertilizer', *Compost Science and Utilization*, vol 13, pp252–261

McKenzie, D. C. and So, H. B. (1989) 'Effect of gypsum on vertisols of the Gwydir Valley, New South Wales. 2. Ease of tillage', *Australian Journal of Experimental Agriculture*, vol 29, pp63–67

NSW Department of Primary Industries (undated) *Farm Enterprise Budget (Broccoli, Canola, Wheat)*, NSW DPI, Orange, Australia

Ogle, S. M., Jay Breidt, F., Eve, M. D., and Paustian, K. (2003) 'Uncertainty in estimating land use and management impacts on soil organic carbon storage for US agricultural lands between 1982 and 1997', *Global Change Biology*, vol 9, pp1521–1542

Pattey, E., Trzcinski, M. K. and Desjardins, R. L. (2005) 'Quantifying the reduction of greenhouse gas emissions as a result of composting dairy and beef cattle manure', *Nutrient Cycling in Agroecosystems*, vol 72, pp173–187

Prentice, I. C., Farquhar, G. D., Fasham, M. J. R., Goulden, M. L., Heimann, M., Jaramillo, V. J., Kheshgi, H. S., Le Quere, C., Scholes, R. J., and Wallace, D. W. R. (2001) 'The carbon cycle and atmospheric carbon dioxide', in J. T. Houghton, Y. Ding, D. J. Griggs, M. Noguer, P. van der Linden, X. Dai, K. Maskell and C. A. Johnson (eds) *Climate Change 2001: The Scientific Basis. Contribution of Working Group I to the Third Assessment Report of the Intergovernmental Panel on Climate Change*, Cambridge University Press, UK

Productivity Commission (Australia) (2007) *Productivity Commission Submission to the Prime Ministerial Task Group on Emissions Trading*, Australian Government Productivity Commission, www.pc.gov.au/research/submission/emissionstrading, accessed 21 August 2008

Rondon, M., Ramirez, J. A. and Lehmann, J. (2005) 'Charcoal additions reduce net emissions of greenhouse gases to the atmosphere', in *Proceedings of the Third USDA Symposium on Greenhouse Gases and Carbon Sequestration*, Baltimore, MD, 21–24 March 2005, p208

Steiner, C., Glaser, B., Teixeira, W. G., Lehmann, J., Blum, W. E. H. and Zech, W. (in press) 'Nitrogen retention and plant uptake on a highly weathered central Amazonian Ferralsol amended with compost and charcoal', *Journal of Plant Nutrition and Soil Science*

Stern, N. (2007) *The Economics of Climate Change: The Stern Review*, Cambridge University Press, Cambridge, UK

Thomas, B. (2008) *Tax vs Trade, or Attitudes in the Carbon Economy*, www.climatebiz.com/column/2008/07/02/tax-vs-trade-carbon-economy?mode=one

UNFCCC (United Nations Framework Convention on Climate Change) (2005) *Decision – CMP.1 Consideration of Commitments for Subsequent Periods for Parties Included in Annex I to the Convention under Article 3, Paragraph 9, of the Kyoto Protocol*, UNFCCC, http://unfccc.int/files/meetings/cop_11/application/pdf/cmp1_00_consideration_of_commitments_under_3.9.pdf, accessed 19 August 2008

UNFCCC (2008) *Kyoto Protocol: Status of Ratification*, http://unfccc.int/files/kyoto_protocol/status_of_ratification/application/pdf/kp_ratification.pdf, accessed 14 August 2008

USDA (US Department of Agriculture) (2007) *New York Agricultural Overview*, National Agricultural Statistics Service, www.nass.usda.gov/Statistics_by_State/New_York/index.asp

Vattenfall (2007) *The Climate Threat: Can Humanity Rise to the Greatest Challenge of our Times?*, www.vattenfall.com/www/ccc/ccc/577730downl/index.jsp

VCS (Voluntary Carbon Standard) (2007) *Guidance for Agriculture, Forestry and Other Land Use Projects*, VCS

Wood, S. and Cowie, A. (2004) *A Review of Greenhouse Gas Emission Factors for Fertiliser Production*, IEA Bioenergy Task 38, www.ieabioenergy-task38.org/publications/GHG_Emission_Fertilizer%20Production_July2004.pdf, accessed 12 August 2008

Wrage, N., van Groeningen, J. W., Oenema, O. and Baggs, E. M. (2005) 'Distinguishing between soil sources of N_2O using a new ^{15}N- and ^{18}O-enrichment method', *Rapid Communications in Mass Spectrometry*, vol 19, pp3298–3306

WRI WBCSD (World Resources Institute, World Business Council for Sustainable Development) (2005) *GHG Protocol for Project Accounting*, WRI WBCSD, www.ghgprotocol.org/files/ghg_project_protocol.pdf

Ximenes, F. A., Gardner, W. D. and Cowie, A. L. (2008) 'The decomposition of wood products in landfills in Sydney, Australia', *Waste Management*, vol 28, no 11, November, pp2344–2354

Yanai, Y., Toyota, K. and Okazaki, M. (2007) 'Effects of charcoal addition on N_2O emissions from soil resulting from rewetting air-dried soil in short-term laboratory experiments', *Soil Science and Plant Nutrition*, vol 53, pp181–188

19

Economics of Biochar Production, Utilization and Greenhouse Gas Offsets

Bruce A. McCarl, Cordner Peacocke, Ray Chrisman,
Chih-Chun Kung and Ronald D. Sands

Introduction

In order for pyrolysis and agriculturally applied biochar to be an important development, they must jointly be an economically attractive alternative. This economic attractiveness could arise from a combination of:

- valuable energy commodity yields (as also discussed in Chapters 8 and 9);
- value arising from biochar as a soil additive (see Chapters 5 and 12);
- valuable greenhouse gas (GHG) offsets generated by offsetting fossil fuels, reducing emissions from use of agricultural inputs and sequestering carbon (C) (see Chapter 18); and
- value arising from other chemical products.

In addition, revenues from these items must offset the economic and GHG costs of raising, harvesting, hauling and storing the biomass feedstock, along with those of employing pyrolysis and then transporting and applying the biochar.

This chapter reports on an analysis approach that assesses the economic and GHG consequences of biochar–pyrolysis production, using a crop residue case as a specific example. Namely, we use a case study involving collection of maize residue and transportation to a large fast or slow pyrolysis facility (in contrast to Chapter 20, which examines small-scale pyrolysis opportunities), yielding both energy products and biochar with the biochar applied to cropland (other biochar systems are discussed in Chapter 9). Specifically, we examine the:

- cost of feedstock harvest, hauling, storage and use, along with implications for nutrient replacement and tillage alteration;
- value of energy production and the costs of associated processes;
- value of biochar application and subsequent implications for crop production;
- GHG-related accounts involving:
  - offsets for displaced fossil fuels;

– emissions saved and increased from fossil fuels and manufactured agricultural inputs employed in the farm-to-pyrolysis facility-to-farm process; and

– sequestration enhancements and losses involved with residue recovery and biochar application.

In examining these factors we realized that many items are uncertain and develop only a preliminary case study on net economic benefits and a simultaneous GHG life-cycle assessment. We also explore how the case study net benefits are affected by variations in assumptions involving alternative feedstocks, pyrolysis facility/operation costs, energy prices, C prices and other factors.

Pyrolysis and biochar

Biochar is produced by pyrolysis (Bridgwater and Peacocke, 2002; Demirbas and Arin, 2002) and, to a limited extent can, also be a by-product of gasification (Bridgwater, 2005). Pyrolysis is the chemical decomposition of organic materials by heating in the absence of oxygen (O) (see Chapters 1, 7 and 8) where:

• Fast pyrolysis involves biomass being rapidly (on the order of 5 to 10 seconds) heated to between 400°C and 550°C.
• Slow pyrolysis involves slower heating to less than 400°C (although other definitions have higher temperatures; see Chapter 8). The biomass is typically in the reactor for at least 30 minutes and possibly several hours.

During pyrolysis biomass is converted into three products:

1 a liquid product that is commonly called bio-oil, pyrolysis oil or bio-crude;
2 a solid char that can be used in a range of applications, including use as a soil additive (then called 'biochar') or as a source of energy in the conversion process;
3 a non-condensable gas product containing carbon monoxide (CO), carbon dioxide (CO_2), hydrogen (H_2), methane (CH_4) and higher hydrocarbons, 'syngas' or 'pyrolysis gas'.

Slow pyrolysis yields relatively more biochar, but less bio-oil. Wright et al (2008) indicate that fast pyrolysis yields about 15 per cent biochar, 70 per cent bio-oil and 13 per cent syngas. Ringer et al (2006) indicate that under slow pyrolysis, about 35 per cent of the feedstock C ends up as biochar, 30 per cent as bio-oil and 35 per cent as syngas (for additional information, see Chapter 8).

In both cases, the bio-oil can then be cleaned and further processed to produce higher-quality fuels (Czernik and Bridgwater, 2004), gasified to produce electricity, or it can be refined to produce chemical feedstocks such as resins and slow-release fertilizers, as well as have selective food chemicals recovered from it (Baum and Weitner, 2006). Each of these products is a potential source of value.

While biochar was initially viewed as a source of energy and can be burned to supply process energy, it can be used in water purification, gas cleaning, metallurgical industries and for charcoal in home cooking. In addition, it has lately been regarded as a potentially valuable soil amendment where it stores C in stable form along with storing nutrients and water (see Chapters 1 to 6, 9, 11, 12 and 18).

Finally, both the energy products and the biochar as a soil additive have GHG implications, displacing fossil fuel use and associated emissions, along with sequestering C (see

Chapter 18). In considering these GHG impacts, one must consider the full life cycle of GHGs released in the farm-to-factory-to-biochar application system.

Examination of a biomass to pyrolysis feedstock prospect

This section examines the economic and GHG value that would arise from producing biochar and other products under fast and slow pyrolysis using agricultural biomass. We present a somewhat general discussion of feedstock possibilities, along with a concrete application using data representative of the case of maize residues as a feedstock. In calculating the value of such a prospect, we consider benefits and costs, first, and then examine implications from changes in the GHG balance.

Costs and benefits

The economic costs and benefits of fast and slow pyrolysis, as well as the associated products, considered are:

- feedstock production and collection;
- value lost by feedstock removal in terms of altered nutrients and tillage on fields from which crop residue was harvested;
- feedstock hauling;
- feedstock storage and pre-processing;
- feedstock processing;
- pyrolysis operation;
- energy sales;
- biochar hauling and application; and
- biochar-induced cropping system gains.

Each is discussed separately below.

Feedstock production and collection

Biomass requires some form of assembly, harvesting, collection and compaction, all of which involve costs (Caputo et al, 2005). In the case of:

- *Urban municipal wastes:* this could involve separation, assembly at a transport point, possibly compaction and then truck loading, and could involve a tipping fee to municipal agencies (NSWMA, 2005). One should also consider the value of saved landfill space (Read et al, 2008), as well as the possible costs of removing or dealing with any materials such as nails or contaminants in the pyrolysis phase. However, there may be cases where these items can be obtained at no cost with the facility collecting a tipping fee in lieu of a disposal fee.
- *Energy crops such as switchgrass or hybrid poplar:* this would involve the costs of the inputs to raise and harvest the commodity, such as seed, rootstock, fertilizer, fossil fuels, equipment, labour and land value, along with movement to a transport point, compaction and loading.
- *Milling residues or processing by-products such as bagasse:* this could involve the cost of buying them away from their current use (or savings in cost if they are now a disposal item), as well as costs of moving to a transport site, compacting and loading along with the amount one might need to pay the processor for access.
- *Logging or cropping residues:* this would involve the inputs to harvest and transport to a hauling site, along with compaction and loading (Polagye et al, 2007), as well as the future productivity losses or nutrient replacement costs from removal (unless the produced biochar is returned to the site from where the biomass originated or other appropriate soil amendment is used).

More specifically, costs for harvesting and moving maize crop residues to the field edge are assumed to equal US$10.91 t^{-1} based on a rice straw feedstock supply study by Fife and Miller (1999). We adjust this up to US$13 after some discussion with Environmental Protection Agency (EPA) personnel and to account for higher energy costs, and we add US$10 for a payment to the farmer.

When considering the use of a feedstock, it is necessary to consider the costs and benefits of that feedstock were it not diverted to pyrolysis. In the case of maize stover, this involves analysis of the net value if it remains in the field. In this case, the items arising are lost nutrients and sequestration from its diversion as well as increased tillage costs due to its presence (note that we are assuming a sufficient amount is left in the field to avoid increased erosion).

Agronomists have argued that when crop residues are removed, this removes nutrients that must be replaced by commercial fertilizers in subsequent production operations. In terms of amount, we employ estimates of nutrient loss after removal of maize residue developed in an Argonne National Laboratory (2006) report. This amounts to 2.7kg needed for replacement of nitrogen (N) per tonne of residue removed, along with 1.6kg of phosphorus (P) and 8.3kg of potassium (K). Based on current costs of these items, we compute the replacement cost for these as US$10.08 t^{-1} of residue removed. This would vary if other feedstocks were used.

Additionally, for a crop such as maize, tillage is partially motivated by a need to handle the large volume of crop residue. We assume that when the crop residue is removed, tillage intensity can be reduced and can credit the difference in cost from conventional to no-till farming at US$20.60 per hectare amounting to US$5.59 t^{-1} removed. The farm gate price then includes the harvest cost, the nutrient replacement, farmer payment and the savings from reduced tillage, and amounts to US$27.59 t^{-1}.

Furthermore, we assume the crop residue yield is 3.75t ha^{-1}, which leaves the remaining quantity of residue for erosion control needs and is motivated by the adjustments in the billion tonne study (Perlack et al, 2005). Consequently, each hectare produces 3.75t of feedstock at a farm gate price of US$27.59 t^{-1}.

The use of other feedstocks would raise different issues and calculation procedures. Specifically, when using:

- *Logging residues:* one would employ essentially the same procedures, examining the extra costs of harvest and hauling to the field edge, but might have to include the cost of on-site chipping and compaction, a differential loss factor in storage and hauling, and a savings in costs for handling residue such as the need for collection and burning, among others.
- *Dedicated energy crops:* one would need to consider the opportunity cost of the land in other usages, such as conventional crop production along with rotation length and differential yields over time.
- *Municipal wastes:* one might encounter cases where firms may pay the pyrolysis plant a tipping fee to take waste materials. Sorting, separation and subsequent disposal of inerts may reduce the income opportunity significantly.

Feedstock hauling and storage

A significant cost element when using some feedstocks is hauling costs. This may well be straightforward when looking at municipal wastes or processing by-products as it merely requires computation of distance and number of truckloads to obtain a total cost. However, when examining energy crops as well as logging residues, the calculation becomes more complex. In particular, one must take into account the size of the feedstock need and the service area required to supply that feedstock. Here we present an approach to this.

First, we consider the size of the operation. A pyrolysis operation using 70,000t yr^{-1} of residue at 3.75t ha^{-1} with 5 per cent loss in hauling and storage requires a land area of 19,600ha for production under a diverse landscape where the proportion of maize cropping area to total land area is close to 20 per cent (as observed in key Iowa maize-producing counties). This implies a substantial hauling effort and associated cost.

We used McCarl et al's (2000) adaptation of French's (1960) procedure to approximate hauling cost, which assumes that the pyrolysis plant is in the centre of a square surrounded by a grid layout of roads. In turn, the hauling cost (H) and average hauling distance ($\bar{D}$) is given by the following formulae:

$$H = (b_0 + 2b_1\bar{D})S / Load$$

and

$$\bar{D} = \sqrt{\frac{S}{640Y}} \qquad [1]$$

where:

$\bar{D}$ is the average distance the feedstock is hauled in miles;

S is the amount of feedstock input for a bio-refinery to fuel the plant, which we assume is 1Mt plus an adjustment for an assumed 5 per cent loss in conveyance and storage;

$Load$ is the truck load size, which we assume to be 20t;

Y is the crop yield (3.75t ha^{-1}, or 1.5t acre^{-1}) multiplied by an assumed crop (maize) density of 20 per cent based on physical size versus maize density in mid-western US states that have a high intensity of maize production;

640 is a conversion factor for the number of acres per square mile;

b_0 is a fixed loading charge per truckload and is assumed to be US$90 per truckload for a 20t truck; and

b_1 is the charge for hauling including labour (per mile) and maintenance costs, which is assumed to equal US$2.20.

This calculation already includes 5 per cent yield loss, a service area of 19,600ha of cropland and an average hauling distance of 14.8km with a cost of US$6.86 t^{-1}.

The hauling cost is sensitive to the case at hand, which would vary across feedstocks and time as petroleum and other input costs change. Note that hauling costs can be cut in half, with much higher yields, as might exist with dedicated energy crops, while they fall about 10 per cent with increased feedstock density. The cost of hauling also has a great impact. Larger volumes increase hauling with, for example, a plant ten times the size experiencing hauling costs that are three times higher. Hauling cost in our case study amounts to about 20 per cent of the feedstock cost and would be reduced by being located close to a municipal waste source (although sorting, pre-treatment and drying costs may be required).

The assumptions used here are reasonable for agricultural commodities, but may not be so in the case of forest logging residues or other product hauling. The US Department of Agriculture (USDA) Forest Service has an alternative calculation procedure that is embedded in the Forest Residues Transportation Model (FoRTS) (USDA, 2008).

Finally, since crop residues such as those from maize are seasonal, we also assume the need for secondary storage and handling to be US$25 t^{-1} based on conversations with EPA personnel (pers comm, 2008). All of this together makes the feedstock cost US$59.44 t^{-1}. Since this and most of the assumptions above would vary with feedstock, a sensitivity analysis is performed across a spectrum of feedstock costs.

Costs of plant operations

Processing biomass into energy costs money. This cost is composed of a fixed and a variable cost component. The fixed cost would be an amortized one-year value of the equipment costs considering purchase price, loan terms, salvage value, etc. The variable cost would involve the costs per unit of production including labour, energy, materials handling etc. Both are highly uncertain given that this is largely a prospective technology that has not been applied at a commercial scale.

In constructing the cost estimate, we assumed the maize stover was delivered in a wet form on a whole basis. The overall system consists of three modules:

- *Module I:* biomass preparation (reception, drying, comminution, storage, feeding);
- *Module II:* fast pyrolysis to a bio-oil product (based on an integrated fluid-bed process using the biochar and syngas for process heat and fluidization, plus recovering the excess biochar for sale);

- *Module III:* electricity generation in a 2 × 7MWe dual fuel diesel engine fuelled by bio-oil and diesel.

For all three modules, costs associated with the system include an annual fixed cost of capital (assuming all of the capital is borrowed), as well as the annual operating costs of the plant. The operating costs include feedstock, labour, utilities, maintenance and overhead. The procedures under which these costs were derived were obtained from Peacocke et al (2006) and Aston University (2002).

A base plant size of 10t hr^{-1} dry feed input was used. The assumed fast pyrolysis process yields and feed properties are given in Table 19.1. The product yields are used in a plant design model to assess the mass and energy balance needed to ensure that the process is optimized for energy efficiency and product yields. The mass and energy balance outputs are employed to size the equipment, which is then costed. The equipment costs are based on actual or published costs in the US at the end of 2007. The lower

Table 19.1 *Fast pyrolysis of maize stover: Summary of modelling assumptions relative to fast pyrolysis at 10t hr^{-1} (dry feedstock basis)*

Feedstock	
Moisture (weight %, dry feed basis)	6.8
Ash (weight %, dry feed basis)	5.9
Reactor temperature (°C)	450
Yields (weight %, dry feedstock basis)	
Biochar	14.8
Organics (pyrolysis liquid)	59.8
Water (of pyrolysis)[1]	11.1
Pyrolysis gases	14.2
Gas yields (weight %, dry feedstock basis)	
CH_4	0.3
CO	3.8
CO_2	10.1

Note: 1 Excludes moisture present in the maize stover, which is recovered in the final liquid product.

Source: chapter authors

Table 19.2 *Summary of primary process inputs and outputs*

	Rate	Units
Process inputs		
Dried maize stover	10.0	$t\,hr^{-1}$
Water in feed	0.7	$t\,hr^{-1}$
Natural gas consumption (preheat burners)	31	$kg\,hr^{-1}$
Cooling water consumption	89	$t\,hr^{-1}$
Diesel for dual fuel engines	83.6	$kg\,hr^{-1}$
Process outputs		
Pyrolysis liquid out (includes water in feedstock)	7.81	$t\,hr^{-1}$
Excess char	444.6	$kg\,hr^{-1}$
Condensate to drain from process	103	$kg\,hr^{-1}$
Stack gases		
CO_2	3161	$kg\,hr^{-1}$
N_2	7321	$kg\,hr^{-1}$
H_2O	593	$kg\,hr^{-1}$
O_2	671	$kg\,hr^{-1}$
NO_x	1.7	$kg\,hr^{-1}$
SO_2	0.7	$kg\,hr^{-1}$
Power		
Gross electrical output	12.9	MW_e
Net electrical output	12.5	MW_e

Source: chapter authors

heating values of the char and recovered pyrolysis liquids are taken as $11.4MJ\,kg^{-1}$ and $16.1MJ\,kg^{-1}$, respectively.

The pyrolysis data arise from experimental data on Iowa maize stover (J. Piskorz, RTI Ltd, Canada, personal communication, 2008). The pyrolysis biochar composition was identical to that in Zabaniotou and Ioannidou (2008), corrected for temperature and ash content. The biochar generated from maize stover is nearly 40 per cent by weight ash, which means that it may not be an ideal fuel for use in the biochar combustor and may have more value as a soil amendment. The process inputs and outputs are given in Table 19.2. All of the pyrolysis gases are used for process heat, fluidizing and are oxidized in the biochar combustor prior to discharge. All the produced pyrolysis liquids are, in turn, used for electrical power generation in dual-fuelled diesel engines, which is an area still under

development. Note that it is also possible to make use of a modified gas turbine, avoiding the need for the diesel as a pilot fuel (alternatively, biodiesel could be used).

The associated estimated total capital costs are given in Table 19.3.

These capital costs are then amortized over the life of the project for use system cost estimation. Plant life is assumed to be 20

Table 19.3 *Total capital investment cost estimates for the three plant modules in US$ million (2007 basis)*

Plant component	Capital cost (US$ million)
Pre-treatment plant cost	3.6
Pyrolysis plant cost	10.6
Power generation capital costs	9.6
Total capital costs	23.7

Source: chapter authors

Table 19.4 *Annual costs of raw pyrolysis liquids production in US$1000 yr^{-1} and variation with delivered feedstock cost*

| | Cost delivered (US$1000 t^{-1} (dry feedstock)) | | | |
	33	44	55	66
Pre-treatment capital cost (annualized)	367	367	367	367
Biomass pre-treatment operating cost	334	334	334	334
Cost pyrolysis capital	1080	1080	1080	1080
Feedstock cost	2310	3080	3851	4621
Utilities – water	3867	3867	3867	3867
Labour	900	900	900	900
Maintenance	423	423	423	423
Overhead	423	423	423	423
Annual liquids production cost	5624	6394	7164	7934

Source: chapter authors

years for 80 per cent availability with an interest rate of 12 per cent. Feedstock preparation costs are assumed to be US$11.35 t^{-1} to dry, comminute, size and store the maize stover prior to pyrolysis. The liquids production costs for different maize stover costs are given in Table 19.4.

This involves the annual use of 70,080t of feedstock yielding 55,000t of bio-oil (including the water from pyrolysis and that in the feedstock), costing between US$102 and US$144 t^{-1} of bio-oil.

Costs for electricity generation consist of fixed and variable costs. The cost components are given in Table 19.5, where the first six rows account for the electricity cost only. In order to obtain total cost, we add the costs from the bio-oil and arrive at an annual total cost. We also divide by the electricity output to obtain a cost per kilowatt hour. Costs between 9.7 and 12.2 US cents kWh^{-1} are above current (2008) US prices for energy; but credits for reductions in greenhouse gas emissions have not yet been applied.

The same cost structure was used for the scenario of a slow pyrolysis plant where we used exactly the same fixed pyrolysis cost for 1t of biomass. For the slow pyrolysis scenario, fixed and operating costs for biomass pre-treatment were reduced by 50 per cent; but the other operating costs were assumed to remain the same per tonne of feedstock. These costs would vary under use of alternative feedstocks depending upon feedstock properties such as water content.

The fixed and operating costs for the modules are transformed into a per tonne feedstock basis by dividing by 70,080 for use in the calculations below.

Selling energy

As mentioned above, the pyrolysis plant yields bio-oil, syngas and electricity. For this case study, the relative yields are assumed to be 70 per cent bio-oil (including the feedstock water) and 13 per cent syngas for fast pyrolysis, and 30 per cent bio-oil and 35 per cent syngas for slow pyrolysis (see Chapter 8).

In the following, an approach is developed to value these items. For simplicity and based on available data, we assumed for both the fast and the slow pyrolysis scenario that the bio-oil and syngas were used in plant operation and electricity generation. In turn, it was assumed that the fast pyrolysis plant produced 1.25MWh t^{-1} of feedstock, while slow pyrolysis produced 25 per cent of the

Table 19.5 *Costs of electricity production in US$1000 yr^{-1} and their variation with delivered feed-stock cost: net electrical output is 12.52MW$_e$ (427.3 US therms)*

	Cost delivered (US$1000 t^{-1} (dry feedstock))			
	33	44	55	66
Capital amortization	978	978	978	978
Labour cost	124	124	124	124
Utilities	1507	1507	1507	1507
Overheads	188	188	188	188
Maintenance	235	235	235	235
Total electricity	3339	3339	3339	3339
Bio-oil cost (from Table 19.4)	5624	6394	7164	7934
Total cost of electricity and bio-oil	9742	10,512	11,282	12,052
Electricity production cost (US cents kWh^{-1})	9.7	10.5	11.4	12.2

Source: chapter authors

electricity of fast pyrolysis or 0.31MWh t^{-1}. In terms of cost, we compute that fast pyrolysis-related generation encounters an operating cost of US$26.64 t^{-1} feedstock with a fixed cost of US$20.18 t^{-1}. For slow pyrolysis, we assumed that the costs per unit of electricity were the same, and since the slow pyrolysis electricity output was only 25 per cent of the electricity generated by fast pyrolysis that the costs of electricity produced by slow pyrolysis were 25 per cent of that produced by fast pyrolysis.

This information is summarized in Table 19.6. At a sale price of US$80 MWh^{-1}, we obtain the sales levels shown in Table 19.6 and observe that both fast and slow pyrolysis lose money based only on energy sales. This may explain why the practice is not in widespread use. However, in order to look at final profitability, one needs to also consider biochar and GHGs as a source of income along with other chemicals. The biochar and GHG aspects are evaluated in subsequent sections.

In general, we could have tried to value the bio-oil using a proxy-products approach as an equivalent to a conventional product. Even though the use of market prices is preferable for the commodities, the infant nature of the pyrolysis oils markets precludes this approach. For example, one could assume that the value of the bio-oil is proportional to the energy content and, thus, might be approximately 25 per cent of the heating oil price.

Net saleable biochar

In this analysis we assume that some of the biochar is used to supply energy for the fast pyrolysis plant, while all of it is sold in the slow pyrolysis plant. In particular, in the fast pyrolysis plant we assume the net yield is 0.0445t t^{-1} feedstock, while for slow pyrolysis we assume 0.35t t^{-1} feedstock.

Biochar as a soil amendment

Lehmann et al (2003) found that the application of biochar to soil led to a reduction of N leaching by 60 per cent and increases of crop productivity by 38 to 45 per cent, which we assume to translate into a 20 per cent saving in fertilizer and 10 per cent savings in irrigation and seeds. Others have found yield increases of up to 140 per cent on poor soils under recommended fertilization (Lehmann and Rondon, 2006).

Table 19.6 *Returns and costs (US$ t⁻¹ feedstock) as well as biochar yields (t t⁻¹ feedstock) for fast and slow pyrolysis as value items are applied*

	Fast	Slow
Feedstock cost	−$59.44	−$59.44
Pyrolysis cost (modules I and II)	−$46.82	−$42.05
Generating cost (module III)	−$43.26	−$10.81
Electricity value	$100.00	$25.00
Net margin (electricity only)	−$49.52	−$87.30
Biochar yield	0.045	0.350
Biochar value	$2.00	$15.75
Biochar haul cost	$0.39	$3.07
Net margin (electricity + biochar)	−$47.91	−$74.63
GHG value	$3.29	$4.55
Net margin all	−$44.62	−$70.08

Source: chapter authors

Since we are using US Corn Belt data, we neglect the irrigation savings (since irrigation is not prevalent there) but assume that biochar applications lead to a 5 per cent yield increase of maize at an application rate of 5t ha⁻¹. For an average baseline maize grain yield of 4.07t ha⁻¹ selling for US$137.50 t⁻¹, the yield increase is US$60 ha⁻¹ yr⁻¹. Nutrients, lime and seed are also replaced. The value of that replacement based on application rates under Iowa crop budgets (Duffy and Smith, 2008) amounts to a saving of US$73.4 ha⁻¹ when biochar is applied. The net value across yield increases and input savings realized for crop production then calculates to US$143.4 ha⁻¹.

The gains from biochar have been shown to persist somewhat permanently after the application as the biochar remains in the soil without rapid degradation. We thus treat this as an annuity capitalized forever at 5 per cent and multiply by 20 to obtain the net present value. However, we assume this gain only occurs the first time that the biochar is applied and that the biochar can be applied ten more times without further gain. Consequently, the net gain calculates to twice (equivalent to 20/10) the annual gain with a

net present value of US$286.80 ha⁻¹. We also assume based on examination of manure application costs that the application of biochar to soil would cost US$20 t⁻¹ for a net value of US$236.80 ha⁻¹. This calculates to a biochar value of US$47.36 t⁻¹ at the field with an assumed application rate of 5t ha⁻¹ or US$32.94 t⁻¹ at the plant after hauling costs are deducted. This value is below the approximate combustion value of the biochar as of this writing (Central Appalachian coal in August 2008 was worth about US$139.30 for a short tonne, which contains 12,500MmBtu t⁻¹, while we assume biochar has approximately 4900MmBtu t⁻¹ or 39.2 per cent of that of the coal, making its combustion value approximately US$54.73 t⁻¹); but the price of coal has escalated radically in recent times (coal having been about US$45 in December 2007, yielding a biochar combustion value of US$17.70 t⁻¹).

The next step is to determine the proportion of land to which biochar can be applied, which varies in different assessments between a few tonnes to several tens of tonnes without universally applicable recommendation (Lehmann and Rondon, 2006). We set the biochar application rate at 5t ha⁻¹. The pyrolysis plants use crop residues from 19,600ha and after a biochar shrinkage of 5 per cent due to less than perfect recovery, conveyance, application, fire and other losses, the pyrolysis plants yield enough biochar annually to treat 3 per cent of the land under fast pyrolysis and 23.75 per cent under slow pyrolysis. (A major issue that this chapter will not try to resolve is that we assume this gain is repeated year after year with no change in hauling cost. In actuality, the biochar may be applied to different fields – even those of other crops or on fields without residue harvest – that are successively further away and may also be applied up to some maximum holding point for the soil. It is also possible that the second application enhances the gains.) Therefore, the value of applying biochar to the land where the residue is harvested calculates to US$7.15 ha^{-1} under fast pyrolysis and US$56.24 ha^{-1} under slow pyrolysis. This amounts to US$2.00 t^{-1} feedstock for fast pyrolysis and US$15.75 t^{-1} for slow.

Hauling biochar to the field

When biochar is applied as a soil supplement, it must be hauled back to the field. In this case, we assume an identical hauling distance to that obtained when calculating the cost for moving the feedstock and similar cost structure, but moving only the amount of the biochar. We also assume a different fleet of trucks is involved employing different handling procedures to control the combustibility of the biochar. Thus, we do not factor in backhauling. Rather, we charge US$1.38 km^{-1} for a round trip and also increase the fixed cost per truckload by 50 per cent. This yields a hauling cost estimate of US$8.78 t^{-1} of biochar when using fast or slow pyrolysis. This biochar hauling cost amounts to US$0.39 t^{-1} of the raw maize residue feedstock under fast pyrolysis and US$3.07 t^{-1} of feedstock when using slow pyrolysis (note this may not be appropriate as the fast pyrolysis biochar bulk density is likely much lower than that of the slow pyrolysis biochar).

In turn, and as summarized in Table 19.6, after adding in the value of the biochar offset by its hauling cost we find that there is a net US$47.91 loss for fast pyrolysis and a loss of US$74.63 for slow pyrolysis.

GHG offset

The net GHG effect is another possible component of value. The pyrolysis with biochar prospect is emitting GHGs based on fossil fuel use during residue harvest, as well as the C consequences of residue removal, nutrient replacement, feedstock hauling, feedstock transformation, biochar hauling and biochar application. It is GHG reducing in that it employs electricity generation from a renewable source, recycling C rather than emitting the C stored in fossil fuels, along with biochar-induced reductions in nutrient use and increases in sequestration.

Residue removal and sequestration loss. In terms of the original fields from where the residue is removed, we assume that the residue removed contains 45 per cent C, of which 2 per cent is taken from the sequestered soil stock by its removal. Thus, we have 0.09t C sequestration reduction per tonne of crop residue removed. Converting these values to CO_2, this results in a loss of 0.033t CO_2 t^{-1} removed. We also assume, based on Kim et al (2008), that this is an impermanent form of C and is only worth 50 per cent of more permanent forms.

Nutrient replacement. Crop residue removal may also cause an increased need for nutrients such as N, P and K, as discussed earlier. This causes additional GHG emissions in the manufacture and use of fertilizers. In order to estimate these impacts, we used the Greenhouse Gases, Regulated Emissions, and Energy Use in Transportation (GREET) assumptions for the GHG releases involved in manufacturing these inputs (Wang, 1999; Argonne National Lab, 2006; Wang et al, 2007), plus the amounts for nitrous oxide (N_2O) emissions calculated after IPCC (2006). This results in increased emissions of 0.019t CO_2 equivalent (CO_2e) when 1t of residue is removed to replace the nutrients therein. We also used the GREET assumption of 0.011t CO_2e t^{-1} of maize residue for fossil fuel emissions during harvest collection and movement to the farm gate.

Feedstock and biochar transport. Hauling emissions also need to be factored in and we did this assuming that a diesel-powered truck was used travelling 2.133km L^{-1} diesel. Overall, hauling calculated to a total travel distance of 480,000km along with 1440km for biochar under fast pyrolysis and 7.960km under slow pyrolysis. This amounted to 0.0021t and 0.0024t CO_2e t^{-1} feedstock removed for fast and slow pyrolysis, respectively.

Plant operation. Fossil fuel is also used in operating the pyrolysis plant. We assume that the operation requires 217t of natural gas and 586t of diesel, with about two-thirds of the 15 per cent yield of biochar burned for fuelling the plant and the slow pyrolysis syngas used for fuel. Using GREET emission factors, we arrive at an estimate that plant fossil use generates an emission level of 0.33t CO_2e t^{-1} feedstock. We reduce the diesel use to 25 per cent for the slow plant since it is used in the generation phase and only 25 per cent of the power is generated under slow pyrolysis.

Fossil fuel offset. Biofuels are recycling C. Namely, as crops grow they absorb CO_2 from the atmosphere and accumulate the C in the body of the plant. At the time of combustion, this C is released. Consequently, the emissions from using the bio-oil and syngas in generating biochar and electricity are recycled C that is not a net addition (as would be the case if fossil fuels were used releasing C

long stored in the ground). As a consequence, we credit for the C that would have been used to generate the electricity yielded by the plant (see Chapter 18). We assume that the electricity replaces electricity that would have been generated in a coal-fired plant. Under the GREET assumptions and the electricity levels given above, this yields an offset rate of 0.765t CO_2 t^{-1} feedstock under fast pyrolysis and 0.191t CO_2 t^{-1} under slow.

Reduced inputs. Application of biochar also reduces input needs at the farm level as a consequence of improved nutrient use (see Chapters 5 and 15), saving the emissions from making and applying nutrients, as well as the N_2O emissions arising from nitrification and denitrification that derive from fertilized fields (see Chapter 13). We compute the saved emissions from this process as 0.004t CO_2e t^{-1} feedstock for fast and 0.028t CO_2e t^{-1} for slow pyrolysis.

Sequestration enhancement. Biochar resides in the soil for a long period of time (see Chapter 11) and consists of approximately 75 per cent C. As such, biochar sequesters the C held in the soil in a manner that overcomes many of the permanence and volatility issues that commonly arise in criticisms of biological sequestration possibilities (see discussion in West and Post, 2002; Post et al, 2004; Smith et al, 2007; Kim et al, 2008). Thus, we credit the total C content of the biochar as a sequestration offset and this amounts to a credit of 0.122t CO_2e t^{-1} feedstock for fast and 0.963t CO_2e t^{-1} for slow pyrolysis.

Net balance. The balance of all C credits is reflected in Table 19.7 and equals a net offset of 0.823t CO_2e t^{-1} of feedstock for fast pyrolysis and 1.113t CO_2e t^{-1} for slow pyrolysis. This amounts to 108 per cent of the coal equivalent emissions for the electricity generated under fast pyrolysis and 595 per cent for

Table 19.7 *Estimated GHG offsets (in CO$_2$e t^{-1} of feedstock) for fast and slow pyrolysis*

Category	Discount	Fast pyrolysis	Slow pyrolysis
Collect feedstock on farm		0.011	0.011
Haul feedstock and biochar		0.002	0.003
Replace lost nutrients on farm		0.007	0.007
Save fuel in tillage		−0.018	−0.018
Operate pyrolysis		0.033	0.033
Reduce nutrients used on farms		−0.004	−0.028
Credit for displacement of coal electricity		−0.765	−0.191
Sequestration lost due to residue removal	0.5	0.033	0.033
Sequestration gain from biochar		−0.122	−0.963
Net GHG effect		−0.823	−1.113

Source: chapter authors

slow pyrolysis. Therefore, the offset efficiency is greater than the power offset due to the sequestration and nutrient offset elements.

C leakage. Also of significance, the feedstock needed for pyrolysis is not dependent upon food crops. Such competition has been the subject of growing recent concern in the context of ethanol and biodiesel production, particularly in terms of leakage in the form of international replacement of lost marketed production and C debts (Fargione et al, 2008; Searchinger et al, 2008). Rather, under pyrolysis, less competition may well exist as by-product residues can be used. In small-scale applications, the heat produced from the pyrolysis unit could also provide energy for on-farm use, such as heat and electricity for lighting, fans, refrigerators, milking machines, etc. No estimates are provided here for this effect.

GHG value. Finally, let us turn our attention to the value of the GHG offset. We can use contemporary prices of about US$4 t^{-1} CO$_2$e on the Chicago Climate Exchange or about US$35 on the European Exchange as indicators of potential future value. We use US$4 in our summary calculations below and consider higher values in the sensitivity analysis section.

Totality of value

Table 19.8 summarizes the calculations in the above sections, yielding a total estimate of value. This indicates for the numerous assumptions made in this chapter that the fast and slow pyrolysis power plants are both unprofitable under current conditions, with the slow plant being less so, largely due to its higher value energy sales, with the biochar value also making a difference to some extent. An investigation of sensitivity to a number of the above assumptions is pursued in the next section.

Table 19.8 *Economic assumption and results summary with economic results reported per tonne of feedstock*

	Fast pyrolysis	Slow pyrolysis
Main assumptions		
Size of plant (L yr^{-1})	70,080	70,080
Yield bio-oil (%)	70	30
Yield syngas (%)	15	35
Yield biochar (%)	15	35
Land used (ha)	19,600	19,600
Average feedstock hauling distance (km)	14.8	14.8
Results (US\$ t^{-1} feedstock)		
Cost of feedstock	−\$59.44	−\$59.44
Value of energy created	\$100.00	\$25.00
Value of biochar	\$2.00	\$15.75
Biochar hauling cost	−\$0.39	−\$3.07
Fixed cost of facility	−\$34.13	−\$21.28
Operating cost of facility	−\$55.95	−\$31.58
GHG market effect	\$3.29	\$4.55
Net value	−\$44.62	−\$70.08

Source: chapter authors

Sensitivity analysis

The above assumption-laden procedure requires a sensitivity analysis to help draw inferences about how critical various factors are. Several investigations were performed, leading to the following results given that all other elements are held constant:

- Fast pyrolysis is profitable as long as the electricity price rises above US\$115 MWh^{-1} while slow pyrolysis requires a price above US\$304 MWh^{-1}. Higher energy prices clearly favour fast pyrolysis.
- Fast pyrolysis becomes profitable when the GHG price is above US\$58 t^{-1} CO_2e, which is substantially above the level of the European price (30 Euros t^{-1} in late August 2008 or US\$41 t^{-1} CO_2e), meaning that European implementations are closer to being profitable than those in

the US if the biochar and GHG incomes can be captured. The CO_2e price would need to rise above US\$71 t^{-1}, or more than 25 per cent above the European price, before slow pyrolysis is profitable.

- There are a wide range of experimental findings on the yield implications of biochar application. We assumed that biochar application increased crop yield by 5 per cent on fields to which it was applied and only led to gains once. Under a more substantial increase of 43 per cent, slow pyrolysis becomes profitable. Fast pyrolysis gains at a much slower rate, requiring a 193 per cent yield increase to become more profitable.
- If biochar prices are high, then the value particularly of slow pyrolysis increases. In other words, when the biochar value exceeds US\$246 t^{-1}, slow pyrolysis

becomes profitable (Chapter 9 reports values in the neighbourhood of US$450 t^{-1}; but this is in a new market and the large quantities arising under large-scale production typically lower such values substantially). Fast pyrolysis requires a value in excess of US$1047 t^{-1}.

- The capital costs of construction are rather uncertain as are, to a lesser extent, the operating costs. Lowering the total plant fixed plus operating cost by 49 per cent or more makes fast pyrolysis profitable. While slow pyrolysis becomes more profitable, the feedstock alone exceeds the value of products under base assumptions and no pure operating cost change can make it profitable.
- It is possible that feedstocks will be available that can be obtained for tipping fees or under other arrangements. If we reduce the feedstock costs, both pyrolysis options become more profitable. For fast pyrolysis, feedstock costs would need to decrease to US$14 or less to be profitable. In the case of slow pyrolysis, this alone cannot make the prospect profitable. Rather, a US$11 t^{-1} fee (a subsidy for operations) would be needed to be profitable.

Omitted factors

The biochar/pyrolysis possibility is one of several ways in which biomass could be used to achieve net reductions in GHG emissions. If cellulosic conversion to ethanol becomes practical and profitable, then this process would compete for biomass feedstocks. There is also the possibility of using crop residues to generate electricity directly. In addition, both biochar production and residue-based generation could be coupled with the CO_2 capture and geologic sequestration. Even though none of these pathways have been implemented at a large scale, the biochar pathway uses technologies that are likely to be available in a relatively short timeframe and, thus, may be an important current action. Cellulosic conversion to ethanol and geologic carbon dioxide capture and storage (CCS) are currently not available.

If the value of crop residue becomes high enough, other sources of biomass, such as switchgrass, fast-growing poplars, logging residues and milling residues, will become available. Future studies should include alter-native feedstocks, as well as the possibility of multiple feedstocks. Additionally, while many factors were considered above, several other factors, such as changes in erosion, water use, water quality and altered air pollution emissions under biofuels versus fossil fuels, were not covered and warrant closer attention in future studies.

A final omitted item meriting discussion involves the nature and dynamic of the crop–biochar production relationship. Very simplifying assumptions were made above on yield increases/nutrient decreases in association with biochar application. It was also assumed that once the biochar was applied, it would permanently enhance yields and lower input requirements. Furthermore, after the first application, it was assumed that no more gains could be achieved. These are undoubtedly not entirely accurate assumptions, and future work might include diminishing returns to applications and dynamics of applications and responses.

Conclusions

Pyrolysis and associated biochar are valuable in terms of nutrient reductions, yield increases, bioenergy products and GHG offsets. These are partly offset by the costs of production, hauling and processing, along with some increases in GHG emissions. An approach was developed for analysing the profitability of such a case and implemented for maize residue.

On balance in our maize residue case study (which is assumption laden, relying on highly uncertain data), we found fast and slow pyrolysis to be currently unprofitable. We find these results particularly sensitive to crop yield enhancement, plant fixed/operating costs, and GHG and energy prices. We do find the value of biochar applied to soil is close to its value as an energy source. However, under current European levels of GHG offset prices, biochar use as a soil amendment in agriculture already exceeds its combustion value.

References

Argonne National Laboratory (2006) *Fuel Cycle Assessment of Selected Bioethanol Production Pathways in the United States*, Report, Argonne National Laboratory, Chicago, IL

Aston University (2002) *Development of Advanced Fast Pyrolysis Processes for Power and Heat*, JORS-CT97-0197, Final report submitted to the European Commission, Brussels

Baum, E. and Weitner, S. (2006) *BIOCHAR Application on Soils and Cellulosic Ethanol Production*, Clean Air Task Force State Climate Network, Boston, MA

Bridgwater, A. V. and Peacocke, G. V. C. (2002) 'Fast pyrolysis processes for biomass', *Renewable and Sustainable Energy Reviews*, vol 4, pp1–73

Bridgwater, T. (2005) 'Fast pyrolysis based biorefineries', Paper presented at the Annual Meeting of the American Chemical Society, Washington, DC, 31 August 2005, http://membership.acs.org/P/PETR/2005-Biorefineries/Presentation-10.pdf

Caputo, A. C., Palumbo, M., Pelagagge, P. M. and Scacchia, F. (2005) 'Economics of biomass energy utilization in combustion and gasification plants: Effects of logistic variables', *Biomass and Bioenergy*, vol 28, pp35–51

Czernik, S. and Bridgwater, A. V. (2004) 'Overview of applications of biomass fast pyrolysis oil', *Energy and Fuels*, vol 18, pp590–598

Demirbas, A. and Arin, G. (2002) 'An overview of biomass pyrolysis', *Energy Sources*, vol 24, pp471–482

Duffy, M. and Smith, D. (2008) *Estimated Costs of Crop Production in Iowa – 2008*, Report, Iowa State University, IA, www.extension.iastate.edu/AGDM/crops/html/a1-20.html

Fargione, J., Hill, J., Tilman, D., Polasky, S. and Hawthorne, P. (2008) 'Land clearing and the biofuel carbon debt', *Science*, vol 319, pp1235–1238

Fife, L. and Miller, W. (1999) *Rice Straw Feedstock Joint Venture, Rice Straw Feedstock Supply Study for Colusa County, California*, Western Regional Biomass Energy Program, Lincoln, NE

French, B. C. (1960) 'Some considerations in estimating assembly cost functions for agricultural processing operations', *Journal of Farm Economics*, vol 62, pp767–778

IPCC (Intergovernmental Panel on Climate Change) (2006) *Guidelines for National Greenhouse Gas Inventories*, IPCC, Cambridge University Press, Cambridge, UK, www.ipcc–nggip.iges.or.jp/public/2006gl/index.htm

Kim, M.-K., McCarl, B. A. and Murray, B. C. (2008) 'Permanence discounting for land-based carbon sequestration', *Ecological Economics*, vol 64, pp763–769

Lehmann, J. and Rondon, M. (2006) 'Biochar soil

management on highly-weathered soils in the humid tropics', in N. Uphoff (ed) *Biological Approaches to Sustainable Soil Systems*, CRC Press, Boca Raton, US, pp517–530

Lehmann, J., da Silva Jr., J. P., Steiner, C., Nehls, T., Zech, W. and Glaser, B. (2003) 'Nutrient availability and leaching in an archaeological Anthrosol and a Ferralsol of the Central Amazon basin: Fertilizer, manure and charcoal amendments', *Plant and Soil*, vol 249, pp343–357

McCarl, B. A., Adams, D. M., Alig, R. J. and Chmelik, J. T. (2000) 'Analysis of biomass fueled electrical power plants: Implications in the agricultural and forestry sectors', *Annals of Operations Research*, vol 94, pp37–55

NSWMA (2005) *NSWMA's 2005 Tip Fee Survey*, NSWMA Research Bulletin 05–3, http://wastec.isproductions.net/webmodules/webarticles/articlefiles/478–Tipping%20Fee%20Bulletin%202005.pdf, accessed 31 August 2008

Peacocke, G. V. C., Bridgwater, A. V. and Brammer, J. G. (2006) 'Techno-economic assessment of power production from the Wellman Process Engineering Ltd and BTG fast pyrolysis processes', in A. V. Bridgwater and D. G. B. Boocock (eds) *Science in Thermal and Chemical Biomass Conversion*, CPL Press, vol 2, pp1785–1802

Perlack, R. D., Wright, L. L., Turhollow, A., Graham, R. L., Stokes, B. and Erbach, D. C. (2005) *Biomass as Feedstock for a Bioenergy and Bioproducts Industry: The Technical Feasibility of a Billion-Tonne Annual Supply*, US Department of Energy and US Department of Agriculture, Forest Service, Washington, DC, US

Polagye, B. L., Hodgson, K. T. and Malte, P. C. (2007) 'An economic analysis of bio-energy options using thinnings from overstocked forests', *Biomass and Bioenergy*, vol 31, pp105–125

Post, W. M., Izaurralde, R. C., Jastrow, J., McCarl, B. A., Amonette, J. E., Bailey, V. L., Jardine, P. M., West, T. O. and Zhou, J. (2004) 'Enhancement of carbon sequestration in US soils', *Bioscience*, vol 54, pp895–908

Read, A. D., Phillips, P. and Robinson, G. (2008) 'Landfill as a future waste management option in England: The view of landfill operators', *Geographical Journal*, vol 164, pp55–66

Ringer, M., Putsche, V. and Scahill, J. (2006) *Large-Scale Pyrolysis Oil Production: A Technology Assessment and Economic Analysis*, National Renewable Energy Laboratory, NREL/TP-510-37779, www.nrel.gov/docs/fy07osti/37779.pdf

Searchinger, T., Heimlich, R., Houghton, R. A., Dong, F., Elobeid, A., Fabiosa, J., Tokgoz, S., Hayes, D. and Yu T.-H. (2008) 'Use of US croplands for biofuels increases greenhouse gases through emissions from land-use change', *Science*, vol 319, pp1238–1240

Smith, G. A., McCarl, B. A., Li, C. S., Reynolds, J. H., Hammerschlag, R., Sass, R. L., Parton, W. J., Ogle, S. M., Paustian, K., Holtkamp, J. A. and Barbour, W. (2007) in Z. Willey and W. L. Chameides (eds) *Harnessing Farms and Forests in the Low-Carbon Economy: How to Create, Measure, and Verify Greenhouse Gas Offsets*, Duke University Press, Durham, NC

USDA (US Department of Agriculture) (2008) *Forest Residue Trucking Simulator (Version 5)*, US Forest Service, www.srs.fs.usda.gov/forestops/biomass.htm, accessed 20 May 2008

Wang, M. (1999) *GREET 1.5 – Transportation Fuel-Cycle Model, Volume 1: Methodology, Development, Use, and Results*, ANL/ESD-39, vol 1, Center for Transportation Research, Argonne National Laboratory, Argonne, IL

Wang, M, Wu, M. and Hong, H. (2007) 'Life-cycle energy and greenhouse gas emission impacts of different maize ethanol plant types', *Environmental Research Letters*, vol 2, article number 024001

West, T. O. and Post, W. M. (2002) 'Soil organic carbon sequestration rates by tillage and crop rotation', *Soil Science Society of America Journal*, vol 66, pp1930–1946

Wright, M. M., Brown, R. C. and Boateng, A. A. (2008) 'Distributed processing of biomass to bio-oil for subsequent production of Fischer-Tropsch liquids', *Biofuels, Bioprocessing, and Biorefining*, vol 2, pp229–238

Zabaniotou, A. and Ioannidou, O. (2008) 'Evaluation of utilization of maize stalks for energy and carbon material production by using rapid pyrolysis at high temperature', *Fuel*, vol 87, pp834–843

20

Socio-economic Assessment and Implementation of Small-scale Biochar Projects

Stephen Joseph

Introduction

Chapter 19 evaluates the financial and environmental costs and benefits of operating large-scale pyrolysis plant at purpose-built central locations and at industrial or waste management sites. This chapter, which should be read in conjunction with Chapter 19, also explores the financial and environmental costs and benefits of pyrolysis technology, but at the household, farm and village level. It discusses the social costs and benefits and local use of the biochar and syngas produced.

In this context, and particularly for small-scale projects in rural areas or in developing countries, the methods used for designing, analysing and evaluating programmes and projects are very different from those used for industrial-scale plants. This chapter takes this into account by including outline descriptions of project design and analysis methodologies as essential precursors to the final evaluation of project costs and benefits.

Perhaps the most important feature of this treatment is that it emphasizes the need to develop programmes that are people centred, responsive and participatory (Schneider, 1999), that are economically, institutionally and environmentally sustainable, and that involve partnership between all stakeholders, including users of the biochar, producers, researchers, extension personnel, government at all levels and donor organizations (Chambers and Blackburn, 1996; Carney, 2002).

At present, there are few such analyses of biochar projects. However, socio-economic studies in related areas can assist the development of suitable methodologies for biochar technology transfer programmes (Smith et al, 1993). They include the introduction of improved biomass cook stoves (Natarajan, 1999), kilns and furnaces, and improved charcoal production techniques (Limmeechokchai and Chawana, 2003). Socio-economic assessments of renewable energy projects, and of improved agricultural and forestry techniques (Upton, 1996), also provide specific insights.

The chapter is divided into two main parts. The first introduces relevant concepts and presents a framework for project design and socio-economic analysis; the second provides a brief case study on the introduction of improved charcoal kilns and low-emissions cooking stoves that also produce biochar as a soil amendment.

Developing a methodology

Developing a framework

Socio-economic analysis at the household, farm or community level involves not just the quantification of the financial impact of biochar technology, but also the broader social, cultural, political and environmental impacts (Hanmer et al, 1997). International efforts have focused on developing a common project framework for aid agencies, and international development agencies have been supporting the development of a common methodological framework whose aim is to ensure projects increase the sustainability of local livelihoods and the security of food, energy and soil health (Davies, 1996). An appropriate methodological framework has been developed by the Sustainable Livelihoods Group (Carney, 1999), as shown in Figure 20.1 below.

This framework is designed to improve our understanding of the livelihoods of lower-income groups who lack the access to resources that is common to middle- and

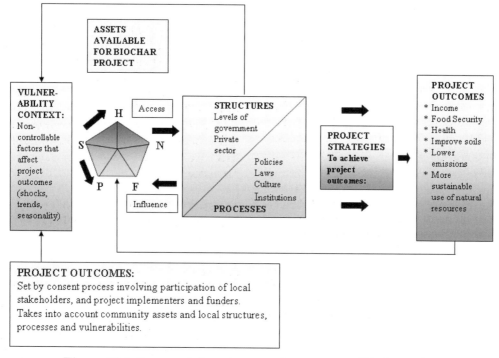

Figure 20.1 *Framework for socio-economic assessment of biochar projects*

Note: H= human capital; S = social capital; N= natural capital; P = physical capital; F = financial capital.

Source: Stephen Joseph

upper-income groups (DFID, 2001). It is now widely used, in part or as a whole, by non-governmental organizations (NGOs), the World Bank and governments (Robb, 1999) for assessing and formulating projects that target rural households and industries.

DFID (2001) notes two important characteristics of this type of framework: it is non-linear and it is people centred. In particular, it:

- provides a checklist of important issues and sketches out the ways in which these link to each other;
- draws attention to core influences and processes; and
- emphasizes the multiple interactions between the various factors that affect livelihoods.

The arrows within the framework indicate different types of relationships, all of which are highly dynamic. None of the arrows implies direct causality, although all imply a certain level of influence.

Figure 20.1 is an adaptation of the DFID framework. The pentagon at the centre of the framework represents the local assets that may be utilized to introduce biochar technology (Moser, 1998). In developing the framework, it is acknowledged that there are many factors that may affect the successful introduction of a technology (Hanmer, 1998). Some, such as droughts and wars, are not easy to predict. Others, such as government regulations, are either stated explicitly (laws) or are implicitly understood by the local community (Davies, 1996). Understanding these factors can assist in both designing a project and in assessing its viability. Project objectives, and strategies to meet these objectives, should be derived from a consensus of all participants as to what is achievable with the given resource base, community needs, potential vulnerabilities, and external and internal structures and processes (Holland and Blackburn, 1998).

The framework can then be used to assist in determining what data should be collected, how it should be collected and how the inevitable complexities can be understood.

Using the framework to collect the data needed for a socio-economic assessment

Ideally, baseline data collection is carried out before the introduction of a new technology and agricultural practice (Ashley et al, 1999). Impact assessment is then based on comparing the system at the end of project implementation with the baseline data gathered before project commencement (Jenkins, 1999). However, if a programme is already under way, socio-economic evaluation should start with an assessment of the existing physical, economic, political, social, cultural and environmental systems.

Assessment of vulnerability context

Many factors affect the lives of village people, farmers and small-scale businesses. When developing a biochar industry, data must be collected in the three categories summarized in Table 20.1. It should be noted that not all shocks will have negative impacts. For example, a sudden increase in the price of fertilizer may provide an incentive for farmers to experiment with biochar.

Assessment of different types of capital: Human, social, natural, physical and financial

Human capital assessment quantifies the skills, knowledge, ability to labour and health of people and enterprises that may directly or indirectly participate in a development project. Data is collected on the amount and quality of labour available, which will vary according to household, farm, enterprise size, skill levels, leadership potential, and health status.

Social capital includes networks and connectedness, membership of more formal-

Table 20.1 *Classes of data to determine vulnerability context*

Trends	Shocks	Seasonality
Population	Human health	Prices
Resource (including conflict)	Natural (e.g. floods, droughts	Production
National and international economy	and severe storms)	Health
Governance (including politics)	Economic (increases in fuel	Employment opportunities
Technological	and fertilizer prices)	
	Conflicts	
	Crop/livestock health	

Source: Stephen Joseph

ized groups (often entailing adherence to mutually agreed or commonly accepted rules, norms and sanctions); and relationships of trust, reciprocity and exchange that facilitate cooperation, reduce transaction costs and may provide the basis for informal safety nets amongst the poor (DFID, 2001). While an understanding of social capital is important for good project design, collecting and analysing data on social capital is difficult and requires considerable time and interpersonal skills.

Natural capital covers the stocks and flows of natural resources (forests, fields, marine life/wildlife, water quality, air quality) that may be required for livelihoods, and from which services such as nutrient cycling, erosion protection and waste assimilation are derived (DFID, 2007). Data will be needed on how, in combination with other assets, natural capital is used to sustain a biochar project and create value for the participants.

Physical capital comprises the basic infrastructure (e.g. transport, secure shelters and buildings, water and sanitation, clean affordable energy and access to communications) and producer goods (tools and equipment used in productive activities) needed to support a particular productive activity (DFID, 2007). It is important to determine if the infrastructure available can actually support the introduction and utilization of biochar technology.

Financial capital includes available stocks such as cash, bank deposits or liquid assets such as livestock and jewellery, and regular inflows of money from sources such as pensions or other transfers from the state, as well as remittances. This information is essential when trying to determine what level of credit or other financial support is required to ensure that local businesses or households can afford the biochar technology (Ledgerwood, 1999).

Assessment of structures and processes

The potential impact of local and national (and, in some cases, international) institutions, organizations, policies and legislation on biochar programmes needs to be ascertained. These may determine the ease with which the biochar programme can gain access to capital and to extension services. It is important to ascertain the different rights and responsibilities between the project participants and institutions and organizations that are directly or indirectly involved (e.g. departments of agriculture, energy or industry, and environmental protection agencies).

The framework (see Figure 20.1) includes feedback loops. There is direct feedback from processes and structures to the *vulnerability context*. Processes (policies), established and implemented through structures, affect trends both directly (e.g. fiscal policy and economic trends) and indirectly (e.g. health policy and population trends) (Carney, 1999). They can also help to cushion the impact of external shocks (e.g. policy on drought relief). Other types of processes are also important, such as well-functioning markets that help to reduce the effects of seasonality by facilitating inter-area trade (DFID, 2001).

Institutions can restrict people's ability to adopt biochar innovations – for example in rigid caste systems (Barry, 1998). More common are policies and regulations that affect the attractiveness of particular livelihood choices through their impact upon expected returns (Ashley et al, 1999). Responsive political structures that implement pro-poor policies, including extending social services into areas in which the poor live, can significantly increase people's sense of well-being. They can promote awareness of rights and a sense of self-control. They can also help to reduce vulnerability through the provision of social safety nets (DFID, 2007).

Tools for collecting and analysing data

Small-scale projects are assessed using both quantitative and qualitative methods (Marsland et al, 1998). These are mentioned briefly with references for further reading. Different tools (Rennie and Singh, 1995) are available to collect and analyse baseline data; but participation of all stakeholders (e.g. households, farmers and charcoal-makers) is essential for effective data collection (Booth et al, 1998).

Macro-economic analysis is important in setting the overall economic context within which a biochar project operates (Agenor and Montiel, 1999). It includes appraisal of how monetary, fiscal, trade and exchange rate conditions affect the price of the goods needed to produce biochar (Ellis, 1992). Similarly, movements in interest rates that can affect the ability of a project to repay loans should be studied. Review of secondary published macro-economic data is, thus, an essential component of the analysis.

In contrast, micro-economic analysis is used to assess decision-making processes within households, farms and small businesses (Bebbington, 1999). Many micro-economic techniques are available for assessing the costs and benefits of new technologies to farmers (Gittinger, 1982) and small industry (Brent, 1990). Relevant examples of their applications include stove programmes (Natarajan, 1999) and renewable energy projects (IT Consultants, 2002). Amongst these techniques, cost-benefit

Table 20.2 *Summary of all impact indicators for the biochar technologies considered*

Environmental impact indicators	Social impact indicators	Economic costs (with assumptions)
Emissions (air, climate change and water)	Community benefits	Resource extraction
Noise	Energy diversification and security of supply	Resource and biochar transportation
Visual	Employment	Materials processing
Effect of biodiversity, soil health, wildlife, erosion, local hydrology	Health	Establishment of crops
Landscape	Political and governance	Cultivation of crops
Planning and costs	Institutional	Processing of crops
Recreation, loss of agricultural land	Tourism	Biochar manufacture
Energy payback		Plant construction, decommissioning

Source: based on IT Consultants (2002)

analysis (CBA) is perhaps the most powerful tool for deciding between alternate strategies; recently, it has included impact indicators of renewable energy technologies (IT Consultants, 2002). Table 20.2 is an example of how these are applied to biochar technology.

To gain a better understanding of the relationship between the livelihoods of the potential project participants and their environment, the above indicators can be expanded by using an environmental checklist procedure (Donnelly et al, 1998). Examples of checklist questions include the following:

- Are forests and fields being degraded, and if so, why? Could biochar help to prevent this? What role do policies and institutions play in that degradation (Hughes and Dalal-Clayton, 1998)?
- What is the contribution of pollution (such as smoke inhalation from stoves) to the ability of women to participate in the introduction of the biochar technology?
- What is the risk that severe floods or droughts could have on the cost of implementing a biochar programme? How much biochar may be removed by floods or strong winds?

Where possible, costs associated with the current environmental issues are determined before ecological economics can be used to analyse the data (Therivel and Partidario, 1996; Daly and Farley, 2004). Similarly, analysis can be undertaken at various scales with different institutions and stakeholder groups to determine their roles in the biochar programmes (Harriss et al, 1995). It is usually built around checklists (DFID, 2001) and seeks to understand the nature of the external environment and the impact of different factors within it, including:

- whether responsibilities (e.g. for service delivery or environmental management)

are sensibly allocated within government and between government and the private sector (including local people) (Mehta et al, 1999);
- roles and strategies: whether organizational structures match functions, and the nature of interaction between organizations and their clients at different levels (North, 1991);
- leadership, management style, incentives (financial and otherwise), organizational culture and their implications for change;
- management systems and their impact upon performance (using key baseline indicators) (Rew and Brustinov, 1998);
- human resource requirements and constraints (DFID, 2001); and
- financial performance and prospects for viability.

Gender analysis can be used to determine the dynamics of gender differences in relation to social relations, division of labour, access to resources, decision-making, networks and specific needs. These are particularly important for assessing the likelihood of conflict between women and men. For example, women may use the biochar stove, but men have the financial means to buy it.

Checklists can also be used to analyse the impact of local governance on biochar projects (Beckhart and Harris, 1987). Suitable questions may include:

- Is political power exercised fairly? If not, how could it affect the project (Hyden, 1998)?
- How efficient, effective and accessible are agricultural, forestry and industry extension workers and are they willing to learn new skills and participate in the project (Hobley and Shields, 2000)?
- Are government organizations that must interface with biochar projects honest, efficient, effective and accessible?
- Could issues of enforcement of basic human, legal and property rights result in

barriers to successful implementation of the project?

The challenge in governance analysis is to differentiate between those factors 'controlled' by the structures closest to communities (e.g. local governments) and those variables determined by higher, and usually more remote, tiers of government (DFID, 2001; Moser, 2001).

Developing objectives, strategies and projects

Participatory project development involves members of the community, researchers and the project implementers jointly analysing data, identifying local needs and resources that can be utilized sustainably, determining barriers to implementation, and assessing the social and cultural strengths of the community. It also involves evaluating the costs and benefits associated with different strategies and technologies. From such analysis, specific project objectives, strategies, organizational structures, budgets and time lines are developed that incorporate principles of sustainability. A detailed monitoring and evaluation methodology is developed to ensure that impacts can be measured both during and at the end of the project, and that project objectives and strategies can be changed if necessary.

Model scenario of a hypothetical village-level biochar project

This model scenario shows how a socio-economic assessment of a biochar programme could be undertaken at village level in a developing country. In the absence of such studies, in practice, it draws on real data from similar studies carried out for improved stove and charcoal kiln projects in a tropical Asian country (Joseph et al, 1990; Edwards et al, 2003; Limmeechokchai and Chawana, 2003).

The approach taken mirrors the hypothetical plant approach of Chapter 19, and adapts data on changes in efficiency and emissions from Feldmann (2007), Limmeechokchai and Chawana (2003) and Edwards et al (2003).

Background

This hypothetical case study is based on a community of 950 people (200 households) that has created a local organization to re-forest common land and to improve water quality. The community has asked a local NGO to help improve land-use practices and soil health and to reduce fuelwood consumption for cooking and charcoal production. The NGO wants to assess if the community's needs can be met by introducing new low-emissions biochar stoves and charcoal kilns. The NGO also wants to determine if this intervention will reduce the burden of women, improve the village income, reduce the incidence of eye and lung disease, and reduce greenhouse gas emissions (Wang and Smith, 1999) while producing both clean heat and biochar. This hypothetical study goes further to examine the feasibility of using trimmings from the forests (when they are better established) to manufacture biochar for agricultural and fuel use.

Before implementing the project, the local NGO undertook a baseline study with a representative group of villagers. The following socio-economic assessment is a summary of the data collected and of the results of the analysis, based on the sustainable livelihood concepts introduced in the previous sections.

Socio-economic assessment

Table 20.3 outlines data (hypothetical) on the vulnerability of the community. Clearly, the community has felt the effects of increases in global temperatures, from changes in local weather conditions, decreases in fuel availability and increases in fuel prices. In particular, women and children now spend three hours per day collecting fuelwood instead of two, resulting in a loss of income from handicraft production and the sale of processed food of about US$20 yr^{-1} in each household. In addition, the use of poorer-quality fuels has increased the frequency of eye and lung infections by 20 per cent in the last two years. The local health authority economist estimates costs to the nation from loss of production and increase in medical costs for each person as US$20 person yr^{-1}.

Drought has affected the availability of disposable household income, credit from local lending institutions and labour. These factors have slowed many development programmes, although it has, in part, been cushioned by income remittances from urban areas.

Table 20.4 summarizes community capi-

tal assets. It shows that although the community has suffered from the impact of climate change, it still has assets that could be used in the project. Community members have embraced modern forms of communication, have internet access and the governance environment is positive. There is a pool of skilled labour and literacy rates are high. An effective community organization is starting a community forest programme, and there are strong micro-enterprise credit systems and effective local agricultural extension services. Within the community there are skilled manufacturers of charcoal and lime who could assist in training women to manufacture biochar in their homes efficiently.

At present, in order to purchase goods and services such as health and education, the community relies on remittances from males who work seasonally or who have moved to local or international urban centres. But the movement of seasonal workers is a major issue in terms of labour availability and inter- and intra-household conflict. Wealth is not distributed evenly: this causes conflict and results in the poorer sections of the community having insufficient time to participate in new development activities.

Table 20.3 *Vulnerability context (assumptions for model scenario)*

Trends	Shocks	Seasonality
Population increasing at 1.5% per year.	Severe drought last year led to low crop and livestock stocks.	Crop prices decrease during harvest (options to preserve crops do not exist).
Average temperature is increasing every year.	Household income decreasing and time taken to collect water and fuel increasing.	Two crops per year when sufficient rain is available.
Inflation of 3% per year.	30% increases in fuel and fertilizer prices.	Onset of wet season sees increase in vector-borne diseases.
Adoption of improved governance practices to ensure continuation of aid and international loans.	Dramatic increase in eye and lung disease caused by shortage of fossil and wood fuels and increased use of dung.	Men are in urban areas when harvesting is finished. Women bear most of the tasks of planting.
Mobile phones and internet increasingly used.		

Source: Stephen Joseph

Table 20.4 *Summary of the assumptions of community assets*

Human	Social	Natural	Physical	Financial
70% literacy	Complex social	20ha of community	School with internet	Average savings
1% higher education	structure that is used	forest	access	US$50 per
10% high-school	to overcome shock,	200ha of degraded	Dispensary	person
educated	but also results in	forest 10km	One deep well	Inflow from
4% trade	conflict, especially	from village	Dirt road to highway	remittance
certification	regarding distribution	Home gardens for	Blacksmithing shop	US$100 yr^{-1}
60% traditional	of assets on death	each household;	Pottery	per person
skills (e.g. pottery,	Strong inter- and	dung and ash used	Bakery	Main agricultural
metal work)	intra-village ties	in garden	Lime kiln	stock: forest,
Traditional medicine	Some conflict	Stream flows in	Little wood available	cattle, tea trees
still practised	over land	wet season	near village (mainly	Gold jewellery is
Wide range of	Support mechanism	High winds in dry	from thinnings from	associated with
agricultural skills	for poor has been	season	community forest);	household wealth
Leaders come from	weakened with	High household	the poor use residues	Three 4-wheel
specific families,	drought	stove emissions	and dung; kerosene	drive vehicles
although mechanism	Conflict arises when	High brick and	for lighting and some	One minivan as a
to replace these if	men return from	charcoal kiln	cooking	taxi
community perceives	seasonal work	emissions		
lack of skill and				
honesty				

Source: Stephen Joseph

Cost-benefit analysis

Avoided emissions from stoves and kilns

A sample survey of households, businesses, local government and NGOs determined the possible costs and benefits of introducing biochar stoves and improved charcoal kilns. Fuel consumption and emissions were measured on 20 stoves. Households were selected at random and one stove was selected from each. Emissions measurements by gas and particle analysis (Zhang et al, 2000) allowed calculation of greenhouse warming commitment (GWC) in g CO_2e (carbon dioxide equivalents) MJ^{-1} heat released based on the following formula:

$$GWC = \sum_i GHG_i \times GWP_i \qquad [1]$$

where GHG_i is the quantity of the ith GHG in question, and GWP_i is the 20-year global warming potential per molecule of that particular GHG relative to CO_2 (Edwards et al, 2003). Fuelwood consumption was measured to be about 5kg per household per day at 12 per cent moisture content (Joseph et al, 1990). CO_2e emissions for the entire household were 2t to 4t CO_2e yr^{-1} (400t to 800t CO_2e yr^{-1} for the entire village) (Zhang et al, 2000) and stove heat transfer efficiency was approximately 19 per cent.

Two families operate two charcoal pit kilns and employ three individuals to help build and load the kilns, which takes about four days. The kilns are fired every month. Each kiln uses about 800kg of wood. The charcoal yield is about 22 per cent, with a total C content of 75 to 85 per cent. Fine charcoal materials without commercial value ('fines'), at about 50kg per kiln firing, can be used without payment. Charcoal sells for about US$150 and US$250 t^{-1} in the dry and wet seasons, respectively, giving a weighted average of US$175 t^{-1}. Greenhouse gas emissions from traditional kilns are 0.77kg to 1.63kg CO_2e kg^{-1} of charcoal produced (Pennise et al, 2001). Thus, total GWC emissions from the two pre-existing kilns are 3.2t to 6.7t CO_2e yr^{-1}.

Women working with local artisans and a combustion engineer designed a biochar metal stove with a secondary combustion chamber to convert 98 per cent of the volatiles to CO_2 and water. Local artisans built them for US$36 each (price ex-factory). Tests showed heat transfer efficiency increases to 29 per cent and fuel consumption fell from 5kg to 3.5kg day^{-1} for each household (Joseph et al, 1990; Limmeechokchai and Chawana, 2003). Biochar production per stove was about 0.75kg day^{-1}. Greenhouse gas emissions (GWC) were reduced by 90 per cent from 0.2t to 0.04t CO_2e yr^{-1} per household (20t to 40t CO_2e yr^{-1} per village), and household air quality improved significantly (reaching levels common with the use of kerosene stoves; Edwards et al, 2003). Women testers found the stove easier and faster to use and estimated that they would have an extra hour each day to tend the gardens, and an extra 30 minutes for cultural, community or family activities.

An improved kiln (with a forced-draught after-burner that will eliminate most products of incomplete combustion) was produced in collaboration with the local bricklayers and charcoal producers and was priced at US$3000 (wholesale price). Data from secondary sources (FAO, 1987; see Chapter 8) used to analyse its costs and benefits showed that the yield of these brick kilns is 30 to 33 per cent, and that the time between firings can be reduced from four weeks to three, increasing annual yields by about 1t or a 50 per cent increase in annual yield. Three per cent of the output of these kilns is fines that can be directly used as a biochar.

Another benefit is that the kiln is permanent and the labour associated with rebuilding pit kilns is saved. Therefore, labour requirements can be reduced by four person days per firing (at US$5 per person day). The after-burner would reduce greenhouse gas emissions by more than 95 per cent. If two kilns were built, the reduction in greenhouse gases (GWC) of the entire village would amount to 0.16t to 0.34t yr^{-1}.

Increased agricultural production

In agronomic trials, samples of biochar fines from pits (from a recent firing) and from the biochar stove were incorporated to grow maize at 6t ha^{-1} (similar to Kimetu et al, 2008). Maize yields are assumed to increase from 3t to 5t ha^{-1}. There appeared to be no significant difference in yields between the biochar produced from the pits and that from the stove. Table 20.5 summarizes the anticipated costs and benefits, based on the following assumptions:

- In year one, 110 households have stoves, increasing to 200 households in year two.
- In year one, the new kiln starts operation in the second half of the year and full output is reached in the second year.
- Kiln and stove lifetime is five years.
- The discount rate set by the government is 12 per cent.
- The benefit of not replacing trees used for firewood is US$10 t^{-1} (Feldmann, 2007) as a community and national benefit.
- Avoided emissions in year one are 50 per cent of those in year two.
- Carbon credits from reduction in emissions from the stoves and kilns are valued at US$23t CO_2e (negotiated by the NGO).
- Carbon credits from burial of biochar and reduction of standing forest is assumed to be zero.
- It is assumed that once biochar is added to soil, its effect on improvement in yields

Table 20.5 Cost-benefit analysis of the project

	Units	1	2	3	4	5
				Years		
Input data						
Biochar from stove	(t yr^{-1})	30.00	54.60	54.60	54.60	54.60
Biochar from kiln	(t yr^{-1})	0.50	0.83	0.83	0.83	0.83
Charcoal from kiln	(t yr^{-1})	6.00	8.32	8.32	8.32	8.32
GHG traditional kilns (GWC)	(t CO$_2$e yr^{-1})	4.90	4.90	4.90	4.90	4.90
GHG new kiln (GWC)	(t CO$_2$e yr^{-1})	0.25	0.25	0.25	0.25	0.25
GHG traditional stoves (GWC)	(t CO$_2$e yr^{-1})	600.00	600.00	600.00	600.00	600.00
GHG new stoves (GWC)	(t CO$_2$e yr^{-1})	30.00	30.00	30.00	30.00	30.00
Reduction in GHG (GWC)	(t CO$_2$e yr^{-1})	287.33	574.65	574.65	574.65	574.65
Increase in wood stock	(t yr^{-1})	109.20	109.20	109.20	109.20	109.20
Increase in maize	(t yr^{-1})	10.17	28.64	47.12	65.60	84.08
Labour rate	(US$ day^{-1})	5.00	5.00	5.00	5.00	5.00
Price maize	(US$ t^{-1})	200.00	200.00	200.00	200.00	200.00
Costs						
Stove	(US$)	7200				
Charcoal kiln	(US$)	6000				
Depreciation (straight line)	(US$)	2640	2640	2640	2640	2640
Maintenance	(US$)	100	660	660	660	660
Kiln labour	(US$)	780	780	780	780	780
Extension + external consultants	(US$)	30,000	20,000	5000	5000	5000
Compliance monitoring and evaluation	(US$)	5000	5000	5000	5000	5000
Total costs	(US$)	51,720	29,080	14,080	14,080	14,080
Income						
Carbon credits stove, kiln	(US$)	6608	13,217	13,217	13,217	13,217
Charcoal sales	(US$)	1050	1456	1456	1456	1456
Savings from increase in trees	(US$)	1092	1092	1092	1092	1092
Increased maize sales	(US$)	2033	5729	9424	13,120	16,815
Reduced medical expenses	(US$)		14250	20,000	28,500	28,500
Income increases labour available	(US$)		4000	4000	4000	4000
Total yearly income	(US$)	10,784	39,744	49,189	61,385	65,080
Total yearly income − costs	(US$)	−40,936	10,664	35,109	47,305	5,1000
Total income − costs	(US$)	103,142				
Internal rate of return	(%)	58				
Net present value calculation	(US$)	−36,550	8501	24,990	30,063	28,939
Discount rate		0.12				
Net present value	(US$)	55,943				

Source: Stephen Joseph

Table 20.6 *Summary of community perception of non-quantifiable costs and benefits of improved stoves, biochar application and improved charcoal kilns*

Environmental benefits and costs	Social benefits and costs	Economic benefits and costs
Benefits:	**Benefits:**	**Benefits:**
• improved air quality in households; • soil easier to till; • reduced smoke from charcoal kiln; • soil retains more water.	• more conducive environment for family interaction; • more time to spend with family and community; • successful project enhances community's self-respect and motivation to undertake similar projects; • successful project brings other agencies to area to impart new skills.	• more food for households; • increase in time and income raises possibility of other economic ventures; • possibility of profitable charcoal business if community forestry programme succeeds.
Costs:	**Costs:**	**Costs:**
• possible increase in extraction of wood from forest for charcoal production as household has the ability to make charcoal an alternative income; • if biochar is not produced correctly. it could have a negative effect on soil.	• possible conflict over distribution of C credits, especially from charcoal kilns; • if the project does not produce financial gains, other environmental projects may not proceed; • time required to learn new skills (biochar production and use); • loss of income if biochar has negative effect on plant growth.	• time required to learn new skills (biochar production and use) • loss of income if biochar has negative effect on plant growth

Source: Stephen Joseph

remains the same over five years. Increase in yields is then calculated on the basis of 6t biochar ha^{-1} and increase from 3t to 5t ha^{-1}. Since biochar is either collected free from the kiln or is produced during cooking, its value is assumed to be US$0.

• Costs to the nation from loss of production and increase in medical costs from eye and lung disease from wood stove smoke are assumed to be US$20 yr^{-1} per person.

The cash flow shows a payback period of less than three years, an internal rate of return greater than 50 per cent and net present value

(NPV) of greater than US$50,000. Under these assumptions, the project is financially as well as economically viable. The principal national economic benefits are reduced incidence of eye and lung disease, on the one hand, and increased maize production, on the other, thus reducing the need for medical services and food imports. Table 20.6 summarizes the non-quantifiable costs and benefits.

The NGO, village leaders, opinion-makers and representatives of households and charcoal-makers discussed the feasibility of the project within the constraints imposed by the drought conditions. They reviewed the survey data, the stove and kiln tests and the agronomic trials, together with the results of the cost-benefit analysis (see Tables 20.5 and 20.6).

All parties concluded that the new technologies and the resultant production of biochar would help them to overcome the burden of drought. Women and children would be healthier from using the new stoves, and would have to spend less time in collecting fuel and cooking food, with more time spent in family and community activities. The improved kilns would result in more income created within the community, less pollution in the surrounding area, and in freeing up labour for other activities.

The community's main concern was their lack of knowledge about how to operate the new stoves and kilns. They were also concerned that the biochar may not be produced to the correct specification. This could then jeopardize the yields of maize. The community thus emphasized the need for considerable assistance from the department of agriculture and for extensive trials at the beginning of the project.

Other concerns included the following: metal workers may not produce a stove with the required quality; kiln operators may not adapt to the new charcoal-producing techniques; the biochar might not be applied to maximum benefit; the biochar produced in the household might be sold as charcoal, which would reduce the income derived from C credits and increased maize production; new kilns could increase the rate of forest depletion; the owners of the charcoal kilns might not allow the fines to be distributed freely and equitably. People expressed uncertainty about how the C credits would be distributed to the villagers and how reliable the income from this source would be. To take these factors into account in the design of the biochar programme, it was agreed that the income from the C credits would be used to employ more young men to plant trees. This, in itself, could generate more C credits. A contract between the charcoal producers and the community would be drawn up and would be administered by the local agricultural extension officer.

Conclusions

A framework and methodology for assessing small-scale biochar projects from a socio-economic point of view are outlined in this chapter. The case study introduces how assessment and planning may be conducted for implementing a biochar project in a developing country. The approach emphasizes the involvement of stakeholders both in the assessment process and in the project design. However, this framework and methodology may be used for introducing biochar within any community. For example, a project to reduce waste on dairy farms in industrialized regions can be undertaken in partnership with all local farmers, the population within a local town and with the local government body. This framework and methodology requires further refinement as experience is gained in biochar project design and implementation.

References

Agenor, P.-R. and Montiel, P. J. (1999) *Development Macroeconomics*, second edition, Princeton University Press, Princeton, NJ

Ashley, C., Elliott, J., Sikoyo, G. and Hanlon, K. (1999) *Handbook for Assessing the Economic and Livelihood Impacts of Wildlife Enterprises*, African Wildlife Foundation, Nairobi, Kenya

Barry, B. (1998) *Social Exclusion, Social Isolation and the Distribution of Income*, London School of Economics, London, UK

Bebbington, A. (1999) 'Capitals and capabilities: A framework for analysing peasant viability, rural livelihoods and poverty'. *World Development*, vol 27, pp2021–2044

Beckhart, R. and Harris, R. T. (1987) *Organizational Transitions: Managing Complex Changes*, Addison-Wesley Series on Organization Development, Addison-Wesley Publishing Company, Inc., Reading, MA

Booth, D., Holland, J., Hentschel, J., Lanjouw, P. and Herbert, A. (1998) *Participation and Combined Methods in African Poverty Assessment: Renewing the Agenda*, DFID, London, UK

Brent, J. (1990) *Project Appraisal for Developing Countries*, New York University Press, New York, US

Carney, D. (1999) *Approaches to Sustainable Livelihoods for the Rural Poor*, ODI Poverty Briefing no 2, ODI, London, UK

Carnie, D. (2002) *Sustainable Livelihood Approaches*, DFID, London, UK

Chambers, R. and Blackburn, J. (1996) *The Power of Participation: PRA and Policy*, IDS Policy Brief, issue 7 (August), IDS, Brighton, UK

Daly, H. E. and Farley, J. (2004) *Ecological Economics*, Island Press, Washington, DC

Davies, S. (1996) *Adaptable Livelihoods: Coping with Food Insecurity in the Malian Sahel*, Macmillan Press, London, UK

DFID (UK Department for International Development) (2001) *Sustainable Livelihoods Guidance Sheet*, DFID, London, UK

DFID (2007) *Distance Learning Guide*, DFID, London, UK

Donnelly, A., Dalal-Clayton, B. and Hughes, R. (1998) *Directory of Impact Assessment Guidelines*, second edition, IIED, London, UK

Edwards, R. D., Smith, K. D., Zhang, J. and Ma, Y. (2003) 'Models to predict emissions of health-damaging pollutants and global warming contributions of residential fuel/stove combinations in China', *Chemosphere*, vol 50, pp201–215

Ellis, F. (1992) *Agricultural Policies in Developing Countries*, Cambridge University Press, Cambridge, UK

FAO (1987) *Simple Technologies for Charcoal Making*, FAO Forestry Paper no 41, Food and Agriculture Organization of the United Nations, Rome, www.fao.org/docrep/X5328e/x5328e00.htm, accessed 16 November 2007

Feldmann, L. (2007) 'Economic evaluation of Uganda stoves program', *Boiling Point*, no 54, p21

Gittinger, J. P. (1982) *Economic Analysis of Agricultural Projects*, John Hopkins University Press, Baltimore, MD

Hanmer, L. (1998) 'Human capital, targeting and social safety nets: An analysis of household data from Zimbabwe', *Oxford Development Studies*, vol 26, pp245–65

Hanmer, L., Pyatt, G. and White, H. (1997) *Poverty in Sub-Saharan Africa: What Can We Learn from the World Bank's Poverty Assessments?* Institute of Social Studies, The Hague, Belgium

Harriss, J., Hunter, J. and Lewis, C. W. (1995) *The New Institutional Economics and Third World Development*, Routledge, London, UK

Hobley, M. and Shields, D. (2000) *The Reality of Trying to Transform Structures and Process: Forestry and Rural Livelihoods*, Working paper no 132, ODI, London, UK

Holland, J. and Blackburn, J. (1998) *Whose Voice? Participatory Research and Policy Change*, IT Publications, London, UK

Hughes, R. and Dalal-Clayton, B. (1998) *Environmental Assessment in Developing Countries*, IIED, London, UK

Hyden, G. (1998) 'Governance and sustainable livelihoods: challenges and opportunities', Paper commissioned by UNDP, www.undp.org/sl/Documents/documents.htm

IT Consultants (2002) *Powering the Island through Renewable Energy: Cost Benefit Analysis for A*

Renewable Energy Strategy for the Isle of Wight to 2010, Intermediate Technology Consultants (ITC) Ltd, Warwickshire, UK

Jenkins, G. P. (1999) 'Evaluation of stake holder impacts in cost benefit analysis', *Impact Assessment and Project Appraisal*, vol 17, pp87–96

Joseph, S., Prasad, K. K. and van der Zaan H. B. (1990) *Bringing Stoves to the People*, Foundation for Wood Stove Dissemination, Nairobi, Kenya

Kimetu, J. K., Lehmann, J., Ngoze, S. O., Mugendi, D. N., Kinyangi, J. M., Riha, S., Verchot, L., Recha, J. W. and Pell, A. N. (2008) 'Reversibility of soil productivity decline with organic matter of differing quality along a degradation gradient', *Ecosystems*, vol 11, pp726–739

Ledgerwood, J. (1999) *Microfinance Handbook – An Institutional and Financial Perspective*, World Bank, Washington, DC

Limmeechokchai, B. and Chawana, S. (2003) 'Reduction of energy consumption and corresponding emissions in Thai residential sector by improved cooking stoves, family biogas digesters and improved charcoal-making kilns options', *Thammasat International Journal of Science and Technology*, vol 8, pp18–26

Marsland, N., Wilson, I., Abeyasekera, S. and Kleih, U. (1998) *A Methodological Framework for Combining Quantitative and Qualitative Survey Methods*, NRI, University of Greenwich and Reading Statistical Services Centre, Chatham, UK

Mehta, L., Newell, M., Scoones, I., Sivaramakrishnan, K. and Way, S. A. (1999) *Exploring Understandings of Institutions and Uncertainty: New Directions in Natural Resource Management*, IDS Discussion Paper no 372, Brighton, UK

Moser, C. (1998) 'The asset vulnerability framework: Reassessing urban poverty reduction strategies', *World Development*, vol 26, pp1–19

Moser, C. (2001) *To Claim Our Rights: Livelihoods Security, Human Rights and Sustainable Development*, ODI, London, UK

Natarajan, I. (1999) 'Social cost benefit analysis of the national programme on improved Chulha in India', Paper presented at the United Nations Food and Agriculture Organization's Regional Wood Energy Development Programme meeting on Wood Energy, Climate, and Health, October, Phuket, Thailand

North, D. C. (1991) *Institutions, Institutional Change and Economic Performance*, Cambridge University Press, Cambridge, UK

Pennise, D., Smith, K. R., Kithinji, J., Rezendi, M. E., Raad, T. and Zhang, J. (2001) 'Emissions of greenhouse gases and other airborne pollution', *Journal of Geophysical Research*, vol 106, pp143–155

Rennie, K. and Singh, N. (1995) *Participatory Research for Sustainable Livelihoods: A Guidebook for Field Projects*, IISD, Winnipeg, Canada

Rew, A. and Brustinov, A. (1998) 'The resolution and validation of policy reform: illustrations from Indian forestry and Russian land privatisation', in D. Mosse, J. Farrington and A. Rew (eds) *Development as Process: Concepts and Methods for Working with Complexity*, Routledge London, UK

Robb, C. (1999) *Can the Poor Influence Policy? Participatory Poverty Assessments in the Developing World*, World Bank, Washington, DC, http://publications.worldbank.org/catalog/content-download?revision_id=1103374

Schneider, H. (1999) *Participatory Governance: The Missing Link for Poverty Reduction*, OECD Development Centre Policy Briefs no 17

Smith, K. R., Gu, S., Huang, K. and Qiu, D. (1993) '100 million improved stoves in China: How was it done?', *World Development*, vol 21, pp941–961

Therivel, R. and Partidario, M. R. (1996) *The Practice of Strategic Environmental Assessment*, Earthscan, London, UK

Upton, M. (1996) *The Economics of Tropical Farming Systems*, Cambridge University Press, Cambridge, UK

Wang, X. and Smith, K. R. (1999) 'Secondary benefits of greenhouse gas control: Health impacts in China', *Environmental Science and Technology*, vol 33, pp3056–3061

Zhang, J., Smith, K. R., Ma, Y., Ye, S., Jiang, F., Qi, W., Liu, P., Khalil, M. A. K., Rasmussen, R. A. and Thorneloe, S. A. (2000) 'Greenhouse gases and other airborne pollutants from household stoves in China: A database for emission factors', *Atmospheric Environment*, vol 34, pp4537–4549

21

Taking Biochar to Market: Some Essential Concepts for Commercial Success

Mark Glover

Introduction

The apparently beneficial properties of biochar (see Chapters 2 to 6 and 12) seem to support immediate investment to bring biochar to full commercialization. Certainly, there are those 'true believers' or 'early adopters' who will invest in the commercial opportunities related to biochar before it is fully proven or established, usually with smaller, but strategic investments. These pioneers are important and must be encouraged; but the biochar sector will need to attract and rely on more traditional sources of investment in order to secure its future for the long term.

For this to happen, the tangible properties and benefits of biochar will need to be presented in a commercially logical context. All of the remarkable properties of biochar need to be verified and taken to market and all the commercial promise and demonstrable benefits presented to potential customers as a viable and cost-effective offer. However, within the context of a carbon (C)-constrained environment, there is potential for over-enthusiastic exploitation that could damage or delay the medium-term commercial prospects for biochar. This has occurred most recently in the first-generation liquid biofuels sector, where the rush to produce the biodiesel and ethanol products neglected to address the genuine sustainability of the actual methods of supply and production for these materials (Giampietro and Ulgiati, 2005). The biochar sector would do well to analyse and understand this experience in order to avoid similar pitfalls and inform a more sustainable commercialization pathway. This is discussed in more detail below in the section on 'Lessons from the first-generation liquid biofuels sector'.

Biochar is positioned to be presented to the market as an important element of the climate change agenda and the new-found attention to sustainability (Mathews, 2008b) as society readjusts the agricultural and industrial practices of the past 200 years. Biochar stands to play a crucial role in the future re-evaluation of biomass as an essential resource in a C-constrained world and will therefore be featured in a number of seemingly disparate agendas, including:

- the urban waste agenda – as the objective moves from waste management to systematic resource recovery and inherent resource value retention (Rhyner et al, 1995);
- the agricultural inputs or supplements sector – as the full C impacts of high-nutrient fertilizers are recognized (Dittrick, 2007);
- the agricultural residues and by-products sector – as land scarcity stimulates the need to optimize the sustainable values of these materials (Tilman et al, 2001);
- the pulp, paper and forest products sector – as by-products, wastes and residues are reassessed as potential profit centres;
- the animal husbandry sector (including biosolids) – as wastes, emissions and effluents are appreciated for their full inherent resource value (Fleming et al, 1998);
- the biofuels sector – as sustainable yields and sources of biomass are applied to the provision of this essential product (Giampietro and Ulgiati, 2005);
- the petrochemical sector – as it is obliged to secure sustainable C-based feedstocks in the face of dwindling fossil fuel reserves;
- the metallurgical industries – as they seek sustainable sources of reductants;
- the stationary energy sector – as it adapts to a C-constrained future and the trend towards optimizing localized or distributed low-carbon energy sources.

Sustainable biochar production is possible (Lehmann, 2007), even probable, as a primary or secondary product for these fast-changing sectors, which will significantly affect the development and commercialization of the biochar sector. Within this framework, the biochar sector will need to demonstrate to the investment community that it is a secure investment and that all risks are strategically managed, and that it will not fail to deliver on the early promise.

The biochar sector could encounter significant long-term challenges if, in the rush to secure research and development funding or early stage project or technology funding, a much more strategic, structured and focused set of principles are not adopted and adhered to. These principles, which are discussed below, derive from the immutable concepts of sustainability that have created the platform for the commercial opportunity in the first place (O'Connell et al, 2005).

Finally, for the biochar sector to reach its full commercial potential, a considerable level of vertical integration along the entire value supply chain (Tan, 2001) will be essential until the sector is sufficiently established and matures to the point where it allows greater levels of individuality, specialization and niche sophistication. The full value/supply chain that could result in sustainable supply and demand for biochar includes, at a minimum, sustainable land-use issues, sustainable biomass yield, constantly evolving technologies, informed customer demand, government policy, intervention or support, a stable global C price signal, and marketing and distribution channels. In a mature sector, each facet can and should undergo incremental development and improvement; but in nascent sectors, such as the entire biochar production and application sector, there are few established protocols, relationships and common understandings.

Because the emerging biochar sector is entirely new, change is the only constant for all stakeholders along the value chain. Commercialization of the sector therefore calls for a widely supported roadmap that can be developed as a consensus document. Its purpose would be to both facilitate the initial success of the sector and to hasten a level of maturity that would encourage sophistication, dynamism and optimization sooner than if the sector left these issues completely to chance.

A roadmap of this type is beyond the scope of this chapter. However, the process would involve a comprehensive review of where the market potential of biochar is, including a detailed customer-segmentation evaluation. An accompanying gap analysis would highlight all the actions and initiatives necessary to attract the capital markets or, in the case of government funding, direct the investment necessary to take biochar to market. Rather than taking a rose-coloured view of biochar and its apparent properties and potential, this chapter examines the opportunities at each stage from the viewpoint of a conservative investor.

It has already been noted that not all investors are conservative and totally risk averse. In fact, some specialize in bold early investment positions. However, the capital required for biochar to reach its full potential as a global product and commodity will require support from the mainstream investment community.

It is also an essential precondition for the successful commercialization of biomass products, in general, and biochar, in particular, that the sustainability context is properly understood, since it is a major driver for the new industry and provides the foundations for a valuable and structured offer to the market. The following will concentrate on summarizing the sustainability and climate change issues and agendas; the inherent properties of biomass and the position that biochar has within that framework; and, finally, the fundamental issues that biochar commercialization should systematically address.

Biochar's positioning in the sustainability and climate change agendas

The commercial properties of biochar have a basic value in a 'business as usual' economy – properties such as tangible soil productivity improvements, even a C sequestration value in jurisdictions where such values are recognized; but these same basic properties have a much greater commercial value in an economy that is proactively managed to internalize environmental and sustainable resource-use externalities. It is therefore important to convey these issues to the investment community in a way that gives them a better understanding.

Biochar is emerging as a product, a service and a concept at precisely the time when issues such as the population of the planet (approaching 9 to 10 billion people), climate change, soil degradation, resource depletion and C-constrained economies are achieving overwhelming worldwide attention. This is a favourable contextual backdrop for the investment community if the benefits of biochar can be cogently and credibly presented. There are two essential messages to focus on that are presented in the following two sections.

Biochar as a sustainable soil productivity enhancer and restorative

First, the investment community needs to understand the future for biomass in a sustainable economy and the role of biomass to provide materials, energy and sequestration products. All the while, the vital differences in philosophy and outcomes between a sustainable economy and business as usual need to be identified, particularly where they present economic opportunities for the (business and) investment community. Within this context, the tangible benefits of biochar as a sustainable way of enhancing and restoring soil productivity (see Chapters 5 and 12) need to be confirmed and described within the integrated opportunity.

Biochar: The long-term and measurable carbon sequestration product

The biochar sequestration story needs to be presented within the framework that being:

- C-positive is part of the problem;
- C-neutral means that the particular activity is no longer part of the problem;
- C-negative is a crucial part of the solution to rising atmospheric carbon dioxide (CO_2) levels.

Therefore, where appropriately sourced biomass can be processed to contribute both essential C-based materials or energy, and with biochar available as a value-adding net sequestration by-product (Lehmann et al, 2006; Laird, 2008), the gross benefits could realize sustainable value well in excess of the more commonly understood 'business as usual' products or outcomes.

The first of the messages – biochar as a sustainable way of enhancing and restoring soil productivity – places biochar in an essential growth sector. Investors will like to be part of the next new sector as long as the claims are substantiated. The second, biochar as a long-term and readily measurable sequestration product, will provide additional revenue in any market or jurisdiction where C is traded or C sequestration outcomes are valued. Within this context, the production of biochar as a vital sequestration product will only occur where the production process also produces C-neutral or even C-negative syngas or bioliquid – but these products are collateral benefits in this biochar context.

The sustainability context for biomass generally

One of the strongest marketing angles for biochar is its integral role in the bio-based economy that is seen to emerge (Bevan and Franssen, 2006). To ensure that the investment community really understands the profound importance and implications of a bio-based economy, the most important issues need to be comprehensively presented in order to clearly outline the extraordinary commercial potential, while emphasizing that bio-business is 'sustainability' business and not business as usual. It also needs to be made clear that, as with the first-generation biofuels, the product is defined as sustainable by the raw material sourcing and subsequent production pathway.

The investment community is comfortable with indexed investments, global trends and relative positioning. They prefer to have appropriate investments in areas that are likely to be the next growth sectors. For positioning biochar in the market, the following arguments could be articulated:

- The planet decarbonized itself all those millennia ago when biomass (phytoplankton, oil and gas/forest, and coal and gas) was transformed into what are now fossil fuels.
- Today's fossil fuels are yesterday's biomass (and sunshine), and these fossil fuels represent a high-energy density that will be difficult and costly to replicate from alternative sources.
- Today's fossil fuel dependence is effectively re-carbonizing the atmosphere to levels never experienced by current civilization (IPCC, 2007).

- The current global attention on climate change will progressively move to introduce measures that provide disincentives to release CO_2 into the atmosphere – incentives to reduce existing atmospheric CO_2 levels or trading mechanisms that will internalize C-cycle impacts within all human activity.
- Against this background, biomass can be seen as the crude, unprocessed and unconcentrated raw material that can provide all the same gas, liquid and solid products that we have produced from fossil resources (Ragauskas et al, 2006). Bio-products are a substantial new industry that will not automatically produce a sustainable outcome. There will be a whole new set of disciplines, economic realities and drivers that will dictate sustainable outcomes (Giampietro and Ulgiati, 2005). Biochar is an integral part of this message. Before focusing on the specific benefits and properties of biochar, the differences between the fossil fuel sector and the replacement biomass sector must be highlighted (Mathews, 2008a). The experience of the first-generation ethanol and biodiesel sectors over the last five to ten years demonstrates that perceived benefits can be offset by total life-cycle costs. What has been observed in the current biofuels sector need not occur in the emerging biochar sector.
- Currently, unrecognized or under-valued biomass resources exist in the agricultural, forest products, animal husbandry and urban waste sectors (e.g. Kaygusuz and Türker, 2002; Hoogwijk et al, 2003). These unrealized assets require only revised value and supply chain management to access markets before any special purpose crops or initiatives are stimulated.

Biomass processing using pyrolysis for the production of potential C-neutral gas, liquid and solid (biochar) products is a new (Lehmann, 2007) but closely integrated sector. It is a sector that must engage in many facets of the existing economy. The ability of the biochar industries to generate sustainable products and outcomes will derive from fully understanding the issues and complexities. The challenge seems to be that the prevailing economic systems have yet to fully appreciate that biomass is a complex and highly differentiated resource (Ragauskas et al, 2006). If we are to avoid 'food for fuel' problems or 'forest to biochar' business models, a working understanding of biomass is essential.

Inherent characteristics of the biomass resource

Biomass is much more than firewood or just another fuel source. Electrical or stationary energy can be provided by hydro, solar, thermal, geothermal, wind, tidal or wave, and even nuclear power in a post-fossil fuels and C-constrained economy. Perhaps fossil fuels with C capture and storage (CCS) (IPCC, 2005) will eventually prove effective. However, only biomass can produce the basic gas, liquids, solids or the C-based chemicals that we currently obtain from fossil supplies.

It is worth noting that during its growth phase, biomass contributes significantly to providing ecosystem services, to the biodiversity of other organisms and even to recreational values. Once harvested, the provision of food, fibre and industrial inputs all provide essential outcomes. The provision of simple heat energy is predominantly a by-product in commercial frameworks where the highest values of biomass are fully recognized.

The basic gas, liquids and solids from biomass may be products in their own right. In most cases, the essential pyrolysis products will be presented as precursors for further refinement into more tightly specified products or reductants (Kamm and Kamm, 2004). The gases may be used to drive the pyrolysis process (Bridgwater and Peacocke, 2000), with surpluses available for synthesizing new products or generating electricity. Liquids and tars will be available for refining into liquid fuels and petrochemical precursors, and the solids, or chars, presented as activated carbon products and metallurgical reductants (coal replacements), with biochar as a soil amendment (Kamm and Kamm, 2004).

The nature of the available biomass, the process technology, local circumstances and prevailing market conditions will all affect the mix of primary and secondary products from biomass processes on a case-by-case basis (see Chapter 9). Biomass resources exist with different ratios of basic chemical constituents, such as lignin, cellulose or carbohydrates (see Chapter 8). For food production, often the reproductive structures are harvested, discarding large amounts of crop residues made up of mainly lignocellulosic materials that may be used as feedstock for energy (O'Connell et al, 2005; Crucible Carbon, 2008).

Within a framework or hierarchy where quite different biochemical fractions of plants are recognized for their specific characteristics, biochar will inevitably be a by-product of a mainstream biomass-processing sector. Biochar is a product that is manufactured to impart certain soil enhancement and soil restorative properties (see Chapters 5 and 12) and to provide net C sequestration and emission reduction (see Chapter 18).

Biomass processing must evolve to more accurately match the properties of the available resources to the required properties of the derived products (Bryant and Downie, 2007). For example, low-ash and homogeneous biomass resources (perhaps single species) might be sustainably applied to filtration products, highly specified manufacturing inputs or metallurgical reductants (Byrne and Nagle, 1997; Langberg et al, 2006). Higher-ash and less homogeneous biomass sources, such as those derived from agricultural residues or urban wastes, could be ideally applied to biochar production where the ash content can provide additional fertilizer effects (Chan et al, 2007; Downie et al, 2007; see Chapter 5).

During low-temperature (<500°C) slow pyrolysis, phosphorus (P), potassium (K) and sulphur (S) typically accumulate on the biochar product in bioavailable form (Hossain et al, 2007). Where pulp and paper sludges are pyrolysed, the ash content contains considerable quantities of calcium carbonate ($CaCO_3$) and bentonite, originally used in the paper-making process. These materials provide valuable liming properties when applied to acid soils, but would be undesirable contaminants if the same biochar was applied as a metal reductant (Van Zwieten et al, 2007). Such differences have to be recognized when designing a commercial biochar product.

Lessons from the first-generation liquid biofuels sector

Liquid biofuels may become particularly important products for the transport sector (Ragauskas et al, 2006). However, the way in which the mainstream investment community worldwide has supported the biofuels sector may create some undesirable outcomes (e.g. Searchinger et al, 2008; Tollefson, 2008). Over the past three to five years, the investment community moved quickly into the liquid biofuels market to support biodiesel and ethanol (Kennedy, 2007; Tollefson, 2008). However, this development has brought rather traditional commercial thinking to a nascent sector that derives much of its current potential by addressing unsustainable outcomes that arose when that same traditional commercial thinking failed to properly account for environmental externalities that have now resulted in the current climate change agendas. This thinking did not understand that biofuels represented an opportunity generated by the emerging sustainability industry, a sector that specifically seeks to address and redress hitherto un-costed and unaccounted for environmental externalities that have driven the climate change debate, in general, and the sustainable resource use and application debate, in particular.

It is informative to acknowledge that our traditional economic approach, which has given us such unprecedented growth over the last 250 years, has also triggered unsustainable climate change, in the most part because the prices have not reflected full ecological or social cost (Stern, 2007). The emergence of C taxes and C trading schemes (see Chapters 18 and 22) are early attempts to place commercial instruments in the market to partially address the internalization of these currently un-costed environmental or social impacts.

A similar argument can be made regarding the competing production of food versus fuel (Hill et al, 2006), whether or not it had an actual effect on food prices and supplies (Tenenbaum, 2008). The first-generation ethanol sector failed to secure the biofuel supply at a price that could be afforded by the transport fuels sector. Rapid technological development in the sector meant that many early plants were, in effect, investing in process technologies that would prove to be suboptimal or outdated well within the projected commercial life of the plants. Early adopters in this nascent sector became high-cost producers as the process technologies developed. The impacts of sharing established fossil-fuel marketing and distribution channels with the new biofuels sector on fossil fuel producers were not adequately considered.

The difference between biofuels projects that are currently not commercially viable or sustainable and the potential to produce biofuels sustainably is in the planning and application. With attention to detail, such projects can demonstrate all of the anticipated benefits, especially where integrated biochar production can provide a C-negative outcome (Mathews, 2008a).

In summary, how liquid biofuels are made is the determining factor in assessing their long-term value as alternatives to fossil fuels. If they are sourced from intensively farmed food-grade feedstocks, their overall benefit to sustainability and reducing the levels of atmospheric CO_2 is likely to be limited. The nascent biochar sector should analyse lessons learned from commercializing biofuels in the past. The customers for biochar will, to a significant extent, be attracted by its prospects for sustainability, so it is vital that biochar is delivered with its sustainability credentials intact.

Biochar commercialization framework

In constructing a sustainable business model for biochar, there are four essential building blocks to the proposition for investment that need specific attention and verifiable assumptions:

1   justification of demand;
2   demonstrable markets and growth opportunities;
3   technological reliability and at least first-order efficiency and cost effectiveness;
4   reliable and sustainable biomass supply or yield.

These factors will define the risk–reward profile for the emerging biomass processing sector, and are discussed in detail below.

Justification of demand

In a sustainable future economy, un-costed externalities will need to be brought into account. However, if an activity has no valid justification of demand and is therefore not undertaken, then all the effort identifying and accounting for collateral externalities will not be necessary. Biochar production should have no difficulty with this initial justification of demand. Nevertheless, biochar production must be sustainable from all aspects to maintain its credentials. Multiple challenges to, for example, health impacts have been voiced (Baveye, 2007) that must be taken seriously and are being addressed by the emerging technology (see Chapter 12).

Ultimately, a sustainable business model will need a community licence to operate. This licence is formally granted through the prevailing approvals and licensing process in any particular jurisdiction – and will therefore be more or less rigorous in various parts of the world (see Chapter 12). Rather than rely on selecting underdeveloped regulatory jurisdictions as business entry points, participation in the sustainability business means always being conscious of the need for the activity, the immediate and collateral impacts of that activity, and mitigating or planning for all and any unintended consequences (externalities) in the final benefit. The ultimate commercial success of the biochar sector will benefit from the systematic observance of these sustainability issues.

The biochar sector may experience commercial competition from products that might look to the less informed assessor to be biochar, but with none or few of the physical and biochemical properties of effective biochar. In these circumstances, the biochar market positioning will benefit from developing reliable industry standards that are controlled by credible organizations. Characterization and classification of biochars is a step in the right direction (see Chapter 7). Attention to this level of detail will help the investment community to engage with and support the nascent biochar sector. In summary, biochar is capable of being positioned as a value-added product with demonstrable benefits that also internalizes externalities.

Markets and growth opportunities

To take biochar to the market, individual project business plans will need to be funded. Central to the investment community is verification of the primary revenue stream generated from the sale and use of biochar.

The primary properties of biochar are as a soil-quality improver (see Chapters 2, 5 and 6). It is both an immediate productivity improver for most soils (Lehmann et al, 2003; Chan et al, 2007) and a restorative of quality following previous overuse or degradation of soil (Kimetu et al, 2008). Under certain soil and management conditions, it may supplement commercial inorganic fertilizer application, so less fertilizer is required to achieve similar crop yields (see Chapters 12 and 18). These properties can be used as a platform for facilitating market-informed discussions about the commercialization of biochar amongst the investment community.

As already stated, the properties of biochar need to be scientifically verified as the foundation value proposition for the market. They also need to be verified in order to establish the appropriate price point for biochar sales and services. In this regard, the nascent biochar sector is at a crossroads, and thoughtful management of the price point issue should be a major focus of any future biochar industry development. On the one hand, the biochar sector could follow the experience of compost products and become a commodity product. On the other hand, all of the demonstrated qualities of biochar could be commercially benchmarked against currently available alternative methods of achieving similar outcomes. A price point could then be established alongside these alternatives, with perhaps a premium for offering multiple sustainable outcomes.

For example, where nutrient retention results (see Chapter 15) or improvements in nutrient-use efficiency are found (see Chapter 5), the commercial value of replacing these nutrients can be readily measured. This would apply to gaseous losses of greenhouse gas from soil as well (see Chapter 13). Where liming values can be achieved by biochar (see Chapter 5), the benefits to acid soils can be benchmarked against commercially applied lime.

The issue of achieving full and fair value in the market for biochar products will be best managed collaboratively by the initial biochar manufacturers. This is an area where a roadmap for developing the biochar industry will be instrumental since the industry may not be able to act collectively from the outset.

The full range of benefits for the customer or land manager need to be detailed, highlighted and justified so that biochar products can be sold for their fair value, and their continued manufacture is stimulated and encouraged. The emerging biochar sector has a few differentiating features from, for example, the industries marketing compost or zeolite; but there are recurring lessons to learn. First, the major difference to the compost sector is that the biochar business will not be a low entry-cost business for those who are doing it properly.

As discussed below, the unit cost of pyrolysis will need to be reduced significantly from today's costs, and carefully controlled pyrolysis processes for commercially relevant flows of biomass (see Chapter 19) at the scale appropriate for a certain system (see Chapter 9) will need to emerge. In some systems, proprietary biochar production will require a significant capital cost, with very specialist technical abilities needed to produce biochar to a volume and quality that supports the commercial promise. However, these barriers to entry to the top table of biochar producers may encourage some operators to put inferior biochar products into the market in order to take advantage of the relatively high market prices achieved by those making genuine biochar products.

Certainly, the biochar sector needs to be structured around the concept of 'market pull' (Luyten, 2003).[1] To do this, all of the immediately valuable properties need to be evaluated and benchmarked for price point against commercially available alternative methods and products that can achieve similar outcomes. The price point also needs to be compared with the net present value of no intervention and the results collated as an important element of the biochar business model that is presented to investors, which could be a focus for the proposed Biochar Industry Commercialization Roadmap.

A vital action item for the sector is to continue to research the precise science of how biochar achieves the range of results that have been demonstrated to date. Only when the science is available will biochar be able to fully optimize its production processes and fully substantiate the offer to market. For example, long-term stability of biochar (see Chapter 11) and the resultant emission reductions (see Chapter 18) needs full scientific verification. Only processes and activities that can remove CO_2 from the atmosphere and sequester it for significant periods of time will be genuinely part of the solution to climate change.

From an investment point of view, any current evaluation of the verifiable market potential for biochar is facing the following challenge: the potential customers may not commit to taking all of a potential plant output without production samples; however, production samples may not be available without a plant, and funding for a pyrolysis plant will depend upon demonstrating a market arrangement. These issues can be overcome with conditional agreements between buyers and sellers and the support of an understanding and knowledgeable investment party who specializes in these start-up projects. However, if the risks and uncertainties can be minimized, the cost of capital will be reduced.

At this point, the issue of optimum investment for the start-up of the biochar sector reverts to the research community since the more that is known of the science of biochar and its manufacture, the smaller the risk will be for the early-stage investors.

The process technology

Technology or process risk is a major concern for the investment community. Many potentially viable business propositions have not been successful when the technology was unreliable, too costly or thermally inefficient to operate.

Another inevitable issue with new technology is that even if it works as planned and produces an acceptable and anticipated product quality, the next generation of technology is certain to be better. This makes it much more difficult to attract the initial project investment (Scotchmer, 1996) since an anticipated reality is that even a completely successful first-generation project will, in effect, create the market opportunity for the second generation of new and improved plants and technologies. These will then compete in the same nascent markets with lower cost, and more efficient and more reliable technology, putting the first-generation

projects in commercial jeopardy, even if at the same time increasing overall innovation (Bessen and Maskin, 2000).

The generic pyrolysis process is well understood and widely employed in a range of industries and applications (Demirbas, 2001; Bridgwater and Peacocke, 2002). However, technology that is specifically tailored to manufacture quality-assured biochar is in its infancy (Lehmann, 2007). In terms of payback periods, the current first-generation slow pyrolysis technologies are externally heated and pyrolysis typically has to allocate at least 10 per cent of the energy gain for driving the thermal process, while the remaining energy can be used externally (Demirbas and Arin, 2002). Biomass with a moisture content of above 50 per cent is typically not used for energy production due to low energy recovery (McKendry, 2002). As shown for a specific case study from Victoria, Australia (Crucible Carbon, 2008), these technologies can have paybacks of 15 to 20 years or a capital intensity value of US$300 to $500 per dry tonne of plant capacity, which in first-generation plants must be mitigated by gate fees. Figure 21.1 suggests an optimum where a capital intensity of approximately US$150 per annual dry tonne of capacity with a realistic CO_2 price of US$30 per tonne were realized, giving a two- to three-year payback period. This payback appears to be in line with the investment community's expectations for such projects (Crucible Carbon, 2008).

For an intermittent period, available technologies for the commercial-scale production of biochar are facing scale-up risks followed by optimization. Promising technologies will attract the enthusiasm of early adopters mentioned at the beginning of the chapter to provide funding for high-risk technology development. The biochar sector needs to demonstrate confidence, professionalism and certainty about its product, especially in the vital early stages. An opportunistic corporate culture established around early projects will

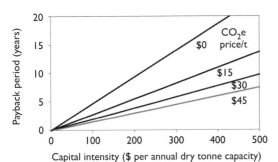

Figure 21.1 *Payback period as a function of the price of C (in CO_2 equivalents)*

Notes: Techno-economic modelling by Crucible Carbon for slow pyrolysis conditions that assume equal generation by weight of biochar, bio-oil and gas during pyrolysis, with the gas used internally to provide the process energy. In the illustrated case, the values assumed for inputs and outputs were biomass US$100 t^{-1} (on a dry weight basis), biochar US$100 t^{-1} and biocrude oil US$300 t^{-1}.

Source: Joe Herbertson (pers comm, 2007)

set the sector back in the eyes of the investment community whose support will be essential if the sector is to achieve its full potential.

Supply and the sustainable yield of feedstock

Of all the key factors that will support the fastest commercialization of the biochar industry, supply and sustainable yield issues are by far the most important, from both a broad sustainability perspective and from the financial and commercial points of view (Faaij, 2008). This will require the sources of biomass selected for biochar production to be appropriate and be able to withstand a comprehensive life-cycle analysis.

The *Sustainability Guide for Bioenergy* commissioned by the Rural Industries Research and Development Corporation (O'Connell et al, 2005) provides some useful structure to the process of determining if a particular biomass source should be sustainably applied for biochar production. The decision-making matrix provided in this

scoping study (see Figure 21.2) highlights that, initially, the sustainability value revolves around a land-use issue before addressing the yield and allocation issues for the various defined fractions of a potential biomass resource (O'Connell et al, 2005, pp22–23). Certification as proof of adherence to certain standards is important in providing assurance of sustainability (Van Dam et al, 2008).

Not only must a defined source of biomass be available to support the direct commercial viability of a particular plant or project (Caputo et al, 2005), but that biomass source must be demonstrably the best and highest use of the resource and, at the same time, retain sustainability credentials that are critical for the optimum commercialization of biochar. In summary:

- Biochar derives much of its cachet by being positioned directly inside the sustainability agenda.
- This positioning, and the resultant commercial potential, requires biochar to be manufactured from sustainable yields of biomass, probably as a significant by-product of an integrated biomass processing operation, such as stalks and stems, rather than fruit or seed.
- The sustainable yield of biomass has no higher net resource value than to be converted to biochar.
- The nascent biomass conversion sector will need to vertically integrate, in the initial stages at least, to ensure that sustainability is maintained.
- The food versus fuel issues will need to be managed until emerging maturity in the sector can support greater levels of specialization and niche operations.

Since the preferred properties of biochar are still being confirmed and the processing techniques and technologies are in a rapid state of development, it is not possible to be definitive on the optimum biomass sources for biochar

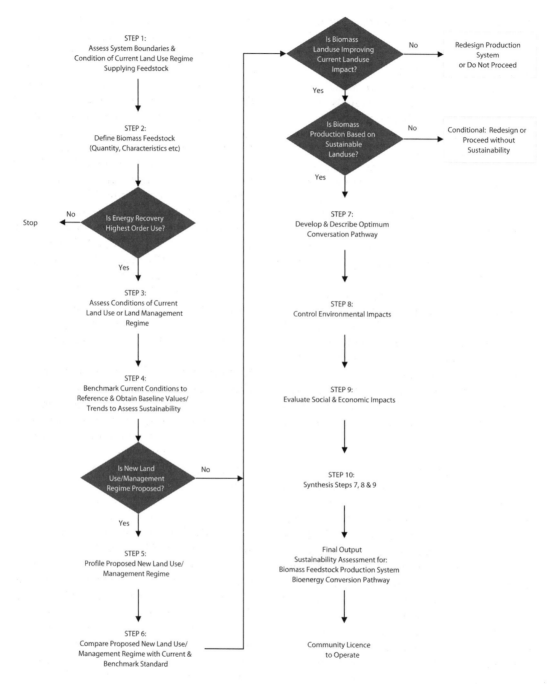

Figure 21.2 *Proposed protocol for developing sustainable land use with bioenergy recovery*

Source: adapted from O'Connell et al (2005)

production. However, we do have some early clues.

Biochar as a by-product

The generic pyrolysis processes when applied to lignocellulosic residuals tend to produce approximately one third gases, one third liquids and one third tars and solids (biochar) in standard applications (see Chapter 8). These proportions can be altered by refining the process to optimize certain fractions (Strezov et al, 2008). The solid biochar product is a minority product or by-product from a gas and/or liquid production enterprise,[2] but can be maximized in production units that do not generate energy (Antal et al, 1996).

There are similarities in the better understood crude oil refining industry. Bituminous residuals are an almost inevitable by-product of the fuels, lubes and petrochemical materials manufacturing processes – but not a single refinery in the world takes in crude oil to produce only bitumen. In fact, if the crude is particularly light, no bituminous residues may be produced at all. This militates against specific biochar crops.

Biomass ash content

Biochar could be made from single-species processing or uniform quality sawdust, hardwood chips or nut shells (see Chapter 8). This type of homogeneous high-quality feedstock (especially nut shells) will tend to be optimally applied to high-quality activated carbons (Heschel and Klose, 1995). Applications where ash content or critical non-C contamination will devalue the product will limit its application in industrial processes (Schröder et al, 2007), such as metal refining, filtration or medical purposes. For example, biochar-type materials as reductants in metallurgical applications have considerable potential (Emmerich and Luengo, 1996; Yalcin and Arot, 2002); but high-ash biochars may lead to slag production or lower metal quality (FAO, 1985), though dependent upon feedstock (Mansaray and Ghaly, 1997). On the other hand, for biochars produced as a soil amendment, high ash contents may even increase the direct nutrient effects (see Chapter 5), even though the effects on surface properties (see Chapter 3) and stability (see Chapter 11) are not fully resolved. Significant liming values may be achieved with biochars that are produced from paper pulp residues (see Chapter 5), which contain high concentrations of calcium carbonate and bentonite. Similarly, high-ash biochars derived from chicken litter (Chan et al, 2007) have high concentrations of K and P that have significant fertilizer value. However, possible metal contamination in the ash would be detrimental and must be carefully quantified and monitored. This can be avoided by choosing appropriate feedstocks such as biomass.

Biomass fraction of urban solid wastes

Urban solid wastes are those surplus materials that emanate from industries and households. In Organisation for Economic Co-operation and Development (OECD) countries, these materials amount to between 700kg and 1000kg per person per year, and some 60 per cent are of biomass or lignocellulosic origin, consisting of wood, wood products, garden residues, paper that has not previously been recycled, cardboard and kitchen residues (Warnken, 2007).

Currently, most jurisdictions focus on recovering a proportion of these materials for compost manufacture (Zurbrügg et al, 2004). Two pertinent issues arise from this practice. First, quality compost cannot be made from materials of indeterminate origin that are likely to be cross-contaminated with other materials or chemicals due to the 'uncontrolled' nature of their origin. Second, most of the organic fraction is not source separated and is still present in the mixed residual waste stream, and may contain unwanted or incompatible materials (Zurbrügg et al, 2004). In addition, the organic fraction derived from urban waste streams may contain specific contaminants by load or species that mean they need to be treated specifically. However, most of this material, most of the time, would seem to be entirely suitable for biochar production because:

- During thermal processing (300°C to 600°C), a wide range of organic compounds that would be critical contaminants in compost are destroyed.
- Pyrolysis processes will have to have comprehensive off-gas management and clean-up systems (Chapter 8).
- Urban solid wastes are typically close to horticultural and agricultural markets where biochar could be of considerable value.

- Biochar is a considerably more valuable product than compost, even if it is made from select fractions of urban solid waste and is more readily transported to diverse or disparate markets due to lower weight and greater product value density (see Chapter 9).

In summary, biochar is not only valuable for all its physical, chemical and biological properties (see Chapters 2 to 6), but can also be presented to the market with impeccable sustainability credentials. Perhaps the single greatest threat to validation of those credentials will derive from the sustainability of the biomass source and yield applied to the product manufacture. Therefore, the route to market for biochar would be much enhanced by strict industry guidelines and sustainability protocols (O'Connell et al, 2005).

Commercial factors and business modelling

The previous chapters have highlighted a wide range of valuable properties of biochar. To prove and demonstrate these properties, commercial volumes of known quality biochar need to be produced to support both the needs of early adopter customers and to provide the solid case study evidence for the broader potential market. This, in turn, will establish a proven price structure and market volume.

In order to produce these volumes of biochar requires the first generation of full-scale commercial plants to be established. To attract the appropriately priced capital for these projects, a reliable business case must be put. The main elements of this must address three key factors:

1 reliable supply issues;
2 process and technical issues, leading to verifiable capital costs and operating

costs assumptions;
3 revenue assumptions from service and product sales.

A risk–certainty assessment of these three foundation issues must present a workable business model for both initial plants and longer-term growth strategies for potential biochar companies. Revenue streams for biochar product sales must initially be considered as unreliable for the purposes of rewarding any capital applied to biochar manufacture. This will require the first-generation commercial-scale biochar plants to provide a waste management service for certain biomass resources in exchange for service or gate fees for their processing (Cartmell et al, 2006). If and when biochar sales and markets can be proven and established, a dependence upon gate fees will be reduced. It is advisable for initial contract conditions to be drafted to reflect this reality.

Initial projects will need to have supply certainty and assured revenue from providing waste management services. However, the limited opportunities to attract gate fees for waste management services will be quickly exhausted in the first round of commercialization, as seen for incineration (Olofsson, 2005). In the second round, a detailed marketing strategy for biochar will need to be systematically implemented and realized around the provision of actual production samples to support trials and successful case study data (see Chapter 9) for the first one to three years of plant operation.

Going forward, the biochar sector will need to both optimize revenue and returns from biochar sales and lower the capital intensity of the process plants so that the projects can afford to pay third parties to produce or collect, store and transport suitable biomass resources for the plant. Typically, costs for shipping the biomass are greater than for shipping the energy products (Searcy et al, 2007), which influences decisions of where to place pyrolysis units.

In certain jurisdictions, C is valued and traded or taxed (see Chapter 18). Therefore, the demonstrable C footprint of biochar production and sequestration needs to be confirmed and valued so that individual project business models can benefit from the additional income stream that will result. In jurisdictions where C is not yet valued or traded, government support in the form of capital grants or market development support could well provide the incremental level of confidence to attract the initial investment at reasonable rates.

This project profile would suggest that investors in first-generation projects would only invest because they share the long-term vision for the biomass conversion sector, generally, and the biochar sector, in particular. Accordingly, business models for first-generation plants will need to come with a well-substantiated and clearly articulated plan, a well-articulated strategy to achieve the full potential for biochar over time, and a highly skilled management team to deliver the strategy.

Notes

1   A market-pull strategy targets the end consumer, using advertising, sales promotions and direct response marketing to pull the customer in.
2   The 'third/third/third' ratio is useful at the planning stage of projects. Different pyrolysis systems and operating conditions will produce different ratios of oil, biochar and gas (Strezov et al, 2008; see Chapter 8). Detailed analysis for project-specific conditions will always be required.

References

Antal, M. J. Jr., Croiset, E., Dai, X., DeAlmeida, C., Mok, W. S.-L. and Norberg, N. (1996) 'High-yield biomass charcoal', *Energy Fuels*, vol 10, 652–658

Baveye, P. (2007) 'Soils and a runaway global warming: Terra incognita', *Journal of Soil and Water Conservation*, vol 62, pp139A–143A

Bessen, J. E. and Maskin, E. (2000) *Sequential Innovation, Patents, and Imitation*, MIT Department of Economics Working Paper no 00-01, http://ssrn.com/abstract=206189 or DOI: 10.2139/ssrn.206189, accessed 19 August 2008

Bevan, M. W. and Franssen, M. C. R. (2006)

'Investing in green and white biotech', *Nature Biotechnology*, vol 24, pp765–767

Bridgwater, A. V. and Peacocke, G. V. C. (2002) 'Fast pyrolysis processes for biomass', *Renewable and Sustainable Energy Reviews*, vol 4, pp1–73

Bryant, D. and Downie, A. (2007) 'Agrichar: Building a commercial venture', Paper presented to the International Agrichar Initiative 2007 Conference, Terrigal, Australia

Byrne, C. E. and Nagle, D. C. (1997) 'Carbonization of wood for advanced materials applications', *Carbon*, vol 35, pp259–266

Caputo, A. C., Palumbo, M., Pelagagge, P. M. and Scacchia, F. (2005) 'Economics of biomass energy utilization in combustion and gasification plants: Effects of logistic variables', *Biomass and Bioenergy*, vol 28, pp35–51

Cartmell, E., Gostelow, P., Riddel-Black, D., Simms, N., Oakey, J., Morris, J., Jeffrey, P., Howsam, P. and Pollard, S. J. (2006) 'Biosolids: A fuel or a waste? An integrated appraisal of five co-combustion scenarios with policy analysis', *Environmental Science and Technology*, vol 40, pp649–658

Chan, K. Y., Van Zwieten, L., Meszaros, I., Downie, A. and Joseph, S. (2007) 'Agronomic values of greenwaste biochar as a soil amendment', *Australian Journal of Soil Research*, vol 45, pp629–634

Crucible Carbon (2008) *Biomass Technology Review: Processing for Energy and Materials*, Sustainability Victoria, Melbourne, www.sustainability.vic.gov.au/resources/documents/Biomass_Technology_Review.pdf, accessed 15 June 2008

Demirbas, A. (2001) 'Biomass resource facilities and biomass conversion processing for fuels and chemicals', *Energy Conversion and Management*, vol 42, pp1357–1378

Demirbas, A. and Arin, G. (2002) 'An overview of biomass pyrolysis', *Energy Sources*, vol 24, pp471–482

Dittrick, P. (2007) 'Biofuels producers confront evolving market unknowns', *Oil and Gas Journal*, vol 105, no 38 pp20–24

Downie, A., Klatt, P., Downie, R. and Munroe, P., (2007) 'Slow pyrolysis: Australian demonstration plant successful on multi-feedstocks', Paper presented to the Bioenergy 2007 Conference, Jyväskylä, Finland

Emmerich, F. G. and Luengo, C. A. (1996) 'Babassu charcoal: A sulfurless renewable thermo-reducing feedstock for steelmaking', *Biomass and Bioenergy*, vol 10, pp41–44

Faaij, A. (2008) 'Developments in international bio-energy markets and trade', *Biomass and Bioenergy*, vol 32, pp657–659

FAO (United Nations Food and Agriculture Organization) (1985) *Industrial Charcoal Making*, FAO Forestry Paper 63, FAO, Rome

Fleming, R. A., Babcock, B. A. and Wang, E. (1998) 'Resource or waste? The economics of swine manure storage and management', *Review of Agricultural Economics*, vol 20, pp96–113

Giampietro, M. and Ulgiati, S. (2005) 'Integrated assessment of large-scale biofuel production', *Critical Reviews in Plant Science*, vol 24, pp365–384

Heschel, H. and Klose, E. (1995) 'On the suitability of agricultural by-products for the manufacture of granular activated carbon', *Fuel*, vol 74, pp1786–1791

Hill, J., Nelson, E., Tilman, D., Polasky, S. and Tiffany, D. (2006) 'Environmental, economic, and energetic costs and benefits of biodiesel and ethanol biofuels', *PNAS*, vol 103, pp11206–11210

Hoogwijk, M., Faaij, A., van den Broek, R., Berndes, G., Gielen, D. and Turkenburg, W. (2003) 'Exploration of the ranges of the global potential of biomass for energy', *Biomass and Bioenergy*, vol 25, pp119–133

Hossain, M. K., Strezov, V. and Nelson, P., (2007) 'Evaluation of agricultural char from sewage sludge', in *Proceedings of the International Agrichar Initiative 2007 Conference*, Terrigal, Australia

IPCC (Intergovernmental Panel on Climate Change) (2005) *Carbon Dioxide Capture and Storage*, IPCC, Cambridge University Press, Cambridge, UK

IPCC (2007) *Fourth Assessment Report: Working Group II Report – Impacts, Adaptation and Vulnerability*, www.ipcc.ch/pdf/assessment-report/ar4/wg2/ar4-wg2-intro.pdf, accessed July 2008

Kamm, B. and Kamm, M. (2004) 'Principles of biorefineries', *Applied Microbiology and Biotechnology*, vol 64, pp137–145

Kaygusuz, K. and Türker, M. F. (2002) 'Biomass

energy potential in Turkey', *Renewable Energy*, vol 26, pp661–678

Kennedy, D. (2007) 'The biofuels conundrum', *Science*, vol 316, p515

Kimetu, J. M., Lehmann, J., Ngoze, S., Mugendi, D. N., Kinyangi, J., Riha, S., Verchot, L., Recha, J. W. and Pell, A. (2008) 'Reversibility of productivity decline with organic matter of differing quality along a degradation gradient', *Ecosystems*, vol 11, pp726–739

Laird, D. A. (2008) 'The charcoal vision: A win–win–win scenario for simultaneously producing bioenergy, permanently sequestering carbon, while improving soil and water quality', *Agronomy Journal*, vol 100, pp178–181

Langberg, D. E., Somervile, M. A., Freeman, D. E. and Washington, B. M. (2006) 'The use of mallee charcoal in metallurgical reactors', Paper presented to the Green Processing Conference, June 2006, Newcastle, Australia

Lehmann, J. (2007) 'Bio-energy in the black', *Frontiers in Ecology and the Environment*, vol 5, pp381–387

Lehmann, J., da Silva Jr., J. P., Steiner, C., Nehls, T., Zech, W. and Glaser, B. (2003) 'Nutrient availability and leaching in an archaeological Anthrosol and a Ferralsol of the Central Amazon basin: Fertilizer, manure and charcoal amendments', *Plant and Soil*, vol 249, pp343–357

Lehmann, J., Gaunt, J. and Rondon, M. (2006) 'Bio-char sequestration in terrestrial ecosystems – a review', *Mitigation and Adaptation Strategies for Global Change*, vol 11, pp403–427

Luyten, H. (2003) 'Quality in the market – technology push versus market pull', *Acta Horticulturae*, vol 604, pp85–93

Mansaray, K. G. and Ghaly, A. E. (1997) 'Agglomeration characteristics of alumina sand–rice husk ash mixtures at elevated temperatures', *Energy Sources A*, vol 19, pp1005–1025

Mathews, J. A., (2008a) 'Biofuels, climate change and industrial development: Can the tropical South build 2000 biorefineries in the next decade?', *Biofuels, Bio-products and Biorefining*, vol 2, pp103–125

Mathews, J. A. (2008b) 'Carbon-negative biofuels', *Energy Policy*, vol 36, pp940–945

McKendry, P. (2002) 'Energy production from biomass (part 1): Overview of biomass', *Bioresource Technology*, vol 83, pp37–43

O'Connell, D., Keating B. and Glover, M. (2005) *Sustainability Guide for Bioenergy: A Scoping Study*, Rural Industries Research and Development Corporation, Barton, www.rirdc.gov.au/reports/AFT/05–190.pdf, accessed 15 June 2008

Olofsson, M. (2005) 'Driving forces for import of waste for energy recovery in Sweden', *Waste Management and Research*, vol 23, pp3–12

Ragauskas, A. J., Williams, C. K., Davison, B. H., Britovsek, G., Cairney, J., Eckert, C. A., Frederick, W. J., Hallett, J. P., Leak, D. J., Liotta, C. L., Mielenz, J. R., Murphy, R., Templer, R. and Tschaplinski, T. (2006) 'The path forward for biofuels and biomaterials', *Science*, vol 311, pp484–489

Rhyner, C. R., Schwartz, L. J., Wenger, R. B. and Kohrell, M. G. (1995) *Waste Management and Resource Recovery*, CRC Press, Boca Raton, FL

Schröder, E., Thomauske, K., Weber, C., Hornung, A. and Tumiatti, V. (2007) 'Experiments on the generation of activated carbon from biomass', *Journal of Analytical and Applied Pyrolysis*, vol 79, pp106–111

Scotchmer, S. (1996) 'Protecting early innovators: Should second-generation products be patentable?', *The RAND Journal of Economics*, vol 27, pp322–331

Searchinger, T., Heimlich, R., Houghton, R. A., Dong, F., Elobeid, A., Fabiosa, J., Tokgoz, S., Hayes, D. and Yu T.-H. (2008) 'Use of US croplands for biofuels increases greenhouse gases through emissions from land-use change', *Science*, vol 319, pp1238–1240

Searcy, E., Flynn, P., Ghafoori, E. and Kumar, A. (2007) 'The relative cost of biomass energy transport', *Applied Biochemistry and Biotechnology*, vol 137–140, pp639–652

Stern, N. (2007) *The Economics of Climate Change: The Stern Review*, Cambridge University Press, Cambridge, UK

Strezov, V., Evans, T. J. and Hayman C. (2008) 'Thermal conversion of elephant grass (*Pennisetum purpureum* Schum) to bio-gas, bio-oil and charcoal', *Bioresource Technology*, vol 99, pp8394–8399

Tan, K. C. (2001) 'A framework of supply chain management literature', *European Journal of Purchasing and Supply Management*, vol 7,

pp39–48

Tenenbaum, D. J. (2008) 'Food vs fuel: Diversion of crops could cause more hunger', *Environmental Health Perspectives*, vol 116, ppA254–A257

Tilman, D., Fargione, J., Wolff, B., D'Antonio, C., Dobson, A., Howarth, R., Schindler, D., Schlesinger, W. H., Simberloff, D. and Swackhamer, D. (2001) 'Forecasting agriculturally driven global environmental change', *Science*, vol 292, pp281–284

Tollefson, J. (2008) 'Advanced biofuels face an uncertain future', *Nature*, vol 452, pp670–671

Van Dam, J., Junginger, M., Faaij, A., Jürgens, I., Best, G. and Fritsche, U. (2008) 'Overview of recent developments in sustainable biomass certification', *Biomass and Bioenergy*, vol 32, pp749–780

Van Zwieten, L., Kimber, S., Downie, A., Joseph, S., Chan, K. Y., Cowie, A., Wainberg, R. and

Morris, S. (2007) 'Paper mill agrichar: benefits to soil health and plant production', in *Proceedings of the International Agrichar Initiative 2007 Conference*, Terrigal, Australia

Warnken, M. (2007) *Stage 3 Report: Infrastructure Requirements for Energy from Waste*, IEA Bioenergy Task 36, www.ieabioenergytask 36.org/Publications/2004-2006/Report% 203_WMAA_EFWD_Stage3.pdf, accessed June 2008

Yalcin, M. and Arot, A. I. (2002) 'Gold cyanide adsorption characteristics of activated carbon of non-coconut shell origin', *Hydrometallurgy*, vol 63, pp201–206

Zurbrügg, C., Drescher, S., Patel, A. and Sharatchandra, H. C. (2004) 'Decentralised composting of urban waste – an overview of community and private initiatives in Indian cities', *Waste Management*, vol 24, pp655–662

22

Policy to Address the Threat of Dangerous Climate Change: A Leading Role for Biochar

Peter Read

The tipping point threat

The fact that anthropogenic climate change is occurring is no longer disputed (IPCC, 2007) and, if the change is dangerous, its avoidance is the agreed ultimate objective of the United Nations Framework Convention on Climate Change (UNFCCC), as stated in its Article 2. Moreover, avoiding extremely dangerous climate change – climate change that carries a risk of passing some tipping point beyond which progress to climatically induced disaster is irreversible – is the first priority, as is called for by Article 3.3. This obliges parties that perceive such a threat to take cost-effective action without delay on account of scientific uncertainty. Time-consuming consensus by the Conference of the Parties, as is the case with the Kyoto Protocol (and with Article 4.2 in the Convention, which provides the legal basis for the Protocol), is not needed under Article 3.3 of the UNFCCC.

That the currently occurring climatic change carries the threat of being thus dangerous is rooted in the fact that climate does not always change smoothly (GRIP,

1993), as has become recognized in recent years. Such smooth change was projected as a very long-term process by the climate models surveyed by the IPCC in the early assessment reports that led to the Kyoto Protocol (IPCC, 1996). Advances in palaeo-climatology have since shown (NAS, 2002) that climate change may occur in sudden jumps, which means that the assumptions that support the Protocol are outdated.

The palaeoclimatic record shows past temperature increases of up to 10°C at polar latitudes (ACIA, 2005) in as short a period as a few decades, with smaller but nevertheless catastrophic temperature changes at lower latitudes. These temperature jumps are associated with sea-level changes of several metres, which occur equally abruptly (Hearty et al, 2007). Such abrupt changes have been attributed to positive feedback processes in the break-up of land-based ice sheets that may be capable of causing rapid transport of very large volumes of polar ice into the oceans, with consequential worldwide sea-level rise (Hansen, 2007).

In part, the consequences of such change are direct – the loss of Greenland's ice cover and consequent sea-level rises of the order of 7m (Church et al, 2001) would destroy coastal ecosystems worldwide and displace hundreds of millions of people living in the fertile coastal regions and river deltas of every continent. But the greater consequence is indirect in the form of the socio-economic system response to such an event, with starvation, land and water hunger, and the desperation of hundreds of millions of environmental refugees offering imminent prospect of conflict, maybe escalating to nuclear war (Wasdell, 2007).

The primacy of this first priority is evident because avoidance of this threatened catastrophe is a *sine qua non* for securing other social and environmental objectives. Such a catastrophe would overwhelm efforts to preserve biodiversity, to combat desertification, to conserve wetlands, to promote sustainable development, to provide clean water and sanitation, and many other desiderata of the multilateral environmental agreements and of the Millennium Development Goals (UN, 2005).

Beyond emissions reductions

Most of the threats of abrupt climate change seem likely to be thermally driven – that is, with regard to the present warming, driven by the *aggregate* of heat inputs due to greenhouse gas levels that have been increasingly elevated by anthropogenic emissions since the Industrial Revolution (Read, 2007). In mathematical terms, this is the integral of the rate of heat input or, with that rate broadly proportionate to the level of greenhouse gases, the double integral of net emissions less (rather slow) natural removals. These threats include methane escapes from thawing tundra, loss of Arctic Ocean summer ice and the collapse of land-based ice sheets. Precursor signs of these are already apparent with, so far, only the heating corresponding to area A in Figure 22.1.

The projection in Figure 22.1 for the next 50 years assumes that everything that could go well with the Kyoto process after 2012 does go well. Not only do the parties find a way of ensuring that all of the major emitting nations – the US, China, India, etc. –

reduce their emissions, but successive agreements under extensions of the Kyoto Protocol result globally in a reduction in man-made emissions to zero in a linear trend over 25 years, starting in 2010. Thus, emissions under the IPCC's SRES A2 Scenario (IPCC, 2000) were multiplied by a percentage that falls at 4 per cent per year from 100 per cent in 2010, 96 per cent in 2011 and so on, until 4 per cent in 2034 and 0 per cent from 2035 on. The resulting profile of emissions was then converted to a profile of levels (i.e. of concentrations) using the Bern model (Joos and Bruno, 1996). These calculations assume a much greater success than global emulation of the British target, widely regarded as very ambitious, of a 60 per cent reduction by 2050. By inspection of Figure 22.1, it is apparent that the cumulative heating increase, to be added to what has cumulated so far, is roughly twice as great for the next 50 years as for the last 50 (during which emissions have mainly taken off) and with no ending in sight in 2058.

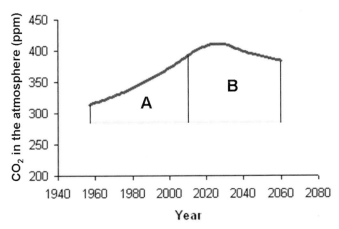

Figure 22.1 *Excess CO_2 over the pre-industrial level for the last 50 years and (assuming emissions fall to zero by 2035 and remain zero thereafter) for the next 50 years (explanation for calculations in text)*

Source: Peter Read

Carbon removals

To prevent this prospective tripling of the aggregate danger metric, it is necessary to go beyond what can be achieved through emissions reductions. This entails large-scale carbon (C) removals from the atmosphere and stocking it somewhere safer (Read and Parshotam, 2007). Thus, we may deduce that the threat of abrupt climate change thrusts negative emissions systems, including, most promisingly, biochar, into a key role in climate change mitigation, rather than being just one of the ways, illustrated by Socolow's 'wedges' of reducing net emissions (Socolow, 2005).

The effectiveness of a C-removals strategy relative to the emissions reductions approach embedded in the cap-and-trade framework created by the Kyoto Protocol is illustrated by comparing its achievement on an ambitious scale with the quite implausible success with reducing emissions as described above.

An ambitious programme of biosphere C stock management (BCSM) (Read, 2007/2008), over the same 25-year period as described for emission reductions above, requires worldwide improvement in the ways that we use land. This is in order to raise its sustainable productivity through financial investments on the scale of prospective global investments in getting oil and other fossil fuels, added to large-scale 'willingness to pay', to avoid catastrophic climate change risks. If enhanced photosynthesis, indeed, takes more carbon dioxide (CO_2) out of the atmosphere than under current land management practice, the fixed CO_2 must be carefully conserved through widespread deployment of C storage systems, such as biochar soil improvement. With enhanced productivity of the land yielding increased supplies of traditional food and fibre, together with biofuel, a large part of the C-rich residues would then also be stocked more safely than in the atmosphere.

It has been shown (Read and Parshotam, 2007) that a trio of technologies, which are available for implementing BCSM could, if pursued on an ambitious scale, return CO_2 levels to ~300ppm by around 2040, as illustrated by line F in Figure 22.2. Line Z is, by definition, the best that can be done by emissions reductions under the 25 years assumption (as shown in Figure 22.1). However, deploying more BCSM could, conceivably, yield lower profiles than F.

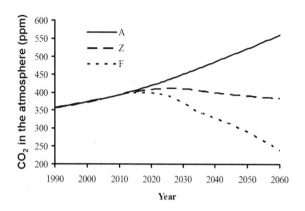

Figure 22.2 *Comparison of zero emission systems and negative emissions systems in mitigating the level of CO$_2$ (in ppm) in the atmosphere*

Notes: The comparison is extended to 2060 only. The usual timeframe for mitigation studies (2100 and beyond) is considered to be too far in the future in relation to the threat of abrupt climate change. Scenarios: A, SRES-A2 business as usual; Z, SRES-A2 with a transition to zero emissions technologies between 2011 and 2035; F, SRES-A2 with a transition to negative emissions technologies over the same period.

Source: data from Read and Parshotam (2007)

In essence, BCSM means large-scale deployment of technologies that remove C from the atmosphere and store it in reservoirs located in the biosphere or lithosphere. It involves enhancing natural aggregate planetary photosynthesis by plants and delaying, or, in part, wholly preventing, the return of C to the atmosphere (typically from wildfire and from oxidation by fungi, bacteria and animals that feed off plant material) through pyrolysis of biomass residues and dispersing the resulting long-lived biochar in the soil.

The economics of biosphere C stock management (BCSM) and biochar

The role of biochar within alternative BCSM technology chains will depend upon the policy incentives in place, together with the economic and commercial factors discussed in Chapters 18 to 21. Here the aim is to discuss the policy opportunity for biochar from the perspective of the prime priority of avoiding dangerous climate change.

Five types of reservoirs have been suggested for stocking C more safely than in the atmosphere:

1   New forestry plantations: this is well understood and, net of prospective sales revenue at harvest, low cost. It can therefore provide a jump start to reservoir filling (Dyson and Marland, 1979). However, it reaches a limit imposed by land availability after which, under commercial exploitation, it acts as an ongoing sink supplying raw material to the other reservoirs in parallel with other annual and perennial crops (Read, 1996)

2   Burying wood where it is grown (Scholz and Hasse, 2008).

3   CO$_2$ capture and storage (CCS): supplying reservoirs in deep geological strata or, through the formation of bicarbonates, in ocean or as insoluble carbonates on land – for example, in worked-out open-cast coal mines (Lackner, 2003). Linked to bioenergy, this yields a negative emissions energy system (Obersteiner et al, 2001, Read and Lermit, 2005).

4   Labile C (Lal, 2004) and biochar storage (Lehmann et al, 2006) in soil reservoirs with co-produced bio-oil and conventional agricultural products storing additional labile C (Read, 2007/2008).

5   New timber structures and other harvested wood products: this provides a reservoir that can grow indefinitely but at

a rate that is limited to substantially less than energy-sector emissions by the finiteness of demand for new structures and by the shortness of the useful life of much harvested wood product as pulp (Winjum et al, 1998).

In addition, the existing fossil C reservoir is maintained *in situ* through technology chains that involve bioenergy and other renewable sources of energy to the extent that they substitute for fossil fuel (Read, 1994). For bioenergy raw material, these can draw on biomass residues from traditional harvesting, processing and consumption of products of the land, as well as residues from harvesting new forestry plantations and supplies from dedicated bioenergy crops, such as sugar cane in tropical regions and switchgrass or short-rotation woody crops in temperate regions (Worldwatch Institute, 2007).

Labile in-soil and above-soil C resulting from soil improvement and productivity also increases under biochar conditioning, as discussed in the body of this book, and constitutes a reservoir that can be augmented and sustained through appropriate management practice for as long as policy incentives remain.

Given that the first and last of the reservoirs are limited by extraneous factors, and that impacts on the fossil fuel and labile soil reservoirs are an outcome of the second and third, the extensive marginal demand for negative emissions involving safe stocking of C from the atmosphere must be met either by bioenergy with carbon storage (BECS), including C storage as carbonates, etc. (Lackner, 2003), or by biochar. These two constitute the candidate backstop technologies for net C removals from the atmosphere. This is subject to the constraint (which *prima facie* appears to be non-binding; Bot et al, 2000) that the aggregate net primary productivity of managed lands, minus priority demands for high-value food and fibre, is

adequate to meet the greater of either energy demands or C removal needs (as revealed by future advances in understanding abrupt climate change).

In considering their relative roles, it may be noted that both BECS and biochar are very immature with regard to their deployment in C stock management, although charcoal burning is, of course, an ancient activity (see Chapter 8). Consequently, relative costing is still speculative (see Chapter 19) and consideration of their relative roles is here based on qualitative aspects, *viz*:

- CCS is dependent upon the availability of geological storage found in sedimentary basins, which are abundant in oil- and gas-producing regions but less so in some of the regions that offer best prospects for enhancing photosynthetic productivity, particularly sub-Saharan Africa (Haszeldine, 2006).
- CCS offers important returns to scale and, if linked to bioenergy, is more likely to be economic in regions with good transportation infrastructure that can support the collection of dispersed supplies of biomass raw material; or in proximity to large cities where food processing, wastes, refuse collection, sewage and some industrial processing provide concentrated sources of organic material (see Chapter 9).
- Particular opportunities arise for BECS from co-firing in fossil fuel facilities that have installed CCS in order to cut emissions while continuing to use low-cost coal (Faaij, 2006).
- CO_2 as fermentation off-gas is available from sugar cane ethanol production and its cheapness may, in regions with a high concentration of sugar cane processing, justify the cost of a gathering pipeline system linked to a suitable geological storage (through which higher-cost CO_2 – for example, captured from the flue

gases of bagasse-fired thermal power plant – could also be carried, if the value of C removals increases).

- CCS imposes an energy cost that reduces the overall plant efficiency and raises the cost of the energy product, while also increasing the throughput of raw material and, consequently, the quantity of CO_2 that needs to be safely stored.

- CCS can be the second (costly) stage of a two-stage BECS strategy, with the first stage (showing a positive return at oil prices over ~US$70 per barrel) being a stand-alone bioenergy system that is designed to be retro-fitted with a second-stage CCS in the event of an imminent threat of abrupt climate change (Read and Lermit, 2005).

- In addition to the two value streams from BECS (energy and C removals), biochar also yields improved soil quality – for example, through better nutrient retention (see Chapter 5), and, hence, is an investment that secures its return through increased harvested crop values.

- Through adjustments to temperature and residence time, pyrolysis provides a trade-off between energy outputs and biochar for soil improvement plus C removals (Worldwatch Institute, 2007; see Chapter 18), which can be used to exploit changing relative prices for C and energy (reflecting changing policy concern over abrupt climate change threats and changing market forces under 'peak oil').

- While fast pyrolysis is a sophisticated industrial process with significant returns to scale (therefore having similar logistic characteristics to those noted in the second point above), certain slow pyrolysis systems are traditional technologies that can be conducted at small scale (e.g. at the village or community level) (see Chapter 8).

These factors lead to an expectation that BECS, linking large-scale bioenergy with CCS, will be deployed mainly in developed countries where CCS infrastructure is in place to enable continued use of cheap fossil fuels in the C-constrained future. In the developing regions of the world, where the bulk of the land and the best climatic conditions for biomass production exist, policy incentives to drive C removals may be expected to result in the widespread adoption of biochar soil improvement based on pyrolysis technologies of a sophistication and scale adapted to local conditions. The potential role of biochar for the removal of CO_2 from the atmosphere and storage in soil of the very large quantities of C implicit in line F of Figure 22.2 thus appears to lie mainly in developing countries. However, community-based social marketing could grow to make a significant contribution to biochar-based BCSM, although linking such activity into a system of formal incentives may prove problematic.

A policy framework for carbon removals: The leaky bucket

We have seen that the threat of abrupt climate change provides motivation to drive C removals forward, and with it a major role for biochar. However, the Kyoto Protocol's cap-and-trade framework for emissions reductions entails rigorous accountability, which holds back difficult-to-measure C removals activity (Grubb et al, 1999). With, at present, only one forestry project worldwide going forward under the Protocol's Clean Development Mechanism (CDM) (Bettelheim, 2008), it has been likened to a silver teaspoon (Read, 2008a) – a strategy bearing high costs and little use for quickly removing CO_2 from the atmosphere.

An alternative for the post-2012 regime is to take land-use change, and perhaps all project-based offsets, out of the account for emissions reductions along with policies and measures that drive such activities and, instead, include these in the emissions cap negotiations. A commitment to easily verified best practices may provide additionality, with low transaction costs yielding a bucket – possibly a leaky bucket since some best practices would be adopted anyway, without incentives to mitigate climate change – that is capable of stimulating an increased volume of C removals.

Under this leaky bucket framework, the evolution of land use towards the sustainable co-production of all human needs for food, fibre and fuel, along with ongoing effective control of CO_2 in the atmosphere, can proceed within the context of mutual gains from trade based on the comparative advantage in photosynthetic productivity of land-rich but otherwise impoverished developing countries. Thus, direct foreign investment in soil improvement in such regions yields both the C mitigation that is the historical responsibility of most fuel-importing countries and the sustainable rural development that is needed in potential biofuel-exporting countries, along with enhanced energy security from the threat presented by volatile prices and dwindling supplies of oil (Blanch et al, 2008).

Such a framework, advanced in response to Article 3.3 of the UNFCCC, can develop initially through bilateral agreements between North and South partners having traditional cultural and trading ties, or in a regional context such as the Asia-Pacific Economic Cooperation (APEC), or through the aegis of, for instance, the group of 8 leading industrialized nations (G8) global bioenergy partnership (Read, 2007/2008). Eventually there can be convergence onto a new Protocol under Article 3.3, complementary to the Kyoto Protocol's focus on emissions reductions.

In reality, the drive to energy security is proceeding independently of climate change concerns, in some cases in climatically counter-productive ways (Fargione et al, 2008; Searchinger et al, 2008). However, to shift this trend into a sustainable path involves commitments by North and South that are far less onerous than the conflictual burden-sharing involved in capping emissions.

It requires exporting country trading partners to commit to objective criteria for sustainable best practice in the production of biofuels and importing country partners to commit to:

- treating biofuels that are produced in an unsustainable way as no different from fossil fuels, thus incurring the C-price related penalties of continued fossil fuel use; and
- imposing an increasing obligation on energy suppliers to invest in biofuel raw material supplies from prospective exporters, rather than, as traditionally done, in fossil fuel extraction.

Obligations on oil companies to include a rising proportion of sustainably produced bio-oils in their refinery feedstock can provide the policy driver for such direct foreign investment in schemes for land-use improvement, diverted from the traditional pattern of investment in petroleum-exporting countries. Such obligations would be discharged subject to independent verification of best practice as a token of additionality, since second best (or worse) practice is, by definition, lower cost. This gives rise to low transaction costs and opens the way, under procedures of simplified CDM, for the large volume of activity that is needed in an effective response to threats of abrupt climate change.

Objective sustainability criteria will evolve with experience and can be incorporated within the best practice standards adopted by the bilateral or wider partnerships. Progressively, these can be made the driver for implementing a range of multilateral environmental agreements (MEAs). For instance, sustainable land use and water planning, supported by official expertise and non-governmental organization (NGO) inputs from partners in the North into capacity-building in the South, can provide conservation areas, migration trails and village-level practices that serve the objectives of the Rio Convention on biological diversity and the Bonn Convention on migratory species, as well as the Helsinki Convention on international rivers and lakes.

Sustainable water management can also be served through the capacity of the major energy firms to manage large-scale projects for desalination and for diversion of a proportion of river waters to irrigation that are currently lost to sea. Diverting from regions of increased rainfall under projected climate change to regions of increasing water shortage can help to greatly increase net photosynthetic production by relaxing water constraints. Such investments can serve both the Ramsar Convention on wetlands preservation and the Convention to Combat Desertification, both currently lacking a mechanism for generating private-sector investment to secure their objectives – and, of course, as noted at the beginning of this chapter, both overwhelmed in the event of an abrupt climate change occurrence.

Food versus fuel and biochar

Finance for BCSM, and therefore the main driver for deploying technology chains that involve biochar, must come from the energy sector (Read, 2008b), and with that a demand to meet raw material requirements of the energy sector for the production of biofuels. Such use of biotic raw materials has come under criticism as being a factor in rising food prices worldwide as well as for deploying technology chains – very far from sustainable best practice – that create a large C debt at the time of initial land-use change and cause indirect effects through stimulating food production on hitherto undisturbed landscapes (Fargione et al, 2008; Searchinger et al, 2008).

In response to these concerns, and other concerns regarding socio-economic impacts and biodiversity issues, the Sustainable Biofuels Consensus (Trindade et al, 2008) distinguishes 'bad' biofuels from 'good' biofuels, including 'second-generation' bioenergy technologies and biochar land-use improvement. Ethanol produced from sugar cane, using the modern fermentation and crop management systems developed in Brazil, is the main 'good' biofuel that is currently available, paying above the going wage and using bagasse wastes to meet process energy needs (J. R. Moreira, personal communication, 2004). In a recent project, this technology is being transferred to Ghana, one of the sub-Saharan African countries that can advance the Millennium Development Goals through economic growth led by exports of 'good' biofuels (Dogbevi, 2008). Sugar cane expansion occurs on *cerrado* land (*miombo* land in sub-Saharan Africa) that is not used for food production and that is plentifully available. It does not occur in rainforest since sugar cane requires a dry season.

In reaching the consensus, it was noted that biofuel obligations in Europe and the US could well be met by expansion of such 'good' sugar cane ethanol in Brazil and sub-

Saharan Africa. Thus, the impact on food prices of such obligations arises entirely from the barriers facing ethanol imports entering just those countries that have imposed the obligations, thus providing protection to 'bad' biofuel production from fodder maize and rape seed (canola) crops. Higher food prices may more likely result from a variety of factors, including:

- high fuel prices (which biofuel supplies serve to ameliorate);
- the shift in developed countries' farm support from production subsidies, with a view to raising the viability of food production elsewhere and supporting sustainable rural development; and
- adventitious extreme weather events that, to the extent they are related to climatic warming, stand to be limited through success with BCSM, including biofuels as the financial driver for biochar soil improvement.

In addition to serving the objectives of several MEAs, the foreign direct investment in the rural economies of numerous developing countries that results from this framework also serves several of the Millennial Development Goals, most obviously poverty relief and, through rural energy accessibility, the lighting and information technology needed to raise educational standards. Although viable food prices initially act negatively on the urban poor, increased rural incomes will generate multiplier effects in these chronically underemployed economies. The resulting economic growth can, with reduced imports of costly petroleum-based fuels (and, eventually, exports of biofuels), expand on a path that is less hampered by a balance of payments constraints. And, where biofuel is linked to biochar in a C removals policy framework, food production may even be increased by raising the productivity of the soil (see Chapter 12), thereby meeting the increased demands for good quality food that arise with better living standards (Worldwatch Institute, 2007).

Conclusions

In this chapter we have looked at the role of biochar from the perspective of a policymaker who intends to mitigate climate change and has no commitment to biochar over other technologies. It is seen as one of several technologies for C removals; but it nevertheless has a key potential role, particularly in many developing countries, as a result of its appropriate technological characteristics and in response to the overriding need to avoid climatic catastrophe.

Thus, avoiding sudden and dangerous climate change requires the removal of C from the atmosphere and its safe storage on, in or deep under the soil. On the soil, in new plantation forestry, provides a short-term response, limited by land availability; but

biochar storage in the soil and BECS, linking bioenergy with CO_2 compression and storage in deep saline aquifers, provide adequate capacity to store the current excess of atmospheric CO_2 and future CO_2 emissions from fossil fuels. Of these, biochar has a key role to play on the bulk of the land areas that will be used for the sustainable production of the biomass raw material, co-produced with food and fibre, that is needed to meet demands for biofuels in an era of dwindling oil and C resources. This key role emerges from consideration of the relative economics of BECS and biochar–bioenergy systems and the lack of geological storages for CO_2 in the main growing regions.

A policy framework to drive this development can hang from Article 3.3 of the UNFCCC, thus avoiding the need for time-consuming consensus that afflicts the Kyoto process. This framework involves bilateral, sectoral or regional agreements that commit energy-sector players in fuel-importing countries to invest in sustainable land-use improvements in prospective biofuel-exporting countries. The latter will deploy biochar soil improvement widely and yield rising supplies of 'good' biofuels, as advanced by the Sustainable Biofuels Consensus. Based on the comparative advantage of many land-rich but otherwise impoverished countries, gains from trade will yield sustainable rural development and other objectives of the Millennium Development Goals. Prospective exporting partners in bilateral or wider agreements will commit to objective standards of environmental sustainability that will be enforced on energy-sector players by conditions on their imports of biofuels and of bioenergy-based products that require them to be produced using 'good' technologies.

Making use of comparative advantage and gains from trade, this framework shifts from sharing the burden of emissions reduction that causes geopolitical conflict to sharing the mutual benefit of soil improvement of a biochar sequestration. Pursued energetically, 'C removals' offer the prospect to escape from climatic catastrophe through the rapid uptake of biochar soil improvement and other C-storing activities. The role of biochar in a climate change regime that is based on C removals could be very large, bringing worldwide benefits to soil quality and to the livelihoods of the people who live on the land. But biochar is in direct competition with CO_2 capture and sequestration and, with its many co-benefits, presents a complex picture that policy-makers and industry managers may find difficult to grasp. Accordingly, it is critical to communicate the concept of biochar sequestration, clarifying where (and where not) it has a role, and developing cost estimates that take account of the prices of the various co-products, as well the costs of inputs, under different production systems.

With the primary objective of avoiding climatic catastrophe secured, the numerous other environmental and socio-economic benefits that accrue from biochar sequestration in soils can be realized. However, from the perspective of the policy-maker, these benefits may be seen as a complication, involving many dimensions of social interaction, in contrast with the one-dimensional solution presented by BECS. Accordingly, if the potential of biochar is to be realized, it requires research and clarification – quantification, where possible – of these benefits.

References

ACIA (2005) *Arctic Climate Impact Assessment*, Cambridge University Press, Cambridge, UK

Bettelheim, E. (2008) 'The UNFCCC in Bali: What does it mean for us?', in *Carbon and Communities in Tropical Woodlands: An International Interdisciplinary Conference*, 16–18 June, 2008, University of Edinburgh School of Geosciences, Edinburgh, UK, pp86–87

Blanch, F., Schels, S., Soares, G., Haase, M. and Hynes, D. (2008) 'Biofuels driving global oil supply growth', *Global Energy Weekly*, 6 June

2008, Merrill Lynch, Pierce, Fenner and Smith, Inc

Bot, A. J., Nachtergaele, F. O. and Young, A. (2000) *Land Resource Potential and Constraints at Regional and Country Levels*, Land and Water Division, FAO, Rome, Italy

Church, J. A., Gregory, J. M., Huybrechts, P., Kuhn, M., Lambeck, K., Nhuan, M., Qin, D. and Woodworth, P. (2001) 'Changes in sea level', in IPCC (ed) *Climate Change 2001: The Scientific Basis*, Cambridge University Press,

Cambridge, UK, pp639–693

Dogbevi, E. K. (2008) 'The biofuel factor, the food crisis and Ghana's participation', *Ghana News Today*, 17 July, www.ghananews today.com/news_readmore.php?id=162

Dyson, F. J. and Marland, G. (1979) 'Technical fixes for the climatic effects of CO_2', in W. P. Elliott and L. Machta (eds) *Workshop on the Global Effects of Carbon Dioxide from Fossil Fuels*, Miami Beach, Florida, 7–11 March 1977, US Department of Energy, US, pp111–118

Faaij, A. (2006) 'Modern options for producing secondary energy carriers from biomass', *Mitigation and Adaptation Strategies for Global Change*, vol 11, pp343–375

Fargione, J., Hill, J., Tilman, D., Polansky, S. and Hawthorne, P. (2008) 'Land clearing and the biofuel carbon debt', *Science*, vol 319, pp1235–1238

GRIP (1993) 'Climate instability during the last interglacial period recorded in the GRIP ice core', *Nature*, vol 364, pp203–207

Grubb, M., Vrolijk, C. and Brack, D. (1999) *The Kyoto Protocol*, RIIA and Earthscan Publications Ltd, London, UK

Hansen, J. (2007) 'Huge sea level rises are coming – unless we act now', *New Scientist*, vol 2614, pp30–34

Haszeldine, R. S. (2006) 'Deep geological CO_2 storage: Principles, and prospecting for bio-energy disposal sites', *Mitigation and Adaptation Strategies for Global Change*, vol 11, pp369–393

Hearty, P. J., Hollin, J. T., Neumann, A. C., O'Leary, M. J. and McCulloch, M. (2007) 'Global sea-level fluctuations during the last interglaciation (MIS 5e)', *Quaternary Science Review*, vol 26, pp2090–2112

IPCC (Intergovernmental Panel on Climate Change) (1996) *Climate Change 1995: The Science of Climate Change. The Contribution of Working Group I to the Second Assessment Report of the Intergovernmental Panel on Climate Change*, Cambridge University Press, Cambridge, UK

IPCC (2000) *Special Report on Emissions Scenarios*, Cambridge University Press, Cambridge, UK

IPCC (2007) *Fourth Assessment Report of the IPCC: Summary for Policy-Makers*, Cambridge

University Press, Cambridge, UK

Joos, F. and Bruno, M. (1996) *A Short Description of the Bern Model*, www.climate.unibe.ch/~joos/model_description/model_description.html

Lackner, K. S. (2003) 'A guide to CO_2 sequestration', *Science*, vol 300, pp1677–1679

Lal, R. (2004) 'Soil carbon sequestration impacts on global climate change and food security', *Science*, vol 304, pp1623–1627

Lehmann, J., Gaunt, J. and Rondon, M. (2006) 'Bio-char sequestration in terrestrial ecosystems – a review', *Mitigation and Adaptation Strategies for Global Change*, vol 11, pp395–419

NAS (National Academic Press) (2002) *Abrupt Climate Change: Inevitable Surprises*, NAS, Washington, DC

Obersteiner, M., Azar, C., Kauppi, P., Möllerstern, M., Moreira, J., Nilsson, S., Read, P., Riahi, K., Schlamadinger, B., Yamagata, Y., Yan, J. and van Ypersele, J.-P. (2001) 'Managing climate risk', *Science*, vol 294, pp786–787

Read, P. (1994) *Responding to Global Warming: The Technology, Economics and Politics of Sustainable Energy*, ZED Books, London and New Jersey

Read, P. (1996) 'Forestry as a medium term buffer stock of carbon', in *World Renewable Energy Conference, Denver, volume III*, pp984–988

Read, P. (2007) 'Comments to "What Next?" IPCC meeting, Berlin, 23 Nov. 07', available at http://ecf.pik-potsdam.de/Events/previous-events/ipcc-conference-1/ipcc_conf_2007/Peter-Read-Berlin%20IPCC%20statement.pdf

Read, P. (2007/2008) 'Biosphere carbon stock management', *Climatic Change*, vol 87, pp305–320

Read, P. (2008a) *Commercial Forestry and LULUCF for a 'Carbon Neutral New Zealand' – the 'Leaky Bucket'*, IPS Working Paper 2008/01, VUW, http://ips.ac.nz/publications/publications/show/218

Read, P. (2008b) 'The energy sector's role in sustainable forest management finance', in *Carbon and Communities in Tropical Woodlands: An International Interdisciplinary Conference*, 16–18 June, 2008, University of Edinburgh School of Geosciences, Edinburgh, UK, pp52–58

Read P. and Lermit, J. (2005) 'Bio-energy with carbon storage (BECS): A sequential decision approach to the threat of abrupt climate change', *Energy*, vol 30, pp2654–2671

Read, P. and Parshotam, A. (2007) *Holistic Greenhouse Gas Management Strategy* (with reviewers' comments and authors' rejoinders), Institute of Policy Studies Working Paper 07/1, Victoria University of Wellington, Wellington, New Zealand, http://ips.ac.nz/publications/publications/list/7

Scholz, F. and Hasse, U. (2008) 'Permanent wood sequestration: The solution to the global carbon dioxide problem', *ChemSusChem*, vol 1, pp381–384

Searchinger, T., Heimlich, R., Houghton, R. A., Dong, F., Elobeid, A., Fabiosa, J., Tokgoz, S., Hayes D. and Yu, T.-H. (2008) 'Use of US croplands for biofuels increases greenhouse gases through emissions from land use change', *Science*, vol 319, pp1238–1240

Socolow, R. (2005) 'Stabilization wedges: An elaboration of the concept', in H. J. Schellnhuber, W. Cramer, N. Nakicenovic, T. Wigley and G. Yohe (eds) *Avoiding Dangerous Climate Change*, Cambridge University Press, Cambridge, UK, pp347–354

Trindade, S. C., Best, G., Earley, J. C., Faaij, A. P. C., Fritsche, U. R., Hester, A., Hunt, S., Iida, T., Johnson, F. X., Kutas, G., Nastari, P. M., Opal, C. A., Otto, M., Read, P., Sims, R. E. H., Tschirley, J. B. and Zarrilli, S. (2008) *Sustainable Biofuels Consensus*, available at www.sef.org.nz/views/Sustainable_Biofuels.pdf

UN (United Nations) (2005) *The Millennium Development Goals Report*, United Nations, New York, available at www.un.org/Docs/ summit2005/MDGBook.pdf

Wasdell, D. (2007) 'Accelerated climate change and the task of stabilisation', in *Planet Earth – We Have a Problem*, All Party Parliamentary Climate Change Group, c/o Colin Challen MP, House of Commons, London, Meridian Programme, London, UK

Winjum, J. K., Corvallis; O. R., Brown, S. and Schlamadinger, B. (1998) 'Forest harvests and wood products: Sources and sinks of atmospheric carbon dioxide', *Forest Science*, vol 44, pp272–284

Worldwatch Institute (2007) *Biofuels for Transport*, Earthscan, London, UK

Index

Note: **Bold** page numbers refer to figures; italic page numbers refer to tables.